M000239813

The Philosophy of Christology

The Philosophy of Christology

From the Bultmannians to Derrida, 1951–2002

HUE WOODSON

WIPF & STOCK · Eugene, Oregon

THE PHILOSOPHY OF CHRISTOLOGY
From the Bultmannians to Derrida, 1951–2002

Copyright © 2022 Hue Woodson. All rights reserved. Except for brief quotations in critical publications or reviews, no part of this book may be reproduced in any manner without prior written permission from the publisher. Write: Permissions, Wipf and Stock Publishers, 199 W. 8th Ave., Suite 3, Eugene, OR 97401.

Wipf & Stock
An Imprint of Wipf and Stock Publishers
199 W. 8th Ave., Suite 3
Eugene, OR 97401

www.wipfandstock.com

PAPERBACK ISBN: 978-1-5326-8153-0
HARDCOVER ISBN: 978-1-5326-8154-7
EBOOK ISBN: 978-1-5326-8155-4

01/31/22

Contents

Preface

This book is as much about a particular history of Christology as it is about a particular philosophy of Christology, such that the particularity of the historical and the particularity of the philosophical hinge, essentially, on *the question of the meaning of Christology*, as that which I have grounded after Rudolf Bultmann's demythologization project. Any history of Christology, in itself, if it intends to be honest, must acknowledge Bultmann, just as it must acknowledge Albert Schweitzer's contributions, which directly influence, to a certain extent, Bultmann and provide a fundamental and lasting paradigm shift in Christological studies at the turn of the twentieth century. Yet, to even evoke Schweitzer and Bultmann, we must inevitably consider, with keen interest, the broad range of voices that emerge throughout the 1950s and well into the 1960s in Germany among "Bultmannians"—those that were Bultmann's former students, proponents of these former students, or contemporary opponents and critics—especially if, when honest, we recognize that Germany is the epicenter of Christological thinking and a substantial amount of post-Bultmann Christological reflection. How this Christological thinking unfolds and how this Christological reflection is laid bare speaks to an unfolding and a laying bare of a history, insofar as, when claiming *a particular history of Christology* here, I am concerned mainly with what develops and arises out of a specific period in time that ultimately requires a philosophizing.

Granted, to even propose a history of Christology, in a general sense, suggests reaching back to the very beginnings of Christological thinking and Christological reflection, from the moment it became understood that Jesus of Nazareth and the Christ of faith share an existentially-theological and theologically-existential relationship—it is one where the former existentializes the theologizing of the latter, just as much as the latter existentializes the theologizing of the former. From those Christological origins, we could certainly give an account of the varied Christological debates throughout the first three centuries in the growth and codifying of the Church, culminating with the Chalcedonian formula. We could even discuss the centuries since the Council of Chalcedon what strands of Christological thinking emerged in Medieval Christianity and disclosed itself in theologizing in the Renaissance, and, for that matter, how these strands informed, eventually, Reformation thought. Since the sixteenth century, we can locate an intensity towards and concentration on the historical Jesus, which does not just calibrate what it means to do Christology, what the limits are to Christological thinking, and what grounds Christological reflection, but also situates an ensuing quest for the historical Jesus—that "quest" and those that contribute to it, along a spectrum of considerations, as "Questors," even after Schweitzer and Bultmann, remain integral to an ongoing "Christologization," I would call it, which fundamentally situates what we mean when we say "historical Jesus" and what we mean when we say "Christ of faith" in a Christological dialectic of Hegelian proportions.

Still, one might ask: why another Christology book? Or, a related question might be something like: what more can be said about Christology that has not been already said? In short, what can another book on Christology offer that is different from the ever-accumulating Christological literature, if we date everything that has been said about Christology to the first century C.E., as followers of the Way sought to explain and make sense out of Jesus of Nazareth and the Christ of faith?

Though such questions are certainly meaningful and not without merit, I think they miss, fundamentally, what remains at stake in Christology. There is a certain suggestion, I believe, that because the subject of Christology has its origins in the first century C.E. and that there, now, in 2020, is an inexhaustive amount of literature and scholarship attempting to conceive of, explain, rationalize, and articulate what Christology is and what Christology means, that the subject matter, itself, is exhaustible. This is certainly far from the truth. Christology, as a subject, and what we do when we engage with the Christological—through Christological thinking and Christological reflection—remains inexhaustible, because of what the Council of Chalcedon sought to "solve" in 451 C.E. over and against other Christological definitions, predicated by creeds, arising previously in the Council of Ephesus (in 431 C.E.), the Council of Constantinople (in 381 C.E.), and the Council of Nicaea (in 325 C.E.).

As much as the Chalcedonian ecumenical council sought to provide a solution to the Christological problem, it is safe to say that the Chalcedonian Creed only presented more problems. We know, indeed, that the Christological debates of the day settled on the compromise that the two natures—or "dyophysitism"—of the person of Jesus Christ are embodied in one existence—or "hypostasis," but this compromise only complicated what Christology is and, in turn, complicated what Christology does. Not only did the Chalcedonian formula complicate what sense can be made out of the relationship between divine nature and human nature to post-Chalcedonian Christological thinking and Christological reflection, but it also complicates what role the problem of the historical Jesus plays in it.

What makes *the problem of the historical Jesus* a "problem"—as that which remains elusive and unsolvable—is that it remains unwieldy and incorrigible. Indeed, there is a certain elusiveness to the notion of a "historical Jesus" to us now, but it is surely not too much to suggest an elusiveness to the same notion at the time of the Council of Chalcedon, which was at least four centuries removed from the lifetime of Jesus. What the "problem" is and does, in *the problem of the historical Jesus*, brings a historical question up against the merely theological one handled explicitly by the Chalcedonian Creed: what can be known about the historical Jesus, if any epistemology of Jesus remains generationally and perpetually fraught with difficulties?

When surmising *the problem of the historical Jesus*, as it is especially evoked in the 1950s and 1960s, it summons an underlying dialectical problem, articulating what remains unresolved epistemologically, historically, and theologically with the Chalcedonian solution. If we view *the problem of the historical Jesus* as problematizing the overarching issue from the spheres of the epistemological, the historical, and the theological, to philosophize *the problem of the historical Jesus* means situating these spheres in a meaningful way against one another, in order to present a narrow task and outline a manageable scope to *the question of the meaning of Christology*.

Indeed, when considering *a particular history of Christology* and *a particular philosophy of Christology*, the very notion of *the problem of the historical Jesus*, as it is made explicit in the 1950s and 1960s, shapes what has occurred at least since the 1970s: a "third" quest for the historical Jesus (circa 1977 with *Paul and Palestinian Judaism* by E. P. Sanders and the coining of the term by N. T. Wright), the Jesus Seminar (1985–2006), the three Princeton-Prague Symposiums on Jesus Research (2005, 2007, 2016), and the three deliberations of the John, Jesus, and History Group in the Society of Biblical Literature (2002–04, 2005–07, 2008–10). Even so, what has occurred in the development of Christological studies since the 1970s has largely overshadowed the voices and efforts of the 1950s and 1960s—though some might argue that this is for good reason, whether suggesting that the various arguments regarding *the problem of the historical Jesus* are methodologically undermined by Bultmann's influences or simply antiquated in their approaches, I maintain that there is a lasting significance in and an enduring importance to the Christological thinking and Christological reflection of the 1950s and 1960s, which, once re-considered, allows us to approach *the question of the meaning of Christology* anew.

To re-consider Christology through an underlining Christological thinking and Christological reflection, we will attend to *a particular philosophy of Christology*—to philosophize Christology requires carefully making it clear what the constitutive elements are: the question and the meaning. That means: we must think through what question we wish to pose and what meaningfulness we wish to seek, so that *the question of the meaning of Christology* becomes calibrated to a particular handling of *the problem of the historical Jesus* and a certain conceptualization of the Christ of faith as its own unique "problem." Philosophizing Christology in any substantive way will require, then, situating the question we wish to pose in relation to the meaningfulness we wish to seek, so that what is disclosed—what is laid bare to us—is *a particular philosophy of Christology* that grounds itself fundamentally in terms of the antecedent importance, however focused, of *a particular history of Christology*.

Acknowledgments

A special thanks to James O. Duke and David J. Gouwens, both of whom ongoingly provide inspiration for me and to whom this book is dedicated.

I am always indebted to the past and present mentorship of Stacy Alaimo, David R. Brochman, Warren Carter, Valerie Forstman, Namsoon Kang, Peter Jones, Joretta Marshall, Kevin J. Porter, Masood Raja, Stephen G. Ray Jr., Timothy Richardson, Kenneth Roemer, Allan Saxe, Jacqueline Vanhoutte, Jim Warren, Kathryn Warren, Jeffrey Williams, Newell Williams, and Kenneth W. Williford. Also, I am thankful for Bob Bernard (*in memoriam*).

I am extremely thankful for the following wonderful friendships developed during my time in seminary at Brite Divinity School at Texas Christian University: Sarah Almanza, Margaret Amos Fields, Kristen Baker-Fletcher, Linda Couser Barnette, Cassandra Bering, Kathy Bouchard, Joel Brown, Will Brown, Ernest Carradine, Casey L. Carter, Douglass Anne Cartwright, Amber Piper Churchill, Erin Dickey, Jennifer Dawson, Paul Fucile, Dre Gardner (*in memoriam*), DeSorrow Golden, Eve Fannin Gorrell, Gary F. Green II, Beth Guy, Dawn Hood-Patterson, Jeff Hood, Kate Hogue, Kevin Howe-Hart, Jennie Huang, Jennifer Jacobson, Chancellor Jenkins, Leah Jordan, Winner Laws, Annelies Moeser, Claudia Moreno-Adams, Johnrice Newton, Lucinda Pritchard Hoad, John O'Neal, Rosemary Redmond, Tomeca Richardson, Nathan Russell, Cody Sanders, Regan Doyle Saoirse, David Schones, Ron Serino, Richard Thomas, Anna Troy, Janet Waggoner, Mark Weathers, John Woodard, and Michael Yandell,

Many thanks to my Tarrant County College family of colleague-friends: Rahma Aboutaj, Cindy Allen, Rebecca Balcarcel, Lisa Benedetti, Jim Baxter, Liz Bradley, Angela Chilton, Adrian Cook, George Edwards, Ryan Ferguson, Angela Jackson-Fowler, Paul Frazier, Curtis Fukuchi, Natalie Garcia, Nicole Hall, Scott Heaton, Kim Tapp Jackson, Leslie Genz

Johnson, Liz Lounsbury, Joël Madore, Erin Mahoney-Ross, Jeff Miranda, LeeAnn Olivier, Melissa Perry, Wendi Pierce, Krista Rascoe, Tony Roberts, Carroll Clayton Savant, Joan Shriver, Steve Smiley, Stacy Thorne Stuewe, Cecilia Sublette, Kristi Ramos Toler, Audrey Haferkamp Towns, Zainah Usman, and Michelle York.

Thanks to my family at Northway Christian Church of Dallas, TX: Jennifer G. Austin, Judd Austin, Sarah Talbott Brown, Ted Brown, Rev. John G. Burton, Chrissy B. Cashion, Gail G. Coburn, Roderick Fisher, Tim Gilger, Paula Hammond, Kim Hetzel, Rev. Derry Henry, Rev. Ruby H. Henry, Emily Hohnstein, Karen S. Hohnstein, Roger Hohnstein, Rev. Virzola Law, Shane Mullin, Andrew Reinhart, Kelsey Reinhart, William Schick, Rev. Cheryl Scramuzza, and Rev. Megan Turner.

Lastly, I am extremely thankful for Samantha Woodson (my wife), Shirley J. Woodson (my mother), and Jeanne McKinnis (my mother-in-law).

Introduction: Questions and Meanings

Placing Christology in context requires properly and purposefully situating *the question of the meaning of Christology* historically, so that, when considering what the Christological can be and what the Christological can do, a certain Christological approach can be definitively laid bare. To project Christology in this manner means thinking, first, about what Christology is and what it does traditionally—by tradition, we can certainly trace a history of Christology and Christological thinking to *the question of the meaning of Christology* as it is rooted from the second to fifth centuries C.E., just as much as *the question of the meaning of Christology* finds another origin in the formation of the New Testament canon itself. Yet, when speaking about tradition, what has been formed as the New Testament canon derives, as we know, from a wide and varied collection of texts dating to the first century C.E., which were either included or excluded from what became known as the New Testament canon.

If we are to say, then, that all these texts—both included and excluded—contain a unified understanding of Christology, the larger *question of the meaning of Christology* remains out of reach. In other words, there is no consensus about what Christology is any more than it is possible to conclude what is Christological across all the texts dated—and written—in the first century as secondary reactions to what the historical Jesus was and did, both in terms of personhood and divinity. Yet, what continues to be at the very heart of a narrower *question of the meaning of Christology* would be: what kind of Christological experiences did Jesus's disciples have in response to what the historical Jesus was and did? That question must be inevitably asked. It becomes a question that was certainly asked from the second to fifth centuries C.E., in the formation of the New Testament itself and in the further development of *the question of the meaning of Christology* itself—the bulk of the debates among the Patristics revolve around

1

matters of Christology, as that which is foundational to what it means to do theology proper.

What is theology proper, if it is nothing more than a methodological frame constructed around *the question of the meaning of Christology*? And what is *the question of the meaning of Christology*, if it is answered by what becomes further defined and stratified by doctrine, dogmatics, and canon?

The question of the meaning of Christology, once asked, not only ties the uniquely historical concerns of the writers of texts dating to the first century C.E. to the concerns of church fathers from the second to the fifth centuries C.E., but it also becomes an ongoing problem through the subsequent centuries. The problem of *the question of the meaning of Christology*, as that which theologically informs every era throughout the Medieval period, positions theologians through the early and late Reformation, calibrates the religious thought throughout the Renaissance and throughout the Enlightenment, and even frames what became known as the first quest for the historical Jesus into the nineteenth century with Friedrich Schleiermacher's *Das Leben Jesu* (1832), translated as *The Life of Jesus*, compiled from Schleiermacher's lectures and David F. Strauss's monograph, *Das leben Jesu kritisch bearbeitet* (1835–36), translated as *The Life of Jesus, Critically Examined* in 1846—though Strauss was influenced by Schleiermacher's "life of Jesus" in a way that was also influenced by Hegel, Strauss' take on Schleiermacher was so roundly rejected and attacked by the "Hegelians" led by Bruno Bauer (1809–82) that it led Strauss to defend himself in *Streitschriften zur Verteidigung meiner Schrift über das Leben Jesu und zur Charakteristik der gegenwärtigen Theologie* (1837), later translated as *In Defense of My 'Life of Jesus' Against the Hegelians*.

Given that Schleiermacher (1768–1834) and Strauss (1808–74) are both concerned with "the life of Jesus," and Strauss' "life of Jesus" is intent on directly criticizing Schleiermacher's lectures, these "lives of Jesus" present biographies of Jesus focusing on historical reconstructions of Jesus's life. Nevertheless, it can be argued, these "lives of Jesus" attend to the problem of *the question of the meaning of Christology* as it contributes to a larger Christological tradition.

ALBERT SCHWEITZER

At the turn of the twentieth century, Albert Schweitzer's *Geschichte der Leben-Jesu-Forschung* (1906), which can be rendered literally as "History of the Life of Jesus Research," but translated as *The Quest of the Historical Jesus* in 1910, became a culmination of the first quest for the historical Jesus while

systematically deconstructing *the question of the meaning of Christology*—
Schweitzer's work followed Martin Kähler's *Der sogenannte historische Jesus
und der geschichtliche, biblische Christus* (1892), translated as *The So-Called
Historical Jesus and the Historic Biblical Christ* (1896), while Schweitzer
was followed by Arthur Drews' *Die Christusmythe* (1909), translated as *The
Christ Myth* (1910). The publications of the three— Kähler (1835–1912),
Schweitzer (1875–1965), and Drews (1865–1935)—effectively and collec-
tively brought an end to the first quest for the historical Jesus, which Ben
Witherington notably details in *The Jesus Quest* (1997).[1] This end, as it were,
is brought more conclusively to bear by Schweitzer in the final section of his
The Question of the Historical Jesus entitled "Results"—as a starting point,
Schweitzer exclaims, "there is nothing more negative than the result of the
critical study of the Life of Jesus."[2]

Here, Schweitzer is addressing the inherent problems, in his view, in
the critical studies of Friedrich Schleiermacher's lectures, *Das Leben Jesu*
and David F. Strauss' *Der Christus des Glaubens und der Jesus der Geschichte*
(1865), translated as *The Christ of Faith and the Jesus of History* 1977, as
an explicit critique of Schleiermacher. In light of what Schleiermacher and
Strauss assess as "the life of Jesus," Schweitzer positions himself in direct
opposition to both views of "the life of Jesus," as two individuals, in Schweitzer's words, "are fond of talking about negative theology."[3] As such, with
Schleiermacher and Strauss certainly in mind, Schweitzer argues:

> Modern Lives of Jesus are too general in their scope. They aim at
> influencing, by giving a complete impression of the life of Jesus,
> a whole community. But the historical Jesus, as He is depicted
> in the Gospels, influenced individuals by the individual word.
> They understood Him so far as it was necessary for them to un-
> derstand, without forming any conception of His life as a whole,
> since this[,]in its ultimate aims[,]remained a mystery even for
> the disciples.[4]

Insofar as Schleiermacher and Strauss, for Schweitzer, present "modern
lives of Jesus" that are, in their respective conceptualization of the historical
Jesus, "too general in their scope," *the question of the meaning of Christology*, as Schweitzer sees it, should be predicated on how "the historical Jesus,
as He is depicted in the Gospels, influenced individuals by the individual
word." Schweitzer views Christological ideas, as far as Jesus of Nazareth is

1. Witherington, *Jesus Quest*, 9–13.
2. Schweitzer, *Quest of the Historical Jesus*, 398.
3. Schweitzer, *Quest of the Historical Jesus*, 398.
4. Schweitzer, *Quest of the Historical Jesus*, 398.

concerned, in light of how, to Schweitzer's point, "[the Gospels] understood Him so far as it was necessary for them to understand, without forming any conception of His life as a whole." This brings Schweitzer to propose that *the question of the meaning of Christology* chiefly depends on:

> The Jesus of Nazareth who came forward publicly as the Messiah, who preached the ethic of the Kingdom of God, who founded the Kingdom of Heaven upon earth, and died to give His work its final consecration, never had any existence. He is a figure designed by rationalism, endowed with life by liberalism, and clothed by modern theology in an historical garb.[5]

Schweitzer's suggestion that Jesus the man "never had any existence" is a fundamental stance towards "the historical Jesus," if we are to say that what the notion of "historical Jesus" hopes to conceptualize is a meaning of defining the existence of Jesus along clear, definitive boundaries. These boundaries, according to Schweitzer, define Jesus as "a figure" tethered to rationalism, liberalism, and modern theology—that which designs, endows, and clothes who Jesus was into what Jesus has become is contingent on what Schweitzer calls "historical garb." To be sure, what Schweitzer believes that Schleiermacher and Strauss respectively accomplish with their "life of Jesus" is something that ignores the fact that Jesus "never had any existence," if we are to take heed to how Jesus is "depicted in the Gospels," just as Schweitzer notes, and "influenced individuals by the individual word." The extent to which Schleiermacher and Strauss, for example, focus on "the life of Jesus," as a quest for the historical Jesus, moves away from how Jesus is "depicted in the Gospels" and even further way from how Jesus "influenced individuals by the individual word."

Though Schweitzer is more explicitly confronting Schleiermacher and Strauss on the issue of "the life of Jesus," the whole of the quest for the historical Jesus, to which Schweitzer makes explicit in the subtitle of *The Quest for the Historical Jesus*, begins with Hermann S. Reimarus (1694–1768) in 1778, with the initially-anonymous, posthumous publications of Reimarus' writings, as published by Gotthold E. Lessing (1729–81). Because of this, as Colin Brown notes in *Jesus in European Protestant Thought: 1778–1860* (1985), "it has been customary to date the quest of the historical Jesus" from Reimarus' work.[6] Schweitzer places the ending period of this quest, just as Schweitzer's subtitle defines, to the work of Georg F. E. W. Wrede (1859–1906), Schweitzer's most immediate contemporary. From Reimarus to Wrede, across various iterations of the quest for the historical Jesus, and if

---

5. Schweitzer, *Quest of the Historical Jesus*, 398.

6. Brown, *Jesus in European Protestant Thought*, 1.

we consider this quest as fundamentally oriented towards *the question of the meaning of Christology* as that which is *par excellence*, Schweitzer concludes:

> Whatever the ultimate solution may be, the historical Jesus of whom the criticism of the future, taking as its starting point the problems which have been recognised and admitted, will draw the portrait, can never render modern theology the services which it claimed from its own half-historical, half-modern, Jesus.[7]

As Schweitzer sees it, whatever can be concluded from any conceptualization of the historical Jesus remains nothing more than a conceptualization, due to "the problems which have been recognised and admitted." Essentially, the manner with which the conceptualization of the historical Jesus is intent on, Schweitzer finds, "draw[ing] the portrait" becomes "the criticism of the future." In this sense, what Schweitzer suggests is that, when theologizing about the historical Jesus as fundamental—even substantive or circumstantial—to how we approach *the question of the meaning of Christology*, such a conflation between what remains unknowable and what is experiential, to Schweitzer's point, "can never render modern theology the services which it claimed from its own half-historical, half-modern, Jesus." In this regard, for the sake of what can be rendered as modern theology, Schweitzer reaches the following point:

> But the truth is, it is not Jesus as historically known, but Jesus as spiritually arisen within men, who is significant for our time and can help it. Not the historical Jesus, but the spirit which goes forth from Him and in the spirits of men strives for new influence and rule, is that which overcomes the world.[8]

This point is definitively made by Schweitzer, insofar as he provides a closed-ended proposition to what can be known and what can be experienced in terms of Jesus. Not only do we see Schweitzer concede to the fact that "Jesus as historically known" is insignificant "for our time," but it becomes apparent that the larger, more important fact that "Jesus as spiritually arisen within men" is what Schweitzer, in so many words, envisions as that which must be at the heart of *the question of the meaning of Christology*. For Schweitzer, what matters to the very task and method undergirding *the question of the meaning of Christology* is "not the historical Jesus," Schweitzer writes, "but the spirit which goes forth from Him and in the spirits of men."

---

7. Schweitzer, *Quest of the Historical Jesus*, 398.
8. Schweitzer, *Quest of the Historical Jesus*, 401.

The conclusion Schweitzer reaches in the "Results" section at the very end of *The Quest for the Historical Jesus* has been well-documented as summarily bringing an end to the history of the scholarly quest into the historical Jesus up to the time of Schweitzer's writing. So much is true, and much credit can be given to Schweitzer for not only re-conceptualizing about 125 years of thinking about the historical Jesus since Reimarus, but also for re-orienting how *the question of the meaning of Christology* can be handled after Schweitzer.

RUDOLF BULTMANN AND AFTER

What follows Schweitzer, it has been traditionally argued—what remains fundamentally attuned to *the question of the meaning of Christology*—was roughly a fifty-year period without a definitive quest for the historical Jesus.[9] Without an emphasis on the historical Jesus, *the question of the meaning of Christology* oriented itself towards the philosophical—what arises, here, is the extent that the philosophical interfaces with the theological comportment of Christology in a way that allows the Christological, in itself, to become a philosophical *question of the meaning of Christology*, particularly through the philosophical-theological work of Rudolf Bultmann (1884–1976).

In the post-"first quest" period, Bultmann published the following texts: *Jesus* (1926), translated as *Jesus and the Word* in 1934, *Neues Testament und Mythologie* (1941), translated in 1953 as part of the *Kerygma and Myth* collection, *Das Evangelium des Johannes* (1941), translated in 1971 as *The Gospel of John*, and *Theologie des Neuen Testaments* (1948), translated in 1961 as *Theology of the New Testament*. Collectively, these texts from Bultmann contribute to a view of theologizing that served as a paradigm shift in how to approach New Testament studies, either from the standpoint of a biblical scholar or a theologian. To be sure, much has been said about Bultmann's significance, not just by those that contemporaneously witnessed Bultmann's "demythologizing" uproot what it meant to do theology after Schweitzer, but also now in the ongoing state of Bultmannian studies. Interest in what Bultmann does to theologizing and means to theology has not waned, now two decades into the twenty-first century, which is, perhaps, exemplified by the 2012 appearance in English of the most definitive biography of Bultmann by Konrad Hammann. With this, there is a continuous strong of English editions of Bultmann's work, all of which have remained

---

9. Witherington, *Jesus Quest*, 9–13.

in print in English, since the first English translation of Bultmann's *Jesus* (1926) as *Jesus and the Word* in 1934.

Whether Bultmann remains in our purview today because of his relationship to Martin Heidegger or to Karl Barth, ongoing work in Heideggerian scholarship and the same in Barthian studies sustains efforts to understand, in one sense, what Heidegger means to Bultmann's work, and, in another sense, what Barth means to Bultmann's work. In a certain sense, Bultmann's work, as that which operates at the intersection of some of the philosophical concerns of Heidegger and some of the theological concerns of Barth, espouses a philosophizing to his work without being a philosopher as much as he injects a systematizing to his work without being a systematic theologian.

By employing his demythologizing to the New Testament, Bultmann's approach to *the question of the meaning of Christology* sought to—with the help of Martin Heidegger's influence on Bultmann's thought in the 1920s, while both were professors at the University of Marburg (Heidegger in Marburg's Philosophy Department, and Bultmann in Marburg's Theology Department)[10]—focus on the facts of Jesus's life and crucifixion, rather than what happened over the course of Jesus's life. By way of Heidegger's influences upon him, Bultmann applies what has come to be known as an existential interpretation to New Testament studies—though the term "existential" need only be used as a manner in which meaning allows for meaningfulness, and not necessarily anything associated with "existentialism."[11]

As a disengagement with history, for Bultmann's demythologization project in particular, Bultmann is interested in existentially interpreting the New Testament, in terms of its inherent mythological elements, through an interpretation into the meaning of Being itself. This meaning, as a question, is precisely Heidegger's philosophical approach, but, through Bultmann's theologizing, the meaning of Being becomes the meaning of Faith itself—Christologically speaking, Bultmann's approach to *the question of the meaning of Christology* is with respect to the meaning of kerygma (or proclamation) in the meaning of Christ, instead of any set of facts particular to the historical Jesus.

Chapter 1 will focus on two of Bultmann's doctoral students: Ernst Käsemann and Günther Bornkamm, as representatives of what I wish to

10. I provide a full account of the relationship between Bultmann and Heidegger in *Heideggerian Theologies* (2018).

11. I use "existential' and "existentialism" carefully here, since, by "existential," I am referring to a means or a vehicle with which interpretation takes place and "existentialism" is more concerned with a philosophical movement, to which a wide variety of thinkers, philosophers, and theologians have been subscribed.

present as the first generation of Bultmannians to grapple with *the question of the meaning of Christology* early in the1950s. Even though the two stand, perhaps, in the closest proximity to Bultmann's influences on them, the two are overshadowed as much by Bultmann himself as they are overshadowed by the broader "second quest" that intensifies in the end of the 1950s. Because of this, this chapter will outline Käsemann's and Bornkamm's respective handlings of "the problem of the historical Jesus," which, though influenced by Bultmann, diverge down theological paths that allow Käsemann and Bornkamm to attend to their own individual interests with what *the question of the meaning of Christology* is. Though both Käsemann and Bornkamm are not as widely known now, what they mean fundamentally as progenitors of the "second quest" is without question—while they both, to an extent, expand on Bultmann's theologizing beyond the scope of demythologizing, this chapter will show that Käsemann and Bornkamm belong to a community of voices that theologically wrestle with the relationship between Jesus of Nazareth and the Christ of faith, and outline a way to engage in Christological thinking and Christological reflection that is uniquely their own. Insofar as Käsemann and Bornkamm belong to the Bultmann-led "Old Marburgers" group, the two participate in both implicit and explicit dialogues with theological interlocutors deeply invested in making meaning out of the problem of the historical Jesus. Indeed, though Käsemann can be viewed as the more influential theologian, this chapter will place Bornkamm on equal theological footing with Käsemann in terms of how both are concerned with making sense of *the question of the meaning of Christology* with respect to how both conceptualize the problem of the historical Jesus.

In Chapter 2, I will broaden the Bultmannian circle beyond Käsemann and Bornkamm to include six theologians that not only expand on *the question of the meaning of Christology*, but also expand the problem of the historical Jesus. Here, I will present the Christological thinking and Christological reflection of James M. Robinson, Erich Dinkler, Ernst Fuchs, Herbert Braun, Oscar Cullmann and Hans Conzelmann. Given that Robinson (American) and Cullmann (French) hail from different traditions than the German theological traditions of the other four, I have collected them within a loosely-tied generation of theologians that are predominantly influenced by Bultmann. Even though Fuchs is the only one of the six that was actually a doctoral student of Bultmann's, with Dinkler having attended Bultmann's classes at Marburg, only Fuchs and Dinkler belonged to the Bultmann-led "Old Marburgers" group as exemplary Bultmannians—nevertheless, this chapter intends to show that Robinson, Braun, Cullmann, and Conzelmann all actively engage in dialogues with the Bultmannian world, in ways that bring them in close proximity to the Christological thinking and Christological reflection that preoccupy Bultmannians, even if, generationally, the four are a level removed from Bultmann himself. What, ultimately, ties the six together, this chapter outlines, is how each carefully attends to *the question of the meaning of Christology* by posing specific questions to and seeking specific meaningfulness in Christology. What begins this chapter is an acknowledgment of Robinson's codifying of the problem of the historical Jesus and programming of *the question of the meaning of Christology* with respect to, Robinson defines in *A New Quest of the Historical Jesus* (1959), "the 'Bultmannian' epoch in German theology"[12] and an underlying "'post-Bultmannian' quest of the historical Jesus."[13] What this chapter shows, then, is that, Robinson's significance is not just in providing a summarization of the state of how Bultmann and Bultmannians have approached the problem of the historical Jesus up to the close of the 1950s, but also in providing a framework that projects the concerns of the 1950s into the 1960s—by beginning with Robinson, this chapter demonstrates what is significant about Dinkler, Fuchs, Braun, Cullmann, and Conzelmann, as embodying what Robinson operationalizes as a "new quest" of the historical Jesus.

Chapter 3 further expands on the community of voices contributing to the problem of the historical Jesus and the underlying *question of the meaning of Christology* by attending to the Christological thinking and Christological reflection of lesser-known interlocutors with more well-known Bultmannians and other theologians contemporary to the 1950s and 1960s. Though, now, these lesser-known theologians have been overshadowed by more well-known theologians of the day, each remains relevant to the very state of the problem of the historical Jesus as a "new quest" outlined by Robinson. Yet, not all of the theologians presented in this chapter are in the purview of Robinson's *A New Quest of the Historical Jesus*—for reasons that will be clearer later in Chapter 3—even though they all populate an ever-expanding, though concentrated commitment to making sense out of the problem of the historical Jesus for *the question of the meaning of Christology*. Of the eleven theologians offered in this chapter, which include the following: Nils A. Dahl, Ernst Heitsch, Peter Biehl, Hermann Diem, Walter Grundmann, Ethelbert Stauffer, Franz Mussner, Johannes Schneider, Ernst Barnikol, Béda Rigaux, and Joachim Jeremias, only about half are cited by Robinson in his programmatic study—still, all, more or less, embark on different theologizing and Christological work by engaging with the problem of the historical Jesus and, in turn, either directly or indirectly engaging

---

12. Robinson, *New Quest of the Historical Jesus*, 9–11.
13. Robinson, *New Quest of the Historical Jesus*, 12–19.

with Bultmann. All are German theologians, with the exception of Dahl (Norwegian) and Rigaux (Belgian), though all fundamentally engage with a German school of theology revolving around Bultmann's influences. This chapter provides four conceptual pairings: Heitsch and Biehl (both of which are mentioned by Robinson), Grundmann and Stauffer (with only Stauffer mentioned by Robinson), Mussner and Schneider, and Barnikol and Rigaux, as a means of juxtaposing approaches to the problem of the historical Jesus and *the question of the meaning of Christology.*

Chapter 4 concentrates on three theologians: Gerhard Ebeling, Friedrich Gogarten, and Paul Althaus by assessing how they each engage in Christological thinking and Christological reflection contextualized with or against Bultmann. These three represent different versions of what a "Bultmannian" is, insofar as each is influenced by Bultmann's theologizing and use that influence to situate themselves toward the problem of the historical Jesus. In this sense, what this chapter illustrates, essentially, is the extent that Bultmann shapes how Ebeling, Gogarten, and Althaus conceive of what the "problem" is in the problem of the historical Jesus and, in turn, what it takes to pose the question to and seek the meaningfulness of Christology, as that which is grounded by *the question of the meaning of Christology.* Bultmann remains the connection point for each of these three theologians, even though the task and scope of how each theologizes diverge down different Christological paths. Similarly, as in Chapter 2, these three theologians are cast in terms of embodying a generation of post-Bultmann theologians, when considering that Bultmann plays such a key role in the heart of how each approaches what is theologically significant and historically relevant to what it means to do Christology.

Chapter 5 explores the development of *the question of the meaning of Christology* mainly from the 1970s up to the present day by carefully working through the contributions of eleven individuals that can be considered either as theologians, philosophers or biblical scholars that pose the question to and seek the meaningfulness of Christology. These eleven figures include: Ferdinand Hahn, Reginald H. Fuller, Fred B. Craddock, Leonardo Boff, Helmut Thielicke, Edward Schillebeeckx, John B. Cobb Jr., Dominic Crossan, N. T. Wright, Ben Witherington, and Craig Keener. Though this chapter comports each individual to *the question of the meaning of Christology,* it does so by acknowledging a shift in the development of Christological thinking and Christological reflection after what has been called "the second quest" of the historical Jesus. Here, this chapter considers the growth and codification of another quest that becomes known as a "third quest," which intensifies by the 1980s with the forming of various groups working through the problem of the historical Jesus. What this chapter illustrates is how *the question of the meaning of Christology* is laid bare, indeed, both within and beyond the concerns of a "third quest," such that the community of voices that comprise this chapter are echoing the similar concerns of Bultmannians in the 1950s.

Chapter 6 constructs *the question of the meaning of Christology* philosophically by framing it as fundamentally understandable within the task and scope of a philosophy of love. Here, this chapter outlines the questions and concerns of a philosophy of love through Jacques Derrida. Making use of an interview Derrida gives as part of the 2002 documentary, *Derrida*, this chapter presents the posing of the question to and the seeking of the meaningfulness of love as that which conceptualizes what is at stake with *the question of the meaning of Christology*, also predicated on how a question is posed and how a meaningfulness is sought. To understand Derrida's approach to the question of the meaning of love, as it comes to Derrida late in life, this chapter implies a deconstructive approach to love that methodologically mirrors Bultmann's demythologization, so that Derrida's approach to the meaning of love is grounded on demythologizing it. This chapter, then, provides a background of key aspects of Derrida's early thought, which comports Derrida's question to and meaningfulness of love to what can be construed as the question to and meaningfulness of Christology—what results is a "Christology of love." In this way, this chapter merges what is important to a philosophy of love with what is important to a philosophy of Christology, by focusing on constitutive elements that attend to the relationship between Jesus of Nazareth and the Christ of faith, the "problem" at the theological core of the problem of the historical Jesus, and what *the question of the meaning of Christology* is and does. Taken together, Derrida, though philosophizing without any concern for theological comportment, is presented as a contributor to *the question of the meaning of Christology* that philosophizes the posing of the question to and the seeking of the meaningfulness of Christology.

Chapter 1

The Question of the Meaning of Christology (I)

Given that Bultmann has become a representative figure in what Alister Mc-Grath refers to as a "disengagement with history" in *The Making of Modern German Christology* (originally published in 1994), this disengagement is the methodological heart of Bultmann's demythologization project. What arises from this disengagement is a de-historicization of what it means to Christology—through Bultmann, *the question of the meaning of Christology* is detached from historicization through an existentialist interpretation applied to the theologizing of the New Testament. In the wake of a "collapse" in the quest for the historical Jesus proclaimed by Schweitzer, Gerd Theissen and Annette Merz, in *Der historische Jesus: Ein Lehrbuch* (1996), translated as the *Historical Jesus: A Comprehensive Guide* in 1998, assert that "the scepticism provoked by these insights was partly absorbed and partly intensified programmatically by [the] theological motives" of Bultmann.[1] To this end, as a consequence of Bultmann, Theissen and Merz write:

> Whereas the (old) liberal quest of the historical Jesus played
> him off against the proclamation of the church, "the new
> quest," which developed in the circle of Bultmann pupils, began
> from the kerygmatic Christ and asked whether his exaltation,

---

1. Theissen and Merz, *Historical Jesus*, 6.

grounded in the cross and resurrection, has any "support" in the proclamation of Jesus before Easter.[2]

Here, Theissen and Merz highlight the difference between what "the quest" was up to Bultmann and how the "new quest" comports itself in a trajectory moving beyond Bultmann. In this, there is also a difference—of both theological and philosophical consequence—in what question is posed towards and what meaning is made in Christology, so that how Bultmann engages in Christological reflection becomes a fundamentally different Christological reflection for "the circle of Bultmann pupils."

Two of these "Bultmann pupils" that are foundational to what the question of the meaning of Christology becomes are: Ernst Käsemann and Günther Bornkamm—for Käsemann and Bornkamm, Theissen and Merz find that "the quest for pre-Easter support for the kerygma of Christ is independent of whether Jesus used [C]hristological titles."[3] Theissen and Merz suggest that "this claim is implicit in [Jesus'] conduct and his proclamation."[4] This is, of course, part and parcel of a Christological reflection, though the conclusions Käsemann and Bornkamm reach are calibrated differently theologically and, by extension, philosophically. In one sense, Theissen and Merz view Käsemann's Christological reflection "as Jesus' criticism of the Law, which puts in question the foundations of all ancient religion, [as] a 'call of freedom.'"[5] In another sense, Theissen and Merz view Bornkamm's Christological reflection "as the immediacy of Jesus by which he is distinguished from the apocalyptic and casuistry of his environment."[6] Together, Käsemann and Bornkamm contribute to a specific post-Bultmannian approach to *the question of the meaning of Christology* as a theological starting point that stands contextually closest to Bultmann and become, then, two essential voices in what it means to do Christology.

ERNST KÄSEMANN

As Bultmann's doctoral student at Marburg, Ernst Käsemann (1906–98), who was "from the very beginning [the] most independent of all of Bultmann's students"[7]—having completed his dissertation in 1931 on Pauline

---

2. Theissen and Merz, *Historical Jesus*, 7.

3. Theissen and Merz, *Historical Jesus*, 8.

4. Theissen and Merz, *Historical Jesus*, 8.

5. Theissen and Merz, *Historical Jesus*, 8.

6. Theissen and Merz, *Historical Jesus*, 8.

7. Hammann, *Rudolf Bultmann*, 248.

ecclesiology[8] entitled *"Leib und Leib Christi"*[9] translated as "Body and Christ's Body" (eventually published in 1937), with his habilitation thesis completed in 1939 on the Epistle to the Hebrews (translated as *The Wandering People of God* in 1984)—initiated what eventually became known as a second quest for the historical Jesus in 1951 with Käsemann's inaugural lecture as professor of New Testament at the University of Göttingen.[10] In 1953, as Gregory W. Dawes notes, Käsemann delivered the lecture to a "reunion of former students of the Marburg theological faculty."[11] This lecture was subsequently published in 1954 as *"Das Problem des historischen Jesus"* or "The Problem of the Historical Jesus" (appearing in *Exegetische Versuche und Besinnungen,* published in 1960,[12] selectively collected in *Essays on New Testament Themes* in 1964)—Käsemann's position differed from Bultmann's, in the sense that Bultmann emphasized a deeply theological interpretation of the New Testament over a historical one, while Käsemann maintained a historical interpretation, believing that the texts of the New Testament provide historical information from which a historical Jesus can be meaningfully constructed.

What resulted in Käsemann's stance on the meaningfulness of the historical Jesus over and against Bultmann's was a "new quest" for the historical Jesus, as Witherington acknowledges.[13] Essentially, to Dawes' point, Käsemann is "responsible for re-opening the question."[14] Though that question, as that which undergirds a "new quest," as Käsemann envisions it, owes its conceptualization to Bultmann's influences on Käsemann, the manner with which Käsemann approaches and articulates *the question of the meaning of Christology* attempts to go further than Käsemann's Bultmannian

---

8. Konrad Hammann tells us that Käsemann's dissertation was recommended by Bultmann for publication in 1932 as part of a series devoted to the "Contributions of Historical Theology." The publisher rejected Käsemann's dissertation for publication not because of the merit of the work, but because the publisher, as Hammann explains, did not normally accept dissertations for publication and held itself to that standard, despite of Bultmann's influence, reputation, and recommendation. Hammann, *Rudolf Bultmann,* 228.

9. Hammann, *Rudolf Bultmann,* 248; Käsemann, *New Testament Questions of Today,* x.

10. This inaugural lecture in 1951 also "addressed the Johannine ethos." As such, though the lecture, more generally, attends to the problem of the historical Jesus, it also attends a problem inherent in the Gospel of John. See "Foreword. Käsemann, *The Testament of Jesus,* xxi.

11. Dawes, *Historical Jesus Question,* 298.

12. This 1960 text is "Band 1," which is the first of two volumes. See the copyright page in the English translation.

13. Witherington, *Jesus Quest,* 9–13.

14. Dawes, *Historical Jesus Quest,* 276.

influences. We find, at the opening of his "The Problem of the Historical Jesus," Käsemann assessing "the present position" in the ongoing discussion about the historical Jesus in the following way:

> It is one of the marks of the upheaval in German work on the New Testament in this last generation that the old question about the Jesus of history has receded rather noticeably into the background. And yet, for about two hundred years before that, the advance of our discipline had been set in motion, impelled on its way[,] and determined in its very essence by this same question.[15]

What Käsemann is undoubtedly wrestling with is *the question of the meaning of Christology*, as that which has become "the old question about the Jesus history." More importantly, Käsemann is grappling with Bultmann's own handling of *the question of the meaning of Christology* in such that way all that Käsemann wishes to render Christologically significance in his Christological reflection "has receded rather noticeably into the background."

By carefully working through his Bultmannian influences such that he is able to more concretely bring *the question of the meaning of Christology* "rather noticeably" to the foreground, Käsemann cites two problems he describes as "the historical element in the Gospels"[16] and the "historification in our Gospels."[17] This follows with Käsemann's considerations of "the significance of the historical element in our Gospel,"[18] then "the embarrassment of historical criticism in the face of our problem,"[19] and finally, "the distinctive element in the mission of Jesus."[20] All things considered, Käsemann comes to this conclusion near the end of his essay: "the question of the historical Jesus is, in its legitimate form, the question of the continuity of the Gospel within the discontinuity of the times and within the variation of the kerygma."[21] This is, at a certain level, a disagreement with Bultmann's notion of kerygma, but, on another level, it becomes Käsemann's own take on and advancement of what kerygma and does, as that which unfolds in "variation." That variation is pivotal for Käsemann's theologizing, particularly in terms of what concretely connects "the discontinuity of the times" with the "continuity of the Gospel"—the latter predicates itself "within" the

---

15. Käsemann, "Problem of the Historical Jesus," 15.
16. Käsemann, "Problem of the Historical Jesus," 18–24.
17. Käsemann, "Problem of the Historical Jesus," 24–29.
18. Käsemann, "Problem of the Historical Jesus," 30–34.
19. Käsemann, "Problem of the Historical Jesus," 34–37.
20. Käsemann, "Problem of the Historical Jesus," 37–45.
21. Käsemann, "Problem of the Historical Jesus," 46.

former, insofar as the former, as a question, is predicated on "the question of the historical Jesus." How Käsemann calibrates and explicates what occurs "within the variation of the kerygma"—and attunes this to *the question of the meaning of Christology*—is through the relationship between "the times" and "the Gospel"—that relationship, as Käsemann sees it, is committed to the understanding of the following:

> The Gospel is tied to [the historical Jesus], who, both before and after Easter, revealed himself to his own as the Lord, by setting them before the God who is near to them and thus translating them into the freedom and responsibility of faith.[22]

Here, Käsemann's notion of "freedom and responsibility of faith" becomes eventually articulated with an emphasis on freedom itself in *Der Ruf der Freiheit* (1968), translated as *Jesus Means Freedom* in 1969. In this sense, Käsemann construes his question of the historical Jesus as that which arises through "the conflict over the challenge of freedom [and] runs all through the church's history."[23] As a result, when speaking about *the question of the meaning of Christology*, as something that is oriented towards and seeks to confront "the conflict over the challenge of freedom," what is questioned and what is made meaningful about Christology, if I made repurpose Käsemann's point, "has constantly to be taken up again in every generation and in every Christian life."[24] To the extent that *the question of the meaning of Christology* is rooted in *Jesus Means Freedom*, it allows Käsemann to come to the following in full measure: "I see the whole of the New Testament as involving the cause of Christian freedom."[25]

The path that Käsemann traverses, then, from 1953 to 1968,[26] includes frequent work in Pauline studies, such as "*Gottesgerechtigkeit hei Paulus*" (1961), translated as "God's Righteousness in Paul" in 1965 as part of the collection, *The Bultmann School of Biblical Interpretation: New Directions?*

---

22. Käsemann, "Problem of the Historical Jesus," 46.

23. Käsemann, *Jesus Means Freedom*, 8.

24. Käsemann, *Jesus Means Freedom*, 8.

25. Käsemann, *Jesus Means Freedom*, 9

26. What can be added to this period, which would revise the beginning marker to 1950, is Käsemann's "*Kritische Analyse von Phil. 2, 5–11*" (1950), translated as "A Critical Analysis of Philippians 2:5–11" in the collection, *God and Christ: Existence and Province* (1968). In it, Käsemann takes care to analyze the term "in Christ," arriving at the notion that such a term presents an understanding of "the existence of the new man." When evoking "in Christ," it speaks to, in Käsemann's view, situating oneself "into obedience, into the freedom of the saved." Käsemann, "A Critical Analysis of Philippians 2:5–11," 87.

(1965),[27] and four Paul-focused lectures delivered from 1965 to 1966, as well as an undelivered lecture dated to 1967, all of which are included in *Paulinische Perspektiven* (1969), translated as *Perspectives on Paul* in 1971. As with two essays included in the collection, Apocalypticism (1969): *"Die Anfänge christlicher Theologie,"* delivered as a paper in 1960, translated as "The Beginnings of Christian Theology"[28] and *"Zum Thema der urchristlichen Apokalyptik,"* delivered as a lecture in 1962, translated as "On the Topic of Primitive Christian Apocalyptic"[29]—both pieces, generally speaking, wrestle with Käsemann's conceptualization of the relationship between primitive Christian history and the development of Christian theology. Even so, in the second of the two pieces, Käsemann's arrival at the conclusion that "mission, the freedom of the Christian church, faith under trial, [are] the different aspects of the *regnum Christi*"[30] directly speaks to Käsemann's concerns with how what I have called *the question of the meaning of Christology* becomes fundamental to Käsemann's call for a "new quest."

Yet, Käsemann wrestles with what the call for a "new quest" means and how theologizing is laid bare in what meaning can be made out of Christology. What is, for Käsemann, a problem is how one theologizes Christological matters, which are undoubtedly at the heart of the general questions Käsemann poses in "The Beginnings of Christian Theology" and "On the Topic of Primitive Christian Apocalyptic" and the more specific Pauline questions disclosed in "God's Righteousness in Paul." While the first two appear in the collection, *The Bultmann School of Biblical Interpretation: New Directions?* and the third appears in *Perspectives on Paul,* all three are re-produced in Käsemann's *Exegetische Versuche und Besinnungen* (1965),[31] selectively collected in *New Testament Questions of Today* in 1969.

One can conclude from the reproduction of "The Beginnings of Christian Theology" and "On the Topic of Primitive Christian Apocalyptic" in the English-translated collections of *Essays on New Testament Themes* and *New Testament Questions of Today* that the two texts are pivotal to Käsemann's overall theologizing and especially crucial to the manner by which we can tease out of Käsemann's theologizing *the question of the meaning of Christology.* In addition to these two texts, two others included in the *New Testament Questions of Today* provide a more complete picture of

27. Käsemann, "God's Righteousness in Paul," 100–110.

28. Käsemann, "Beginnings of Christian Theology," 17–46.

29. Käsemann, "On the Topic of Primitive Christian Apocalyptic," 99–133.

30. Käsemann, "On the Topic of Primitive Christian Apocalyptic," 133.

31. This 1965 text is the second edition of "Band 2," which is the second of two volumes. See copyright page for the English translation.

Käsemann's Christological reflection: "*Neutestamentliche Fragen von Heute*" (1957), translated as "New Testament Questions of Today" and "*Sackgassen im Streit um den historischen Jesus*" (previously unpublished and undated), translated as "Blind Alleys in the 'Jesus of History' Controversy." These four texts, then—as well as the whole *New Testament Questions of Today* volume—provide an even broader picture of Käsemann's approach to and articulation of *the question of the meaning of Christology*. To be sure, in the Preface to *New Testament Questions of Today*, when Käsemann explains that "[his] labours in these essays are concerned with the multiplicity and range of New Testament proclamation,"[32] there is also a multiplicity and range to the four texts I have pointed out. If we can say that this underlining multiplicity and range can be thematically expressed in *the question of the meaning of Christology*, we find, too, that Käsemann's Preface acknowledges his role in the "new quest" movement. To this, with Bultmann's influences on Käsemann, what Käsemann reminds us is, given what the "new quest" initiated in 1951 proposes, that "controversy seems to me most meaningful when carried on with the strongest protagonist available and with one's closest intimates."[33] If Bultmann is "the strongest protagonist available" and Bultmann's students are Käsemann's "closest intimates," and what remains, ultimately, at stake is *the question of the meaning of Christology*, the way the question is posed and the way its meaningfulness is sought is determined by the self-determining effects of Christological reflection. It is out of this self-determination at the heart of what Christological reflections determines that a disagreement arises between Bultmann as "the strongest protagonist available" and Bultmann's students as Käsemann's "closest intimates," but also between Käsemann and Käsemann's "closest intimates," which Käsemann is able to survey in this way:

> Disagreement is in this case the outward form of gratitude in the critical field, and is primarily designed to indicate those who must at all costs be heard and heeded. I do not really mind what effect it has on others, unless it is to drive them likewise to critical thought. There can, of course, be no true fellowship without the tensions and agonizings which are the inevitable price of freedom in human relationships.[34]

Out of the disagreement with *the question of the meaning of Christology* at the juncture of what defines and is defined by Christological reflection, what becomes all the more evident is what fundamentally grounds the "new

32. Käsemann, *New Testament Questions of Today*, ix.

33. Käsemann, *New Testament Questions of Today*, ix.

34. Käsemann, *New Testament Questions of Today*, ix.

quest." It is through this way that, as Käsemann surmises, different variations on *the question of the meaning of Christology* and different manners with which Christological reflection takes place, such that these differences, as those that emanate from a theological commonplace—from this situational theologizing, to Käsemann's point, something must "drive them likewise to critical thought." It is from "the tensions and agonizings," if I may re-appropriate Käsemann's words, that Käsemann eventually navigates how he poses the question to and how he seeks the meaningfulness of Christology towards a Christological reflection that matures with complexity by "New Testament Questions of Today."

"New Testament Questions of Today," Käsemann informs us, was originally dedicated to Friedrich Gogarten on the occasion of Gogarten's seventieth birthday in 1957. This dedication is significant for two reasons, when considering the dating along two fronts of textual transmission. First, Käsemann's text follows up on Gogarten's *Entmhyhologisierung und Kirche* originally published in 1953 and translated as *Demythologizing and History* in 1955, whereby Käsemann situates himself as presenting a dedication in hindsight to Gogarten's work. In another sense, though, if we think about the second life of the text in the collection that bears its name, Käsemann's text can be seen to foreshadow Gogarten's *Jesus Christus Wende der Welt* originally published in 1967 and coincidently rendered in English to point towards the "basic questions concerning Christology." Whether viewing the implications of Käsemann's text with respect to the former or the latter, it is safe to assume that Käsemann considers Gogarten as someone that is wrestling with the questions concerning the New Testament of the day—for Käsemann, Gogarten is undeniably a representative figure with respect to the endeavors confronting what is being made of the "new quest," as that which concerns itself with *the question of the meaning of Christology*. Käsemann makes this point, indeed, in his first footnote that provides the reader with a contextualization of what "New Testament Questions of Today" offers the reader both as a window into 1957 and the contemporary period of 1965—Käsemann provides the following explanation:

> Even though I should describe the German situation today in considerably different terms, nevertheless the essay delineates in programmatic form the nexus of problems, out of which the investigation that follows have grown during the last decade.[35]

Not only is Käsemann making an account for the particular time in which he writes the essay, but he also recognizes the extent that the concerns,

35. Käsemann, *New Testament Questions of Today*, 1.

questions, and interests from which the essay sprang forth "have grown during the last decade." There is something quite significant in what Käsemann says here, even if it is minimized into a footnote that can be easily passed over. Clearly, Käsemann is speaking about the development of the "new quest" which broadened in scope through the 1950s, perhaps reaching something of an intellectual height sometime around 1957, but it has begun to wane by the reproduction of the essay in 1965. What Käsemann is reminded of, with respect to *the question of the meaning of Christology* in 1957 and what *the question of the meaning of Christology,* becomes in 1965 as "considerably different," even if, Käsemann maintains, "the essay delineates in programmatic form the nexus of problems" which largely remain central to "the German situation [of] today." That situation, of course, is how one asks the question and seeks the meaning necessary for meaningful Christological reflection. For Käsemann, at the very center of this Christological reflection is:

> The theological crisis of which Bultmann's work has enabled us to become freshly aware has been endemic in Protestantism for the last two hundred years. Bultmann the exegete has outlined the dimensions of it, Bultmann the systematic theologian has sought to open up ways by which it may be overcome.[36]

Here, it will prove important to understand what distinction Käsemann makes between "the exegete" and "the systematic theologian," and the extent that either brings different tasks and methods to the investigation into *the question of the meaning of Christology.* In particular, when couching this distinction in what Käsemann understands Bultmann to be, I want to affirm Käsemann's characterization of Bultmann's role as "the exegete," while challenging the notion of Bultmann being "the systematic theologian." While I do not think it is helpful or even reasonable to call Bultmann a systematic theologian, insofar as "the manner in which Bultmann conceptualizes kerygma and the primordiality of being become essential to a brand of New Testament theology that is not necessarily systematic in nature,"[37] I do believe Käsemann makes an excellent point about how Bultmann "has sought to open up ways by which [theological crisis] may be overcome." That theological crisis, of course, is with *the question of the meaning of Christology,* which with Bultmann wrestles more authentically and meaningfully as "the exegete"—similarly, Käsemann, as "the exegete has outlined the dimensions of" *the question of the meaning of Christology* and, just as removed from the

36. Käsemann, *New Testament Questions of Today,* 11.

37. Woodson, *Heideggerian Theologies,* 88.

characterization of being a systematic theologian as Bultmann, I submit, is how Käsemann, too, seeks "to open up ways by which [*the question of the meaning of Christology*] may be overcome."

One way that *the question of the meaning of Christology* manifests itself, as that which is predicated by Christological reflection, is through the problem of the historical Jesus. Yet, Käsemann makes it clear that, even after outlining the dimensions of it and seeking to open up ways by which it may be overcome, Käsemann reflects upon his own approach to *the question of the meaning of Christology* in the following way:

> I am not specially anxious to embark on the problem [. . .] of the historical Jesus and the relation of his proclamation to that of his first disciples. However, we have to postulate that, according to all the indications, violent controversies are to be expected on this point.[38]

The extent that "we have to postulate" *the question of the meaning of Christology*, then, in despite of "violent controversies [that] are to be expected on this point" from Christological epistemologies yielded from Christological reflection, Käsemann believes that this holds true:

> The story of the "quest of the historical Jesus" should really have convinced anyone who is capable of drawing any conclusions at all from so long and laborious a history [. . .] Only the proclamation of Jesus can enable us to encounter the historical Jesus and to comprehend his history. It is therefore meaningful to put this proclamation to the question concerning its relationship to the proclamation of the community.[39]

If, as Käsemann claims, it is "only the proclamation of Jesus [that] can enable us to encounter the historical Jesus and to comprehend his history," such a sentiment comes from Christological reflection and having approached, understood, and articulated *the question of the meaning of Christology* itself. It is the posing of the question to and the seeking of the meaningfulness of Christology that allows Käsemann to conclude, through Christological reflection, that there is meaningfulness in "put[ting] this proclamation to the question concerning [the historical Jesus'] relationship to the proclamation of the community." Given that Christological reflection of this sort is as temporal as it is historical, such that the temporality and historicity with which Käsemann is able to situate himself existentially to the matters of Christology, in terms of what has come before and has yet to come, how Käsemann

---

38. Käsemann, *New Testament Questions of Today*, 11.
39. Käsemann, *New Testament Questions of Today*, 12.

works through *the question of the meaning of Christology* is based on a contemporary existentializing—this is articulated by Käsemann, I submit, at the very end of "New Testament Questions of Today," as: "it is precisely in the open state of all the fundamental questions today that I should myself see the characteristic mark and the promise of our situation."[40]

What follows "New Testament Questions of Today" in the collection of the same name is "*Sackgassen im Streit um den historischen Jesus*," translated as "Blind Alleys in the 'Jesus of History' Controversy." While Käsemann makes it clear that the former text is dated to 1957, Käsemann, curiously, does not provide a date for the latter—all that Käsemann notes is that "Blind Alleys in the 'Jesus of History' Controversy" is an unpublished lecture.[41] Though this undated and previously unpublished lecture is related to the "New Testament Questions of Today" text, it remains difficult to determine, when viewed at face value, if the undated and previously unpublished lecture was influenced by or influenced the "New Testament Questions of Today" text—though it is apparent that the undated and previously unpublished lecture was actually delivered at some point in time, oddly enough, Käsemann does not make this explicit. Not only does this lack of dating make the "Blind Alleys in the 'Jesus of History' Controversy" text stand out in the *New Testament Questions of Today* collection—as the only one without specific dating—but the text also stands out in length at 43 pages, as the longest text included in the *New Testament Questions of Today* collection.

What remains significant about the "Blind Alleys in the 'Jesus of History' Controversy" text is that, in it, Käsemann contributes to *the question of the meaning of Christology* through a Christological reflection on "Jesus of History." From the opening line in the text, Käsemann proclaims this:

> Anyone who has followed the debate about the historical Jesus during the last decade must have been astonished or even horrified to observe how, as in a volcanic area, the earth was suddenly everywhere spewing forth fire, smoke and differently-sized masses of lava, where, for a generation past, pleasant gardens had been planted on the slopes of ancient craters.[42]

Though Käsemann appears to be hyperbolic here, he is attempting to characterize what is at stake with *the question of the meaning of Christology* and how, to a certain extent, Christological reflection that poses the question of and seeks the meaningfulness to Christology "must have been astonish[ing] or horrif[ying] to observe." As much as this is Käsemann's own reflection

40. Käsemann, *New Testament Questions of Today*, 22.
41. Käsemann, "Blind Alleys," 23.
42. Käsemann, "Blind Alleys," 23.

about "the debate about the historical Jesus during the last decade"—which, as an admission, possibly allows us to roughly date this text to the 1960s—he recognizes that such a debate has evolved into a broader controversy about what *the question of the meaning of Christology* is, how one is to arrive at it, and why it is immensely important. Calling this debate a controversy in one sense and, in another sense, something of a "volcanic area," Käsemann certainly views what he has awakened into a "new quest" as that which is necessarily. What makes it necessary, I submit, is that it moves beyond Bultmann and out of any Bultmannian view, insofar as Käsemann himself attempts to access what the landscape of *the question of the meaning of Christology* has come to. Käsemann sees this questioning as calling forth and being called forth by a more contemporary Christological reflection. For Käsemann:

> The "new question" only merits being called "new" because the theological relevance of the historical element has become, to a quite unprecedented extent, an acute and decisive problem which no one has really succeeded in mastering.[43]

The relationship between how this "new question" is posed and what is "an acute and decisive problem" that arises from seeking meaningfulness hinges on a Christological reflection that must, in itself, be methodological. In this sense, when considering *the question of the meaning of Christology* and the manner by which it materializes from Christological reflection, Käsemann is aware that some methodology is required, if for no other reason, I submit, than to provide a direction to the task and scope of Christological reflection—a method provides a focused and concentrated means of actually allowing the question of the meaning of Christology to be authentically posed and authentically sought. Yet, even so, Käsemann reminds us that there are always "polemics" at play as "an inevitable concomitant of this method"[44]—these polemics are between opposing ways of questioning and means of seeking Christology, such that, even if we debate *the question of the meaning of Christology* from differing Christological reflections, our polemics, nevertheless, "may well recall us from some blind alleys with which we are threatened."[45] For Käsemann, these "blind alleys" not only threaten the possibility of Christological reflection—its very breadth, very meaningfulness, and very questionability—but they also threaten any possibility of approaching, understanding, and articulating *the question of the meaning of Christology.*

43. Käsemann, "Blind Alleys," 23.
44. Käsemann, "Blind Alleys," 24.
45. Käsemann, "Blind Alleys," 24.

This is Käsemann's warning—the pitfalls of "blind alleys"—not just with respect to how far the "new quest" has gone into the post-Bultmannian era, but also with respect to how far the "new quest" still must go—and though Käsemann situates himself between what has come before him and what lies ahead, he recognizes that "no one has really succeeded in mastering" *the question of the meaning of Christology*. He also recognizes that "any methodology which is not based on rigid principles can only learn from errors committed in the past and see in them ways which it might have taken for itself but which others have explored already."[46] While what he means by "methodology" surely implies that Bultmann's methodology of demythologizing is, to reconsider Käsemann's point, "based on rigid principles," Käsemann tells us, in a rather explicit way, that he wishes *the question of the meaning of Christology* avoids "methodology," insofar as Christological reflection presents a more authentic thinking towards a kind of thought that thinks what is true of, in, and with Christology. It is on this point, as Käsemann thinks the kind of thought necessary to think through *the question of the meaning of Christology* as a "new quest," that Käsemann concludes, through a Christological reflection laid explicitly bare, that "methodology by itself is not sufficient to guarantee the correctness of interpretation and this is true even of the existentialist methodology."[47]

Not only can we view Käsemann's acknowledgement of an "existentialist methodology" as a not-so thinly-veiled reference to Bultmann's theologizing, but we can also view this as implicitly pointing to a larger cognizance of those that even Käsemann sees as comprising of a Bultmannian school of theologizing. More than that, it may be possible to read Käsemann, here, as providing a larger commentary on state of existentialism itself—I am speaking not just about Bultmann's existentialist tendencies in his theologizing of the New Testament, but also about how Heidegger's so-called philosophical existentialist influences serve upon Bultmann, and to whatever extent it may be possible to see in Käsemann a co-critique of Bultmann and Heidegger. This seems certainly plausible given when Käsemann is writing "Blind Alleys in the 'Jesus of History' Controversy" text, if we can say, of course, that there is a strong likelihood that the text can be dated to the 1960s.

Even without what can be dated with specificity, there is little doubt that Käsemann's sentiments towards existentialist methodology can be contextualized alongside not just how the theological landscape begins to shift away from the centrality of Bultmann, but also how the philosophical landscape is similarly shifting away from existentialism's centrality. These

46. Käsemann, "Blind Alleys," 24.
47. Käsemann, "Blind Alleys," 65.

sentiments, of course, initiated by Käsemann's approach to *the question of the meaning of Christology*, as that which resists and eludes what can be guaranteed and deemed correct by so-called existentialist methodology.

It would seem, then, that Käsemann finds "blind alleys" in what existentialist methodology portends to do—both theologically for Bultmann and philosophically towards Heidegger[48]—and is aware that *the question of the meaning of Christology* can be compromised by such a methodology. What is compromised, for Käsemann, is the extent that Christological reflection, in itself, cannot be "guarantee[d] the correctness of interpretation," when what is made meaningful about Christology gathers is meaningfulness through the inadequacy of an "existentialist methodology." Indeed, what concerns Käsemann is how theologizing about the New Testament, particularly for the sake of *the question of the meaning of Christology*, is hampered by an "existentialist methodology"—given that an existentialist methodology is intent on providing a way to interpret meaningfulness, and the extent that Bultmann's demythologizing, as an "existentialist methodology," attempts to interpret meaningfulness in what it means to do Christology, it seems to me that, for Käsemann, whatever meaningfulness can be yielded existentially does not make a sufficient enough account for what is made meaningful through Christological reflection. In effect, if we view what Christologically matters to Käsemann in terms of what unfolds and discloses itself through Christological reflection, it stands to reason why Käsemann considers what unfolds and discloses itself through existentialist methodology—of Bultmann, in particular—is "by itself is not sufficient."

In *The Making of Modern German Christology: 1750–1990* (1994), Alister E. McGrath provides the following context:

> In the aftermath of the Second World War, growing anxieties concerning the reliability of Bultmann's approach were voiced. It seemed to an increasing number of writers, within the fields of both New Testament and dogmatic studies, that Bultmann had merely cut a Gordian knot, without resolving the serious historical issues at stake.[49]

From here, McGrath further contextualizes the following way:

48. I have intentionally used "towards" rather than "for," in order to emphasis that Heidegger was absorbed into what became existentialism and, then, whatever can be meant by "existentialist methodology." Heidegger, himself, resisted this classification, even if, as is customary, to situate what can be meant by "existentialism" to Heidegger's *Being and Time*. Such a situatedness in terms of such a classification must be carefully laid bare, insofar as it is helpful to what influences Heidegger's philosophizing serves on Bultmann's theologizing.

49. McGrath, *Making of Modern German Christology*, 179.

The considerable emphasis given to the kerygma by the Bultmannian school served only to heighten, rather than to resolve,
[Christological] questions. This concern lay behind the criticism
of Bultmann by a cluster of writers [. . .] of Ernst Käsemann,
reflecting new trends in New Testament scholarship, focusing especially on the renewed interest in the "historical Jesus
question."[50]

Here, McGrath—and rightfully so—places Käsemann at the very forefront
of "the renewed interest" towards *the question of the meaning of Christology*.
Indeed, what brings Käsemann to this "renewed interest" is Käsemann's own
Christological reflection that, in itself, hopes "to resolve" what is laid bare
Christologically. In this way, as McGrath describes, Käsemann "reawaken[s]
interest in the historical dimensions of Christology, in response to Bultmann's programme of detachment from the issues of history."[51] Essentially,
Käsemann is concerned with attaching what it means to do Christology to
"issues of history."

While McGrath acknowledges that "the full importance" of Käsemann's lecture on the problem of the historical Jesus—which McGrath dates
to October 1953—is evident "only if it is viewed in the light of the presuppositions and methods of the Bultmannian school up to this point,"[52] McGrath
offers only the briefest survey of Käsemann's significance. An important
part of this significance, for McGrath, rests in the following:

It must be stressed that Käsemann is not suggesting that a new
inquiry should be undertaken concerning the historical Jesus in
order to provide historical legitimation for the *kerygma*, still less
is he suggesting that the discontinuity between the historical Jesus and the proclaimed Christ necessitates the deconstruction
of the latter in terms of the former.[53]

On this point, McGrath continues, "rather, Käsemann is pointing to the
theological assertion of the identity of the earthly Jesus and the exalted
Christ being *historically grounded* in the actions and preaching of Jesus
of Nazareth."[54] Note the emphasis McGrath places on "theological" and
"historically grounded." The relationship, here, between what arises from a
"theological assertion" and what arises from what is "historically grounded"

---

50. McGrath, *Making of Modern German Christology*, 179.

51. McGrath, *Making of Modern German Christology*, 184.

52. McGrath, *Making of Modern German Christology*, 184.

53. McGrath, *Making of Modern German Christology*, 184.

54. McGrath, *Making of Modern German Christology*, 184.

speaks to, I submit, how Käsemann envisions *the question of the meaning of Christology*—it is the extent that Käsemann's "new inquiry," as such, tempers "the identity of the earthly Jesus" with "the exalted Christ," so that one existentializes the other, for the sake of existentializing what it means to engage in Christological reflection in all of its dimensions and complexities. Not only does this allow us to see, in light of McGrath, that Käsemann is not conceiving of a "discontinuity between the historical Jesus and the proclaimed Christ," or even that some kind of deconstruction must take place "of the latter in terms of the former," but it also allows us to see how Käsemann sees an inextricable link between the two—to be sure, this continuity comes by way of Christological reflection, predicated by what is Christologically laid bare by *the question of the meaning of Christology*.

Because there is no true deconstruction here, to McGrath's point, I view Käsemann's engagement in a reconstruction of "the proclaimed Christ" in terms of "the historical Jesus." This reconstruction is constructed with how Käsemann "point[s] to the theological assertion of the identity of the earthly Jesus," insofar Käsemann is also pointing to, in McGrath's words, "the exalted Christ being *historically grounded* in the actions and preaching of Jesus of Nazareth." By attending to both "the identity of the earthly Jesus," as that which is theologically asserted, as well as "the exalted Christ," as that which is historically grounded, both calibrate what *the question of the meaning of Christology* is for Käsemann—nevertheless, Käsemann's use of what matters theologically and what matters historically is carefully measured, to which McGrath agrees, suggesting that:

> Käsemann has no intention of travelling along this historically and theologically discredited route. He insists that our only access to the Jesus of history is through the proclamation of the community of faith. There is no possibility of reconstructing any other "historical Jesus" than that which is presented to us by the *kerygma*. [. . .] A return of history is theologically legitimate, on account of the continuity between the historical Jesus and the Christ of faith.[55]

This idea of "a return to history" heads McGrath's understanding of how Käsemann situates himself theologically to Bultmann, with Bultmann belonging to an understanding rooted in "a disengagement with history."[56] In one sense, as McGrath finds, Käsemann's "return to history" approach to *the question of the meaning of Christology* is fundamentally different from Bultmann's disengagement with history, and, in another sense, at the same

---

55. McGrath, *Making of Modern German Christology*, 185.
56. McGrath, *Making of Modern German Christology*, 154–178.

time, Käsemann positions what he wants to do Christologically in terms of a quest for the historical Jesus in contrast to what the earlier quest a century earlier than Käsemann's intended to do.

Consider how, in the following, McGrath explains the manner with which Bultmann and Käsemann situate themselves:

> It will be clear that the "new quest of the historical Jesus" is qualitatively different from the discredited quest of the nineteenth century [. . .] Where the older quest had assumed that the discontinuity between the historical Jesus and the Christ of faith implied that the latter was potentially a fiction, who required to be reconstructed in the light of objective historical investigation, Käsemann stresses that such reconstruction is neither necessary nor possible.[57]

This notion of the difference between the quests is similarly articulated by Thiessen and Merz, wherein, like Thiessen and Merz, what grounds the quests to *the question of the meaning of Christology* is either viewing a discontinuity or continuity "between the historical Jesus and the Christ of faith." If this fundamental continuity modulates Käsemann's Christological reflection, it stands to reason, then, that, as McGrath explains, "the scene was thus set for an informed return to history as the ultimate foundation of Christology."[58]

With this remaining in Käsemann's purview, the "Blind Alleys in the 'Jesus of History' Controversy" text is clearly Käsemann looking back on and anticipating the future of *the question of the meaning of Christology*. In it, Käsemann ascribes to a task and scope to what can be meant by the "new quest" for the historical Jesus, as that which attends to *the question of the meaning of Christology*. There is little doubt, though unmentioned, that Käsemann is reckoning with, seemingly from the 1960s, how his initiation of the "new quest" gave rise to Günther Bornkamm's *Jesus von Nazareth* (1956)—with Bornkamm (1905–90), like Käsemann, also being one of Bultmann's doctoral students—and James M. Robinson's aptly-titled, *A New Quest for the Historical Jesus* (1959). In close proximity to Bornkamm's and Robinson's respective historical studies, two decidedly and overtly Christological works appeared, focused on *the question of the meaning of Christology* in light of the proclivities of a "new quest" for the historical Jesus: Herbert W. Braun's "The Meaning of New Testament Christology" (finished in June 1956) and Oscar Cullmann's *Die Christologie des Neuen Testaments*, originally published in 1957, with earlier portions delivered in March 1955,

---

57. McGrath, *Making of Modern German Christology*, 185.

58. McGrath, *Making of Modern German Christology*, 187.

and eventually translated as *The Christology of the New Testament* (1959). In a certain sense, Robinson (1924–2016), Braun (1903–91) and Cullmann (1902–99) all expand upon Käsemann's "new quest" for the historical Jesus.

GÜNTHER BORNKAMM

Before considering Robinson's contributions to *the question of the meaning of Christology*, and, still, setting aside, for the moment, what Braun and Cullmann provide in the questioning and meaningfulness of Christology, we shall consider Bornkamm, as an expansion of Käsemann's handling of *the question of the meaning of Christology*—what Bornkamm contributes to the development of *the question of the meaning of Christology* is a Christological reflection that wrestles with how one poses the question of and one seeks the meaning to Christology through the meaningfulness of the problem of the historical Jesus.

Like Käsemann, Bornkamm was a doctoral student of Bultmann's at Marburg—and also like Käsemann, Bornkamm completed his dissertation in 1931, but did so on the apocryphal Acts of Thomas, entitled "*Mythos und Legende*," translated as "Myth and Legend."[59] However, unlike Käsemann, Bornkamm would go on to complete his habilitation thesis at the University of Königsberg, under the direction of Julius Schniewind, "with an investigation of the confession of faith in earliest Christianity."[60] Nevertheless, when comparing Bornkamm to Käsemann, Konrad Hammann explains, in a brief account of Bornkamm, that "in [Bornkamm's] case as well, a lasting friendship with Bultmann developed from having been [Bultmann's] student."[61] Because of this, Bornkamm is part of the same rather small circle of Bultmannians to which Käsemann belongs—in fact, there is no question that Bornkamm is one of Käsemann's "closest intimates" that Käsemann mentions in prefatory matter to Käsemann's *New Testament Questions of Today* collection. Yet, it seems to me, Bornkamm is much more obscure figure within Bultmannian circle of Marburg students—though Bornkamm provides an understanding and use of Bultmann's demythologizing, as that which directly influences Bornkamm as it does Käsemann, Bornkamm's handling of *the question of the meaning of Christology* remains noteworthy.

Bornkamm's most important text, *Jesus von Nazareth* (1956), translated as *Jesus of Nazareth* in 1960, is an excellent starting point to laying bare what *the question of the meaning of Christology* is for Bornkamm. Before

59. Hammann, *Rudolf Bultmann*, 245.
60. Hammann, *Rudolf Bultmann*, 245.
61. Hammann, *Rudolf Bultmann*, 245.

proceeding with *Jesus of Nazareth*, I will begin, however, with a text that predates and anticipates it, as that which sets the stage for Bornkamm's Christological reflection: "End-Expectation and Church in Matthew," which is included in the collection, *Überlieferung und Auslegung im Matthäusevangelium* (1960), translated as *Tradition and Interpretation in Matthew* in 1963. Along with two studies from dissertations submitted to the University of Heidelberg by Bornkamm's doctoral students, Gerhard Barth from 1955 and Heinz Joachim from 1957, Bornkamm informs us in the preface to the collection that, with his "End-Expectation and Church in Matthew" in tow, there is "[a] unity in method of approach and thesis" to the three texts.[62] The three texts, for Bornkamm, speak to "how fruitful and rewarding a careful investigation of Matthew's way of working and his theology can be."[63] Bornkamm's "End-Expectation and Church in Matthew," which appears as three previous versions in 1948, 1954, and 1955[64] before its presentation for inclusion in the *Tradition and Interpretation in Matthew* collection, leads this investigation of Matthew, such that it orients the collection, Bornkamm says:

> On the question at issue, the methods and aim of our enquiries, their relationship to the form-critical research into the Synoptic Gospels, and to the recent investigation into the theology of the historical work of Luke, and the Gospel of Mark.[65]

Yet, another question at issue, as that which fundamentally grounds "form-critical research into the Synoptic Gospels" for Bornkamm, is *the question of the meaning of Christology*, which is more apparent in Bornkamm's text than his two students' respective texts. As much as Bornkamm's "End-Expectation and Church in Matthew" hopes to expand upon the meaningfulness of "form-critical research" to the theologizing of the New Testament—if we see Bornkamm as extending a new direction to Bultmann's work on form criticism, marked by Bultmann's *Die Geschichte der synoptischen Tradition* (1921), translated as *History of the Synoptic Tradition* in 1963, which is the same year as the *Tradition and Interpretation in Matthew* collection appeared in English translation—the second half of Bornkamm's four-part "End-Expectation and Church in Matthew" text devotes itself to

---

62. Bornkamm, "End-Expectation and Church in Matthew," 9.
63. Bornkamm, "End-Expectation and Church in Matthew," 9.
64. Bornkamm, "End-Expectation and Church in Matthew," 9.
65. Bornkamm, "End-Expectation and Church in Matthew," 9.

posing two questions that delineate two meanings for Christology: law[66] and ecclesiology.[67]

In the section entitled "Christology and Law," Bornkamm predicates a Christological reflection on Matthew, in terms of Bornkamm's selection of passages, proposing that:

> All these passages, in which Matthew (to some degree also his sources) interprets theologically the received tradition, aim at the distinction between the earthly lowliness of Jesus and his future appearance in glory for the judgment.[68]

Here, what is notable is Bornkamm's rearticulation of the historical Jesus into "the earthly lowliness of Jesus," which he sees, in terms of what the problem of the historical Jesus is, as a distinction between what can be meaningfully understood about "the earthly lowliness of Jesus" and what can be meaningfully understood about "[Jesus'] future appearance in glory for the judgment." That distinction, for Bornkamm, is the relationship between Christology and law—it is a Christological reflection on the meaningfulness of Christology itself for itself and the meaningfulness of Christology towards the law. The question, as Bornkamm sees it, is not just about what *the question of the meaning of Christology* does for what matters about the historical Jesus for Christ, but it is also about what *the question of the meaning of Christology* does for what matters about Christ for law. To this problem, as that which becomes an underlining projection of *the question of the meaning of Christology*, Bornkamm concludes rather deftly that "the earthly function of Jesus as Messiah—apart from his miracles, to which Matthew, of course, allows considerable space, although they take second place to this teaching [. . .] is above all *interpretation of the law*."[69]

As a means of building on the relationship between Christology and law, such that the way we pose the question to and seek the meaning of Christology traverses through the meaningfulness of law, Bornkamm's Christological reflection is oriented towards ecclesiology in the section entitled "Ecclesiology and Christology"—in it, Bornkamm begins with the following assessment about Matthew: "no other Gospel is so shaped by the thought of the Church as Matthew's, so constructed for use by the Church; for this reason it has exercised, as no other, a normative influence in the later Church."[70] Insofar

---

66. Bornkamm, "End-Expectation and Church in Matthew," 32–38.
67. Bornkamm, "End-Expectation and Church in Matthew," 38–51.
68. Bornkamm, "End-Expectation and Church in Matthew," 35.
69. Bornkamm, "End-Expectation and Church in Matthew," 35.
70. Bornkamm, "End-Expectation and Church in Matthew," 38.

as Bornkamm continues, "statements in which the eschatological self-consciousness of primitive Christianity is expressed run through the whole Gospel," Bornkamm locates the use of terms like ἐκκλησία and βασιλεία—these terms become, for Bornkamm, the centerpieces of a broader ecclesiology to Matthew.[71] What arises from this, Bornkamm explains, is:

> It must be agreed from the beginning that in spite of all these passages only the most meagre beginnings of a real ecclesiology, centred in the Church as an independent, empirically circumscribed entity, are to be found in Matthew's Gospel [nevertheless] there is no similar number of ecclesiological concepts and words corresponding to the wealth of Christological titles and statements.[72]

Insofar as what arises, for Bornkamm, is a "Christology of the Gospel,"[73] how this reconciles with what the Church is with respect to what Jesus is brings Bornkamm to find:

> The Church after Easter with its life and the office of the keys sanctioned by Jesus, is thus subjected to the law of the life and suffering of the earthly Jesus. If the decisions made by the Church are to be valid in the coming judgment it is clear that the forgiving and retaining of sins is thereby placed under the same standard as that of which [. . .] speaks: imitation in suffering and life-devotion.[74]

Bornkamm, then, concludes: "the conception of the Church expressed in [Matthew] 16.17–19 finds its counterpart and basis in the Christology of the context of [Matthew] 16.13–28."[75] This raises questions, of course—all of these questions revolve around *the question of the meaning of Christology.* For Bornkamm:

> All these are questions which can by no means be disposed of wholesale as hopeless and theologically of no consequence, and in a cheap sort of way be sacrificed in the interests of the "kerygma" or the "doctrinal concept" of the Gospel. If we have excluded these questions it is only because the investigation of our problem, which could not be carried through without a

---

71. Bornkamm, "End-Expectation and Church in Matthew," 38.
72. Bornkamm, "End-Expectation and Church in Matthew," 39.
73. Bornkamm, "End-Expectation and Church in Matthew," 39–40.
74. Bornkamm, "End-Expectation and Church in Matthew," 48.
75. Bornkamm, "End-Expectation and Church in Matthew," 49.

deliberate concentration, is also an indispensable presupposition for the answering of those questions.[76]

Though, here, Bornkamm ends "End-Expectation and Church in Matthew," perhaps as a way to allow its Christological reflection to remain open-ended, he immediately follows it—in the *Tradition and Interpretation in Matthew* collection—with very brief, but oddly undated essay, "The Stilling of the Storm in Matthew," which, it seems to me, was written precisely for the *Tradition and Interpretation in Matthew* collection. Even as a transitional piece that allows Bornkamm to move from his study to those of his two students, Bornkamm writes the following:

> It has increasingly become an accepted result of New Testament enquiry and a principle of all Synoptic exegesis that the Gospels must be understood and interpreted in terms of kerygma and not as biographies of Jesus of Nazareth, that they do not fall into any category of the history of ancient literature, but that in content and form as a whole and in matters of detail they are determined and shaped on the basis of faith in Jesus Christ.[77]

Here, this anticipates what *the question of the meaning of Christology* becomes for Bornkamm in his inarguably seminal text, *Jesus of Nazareth*, as that which is ostensibly considered, Michael B. Metts writes of Bornkamm, as the first "full treatment of the historical Jesus" produced by a "New Quest scholar."[78]

Bornkamm's *Jesus von Nazareth* (1956), translated as *Jesus of Nazareth* in 1960, as Helmut Koester details in the 1995 forward to the second English edition of the work, "became the landmark of a new interest in the historical Jesus."[79] Koester's assessment is important, given that, like Bornkamm, Koester was one of Bultmann's doctoral students—Bultmann's last one, in fact, before retiring from Marburg—and because Koester is able to contextualize the significance of *Jesus of Nazareth* against the broader "interest in the historical Jesus," as that which Käsemann initiated. Though Koester positions Bornkamm within a Bultmannian influence and traces that influence ultimately to Schweitzer's "critical assessment of nineteenth-century attempts to reconstruct the life and message of the historical Jesus [that] appeared at the beginning of the twentieth-century,"[80] it is, nonetheless,

76. Bornkamm, "End-Expectation and Church in Matthew," 50.

77. Bornkamm, "Stilling of the Storm in Matthew," 52.

78. Metts, "Neglected Discontinuity Between Early Form Criticism and the New Quest," 82.

79. Koester, "Foreword," 3.

80. Koester, "Foreword," 3.

notable that Koester does not mention Käsemann by name. This is a curious omission. Instead, Koester highlights Robinson's 1959 contribution to
"discuss[ing] programmatically" what Bornkamm's *Jesus of Nazareth* laid
bare and the extent that Robinson reacts to how "[a] new interest in Jesus
was hailed" after the success of Bornkamm's book.[81] What is also laid bare,
I believe, is part of the reason why Koester does not acknowledge Käsemann—Koester's purpose for referring to Robinson, it seems to me, is, once
primarily tying Robinson to the development of the "new quest," to secondarily tying Robinson to the translation of the first English edition of *Jesus of
Nazareth* in 1960, to which Robinson provides a "Translator's Preface."

In doing so, Koester undoubtedly uses Robinson to portray a co-
significance to *Jesus of Nazareth*—on one hand, Bornkamm's book is significant to the origins of the "new quest" in the heart of the 1950s, but, on the
other hand, Bornkamm's book is significant to what Robinson "discuss[es]
programmatically" into his survey of the "new quest" that becomes projected into the 1960s. To both points perhaps, Koester adjudicates the dual
significance of Bornkamm's *Jesus of Nazareth* by proclaiming "Bornkamm's
book about Jesus of Nazareth, however, eschews any and every attempt to
write a 'life' of Jesus."[82] Koester furthers this with:

> The "new quest," as it is represented by this work, did not arise
> from a suddenly awaking, fresh curiosity that wanted to know
> more about the life, consciousness, and personality of the his-
> torical Jesus. What is central for the writing of a biography, and
> what had dominated the original quest for the historical Jesus,
> namely the inquiry into the social and psychological motiva-
> tions of the work, life, and the fate of the historical person, did
> not play any role in the beginning of the quest.[83]

What Koester makes clear in the significance of Bornkamm's *Jesus of Nazareth* for the significance of the "new quest" is that, in my view, Bornkamm
influences just as much as he is influenced by what we call the "new quest."
The movement therein towards how *the question of the meaning of Christology* lends itself to how, to Koester's point, we can "know more about the life,
consciousness, and personality of the historical Jesus." To the extent that
what Bornkamm provides "[does] not arise from a suddenly awaking, fresh
curiosity," Bornkamm's approach to *the question of the meaning of Christology* comes by way of a Christological reflection on the meaningfulness of
the historical Jesus. That meaningfulness, as that which brings us closer to

81. Koester, "Foreword," 3.
82. Koester, "Foreword," 4.
83. Koester, "Foreword," 4.

posing a particular question and seeking a particular meaning, is only hollowed out in approaching the historical Jesus in terms of the interests in the quest that had come before Bornkamm concentrated on a Christological biography, which, as Koester tells us, becomes "namely the inquiry into the social and psychological motivations of the work, life, and the fate of the historical person." Just as Koester explains, "what is central for the writing of a biography [. . .] did not play any role in the beginning of the quest," because Bornkamm—in a position that converges fundamentally with Schweitzer, at least in principle—believes that such a biography of Jesus, *per se*, is remains largely impossible and untenable.

This is so, too, Koester conditions, "even if the Gospels of the New Testament can be understood in some way as biographies."[84] Yet, for Bornkamm, Koester considers," the new quest renounced any biographical interests."[85] In renouncing and resisting "biographical interests," and attuning to *the question of the meaning of Christology* itself, Bornkamm, Koester surmises within the broader concerns of the "new quest" movement, "[is] motivated by a theological question, namely, the search for the historical foundation of the Christian proclamation, the kerygma of the early church."[86] Thusly, Koester concludes:

> Bornkamm's entire effort is born out of a commitment that conjoins critical analysis to the continuing bond that ties a believing community to the origin and ground of its faith. Without this bond, research in the historical Jesus may once more become an exercise in futility. But if this bond is respected, Bornkamm's book remains an example of responsible and possible research in the question of the historical Jesus.[87]

The contextualization of Bornkamm's approach to "responsible and possible research in the question of the historical Jesus" will prove beneficial when considering Bornkamm's handling of *the question of the meaning of Christology* as grounded on "responsible and possible research."

Bornkamm begins his "Author's Preface," dated to June 1956, with the following: "in recent years scholarly treatment of Jesus of Nazareth, his message and history, have become, at least in Germany, increasingly rare."[88] Not only does this, in one sense, serve to situate Bornkamm to the historical treatment of Jesus as a question and meaning that predates Bornkamm,

84. Koester, "Foreword," 4.

85. Koester, "Foreword," 4.

86. Koester, "Foreword," 4.

87. Koester, "Foreword," 4.

88. Bornkamm, *Jesus of Nazareth*, 9.

but he also, in another sense, comports himself to the path that lies ahead, particularly within the German tradition from which Bornkamm hails. To this end, Bornkamm's comportment to *the question of the meaning of Christology* is one that presents a Christological reflection that is modulated by a "scholarly treatment of Jesus of Nazareth, his message and history." As such, Bornkamm asserts:

> This book is intended to inform not only professional theologians on such questions, uncertainties and findings of historical research, but also the laymen who wish, so far as possible, to arrive at an historical understanding of the tradition about Jesus and are not content with edifying or romantic portrayals.[89]

By positioning himself within a discontentment "with edifying or romantic portrayals" of Jesus of Nazareth, what Bornkamm is undoubtedly concerned with is providing an existentialist interpretation of Jesus of Nazareth. Yet, if we can call it an "existentialist interpretation," perhaps tying what Bornkamm wishes to interpret to what Bultmann wishes to interpret, it may be very well likely that even an existentialist interpretation brings forth, in itself, "edifying or romantic portrayals." Because of this, if we pay closer attention to what Bornkamm wishes to make meaningful about Jesus and how that meaningfulness is always oriented towards an authentic and concrete approach to *the question of the meaning of Christology*, it stands to reason that Bornkamm finds "no one is any longer in the position to write a life of Jesus."[90] To this point, Bornkamm concedes:

> This is the scarcely questioned and surprising result today of an enquiry which for almost two hundred years has devoted prodigious and by no means fruitless effort to regain and expound the life of the historical Jesus, freed from all embellishment by dogma and doctrine.[91]

Bornkamm goes on to ask:

> Why have these attempts failed? Perhaps only because it became alarmingly and terrifyingly evident how inevitably each author brought the spirit of his own age into his presentation of the figure of Jesus.[92]

---

89. Bornkamm, *Jesus of Nazareth*, 10.
90. Bornkamm, *Jesus of Nazareth*, 13.
91. Bornkamm, *Jesus of Nazareth*, 13.
92. Bornkamm, *Jesus of Nazareth*, 13.

In combatting this problem, Bornkamm intends to, I submit, attune him-self to *the question of the meaning of Christology* through a Christological reflection, which looks "[. . .] for a genuine, historical enquiry, enabled by a sharper criticism even of the presuppositions and ideals provided by its own age, to start afresh on the old task and to better purpose."[93] Neverthe-less, Bornkamm questions how "to start afresh on the old task" and what can be attained by a "better purpose." Engaged in Christological reflection predicated on what Bornkamm perceives is at stake for Christological ques-tioning, Bornkamm asks:

> Has all the life gone out of research? Does it lack today a sympa-thetic exponent? If that is so we would have reason to speak of a scholarly fade-out, in which research has perhaps found itself the victim of its own hypercriticism. In truth this state of affairs has deeper causes, and compels us to affirm the futility of any renewal of attempts at Lives of Jesus now or in the future.[94]

Though all true—if we place an emphasis on Bornkamm recognition of "the futility of any renewal of attempts at Lives of Jesus"—it seems to me that Bornkamm, by wrestling with *the question of the meaning of Christology* through Christological reflection, wishes to reconceptualize, re-orient, and re-cast what can be made meaningful by presenting a "life of Jesus." The question is: what does this look like, "now or in the future"? If, unlike pre-vious "attempts," Bornkamm maintains the "futility" in previous "attempts at Lives of Jesus," Bornkamm fundamentally holds himself to the existen-tializing sentiment that "because the earthly Jesus is for the Church at the same time the Risen Lord, his word takes on, in the tradition, the features of the present."[95] What "the earthly Jesus" means for "the Church" will re-quire Bornkamm carefully locating what "the earthly Jesus" is and, in turn, what "the Church" is—this will lead Bornkamm, while working through *the question of the meaning of Christology*, to ascertain what role Paul has in Christological reflection.

In two collections, *Das Ende des Gesetzes* (1958) and *Studien zu An-tike und Urchristentum* (1959), which selectively make up, in translation, the collection, *Early Christian Experience* in 1969, Bornkamm develops, through various Pauline studies that ultimately contribute to a theologiz-ing about the New Testament, a connection between Paul and Christ. What results in this, is a Christological reflection that utilizes a Pauline reflec-tion—by theologizing the significance of Pauline texts for what it means to

93. Bornkamm, *Jesus of Nazareth*, 13.

94. Bornkamm, *Jesus of Nazareth*, 13.

95. Bornkamm, *Jesus of Nazareth*, 17.

theologize the New Testament, Bornkamm considers how this significance existentializes *the question of the meaning of Christology*. One text, in particular, "Christ and the World in the Early Christian Message," Bornkamm begins with:

> It is a strange historical juncture that the history of the gospel of Jesus Christ had its beginnings on the soil of the European continent in a place that was also of supreme significance for the history of the Roman Empire and thereby for the history and culture of the West.[96]

Here, through this Christological reflection, predicated on an understanding of what the meaning of historicity is for *the question of the meaning of Christology*, Bornkamm places Paul—from Bornkamm's historicizing of Paul, Bornkamm is able to historicize Christology. Essentially, it is the meaningfulness of Paul to "the history and culture of the West" that calibrates and is calibrated by the meaningfulness of Christology itself. In this sense, for Bornkamm, the posing of the question of and the seeking of the meaning to Christology lays bare, I submit, as Bornkamm tells us, "faith in the lordship of Jesus Christ over the world, established in the resurrection and exaltation, characterizes the course and goal of the Pauline mission."[97]

Insofar as the meaningfulness of Christology affirms "the course and goal of the Pauline mission," Bornkamm concludes, too, that the reverse is true: "Paul must also proclaim the lordship of Jesus Christ."[98] For Bornkamm, then, *the question of the meaning of Christology* can be grounded by as much as it grounds Paul's own Christological reflection—it is through Bornkamm's Christological reflection on Paul's Christological reflection that Bornkamm comes to the following conclusion near the very end of "Christ and the World in the Early Christian Message," ultimately grounded on Paul's epistle to the Romans: "the question whether the gospel of Jesus Christ will stand the test in contrast to this summons of the world and of man and not come to nought is decided for Paul."[99]

Yet, given where Bornkamm concludes in "Christ and the World in the Early Christian Message," Bornkamm complicates the relationship between Paul and Christ in its relation to my overarching *question of the meaning of Christology* in "The Significance of the Historical Jesus for Faith" included in the collection, *Die Frage nach dem historischen Jesus* (1962), translated

---

96. Bornkamm, *Early Christian Experience*, 14.
97. Bornkamm, *Early Christian Experience*, 16.
98. Bornkamm, *Early Christian Experience*, 25.
99. Bornkamm, *Early Christian Experience*, 26.

as *What Can We Know About Jesus?* in 1969. Dated to 1960, and eventually, as explained in the Foreword to the *What Can We Know About Jesus?* collection, "represent[ing] lectures given at a seminar conducted by the Evangelical Academy of Tutzing on the subject of 'Jesus of Nazareth'"[100] in 1961, Bornkamm's "The Significance of the Historical Jesus for Faith" immediately professes a concern with historicity. That history, according to Bornkamm, "is crucial for the very meaning of our [Christological] question and which at the same time assigns a definite standpoint to us who pose this question."[101]

Just as Bornkamm situates "Christ and the World in the Early Christian Message" with respect to the role that history plays in what can be laid bare through Christological reflection about what kind of Christological reflection can be located in Pauline theologizing through his letters, Bornkamm makes the following admission:

> The somewhat surprising and remarkable fact remains that no word is spoken by Paul, by the Epistles to the Hebrews, or, indeed, by any of the New Testament letters, that would identify the Christ here proclaimed with that teacher and prophet from Nazareth [. . .] Conversely, we cannot easily rediscover in the gospels the fulness and variety of the post-resurrection message of redemption.[102]

From such a claim, Bornkamm arrives at what he calls "two heretical possibilities" to which Bornkamm surmises that "throughout the history of the Christian faith" has opposed.[103] Bornkamm explains these "heretical possibilities" as:

> One of these already meets us in primitive Christianity and the early church in the form of a faith in Christ which gave up the earthly historical figure of Jesus and sacrificed it to a Christ myth [. . .] The other [. . .] the earthly historical Jesus alone is representative, while the message of the apostles appears as alien, falsified and distorted.[104]

Here, as Bornkamm sees it, a problem disclosed itself—it is a problem at the juncture of the relationship between "two heretical possibilities." What arises is a problem that which speaks to *the question of the meaning of Christology,*

100. Rieger, "Foreword," 7.

101. Bornkamm, "Significance of the Historical Jesus for Faith," 69.

102. Bornkamm, "Significance of the Historical Jesus for Faith," 70.

103. Bornkamm, "Significance of the Historical Jesus for Faith," 71.

104. Bornkamm, "Significance of the Historical Jesus for Faith," 71.

In Bornkamm's view, "this problem of the historical Jesus represents the question about Jesus as he is made known and presented by the scientific investigation of history alone."[105] If, at the heart of what Bornkamm means by this, there is *the question of the meaning of Christology*, Christological reflection is what allows us to confront Jesus "as he is made known and presented by the scientific investigation of history alone." In doing so, as a means of positioning ourselves closer to *the question of the meaning of Christology*—as a means of posing the necessary question and seeking the necessary meaningfulness—Bornkamm's notion that "we are concerned here not with remnants of the tradition but with Jesus' message and history as a whole and with the understanding of the tradition both in the gospels and in the apostolic testimony"[106] speaks to a Christological understanding that is both an understanding of Jesus and a self-understanding.

Even so, if we approach *the question of the meaning of Christology* in terms of how it modulates the understanding of Jesus with our own self-understanding, the following from Bornkamm holds true:

> Proper understanding does not depend upon whether we are successful in constructing a life of Jesus out of the multitude of reports or a system of doctrine out of all traditional or critically examined words of Jesus [. . .] Jesus is wholly present there and steps forth powerfully from them in his historical originally and uniqueness.[107]

If we see this "proper understanding" as pivotal to one's Christological reflection as that which fundamentally underwrites what *the question of the meaning of Christology* comes to represent, the same can be said of the acknowledgement of "Jesus [being] wholly present there." The means by which "Jesus is wholly present there" points to a thereness to one's Christological reflection, as that which is underwritten by the thereness of *the question of the meaning of Christology*. This thereness, then, both in terms of Bornkamm's notion of "proper understanding" and how "Jesus is wholly present," is framed by what faith is and what faith does. As a result, Bornkamm finds, "for faith[,] everything depends upon the identity between Jesus and the Christ, if it is not to lose itself in reliance upon a mythical figure."[108]

The "Identity between Jesus and the Christ" becomes the means by which we locate our own identity through Christological reflection and

---

105. Bornkamm, "Significance of the Historical Jesus for Faith," 72.

106. Bornkamm, "Significance of the Historical Jesus for Faith," 77.

107. Bornkamm, "Significance of the Historical Jesus for Faith," 81.

108. Bornkamm, "Significance of the Historical Jesus for Faith," 84.

self-understanding, insofar as we see, too, our identity manifested in *the question of the meaning of Christology*. Theologizing about Jesus and theologizing about Christ, in terms of their co-significance, affords us with the existential opportunity to develop a Christological identity through how we interpret the meaningfulness of how history has come to bear on us and how we, in turn, allow history to be laid bear to our posterity. In this, what it means to engage in Christological reflection is always-already an engagement with our historicity, such that history informs what *the question of the meaning of Christology* is. On this point, then, we can consider Bornkamm:

> It is a history which is only understood in encounter and whose essence is only expressed in the proclaimed word [. . .] He himself speaks this word in the Gospels, the word to which God's Yea and Amen have resounded in the cross and resurrection. In this sense the Gospels lead us back to the beginning, so that faith should not be satisfied with some merely past event, nor even rest content with some so-called "saving realities."[109]

Here, what Bornkamm outlines is a delicate balance that must be struck between the past and the present as a means of projecting an existentializing future. As meaningfully as Christological reflection must reckon with "some merely past event" and the notion of "saving realities," as two existentializing aspects of what history is, *the question of the meaning of Christology*, if we understand Bornkamm, must be tempered by the existentializing, atemporal modulation of faith.

Appearing contemporaneously to "The Significance of the Historical Jesus for Faith," Bornkamm's "Myth and Gospel: A Discussion of the Problem of Demythologizing the New Testament Message" broadens how we can understand Bornkamm's approach to *the question of the meaning of Christology*, as that which is, for Bornkamm, filtered through Bornkamm's influence by and challenge of Bultmann. In "Myth and Gospel," presented in the *Kerygma and History: A Symposium on the Theology of Rudolf Bultmann* collection (1962), the editor of the volume, Carl E. Braaten characterizes, in "A Critical Introduction," Bornkamm's "Myth and Gospel" as "evaluat[ing] more positively the function of the historical-critical methods for theological work."[110] As a "leading disciple" of Bultmann—alongside Käsemann—Braaten also notes, which is certainly worth mentioning even if Braaten footnotes this information, "[Bornkamm] speaks with the authority of one who knows Bultmann's thought from within, and therefore his criticisms of

---

109. Bornkamm, "Significance of the Historical Jesus for Faith," 86.
110. Braaten, "Critical Introduction," 19.

Bultmann are felt to be fair and soundly based on firsthand knowledge."[111] Out of these "criticisms of Bultmann," Bornkamm not only is able to ascertain Bultmann's handling of *the question of the meaning of Christology*, but Bornkamm is also able to give voice to his own handling of the question. Insofar as Bornkamm sees how Bultmann works through *the question of the meaning of Christology* in terms of the concept of myth, Bornkamm finds that "Bultmann's concept of myth, his persistent differentiation between nature and existence, world and man, are burdened by such a concept."[112] Bornkamm continues:

> Even the majority if [Bultmann's] opponents are in no better position, however, for they either totally deny him the right to his concern, or at least snatch this and that from his grasp [. . .] and once more attempt to secure them "historically." Thus the question of faith is always fatally captive to the alternative whether this or that event has occurred in such a way or not.[113]

On this point, Bornkamm contends:

> Faith thereby makes known that the reality which encounters it in the word is the transcendent reality of the risen Lord which touches me together with my world, but now in such a way that transcends, abolishes and at the same time renews my own understanding of the world and myself.[114]

An "understanding of the world" and an understanding of "myself," both of which attune and are attuned by Christological reflection, is the means by which *the question of the meaning of Christology* presents itself to us.

This leads Bornkamm to the Christological question, as that which is grounded on this: "how are the Christological expressions of the New Testament to be correctly understood?"[115] After beginning with the means by which the New Testament Christology may not be understood and developed Bornkamm highlights problems inherent in the theologizing of Oscar Cullmann's *Christ and Time* (1950) and Ethelbert Stauffer's *New Testament Theology* (1955)—which will both be explained later. In this sense, Bornkamm suggests, if following on with what he understands as *the question of the meaning of Christology*, that neither Cullmann nor Stauffer—in terms of either of their respective Christological reflection—adequately

111. Braaten, "Critical Introduction," 18.

112. Bornkamm, "Myth and Gospel," 187.

113. Bornkamm, "Myth and Gospel," 187.

114. Bornkamm, "Myth and Gospel," 189.

115. Bornkamm, "Myth and Gospel," 189.

work out or work through *the question of the meaning of Christology*, insofar as what it means to do New Testament Christology may not be understood and developed on Cullmann's and Stauffer's terms alone. Consequently, Bornkamm believes, "as to the way in which the New Testament message of Christ should be interpreted, what is most significant is to be learned from the New Testament itself and especially from the theology of Paul."[116] With this in mind, Bornkamm arrives at the following question: how does [Paul] interpret the Christian tradition handed down to him?"[117] Indeed, this question arises from Bornkamm's own Christological reflection, which, in itself, attends to the larger *question of the meaning of Christology* in a way that, as Bornkamm sees it, poses the most optimal question of and seeks the most optimal meaning to Christology itself. Setting aside Bornkamm's critiques of and problems with how Cullmann and Stauffer respectively approach *the question of the meaning of Christology*, Bornkamm is tempered by the fact that "[Paul] neither narrates merely a story of Jesus, nor develops a Christ myth."[118] Not only does this allow Bornkamm to return to Bultmann, but it also allows Bornkamm to question, "should we follow [Bultmann] in interpreting the [C]hristological utterances merely as an expression of the Christian self-understanding?"[119] To be sure, "Christian self-understanding" grounds and is grounded on Christological reflection. To this, Bornkamm concludes, "it seems to me that such a procedure is opposed by the fact that Paul does not merely develop Christology as the doctrine of law and gospel, but also develops the doctrine of justification as Christology."[120]

Where Bornkamm ends in "Myth and Gospel" is precisely where he seemingly resumes towards the end of *Paulus* (1969), translated as *Paul* in 1971. Though concentrating on Paul, Pauline letters, and Pauline theology, Bornkamm's theologizing of Paul allows him to theologically conclude with a relationship between Paul and Jesus.[121] What is, in effect, in *Paul*, a Pauline reflection becomes a Christological reflection—for Bornkamm, what ties the two is an underlying *question of the meaning of Christology*, culminating with an appendix section entitled "Christology and Justification."[122] Yet, as it is made evident in "Myth and Gospel," Bornkamm finds an inextricable link between Pauline reflection and Christological reflection, so that what it

116. Bornkamm, "Myth and Gospel," 190.
117. Bornkamm, "Myth and Gospel," 190.
118. Bornkamm, "Myth and Gospel," 190.
119. Bornkamm, "Myth and Gospel," 191.
120. Bornkamm, "Myth and Gospel," 191.
121. Bornkamm, *Paul*, 228–239.
122. Bornkamm, *Paul*, 248–249.

means to do Pauline reflection is always-already a Christological reflection, and vice versa—what one means to the other, as Bornkamm contends in both "Myth and Gospel" and *Paul*, is determined by a doctrine of justification. It is to this end that Bornkamm brings himself to maintain—particularly if viewing how "Myth and Gospel" is brought to bear on *Paul*—that there is an "indissoluble connection in the Pauline theology between Christology and the doctrine of justification."[123]

All in all, through a thematic relationship between "Myth and Gospel" and *Paul* on the notion of what Pauline theology means to the "connection" between Christology and the doctrine of justification, what makes this "connection" possible is the extent that Pauline theology is chiefly concerned with *the question of the meaning of Christology*. As, I submit, Bornkamm sees it, Pauline theology is oriented towards posing the question of and the seeking the meaning to Christology through a Christological reflection tempers by the doctrine of justification.

Bornkamm further complicates how he conceives of *the question of the meaning of Christology* in *Bibel: Das Neue Testament. Eine Einführung in seine Schriften im Rahmen der Geschichte des Urchristentums* (1971), translated as *The New Testament: A Guide to Its Writings* in 1973. In a way that allows Bornkamm to circle back to the Christological reflection inherent in *Jesus of Nazareth*, which Christologically traverses how Bornkamm carefully attends to the "indissoluble connection in the Pauline theology between Christology and the doctrine of justification" of his *Paul*, Bornkamm's *The New Testament: A Guide to Its Writings* Christologically contends that: "there is no direct road from the 'historical' Jesus to the story narrated in the Gospels, still less to what the later doctrine of the church since the New Testament affirms about this Jesus."[124] Not only does this, then, speak to what is at the core of Bornkamm's sense of *the question of the meaning of Christology*, but it also specifically lays bare the sense that the Gospels become what Bornkamm refers to as "the Gospel according to Paul,"[125] such that "[Paul] relates everything to the Christ event."[126]

123. Bornkamm, *Paul*, 249.

124. Bornkamm, *New Testament*, 15–16.

125. Bornkamm, *New Testament*, 73–116.

126. Bornkamm, *New Testament*, 77.

Chapter 2

The Question of the Meaning of Christology (II)

Together, Ernst Käsemann and Günther Bornkamm methodologically frame *the question of the meaning of Christology* in terms of a re-historicization of Christological thinking. What they frame respectively are two kinds of theologizing that spring forth from the influence Bultmann's theologizing directly serves upon them, particularly if we can view the two as first-generation Bultmannians. It is in this sense that it is possible to say that Käsemann and Bornkamm lay the groundwork for whatever can be surmised as a Bultmann School of Interpretation—the hermeneutical and theological directions they respectively take are immediately laid bare by both of their 1931 Marburg dissertations, as supervised by Bultmann. As they both engage the problem of the historical Jesus and eventually present monographs on Jesus—Käsemann's *Jesus Means Freedom* and Bornkamm's *Jesus of Nazareth*—the extent that they both become progenitors of a "new quest" for the historical Jesus is only made possible by how closely the two stand to Bultmann as Bultmann's doctoral students and, in turn, how the progression of their respective careers develop out of their ties to the "Old Marburgers" throughout the 1950s and their personal relationships with Bultmann himself with correspondence well into the 1960s.[1]

In order to understand the roles that Käsemann and Bornkamm respectively have with respect to what *the question of the meaning of*

---

1. Hammann, *Rudolf Bultmann*, 516.

Christology becomes after Bultmann, it requires thinking about these roles programmatically within a larger *question of the meaning of Christology*, as that which further unfolds throughout the 1950s and 1960s as other figures emerge. In building on the task and broadening the scope set forth by Käsemann and Bornkamm, these other figures coalesce around a means of doing Christological reflection that espouse a kind of Christological thinking that attempts to authentically think on and about the problem of the historical Jesus: a new quest.

JAMES M. ROBINSON

Let us now consider Robinson, with his *A New Quest for the Historical Jesus*—not only does Robinson announce what the "new quest" is by name, but he also attempts to purposefully codify the "new quest" into a systematic study of key figures and texts associated with what was, by Robinson's time, a new movement approaching *the question of the meaning of Christology.* Accordingly, in the introduction to Robinson's monograph, Robinson proclaims that it "is intended as a programmatic essay."[2] As such, Robinson clarifies by indicating that the monograph is "a contribution to basic thought about the unfulfilled task of New Testament scholarship."[3] While true, Robinson casts this work in terms of having a "point of departure [that] is not in the relatively untroubled and uninterrupted quest of the historical Jesus going on in French and Anglo-Saxon scholarship."[4] This is an important point, not just for the sake of the Jesus-quest scholarship Robinson believes is "relatively untroubled and uninterrupted," but for the sake of Robinson's own lineage in that scholarship—Robinson wishes to work outside of the theological tradition from which he hails. For Robinson, the task of his "programmatic essay" is, ultimately, as he rightly concedes, "based upon the conviction that this continuation of the nineteenth-century German quest ought probably to be interrupted or at least disturbed."[5] Because of this, Robinson aligns himself with the trajectory of the German quest—over and against the respective French and Anglo-Saxon quests—which "is recognized in its full significance only when one observes that it forms a central thrust in a second 'post-Bultmannian' phase of post-war German theology."[6] Insofar as "the first phase of post-war German theology," Robinson writes,

2. Robinson, *New Quest for the Historical Jesus*, 9.
3. Robinson, *New Quest for the Historical Jesus*, 9.
4. Robinson, *New Quest for the Historical Jesus*, 9.
5. Robinson, *New Quest for the Historical Jesus*, 9.
6. Robinson, *New Quest for the Historical Jesus*, 10.

"was the rise of the Bultmannian position to the centre of debate," as it is pertains to the German quest, but also a broader quest that cuts across all traditions, Robinson enumerates the key figures of what is methodologically a "new quest" as Ernst Käsemann, Günther Bornkamm, Erich Dinkler (1909–81), Ernst Fuchs (1903–83), and Hans Conzelmann (1915–89).[7] In light of these "pupils of Bultmann," Robinson rightly highlights the leading role Käsemann has, having "moved beyond a recognition of the validity of much of Bultmann's position, to argue that something *can* be known about the historical Jesus."[8] Robinson goes on to characterize Käsemann's stance as being grounded on the fact "that we must concern ourselves with working [the historical Jesus] out, if we do not wish ultimately to find ourselves committed to a mythological Lord."[9]

Through Käsemann's fundamental stance in relation to what remained undone by Bultmann and what was left in flux following Schweitzer, Robinson concludes, "Käsemann's initial proposal of a new quest arose from the problem of the relation to Jesus' *message* to the Church's *kerygma*."[10] To this end, "the proposal of a new quest of the historical Jesus," Robinson explains, "originally made within the context of the 'post-Bultmannian' direction of leading pupils of Bultmann, has broadened itself."[11] This broadening, as Robinson describes, became acknowledged "in traditionally conservative circles, but also by support from the Barthian side as well as from Bultmann himself."[12] In a footnote to this point, Robinson adds that, in response to Käsemann's proposal for a "new quest" and how this broadened theologically across the larger German school of theology, a "rapprochement"[13] occurred between two kinds of German theologizing at the time—Robinson cites these two camps in the following way: "German New Testament scholars largely operating upon Bultmannian presuppositions and German systematic theologians largely operating upon Barthian presuppositions."[14] With this "rapprochement" in mind, Robinson writes:

> It is in this relatively propitious setting that this present work
> is presented, as a contribution to the new quest both by a

7. Robinson, *New Quest for the Historical Jesus*, 10–11.

8. Robinson, *New Quest for the Historical Jesus*, 12.

9. Robinson, *New Quest for the Historical Jesus*, 12–13.

10. Robinson, *New Quest for the Historical Jesus*, 14.

11. Robinson, *New Quest for the Historical Jesus*, 24.

12. Robinson, *New Quest for the Historical Jesus*, 24.

13. Robinson, *New Quest for the Historical Jesus*, 24.

14. Robinson, *New Quest for the Historical Jesus*, 24.

clarification of its nature, and by an initial participation in the work of the new quest at a few significant points.[15]

What Robinson wishes to present "by a clarification of its nature" is the very *question of the meaning of Christology*, as a question and as a meaning to which Robinson hopes to situate as "an initial participation in the work of the new quest."

By 1965, Robinson's participation in and contribution to the work of the new quest became channelled into an introductory essay, entitled "For Theology and the Church," for the *Journal for Theology and the Church*, which "reflects the title of the German journal, the *Zeitschrift für Theologie und Kirche*, from whose pages some its contents are drawn."[16] Recognizing that the *Zeitschrift* was "in the forefront of German theology," Robinson suggests that his intention for this introductory essay is "to clarify [the dialectic relation between theology and the church] and at the same time to provide a survey of the course of the *Zeitschrift für Theologie und Kirche* out of which the *Journal for Theology and the Church* emerges."[17] For Robinson, given that "the issue involved in this dialectic will not remain abstract, nor will the history of the [*Zeitschrift für Theologie und Kirche*] remain immaterial,"[18] what becomes *The Bultmann School of Biblical Interpretation* collection acts as the first-volume representation of what Robinson presents as "the programmatic essays leading to most of the new trends characterizing German theology today."[19] Undoubtedly, Käsemann's work, with which Robinson is keenly aware, is at the leading edge of, in Robinson's words, "most of the new trends characterizing German theology" at the time, particularly as that which revolves around, I submit, *the question of the meaning of Christology*.

Because of this, while Robinson's introductory essay leads *The Bultmann School of Biblical Interpretation* collection—just as another essay by Robinson leads a 1968 translation of Schweitzer's *The Quest of the Historical Jesus*[20]—the collection includes pieces by three key figures Robinson earlier highlights in *A New Quest for the Historical Jesus*: Käsemann, Dinkler, and Fuchs. Setting aside Käsemann's "God's Righteousness in Paul"—which I have previously discussed—Dinkler's "Comments on the History of the

15. Robinson, *New Quest for the Historical Jesus*, 25.

16. Robinson, "For Theology and the Church," 1.

17. Robinson, "For Theology and the Church," 1.

18. Robinson, "For Theology and the Church," 1.

19. Robinson, "For Theology and the Church," 1.

20. The very thorough 23-page introduction to *The Quest of the Historical Jesus* can be seen as a companion piece to Robinson's introductory essay to *The Bultmann School of Biblical Interpretation* collection.

Symbol of the Cross" (translated from *"Zur Geschichte des Kreuzsymbols,"* originally published in 1951) and Fuchs' "Must One believe in Jesus if He wants to Believe in God?" (translated from *"Muß man an Jesus glauben, wenn man an Gott glauben will?"* originally published in 1961) both directly speak to *the question of the meaning of Christology.* Käsemann, Fuchs, and Dinkler, in particular, speak to *the question of the meaning of Christology,* when grounding what is being asked and what is being sought to Bultmann's direct influences on the three, and how the three belong to a "Bultmann School of Interpretation"—especially, a more intimate Bultmannian circle of students that had their respective dissertations at Marburg directed by Bultmann (to which we can include Bornkamm), even though Bultmann did not direct Dinkler's dissertation nor his habilitation thesis. Though, given the figures collected in *The Bultmann School of Biblical Interpretation* collection (to the exclusion of Bornkamm), Helmut Koester is included in this more intimate circle, having had his dissertation directed by Bultmann in 1954,[21] with Käsemann in our purview now, we shall make accounts for Dinkler and Fuchs.

ERICH DINKLER

It is no coincidence that Dinkler's piece is immediately followed by Fuchs' piece in *The Bultmann School of Biblical Interpretation* collection—both, at one time, were students of Bultmann's at Marburg. Dinkler's apprenticeship to Bultmann is different from how Fuchs' was under tutelage of Bultmann. To be clear, Dinkler completed his dissertation in 1932 at the University of Heidelberg with *Die Anthropologie Augustins* (or "Augustine's Anthropology"), eventually working in the field of Christian archaeology at Marburg and completing his *habilitationsschrift* with Hans von Soden in 1936. Nevertheless, Dinkler was one of a handful of Marburg students, Konrad Hammann points out, that "belonged to Bultmann's *Graeca* [. . .] this group [meeting] at Bultmann's home every Thursday evening to read the classics of Greek antiquity with him."[22] Though Bultmann's *Graeca* began meeting in the 1920s and continued meeting for "about fifteen years," judging from Hammann's rare account of this and the time when Dinkler was a student at Marburg, Dinkler likely participated in the group sometime in the early 1930s. Not only was Dinkler not one of Bultmann's doctoral students at the

---

21. Helmut Koester (1926–2016) was the Bultmann's last doctoral student, according to Konrad Hammann. See Hammann, *Rudolf Bultmann*, 240.

22. Hammann, *Rudolf Bultmann*, 242.

time—just as others in the group such as Hans-Georg Gadamer[23] and Gerhard Krüger[24] were not—but, "after 1945,"[25] as Hammann details:

> [Bultmann] assigned some of [his unpublished papers] to Erich Dinkler, whom [Bultmann] charged with going over the manuscript of his lectures on Second Corinthians and preparing it for the press, as well as readying for publication his lecture course on theological encyclopedia.[26]

Hammann notes that Dinkler was unable to see the manuscript for "theological encyclopedia" all the way to publication, since Dinkler died in the editorial process. Yet, Dinkler was able to complete the editorial work on "the manuscript of [Bultmann's] lectures on Second Corinthians," which was originally published in 1976 (and translated into English in 1985) and, additionally, Hammann explains in a footnote, "Dinkler received Bultmann's lectures on *Romans*."[27] What is the most notable, important and substantial of all Dinkler's editorial work is on *Exegetica*, published in 1967, which remains untranslated—to this, Hammann explains:

> The initiative for publishing a volume of Bultmann's most important exegetical essays came from Erich Dinkler. He also consulted with [Bultmann] in selecting the studies that were reprinted in *Exegetica*. This collection was not meant to resemble a museum archive or to provide a glimpse into Bultmann's research on the New Testament [. . .] instead, Dinkler selected exegetical works and studies in the history of religions that he regarded as relevant to contemporary scholarly discussion.[28]

Being that Dinkler editorially structures *Exegetica* chronologically, culminating with essays dealing with, Hammann describes, "topics surrounding

---

23. Martin Heidegger's doctoral student up to 1928 and then a lecturer in the 1930s at University of Marburg.

24. Martin Heidegger's doctoral student up to 1929, though Heidegger, by 1928, left University of Marburg for University of Freiburg. It would not be too much to assume that Heidegger's leaving for Freiburg allowed Krüger to more firmly become rooted in Bultmann's circle of students and colleagues well into the 1930s, when surmising this from the photograph of Bultmann and Krüger leaving a meeting of Marburg theologians in February 1937, presented by Konrad Hammann. See Hammann, *Rudolf Bultmann*, 251.

25. Hammann, *Rudolf Bultmann*, 218.

26. Hammann, *Rudolf Bultmann*, 479.

27. Hammann, *Rudolf Bultmann*, 480.

28. Hammann, *Rudolf Bultmann*, 480.

the issue of the significance of the historical Jesus,"[29] there is no doubt that Dinkler hopes *Exegetica* would contribute to the ongoing *question of the meaning of Christology*, as that which throughout the 1960s would be predicated on "the new quest," which was, to Hammann's point, a "contemporary scholarly discussion." Given that Dinkler, Hammann is careful to remind us, "who, though Hans von Soden's student, increasingly became Bultmann's trusted theological partner,"[30] we might wonder, too, if Dinkler's contribution to *the question of the meaning of Christology*, as it has been asked and sought by Käsemann and Bornkamm, surveyed by Robinson, and articulated by Fuchs, Ebeling, as well as Braun and Cullmann, and situated between Gogarten and Althaus, is, in itself, speaking to us through his editorial work on Bultmann's *Exegetica*.

Exegetica, under Dinkler's stewardship, interestingly follows Gogarten's *Jesus Christus Wende der Welt* (1966), such that both become contemporaneous expressions of Bultmann's participation in *the question of the meaning of Christology* at the height of the "new quest" for the historical Jesus. Like Gogarten, Dinkler similarly defends Bultmann forthrightly, though Dinkler does so from a position that remains more fundamentally backgrounded than Gogarten's—while Gogarten can be seen as an interpreter of Bultmann's relevance towards *the question of the meaning of Christology*, Dinkler is a presenter of Bultmann's relevance.

The problem with Dinkler, I submit, is how relatively obscure Dinkler remains with respect not just to Gogarten but also with respect to the rest of his Bultmannian contemporaries. Unlike others strongly associated with Bultmann in the 1930s, to the best of my knowledge, all of Dinkler's major monographs produced in the 1950s or 1960s remain untranslated. Dinkler's arguably most significant work, *Signum crucis: Aufsätze zum Neuen Testament und zur christlichen Archäologie* (1967) goes unreferenced and unmentioned by Hammann—two of the four texts Hammann cites are Dinkler's editorial work, another is Dinkler's article on Bultmann, and the fourth is part of a collection to which Dinkler contributes pieces. Consequently, Dinkler becomes a more peripheral figure in relation to the more rounded composites Hammann draws of Dinkler's Bultmannian contemporaries, such as Käsemann, Bornkamm, and Fuchs. Dinker is so peripheral, in fact that, aside from Dinkler's involvement in Bultmann's *Graeca* in the 1930s and Dinkler having been assigned editorial work on various Bultmann projects in Bultmann's post-retirement period after 1954, the only other thing of note that Hammann cites is "[Dinkler] was called up to the [German]

---

29. Hammann, *Rudolf Bultmann*, 480.
30. Hammann, *Rudolf Bultmann*, 516.

armed forces" presumedly in 1939.[31] What is notable about this is that it is, in one sense, provided in passing to the reader, and in another sense, only spawns more questions when connecting Dinkler's conscription to the only picture Hammann provides of Dinkler in seemingly Nazi-styled uniform.[32] Hammann does not explain Dinker's picture, nor does Hammann explain Dinkler's notable absence from a group picture of the "Old Marburgers," dated to October 1949—Dinkler's absence is made all the more noticeable, I believe, with the presence of Dinkler's most immediate Bultmannian contemporaries Käsemann, Bornkamm, Fuchs, and Ebeling.

All told, when grouping Dinkler with his Bultmannian contemporaries, Dinkler is curiously a lesser-known compatriot. Yet, Dinkler is an essential participant in *the question of the meaning of Christology*, which is evident by Dinkler's inclusion in *The Bultmann School of Biblical Interpretation* collection. This essentiality is made even more apparent with Dinkler's inclusion in this first of the seven collections[33] comprising of the *Journal for Theology and the Church* series, as well as, Robinson informs us, Dinkler's inclusion on the editorial board in 1950 for the original German version of the series appearing as *Zeitschrift für Theologie und Kirche*, with Ebeling as the earliest editor.[34]

Dinkler's "Comments on the History of the Symbol of the Cross," as it is included in *The Bultmann School of Biblical Interpretation* collection, though published in 1951, originally existed, as Dinkler places in a footnote, as part of "an unpublished '*Festschrift*' by friends and pupils" commemorating Friedrich Matz, a Marburg archaeologist.[35] While the commemoration occurred in 1950, it is unclear—since Dinkler does not tell us so—if the text was written that year or sometime earlier. That set aside, what does become clear, though, is that "Comments on the History of the Symbol of the Cross" contributes to Dinkler's broader archaeological perspective grounded on and cultivated by his work in Christian archaeology—the text certainly speaks to and extends upon Dinkler's Marburg *habilitationsschrift* with Hans von Soden in 1936, but, here, judging from the title alone, is focused on *the question of the meaning of Christology* by considering the meaning of the symbolic iconography of cross.

---

31. Hammann, *Rudolf Bultmann*, 361.

32. Hammann, *Rudolf Bultmann*, 243.

33. The seventh (and final) collection, published in 1970, is entitled *Schleiermacher as Contemporary*.

34. Robinson, "For Theology and the Church," 17.

35. Dinkler, "Comments on the History of the Symbol of the Cross," 124.

This meaning, Dinkler writes, "show[s] that this 'earliest monument of Christianity' is a Jewish and not a Christian monument."[36] On this point, Dinkler concludes with his emphasis included, "*the sign of the cross has its home in Judaism* and can be found repeatedly, especially on ossuaries and tomb inscriptions."[37] What Dinkler is challenging is the historicity of the cross as a Christological symbol grounding Christological reflection itself— with this in mind, Dinkler notes, "for the present the question remains open as to whether one should then speak of the cross as a symbol or [. . .] of a pre-symbolic sign which expresses no more than, 'He was crucified.'"[38] This not only questions the very meaning of Christology as that which Christological reflection seeks, but is also brings about another way to ask the question of Christology as that which allows us to enter Christological reflection. Following on Eleazar Sukenik's dating of "Jesus inscriptions and crosses" appearing on the chamber tomb of Talpioth that "was in use from the first century B.C. till 50 A.D.,"[39] Dinkler suggests the implications of Sukenik's thesis. For Dinkler, "if this thesis could be proven it would indeed be gratifying for New Testament scholarship to have an inscribed monument witnessing to a pre-Pauline *theologica crucis*, no matter how this would have to be qualified."[40] Here, the term "*theologica crucis*," as it originates in Martin Luther's theologizing, speaks of a theology of the cross or, more aptly "staurology." To this, Dinkler's handling of *the question of the meaning of Christology*, as that which arises from Christological reflection, comes by way of what can only be called staurological reflection. More importantly, for Dinkler, this becomes predicated by an archaeological reflection on the staurological, insofar as Dinkler's understanding of Sukenik's thesis "would also be revolutionary for Christian archaeology."[41]

What is at stake for Dinkler's approach to and articulation of *the question of the meaning of Christology* can be described substantively and meaningfully in the following way:

> For, until now, in the field of archaeology it has been an absolute dogma that the symbol of the cross makes its first appearance in the age of Constantine, and that this appearance is directly connected with the finding of the relic of the cross ascribed to the Empress Mother Helena. Does this common opinion now have

36. Dinkler, "Comments on the History of the Symbol of the Cross," 126.
37. Dinkler, "Comments on the History of the Symbol of the Cross," 126.
38. Dinkler, "Comments on the History of the Symbol of the Cross," 132.
39. Dinkler, "Comments on the History of the Symbol of the Cross," 132.
40. Dinkler, "Comments on the History of the Symbol of the Cross," 132.
41. Dinkler, "Comments on the History of the Symbol of the Cross," 132.

to be corrected by taking cognizance of the fact that the sign of
the cross was already affixed to graves of Christians prior to the
time of the Pauline epistles?[42]

The answer to this question is yes. Indeed, the "common opinion" about
and the "absolute dogma" towards "the symbol of the cross," as far as Dinkler is concerned, needs "to be corrected." That correction, as such, intends
to re-conceptualize what the symbol of the cross means for Christological
reflection and, in turn, *the question of the meaning of Christology*. It is a correction to the historicity with which we come to understand the symbolism
of the cross, as that which tradition tells us originates with Constantine.
To Dinkler, such a correction reorients us to not just what tradition has
come to represent, but also how that representation has shaped how we
understand ourselves as a product of the historicity from which we come.
If the Constantine narrative is extracted from our historicity and from the
development of our tradition, along with the very meaning of the cross itself, only then, as Dinkler does, do we come to "the cognizance of the fact
that the sign of the cross" pre-dates the Constantine narrative all-together.
If, Dinkler tells us, the meaning of the cross was made meaningful when it
"was already affixed to graves of Christians prior to the time of the Pauline
epistles," the question is this: does this change how we ask the question of
and seek the meaning for Christology? In other words, what kind of staurological reflection positions us towards a Christological reflection that, then,
positions us to *the question of the meaning of Christology*?

Dinkler is, undoubtedly, particularly interested and deeply invested in
reverse-engineering this question. Though predominantly informed by how
the possibilities of Sukenik's thesis becomes "revolutionary for Christian archaeology," it brings Dinkler to conclude:

> The course of our investigation has already illustrated the prox-
> imity of [Judaism and Christianity] through the question of
> whether the frequently found cross signs are Jewish or Chris-
> tian. But nevertheless, it must now be stated that our assertion
> of the existence of a Jewish cross symbol does *not* imply that the
> *origin of the Christian cross symbol* has been disclosed.[43]

Rather, Dinkler finds that "there is no direct continuity between the two
symbols [wherein] only *indirect connections* can be shown to exist."[44] What
this means is that Dinkler does not wish to conflate the historicity of "a

---

42. Dinkler, "Comments on the History of the Symbol of the Cross," 132–133.

43. Dinkler, "Comments on the History of the Symbol of the Cross," 145.

44. Dinkler, "Comments on the History of the Symbol of the Cross," 145.

Jewish cross symbol" with that of "the origin of the Christian cross symbol," to the extent that there is a cross-pollination of the symbolism of the former into the symbolism of the latter. It is not to say, Dinkler believes, "a Jewish cross symbol" stands so close to the "origin of the Christian cross symbol" that the former is responsible for the making of the latter—or that the former is an antecedent to the latter and, thusly, antecedent to what staurological reflection means for Christological reflection and *pre forma* to *the question of the meaning of Christology*. Dinkler explains this further:

> The migration and transformation of symbols and myths from one religion to another is a hermeneutical problem not only for theology but also for archaeology and the history of art. Continual reciprocal interpretation of literary and of monumental evidence is necessary in order clearly to distinguish that which is constant from that which is variable in the migration and changes of symbols and myths.[45]

What this means, then, is that, when considering the relationship between the Judaic meaning of the cross and how the symbol of the cross arises in Christianity, "there is no mere acceptance, no simple migration of the symbol"[46] of the former unto the latter. What this subsequently means for Dinkler's approach to and articulation of *the question of the meaning of Christology* is, through a staurological reflection informing his Christological reflection, he deduces that "the Christian symbol of the cross is a new beginning."[47]

ERNST FUCHS

As a doctoral student of Bultmann's at Marburg—having arrived in 1924[48]—Fuchs completed his dissertation in 1930 under the direction of Bultmann, entitled *Das Verhiltnis des Glaubens zur Tat im Hermas*, translated as "The Relation of Faith to Deed in the Shepherd of Hermas."[49] As with this early study, Fuchs' primary concern is with the role that hermeneutics plays in the approach to theologizing itself. Not only is this influenced by Bultmann, but it is also influenced by Karl Barth and dialectical theology, as well as,

---

45. Dinkler, "Comments on the History of the Symbol of the Cross," 145.
46. Dinkler, "Comments on the History of the Symbol of the Cross," 145.
47. Dinkler, "Comments on the History of the Symbol of the Cross," 145.
48. Hammann, *Rudolf Bultmann*, 246.
49. Hammann, *Rudolf Bultmann*, 246.

while at Marburg, philosophy courses Fuchs took from Heidegger[50]—in this sense, Bultmann, Barth, and Heidegger all allow Fuchs to contextualize and develop a hermeneutical approach to theologizing beginning with Fuchs' 1930 dissertation,[51] which became key to the notion of "the new hermeneutic," which is especially laid bare in Fuchs' *Hermeneutik* (1969) and presented by an expansive "prolegomena" that makes explicit use of Barth, Martin Kähler, Bultmann, Heidegger, and Gogarten.[52]

Fuchs' *Hermeneutik* expands upon the three texts included in Fuchs' *Gesammelte Aufsätze* (1965): *Zum hermeneutischen Problem in der Theologie: Die existentiale Interpretation, Zur Frage nach dem Historischen Jesus*, and *Glaube und Erfahrung: Zum christologischen Problem im Neuen Testament*. All three consider different aspects to the role that hermeneutics plays as a "problem" to what it means to theologize—the first, the manner of existential interpretation as a hermeneutical problem, the second, the notion of the historical Jesus as a historical problem, and the third, the meaning of Christology as a problem for the New Testament. All, then, as constituents of how Fuchs more broadly handles *the question of the meaning of Christology*, if we are to say that each of the three texts, along with *Hermeneutik*, interpolate how Fuchs poses the question to and seeks the meaningfulness of Christology through a Christological reflection that wrestles with "the hermeneutical problem" inherent in Christological thinking itself.

Throughout the 1950s, Fuchs contributes in various ways to the shifting and evolving state of Christology after Bultmann, particularly after Käsemann's initiation of a "new quest." As one of the key post-Bultmannians—by this, we can simply say that Fuchs was a major figure within the circle of theologians directly influenced by Bultmann and was among a relatively small group of theologians that belonged to the "Old Marburgers"—though Fuchs has a close tie to Bultmann, he also has a close tie to Ebeling (which will be discussed later), which has been captured in a photo dating to October 1949, documenting a meeting of the "Old Marburgers."[53] But, of course, like Ebeling, when considering how Fuchs is aligned to Bultmann theologically, Charles C. Anderson, in his *Critical Quests of Jesus* (1969), considers Fuchs as a critic within Bultmann's circle. Even so, given Anderson's

50. Hammann, *Rudolf Bultmann*, 246.

51. Konrad Hammann notes that Bultmann that Fuchs' dissertation could not be included in the Investigations into the Religion and Literature of the Old and New Testament series, "for it suffered from its author having depended too heavily in language and style on Heidegger's existentialist analysis." See Hammann, *Rudolf Bultmann*, 246.

52. Fuchs, *Hermeneutik*, 3–87.

53. This photo has been reproduced in Konrad Hammann's biography of Bultmann. See Hammann, *Rudolf Bultmann*, 392.

reference to Fuchs, Anderson admits that "some would consider it inappropriate to include Fuchs and Ebeling in a chapter on the new quest."[54] The term "inappropriate" may be a bit strong here—I would venture, instead, to say "limiting," as in, perhaps, it is limiting to consider Fuchs only within the task and scope of the "new quest." Anderson suggests that, for Fuchs and Ebeling, "they go beyond the position of the other scholars [of the new quest] to deal with an existentialist interpretation of the New Testament rather than an existentialist interpretation of the kerygma."[55] This is, as Anderson is correct to characterize, a "theological position at which they arrive [that] has been called by some the 'New Hermeneutic.'"[56] That theological position, as such, becomes essential, nonetheless, to how Fuchs (and Ebeling) contribute to *the question of the meaning of Christology* as it resides within Life-of-Jesus research.

If we are to tie Fuchs' work on *the question of the meaning of Christology* to Life-of-Jesus research, we find in Craig A. Evans' comprehensive *Life of Jesus Research* (1996) that Fuchs earliest contribution to Life-of-Jesus research—or what is known as "*Jesu Forschung*"—is "*Jesu Selbstzeugnis nach Matthäus 5*" (1952).[57] There are two problems with Evans' reference to this Fuchs article, which can be rendered as "Jesus' Self-Testimony to Matthew 5": first, the article was actually published in 1954,[58] and secondly, the article is not the earliest Fuchs piece that attends to the matters of Christology. Though Fuchs' "*Jesu Selbstzeugnis nach Matthäus 5*," Evans tells us, "argues that Jesus' manner of teaching, as seen in Matthew, is an important aspect of Jesus' self-testimony,"[59] it is predated by Fuchs' "*Warum fordert der Glaube an Jesus Christus von un sein Selbstverständnis?*" (1951), which can be rendered as "Why Does Faith in Jesus Christ Require Us to Understand Ourselves?" In this earlier article, as the title suggests, Fuchs constructs a relationship between what it means to understand faith and what it means to understand ourselves—Fuchs uses this relationship to mitigate the larger question of where we can locate faith, either in the resurrection or in demythologization.[60] Faith, then, becomes pivotal to Fuchs' "*Die Frage nach dem historischen Jesus*" (1956)—Evans tells us that, in this text, Fuchs

---

54. Anderson, *Critical Quests of Jesus*, 181.

55. Anderson, *Critical Quests of Jesus*, 181.

56. Anderson, *Critical Quests of Jesus*, 181.

57. Evans, *Life of Jesus Research*, 23.

58. The article did not appear in volume 49 of *Zeitschrift für Theologie und Kirche*, as noted by Evans, but, instead, it appeared in volume 51.

59. Evans, *Life of Jesus Research*, 23.

60. Fuchs, "*Warum fordert der Glaube an Jesus Christus von un sein Selbstverständnis?*," 342.

understands that "Christology is to be found in Jesus' attitude and conduct toward sinners [and] faith in Jesus is to repeat Jesus' decision to have faith."[61] What follows this is *"Glaube und Geschichte im Blick auf die Frage nach dem historischen Jesus: Eine Auseinandersetzung mit G. Bornkamms Buch über 'Jesus von Nazareth'"* (1957), which can be literally rendered as "Faith and History in View of the Question of the Historical Jesus: A Confrontation with G. Bornkamm's Book about 'Jesus of Nazareth'"—this is simply a review, though fairly lengthy, of Bornkamm's 1956 book. What follows, then, is *"Jesus und der Glaube"* (1958), which can be rendered as "Jesus and Faith"—Evans explains that this text "considers the question of how faith of Jesus becomes faith *in* Jesus [and] concludes that in taking Jesus' faith upon oneself, one believes in Jesus (i.e. in Jesus' understanding of faith in God)."[62] What follows, then, is *"Was wird in der Exegese des Neuen Testaments interpretiert?"* (1959), which can be rendered as "What is Interpreted in the Exegesis of the New Testament?"

Each of the texts appearing in 1951, 1954, 1956, 1957, and 1958 are all collected in Fuchs' *Zur Frage nach dem Historischen Jesus* (1960)—what this demonstrates is that each of the texts contribute to Fuchs' approach to the "new quest" and what can be understood as the historical Jesus. More importantly, if seeing each of the texts as ascribing to Fuchs' handling of *the question of the meaning of Christology*, each presents, I submit, an approach to Christological reflection, though Fuchs' engages in a Christological thinking that frequently considers and reconsiders faith, as that which is existentialized and existentializes us.

When considering *the question of the meaning of Christology*, Fuchs situates himself with respect to this question of Jesus and this Christological meaningfulness in *"Das Neue Testament und das hermeneutische Problem"* (1961), which Evans describes as a piece where Fuchs "explores the new quest's relationship to the old quest [and] argues that the Gospels are concerned with the historical Jesus."[63] Here, Fuchs engages in a Christological reflection on how the "new quest" situates itself in terms of where the old quest discontinued itself. Writing relatively concurrently to this, in *"Muß man an Jesus glauben, wenn man an Gott glauben will?"* (1961),[64] which was translated as "Must One Believe in Jesus if He Wants to Believe in God?" (1965), Fuchs further his Christological reflection by explaining:

61. Evans, *Life of Jesus Research*, 27.

62. Evans, *Life of Jesus Research*, 30.

63. Evans, *Life of Jesus Research*, 39.

64. This text appears again in Fuchs' collection, *Glaube und Erfahrung: Zum christologischen Problem im Neuen Testament* (1971).

> One must not believe in Jesus if he wants to believe in God, but
> one is invited to believe in him, since God speaks with us in the
> person of Jesus, in that he also makes us persons and thus keeps
> us by his side. Then our life is not idle talk but a conversation
> with God.[65]

Coming to this conclusion, as that which wrestles with *the question of the
meaning of Christology*, this lays the foundation for Fuchs' contribution to
the new quest for the historical Jesus, as initiated by Käsemann and an-
nounced by Robinson. How Fuchs reaches the sentiment that "one is invited
to believe in [Jesus] since God speaks with us in the person of Jesus" is
furthered—albeit, culminated—in *Zur Frage nach dem Historischen Jesus*,
translated and truncated[66] as *Studies of the Historical Jesus* in 1964.[67] In the
preface to the English edition of it, Fuchs notes:

> I am convinced that the question of the immediate meaning of
> Jesus for us cannot be answered apart from the question of the
> 'historical' Jesus. We are not interested in exchanging this Jesus
> for some idea about Jesus. The New Testament—particularly in
> the Gospels—claims to talk of Jesus himself. We must therefore
> attempt to examine, and indeed to fulfil this assertation on the
> part of the New Testament.[68]

Insofar, as Fuchs finds, "the question of the immediate meaning of us" is
inextricably linked to "the question of the historical Jesus," there is a co-
dependency between the two questions. What links these two, I argue, is *the
question of the meaning of Christology*. Nevertheless, what exists as a triangular sort of questioning for Fuchs directly promotes additional questions,
some of which Fuchs asks in relation to what role the text itself has in the
triangular meaningfulness of Christology. To this, Fuchs writes, "those who
ask these questions are confronted by the 'hermeneutical problem [while]
this problem is not exhausted in the technical question of how we translate,
or how we explain words."[69] Yet, Fuchs goes on to say:

> Historical reconstruction is not enough to render the New
> Testament comprehensible. We do not abandon the historical

65. Fuchs, "Must One Believe in Jesus if He Wants to Believe in God?," 168.

66. The German version of the text, numbering 458 pages, is nearly twice as long
as the length of the English translation, which is 228 pages.

67. A more literal translation of *Zur Frage nach dem Historischen Jesus* would be
The Question of the Historical Jesus.

68. Fuchs, *Studies of the Historical Jesus*, 7.

69. Fuchs, *Studies of the Historical Jesus*, 8.

question. However, we do guard against the naïve opinion that it might be possible to understand the New Testament without reflecting on its purpose.[70]

This hermeneutical problem orients Fuchs throughout his *Zur Frage nach dem Historischen Jesus*—the inadequacy of "historical reconstruction" and the necessity of "the historical question" illustrates the dimensions and parameters of the hermeneutical problem, especially as it speaks to the construction of *the question of the meaning of Christology*.

Given that Fuchs' remarks, here, about the hermeneutical problem in the preface to the English edition is not included in the original German edition, and given the fact that these remarks serve as an expansion on the 1960 text, Fuchs further expands the 1960 text with the inclusion of a tenth and "final study" in the 1964 text—to the original nine studies—which Fuchs notes "appears in substantially the same form" in 1961–62.[71] The "final study," entitled, "The Essence of the 'Language-Event' and Christology," Fuchs begins by summarizing Bultmann's view about the historical Jesus "as theologically irrelevant," insomuch as "[Bultmann's] main argument is that the enquiry into the historical Jesus cannot and indeed should not contribute to faith in Jesus Christ."[72] Fuchs counters Bultmann's view, coming to the understanding that "the quest of the historical Jesus then reveals to us our own time as a time conditioned by the situation of the preaching of faith."[73] This situation, as Fuchs defines it, is signified by a hermeneutical problem and, more importantly, it becomes the situation "in which the being of others strives after an adjustment with my being."[74] Fuchs, then, suggests that "situation is the essence of the 'language-event,' to which Christological reference, ultimately, refers.[75] It is with this that, for Fuchs, "the concept of the situation, which is understood as the essence of the 'language-event,' is able to reveal that Jesus' person belongs to the content of his proclamation."[76]

As with Fuchs' concern with what he refers to as "the hermeneutical significance of the 'situation'" of the language-event, as that which, at its essence, with what I have called *the question of the meaning of Christology*, allows for a way to resolve an underlining hermeneutical problem

70. Fuchs, *Studies of the Historical Jesus*, 8.

71. Fuchs, *Studies of the Historical Jesus*, 8.

72. Fuchs, *Studies of the Historical Jesus*, 213.

73. Fuchs, *Studies of the Historical Jesus*, 227.

74. Fuchs, *Studies of the Historical Jesus*, 222.

75. Fuchs, *Studies of the Historical Jesus*, 222.

76. Fuchs, *Studies of the Historical Jesus*, 222.

associated with proclamation, Fuchs similarly uncovers a significance in the relationship between the New Testament and the hermeneutical problem in an essay of the same name. If we can say that the New Testament encompasses "the essence of the language-event," insofar as this presents a hermeneutical problem predicated on how proclamation is brought forth from the language-event in terms of what is, to Fuchs' point, "required by faith,"[77] what role the historical Jesus meaningfully plays in this process, how we meaningfully attend to it, and why we must do so meaningfully becomes a broader, unavoidable negotiation, when we are meaningfully confronted with what meaning we are to gather from the accounts of the New Testament evangelists. Fuchs addresses this in "The New Testament and the Hermeneutical Problem" (1961), which later appears in *The New Hermeneutic* (1964) collection—becoming one of the two "focal essays" in the collection (with Ebeling's essay as the other), such that Fuchs' essay contributes to Fuchs' and Ebeling's joint venture into what becomes known as "The New Hermeneutic," Fuchs presents us with the following:

> Much of what [the New Testament evangelists] say does not stand up under historical criticism. But *they all have in mind the historical Jesus*, that man who, at the time when he was crucified, had lived and had been known and loved by men such as Peter.[78]

The emphasis Fuchs makes is not just significant but telling. The extent that, for Fuchs, all the New Testament evangelists "have in mind the historical Jesus" suggests that New Testament theologizing itself must be focused on the historical Jesus. This explicitly disagrees with Bultmann's understanding of kerygma, of course, but it also places the "new quest," as initiated by Käsemann, at the very epi-center of theologizing about the New Testament now. Fuchs makes this case for the importance of the "new quest" through what can be ascertained as his understanding of *the question of the meaning of Christology* in this manner:

> In any case, we cannot deny that *the Gospels intended to include the historical Jesus in the kerygma* and that for this purpose they appealed to what he said and did. This is true in principle, as well as in detail, of both the Gospel of John and the other three. *Could our conception of the historical be in need of correction? This is indeed my opinion.*[79]

---

77. Fuchs, *Studies of the Historical Jesus*, 219.
78. Fuchs, "New Testament and the Hermeneutical Problem," 115.
79. Fuchs, "New Testament and the Hermeneutical Problem," 115.

To the extent that "our conception of the historical [is] in need of correction," Fuchs acknowledges the weight of the hermeneutical problem on what can be meant by and articulated through *the question of the meaning of Christology*, when directing ourselves to what role kerygma plays in what can be gathered from the Gospels as that which allows us to theologize about the New Testament now. On the one hand, this is, again, Fuchs' disagreement with Bultmann's understanding of kerygma, but it is also, on the other hand, Fuchs' disagreement with Käsemann.

Published contemporaneously with "The New Testament and the Hermeneutical Problem," Fuchs explicitly challenges Käsemann's "The Beginnings of Christian Theology" in Fuchs' *"Uber die Aufgabe einer christichen Theologie"* (1961), translated as "On the Task of a Christian Theology" in the *Apocalypticism* collection. Fuchs levels his critique of Käsemann, when particularly viewed in the purview of Fuchs' own wrestling with and need to clarify *the question of the meaning of Christology*, in the following way:

> I find that Käsemann, despite his justified objection to the confusing of Jesus with a Christ-idea, has himself become entangled in a framework of the history of ideas, even if it be concretely expressed in terms of the history of motifs.[80]

Though Fuchs' critique, here, is specifically couched in Käsemann's defining "the eschatological revelation as an apocalyptic mode of existence," insomuch as, in Fuchs' view, Käsemann's Christological reflection predicated on an eschatological reflection "eliminate[s] Jesus by turning Jesus into an apocalyptic figure, that is, by using apocalyptic to get rid of him."[81] This, indeed, is Fuchs' awareness of the hermeneutical problem inherent in what Fuchs considers as a guiding principle to Käsemann's "The Beginnings of Christian Theology"—as a result, what we find in Fuchs, as that which Fuchs calls "the task" of what it means to theologize the New Testament now, is a need to develop a praxis to *the question of the meaning of Christology*, which, in itself, is not, to Fuchs' criticism of Käsemann, "entangled in a framework of the history of ideas" that, I submit, makes the hermeneutical problem all the more untenable.

HERBERT BRAUN

Fuchs' articulation of the manner with which the hermeneutical problem comports itself to the New Testament theologizing of the evangelists and to

---

80. Fuchs, "On the Task of a Christian Theology," 76.
81. Fuchs, "On the Task of a Christian Theology," 76.

theologizing about the New Testament today becomes similarly and relatively contemporaneously integral to Braun's "*Die Problematik einer Theologie des Neuen Testaments*" (1961), translated as "The Problem of a New Testament Theology" in *The Bultmann School of Biblical Interpretation* collection in 1965. While working in such a close proximity to Fuchs' work—and taking into account that Braun's aforementioned article directly follows Fuchs' "Must One believe in Jesus if He wants to Believe in God?" in the aforementioned collection—Braun suggests that there is a "double aspect" to what he considers as "the problem of a theology of the New Testament."[82] Braun explains this first underlining problem in the following way:

> The authors of the New Testament make statements dealing with man's salvation and with his relation to God which cannot be brought into harmony with one another, and which prove by their disparateness that their subject matter is not what they state, *expressis verbis*, in mutual contradiction.[83]

Proceeding from this first problem is, as Fuchs expresses at the conclusion of *Studies of the Historical Jesus*, "the language-event," as that which attempts to settle the multitude of New Testament "statements dealing with man's salvation and with his relation to God." This is mitigated by *the question of the meaning of Christology*, if we can say this makes an account for and cumulatively articulates that "which cannot be brought into harmony with one another." To the same degree of mitigation, *the question of the meaning of Christology*, as what it means to do New Testament theologizing now, which Fuchs attends to by bringing together "the language-event" and what Christology is in itself, allows Fuchs considers the second underlining problem along these lines:

> On the other hand, if one conceives of theology in the narrower sense—as doctrine concerning the deity—it is clearly seen that the New Testament reckons naively with the existence of a deity [. . .] The New Testament is thus alienated from us who are no longer able to make such a proposition.[84]

In light of this second underlining problem, and in the purview of the first that Fuchs highlights, though Fuchs assesses these two problems separately in order to propose that "[an] effort [can] be made to break through this two-fold problem,"[85] an essential means of understanding Fuchs' sense of

---

82. Braun, "Problem of a New Testament Theology," 169.
83. Braun, "Problem of a New Testament Theology," 169.
84. Braun, "Problem of a New Testament Theology," 169.
85. Braun, "Problem of a New Testament Theology," 169.

a possible "break through" in "The Problem of a New Testament Theology" can be further and more completely contextualized in relation to another earlier article by Fuchs dating to 1956: "The Meaning of New Testament Christology."

Originally published as "*Der Sinn der neutestamentlichen Christologie*" (1957) in *Zeitschrift für Theologie und Kirche*, though not included until the collection, *God and Christ: Existence and Province* (1968)—which, coincidently, is four years after Fuchs' English translation of *Studies of the Historical Jesus* and just a year before the appearance of Braun's *Jesus, der Mann aus Nazareth und seine Zeit* (1969), translated as *Jesus of Nazareth: The Man and His Time* in 1979—Braun's "The Meaning of New Testament Christology" establishes two very important points in the development of what is essential to *the question of the meaning of Christology*, not only in the evolution of what Christological thinking was by 1956, but also Braun's own approach to Christological reflection. In *Life of Jesus Research* (1996), Craig A. Evans explains that Braun's "The Meaning of New Testament Christology": "argues that although there is little historical Jesus material that appears in Paul and the Johannine writings, there is [an] essential agreement in these diverse traditions."[86]

For Braun, Christology in the New Testament is played out meaningfully in either a non-programmatic way or a programmatic way. In the first sense, Braun suggests that "statements about Christ appear for the most part in a non-programmatic way, and therefore not as a separate point of doctrine which represents an end in itself."[87] Yet, Braun goes on to explain, in light of what he ascertains to be a non-programmatic way, a second aspect presents itself "where Jesus is spoken of in a programmatic and schematic way, as in the gospels, it can clearly be seen—this is the second fact—that the honorific statements about Jesus increase in the course of the development of this material."[88] Together, what Braun identifies is two way to consider what Christology is—this, in turn, leads Braun to ask: "what then is the meaning of Christology?"[89]

Posing this question, as Braun does, in the very opening of the article, Braun footnotes a means of contextualizing how he poses the fundamental question of the piece, while contextualizing, in a broader sense, *the question of the meaning of Christology* itself. Not only does Braun concede that this article was finished in June 1956 and that, according to his footnote,

---

86. Evans, *Life of Jesus Research*, 27.
87. Braun, "Meaning of New Testament Christology," 89.
88. Braun, "Meaning of New Testament Christology," 89.
89. Braun, "Meaning of New Testament Christology," 89.

"was later made the basis of a course of lectures," he acknowledges both Bornkamm's and Cullmann's work, as texts that he "can refer here only in passing."[90] Indeed, in the years between the original conception of the article and its later appearance in 1968 in the *God and Christ* collection, Braun seemingly recognizes the limitations of what can be derived from *the question of the meaning of Christology* in his "The Meaning of New Testament Christology," particularly when envisioning, by 1968 at least, that "a more explicit discussion," he footnotes, "would go beyond the range of the present article."[91]

Nevertheless, Braun's article sets the stage for the founding of a "new quest" of the historical Jesus, not just in relation to Käsemann's break from Bultmann, but also as an ideological bridge to Cullmann's work. It is difficult to determine if Braun envisions his "The Meaning of New Testament Christology" as being situated between Käsemann and Cullmann, given that Braun refers to the English translations of both men's respective works over the earlier and original German editions. Though it is also difficult to ascertain Braun's understanding of Käsemann as a beginning point of a new phase into the study of *the question of the meaning of Christology*, Braun's reference to Käsemann, nonetheless, implies something significant, just as Braun is seemingly interested in what manner the concerns of his "The Meaning of New Testament Christology" article can speak to the concerns of Cullmann's *The Christology of the New Testament*—without such a conversation being possible, Braun certainly views Cullmann as expanding upon or extending what Braun originally does in "The Meaning of New Testament Christology" article.

OSCAR CULLMANN

What seems to stand behind Braun's approach to *the question of the meaning of Christology*, if holding to Braun's own question at the end of the introductory remarks to his article, is one of Cullmann's opening remarks to *The Christology of the New Testament*, which is outlines Cullmann's approach to *the question of the meaning of Christology* as follows:

> If theo-logy is that science whose object is God, [*theos*], then Christology is that science whose object is *Christ*, his person, and his work. Christology is usually considered as a sub-division of theology in the etymological sense. This custom has

90. Braun, "Meaning of New Testament Christology," 89.
91. Braun, "Meaning of New Testament Christology," 89.

frequently influenced the historical representation of the first Christians' faith to the extent that one begins by stating their thoughts about *God*, and speaks only in the second place of their Christological convictions.[92]

Here, just as Braun is likely aware, Cullmann aligns a fundamental understanding of Christology alongside a fundamental understanding of theology itself. Both are, for Cullmann, oriented towards the "science" of an object—for theology, it is God, while, for Christology, it is "Christ, his person, and his work." The extent to which Christology "is usually considered as a subdivision of theology in the etymological sense" points to, as Cullmann does, the fact that the study of Christ is part and parcel of the study of God. In other words, when one studies Christology, one does so simultaneously with how one studies theology, and, when one attends to the matters of theology, one cannot do so without attending to the matters of Christology, as that which sheds theological light on what theology is in itself and does in itself.

Even so, Cullmann wishes to draw a difference between the relationship between theology and Christology in the modern twentieth century and how theology-Christology relations were originally conceived of etymologically, to decenter, in Cullmann's words, how "one begins by stating their thoughts about *God*, and speaks only in the second place of their Christological convictions." Because of this, Cullmann re-centers to *the question of the meaning of Christology* to the question of the meaning of theology itself, making it necessarily clear that "early Christian theology is in reality almost exclusively Christology."[93] To this, Cullmann subsequently adds, "as [early Christian theology] concentrated its whole theological interest for several centuries on Christological discussions, the early Catholic Church remained close enough to the early Church."[94] For Cullmann, then, because *the question of the meaning of Christology* is tied so intimately to the question of the meaning of theology itself, insofar as "early Christian theology," as such, is "almost exclusively Christology," as such, any contemporary understanding of what Christology is and does must be intimately tied—albeit conceptually and ideologically, for existential purposes—to the early Church's understanding of what Christology is and does.

Thinking of *the question of the meaning of the Christology* as a science, to Cullmann's point, such that Cullmann comes to the conclusion that, at the very outset of his work, "We have described Christology as the science

92. Cullmann, *Christology of the New Testament*, 1.

93. Cullmann, *Christology of the New Testament*, 2–3.

94. Cullmann, *Christology of the New Testament*, 3.

whose object is the person and work of Christ."[95] With this in mind, and what I have articulated as *the question of the meaning of the Christology*, Cullmann articulates the following imperative of sorts: "now we ask to what extent a *problem* confronted the first Christians in this respect and exactly what [Christology] it is."[96] As Cullmann suggests, the problem with respect to *the question of the meaning of the Christology* is a historical problem, which confronts "the first Christians" as much as it confronts us—just as "the first Christians" wrestled with "exactly what [Christology] is," we, too, wrestle with the same issue. The difference, of course, is that "the first Christians" wrestled with one another, to the extent that, as we know, well-documented controversies arose about *the question of the meaning of Christology*. Though these controversies were not only about "what [Christology] is," to continue with Cullmann's point, but it was also about *how* Christology is, and *why* Christology is, and even *for whom* Christology is. Essentially, the what-question became, for "the first Christians," a how-question (how does Christology work?), a why-question (why has Christology happened?), and a for whom-question (for whom does Christology work?).

It is through these multi-dimensional questions, as Cullman writes, that the "so-called Christological controversies refer almost exclusively to the *person* or *nature* and that of God; on the other hand, to the relation which exists in Christ himself between his divine and his human nature."[97] Whether we are speaking about *the what, the how, the why*, or *the for whom*, we are speaking about *the question of the meaning of Christology* at the juncture, if you will, of the question of the meaning of the person of nature and the question of the meaning of nature of the divine. It is a controversy over what can be meant by person, by nature, and by divine. But, what Cullmann recognizes, too, that these questions are always questions hoping to understand and explain, in Cullman's words, the relation which exists in Christ himself between his divine and his human nature." It is a controversy that attempts to mitigate or adjudicate *the question of the meaning of Christology* from the standpoint of Christ's divinity and another standpoint associated with Christ's human nature. More than that, it is a controversy over how one fundamentally situates themselves to *the question of the meaning of Christology* from the standpoint of Christ's divinity and how this differs fundamentally from another standpoint concerned with Christ's human nature. Still, beyond this, it is about why we even speak of Christ's divinity over and against Christ's human nature—why is one standpoint different

95. Cullmann, *Christology of the New Testament*, 3.
96. Cullmann, *Christology of the New Testament*, 3.
97. Cullmann, *Christology of the New Testament*, 3.

from another? And lastly, for whom do we think about and explain Christ's divinity rather than Christ's human nature—for whom does it matter that one is upheld or advanced over the other? The problem, here, too, is that the multi-dimensional way that we ask *the question of the meaning of Christology* does more to bring together what we mean by divinity and what have we mean by human nature, rather than settle differences and relegate both to ideological corners. That is to say, when we speak about Christ, we are always-already speaking about both divinity and human nature, in much the same way as we are speaking of a historical Jesus—the qualify Jesus as "historical" does little to tame the fact that we are always-already speaking about divinity and human nature simultaneously.

The complicity of *the question of the meaning of Christology* is not lost on Cullmann, if carefully parsing Cullmann's concluding "the New Testament hardly ever speaks of the person of Christ without at the same time speaking of his work."[98] Given that this means that *the question of the meaning of Christology* is always a co-articulated question about "the person of Christ" and "his work," when we separate the two, we do injustice to the spirit of the question itself and commit violence to the meaning we hope to derive from the spirit of the question. All dimensions of this question—*the what, the how, the why,* and *the for whom*—make *the question of the meaning of Christology* all the more a contemporary articulation, ultimately divorced from what would have been articulated by the first Christians, just as much as what was articulated by the first Christians becomes divorced from the fathers associated with the early Church. If there is, Cullmann finds, "a difference between the way in which the first Christians and the later Church understood the Christological problems,"[99] what kind of difference is there between both parties and what attempts to be articulated now?

Are we not, now, concerned with Christological problems? Is there not still, now, a concern with *what* can be said about Christology, *how* Christology can be said as such, *why* we might say what is said through the term "Christology," and *for whom* do we direct what can be said with the term "Christology"?

Let us ask it this way: even from a contemporary understanding, what is it about the most ancient understandings of Christology—those of the first Christians and those of the early Church—that speaks to our own *what*? How do the ancient understandings of Christology address our own *how*, now? In surmising the *why* behind these ancient understandings, why do we come to our own understandings, now? If know *for whom* the ancient

---

98. Cullmann, *Christology of the New Testament*, 3.
99. Cullmann, *Christology of the New Testament*, 4.

understandings of Christology spoke, can be meaningfully ascertain our own *for whom*, now?

Cullmann's interests in how *the question of the meaning of Christology* is handled between ancient understandings and our own now is culminated in Cullmann's *Christology of the New Testament*, particularly in relation to Cullmann's earlier works: *Christus und die Zeit* (1946), translated as *Christ and Time* in 1951, and *The Early Church* (1956). For instance, as noted by the translator of *Christ and Time*, "[Cullmann] has dealt in a scholarly and vital way with a central issue of Biblical study and Christian theology."[100] Insofar as the "central issue" pivots on *the question of the meaning of Christology*, the translator of *Christ and Time* goes on to note that "[Cullmann] sharpens the issues between himself and such noted scholars as Rudolf Bultmann, Karl Barth, Emil Brunner, and Martin Werner."[101] While Barth, Brunner, and Werner[102] all hail the same Swiss school theology as contemporaries each wrestling with what role history plays in *the question of the meaning of Christology*, Bultmann's view of history adds another dimension to how Cullmann conceives of and confronts the issue for the sake of the establishment of Christological ideas. With all four figures at hand, Cullmann concedes in the introductory chapter to the third edition of *Christ and Time*, that "[the book] is a not a philosophy of history, as some erroneously concluded [. . .] but only as an analogy to the perspective of redemptive history."[103]

This analogy between "Christ" and "time" for Cullmann unmistakably bears a striking resemblance to Heidegger's own analogy between "being" and "time," particularly since Cullmann's *Christus und die Zeit* originally appears in German almost twenty years after Heidegger's *Sein und Zeit* originally appeared in 1927. What makes this resemblance between Cullmann and Heidegger all the more noticeable is that the third edition to the translated version of *Christus und die Zeit* as *Christ and Time* appears in 1962, with Cullmann's introductory chapter dated to Summer 1962—this is the same year that *Sein und Zeit* first appears as *Being and Time* in English, having been translated by John Macquarrie and Edward Robinson. The

---

100. Cullmann, *Christ and Time*, vii.

101. Cullmann, *Christ and Time*, vii

102. Martin Werner (1887–1964), Albert Schweitzer's friend, and Karl Barth's colleague, has been criticized, according to Alister McGrath (who coincidently published one of the rare studies of Emil Brunner's thought), for Werner's having "merely reasserted Schweitzer's ideas at a time when they were regarded as outdated, and made them the central platform of his ambitious explanation of the origins of dogma." McGrath, *A Scientific Theology*, 59.

103. Cullmann, *Christ and Time*, 8.

close proximity of Heidegger's *Being and Time* to Cullmann's *Christ and Time* in terms of the possibility that the former served as an influence on the latter seems rather straightforward, if we can say, to a certain extent, that the relationship Heidegger sees between *"sein"* and *"zeit"* marks a similar relatedness between what Cullmann sees between *"Christus"* and *"zeit."* At best, Heidegger's so-called existentialist analysis towards philosophizing influences Bultmann's existentialist interpretation towards New Testament theologizing which, in turn, brings a disagreement between Bultmann and Cullmann on how a "historical-critical approach to New Testament"[104] informs theologizing. To this point, when pitting Bultmann against Cullmann with respect to an existentialist Christology, Ed. L. Miller and Stanley J. Grenz, in the co-authored *Fortress Introduction to Contemporary Theologies* (1998)—which is, itself, co-dedicated to Cullmann—explain the Bultmann-Cullman relation in the following way: "[given] of all the critical responses to Bultmann, none was more systematic, sustained, and influential than that of Oscar Cullmann."[105] Miller and Grenz explain that Cullmann comes to "quite different conclusions from Bultmann's,"[106] even if, indeed, Cullmann makes some use of Heidegger through Bultmann to arrive at Cullmann's "different conclusions." Still, to the best of my knowledge, no other scholarship draws a direct relationship between Heidegger and Cullmann without Bultmann playing an intermediary part, even if what we see in the title of *Christ and Time* is an obvious appropriation of Heidegger's title of *Being and Time.* Nevertheless, in challenging Bultmann's theological handling of history, Miller and Grenz write, "[Cullmann] argued, for example, that considerable and reliable information can be recovered from the New Testament and related literature about the historical Jesus and his teaching."[107] This, of course, speaks to how Cullmann comes to *the question of the meaning of Christology.* While Bultmann largely argues against the possibility that any information—however limited or unreliable—"can be recovered," such that Bultmann's theologizing of *the question of the meaning of Christology* does not think information about the historical Jesus "can be recovered" either and rejects, in 1948, Cullmann espousal of a *"Heilsgeschichte"* in *Christ and Time,*[108] how Cullmann theologizes *the question of the meaning of Christol-*

---

104. Miller and Grenz, *Fortress Introduction to Contemporary Theologies*, 48.

105. Miller and Grenz, *Fortress Introduction to Contemporary Theologies*, 48.

106. Miller and Grenz, *Fortress Introduction to Contemporary Theologies*, 48.

107. Miller and Grenz, *Fortress Introduction to Contemporary Theologies*, 48.

108. Robert W. Funk cites three texts in which Bultmann rejects Cullmann: first, in *Existence and Faith*, secondly in two places in *Kerygma and Myth*, and thirdly in *Jesus Christ and Mythology.* The first of these, from 1948, is by far the most direct and explicit of the three. Funk, *Language, Hermeneutic, and Word of God*, 21.

ogy reconsiders, re-appropriates, and re-casts the problem of history and the meaningfulness of historicity towards Christological reflection. Cullmann's *"Heilsgeschichte"*—which can be rendered as either "saving history" or "history of salvation"—as that which grounds Cullmann's understanding of *the question of the meaning of Christology*, is not only at the heart of Cullmann's argument in *Christ and Time*, but it also later finds its way into *Heil als Geschichte* (1965), translated as *Salvation in History* in 1965.

As much as Bultmann disagrees with Cullmann in *"Heilsgeschichte und Geschichte"* (1948)—which, while originally subtitled as "A Review of Oscar Cullmann, *Christ and Time*,"[109] is translated as "History of Salvation and History" in Bultmann's collection, *Existence and Faith* in 1960—opposing "the picture that Cullmann draws of the early Christian conception of time and history,"[110] Robert W. Funk, in his *Language, Hermeneutic, and Word of God* (1966), characterizes Bultmann's opposition to Cullmann in the following way:

> [Bultmann] was concerned in this move to make it clear that faith does not permit itself any extrinsic basis in objective facts, certainly not in objective "saving facts." He was moved to point out, furthermore, that the language of faith, when it pictures God's acts mythologically, obscures the true character of faith precisely by its objectifying tendencies.[111]

Yet, given Funk's take on Bultmann's criticism of Cullmann and what Bultmann, himself, articulates about that criticism, Cullmann characterizes, in 1962—directly responding to Bultmann but predating Funk—is a kind of theologizing based on the following stance:

> I still maintain that the New Testament never speculates about God's eternal being, and since it is concerned primarily with God's redemptive activity, it does not make a philosophical, qualitative distinction between time and eternity. It knows linear time only; hence it is wrong to state that I show the authors of the New Testament to have made an article of faith out of linear time. It is a frame, within which they spoke of God's deeds [. . .] starting always from that which the whole message of the New Testament is about: God's redemptive activity.[112]

109. Bultmann, "History of Salvation and History," 226.

110. Bultmann, "History of Salvation and History," 226.

111. Funk, *Language, Hermeneutic, and Word of God*, 21.

112. Cullmann, *Christ and Time*, 10–11.

This notion of what Cullmann calls "God's redemptive activity" becomes a means of theologizing the New Testament, but it also becomes the very manner by which Cullmann eventually arrives at the kind of theologizing evident in *Christology of the New Testament*. In this sense, then, "God's redemptive activity"—which counters how Bultmann surmises the act of God—grounds how Cullmann understands and approaches *the question of the meaning of Christology*. What is laid bare in *Christ and Time* is the posing of a particular question to and the seeking of the specific meaning of Christology. By this, Cullmann's Christological reflection explores, Cullmann tells us towards the end of the original introduction to *Christ and Time*, "the unique element in the Christian conception of time as the scene of redemptive history is of a twofold character, and we desire to distinguish the two sides."[113] Cullmann presents the first part of this twofold character—the first of "two sides"—in these terms:

> Salvation is bound to a *continuous time process* which embraces past, present, and future. Revelation and salvation take place along the course of an ascending time line. [. . .] we must show how according to the Primitive Christian view revelation and salvation actually "occur" in a connected manner during the continuous time process.[114]

In building on this first part of the two-fold character, Cullmann describes the second part as this:

> It is characteristic of [the continuous time process] of time as the scene of redemptive history that all points of this redemptive line are related to the *one historical fact* at the mid-point, a fact which precisely in its unrepeatable character, which marks all historical events, is decisive for salvation, This fact is the death and resurrection of Jesus Christ.[115]

Here, Cullmann's "fact," as that which is based on the facticities of "the death and resurrection of Jesus Christ," is precisely what Bultmann criticizes as, in Bultmann's words, an "objective 'saving fact.'" Insofar as Bultmann disagrees with the possibility of an "extrinsic basis in objective facts," Cullmann conceives of a redemptive history that informs what it means to engage in Christological reflection and how, then, what it means to do Christology must contend with the two-fold character which Cullmann emphasizes as "a continuous time process" and "one historical fact."

113. Cullmann, *Christ and Time*, 32.
114. Cullmann, *Christ and Time*, 32.
115. Cullamnn, *Christ and Time*, 32–33.

To this end, Cullmann's handling of *the question of the meaning of Christology* is interpolated by understandings of temporality and historicity that are, despite Bultmann's vociferous opposition to Cullmann, decidedly post-Bultmannian. By contrast, Cullmann opposes Bultmann and Bultmannians explicitly in "Out of Season Remarks on the 'Historical Jesus' of the Bultmann School" (1961) wherein, as Evans characterizes, Cullmann "argues that the existentialist approach to [the] hermeneutics of Bultmann and [his] pupils hinders the efforts of the new quest, a quest which is otherwise appropriate and necessary."[116]

Given that Cullmann's overall approach is influenced by, a response to, and an expansion of Bultmann's meaning of Christology into a broader concern for the meaning of the historical Jesus, the same can be said of Käsemann's and Braun's own respective takes on *the question of the meaning of Christology* and how this fundamentally guides one's comportment to the fundamentals of the "new quest." What positions Käsemann and Braun respectively in relation to the Bultmann extends from the 1950s well into the 1960s—while Käsemann's *Jesus Means Freedom* in 1972, challenges Bultmann's historicizing, so too does Braun's *Jesus of Nazareth* in 1979. For Käsemann, in *Jesus Means Freedom*, *the question of the meaning of Christology* revolves around the understanding that "if the history of Jesus has any relevance at all, we cannot slink past this 'fact' without endangering everything else and at least robbing it of its concrete relation to Jesus' life, and so making it unintelligible."[117] On the other hand, for Braun, *the question of the meaning of Christology* revolves around an understanding of the history of Jesus, just as Käsemann maintains, but is largely grounded, in terms of the most of Braun's *Jesus of Nazareth*, to the teachings of Jesus.

HANS CONZELMANN

Like Cullmann, Hans Conzelmann attends to the concept of "*Heilsgeschichte*"—or "salvation history"—situating it with respect to Conzelmann's reading and interpretation of the Gospel of Luke. Similarily to how Cullmann's *Christ and Time* lays bare Cullmann's understanding of "*Heilsgeschichte*," the same is laid bare in Conzelmann's *Die Mitte der Zeit: Studien zur Theologie des Lukas* (1954), which can be literally rendered as "The Middle of Time" but is translated as *The Theology of St. Luke* in 1960.

While *The Theology of St. Luke* is considered as one of Conzelmann's major works, Conzelmann's other major contributions involve

116. Evans, *Life of Jesus Research*, 38.
117. Käsemann, *Jesus Means Freedom*, 17.

commentaries such as: *Die Apostelgeschichte* (1963), translated as *Acts of the Apostles: Commentary on the Acts of the Apostles* in 1987 and *Erste Brief an die Korinther* (1969), translated as *1 Corinthians: A Commentary in the First Epistle to the Corinthians* in 1975, with New Testament surveys such as: *Grundriss der Theologie des Neuen Testaments* (1967), translated as *An Outline of the Theology of the New Testament* in 1979, *Geschichte des Urchristentums* (1969), translated as *History of Primitive Christianity* in 1973, and *Arbeitsbuch zum Neuen Testament* (1975), translated as *Interpreting the New Testament* in 1988.

Yet, situated in between *The Theology of St. Luke* in the 1950s and the commentaries and surveys published largely across the 1960s is a small, but significant text that directly contributes to Conzelmann's own take on *the question of the meaning of Christology*: "*Jesus Christus*" (1959), originally published as an article in the multi-volume, *Die Religion in Geschichte und Gegenwart: Handwörterbuch für Theologie und Religionwissenschaft*. Translated as *Jesus*—but not until 1973—the original article, as explained in the Editor's Introduction to the English translation, is acknowledged by Norman Perrin in *Rediscovering the Teaching of Jesus* (1967) in the following way:

> The importance of this article is that Conzelmann successfully attempts a presentation of the current situation in life of Christ research, as seen from the perspective of the radical acceptance of the form-critical view of the sources characteristic of the Bultmann school, and so achieves a presentation of the factors involved in this research that should become a standard, a basis for future work as the perspective from which he starts becomes even more widely accepted.[118]

On the point, Perrin comes to say:

> In passing, may we say that it is an article which demands both translation into English and presentation in a form more readily accessible than that of an article within the pages of a multi-volume learned encyclopedia.[119]

Though Perrin makes this assertion "in passing," the sentiment, nonetheless, is far from passing. It speaks to the unique situation that Conzelmann's article is placed—it is originally written during the 1950s with the rise of voices contributing to the "new quest" for the historical Jesus, with its importance not acknowledged until the height of "new quest" at the end of

118. Perrin, *Rediscovering the Teaching of Jesus*, 42.
119. Perrin, *Rediscovering the Teaching of Jesus*, 42.

the 1960s, and, of course, the fact that it is not translated into English until the "new quest" was already mostly out of vogue. Though Perrin would certainly not have imagined it would take another six years for its English translation to appear, Perrin undoubtedly recognizing that Conzelmann's modest article is a participant—however obscured, to Perrin's point, "within the pages of a multi-volume learned encyclopedia"—to the Christological matters brought to bear by Käsemann as early as 1951. Perrin sees Conzelmann's article as being, in one sense, an active theological voice in *the question of the meaning of Christology*, but also a relatively passive historical artifact documenting the state of the "new quest" by 1959.

By pointing out what Perrin says about Conzelman's article, the editor of the English translation of the article seems to recognize that Conzelmann's contribution to the "new quest" has become long overdue. There is some irony, perhaps, given that Perrin also, by 1967, believed the contributions of the article were also long overdue—indeed, Perrin tells us that not only does the article "demand" translation into English, but it also "demands [. . .] presentation in a form more readily accessible than that of an article." Perrin's vision is ultimately brought to fruition by the book form of *Jesus*, even though it remains remarkable that, if it had not been for Perrin, Conzelmann's contribution to *the question of the meaning of Christology*, as that which owes its lineage to Käsemann and deserves a seat at the Christological table of the 1950s, what Conzelmann has to say would have remained resigned to the obscure (though noteworthy) pages of *Die Religion in Geschichte und Gegenwart: Handwörterbuch für Theologie und Religionwissenschaft* (known as the *RGG*).[120] For that matter, the "Jesus Christus" article would have remained overshadowed by Conzelmann's *The Theology of St. Luke* and Conzelmann's commentaries and surveys published largely across the 1960s.

In light of Perrin's characterization of it, the editor of the English translation of the article, John Reumann concludes:

> The encyclopedia article on "Jesus Christ" thus derives importance from its place of publication, *RGG*, and from the significance of its author, but Professor Conzelmann's stance and certain features of his presentation also help account for the meaningfulness which Professor Perrin and others see in it.[121]

---

120. The editor of the English translation of Conzelmann's article into *Jesus* tells us that, though "for several years plans have been under way for such [an English] version, to be called the Chicago Encyclopedia of Religion [. . .] the article on 'Jesus Christ' by Conzelmann will not appear in the Chicago publication." Conzelmann, *Jesus*, vi.

121. Conzelmann, *Jesus*, viii.

Given the meaningfulness that can be seen in Conzelmann by Perrin, we see Reumann locating the same meaningfulness in Conzelmann in the following way: "Conzelmann not only accepts, he applies the results of the critical-historical approach to the life of Jesus which developed over precisely the period in this century that the three editions of *RGG* cover."[122] By applying "the results of the critical-historical approach," Conzelmann approaches *the question of the meaning of Christology* in terms of "the life of Jesus," as that which "developed" through an ongoing Christological reflection "over precisely the period" marked by Schweitzer's *The Quest for the Historical Jesus* (1910). What has unfolded since Schweitzer, of course, are various iterations of *the question of the meaning of Christology* tempered by variations of Christological reflection, such that, once *the question of the meaning of Christology* traverses Bultmann's Christological reflection until the Christological reflection that informs Käsemann's ideological shift of a "new quest" with respect to *the question of the meaning of Christology*, it becomes all the more apparent, as Reumann asserts, "Conzelmann's article can be called a fruit of the new quest of the historical Jesus, for it appeared when in many ways that quest was at its height."[123] Reumann goes on to say:

> It was in this situation of the new quest that Conzelmann had to write his encyclopedia article. He was generally in sympathy with the quest's intent [. . .] However, he did not produce a "life" (like those of Bultmann or Bornkamm, other than this article) and soon announced his withdrawal from the quest and, like Käsemann, his dissatisfaction with much that was put forth under the guise of this endeavor. In many ways, however, Conzelmann's "Jesus Christ" represents a highwater mark of the new quest in its general representation of the position of the Bultmann school on the topic.[124]

It is through Conzelmann's "sympathy" with and his representing "a high-water mark" of the new quest that brings Conzelmann's interest with *the question of the meaning of Christology* as an expansion of those that belonged to Bultmann's circle. In this sense, if recognizing, to Reumann's point, that Conzelmann puts forth a "general representation of the position of the Bultmann school on the topic" of Christology, we view Conzelmann as a participant in the Bultmann School of Interpretation, insofar as "it deserves to be mentioned that," Reumann writes, "like most Bultmannites, Conzelmann does not follow a narrow party line but exhibits real independence

122. Conzelmann, *Jesus*, viii.
123. Conzelmann, *Jesus*, viii.
124. Conzelmann, *Jesus*, ix–x.

of outlook. (This is a characteristic of Bultmann's pupils generally.)"[125] As a result, through an independent Christological reflection rooted on *the question of the meaning of Christology*, Conzelmann's theological position, in Reumann's view, places "[an] emphasis on preaching (proclamation) as that which contemporizes Jesus for us today."[126]

In the last section of Conzelmann's *Jesus*, entitled "The Historical Jesus and Faith (Jesus of Nazareth and Jesus Christ)," Conzelmann situates his study more firmly within the circle of voices devoted to the "new quest" and *the question of the meaning of Christology* throughout the 1950s. The "literature" Conzelmann cites for this section includes texts from Ernst Fuchs (1952, 1956, 1957, 1958), Ernst Käsemann (1954), Nils Dahl (1955), Ernst Heitsch (1956), Peter Biehl (1956/1957), Hermann Diem (1957), Franz Mussner (1957), Johannes Schneider (1958), Gerhard Ebeling (1958), Joachim Jeremias (1958), and James M. Robinson (1959).[127] With all in tow, Conzelmann makes the following conclusion: "in terms of historical presentation, what happens after the crucifixion of Jesus is no longer the history of Jesus but the history of its consequences."[128] What arises from "the history of [the crucifixion's] consequences" is what Conzelmann cites as a theological question—one that is rooted in, but also filtered through and oriented by *the question of the meaning of Christology*—and he explains that:

> The theological question can be stated thus: how can a historical event be the *eschatological* event and encounter a person as such today? The answer is to be given by referring to proclamation: it can be present when *preached*. This possibility is then to be distinguished on principle from the historically comprehensible consequences of a personality.[129]

On this point, Conzelmann proceeds from Christological reflection and Christological thinking to the construction of *the question of the meaning of Christology* in terms of the posing of the question itself and the meaningfulness that lies therein, by taking us through it in the following methodical way:

> Now precisely in this framing of the question, further historical inquiry is not opposed, but is required. However, it no longer has as its aim that of giving faith its content—that it receives

125. Conzelmann, *Jesus*, x.
126. Conzelmann, *Jesus*, x.
127. Conzelmann, *Jesus*, 87–88.
128. Conzelmann, *Jesus*, 88.
129. Conzelmann, *Jesus*, 89.

through preaching. Rather its purpose is to keep us from losing sight of the historicity of the revelation and to confirm the fact that revelation is not a body of teaching, but a historical and historically encountered act.[130]

The extent that historical inquiry, as Conzelmann conceives it, "is required," this attends to "the historicity of the revelation" as that which is "a historical and historically encountered act." We can note here that Conzelmann is referencing different contexts of the meaning of history, which situates its meaningfulness as a network of understanding or, perhaps, a web of belief— it is an understanding of and a belief in the existentiality of the revelation as something that is existentially encountered as an existential act. Indeed, the meaning of history arches towards the existentiality of itself—the existentiality of history is its own meaningfulness, but what is construed existentially must be reified, sustained, and existentialized. To this, Conzelmann writes, "in dogmatic terms, this means that the belief that Jesus is true man is a tenet of faith which must be concretized time and again."[131]

Given the degree that "the belief that Jesus is true man" and the manner in which this, in itself, is "a tenet of faith," *the question of the meaning of Christology*, I submit, is laid bare by Conzelmann, as that which becomes represented by the problem of the historical Jesus. In this way, Christological reflection becomes dialectical reflection and, in turn, Christological thinking is dialectical thinking. Conzelmann views this as:

> The fact that the relationship of Jesus the preacher to the Christ who is preached has generally become a problem, indeed the central problem, of New Testament theology presupposes the origin of modern historical consciousness and, as a result of that, consideration of the biblical texts as historical sources.[132]

This eventually brings Conzelmann to say, through a concluding flourish:

> Only if one includes the event of proclamation in the problematic does he avoid the risk which today, as ever, threatens, viz., that once again in our day a picture of Jesus is made the basis of faith, a picture which is again psychologically based.[133]

130. Conzelmann, *Jesus*, 89.
131. Conzelmann, *Jesus*, 89.
132. Conzelmann, *Jesus*, 90.
133. Conzelmann, *Jesus*, 96.

Chapter 3

The Question of the Meaning
of Christology (III)

If we recall the last section of Conzelmann's *Jesus*, which lists "literature" that contribute to Conzelmann's characterization of the "new quest" by 1959, Conzelmann contextualizes his approach with what I refer to as *the question of the meaning of Christology* in terms of the following figures: Fuchs (1952, 1956, 1957, 1958), Käsemann (1954), Dahl (1955), Heitsch (1956), Biehl (1956/1957), Diem (1957), Mussner (1957), Schneider (1958), Ebeling (1958), Jeremias (1958), and Robinson (1959).[1] Insofar as Conzelmann's *Jesus* owes what it is to Conzelmann's "*Jesus Christus*," another Conzelmann article that participates in not just how Conzelmann positions himself to Life-of-Jesus research and, to a certain extent, how Life-of-Jesus research interpolates Conzelmann is: "*Zur Methode der Leben-Jesu-Forschung*" (1959)—published in the same year as "*Jesus Christus*," the latter article has a distinctly different textual transmission from "Jesus Christus," providing a more explicit assessment of *the question of the meaning of Christology*, rather than what can be implicitly drawn from "*Jesus Christus*."

Though originally published in *Zeitschrift für Theologie und Kirche*, in an October 1959 issue, "*Zur Methode der Leben-Jesu-Forschung*" was translated as "The Method of the Life of Jesus Research" as part of the Carl E. Braaten and Roy A. Harrisville co-edited collection, *The Historical Jesus and the Kerygmatic Christ* (1964). Eventually, however, "*Zur Methode der*

---

1. Conzelmann, *Jesus*, 87–88.

Leben-Jesu-Forschung" would be reprinted untranslated in Conzelmann's collection, *Theologie als Schriftauslegung* (1974)—we can note that this lattermost version appears only a year after Conzelmann's *Jesus* appears in translation in 1973. As with what arises in the *Jesus* text, but more narrowly in *"Zur Methode der Leben-Jesu-Forschung,"* Conzelmann references Robinson (1959), Bultmann (1950),[2] Barth (1955),[3] Käsemann (1954), Ebeling (1958), and Fuchs (1956, 1958). By way of what is excluded from it and what has been included in it, Conzelmann's *"Zur Methode der Leben-Jesu-Forschung"* has a narrower purpose than what we find in *Jesus* or even *"Jesus Christus."*

Conzelmann's *"Zur Methode der Leben-Jesu-Forschung,"* as Craig A. Evans explains in *Life of Jesus Research: An Annotated Bibliography* (1996), "defends the necessity of the quest of the historical Jesus; identifies several areas where important gains have been made."[4] Because of this, what becomes apparent about *"Zur Methode der Leben-Jesu-Forschung"* is that Conzelmann wishes to place himself alongside the figures he highlights in *Jesus*—in this way, through *"Zur Methode der Leben-Jesu-Forschung,"* we can situate Conzelmann more closely to *the question of the meaning of Christology* as it unfolds itself specifically for him, but also as it unfolds itself individually through a "method" oriented towards the Life-of-Jesus research of those that are acknowledged in Conzelmann's *Jesus*.

NILS DAHL

Though Nils Alstrup Dahl (1911–2001), a Norwegian theologian, is undoubtedly an important figure in the "new quest" for the historical Jesus in the 1950s—having been explicitly recognized by both Conzelmann and, later, Ebeling and Joachim Jeremias[5]—Dahl remains, oddly enough, largely overlooked and forgotten in contemporary surveys of the period by Alister McGrath's *The Making of Modern German Christology* (1994), both of Gregory W. Dawes' monographs (2000 and 2001), Theissen and Merz's co-authored, comprehensive *The Historical Jesus* (translated in 1998), Ben Witherington's *The Jesus Quest* (second edition in 1997) and even Craig S. Keener's exhaustive *The Historical Jesus of the Gospels* (2009). To the best of

2. This reference is to Bultmann's *"Das Problem der Hermeneutik"* (1950), which is later included in Bultmann's collection, *Glauben und Verstehen II* (1952).

3. This reference is to Barth's Church *Dogmatics 4.2.*

4. Evans, *Life of Jesus Research*, 32.

5. Joachim Jeremias, in his *"The Problem of the Historical Jesus"* (1964), mentions Dahl's article in a lengthy footnote.

my knowledge, with the exception of Evans' invaluable monograph *Life of Jesus Research: An Annotated Bibliography*, all scholarship into the development of *the question of the meaning of Christology* of the 1950s[6]—at least, that is to say, what has been produced in the last thirty years—has curiously omitted Dahl from its purview. This is even so of Paul N. Anderson's forward to the re-publication of Käsemann's *The Testament of Jesus* (2017), wherein Dahl is not mentioned among those that "kick-started the 'New Quest of Jesus.'"[7] It seems, then, that one would need to go as far back as the 1960s to find Dahl mentioned alongside Käsemann and Bornkamm,[8] as key figures challenging and taking Bultmann in new interpretative directions in the 1950s. Norman Perrin's *Rediscovering the Teaching of Jesus* (1967), in my view, is the last to address Dahl by name, rightly situating Dahl's voice within the small circle of Christological thinkers hoping to make sense out of and recast the historical Jesus.[9] Before Perrin, there is only the Carl A. Braaten and Roy A. Harrisville co-edited *Kerygma and History* collection (1962), in which Dahl is included with Bornkamm.

I do not presume to know precisely why Dahl has been lost to posterity, since, at least, the late 1960s. Suggesting a particular reason, now, will only take us too far afield from the implications of what has been lost. What remains apparent, at this juncture, is that, somehow, barely a decade after Dahl's "The Problem of the Historical Jesus" first appeared in German as *"Der historische Jesus als geschichtswissenschaftliches und theologisches Problem"* in 1955, the article became marginalized—this largely-forgotten article, which would have remained forgotten, if not for Conzelmann, Ebeling, the *Kerygma and History* collection, and Perrin, provides an important benchmark in the very beginning of *the question of the meaning of Christology* in the 1950s, as that which would further evolve by the 1960s.

Just as Perrin notes in his annotated bibliographies included in *Rediscovering the Teaching of Jesus*, Dahl's "The Problem of the Historical Jesus" originally appeared in Norwegian as, Craig A Evans' cites, *"Problemet dem*

6. Craig A. Evans' *Life of Jesus Research: An Annotated Bibliography* (1996) is, to be clear, the exception, though, keeping in mind, that it is just a bibliography of works presented chronologically, associated the history of "Life of Jesus" research. Evans provides only brief statements about each entry in his bibliography, which put forth only the briefest distillation of each entry's argument. In such brevity, there remains no detailed explication.

7. Anderson, *The Testament of Jesus*, xix.

8. As it is included in the Craig A. Evans edited, *The Historical Jesus: Volume 1* (2004), Joachim Jeremias' "The Problem of the Historical Jesus" is re-published, with Jeremias' lengthy footnote, wherein we find Käsemann's and Dahl's respective articles mentioned in close, chronological proximity.

9. See Norman Perrin's *Rediscovering the Teaching of Jesus* (1967).

historiske Jesus" in 1953.[10] In fact, as explained in a footnote by the editors of the *Kerygma and History* collection, "[the] essay originally appeared in a collection of lectures entitled *Rett laere og kjetterske meninger.*"[11] Given that the essay first appears in 1953, this is significant, since it pre-dates Käsemann's initial 1954 publication of "The Problem of the Historical Jesus"—we can further note, of course, that Dahl's and Käsemann's texts respectively share the same title—and can be dated just after Käsemann's 1951 inaugural lecture at Göttingen and contemporaneously to the 1953 presentation of the essay to the "Old Marburgers." Whether or not it is possible to say that either Dahl is influenced by Käsemann or Käsemann by Dahl, there is an undeniable kinship between the two as companion pieces, even though whatever significance either holds on the other remains largely dependent on hindsight, rather than anything that, to the best of my knowledge, can be derived contemporarily to Dahl's and Käsemann's time.

In summarizing Dahl's "The Problem of the Historical Jesus," Perrin describes it as "offer[ing] a good discussion of the problems of current Life of Christ research in general."[12] In this way, like Conzelmann's *Jesus*, Dahl attempts to provide what is, essentially, an assessment of the state of *the question of the meaning of Christology* with respect to "Life of Christ research." Though this is fundamentally similar to Conzelmann's task, the scope of Dahl's article is cast differently—this different scope is predicated, at least in part, on Dahl's Norwegian background, which Perrin further conceives of as "[Dahl's] confessedly conservative" approach.[13]

Be that as it may, Dahl's sense of what is a Christological "problem," as it pertains to Dahl's understanding of the historical Jesus, undoubtedly echoes Käsemann's notion of a Christological problem. Yet, setting aside any possibility of precisely knowing whether what Dahl highlights is influenced by Käsemann or if what the latter highlights is influenced by the former, Dahl begins "The Problem of the Historical Jesus" in a way that both encapsulates and anticipates what is at stake for *the question of the meaning of Christology* with this:

> The historical Jesus has become a problem for us. That does not mean that Jesus generally or primarily is a problem. Whatever the problem, we have a direct impression of Jesus as his figure encounters us in the Gospels [. . .] The *problem* of the historical Jesus first arises in connection with critical reflection which

10. Evans, *Life of Jesus Research*, 18.

11. Dahl, "Problem of the Historical Jesus," 139.

12. Perrin, *Rediscovering the Teaching of Jesus*, 102.

13. Perrin, *Rediscovering the Teaching of Jesus*, 102.

raises the question as to what can be ascertained about Jesus in purely historico-scientific fashion.[14]

Indeed, the fact that "we have a direct impression of Jesus" becomes, in itself, a problem when reconciling that impression with what is inherently problematic about "figure encounters us in the Gospels." What makes both issues a problem—to the extent that both collide into a problem with *the question of the meaning of Christology*—is how they lay bare what role history plays Christologically. In one sense, to even say "we have a direct impression of Jesus" is always tempered by history, insofar as whatever is "direct" and whatever impression is made possible is filtered through history. Still, in another sense, to even be aware of what "figure encounters us in the Gospels" means we must also be aware of what must be interpreted out of the history depicted for us and interpreted into the history that we, ourselves, occupy in the present. In both senses, history shapes the meaningfulness of what our "direct impression of Jesus" is and how that "figure encounters us in the Gospels." These two problems—which are really two sides of the same issue—is brought before us through Christological reflection, which allows what is problematic to come to the fore.

Through Christological reflection on the "problem" of the historical Jesus, Dahl begins to interrogate more closely the concept itself—that is to say, what is meant by the term "historical Jesus," if this concept, for Dahl, is integral, to approaching, understanding, and developing *the question of the meaning of Christology*:

> The concept of the "historical Jesus," as I use it here, designates Jesus as the object of methodical, critical, historical research, and the picture of him which can be drawn by such research. It is this historical Jesus which has become a problem for us.[15]

Though Dahl tells us that "historical Jesus," as a term is in reference to how he "use[s] it here," we know, too, that Käsemann is using the same term relatively contemporaneously. What we also know is that the problem, as Käsemann sees it, is fundamentally analogous to Dahl's conception of it, particularly if we can see that, for Dahl, the meaning of "historical Jesus" conceptualizes a specific designation. Indeed, Käsemann is ascribing to a designation, too. For Dahl, when we speak of "historical Jesus," he is referring to that which "designates Jesus as the object of methodical, critical, historical research." This is precisely what can be teased from Käsemann and, in short order, what Bornkamm designates. Insofar as Käsemann, Bornkamm,

---

14. Dahl, "Problem of the Historical Jesus," 138.
15. Dahl, "Problem of the Historical Jesus," 138.

and even Dahl all designate what they mean by "historical Jesus" similarly, what Dahl sees as "the picture of [Jesus] which can be drawn by" research speaks for Käsemann's and Bornkamm's respective interests in what conclusions can be drawn from methodical, critical, and historical research about what can be meant by "historical Jesus" itself.

What can be meant by "historical Jesus" is construed differently between Käsemann, Bornkamm, and Dahl, even though they all agree that, to Dahl's point, "this historical Jesus which has become a problem for us." Since Bornkamm is not yet in Dahl's purview, we can, perhaps, surmise that the "us" of which Dahl speaks may be an implicit acknowledgment of Käsemann. This is just a best guess, of course. Even if provable—or even disprovable—Dahl seemingly wishes to carve out his own articulation of the "problem" and what is "problematic," whether we can view this either in light of or in the shadow of Käsemann. After having elucidated what is meant by "historical Jesus" itself, Dahl explains precisely what he sees as the "problem" in what we mean when we say "the problem of the historical Jesus";

> The problem concerns not only the question whether it is at all possible to give a scientifically founded and tenable description of the life of Jesus; it also involves the question concerning the relevance of such a description for theology and the Church.[16]

On this point, "for theology and the Church," we see in Dahl, something that will remind us of the series of volumes associated with the *Journal for Theology and the Church*. Though according to Robert W. Funk, the journal "was conceived in a late night conversation with Gerhard Ebeling during the First Drew Consultation on Hermeneutics in 1962,"[17] with the first two volumes appearing in 1965, James M. Robinson's introduction to the journal, as it appears in *The Bultmann School of Interpretation* volume, wishes to clarify the means by which the journal hopes to focus on the "dialectic nature" of what "theology [is] in relation to the church"[18] and situate "the journal in the forefront of German theology since World War II."[19] How Funk and Robinson characterize what the task and scope of the *Journal for Theology and the Church* are locates its origins—in Robinson's case more explicitly—in Käsemann's "The Problem of the Historical Jesus," as

---

16. Dahl, "Problem of the Historical Jesus," 139.

17. Funk, "Forward," ix.

18. Robinson, "For Theology and the Church," 1.

19. Robinson, "For Theology and the Church," 1.

a programmatic essay, Robinson writes, "leading to the most of the new trends characterizing German theology today."[20]

Not only do we see, from Robinson, that "the new trends characterizing German theology today"—as in 1965—purposely narrows its perspective, but it also does so to the exclusion of anything outside of what was considered as "German theology" of the time. It is in this regard that we see how Dahl's "The Problem of the Historical Jesus," hailing from what can only be described, if attending to what could possibly be characterized at the time, as a Norwegian theology, would have been outside of an awareness of what "most of the new trends" were. Still, what remains curious is that, when Dahl's "The Problem of the Historical Jesus" did appear in German in 1955, it was published in the journal, *Kerygma und Dogma: Zeitschrift für theologische Forschung und kirchliche Lehre*. Like the *Journal for Theology and the Church*, the *Kerygma und Dogma* journal sought to place "theology in relation to the church" just as Robinson hopes to do for the *Journal for Theology and the Church*—this stands to reason, I submit, why *Kerygma und Dogma* publishes Dahl's "The Problem of the Historical Jesus" in what was, in fact, the journal's first year in publication in 1955. However, though it does not completely explain why Dahl's "The Problem of the Historical Jesus" goes unacknowledged by Robinson, I believe it does possibly explain, nonetheless, why Dahl's article never appears in *the Journal for Theology and the Church*—I submit two possible reasons: firstly, with the content of the *Journal for Theology and the Church* inspired by the earlier *Zeitschrift für Theologie und Kirche (ZthK)*, which began publishing in 1891, the *ZthK* never publishes Dahl's article, and secondly, given that the *Kerygma and History* collection appears in 1962 with an English translation of Dahl's article, it is plausible that the article was not granted re-published by the original publisher of *Kerygma und Myth* for the *Journal for Theology and the Church*, having appeared some three years later in 1965.

Indeed, the exclusion of Dahl by Robinson's recount in the introduction to the *Journal for Theology and the Church* is notable. I believe it is intentional, if recognizing that Robinson is casting his net with respect to only German theology, with the *Kerygma und Dogma* journal going unacknowledged. Nevertheless, as Robinson outlines the purpose of the *Journal for Theology and the Church* as "carry[ing] through the 'word event,' as Ebeling puts it, which is the hermeneutical work of theology and the church," this same purpose can be located in Dahl. To this end, it is safe to say that Dahl's conception of "the hermeneutical work of theology and the church" hopes to bring, just as Robinson writes, "theology in relation to the church," by, to

---

20. Robinson, "For Theology and the Church," 1.

Dahl's particular point, "contribut[ing] to the clarification of the historico-scientific and theological problem."[21]

As Robinson provides, which Conzelmann expounds on more exhaustively, Dahl provides a "history of the problem" as to the concept of "the historical Jesus."[22] After this historical survey of what I maintain as *the question of the meaning of Christology*, Dahl's presentation of "the historico-scientific problem" culminates with the following conclusion:

> No one can maintain that historical research has access only to the preaching of Jesus and not to his life. Rather, we must state that an historical understanding of his preaching can be attained only when it is seen in connection with his life, namely with the life which ended on the cross.[23]

What arises from this is what Dahl denotes as "the theological problem," which, ultimately, culminates with another conclusion—it is on the following point, Dahl ends the article:

> We must expect of dogmatic work in Christology that it not avoid the problem of the historical Jesus, but really have a concern for a better solution than the historical Life-of-Jesus theology and the dehistoricizing kerygma-theology.[24]

Here, we see Dahl is just as suspicious of what he calls "Historical Life-of-Jesus theology" as much as he is of "the dehistoricizing kerygma-theology," with an interest and deep investment, nonetheless, with "hav[ing] a concern for a better solution" to the problem of the historical Jesus.

ERNST HEITSCH AND PETER BIEHL

By providing what is inarguably the most exhaustive bibliography of texts directly and indirectly associated with—to borrow the title from James M. Robinson's monograph—studies into the historical Jesus, Craig A. Evans' *Life of Jesus Research* (1996), as part of the *New Testament Tools and Studies* series, is an essential resource. More so than anything that has been published before it or since, Evans' book, as a professed annotated bibliography, makes accessible so many otherwise unnoticed contributions to the history of the "life of Jesus" research—though comprehensive to the immensely

---

21. Dahl, "Problem of the Historical Jesus," 139.

22. Dahl, "Problem of the Historical Jesus," 139–150.

23. Dahl, "Problem of the Historical Jesus," 159.

24. Dahl, "Problem of the Historical Jesus," 171.

important periods of 1951–1955 and 1956–1960, with which we are reminded about all of the major contributors whose respective texts appear in close proximity to Käsemann's "The Problem of the Historical Jesus" of 1954, there are, indeed, several otherwise minor and lesser-known voices that would have remained largely forgotten, albiet marginalized, in Käsemann's shadow, if not for Evans' *Life of Jesus Research*. However, there are two voices worth noting that cross-pollinate Evans' *Life of Jesus Research* and to which direct references are made by Conzelmann and, later, Ebeling: Ernst Heitsch (1928–2019) and Peter Biehl (1931–2006)—both publish, in close proximity to one another, articles devoted to the question of the historical Jesus and the meaningfulness of the "new" quest involved, as those that lay bare *the question of the meaning of Christology.*

Let us consdier Heitsch first. Published in *Zeitschrift für Theologie und Kirche*, though still remaining untranslated, Heitsch's "*Die Aporie des historischen Jesus als Problem theologischer Hermeneutik*" (1956), which Evans describes as an article that "criticizes Bultmann; argues that the historical aspect of Jesus has been neglected."[25] This sort of argument, if placing it in context, appears in the same year as Bornkamm's *Jesus von Nazareth*, Fuchs' "*Due Frage nach dem historischen Jesus*," and Grundmann's *Die Geschichte Jesu Christi*. Rendered as "The Difficulty of the Historical Jesus as a Hermeneutical-Theological Problem," Heitsch begins with the following footnote on its title:

> *Die folgenden Gedanken sind erwachsen und haben sich geklärt in Gesprächen mit Herrn Professor Käsemann. Wenn ich nicht der theologischen Problematik vorbeirede, so verdanke ich das seiner immer erneuten Bereitwilligkeit, mit der er auf meine Fragen einging.*[26]

Here, Heitsch can be rendered in this way:

> The following thoughts have developed and have cleared themselves up in conversations with Mr. Professor Käsemann. If I do not talk through the theological problems, I owe it to [Käsemann's] constant willingness with which he answered my questions.

In this footnote, which functions as something of a disclaimer to what Heitsch intends to present in the article, the fact that Heitsch tells us that his thoughts "have developed and have cleared themselves up in conversations

---

25. Evans, *Life of Jesus Research*, 27.

26. Heitsch, "*Die Aporie des historischen Jesus als Problem theologischer Hermeneutik*," 192.

with" Käsemann is a significant admission. In one sense, while it allows us to place Heitsch in close proximity theologically to Käsemann, it also lays bare that the fundamentals to Heitsch's Christological reflection owes itself to Käsemann's own Christological reflection, insofar as the manner by which Käsemann approaches *the question of the meaning of Christology* informs, at Heitsch's own admission, how Heitsch approaches the question of and the meaningfulness to Christology. It is certainly not too strong a thing to say that Heitsch is influenced by Käsemann—in other words, Käsemann allows Heitsch to position himself to the question of the meaning of Christology in terms of what the problem of the historical Jesus was by 1956. Given that Käsemann's "*Das Problem des historischen Jesus*" first appeared in 1954, as a version of what Käsemann presented to the "Old Marburgers" the previous year, and is, to Evans' point, "credited with launching the new quest,"[27] it stands to reason that Käsemann would influence Heitsch—this is only made all the more explicit when considering that Heitsch cites the 1954 Käsemann article early in Heitsch's article and, again, Heitsch cites the same Käsemann article very early in another article, "*Über die Aneignung neutestamentlicher Überlieferung in der Gegenwart*" (1957), which can be rendered as "On the Appropriation of the New Testament Tradition in the Present," as something of a follow-up to "*Die Aporie des historischen Jesus als Problem theologischer Hermeneutik.*"

Insofar as, Heitsch writes, he will "not talk through the theological problems," and that Käsemann helped him work through and answer his questions, we can view these "questions" being "answered," I submit, as relating to the larger *question of the meaning of Christology*. Essentially, if we see Käsemann as being an interlocutor for Heitsch on matters of Christological thinking, we see Heitsch coming to terms with what is at stake in his Christological reflection, as that which explicitly lays bare the "*Aporie*" or the "difficulty" of what it means to engage with the problem of the historical Jesus. The fact that Heitsch acknowledges this difficulty is not new, since we see, just within the same year as Heitsch's "*Die Aporie des historischen Jesus als Problem theologischer Hermeneutik*" appears, Grundmann, Fuchs, and Bornkamm also wrestling, to different extents, the "difficulty" that arises in the problem of the historical Jesus. It is, which Heitsch points out in the title to his article, an issue with theological hermeneutics—the problem of the historical Jesus, as such, comes to bear through the problem of theological hermeneutics. This, of course, is certainly not lost on Bornkamm, Fuchs, nor Grundmann any more than it is out of the purview of those immediately following Hietsch: the likes of Braun, Conzelmann, or Diem (which

---

27. Evans, *Life of Jesus Research*, 25.

we will discuss shortly), who all engage in some version of Life-of-Jesus research and produce articles that appear in 1957.

There is a difference, however, in how *the question of the meaning of Christology* is handled by Heitsch, given the background from which Heitsch's theologizing comes. Heitsch's academic background and research interests were in classical philology and, by extension, he specialized in ancient Greek philosophy, having written commentaries on Plato. Nevertheless, along with classical philology, Heitsch studied philosophy and theology at the University of Göttingen, beginning in 1948 and throughout the 1950s—it was at the University of Göttingen, it seems, that Heitsch came in contact with Käsemann, who taught at Göttingen from 1951 to 1959. This seems to be how Heitsch becomes drawn into Life-of-Jesus research, though I do not presume to know what sort of relationship Heitsch had with Käsemann or if Heitsch was one of Käsemann's Göttingen students, during the years before Heitsch became an adjunct professor at Göttingen in 1960. Similarly, it is difficult to say if Heitsch, by way of Käsemann, was secondarily involved with other Bultmannians—to the best of my knowledge, with Heitsch's "*Die Aporie des historischen Jesus als Problem theologischer Hermeneutik*" as the only contribution to Life-of-Jesus research, I would venture to say that, given the rest of Heitsch's scholarly output, the article is more of an outlier, rather than anything in which Heitsch had any sustained interest.

One can only guess, judging from what seems to be implied in Heitsch's footnote to "*Die Aporie des historischen Jesus als Problem theologischer Hermeneutik.*" Still, I find in Heitsch a fundamental articulation of the dimensions and complexity of the "difficulty" one is faced with when assessing what is problematic about the problem of the historical Jesus and how this problematizes *the question of the meaning of Christology*. Heitsch describes what is at stake in the following way:

> *Der Historiker im weiteren Sinne sieht sich einer Traditionsmasse gegenüber, die erm it den Mitteln seiner jeweiligen Disziplin zu verstehen sucht. Sofern der Neutestamentler Literahistoriker ist, gilt dementsprechend für ihn, daß er seine Text emit den heute entwickelten Interpretationsmethoden zum Sprechen bringt. Er unterstellt sich somit den Aufgaben jeder philologischen Wissenschaft.*[28]

Here, Heitsch can be rendered as follows:

28. Heitsch, "*Die Aporie des historischen Jesus als Problem theologischer Hermeneutik,*" 192.

> The historian in the broader sense faces a traditional mass that he tries to understand with the means of his respective discipline. If the New Testament literary historian is, the same applies to him that he brings his texts to speak with the interpretation methods developed today. He subordinates himself to the tasks of every philological science.

Though Heitsch speaks about "the historian" more generally and then proceeds to specifically discuss "the New Testament literary historian," we see that Heitsch characterizes these two persons as engaged in different tasks and oriented towards different goals in terms of scope. Yet, both, as Heitsch points out, subordinate themselves "to the tasks of every philological science." What we can take this to mean, then, is that, for Heitsch, whether one is a historian "in the broader sense" or a New Testament literary historian in the narrower sense, both confront and are confronted by "philological science"—in this, what it means to do Christology depends on what it means to do philology. All told, Heitsch sees the problem of the historical Jesus as a philological problem, such theological hermeneutics contextualize *the question of the meaning of Christology.*

Now, let me consider Biehl. Like Heitsch, Biehl was associated with Göttingen, having been appointed to Göttingen's education department as a professor of evangelical religious education from 1969 to 1996. While Heitsch left Göttingen two years before Biehl began there, both men retire in 1996: Heitsch retiring from the University of Regensburg, and Biehl, of course, from Göttingen. Like Heitsch, Biehl is explicitly interested in the problem of the historical Jesus, approaching the subject relatively contemporaneously to Heitsch.

Published in *Theologische Rundschau* though still remaining untranslated, Biehl's "*Zur Frage nach dem historischen Jesus*" (1957/1958),[29] which can be rendered as "On the Question of the Historical Jesus," is, as Evans briefly describes in the bibliographies of *Life of Jesus Research*, focused on "examin[ing] the views of R. Bultmann, H. Diem, E. Heitsch, E. Käsemann, N. Dahl, and E. Fuchs."[30] This is certainly what Biehl makes explicit before actually beginning the article itself—all of the figures Evans mentions are noted by Biehl, along with one that Evans does not mention: Walter Kümmel.[31]

29. Though both Conzelmann and Ebeling date this article to "1956/1957," the volume and issue number in which the article appears in *Theologische Rundschau* is dated 1957/1958.

30. Evans, *Life of Jesus Research*, 9.

31. This text is dated to 1940, while nearly all of the other texts to which Dahl refers belong to a small window between 1954 to 1956. An outlier in this is a second

What Biehl accomplishes, then, is a front-loading of texts which both inform how he wishes to approach "the question of the historical Jesus" and allows him to situate himself in what he acknowledges as an ongoing "question" marked by an ongoing discussion. Beginning with Bultmann, as Biehl does, is not so much about allowing Bultmann to be a chronological starting point as it about viewing Bultmann as an ideological starting point for the "problem" itself. The two Bultmann texts that Biehl point out (from 1936 and 1954) present the task and outline the scope, with which Diem, Käsemann, Dahl, Heitsch, and Fuchs are all oriented. By positioning himself in a way that not only follows all the figures in Biehl's purview, but, more importantly, follows Bultmann in particular—at the time of the publication of Biehl's "On the Question of the Historical Jesus," Biehl was already working as Bultmann's personal assistant at Marburg, doing so from 1956 to 1969. Insofar as Biehl uses Bultmann as a starting point in Biehl's contextualization of "the question of the historical Jesus" as that which modulates *the question of the meaning of Christology*, where Biehl begins is with Bultmann's Christological reflection on the historical Jesus through a theologizing of Pauline thought—both of the Bultmann texts and the Kümmel text (dated to 1940) are concerned with what Jesus-Paul relations mean Christologically.

Like Conzelmann, Biehl's presentation of what is laid bare before him and how all has come to bear on what he intends to say on the matter of "the historical Jesus"—the difference, however, is that Biehl sets a specific tone predicated on the following, which Biehl cites directly from the outset of Fuchs' "The Question of the Historical Jesus" (1956): *"Die Frage nach dem historischen Jesus ist da, seit es eine sich ihrer Aufgabe bewußt gewordene neutestamentliche Wissenschaft gibt."*[32] This can be rendered as: "the question of the historical Jesus has been there since New Testament science became aware of its task." In it, Biehl suggests that New Testament theologizing itself is a theologizing of the question of the historical Jesus—what this means, then, is to even engage in the act of theologizing we are always-already engaging in the act of approaching the question of the historical Jesus. Essentially, to say that the question of the historical Jesus, as it is by circa 1957, "has been there" from the very moment that New Testament theologizing "became aware of its task," Biehl is acknowledging that the posing of the question to and the meaningfulness of Christology is not novel to 1957—it is not even novel to the recent memory of Biehl's day. Rather, the question of the historical Jesus, at its most fundamental, for Biehl, is imbued

---

text authored by Bultmann, dated to 1936.

32. Biehl, *"Zur Frage nach dem historischen Jesus,"* 54.

in the very making of the New Testament itself and pre-wired in the theologizing that exudes from it.

If we are always-already working through the question of the historical Jesus, we are also always-already working through *the question of the meaning of Christology*—the very science of the New Testament is also the science of Christological reflection, Christological thinking, and what it means to do Christology.

With the notion of "science" in mind, Biehl points to Dahl's "*Problemet dem historiske Jesus*" from 1953 as a grounding point, rather than Käsemann's "*Das Problem des historischen Jesus.*" This grounding point, for Biehl, is the theologizing from which the "new quest" projects itself. Beginning with Dahl is a noticeable ideological shift, even for Biehl in 1957/1958, since it is safe to say that, by this time, there was some general consensus that Käsemann—following on this ideological shift, Biehl finds that: "*Dahl skizziert noch einmal den Weg dieser Wissenschaft [. . .], der über den noch heute aktuellen Streit zwischen M. Kähler und W. Herrmann in unsere Situation führt.*"[33] Here, we can render Biehl's words as: "Dahl once again outlines the path of this science [. . .] which leads into our situation about the dispute between M. Kähler and W. Herrmann that is still relevant today." While we see Biehl interested in Dahl as someone that "outlines the path of [the] science" of New Testament theologizing and, I submit, that which articulates itself as *the question of the meaning of Christology*, we also see that Biehl is deeply invested in the situation of the day—what Biehl calls "our situation"—which Biehl situates as a "dispute" between contemporaries Martin Kähler and Wilhelm Herrmann (1846–1922).[34] This dispute, as Biehl sees its relevance even in circa 1957, is with respect to Kähler's understanding of what matters historically about Jesus and Herrmann's liberal theology.

Ultimately, Biehl's handling of *the question of the meaning of Christology* is calibrated by the Kähler-Herrmann dispute, as that which lends itself to the state of Life-of-Jesus research, which Biehl explains in the following way:

> *Diese ist dadurch gekennzeichnet, daß die genuin liberale Frage*
> *nach dem historischen Jesus wieder zunehmend an theologischem*
> *Gewicht gewinnt, paradoxerweise freilich in einer Zeit, in welcher*
> *der Liberalismus kirchlich weitgehend ausgeschaltet ist, und im*

---

33. Biehl, "*Zur Frage nach dem historischen Jesus,*" 54.

34. As a professor at the University of Marburg and remaining there for the duration of his professional career, Herrmann taught Rudolf Bultmann, Karl Barth, and John Gresham Machen (1881–1937).

Gegenschlag zu einer auf dem Boden des Liberalismus erwach-
senen historischen und theologischen Kritik.[35]

Here, Biehl can be rendered in the following way:

> This is characterized by the fact that the genuine liberal ques-
> tion about the historical Jesus is gaining increasing theological
> weight again, paradoxically, indeed, at a time when liberalism is
> largely shut out of the church, and in opposition to a historical
> and theological criticism that developed on the basis of liberal
> criticism.

It is out of this "dispute" that Biehl's Christological reflection charts his
Christological thinking about posing the question to and seeking the meaningfulness of Christology itself. Biehl's wish, then, is to negotiate between
the two—between Kähler and Herrmann—as a means of understanding
what the task and scope of Christology should be and in what manner that
task and scope should be, in itself, shaped by the perennial problem of the
historical Jesus.

HERMANN DIEM

To a certain extent, like Biehl, Hermann Diem (1900–75) is intent on nego-
tiating a similar "dispute," but one that is more firmly rooted in the relationship between dogmatic and biblical theology, particularly as a debate arising
in the 1950s. Just as Sylvester P. Schilling details in *Contemporary Continental Theologians* (1966)—in, to the best of my knowledge, is one of the few
assessments of Diem's theologizing—Diem is "among the theologians most
positively influenced by Karl Barth [and] has addressed himself more vigor-
ously to the central issues in the current theological debate" of the day.[36]
Though Diem is noted for, Schilling writes, "the exceptional distinction of
having been named to a German university professorship in middle age,
directly from the pastorate, without the usual requirement of 'habilitation'
through postdoctoral dissertation,"[37] the same sort of "exceptional distinction" can be used to characterize Barth's own ascension into academia from
his own pastorate in the village of Safewil in Switzerland—it seems to me
that this becomes a foundational part of the influence Barth has on Diem.

Yet, it is through Barth's break with liberalism and, more particularly,
liberal theology of his own chief influence, Wilhelm Herrmann, as early as

---

35. Biehl, *"Zur Frage nach dem historischen Jesus,"* 54.
36. Schilling, *Contemporary Continental Theologians*, 41.
37. Schilling, *Contemporary Continental Theologians*, 41.

1914, which positions Diem theologically through Diem's theological association with Barth. This positioning by way of Barth also, subsequently, place Diem positionally in relation to Bultmann and the Bultmannians, due to Barth's own relations. Insofar as Diem conceives of the opposition between Barth and Bultmann (and the Bultmannians) as an opposition between the matters of dogmatics and those of exegesis, Schilling considers Diem's need "to bring the divergent positions into renewed discussion with each other [which] has been a major concern of [Diem's] theological labor."[38] Schilling goes on to say:

> His intention is not to chart a mediating path between them, but to discover a way by which the conflicting questions and answers may be so formulated that comparisons may again become possible. In pursuing this purpose he inevitably discloses and develops his own theological standpoint.[39]

Schilling situates Diem's "theological standpoint" in the following way, which becomes immensely important in how we can understand Diem's approach to *the question of the meaning of Christology* as an off-shoot of how we can conceive of, with the help of Schilling, Diem's theological standpoint:

> In the debate between dogmatic and biblical theology two questions have emerged: (1) What is the right relationship between dogmatics and exegesis? (2) What is the essential task of dogmatics itself? Diem finds a valuable approach to both questions in the examination of a problem which is important to both Barth and Bultmann—the meaning of the historical Jesus for the preaching and doctrine of the church.[40]

Schilling correctly notes that the term "historical" towards "the meaning of the historical Jesus" is a term that Diem avoids—Schilling footnotes this disclaimer as: "Diem prefers the term *earthly Jesus* to avoid the ambiguity involved in [the] current use of the word *historical*."[41]

It is, to this end, Diem's consideration of "the earthly Jesus" with respect to "the Christ of faith," which can be generally characterized, Schilling writes, in this way:

> In Diem's view, the starting point as well as the historical locus of all Christian theology is the self-proclamation of Jesus in the Gospels. However, this self-proclamation comes to us not as an

38. Schilling, *Contemporary Continental Theologians*, 44.
39. Schilling, *Contemporary Continental Theologians*, 44.
40. Schilling, *Contemporary Continental Theologians*, 44.
41. Schilling, *Contemporary Continental Theologians*, 44.

objective historical report, but as part of the early church's proc-lamation of Jesus as the Messiah.[42]

This "starting point" for Diem is laid bare in Diem's "*Der irdische Jesus und der Christus des Glaubens*" (1957), included in the Helmut Ristow and Karl Matthiae co-edited collection, *Der historische Jesus und der kerygmatische Christus* (1960), and later included in translatiom as "The Earthly Jesus and the Christ of Faith" in *Kergyma and History* (1962).

As Evans explains in *Life of Jesus Research*, Diem's "*Der irdische Jesus und der Christus des Glaubens*": "criticizes Bultmann arguing that historical involves more than only what can be verfified."[43] This brings Diem into the ongoing discussions into the problem of the historical Jesus. In this way, what we find in Diem's argument is something that implicitly dialogues with Käsemann's own critique of Bultmann, arising from, as Evans describes Käsemann's "*Das Problem des historischen Jesus*," Käsemann's own "dissati-fication with Bultmann's position"[44] on what was, by 1954 for Käsemann, a glaring problem. This problem, by 1957 for Diem remained a critical com-ponent of the Christological reflection of Butlmannians led by Käsemann's call for a "new quest."

Though it might be too strong a claim to say that Diem was among the Bultmannians—to the best of my knowledge, there has been no claim in this regard—Diem was, nonetheless, deeply ensconced theologically with Käsemann, as well as the small group of theologians that belonged to the "Old Marburgers" by 1949. Diem can be found in a group picture captur-ing a meeting of the "Old Marburgers" dated precisely to October 1949, which includes, most notably, Bultmann, Gadamer, Ebeling, Käsemann, Bornkamm, and Fuchs.[45] This picture shows not so much Diem's alignment with Bultmann—since we do find, of course, several others in the picture that disagree with Bultmann theologically—but, rather, it does shows Di-em's alignment with those that became known as Bultmannians, which, in itself, is rather interesting given Diem's earlier Barthian influences. Yet, what ties Diem to the Bultmannians, *per se*, is his relationship with Käsemann, as that which can be pinpointed to ties both had to the University of Tübingen. By the time Käsemann began teaching at Tübingen in 1959, Diem began

---

42. Schilling, *Contemporary Continental Theologians*, 44.

43. Evans, *Life of Jesus Research*, 28.

44. Evans, *Life of Jesus Research*, 25.

45. Diem can be seen, in the picture reproduced in Konrad Hammann's biography on Bultmann, prominently standing to the extreme left of the second row of the rather large group photo, with Bultmann among the few seated in the front row. Hammann, *Rudolf Bultmann*, 392.

teaching there two years earlier in 1957 eventually becoming Tübingen rector by 1964, and continuing at Tübingen until his death in 1975 (Käsemann would retire from Tübingen in 1971).

The fact that Diem's paths crossed with Käsemann certainly gives a necessary context to how Diem approaches *the question of the meaning of Christology* by 1957. Given that Diem is noted for a monograph on Kierkegaard that originally appeared in 1950, Diem's *"Der irdische Jesus und der Christus des Glaubens"* stands out in Diem's body of work and is, to be sure, Diem's one and only contribution to Life-of-Jesus research in the 1950s. As such, Diem's *"Der irdische Jesus und der Christus des Glaubens"* can be contextualized as following Bornkamm, Fuchs, Grundmann and Heitsch, all appearing in 1956, and Braun, Conzelmann's *"Gegenwart und Zukunft in the synoptischen Tradition,"* Fuchs, Käsemann's *"Neutestamentliche Fragen von heute,"* and Mussner, all appearing in 1957.

It is with this context that the opening of Diem's *"Der irdische Jesus und der Christus des Glaubens"* all the more stands out, even in translation as the following:

> Ever since the penetration of historical-critical thought into theology there has been inquiry into the relationsip between the historical Jesus and the Christ of faith. If I feel compelled to break with this usual formulation of the question and inquire into the *earthly* rather than the historical Jesus, it is because that is the more relevant and comprehensive way of putting the question. It is only within this formulation of the question that the subordinate question regarding the historical Jesus can be properly put and answered.[46]

Here, we can note the emphasis Diem places on "earthly" over "historical"— Schilling, again, points this out for us, though Diem couches the reason for this in terms of what allows for a "more relevant and comprehensive way of putting the question." What this question is, I submit, is *the question of the meaning of Christology*—it is this question, for Diem, that gives more of an account for the ramifications of the "earthly Jesus" rather than a "historical Jesus."

We need not see in Diem's preference an issue of semantics in his favoring of the former over the latter. Rather, Diem views the notion of an "earthly Jesus" as key to the formulation of *the question of the meaning of Christology* itself. It is by what is meant by saying "earthly Jesus" that, as Diem finds it, "the subordinate question regarding the historical Jesus can be properly put and answered." In other words, it is by working through

---

46. Diem, "Earthly Jesus and the Christ of Faith," 197.

the "subordinate question regarding the historical Jesus" that we are able to come to the more immediate, existential question regarding the "earthly Jesus." Christological reflection makes this happen, where by Christological thinking allows us to think through the notion of the historical Jesus to arrive at the notion of the earthly Jesus—it is by speaking of what is "earthly" about Jesus that we can make better sense of what is "historical" about Jesus. To this end, Diem explains:

> The question of the relation of faith to the earthly Jesus is thus the prior question because it existed even before there was a New Testament, and hence even before there was a historical criticism of the New Testament. This question was already addressed to the eyewitnesses of Jesus' life.[47]

Diem considers this as the "decisive question,"[48] which, later, allows Diem concludes that:

> We must now gain final clarity concerning what historical question of truth is actually to be put to the Gospels, for without an answer to this question the relationship of the historical to the theological question of truth cannot be determined.[49]

This "historical question of truth" is precisely *the question of the meaning of Christology*, insofar as the posing of the question to and seeking the meaningfulness of Christology is predicated on what is existentially laid bare in the Gospels in a way that existentializes us. Yet, Diem warns us that "before the historical question of truth can be posed [. . .] we must first determine what is the object of historical-critical research when we inquire into the story of the earthly Jesus."[50]

If it is in this vain, for Diem, that *the question of the meaning of Christology* "can be posed," Diem makes the following assessment:

> In pursuit of the discovery of the kerygmatic character of the Gospels an alternative question has been raised, i.e., whether this object is the life or the preaching of Jesus. No one, of course, has quite succeeded with this alternative, but that theology which regards historical research into the life of Jesus as a failure inquires first into the kerygma of Jesus.[51]

---

47. Diem, "Earthly Jesus and the Christ of Faith," 197.
48. Diem, "Earthly Jesus and the Christ of Faith," 197.
49. Diem, "Earthly Jesus and the Christ of Faith," 201.
50. Diem, "Earthly Jesus and the Christ of Faith," 201.
51. Diem, "Earthly Jesus and the Christ of Faith," 201.

By considering those that trace an "alternative question" for the sake of what Diem wishes to designate to a school of "kerygma-theology," Diem characterizes:

> Those theologians who are of the opinion that they can carry on the Life-of-Jesus research by using new and especially Jewish sources, and whom we call the "theological right wing" as to their origin, do not intend and indeed cannot disregard the kerygmatic character of the Gospels.[52]

Given the significance of "the kerygmatic character of the Gospels," Diem finds that, as unavoidable as that "kerygmatic character" is, other theologians theologizing the Gospels to lay bare *the question of the meaning of Christology,* "are afraid [that] this proclamation will become merely a general truth when loosed from history, or at least when the historical knowledge of this history is declared to be theologically irrelevant."[53] On this point, Diem suggests that "for that reason they are interested in the historically ascertainable event-character of this history and concentrate their work upon it."[54]

Though Diem resists explicitly referencing the theologians of whom he is speaking—and we see throughout "*Der irdische Jesus und der Christus des Glaubens*" and the translated version appearing in the *Kerygma and History* collection that there are interestingly no footnotes or citations—it is relatively clear which theologians "are interested in the historically ascertainable event-character." What Diem terms as "event-character" is a recognizable take, I submit, on Ebeling's notion of "word-event" and Fuchs' notion of "language-event," as well as how Bornkamm and Conzelmann respectively conceive of "event." If we can say, then, that, in Diem's view, Ebeling, Fuchs, Bornkamm, and Conzelmann, as a composite of a larger trend by 1957, "are afraid," Diem says, "this proclamation will become merely a general truth when loosed from history," Diem wishes to more meaningfully handle the relationship between proclamation and history, for the sake of disclosing a specific "truth" couched in *the question of the meaning of Christology.*

In attending to proclamation in terms of "kerygma" as "preaching" and history in terms of the historical as "earthly," as both come to bear on Diem's sense of "the earthly Jesus" means in relation to the "Christ of faith," Diem arrives at the following conclusion:

---

52. Diem, "Earthly Jesus and the Christ of Faith," 201.

53. Diem, "Earthly Jesus and the Christ of Faith," 201.

54. Diem, "Earthly Jesus and the Christ of Faith," 201.

> Only the historical interval which separates from the preach-
> ing of the earthly Jesus would be removed and the way opened
> up on which the earthly Jesus will encounter us in the *Christus
> praedicatus*. But not even the most positive results of historical
> research concerning that continuity could guarantee us that he
> really will or actually must encounter us here [. . .] this encounter
> can only come about when the Church simply dares to *preach*
> the Christ of the Scriptures in order that he may demonstrate
> himself to be the living and present Christ.[55]

Here, the emphasis Diem places on "*Christus praedicatus*" is important
to what he means by "encounter" and, more aptly, what "must encounter
us here." The notion of "*Christus praedicatus*" or the "proclaimed Christ"
predicates itself on *the question of the meaning of Christology*, as that which
is foundationally about posing the question and seeking the meaningfulness of Christology—if the posing and seeking are both about an encounter
and this encounter, Diem writes, "can only come about when the Church
simply dares to *preach* the Christ of the Scriptures," the act of preaching (or
the "*kerygma*" itself), through a Christological reflection, is what ties the
meaning of "the earthly Jesus" to the meaning of "the Christ of faith" in a
way that existentializes how this dual identity demonstrates itself "to be the
living and present Christ."

In light of "The Earthly Jesus and the Christ of Faith," Diem's understanding of the relationship between the act of preaching and *the question
of the meaning of Christology* can be also found in a text that pre-dates "The
Earthly Jesus and the Christ of Faith": *Dogmatik: Ihr Weg zwischen Historismus und Existenzialismus* (1955), which can be literally rendered into
"Dogmatics: Your Way Between Historicism and Existentialism." In a way,
"The Earthly Jesus and the Christ of Faith" can be seen as an expansion or
a more focused treatment of what originally appears in *Dogmatik: Ihr Weg
zwischen Historismus und Existenzialismus*—however, it is possible to view
"The Earthly Jesus and the Christ of Faith" as influencing the translation of
Dogmatik: Ihr Weg zwischen Historismus und Existenzialismus into simply
Dogmatics in 1959. Though, to be sure, there are two specific sections in
Dogmatics of relevance—one, entitled, "The Meaning of the Historical Jesus
for the Preaching, Doctrine and Faith of the Church" and the other, entitled,
"The History of Jesus Christ Who Is his Preaching Reveals and Authenti-
cates Himself." The two, perhaps more explicitly than the other sections that
make up *Dogmatics*, jointly demonstrate how Diem uses "The Earthly Jesus
and the Christ of Faith" to thematically expand on them by 1957, while we

---

55. Diem, "Earthly Jesus and the Christ of Faith," 211.

can see, too, with Diem's participation in the 1959 translation with an "Author's Foreword," Diem seemingly interested in allows the two specific sections along with the rest of Dogmatics to contextually expand "The Earthly Jesus and the Christ of Faith."

WALTER GRUNDMANN AND ETHELBERT STAUFFER

Given the bibliographies of Evans' *Life of Jesus Research*, if focusing on just a handful of relatively minor, but still signficant, figures listed in the "general discussion" section devoted to 1956–60 with which Bornkamm's *Jesus of Nazareth* prominantly leads and marks the beginning of the period,[56] I want to highlight the two individuals, by attending to how both approach *the question of the meaning of Christology*, and the means by which both situate themselves Christologically respectively in terms of their own Christological reflection: Walter Grundmann (1906–76) and Ethelbert Stauffer (1902–79).

As noted by Evans, Walter Grundmann's *Die Geschichte Jesu Christi* (1956), which can be translated as "The History of Jesus Christ," is "a massive study [that] systematically investigates the events in the life and minstry of Jesus [and] covers all of Jesus' teaching."[57] In it, Evans tell us, Grundmann "regards the gospels as essentially reliable."[58] Though Evans' remarks are extremely brief, they encapulate how Grundmann attends to *the question of the meaning of Christology* by following Bornkamm into a reassessment of the importance of the "historical Jesus," with special emphasis, of course, on what can be meant by term "historical" itself. For Grundmann, he is, indeed, situating himself Christologically in a post-Bultmannian perspective, though not a "post-Bultmannian," but he comes to what can be made meaningful about "the historical" through a specific kind of Christological reflection—the theological significance of Grundmann's Christological reflection is, in large part, what reduces Grundmann to some of the most minor of voices, despite how, to Evans' point, "massive" a study *Die Geschichte Jesu Christi* is.

In a certain sense, *Die Geschichte Jesu Christi* is a culmination of Grundmann's Christological thinking, which, when considering how Grundmann's Christological reflection can be accounted for, include companion works: the pamphlet, *Wer ist Jesus von Nazareth?* (1940), which can be rendered as "Who is Jesus of Nazareth?" and the book, *Jesus der Galiläer*

56. Evans, *Life of Jesus Research*, 21.

57. Evans, *Life of Jesus Research*, 21.

58. Evans, *Life of Jesus Research*, 21.

und das Judentum (1941), which can be rendered as "Jesus the Galilean and Judaism." Like *Die Geschichte Jesu Christi, Jesus der Galiläer und das Judentum* has remained untranslated, though a translation of *Wer ist Jesus von Nazareth?* appears in excerpt in the collection, *A Church Undone: Documents from the German Christian Faith Movement* (2015), edited by Mary M. Solberg. Though, by and large, assessments of either work, like *Die Geschichte Jesu Christi*, are relatively sparce, Solberg characterizes the *Wer ist Jesus von Nazareth?* pamphlet in the following way:

> The pamphlet makes many of the same points [*Jesus der Galiläer und das Judentum*] does, arguing that Jesus was not only not a Jew but was deeply anti-Jewish. [Jesus'] understanding of God and the kingdom of God was diametrically opposed to Jewish ideas.[59]

What becomes apparent in Grundmann's handling of the historical Jesus, if thematically connecting the pamphlet to the companion book, is that, according to Sean Feyne in the opening pages of his *Jesus, a Jewish Galilean* (2010), is "the most shocking example of [. . .] a manipulation of [historical] evidence."[60] There is no doubt that Solberg would agree with this, since Grundmann's "manipulation," given Solberg's translation of the *Wer ist Jesus von Nazareth?* pamphlet, appears in in the methodological trajectory of Grundmann's "preliminary question" to the implications of Christology on Germany and with respect to the German people is fundamentally invested in Grundmann's belief that "the German people have struggled against the Jews for liberation from [Jewish] subversion of Germany's life and essence."[61]

What remains significant about Grundmann—which Evans does not mention, and which is, in my view, the reason why Grundmann's voice is especially marginalized, even now, with *Die Geschichte Jesu Christi* remaining untranslated (along with the most of Grundmann's work)—is to due Grundmann's anti-Semitism, membership in the Nazi party from 1930 on, and his participation with the German Christians beginning, at least, in 1933.

One of the few assessments of the implications of Grundmann's theologizing through the politicization of his Nazism is brought forth Susannah Heschel's "Nazifying Christian Theology" (1994)—in it, Heschel reassesses what role anti-Semitism played in the theologizing of the German

---

59. Solberg, *Church Undone*, 454.

60. Feyne, *Jesus, a Jewish Galilean*, 6.

61. Grundmann, *Who is Jesus of Nazareth?*, 456.

Christians, to which Grundmann belonged, and pointing out the incorrect historical assumption that the German Christians "underwent a dissolution at the end of 1933."[62] In her *The Aryan Jesus: Christian Theologians and the Bible in Nazi Germany* (2008), Heschel reminds us that Grundmann "composed the 'Twenty-Eight Theses' of the German Christian movement"[63]—it was published in 1934. In doing so, Heschel writes, "[Grundmann] stated that Jesus transcended human categories of such as race and thus could be labeled neither as Jew or as Aryan."[64] However, Robert P. Erickson contends in *Complicity in the Holocaust* (2012) that, particularly throughout the 1930s and 1940s, Grundmann "took up the most difficult and most important task [of] set[ting] out to prove an 'Aryan Jesus.'"[65] Seemingly with Erickson's argument in mind, Heschel makes it clear that:

> Grundmann presented Jesus's teachings as standing in absolute opposition to Judaism; theirs was a religion of law, his was a religion of intimacy with God. The goal of Jesus, [Grundmann] claimed, was to bring an end to Judaism, but instead he fell victim to the Jews, a violent and degenerate people.[66]

Heschel continues:

> Grundmann did not engage in any new research or present new evidence in making his claims, but rather drew on existing arguments by scholars and demagogues, despite knowing that those arguments did not meet scholarly standards. Yet, there were enough theologians of importance who had participated in the discussions about Jesus as Aryan to make it possible for Grundmann to rest his case in their shoulders.[67]

All of these views on Jesus—part and parcel of Grundmann's Christological reflection, in terms of what orients him to *the question of the meaning of Christology*—fundamentally inform Grundmann's Nazi-era writings. However, Heschel notes that "Grundmann never discussed his Nazi-era writings apart from an allusion in the preface of *Die Geschichte Jesu Christi*."[68] This

62. Heschel, "Nazifying Christian Theology," 587–605.

63. Heschel, *Aryan Jesus*, 152.

64. Heschel, *Aryan Jesus*, 152.

65. Erickson, *Complicity in the Holocaust*, 123.

66. Heschel, *Aryan Jesus*, 152.

67. Heschel, *Aryan Jesus*, 152.

68. Heschel, *Aryan Jesus*, 265.

seems so, when considering Heschel alongside Erickson's assertion that "after 1945, [Grundmann] dropped the Aryan portion of his argument."[69]

In reproducing what is an otherwise untranslated passage from Grundmann's prefatory comments, Heschel demonstrates, through Grundmann's reference to himself in third-person, that Grundmann was aware how his earlier work, in its perceived strengths and weaknesses, modulate the Christological thinking of *Die Geschichte Jesu Christi*. Heschel characterizes Grundmann's self-reflection—as a Christological reflection—as that which "solely refers to the depiction of Jesus, not of Judaism, which he continued to describe in denigrating language."[70] Even so, it is all the more remarkable that, according to Heschel, "Grundmann's Nazi involvements were known but rarely mentioned by his academic colleagues."[71]

It is for this reason, I submit, that Grundmann has been relatively marginalized. Though Evans presents one of the rare pieces of scholarship that reference Grundmann, it would seem that the marginalization of Grundmann can be seen even in Conzelmann in 1959, insofar as Conzelmann lists Grundmann among "Jesus-of-Life Research" without addressing Grundmann's kind of theologizing.[72] While this can certainly be traced to Grundmann's Nazi involvement more so than his activities with the German Christians—with Paul Althaus aligning himself with Nazism, too, but, still referenced frequently by post-Bultmannians primarily due to Althaus' criticisms of Bultmann—another figure with some of the same proclivities towards Nazism and the German Christians movement, which has not become quite as marginalized as Grundmann is: Ethelbert Stauffer.

Though Stauffer was apparently never an active member of the Nazi Party as Grundmann was, Stauffer's activities with the German Christians, nonetheless, as they do Grundmann, inform and are informed by Stauffer's handling of *the question of the meaning of Christology*. In close proximity to Grundmann's still untranslated, *Die Geschichte Jesu Christi*, Stauffer's contemporaneously produced, *Jesus: Gestalt und Geschichte* (1957), which has been translated as *Jesus and His Story* in 1960, is described by Evans as "marshall[ing] background materials as evidence of the historical reliability of the gospels [and] defends the historicity of virtually all gospels details."[73]

In addition to *Jesus: Gestalt und Geschichte*, we find just two years later, another Stauffer article, *"Neue Wege der Jesusforschung"* (1959), which can

---

69. Erickson, *Complicity in the Holocaust*, 125.

70. Heschel, *Aryan Jesus*, 265.

71. Heschel, *Aryan Jesus*, 265.

72. Conzelmann, *Jesus*, 4–11.

73. Evans, *Life of Jesus Research*, 23.

be rendered as "New Ways of Jesus-Research," appearing in the still un-translated collection, *Gottes ist der Orient*. Even though, as Evans explains, Stauffer's *"Neue Wege der Jesusforschung"* is an "assessment of major trends in the new quest," it is safe to say that it does not include Stauffer's own Christological reflection towards *the question of the meaning of Christology* insofar as it only provide an overview of the various approaches to the question to and meaningfulness of Christology. In a certain sense, when thinking about this text contemporaneously to Robinson's *A New Quest of the Historical Jesus* published the same year, Stauffer is accomplishing the same task as Robinson, though in a smaller scale than Robinson. Still, while both present comparative studies of, to Evans' point, "the major trends" in thinking through *the question of the meaning of Christology*, we must not mistake the broader intent of Robinson's "assessment" for what can be sur-mised from Stauffer's "assessment."

Stauffer's specific stance towards the historical Jesus, as that which is predicated on his Christological reflection, is shared by Grundmann, insofar as, as Heschel aptly points out, Stauffer and Grundmann were colleagues in German Christian movement and "comrades from the Nazi era."[74] To the extent that Stauffer-Grundmann relations were based on "collaborat[ing] after the war [and] praising each other's work,"[75] in the form of a review, or a *"Rezension,"* whereby, in one such case, Heschel notes that, in 1958, "Grundmann published a very positive review in the prestigious journal, *Theologische Literaturzeitung*," of *Jesus: Gestalt und Geschichte*.[76] This is certainly true, and it is also true that, in the following year, in 1959, Stauffer gives a positive review of Grundmann's *Die Geschichte Jesu Christi*—in his review of Grundmann, Stauffer places Grundmann alongside Bornkamm, himself, and Barnikol within the context of *Jesusforschung*.[77]

With Stauffer-Grundmann relations, in particular, in mind, Heschel describes Stauffer's *Jesus: Gestalt und Geschichte* thusly:

> Basing his argument on the Gospel of John, which had been fa-vored by the German Christians for its hostility to Jews, Stauffer reiterated the German Christian view of Jesus as a lonely fighter against the Jewish legalistic pseudo-piety he opposed. Although Stauffer cited Rabbinic texts extensively, he used them not to contextualize Jesus's teaching nor to demonstrate his Jewishness,

---

74. Heschel, *Aryan Jesus*, 264.

75. Heschel, *Aryan Jesus*, 264.

76. Heschel, *Aryan Jesus*, 264.

77. Stauffer, "Grundmann, Walter, Die Geschichte Jesu Christi," 186.

but to present a contrasting, negative picture of the Jewish background against which Jesus fought.[78]

These Christological ideas become more focused in Stauffer's *Die Botschaft
Jesu* (1959), which can be rendered as "The Message of Jesus." In it—though
it remains untranslated—Heschel tells us that Stauffer argues "that obedience to commands had led Christians to commit murder through the
centuries."[79] Heschel goes on to say: "Jesus, according to Stauffer, tried to
liberate his followers from moral duties of the Old Testament, advocating
instead [for] a 'free conscience,' an argument close to Grundmann's."[80]

Though the respective theologizing of Stauffer and Grundmann were
aligned, particularly with respect to their involvement with the German
Christians, the fact that Stauffer was not as actively involved with the Nazi
Party—that is to say, Stauffer is believed to have not been an active member[81]—allowed Stauffer to avoid close scrutiny of his political dealings after
World War II based on, as Heschel argues in "Confronting the Past: Post-
1945 German Protestant Theology and the Fate of the Jews" (2010), "the
naïve assumption [. . .] that those who had expertise in rabbinical texts must
have been sympathetic to Judaism, or at least uninvolved in Nazi activities."[82]
Because of this, Stauffer's status as a German Christian, rather than any status that can be bestowed as a member of Nazi Party, allows Stauffer to be
not as marginalized as Grundmann, when considering that Stauffer (and
not Grundmann) is mentioned by Ebeling as early as 1958. Thusly, it would
seem that it is Stauffer (and not Grundmann) that remained in the purview
of the post-Bultmannians, since Stauffer's *Jesus: Gestalt und Geschichte*,
rather than Grundmann's *Die Geschichte Jesu Christi*, seems to contribute to
the problem of the historical Jesus and the underlying *question of the meaning of Christology* in a way that is not as racialized and politicized. Though
Stauffer, in writing in such close proximity to Bornkamm, acts as roughly
as a methodological companion piece to Bornkamm, we must not forget
that Stauffer's intentions with the historical Jesus and towards approaching *the question of the meaning of Christology* remains ultimately concerned
with contruing an ideological alignment between German Protestantism
and the *Führerprinzip* of Nazism. Keeping this in mind, we find that, especially for post-Bultmannians and those that were actively involved with the

78. Heschel, *Aryan Jesus*, 264.

79. Heschel, *Aryan Jesus*, 264.

80. Heschel, *Aryan Jesus*, 264–65.

81. Even though this is most believed to be true, Heschel points out that Stauffer
has been accused of engaging in Nazi activities. Heschel, "Confronting the Past," 58.

82. Heschel, "Confronting the Past," 58.

Confessing Church during the 1930s, Stauffer's *Jesus: Gestalt und Geschichte* is handled with care— by 1959, Conzelmann also acknowledges Stauffer, like Grundmann, but does not directly address Stauffer's theologizing.[83]

Still, it must not be lost on us that Stauffer's *Jesus: Gestalt und Geschichte* was translated in 1960 as *Jesus and His Story*. If we render *Jesus: Gestalt und Geschichte* literally, it is closer to "Jesus: Figure and History," so it would seem the title given to the 1960 translation wishes to contribute to the 1960s wave of the "new quest"—with the text translated twice: in the U.K. in 1960 and again in the U.S. in 1970. Two other texts contributing to Stauffer's Christological thinking: one, first translated in 1953, *New Testament Theology* (originally published in German as *Die Theologie des Neuen Testaments* in 1948), and the other, first translated in 1955, *Christ and the Caesars* (originally published in German as *Christus und die Caesaren* in 1948), both inform the trajctory of Stauffer's *Jesus: Gestalt und Geschichte* into Christological thought and what it means to present *the question of the meaning of Christology* in the 1960s.

Indeed, much has been discussed about Stauffer's *Jesus: Gestalt und Geschichte*, if we acknowledge, just as most (if not all) theologians engaged in Christological thinking contemporaneously and in posterity to Stauffer, that *Jesus: Gestalt und Geschichte* is the center-piece of Stauffer's theologizing, but also the center-piece of Stauffer's Christological reflection. We can glean this, for example, from Conzelmann's and Evans' references to the work in their respective bibliographies and, more importantly, the extent that Stauffer was in the purview of most (if not all) of the post-Bultmannians becomes something that can be gleaned from Ebeling's reference to Stauffer. What places Stauffer in the purview of the post-Bultmannians, in particular, is Stauffer's critcisms of Bultmann—in *Critical Quests of Jesus* (1969), in one of the most important accounts of Stauffer's significance, Charles C. Anderson places Stauffer to the "right" of Bultmann, insofar, with Stauffer in tow, there is "with all the critics to [Bultmann's] right a feeling that Bultmann has not done justice to the question of history as it relates to the Christian faith."[84] Even so, Anderson makes the following assessment:

> If anyone should have come from such a national and theological environment as would make him willing to engage Bultmann in debate, that would have been Stauffer [. . .] It is therefore some-what surprising that he takes as little notice of Bultmann and the

83. Conzelmann, *Jesus*, 4–11.

84. Anderson, *Critical Quests of Jesus*, 121.

Bultmannians as he does. This is no doubt part of the reason of their extreme irritation with him.[85]

Here, what we find in Anderson is the sense that, as a critic of Bultmann, Stauffer comes to this role without being "willing to engage Bultmann in debate." This is, indeed, as Anderson points out, "somewhat surprising," but it is, perhaps, due to Stauffer's intent with *the question of the meaning of Christology.*

It may not be too far-fetched to say, then, that Stauffer's lack of concern with debating Bultmann was out of Stauffer's own disinterest in theological debate in general. If Stauffer's concern was with ultimately with how German Protestantism could be ideologically aligned with the the the *Führerprinzip* of Nazism—if viewed this way, I disagree with Anderson: it is not at all surprising that Stauffer, in Anderson's words, "takes as little notice of Bultmann and the Bultmannians as he does." In fact, I think what Stauffer is aware of is much more than Anderson proposes—Stauffer's broader intent may not be with Bultmann or the Bultmannians, but it is clear that Stauffer does take notice to how Bultmann and the Bultmannians influence the Christological trends of the day.

Consider, for the moment, how Anderson characterizes how Stauffer comports himself Christologically and, at the time, with respect to what is the ongoing problem of the historical Jesus, with this:

> As to the possibility of knowing the historical Jesus, he acknowledges the contention of the critical school that there is back of the Gospels a "theological and church-oriented bias" that is much earlier than the time of the writing of the Gospels themselves. The important question, consequently, for Stauffer is how one may separate the historical elements in the Gospels from the dogmatic elements.[86]

This "important question," I submit, becomes, for Stauffer, *the question of the meaning of Christology.* It is through Christological reflection that Stauffer is able to "separate the historical elements in the Gospels from the dogmatic elements," such that, through Christological thinking, Stauffer is able to arrive at a way to pose the question politically and seek the meaningfulness of Christology politically—it is for this reason, I submit, that Stauffer is unbothered with debating Bultmann or, for that matter, debating the post-Bultmannians.

---

85. Anderson, *Critical Quests of Jesus,* 122.

86. Anderson, *Critical Quests of Jesus,* 122.

Even though there is a particular political intent to what Stauffer does Christologically, Stauffer's Christological thinking cannot be limited to *Jesus: Gestalt und Geschichte*. Not only does Anderson limit Stauffer thusly—as do plenty others that assess Stauffer's theologizing mainly and predominantly in terms of *Jesus: Gestalt und Geschichte*—what has been frequently overlooked by what is believed to be the scope of Stauffer's Christological thinking and the assumed as the fullest extent that Stauffer approaches and conceptualizes *the question of the meaning of Christology* is a lesser known, largely forgotten, and still untranslated text: Stauffer's *Jesus war ganz anders* (1967).

Published ten years after *Jesus: Gestalt und Geschichte*, the Christological position Stauffer takes in his *Jesus war ganz anders*, which can be rendered as "Jesus Was Very Different," speaks to a fundamentally different handling of *the question of the meaning of Christology* for Stauffer. This difference, it seems, appears to pull Stauffer away from the role of critic of Bultmann and more firmly into the role of a post-Bultmannian of sorts—it is a Christological difference, in fact, wherein Stauffer attempts to handle Bultmann's demythologizing in a way that, to my mind, situates Bultmann on the side of the "new quest," rather than Bultmann's own situating of himself between what ended with Schweitzer and was taken up anew by Käsemann.[87] To be sure, it is Stauffer's *Jesus war ganz anders* that more authentically brings to the fore Stauffer's contribution to the "new quest" than what can be surmised from *Jesus: Gestalt und Geschichte*. This certainly becomes clear from Evans' account of *Jesus war ganz anders*—in what is, essentially, one of the only (if not, the only), however brief, assessments of Stauffer's *Jesus war ganz anders*,[88] Evans explains that Stauffer "claims that Jesus was the 'demythologizer' of his time, a man of protest [and] what is characteristic of Jesus is his uniqueness—he cannot be put into a commonly recognized category."[89] Here, we can see that, instead of demythologizing the new testament as Bultmann does, or challenging what can be made meaningful Christologically through demythologization by post-Bultmannians, Stauffer's view of Jesus as a "demythologizer" attends to a Christological reflection in which the historical Jesus fundamentally modulates *the question of the meaning of Christology*.

87. As early as 1952, in Stauffer's "*Entmythologisierung oder Realthelologie?*," as it appears in the collection, *Kerygma und Mythos II*, Stauffer provides an assessment of Bultmann's demythologization project.

88. I want to note, here, that Conzelmann's *Jesus* also cites Stauffer's *Jesus war ganz anders* in Conzelmann's "Further Reading" section within the category of devoted to "Lives of Jesus." See Conzelmann, *Jesus*, 103.

89. Evans, *Life of Jesus Research*, 58.

FRANZ MUSSNER AND JOHANNES SCHNEIDER

In the section of Conzelmann's *Jesus* entitled, "The Historical Jesus and Faith (Jesus of Nazareth and Jesus Christ)," among the most minor contributors to Christological thinking in the late-1950s are: Franz Mussner (1916–2016) and Johannes Schneider (1895–1970).

Though the two go curiously unreferenced by Anderson in, though notable, both *Critical Quests of Jesus* (1969) and *The Historical Jesus: A Continuing Quest* (1972), we find them appear in Evans' *Life of Jesus Research* (1996)—while Evans, of course, provides us with an exhaustive annotated bibliography, when considering Ben Witherington's *The Jesus Quest* (1997) and *The Many Faces of the Christ* (1998), Gregory Dawes' *The Historical Jesus Question* (2001), and Craig Keener's immensely comprehensive, *The Historical Jesus of the Gospels* (2009) and recent, *Christobiography* (2019), we, again, note that both Mussner and Schneider are oddly missing.

The fact that Mussner and Schneider are directly referenced by Conzelmann and that the two published texts in German—Mussner in 1957 and Schneider in 1958—are in such close proximity to Conzelmann's *Jesus* remains significant to how it construes *the question of the meaning of Christology* with respect to how the same question and meaning respectively unfolds in Mussner and Schneider. This signficance is definitely not lost on Evans. What makes this significance all the more apparent is in the fact that neither text from Mussner nor from Schneider had been translated in 1959—both untranslated texts, for Conzelmann, focus on approaches to the historical Jesus, as that which inform Mussner's and Schneider's approaches to *the question of the meaning of Christology* and, in turn, inform Conzelmann's conceptualization of the question and meaning themselves.

The text in question for Conzelmann—and likewise for Evans—is Mussner's "*Der historische Jesus und der Christus des Glaubens*" (1957), which can be rendered as "The Historical Jesus and the Christ of Faith." As noted by both Conzelmann and Evans, the text first appears in the journal, *Biblische Zeitschrift*, in, judging from its associated bibliographical information, is the journal's first issue. For Conzelmann, the text is directly contributive to Conzelmann's understanding of the relationship between the "historical Jesus" and "faith"—or what Conzelmann parenthetically notes as the relationship between "Jesus of Nazareth" and "Jesus Christ"—and is characterized, in Evans' words, as "argu[ing] that a picture of the historical Jesus, one that is relevant for faith, can be recovered from the Gospels, despite their kerygmatic orientation."[90]

---

90. Evans, *Life of Jesus Research*, 28.

Similarly to Grundmann's and Stauffer's respective takes on the reliability of the Gospels to how the historical Jesus can be conceptualized, we see Mussner following this claim contemporaneously, if attending to Evans' recognition that Mussner is Christologically focused on what "can be recovered from the Gospels." Indeed, any fundamental agreement between Mussner and the likes of Grundmann and Stauffer on how one can historically calibrate *the question of the meaning of Christology* must be carefully articulated. We know, of course, that Grundmann and Stauffer, coming from Protestant backgrounds, hoped to synthesize Protestantism with the *Führerprinzip* of Nazism—thinking about what theologically informed Grundmann and Stauffer towards their Nazi proclivities, we find, in Mussner, a Roman Catholic background, even though, like Grundmann and Stauffer, Mussner uses his theological proclivities to orient how he approaches *the question of the meaning of Christology*. The difference, I submit, even if Mussner attends to the same belief in the reliability of the Gospels as Grundmann and Stauffer do, remains in the Christological thinking Mussner engages in when arriving at *the question of the meaning of Christology*, as that which surmises what the historical Jesus brings to a Christological picture, to Evans' point, "that is relevant for faith."

In terms of what is theologically relevant and how that theological relevance matters, along with how faith, itself, is Christologically conceptualized, what Mussner lays bare in how he conceives of the relationship between "Jesus of Nazareth" and "Jesus Christ" occurs through a critiique of Bultmann's demythologization. This brings Mussner closer to Stauffer's own critique of Bultmann, insofar as we are able, through Anderson, see that both Stauffer and Mussner belong to "critics to the right of Bultmann."[91]

Given that Anderson does not mention Mussner as someone who is to the right of Bultmann, or even mention Mussner at all, I maintain that Mussner can be situated theologically in relation to Bultmann, since, just as Anderson writes, Mussner, in a certain sense, is one "who write[s] in conscious opposition to Bultmann."[92] As Anderson is right to say that this sort of criticism "cannot be treated as Stauffer has been," the means by which it is possible to place Mussner as someone who is to the right of Bultmann comes through the means by which Mussner, as others to the right, "deal with [demythology] only on the points at which they find themselves in opposition to Bultmann."[93] To be sure, we can glean, even from Evans' very brief account of Mussner, that Mussner is concerned with what sense can

91. Anderson, *Critical Quests of Jesus*, 121–39.

92. Anderson, *Critical Quests of Jesus*, 128.

93. Anderson, *Critical Quests of Jesus*, 128.

be made out of the meaning of "kerygmatic" and what kerygma, in itself, means for how we understand and come to terms with, in Evans' words, "[the] picture of the historical Jesus." Though subtle, Evans seems to recognize that Mussner's "picture," as it were, is developed in relation to what influences Bultmann has on Mussner resistance to "kerygmatic orientation."

Yet, while Conzelmann's awareness of the text was limited to its *Biblische Zeitschrift* publication, Conzelmann does not give any indication of what relationship exists between Mussner's work and Bultmann's demythology. Though Evans implies this, Evans is not explicit enough in his brief account for us to glean any Mussner-Bultmann relations. For that matter, while Conzelmann gives us the impression that Mussner's "*Der historische Jesus und der Christus des Glaubens*" remained untranslated by 1959, as well as by 1973, with the translation of Conzelmann's *Jesus*, Conzelmann also gives us the impression that the Mussner article was only published once in 1957. It is from Evans' thorough bibliographic information that we, instead, find out that Mussner's "*Der historische Jesus und der Christus des Glaubens*" was re-published and reprinted in the Herbert Vorgrimler edited, *Exegese und Dogmatik* (1962), collection of essays that includes two works from Karl Rahner—curiously, the collection itself, though unmentioned by Evans, was eventually translated into English as *Dogmatic vs. Biblical Theology* in 1965.

Setting aside the problems with the pagination of the text,[94] it is clear that Mussner's "*Der historische Jesus und der Christus des Glaubens*" bears immense significance to Vorgrimler within the circle of Roman Catholic theologizing, perhaps in spite of what influences Bultmann serve on how Mussner approaches *the question of the meaning of Christology*. By saying that Bultmann casts an influence on Mussner, I want to point our attention to how Mussner's "*Der historische Jesus und der Christus des Glaubens*" may likely be an expansion or even a re-asessment of Mussner's habilitation thesis, "*Christus, das All und die Kirche: Studien zur Theologie des Epheserbriefes*" from 1952 at the University of Münich—rendered as "Christ, the All and the Church: Studies in Theology of the Letter to the Ephesians" and published by *Trierer Theologische Studien* while Mussner served on the faculty at the University of Trier, Mussner's habilitation thesis situates itself Christologically by thinking critically through Bultmann's demythologization project.

If we can view this thesis as foundational to Mussner's Christological thinking in "*Der historische Jesus und der Christus des Glaubens*," the 1957

---

94. While Evans' detailing of the text's bibliographic information with respect to its *Biblische Zeitschrift* publication, shows a pagination of 224–52, while Conzelmann's bibliographic information to the same text, within the same *Biblische Zeitschrift* publication, shows a pagination of 257–75.

article becomes, in itself, foundational to the Christological thinking that Mussner lays bare in another article that only Evans mentions in his bibliographies: "*Der 'historische' Jesus*" (1960), published in *Trierer Theologische Zitschrift* (*TTZ*). Insofar as "*Der 'historische' Jesus*" is included in *Der historische Jesus und der Christus unseres Glaubens* (1962), Evans tells us that, in it, Mussner "argues that the Gospel witness is historically accurate, and that its witness should be presupposed by Christian faith."[95]

However, given that "*Der 'historische' Jesus*" articulates what Mussner's view of the historical Jesus means for "the Gospel witness," the text lays itself bare Christologically in *Die Johanneische Sehweise und die Frage nach dem historischen Jesus* (1965), which is interestingly omitted from the purview of Evans' bibliographes of *Life of Jesus Research*. Be that as it may, *Die Johanneische Sehweise und die Frage nach dem historischen Jesus*, translated as *The Historical Jesus in the Gospel of St. John* in 1966—one of only a handful of Mussner's works to even appear in English[96]—is brought to bear in Mussner's "*Methodologie der Frage nach dem historischen Jesus*" (1974), roughly rendered as "Methodology of the Question of the Historical Jesus," which, as Evans notes, is included with five other essays in the still untranslated collection, *Rückfrage nach Jesus: zur Methodik und Bedeutung der Frage nach dem historischen Jesus* (which can be rendered as *Query about Jesus: Method and Meaning of the Question about the Historical Jesus*).[97]

Just as Mussner turns to the Gospel of John to situate his understanding of the historical Jesus and, from this, construes an approach to *the question of the meaning of Christology*, Johannes Schneider does the same thing in the posthumously published, *Das Evangelium nach Johannes* (1976), which remains untranslated as of 1988.

While Mussner comports the historical Jesus to "the Gospel's witness" in Mussner's *The Historical Jesus in the Gospel of St. John*, I submit, the same can be said of Schneider's handling of *Das Evangelium nach Johannes*. There is, of course, a difference between the theologizing of Mussner and that of Schneider, when recognizing Mussner's Roman Catholicism in relation to Schneider's Baptist background—this difference in theologizing is evidenced in Schneider's "*Taufe in der Neuen Testament*" lecture, delivered in October 1955, translated as *Baptism and Church in the New Testament* in 1957. Indeed, the very possibility of viewing what role the historical Jesus plays in Schneider's *Das Evangelium nach Johannes*—in the way that the

---

95. Evans, *Life of Jesus Research*, 36.

96. One of the Mussner's most significant works to have appeared in English is: *Tractate on the Jews: The Significance of Judaism for Christian Faith* (1984).

97. Evans, *Life of Jesus Research*, 71.

historical Jesus figures into Mussner's theologizing—as that which expresses how Schneider approaches *the question of the meaning of Christology*, requires us to see that what is laid bare in Schneider's *Das Evangelium nach Johannes*. This comes by way the Christological thinking made explicit in Schneider's "*Die Frage nach dem historischen Jesus in der neutestamentlichen Forschung der Gegenwart*" (1958), which can be rendered as "The Question of the Historical Jesus in Contemporary New Testament Research." Though currently untranslated, Evans explains that the text provides a "critical assessment of the new quest, in which it is concluded that the new research should result in a history of Jesus."[98]

If, to Evans' characterization Schneider's belief that "new research" associated with the new quest "should result in a history of Jesus," it would seem, then, Schneider is interested in the extent that there exists a historical reliability to the New Testament, from which "a historical Jesus" can be gleaned as a representation of the "history of Jesus." This speaks, of course, to how Schneider conceives of, in line with the title of the 1958 article, how "the question of the historical Jesus" can be ascertained from "contemporary New Testament research." Essentially, if the New Testament lays bare "the question of the historical Jesus," this must be disclosed through research, which is precisely what Schneider is arguing—it must be through a research that grounds and is grounded by *the question of the meaning of Christology*, such that, as Schneider attends closely to a Christological thinking modulated by Christological reflection, "the history of Jesus" discloses itself. In this sense, we should take special note to Evans' characterization of what Schneider is doing as hinging on "should"—it is not that, to Evans' point, a "critical assessment of the new quest," at the point of its conclusion, or in terms of how it eventually concludes itself of its own methodological, theological and Christological volition, brings about a "new research" that will "result in a history of Jesus" or is "result[ing] in a history of Jesus." The emphasis, here, is on "should," which suggests, in Evans' view of Schneider, that Schneider believes that the new research that predicates the new quest cannot, may not, or will not "result in a history of Jesus."

For Schneider, the only means by which "new research" can "result in a history of Jesus" is through an undergirding proposition of a historical reliability to the New Testament. Not only does this fall in line with Mussner's fundamental argument in both "*Der historische Jesus und der Christus des Glaubens*" and "*Der 'historische' Jesus*," it also allows us to place Schneider's theologizing in close proximity to the theologizes of Grundmann and Stauffer. This seems so, if only by aligning Schneider (and Mussner),

98. Evans, *Life of Jesus Research*, 31.

Grundmann, and Stauffer as, to Anderson's point, positioning themselves ideologically to the right of Bultmann. That ideological alignment is made all the more explicit, perhaps, when considering Grundmann's review of Schneider's "*Die Frage nach dem historischen Jesus in der neutestamentlichen Forschung der Gegenwart*" in 1959 in *Theologische Literaturzeitung*.[99]

In Grundman's review of Schneider's "*Die Frage nach dem historischen Jesus in der neutestamentlichen Forschung der Gegenwart*,"—which points out, as Evans does, that the text originally appeared as part of a commemoratory lecture "*Festvorlesung*" celebrating the birthday ("*Geburtstag*") of Erich Fascher—we find, through Grundmann, not just a means of understanding the specifics of Schneider's approach to the question of the historical Jesus, but we also gain significant insight into the larger context in which Schneider is writing. To this end, Grundmann's evaluation sheds some important light on how we might position Schneider within the scope of *the question of the meaning of Christology*, to which Grundmann introduces as: "*Anknüpfend an die systematisch bestimmten Ausführungen von Paul Althaus will [Schneider] zur Geltung bringen, was [. . .] Forschung zu dieser Frage beigetragen wird.*"[100] Here, we can render Grundmann in the following way: "Based on the systematically determined statements by Paul Althaus, [Schneider] wants to show what [. . .] research is being contributed to this issue."

Insofar as Schneider expands upon Paul Althaus—with "systematically determined statements" predicated on Althaus' *Das sogenannte Kerygma und der historische Jesus* (1958)—Grundmann tells us that the kind of research that Schneider is involved with and contributes is directed towards the issue of kerygma. It is the issue of kerygma, I submit, as that which modulates *the question of the meaning of Christology*, not only foes Althaus and Schneider, but also for Grundmann himself. For Grundmann's take on Schneider, Schneider's approach to *the question of the meaning of Christology* occupies the same space as Althaus' *Das sogenannte Kerygma und der historische Jesus*, which was published the same year as Schneider's own article. Similarly, just as Althaus makes it clear in the subtitle of *Das sogenannte Kerygma und der historische Jesus*, we certainly see Schneider providing criticism about what kerygma means for theological thinking, but also Christological reflection, just as Althaus's subtitle makes explicit, *Zur Kritik der heutigen Kerygma-Theologie*, which can be rendered as "for criticism of

---

99. Grundmann, "Schneider, Johannes, *Die Frage nach historischen Jesus un der neutestamentlichen Forschung der Gegenwart*," 103–5.

100. Grundmann, "Schneider, Johannes, *Die Frage nach dem historischen Jesus in der neutestamentlichen Forschung der Gegenwart*," 103.

Kergyma-Theology today," there is no doubt, as Grundmann is fully aware, that Schneider finds Christological problems in "kerygma-theology."

With both Althaus and Schneider in mind, and the extent that the very conceptualization of "kerygma-theology" theologically stunts Christological reflection and minimizes what sense can be made out of *the question of the meaning of Christology*, Grundmann goes on to say:

> *Schneider geht davon aus, daß die Leben-Jesu-Forschung durch die Kerygma-Theologie abgelöst worden ist, die mit Martin Kähler beginnt und deren profiliertester und radikalster Vertreter Rudolf Bultmann ist.*[101]

Grundmann's words can be rendered thusly:

> Schneider suggests that the Life of Jesus research has been replaced by kerygma-theology, which begins with Martin Kähler and whose most prominent and radical representative is Rudolf Bultmann.

Here, in attending to Grundmann's characterization that Schneider "*geht davon*," which could be rendered as "assumes," we may, indeed, think of the world "suggests," or even "proposes," since "assumes" has, however subtle, a negative connotation to Grundmann's remarks on Schneider. I do not think Grundmann believes "Schneider assumes," insofar as "assumes" also points to the possibility that Schneider, in Grundmann's view, could be wrong about the sentiment that "the Life of Jesus research has been replaced by kerygma theology." Indeed, I submit, "assume" is a bit strong and misleading, given that, particularly by the end of the 1950s, in which Schneider and Grundmann are both writing, there is undoubtedly an ideological shift in the Life of Jesus research and how it comports itself to the problem of the historical Jesus, and there is also undoubtedly an origin to this in Käsemann, and this is also undoubtedly compounded by Käsemann and other post-Bultmannians wrestling with what "has been replaced by kerygma-theology." It is in this way that, Grundmann rightly explains, through directly quoting Schneider, there arises a "*Diskussion der Frage nach dem historischen Jesus weithin eine Auseinandersetzung mit Bultmann ist.*"[102] From this, Schneider's comments, seen through Grundmann, can be rendered as: "discussion of the question of the historical Jesus is largely a confrontation with Bultmann."

---

101. Grundmann, "Schneider, Johannes, *Die Frage nach dem historischen Jesus in der neutestamentlichen Forschung der Gegenwart*," 103.

102. Grundmann, "Schneider, Johannes, *Die Frage nach dem historischen Jesus in der neutestamentlichen Forschung der Gegenwart*," 103.

If Schneider's interest is with the degree to which "Life of Jesus research has been replaced by kerygma-theology," as Grundmann explains, Schneider's situatedness to *the question of the meaning of Christology* is, as a point of necessity, just as Schneider describes, "largely a confrontation with Bultmann." What necessitates Schneider's approach to Bultmann as that which informs his approach to *the question of the meaning of Christology* stands to reason why Grundmann would conclude the following: "*Bei ihm setzt darum Schneiders Referat ein*,"[103] which can be rendered as "That's why Schneider uses his presentation."

Schneider's "presentation," as that which is "largely a confrontation with Bultmann," situates itself, Grundmann informs:

> [Schneider] *versteht Bultmanns Arbeit an der Jesustradition als "eine Reduzierung seines Wesens, seiner Person und seiner Verkündigung" und zieht als zustimmende Zeugen für diese These Dahl, Karl Barth und Stauffer heran.*[104]

Here, allow me to render Grundmann's remarks with Grundmann's citing of Schneider's words, in the following manner, by substituting "*seines*" and "*seiner*" for "Jesus's" for the sake of emphasis and clarity:

> [Schneider] understands Bultmann's work on the Jesus-Tradition as "a reduction of [Jesus's] nature, [Jesus's] person and proclamation" and uses Dahl, Karl Barth, and Stauffer as supporting witnesses for this thesis.

The extent that Grundmann finds Schneider's argument situated on how Schneider "understands Bultmann's work on the Jesus-Tradition" is precisely what centers Grundmann's own work. Just as Grundmann acknowledges, if Schneider sees Bultmann's theologizing as "a reduction of [Jesus's] nature, [Jesus's] person and proclamation," so too does Grundmann, and even Stauffer. To Grundmann's point, in an effort to present "supporting witnesses for this thesis," Schneider not only "uses" Stauffer, but also Dahl, particularly if we are reminded that both Stauffer and Dahl are writing contemporaneously to Schneider (and Grundmann, for that matter).

But, what about Grundmann's reference to Karl Barth? Here, it seems that Grundmann is recognizing Schneider's use of both parts of the fourth volume of Karl Barth's *Church Dogmatics*, which first appear in 1959— given that Barth's fourth volume of *Church Dogmatics*, subtitled, *Doctrine*

---

103. Grundmann, "Schneider, Johannes, *Die Frage nach dem historischen Jesus in der neutestamentlichen Forschung der Gegenwart*," 103.

104. Grundmann, "Schneider, Johannes, *Die Frage nach dem historischen Jesus in der neutestamentlichen Forschung der Gegenwart*," 103.

of Reconciliation, is devoted to, as its subtitle informs us, "Jesus Christ the True Witness" and the extent that Barth certainly disagreed with Bultmann, it certainly makes sense that Schneider would use Barth, too, as a "supporting witness" against Bultman's "work on the Jesus-Tradition." Even with the "supporting witnesses for [Schneider's] thesis" in tow against Bultmann, Grundmann further contextualizes Schneider carefully along these lines:

> *Die Frage nach dem historischen Jesus ist einerseits im Kreis der Schüler Bultmanns in Fluß gekommen andererseits haben Forscher anderer Herkunft ihrerseits neue Fragestellungen aufgeworfen, über die Schneider ebenfalls berichtet.*[105]

Grundmann's words that be rendered in this way:

> On the one hand, the question of the historical Jesus has flowed in the circle of Bultmann's students, on the other hand, researchers from other backgrounds have in turn raised new questions, which Schneider also reports.

Positioning Schneider thusly, Grundmann seems to suggest that Schneider's opposition to Bultmann and "the circle of Bultmann's students" has allowed Schneider to raise "new questions," especially one that generally rooted in *the question of the meaning of Christology*.

Grundmann's sense of this—*the question of the meaning of Christology*—not just in Schneider but in Grundmann's own work, or even Grundmann's collaborator, Stauffer, or even Grundmann's own awareness of how Dahl and Barth are "supporting witnesses" is made all the more explicit with Grundmann's evoking Conzelmann by name, seemingly with respect to Conzelmann's contribution to *the question of the meaning of Christology* in "*Jesus Christus*," which appears in the interim between Schneider's "*Die Frage nach dem historischen Jesus in der neutestamentlichen Forschung der Gegenwart*" and Grundmann's review of Schneider—that is, if we can say, with any degree of certainty, that, though we can tell from the Conzelmann's 1959 article that he is aware of Schneider's 1957 piece, we can only assume that Grundmann is also aware of Conzelmann's 1959 article. Yet, in inserting Conzelmann into the conversation, Grundmann tells us:

> *Hans Conzelmann hat jüngst darauf aufmerksam gemacht, daß Bultmann und seine Mitarbeiter von dem "Bruch" her denken, "der zwischen dem historischen Jesus und der Gemeinde liegt"; "aber so selbstverständlich uns dieser Ansatz erscheinen mag, wir*

---

105. Grundmann, "Schneider, Johannes, *Die Frage nach dem historischen Jesus in der neutestamentlichen Forschung der Gegenwart*," 103.

> *müssen uns klar sein, daß er außer einigen Mitteleuropäern nur wenigen einleuchtet.*"[106]

Here, Grundmann can be rendered as:

> Hans Conzelmann recently made it clear that Bultmann and his (co-workers) think of the "break" that "lies between the historical Jesus and the Church"; "but as self-evident as this approach may seem to us, we have to be clear that apart from some Central Europeans it only makes sense to a few."

Note, here, that Grundmann provides two cited quotations: one from Conzelmann, the other from Schneider. What we find in Grundmann's citation, though incomplete from Conzelmann, is a reference to Conzelmann's *"Gegenwart und Zukunft in der synoptischen Tradition"* (1957), published in *Zeitschrift für Theologie und Kirche*,[107] having appeared relatively contemporaneously to Schneider's article. Translated as "Present and Future in the Synoptic Tradition" in 1968, it behooves us to emphasize that what Conzelmann means by "tradition" in the article's title, which Conzelmann himself footnotes, is couched in the question of the historical Jesus by 1957.[108]

  With respect to Schneider's notion of whatever "break" Bultmann and Bultmannians believe exists "between the historical Jesus and the Church," the fact that Schneider believes, too that such a break "only makes sense to a few" is what Schneider fundamentally disagrees with, to which Grundmann cosigns. Grundmann, then, tells us that Schneider employs Ernst Heitsch—who, only a year before Schneider, publishes *"Die Aporie des historischen Jesus als Problem theologischer Hermeneutik,"* with which Grundmann is as seemingly familiar as Schneider—and Heitsch's characterization of what is accomplished by the "break" Bultmann and Bultmannians place conclusively "between the historical Jesus and the Church." Directly quoting Schneider, Grundmann informs us that Heitsch wishes "to demonstrate the transition from history to kerygma not only in a factual but also in its historical continuity" (which I have rendered from the following: *"den Übergang von der Historie zum Kerygma nicht nur in sachlicher, sondern gerade auch in seiner geschichtlichen Kontinuität aufzuweisen"*).[109]

---

106. Grundmann, "Schneider, Johannes, *Die Frage nach dem historischen Jesus in der neutestamentlichen Forschung der Gegenwart*," 103.

107. Conzelmann, *"Gegenwart und Zukunft in der synoptischen Tradition,"* 277–96.

108. Conzelmann, *"Gegenwart und Zukunft in der synoptischen Tradition,"* 277.

109. Grundmann, "Schneider, Johannes, *Die Frage nach dem historischen Jesus in der neutestamentlichen Forschung der Gegenwart*," 103.

Overall, after acknowledging that "Schneider consecutively discusses the voices from Bultmann's circle, Käsemann, Bornkamm, Ernst Fuchs" (which can be rendered from "*Schneider bespricht nacheinander die aus dem Kreis um Bultmann laut gewordenen Stimmen*"), at the close of Grundmann's review of Schneider, Grundmann makes this clear:

> *Schneiders klares und übersichtliches Referat, zu dem wir eine Reihe von Anmerkungen gaben, ist geeignet, die weitere Erörterung durch die Herausarbeitung der verschiedenen Positionen zu fördern. Dafür gebührt ihm unser Dank.*[110]

We can render Grundmann's final words as:

> Schneider's clear and concise presentation, to which we made a number of comments, is apt to require further discussion by working out the various positions. Our thanks go to him for that.

What Grundmann is thankful for, it seems, is Schneider's contribution to the state of *the question of the meaning of Christology* through the problem of the historical Jesus by 1959, given all the other assessments presented in close proximity to Schneider's. But, to a certain extent, if we can say that Schneider is as firmly to the right of Bultmann as Grundmann is, there is no doubt that Grundmann is likely thankful for Schneider's voice adding to the like of Mussner and Stauffer.

ERNST BARNIKOL AND BÉDA RIGAUX

Returning to the bibliographies of Evans' *Life of Jesus Research*, if continuing to focus on just a handful of relatively minor figures listed in the "general discussion" section devoted to 1956–1960 with which Bornkamm's *Jesus of Nazareth* prominantly leads and marks the beginning of the period,[111] I want to consider two theologians: Ernst Barnikol (1892–1968) and Béda Rigaux (1899–1982).

To the best of my knowledge, Evans contains the only scholarship referencing Barnikol and Rigaux. From this, we can certain question why both go unacknowledged by both Conzelmann and Anderson—while, on one hand, we can surely say that both of Anderson's relatively-narrow perspectives in *Critical Quests of Jesus* (1969) and *The Historical Jesus: A*

---

110. Grundmann, "Schneider, Johannes, *Die Frage nach dem historischen Jesus in der neutestamentlichen Forschung der Gegenwart*," 105.

111. Evans, *Life of Jesus Research*, 21.

Continuing Quest (1972) are more interested in major voices or contributors to the problem of the historical Jesus, Conzelmann, on the other hand, provides a more inclusive perspective of both major and minor voices, particularly those that appear in close proximity to Conzelmann's *"Jesus Christus"* (1959). Essentially, even though it need not surprise us that some minor figures writing on the problem of the historical Jesus in the 1950s fall outside of Anderson's purview, it would seem that Conzelmann's interest is in providing the most inclusive array of voices leading up to Conzelmann's *"Jesus Christus"*—yet, it is clear that, somehow, in a way that remains laregly unanswerable, why Conzelmann completely misses Barnikol and Rigaux.

Indeed, I concede that Conzelmann's "Jesus Christus" is not nearly as exhaustive as the bibliographies included in Evans' *Life of Jesus Research.* Even if we compare Conzelmann to Evans only with respect to the entirety of the 1950s, we will find numerous texts omitted from Conzelmann's purview—this is especially the case when looking only at texts that appear in the year just prior to Conzelmann's *"Jesus Christus."* The two that stand out, I maintain, are Barnikol and Rigaux, insofar as both, though omitted from Conzelmann's purview, not only directly contribute to the position in which Conzelmann situates himself by 1959, but also immediately orient the task and scope of *the question of the meaning of Christology* at the close of the 1950s.

Let us first consider Barnikol's *Das Leben Jesu der Heilsgeschichte* (1958)—though it is still currently untranslated, the title can be rendered as "The Life of Jesus in Salvation History." I want to bring our attention, first, to Barnikol's use of the term *"Heilsgeschichte,"* which, I submit, is evoked similarly to Cullmann's *Christ and Time* (1951), originally appearing in German in 1946 and Cullmann's later work, *Salvation in History* (1965). Insofar as Cullmann's later work attempts to clarify his earlier position on *"Heilsgeschichte"*—if, as Cullmann makes explicit, the later work arises as a way to counter the criticism Cullmann received from *Christ and Time*—it seems to me that Barnikol is directly reacting to Cullmann's use of the term, how the term, for Cullmann's *Christ and Time,* casts a specific view of Christological reflection, and the extent that Cullmann's Christological thinking through *"Heilsgeschichte"* allows him to conceive and make sense out of *the question of the meaning of Christology.*

How Cullmann theologizes the New Testament traverses, in the introduction to *Christ and Time,* the Gospels of Luke and John, insomuch as there is a "unified Christ line"[112]—this leads Cullmann, he makes clear, to "investigate in all their complication and range the *basic presuppositions of*

112. Cullmann, *Christ and Time,* 25.

all New Testament theology, that is, the New Testament conception of time and history."[113] In direct contrast to Cullmann's conception, Barnikol's *Das Leben Jesu der Heilsgeschichte,* not only counters what can be meant by history and time, but challenges the role that the Gospels play in relation to them. In what is a rare account of Barnikol's contribution to *the question of the meaning of Christology* through the problem of the historical Jesus, Evans tells us that Barnikol's *Das Leben Jesu der Heilsgeschichte* is a "massive study" that:

> Examines some 158 pericopae (mostly from Mark and Q); dates the Synoptics very late (105 CE for Mark; 119 CE for Matthew; 125 CE for Luke); regards "high [C]hristology" as inauthentic tradition; views Jesus as prophet and teacher.[114]

Setting aside Barnikol's dating of the Gospels—which is, in itself, of a minority opinion that is outside of the mainstream or general historical consensus—the fact that Barnikol focuses so heavily on Mark is noteworthy, if for no other reason than to pit what Barnikol emphasizes against what Cullman seems to emphasize with Luke and John. Moreover, what arises from Barnikol's meticulous study of Mark, as a means to ground Barnikol's theologizing of the New Testament, is a rejection of "high Christology," especially if Cullmann's take on *"Heilsgeschichte"* is, in fact, a kind of high Christology. To Barnikol, high Christology, as Evans says, abides to an "inauthentic tradition."

It would seem, then, that, for Barnikol, *"Heilsgeschichte"* only matters to what can be surmised as "the life of Jesus," insofar as *"Heilsgeschichte"* is able to lay bare Barnikol's belief in "Jesus as a prophet and teacher." To this end, what we find in Barnikol's Christological thinking is a relatively low Christology. Yet, I want to be very careful here—we must not confuse whatever Christology means to Barnikol and however Barnikol envisions *the question of the meaning of Christology* with other more definable low Christologies of a more philosophical bent.[115] Barnikol's approach to Christology in general has been largely dismissed—in the rare instances that Barnikol is evoked, Barnikol's presentation of his "Life of Jesus" has been heavily criticized, for example, in Iosif A. Kryvelev's *Christ: Myth or Reality* (1987)[116] and Petr Pokorný's "Jesus as the Ever-Living Lawgiver in the Let-

---

113. Cullmann, *Christ and Time,* 26.

114. Evans, *Life of Jesus Research,* 29.

115. By this, if we call Bultmann and Tillich, for instance, as embarking on low Christologies, there is no doubt in my mind that Barnikol's Christology.

116. Kryvelev, *Christ: Myth or Reality,* 186.

ter of Mara bar Sarapion" (2012).[117] In both cases, as with how George A. Wells takes Barnikol to task in *Cutting Jesus Down to Size* (2009),[118] the criticism leveled at Barnikol is not just with respect to the conclusions Barnikol reaches, but it also with respect to the way Barnikol goes about the process of theologizing itself.

To simply view, to Evans' point, "Jesus as prophet and teacher" encapulates Barnikol's conceptualization of the "Life of Jesus" in a way that was largely out of step with other research in Barnikol's time. However "massive" a study Barnikol's *Das Leben Jesu der Heilsgeschichte* is, Barnikol's study methodologically pales in comparison to other texts by Stauffer, Althaus, Ebeling, and Fuchs produced contemporaneously to Barnikol. Even though *Das Leben Jesu der Heilsgeschichte* appears very late in Barnikol's career and, before it, Barnikol was considered as an authority on Bruno Bauer,[119] what Barnikol contributes to *the question of the meaning of Christology* is far from negligible, even if it has become marginalized. Even if others engaging in Christological thinking of the day, to the best of my knowledge, never mention Barnikol at all, in a certain sense, what we have in Barnikol is a snapshot in time—similarly, what contemporaneously happens to Rigaux not only shows that what Rigaux contributes to the *question of the meaning of Christology* is also far from negligible, while also marginalized, and speaks to a particular snapshot in time.

The reason why Rigaux is never mentioned by others engaging in the Christological thinking of the day remains, I am afraid, largely and frustratingly unanswerable. For reasons, perhaps, that are different from what happens to Barnikol, it is possible to suppose that Rigaux's Belgian background is certainly the most immediate factor. From this, the fact that, for most of his academic career, Rigaux was affiliated Belgium's largest French-speaking university, the University of Louvain (also known as *Université catholique de Louvain*), seems to be what likely marginalized Rigaux from the predominantly-German handling of Life of Jesus research in the 1950s—insofar as we can say that most of the leaders on *the question of the meaning of Christology* hail from German protestantism and tend to be Marburgers, we can see that the Catholicism theologically-informing Rigaux's Christological thinking is outside whatever we can surmise to be mainstream.[120]

117. Pokorný, "Jesus as the Ever-Living Lawgiver in the Letter of Mara bar Sarapion," 135.

118. Wells, *Cutting Jesus Down to Size*, 138–39.

119. This is, in particular, grounded on Barnikol's *Bruno Bauer Studien and Materialien* (1972).

120. In addition to Rigaux, an article by Lucien Cerfaux (1883–1968) in 1959 and another by Karl Rahner in 1970, as pointed out by Evans, also contribute to the problem

When considering that Conzelmann, it seems to me, attempts to represent a mainstream understanding of the various handlings of *the question of the meaning of Christology*—even though Conzelmann concentrates on the state of the problem of the historical Jesus up to 1959—Conzelmann never acknowledges Rigaux. This seems to speak to, I submit, Conzelmann's own interest in what his German tradition contributes to the Christological thinking directed towards the historical Jesus. If we maintain that the degree that Rigaux is outside even Conzelmann's sense of the mainstream problematizing of the historical Jesus, we may be able to ascertain that what places Rigaux outside of Conzelmann's mainstream is not only because Rigaux is outside the Protestant tradition as a Catholic, or even that Rigaux is outside the German school as a French Belgian, but more precisely because of the specific argument Rigaux makes.

In his "*L 'historicité de Jésus devant l'exégèse récente*" (1958), which can be rendered from the French as "The Historicity of Jesus in the Face of Recent Exegesis," Evans explains Rigaux's argument as one where Rigaux "argues that Bultmann's following has defected, [Bultmann's] influence has waned, and that the Gospels do give us a reliable picture of the historical Jesus."[121] What is immediately apparent in Rigaux's title is that Rigaux wishes to constitute his understanding of "the historicity of Jesus" over and against the problem of the historical Jesus. To point to a "historicity," in my view, certainly contends that there is a relationship between the meaning of Jesus of "history" and the meaning of the history of "Jesus," such that Rigaux's conceptions of Jesus of Nazareth and the Jesus of faith are without conflict and are inextricably linked theologically and Christologically, since the Gospels, in effect, are historically reliable and collectively settle the problem of the historical Jesus. The extent that, as Evans ascertains, Rigaux believes that "the Gospels do give us a reliable picture of the historical Jesus" is, to be sure, an opinion shared by others, such as Grundmann, Stauffer, and Mussner. In this way, we can align Rigaux with critics to the right of Bultmann on the matter of what is historically-reliable in the Gospels and how this serves *the question of the meaning of Christology*.

Given Evans' characterization, we can see that Rigaux's critique of Bultmann ventures into an attack on Bultmann. Indeed, Bultmann, particularly by 1958, was certainly not without his critics—to be sure, Anderson tells us in *Critical Quests of Jesus* (1969) that this criticism came from Bultmann's left, Bultmann's right, and within Bultmann's circle of

---

of the historical Jesus from the standpoint of Catholic theologizing on *the question of the meaning of Christology*. See Evans, *Life of Jesus Research*, 31; 64.

121. Evans, *Life of Jesus Research*, 30.

Bultmannians[122]—however, there is something especially venomous about Rigaux's assertion that, Evans summarizes, "Bultmann's following has defected" and, for that matter, "[Bultmann's] influence has waned." Through what can only be perceived as an attack on Bultmann, what Rigaux seemingly suggests—by way of our reliance on Evans' characterization of "*L 'historicité de Jésus devant l'exégèse récente*"—is that, by 1958, Bultmann's kind of theologizing has lost its significance, insofar as what demythologizing means to *the question of the meaning of Christology* has become less important. It is probably not too much to say that, for Rigaux, by 1958, Bultmann is a diminishing figure that may have entered the 1950s with a sizable influence on the likes of Käsemann and Bornkamm, but has reached the close of the 1950s defecting followers and waning influence.

It is easy to simply disagree with Rigaux, if attending to the facts on the ground throughout the 1950s up to 1958, when we think about how many figures have been influenced by Bultmann—those that come from within Bultmann's immediate circle and those coming from outside it. To say that anyone "has defected" and that any influence "has waned" misses four very important facts that are worth listing carefully, thanks to Evans' bibliographies in *Life of Jesus Research*. First, from 1951 to 1955, a little more than 20 articles appear by a combination of Bultmann's followers and others that have inserted themselves in the discussion solicited by Bultmann's followers. Secondly, from 1956 to 1958—the year Rigaux's article first appeared—roughly about 20 articles appeared, again by a combination of Bultmann's followers and others influenced by those followers. Thirdly, when looking at the period from 1956 to 1960, some 40 articles appear—which is twice as many as the same previous period—all by both Bultmann's followers and those that employed themselves as interlocutors with Bultmann's followers. And lastly, in the same calendar year that Rigaux's article appeared, more than 10 articles appeared, including pieces by Althaus, Ebeling, Fuchs, Jeremias, and Schneider and Barnikol. What all have in common, when considering what Evans' rather comprehensively includes in his bibliographies, is the subject of the problem of the historical Jesus, and what this means to doing Christology. What is clear from Evans' compilations is that there is an increasing interest in what was laid bare by Bultmann in 1940s, and that interest only gains momentum by 1958 and through to the end of the decade in 1960.

Now, given what is made explicit by this evidence, we should probably consider Rigaux's claims, through Evans, more thoroughly from Rigaux's specific theological perspective rather than what is generally taking place

122. Anderson, *Critical Quests of Jesus*, 121–200.

theologically. Suffice it to say: Rigaux's experience of Bultmann, Bultmann's followers, and who has "defected" and what has "waned" are obviously situated more firmly within the narrow context of Rigaux's Belgian experience at French-speaking University of Louvain. Indeed, Rigaux's context is unlike anything that can be extended more generally to what is happening contemporaneously in Germany.

Because of this, we should ask two things of Rigaux: whom does he consider as Bultmann's "following" and who at does he consider as "influence"—based on what is happening contemporaneously in Germany, it is certainly conceivable to view Rigaux's understanding of Bultmann, Bultmann's followers, and the development of *the question of the meaning of Christology* by 1958 as largely out of touch, misunderstood, and mischaracterized.

Yet, what we find, through Rigaux, is the extent that *the question of the meaning of Christology* was grounded more in Germany's Christological thinking at the time than anywhere else. This is certainly confirmed by James M. Robinson in his well-known monograph, *A New Quest of the Historical Jesus* (1959). However, in the same year that Rigaux's article appeared, Robinson also publishes the relatively modest, "The Quest of the Historical Jesus Today" (1958) in *Theology Today*, which, Evans tells us, provides an explanation and defense of the new quest."[123] While this earlier text can certainly be seen the basis for what Robinson expands into *A New Quest of the Historical Jesus*, it is clear that Robinson's very thorough survey of and programmatic approach to the "new quest" is purposely situated on how the "new quest" unfolds in Germany. At the outset of "The Quest of the Historical Jesus Today," Robinson explains that his article assesses "a trend in contemporary German scholarship which is seeking to re-open the quest of the historical Jesus."[124] Though never acknowledging Rigaux, even if we can see an engagement with what Rigaux misunderstands and mischaracterizes, Robinson makes it explicit that it is within German circles that the new quest's "development is significant because it takes place where the questioning of such a quest has been most fully sensed."[125]

Rigaux's "*L 'historicité de Jésus devant l'exégèse récente*," to Robinson's point, merely provides a survey that "has [not] been most fully sensed." We can assign the re-appropriation of Robinson's words to another text that is less than half the length of "*L 'historicité de Jésus devant l'exégèse récente*"

---

123. Evans, *Life of Jesus Research*, 31.

124. Robinson, *New Quest of the Historical Jesus*, 183.

125. Robinson, *New Quest of the Historical Jesus*, 183.

but published in the same year: "*Jésus-Christ devant l'histoire et la dialectique*," which can be rendered as "Jesus Christ in the Face of History and the Dialectical."[126] Nevertheless, when making sense of Rigaux's position on the problem of the historical Jesus as that which, to re-appropriate Robinson again, is not "fully sensed." This, as Robinson expounds on in *A New Quest of the Historical Jesus*, is in spite of "the relatively untroubled and uninterrupted quest of the historical Jesus going on in French" scholarship of the day.[127] This point, Robinson footnotes, revolves around "the standard treatment of the quest" with respect to French-speaking theologians that are antecedents to Rigaux.[128] To whatever degree we can say that Rigaux's "*L 'historicité de Jésus devant l'exégèse récente*" contributes to what was standard treatment of the quest in Belgium up to 1958, I submit that there is a strong likelihood that Rigaux's general characterization of the quest since Schweitzer (and since Bultmann) was controversial in French-speaking Belgian theological circles and among French-speaking theologians. Whatever controversy laid bare by Rigaux about the state and relevance of the "new" quest and what it meant for *the question of the meaning of Christology* by 1958, it seems that Rigaux's perspective was challenged, rather indirectly, by a concerted use of Robinson among French-speaking theologians interested in Bultmann and the Bultmannians—this seems the case, perhaps, when considering that Robinson's *A New Quest of the Historical Jesus* was translated into French as *Le kérygme de l' Église et le Jésus de l' histoire* in 1961,[129] even though, as Evans notes, Robinson "complained that the French translation was neither authorized, nor well done."[130]

Though "*L 'historicité de Jésus devant l'exégèse récente*," as far as I can tell, largely remained out of the purview of the Bultmannians that Rigaux claims have "defected" and out of the purview of others influenced by what Bultmann lays bare, which is an influence that Rigaux claims "has waned," Rigaux publishes a series of monographs under the subtle, *Pour une histoire de Jesus* which we can be translated as "For a History of Jesus": *Témoignage de l'évangile de Marc: Pour une histoire de Jesus 1* (1965), *Témoignage de l'évangile de Matthieu: Pour une histoire de Jesus 2* (1967), *Témoignage de l'évangile de Luc: Pour une histoire de Jesus 4* (1970), and *Témoignage*

126. This shorter text appears to be related to the larger text, insofar as it is, perhaps, based on "*L 'historicité de Jésus devant l'exégèse récente*."

127. Robinson, *New Quest of the Historical Jesus*, 9.

128. Robinson, *New Quest of the Historical Jesus*, 9.

129. A year earlier, in 1960, Robinson's *A New Quest of the Historical Jesus* was translated into German as *Kerygma und historischer Jesus*.

130. Evans, *Life of Jesus Research*, 33.

de l'évangile de Jean: Pour une histoire de Jesus 5 (1974).[131] Of these four, only two were translated into English: *Testimony of Saint Mark* (1966) and *Testimony of Saint Matthew* (1968)—from these translations, we find that "*Témoignage*" can be translated as "testimony," but we must be careful to note that Rigaux is not providing us with commentaries on the Gospels in the strictest sense of what commentaries are. This has not gone unnoticed in reviews of each of Rigaux's volumes of *Témoignage*, with the exception of Rigaux's fifth volume, which, to the best of my knowledge, was not reviewed. Across the reviews—one from 1966 on the first volume, three on the second volume (two in 1969 and one in 1970), and one from 1971 on the fourth volume—there is a general consensus, which revolves around, as Neil J. McEleney explains in 1969, Rigaux performing an "extended analysis"[132] directed towards, as Marcel Fallet writes in 1970, "*une contribution á la rédaction d'une histoire de Jésus*" (translated as "a contribution to the writing of a history of Jesus").[133]

In a certain sense, these four texts are significant due to their size in relation to "*L 'historicité de Jésus devant l'exégèse récente*"—the first is approximately 200 pages in length, the second is a little more than 300 pages, the fourth is a little less than 500 pages, and the fifth is around 200. Additionally, all four texts hold a significance over "*L 'historicité de Jésus devant l'exégèse récente*" as, perhaps, expansions of what Rigaux believes to be the "historicity of Jesus" into more explicit variation on the "history of Jesus," through focusing on the Gospels of Mark (in 1965), Matthew (in 1967), Luke (in 1970), and John (in 1974). Towards each of the four gospels, Rigaux, I submit, is attempting to provide essentially four answers to *the question of the meaning of Christology*, which ultimately attend, as we have found in Grundmann's, Stauffer's, and Mussner's suggestions, to the historical reliability of the Gospels. Rather than synthesizing that reliability into one Christological reflection that lends itself to one kind of Christological thinking, Rigaux's presentation—with "*L 'historicité de Jésus devant l'exégèse récente*" functioning as a preliminary text—attends to the notion that there are four histories of Jesus and, because of this, there is a multiplicity to what can be meant by "the historical Jesus" and what, exactly, is at the forefront of the problem therein.

131. The third in this series of texts is a noticeable departure from the prevailing theme others authored by Rigaux. Authored by Lucien Cerfaux, it is entitled *Jésus aux origines de la tradition* (1968).

132. McEleney, "Béda Rigaux, *Témoignage de l'évangile de Matthieu (Pour une histoire de Jesus II*: Bruges: Desclée de Brouwer, 1967)," 601.

133. Fallet, "*Témoignage de l'évangile de Matthieu: Pour une histoire de Jesus II* by Béda Rigaux," 120.

JOACHIM JEREMIAS

Given that the body of work associated with Joachim Jeremias (1900–1979) is eclectic between writings on the Hebrew Bible and New Testament, but also in terms of varied approaches to research on Judaic and Rabbinic texts and research on an array of New Testament problems, his most important—and only—contribution to *the question of the meaning of Christology* through life of Jesus research into the perennial problem of the historical Jesus is the short essay, "The Present Position in the Controversy Concerning the Problem of the Historical Jesus" (1958). Translated in English within *The Expository Times*, though numbering barely eight pages in length, Evans dessribes it as: "[a] concise presentation of the problems and proposals of the new quest [which] argues that the quest of the historical Jesus is the most important task of New Testament scholarship."[134]

Setting aside the argument Jeremias makes in the essay for now, the textual transmission of the essay is worth detailing first. As Evans tells us, Jeremias' essay originally appeared in German as *"Der gegenwärtigen Stand der Debatte um das problem des historischen Jesus"* in *Wissenschaftliche Zeitschrift der Universität Greifswald* in a 1956/1957 edition, but would appear again in the Helmut Ristow and Karl Matthiae co-edited, *Der historische Jesus und der kerygmatische Christus* (1960)[135]—while the earlier 1956/1957 version is roughly the same length as the 1958 version, the 1960 version, as it appeared in the co-edited collection, was expanded to some 14 pages in length, nearly doubling both of the earlier versions. Jeremias revised and expanded the 14-page version to 23 pages and changed the title to *Das Problem des historischen Jesus* (1960), as part of a monograph series entitled *Calwer Hefte zur Förderung biblischen Glaubens und christlichen Lebens*. It is this lattermost version that has been translated into *The Problem of the Historical Jesus* in 1964—in the introduction to this 1964 translation, John Reumann places Jeremias' text in the following context:

> Even those who take a very different tack from Professor Jeremias in the New Quest recognize his presentation as a very useful summary of the past history and present situation in *Leben-Jesu-Forschung*. For almost any reader, the essay is a good starting-point for delving into one of the frontier areas in current biblical and theological study.[136]

---

134. Evans, *Life of Jesus Research*, 30.

135. Evans, *Life of Jesus Research*, 30.

136. Reumann, "Introduction," vii.

Here, we can think of Reumann's understanding of Jeremias as providing "a good starting-point" in terms of Robinson's "The Quest of the Historical Jesus Today" (1958), with his *A New Quest for the Historical Jesus*, having, itself, appeared the following year in 1959, along with Conzelmann's "*Jesus Christus*" and "*Zur Methode der Leben-Jesu-Forschung*," both in 1959. What we have in Jeremias' *The Problem of the Historical Jesus* is something that not only pre-dates Robinson's Conzelmann's respective surveys, but also more firmly roots, to Reumann's point, "the past and present situation in *Leben-Jesu-Forschung*" within a distinctly German context and German tradition of the time. Indeed, Robinson's survey speaks about the German tradition from outside the tradition, though Conzelmann, by contrast, hails from the same German tradition as Jeremias. Nevertheless, as important as Robinson's characterization of the "new" quest for the historical Jesus is at the time—perhaps more so than Conzelmann's, if we can say that, if limiting ourselves to 1959, Robinson's survey had more reach than Conzelmann's—Jeremias' earlier characterization accomplishes the same task as Robinson and Conzelmann. The real significance of Jeremias orients what Robinson and Conzelmann ultimately present, insofar as we can say that Robinson's and Conzelmann's respective surveys are both directly influenced by Jeremias.

What influences Jeremias, as one who wishes to make sense out of what influences Käsemann and other Bultmannians, are "three factors," Reumann writes, "[that] emerged [between 1900 and 1940] which caused many scholars to reverse the optimistic hopes of the previous century."[137] This resulted, by 1940 and in the years that followed, with the conclusion that, Reumann explains, "for scientific as well as for theological reasons, no biography of Jesus could be written."[138] This is precisely where Bultmann comes into play, and the extent that these factors were relayed by Bultmann to those that became Bultmannians. In light of what is brought to bear by Bultmann, Reumann details these factors as: "the rediscovery of eschatology,"[139] "the emergence of form criticism after the First World War,"[140] and "the changed understanding of history."[141] Given what can be surmised from these three factors and what they collectively mean for theologizing and, in turn, what is means to engage in Christological thinking, Reumann places this into a narrower context:

137. Reumann, "Introduction," xi.
138. Reumann, "Introduction," xi.
139. Reumann, "Introduction," xi.
140. Reumann, "Introduction," xiii.
141. Reumann, "Introduction," xiv.

These three factors, then, help to account for what must be called the prevailing view, at least in German theological circles, until about 1953. This view rejected, on scientific and theological grounds, the possibility and even the desirability of a life of Jesus and exulted in this situation, seeing in it a defense of what "faith" really must mean. Professor Jeremias finds both strengths and dangers in such a position.[142]

Reumann goes on to say:

> As to Professor Jeremias' own position in this discussion, it is clear that he is not part of the Old Quest, for he is quite aware of its failures. He is likewise not an enthusiast for "kerygma-theology," for he is concerned to separate the gospel of Jesus from the kerygma of the early church.[143]

The fact that Jeremias is "not part of the Old Quest" should not be at all surprising, given where Jeremias enters into the ongoing discussion in life of Jesus research in the late 1950s. Even so, as much as Jeremias is concerned with *the question of the meaning of Christology*, it should not be surprising, too, that how Jeremias approaches the problem of the historical Jesus is certainly too far afield from what arose and waned after the "Old Quest," particularly after the Bultmann's influences on what it means to do Christology and what is laid bare by Christological thinking throughout the 1940s. Even so, Reumann reminds us that Jeremias was "not an enthusiast for 'kerygma-theology,'" insofar as it is possible to place Jeremias within Bultmann's most intimate circle. Yet, Reumann writes, we need to be careful when placing Jeremias in such close proximity to Bultmann or even within the circle of Bultmannians—to this extent, Reumann holds to this characterization of Jeremias:

> I should not even classify him as part of the "New Questors," for Professor Jeremias never abandoned the task or gave up hope the way the Bultmann school did. I should call his position that of "discerning continuity" with what is worthwhile in past research. [. . .] In many ways, Professor Jeremias fits into the company of those who think of the quest as "continued," and his present essay describes the "why" and "how" for a continuing quest.[144]

---

142. Reumann, "Introduction," xv.

143. Reumann, "Introduction," xvii.

144. Reumann, "Introduction," xvii–xviii.

If the way that Jeremias approaches *the question of the meaning of Christology*, through his characterization of the state of the problem of the historical Jesus by 1958 is with a "discerning continuity," the same can be said about what Robinson and Conzelmann respectively lay bare in their own surveys. Yet, as Reumann sees it:

> As Professor Jeremias unfolds the topic, that study of the Jesus of history involves us in questions not only about the historical method but also about our understanding of revelation, ourselves, and our concept of God. Such a discovery would not surprise the authors of the gospels [. . .] Such an understanding of what telling the story of Jesus involves, immediately implies far more than straight reporting.[145]

Essentially, Jeremias recognizes the complexity, the difficulty and all the nuances to *the question of the meaning of Christology*, as that which situates and is situated by the problem of the historical Jesus. Though Jeremias' survey is comparatively longer than Robinson's "The Quest of the Historical Jesus," but certainly shorter than Conzelmann's "*Jesus Christus*," Jeremias provides us with the earliest, most comprehensive presentation of all of the key scholarship contributing to what had become a "new quest" by 1958.

At the opening of his *The Problem of the Historical Jesus*, as its most revised vision of the task and scope of the "new quest," Jeremias begins with the following: "to anyone who is not aware of the controversy, the question whether the historical Jesus and his message have significance for the Christian faith must sound absurd."[146] With respect to "controversy" in particular, a lengthy footnote citing, "among the more pertinent books and articles in the extensive literature on the subject [of the controversy]," include Martin Kähler (1892) as a beginning point, then proceeding relatively chronologically with Albert Schweitzer (1906), Rudolf Bultmann (1948–53), Ernst Käsemann (1954), Nils A. Dahl (1955), Thomas W. Manson (1956),[147]

145. Reumann, "Introduction," xviii.

146. Jeremias, *Problem of the Historical Jesus*, 1.

147. The inclusion of Thomas W. Manson (1893–1958) may be misleading here. The date of 1956 refers to the collection, *The Background of the New Testament and Its Eschatology*, in which Manson's text appears, though the text itself is likely not dated to 1956. My suspicion is that the text was written sometime in the 1940s, alongside Manson's "The Life of Jesus: A Study of the Available Materials" (1943) and the lecture, "The Quest of the Historical Jesus—Continued" (delivered in 1949). Though both texts are included in Manson's posthumous collection, *Studies in the Gospels and Epistles* (1962), it seems to me that three texts thematically belong to the same contemporaneous period of time. Admittedly, tying the text that appears in the 1956 collection to the other two more explicitly dated to 1943 and 1949 is, at this point, a theory. Yet, quite plausible, given the obscurity of Manson by the dominance of German scholarship in

Ernst Heitsch (1956), Ernst Fuchs (1956), Jeremias, himself (1947),[148] Béda Rigaux (1958–59),[149] Paul Althaus (1958), James M. Robinson (1959), Rudolf Schnackenburg (1959),[150] Hans Conzelmann (1959),[151] and Gerhard Ebeling (1963). This list of "pertinent books and articles" ends with a second text from Bultmann entitled, *Das Verhältnis der urchristlichen Christusbotschaft zum historischen Jesus* (1960), which was not only translated for the Carl E. Braaten and Roy A. Harrisville co-edited, *The Historical Jesus and the Kerygmatic Christ* (1964), as Jeremias notes, but also re-published as part of the Craig A. Evans edited, *The Historical Jesus: Volume 1* (2004)— this is followed by an advisement that "much of what has been written in the controversy in the last decade (mostly in German) may be gathered from this essay and its notes."[152]

The reference made to Bultmann's *Das Verhältnis der urchristlichen Christusbotschaft zum historischen Jesus* is worth parsing for a moment. As it is footnoted, the text is dated to 1960, though, as noted, it eventually appears in translation in 1964. What must be made more specific, I submit, beyond the 1964 collection in which the text appears: *The Historical Jesus and the Kerygmatic Christ*—what must be made clearer is why Bultmann's text, as it is referred to in relation to what Jeremias means by "controversy," is referred to at all. Translated as "The Primitive Christian Kerygma and the Historical Jesus"—which goes unacknowledged—Bultmann begins with the following declaration of sorts:

> The question concerning the relation of the primitive Christian message about Christ to the historical Jesus has become relevant today in a new way. In the period of the Life-of-Jesus research (or of the so-called liberal theology) the question had been controlled by the desire to free the picture of the historical Jesus

the Life of Jesus research more generally over what Robinson, by 1962, relegates to Anglo-Saxon scholarship, to which Manson belongs.

148. Here, Jeremias is cited with the text, *Die Gleichnisse Jesu*, translated as *The Parable of Jesus* in 1962. Another Jeremias text would have been a better contributor to the "controversy" in question: the earlier version of what was translated into *The Problem of the Historical Jesus*. I am speaking about, of course, Jeremias' "The Present Position in the Controversy Concerning the Problem of the Historical Jesus," translated in 1958 from the original version that appeared in 1956–57.

149. I want to note here this references the shorter of two texts Rigaux publishes circa 1958, with the larger text, "*L 'historicité de Jésus devant l'exégèse récente.*" This larger text that goes unreferenced by Jeremias is the only text that is, indeed, referenced in Evans' *Life of Jesus Research* as Rigaux's contribution to the problem of the historical Jesus.

150. Schnackenburg's "*Jesusforschung und Christusglaube*" (1959).

151. Conzelmann's "*Jesus Christus*" (1959).

152. Jeremias, *Problem of the Historical Jesus*, 2.

from the dogmatic overlay which had concealed it in the primitive Christian message, in the "kerygma." For that reason the
emphasis lay upon establishing the difference between Jesus and
the kerygma. Today the situation is reversed. The emphasis lies
on elaborating the unity of the historical Jesus and the Christ of
the kerygma.[153]

Stopping here, we see that Bultmann, indeed, is inserting himself into the
Life-of-Jesus research of the day. Given that the text is actually dated earlier
than 1960, as it has been footnoted in Jeremias—more accurately dated to
1959—it seems to me that referencing Bultmann fundamentally contextualizes Jeremias—we can infer this from the deference made to Bultmann.
What must be unpacked, however, is what is specifically behind this deference, and what Bultmann means for Jeremias more generally.

As Konrad Hammann explains, the Bultmann text in question was
originally, first, a seminar Bultmann presented at Syracuse University in
Spring 1959, then delivered again on July 25, 1959 at Heidelberg.[154] The
text itself, Hammann details, "offered one last opportunity [for Bultmann]
to examine" the problem of the historical Jesus.[155] In it, Bultmann, Hammann writes, "took into consideration the most important contributions
to the discussion that had appeared up to that time."[156] While Hammann
tells us that Bultmann "was able for the first time to discuss essays, by
Hans Conzelmann, Gerhard Ebeling, and Ernst Fuchs,"[157] in the German
version of the text that appears in Bultmann's collection, *Exegetica* (1967),
we find Bultmann referencing many of the voices Jeremias does, but with
the exclusion of, notably, Rigaux, Manson, and Schnackenburg. Given that
Bultmann includes Biehl (1957), Bornkamm (1956), Braun (1957), Diem
(1957)—which goes unreferenced in Jeremias—Bultmann chiefly concentrates on all texts associated, one way or another, with the problem of the
historical Jesus published from 1956 to 1959, all of which hail from German
theologizing of the problem.[158] In doing so, Hammann describes Bultmann's
Das Verhältnis der urchristlichen Christusbotschaft zum historischen Jesus
as "seek[ing] to show that the historical and material relation between the
historical Jesus and the earliest Christian kerygma are to be distinguished

153. Bultmann, "Primitive Christian Kerygma and the Historical Jesus," 211.

154. Hammann, *Rudolf Bultmann*, 459.

155. Hammann, *Rudolf Bultmann*, 459.

156. Hammann, *Rudolf Bultmann*, 459.

157. Hammann, *Rudolf Bultmann*, 460.

158. Bultmann, *Das Verhältnis der urchristlichen Christusbotschaft zum historischen
Jesus*, 445.

from one another."[159] As a sort of encapsulation of the state of Life-of-Jesus research, Bultmann, true enough, as it is footnoted in Jeremias, gathers together "what has been written in the controversy," more specifically within the three years of Bultmann's seminar/lecture—how Bultmann sees this "controversy" undoubtedly directly affects and grounds how Jeremias approaches his own assessment of the "controversy" by 1964.

Even so, the footnote to Jeremias' notion of "controversy" explains that James M. Robinson's *A New Quest of the Historical Jesus* and Reginald H. Fuller's *The New Testament in Current Study* (1962) "are, on the whole, favorable to the Bultmannian outlook but try to reach a position of their own beyond him."[160] With all the contributing voices to what Jeremias calls "the controversy" gathered, Jeremias explains, with respect to "the question whether the historical Jesus and his message have any significance for the Christian faith," that, generally speaking, "no one in the ancient church, no one in the church of the Reformation period and of the two succeeding centuries thought of asking such a question."[161] Jeremias goes on to say, in a way that certainly deserves careful consideration:

> How is it possible that today this question is being asked in all seriousness, that it even occupies a central place in New Testament debate, and that in many quarters, it is being answered with a decisive negative? For a widely held theological position maintains that the historical Jesus and his message have no, or at least no decisive, significance for the Christian faith.[162]

From here, Jeremias asking the following questions:

> (1) Why is such a point of view possible? How has it arisen? What is its basis? (2) What can be said by way of criticism of this view? and (3) What is the relation between the good tidings of Jesus and the proclamation of the church?[163]

It is with these questions that Jeremias' ends his initial section to highlight, essentially, what the complete contextualization of the problem of the historical Jesus, namely, is—this becomes what directs Jeremias toward his own understanding of *the question of the meaning of Christology*.

After providing, just as Evans describes, a "concise presentation of the problems" brought forth from Reimarus to Bultmann, in a section entitled

---

159. Hammann, *Rudolf Bultmann*, 460.

160. Jeremias, *Problem of the Historical Jesus*, 1.

161. Jeremias, *Problem of the Historical Jesus*, 1.

162. Jeremias, *Problem of the Historical Jesus*, 1–2.

163. Jeremias, *Problem of the Historical Jesus*, 2.

"The Crucial Significance of the Historical Jesus," Jeremias asks a fundamental question: "what can be said by way of criticism of the position which
we have outlined?"[164] Though this question postulates the cumulative position with which Jeremias finds himself in his own positioning within a
Christological reflection and attends to *the question of the meaning of Christology*—to this point, as Jeremias says, "what can be said by way of criticism"
is what Jeremias understands as "the necessity of historical study."[165] To this
end, Jeremias makes it clear that "without a doubt it is true to say that the
dream of ever writing a biography of Jesus is over."[166] However, Jeremias
admits:

> It would be disastrous if we were unwilling to heed critical
> scholarship's salutary caution regarding uncritical use of the
> gospels. Nevertheless we *must* go back to the historical Jesus and
> his message. We cannot bypass him.[167]

Note, here, Jeremias' emphasis on "must," which is, again, emphasized to the
following extent:

> We must continually return to the historical Jesus and his mes-
> sage. The sources demand it; the kerygma, which refers us back
> from itself, also demands it. [. . .] We need to know who the
> Jesus of history was, and what was the content of his message.[168]

Because of this, Jeremias recognizes:

> Indeed, it is precisely at this point that the latest theological de-
> velopments push on beyond Bultmann's theology of the keryg-
> ma. It is now generally acknowledged that the problem of the
> historical Jesus must be taken seriously, and thus the situation
> in present-day New Testament studies is not so heterogeneous
> as it might seem at first sight.[169]

The point that Jeremias takes is one that marks an important assessment—it
is not just about what *the question of the meaning of Christology* means, but
it also about what *the question of the meaning of Christology* does. To be sure,
if, as Jeremias says, "it is now generally acknowledged that the problem of
the historical Jesus must be taken seriously," what this means, too, is that *the*

164. Jeremias, *Problem of the Historical Jesus*, 12.

165. Jeremias, *Problem of the Historical Jesus*, 12.

166. Jeremias, *Problem of the Historical Jesus*, 12.

167. Jeremias, *Problem of the Historical Jesus*, 12.

168. Jeremias, *Problem of the Historical Jesus*, 13–14.

169. Jeremias, *Problem of the Historical Jesus*, 21.

question of the meaning of Christology must also be taken seriously, especially if we view the question being posed and the meaning being made as essential to what it means to do Christological thinking through Christological reflection. In this way, because there is nothing heterogeneous about "the situation in present-day New Testament studies" that attends to the problem of the historical Jesus, there is also nothing heterogeneous about *the question of the meaning of Christology*, if we understand that the posing of the question and the meaningfulness of the meaning is "not so heterogeneous." What this must mean, then, for Jeremias—in a way that predates both Robinson's and Conzelmann's own assessments—is that there is a homogeneity to what it means to engage with the problem of the historical Jesus and, in turn, a homogeneity to *the question of the meaning of Christology* too. Jeremias speaks to this underlying homogeneity with respect to "the challenge of faith," as that which is presented through "the words and acts of Jesus,"[170] which, accordingly, should be part and parcel of any Christological reflection working towards and through *the question of the meaning of Christology*. To this particular end, Jeremias makes the following summation:

> When we read the gospels, even when we read them critically, we cannot evade this challenge. This claim to divine authority is the origin of Christianity, and hence study of the historical Jesus and his message is no peripheral task of New Testament scholarship, a study of one particular historical problem among many others. It is *the* central task of New Testament scholarship.[171]

---

170. Jeremias, *Problem of the Historical Jesus*, 21.

171. Jeremias, *Problem of the Historical Jesus*, 21.

Chapter 4

The Question of the Meaning
of Christology (IV)

Given what has been covered so far in the previous chapters, in terms of
the special recognition given to the multitude of voice contributing, in one
way or another, to the conception, development, and casting of *the question
of the meaning of Christology*, this chapter will focus on just three figures
that, until now, have only been referenced in passing, in relation to what has
already been discussed: Gerhard Ebeling (1912–2001), Friedrich Gogarten
(1887–1967), and Paul Althaus (1888–1966).

What, I submit, is important to note about Ebeling, Gogarten, and
Althaus is that each of them, in some form or fashion, can be considered
as "Bultmannians"—I use this term, now, simply to characterize the fact
that each theologize what Bultmann has already laid bare and, for that
matter, present a Christological thinking and enter a Christological reflection that both owe themselves to Bultmann's handling of *the question of
the meaning of Christology* in the 1940s. By calling Ebeling, Gogarten, and
Althaus as "Bultmannians" should also point to the fact that none of them
would have entered into the concerns of the "new quest" had it not been
for what Bultmann began and what, in turn, Käsemann attempts to man-
age by 1951. Now, it is important to be careful here: I do not mean to say
that Ebeling, Gogarten, and Althaus are "Bultmannians" in the sense that
they directly learned how to theologize from Bultmann, or were doctoral
students of Bultmann's at Marburg. This is certainly true of the respective

academic backgrounds for each, if none of them had Bultmann as a *Doktorvater*, though only Ebeling, to the best of my knowledge, belonged to the Bultmann-led "Old Marburgers." Yet, we can still thematically, theologically, and Christologically cast Ebeling, Gogarten, and Althaus in relation to Bultmann, as either being a critic of Bultmann from within Bultmann's circle (Ebeling), or a proponent or apologist for Bultmann (Gogarten), or a staunch, adamant opponent of Bultmann (Althaus).

Though Ebeling, Gogarten, and Althaus have different tasks and scopes to how they confront Bultmann and, in turn, conceive of what is fundamental to *the question of the meaning of Christology*, we must not minimize the role Bultmann plays in each of their respective theologizing in general and, more narrowly, how each attends to the posing of the question to and the seeking of the meaningfulness of Christology. In this sense, considering Ebeling, Gogarten, and Althaus, I intend to not just interpolate Bultmann's theologizing in the 1940s, or even what each brings to working through their respective "Bultmannianism" and the intensification of the "new quest" throughout the 1950s, but, more importantly, to interpolate *the question of the meaning of Christology* itself.

GERHARD EBELING

In addition to how Käsemann and Braun respectively choose to position themselves Christologically to Bultmann beginning in the 1950s, Gerhard Ebeling was also a student of Bultmann's at Marburg, though Ebeling did not ultimately complete his dissertation under Bultmann. Though Ebeling was later a student of Emil Brunner at the University of Zürich, Ebeling eventually completed his dissertation at Zürich in 1938 under the direction of Fritz Blanke, entitled *Evangelische Evangelienauslegung, eine Untersuchung zu Luthers Hermeneutik*, translated as "Evangelical Interpretation of the Gospels: An Investigation of Luther's Hermeneutic." This earliest interest in the "hermeneutic" eventually brings Ebeling and Fuchs together as the two chief proponents captured both by *The New Hermeneutic* (1964) as a volume in the New Frontiers in Theology series[1] and, later, as the "main perspectives" of Cornelius Van Til's *The New Hermeneutic* (1974).[2]

Though Ebeling was not one of Bultmann's doctoral students—as Fuchs, Käsemann, and Bornkamm all were—Ebeling, nonetheless, is considered as a Bultmannian, not just because of his connections to Fuchs, but

1. Ebeling and Fuchs provide "focal essays" that guide the task and scope of the volume.

2. Van Til, *The New Hermeneutic*, 1–18.

also because of Ebeling's own connections to Bultmann himself. Along with Fuchs, Käsemann, and Bornkamm, Ebeling belonged to the Bultmann-led group known as the "Old Marburgers"—in Konrad Hammann's biography on Bultmann, Hammann reproduces a group picture from a meeting of the "Old Marburgers" dated to October 1949.[3] By the time Ebeling and Fuchs, together, develop a theologizing that comes to be called "the new hermeneutic," Ebeling and Fuchs respectively contribute "focal essays" that set the task and scope of *The New Hermeneutic* collection,[4] with Ebeling's essay entitled "Word of God and Hermeneutic"—this essay is alternatively-entitled "Word of God and Hermeneutics" for Ebeling's collection, *Wort und Glaube* (1960), translated as *Word and Faith* (1963), which is, coincidently, in part, dedicated to Fuchs.[5]

James M. Robinson expansively captures the relationship between Ebeling and Fuchs in "Hermeneutic Since Barth," which, as a survey providing direction for *The New Hermeneutic* collection, places Ebeling and Fuchs in the broader issue of hermeneutics, including references to Bultmann, Heidegger, and Gadamer.[6] For Robinson, this holds true:

> It is a central recognition of the new hermeneutic that language itself says what is invisibly taking place in the life of a culture. An instance of this would be the sudden re-emergence of the term *Hermeneutik* within post-Bultmannian German theology.[7]

Though, to Robinson's point, Ebeling and Fuchs emerge from within post-Bultmannian German theology," they do so, as Laurence W. Wood tells us in *Theology as History and Hermeneutics* (2005), by "intend[ing] to move beyond the existentialist exegesis (demythologizing) of their teacher, Rudolf Bultmann."[8] While taking an account for Bultmann's own adaptation of Heidegger, Wood continues:

> Ebeling and Fuchs adapted the later Heidegger's ontological investigation of authentic language, which discloses Being, i.e., language lets Being be. The change of emphasis was thus from

3. Hammann, *Rudolf Bultmann*, 392.

4. There is a photo of the two—Ebeling and Fuchs—on the reverse jacket of the book. The two men sit on the same side of the table, with Fuchs captured speaking while Ebeling listens. The photo is undated and uncredited, though it is possible to assume the photo was taken, perhaps, sometime in the 1960s, judging from the Fuchs' affiliation with the University of Marburg and Ebeling's with the University of Zurich.

5. See the dedication page for *Word and Faith*.

6. Robinson, "Hermeneutic Since Barth," 1–77.

7. Robinson, "Hermeneutic Since Barth," 39.

8. Wood, *Theology as History and Hermeneutics*, 116.

"existence" in Bultmann to "language" in Ebeling and Fuchs
[. . .] the emphasis was upon the distinction between everyday
language corrupted by the subject-object split and the uncorrupted language of being.[9]

Here, from Wood, with Robinson in mind, we can see how closely Ebeling stands with Fuchs in terms of what "the new hermeneutic" means for
theologizing. But also, since Wood and Robinson show us how Ebeling and
Fuchs transcend what theologizing has meant when working "within post-
Bultmannian German theology," Ebeling's and Fuchs' joint concerns with
language, in one sense, speak to what meaning can be made in theologizing
and how that meaningfulness can be laid bare by, to Wood's point, "authentic
language" or "the uncorrupted language of being." In another sense, if what is
made meaningful by the new hermeneutic is the extent that, Wood explains,
"language itself says what is invisibly taking place in the life of a culture," how
Ebeling and Fuchs conceive of the new hermeneutic tempers *the question of
the meaning of Christology*—this is especially so, if we are to say that how we
pose the question of Christology and seek the meaning of Christology comes
through a Christological reflection predicated on the new hermeneutic.

Given that "Word of God and Hermeneutic," Ebeling notes in both
versions of the essay, was "read" at three conferences on three separate
occasions in the consecutive months of April 1959, May 1959, and June
1959, Ebeling directly references Fuchs.[10] Though Ebeling does not mention
whether the essay in its conference paper form was ever modified across
the three times it was "read" at the conferences or if Ebeling maintained its
content across the three occasions he delivered it. For that matter, Ebeling
does not mention how this previous conference paper form compares to the
essay as it appears in *The New Hermeneutic* and *Word and Faith*. However
impossible it may be to determine this—or if such differences in the textual
transmission of the text even matter—Ebeling notably tells the reader in the
essay's first footnote the following:

How profoundly I agree with Ernst Fuchs and how much I owe
to him from many years' exchange of views can be seen from
the many connections between this paper and the recently published first volume of the collected essays of Ernst Fuchs: *Zum
hermeneutischen Problem in der Theologie[:] Die existentiale
Interpretation*.[11]

9. Wood, *Theology as History and Hermeneutics*, 116.

10. Ebeling, "Word of God and Hermeneutic," 78; Ebeling, "Word of God and
Hermeneutics," 305.

11. Ebeling, "Word of God and Hermeneutic," 78; Ebeling, "Word of God and

Ebeling's "exchange of views" with Fuchs on the nature of theologizing tempered by how one handles the hermeneutical problem certainly brings Ebeling in proximity with Fuchs' own relationship with Bultmann. Just as Ebeling acknowledges the "many years" of dialogue with Fuchs and "the many connections," for Ebeling, arising between Ebeling's "Word of God and Hermeneutic" and Fuchs' *Zum hermeneutischen Problem in der Theologie*—culminating with "The New Testament and the Hermeneutical Problem," as the other "focal essay" of *The New Hermeneutic*—Ebeling undoubtedly recognizes "the many connections" between him and Bultmann, particularly by way of Fuchs, which, of course, arise "from many years' exchange of views" with Fuchs.

Ebeling dialogues with Bultmann on the problem of historicity and the notion of kerygma, as that which fundamentally calibrates Ebeling's understanding of *the question of the meaning of Christology*, particularly in Ebeling's lectures from Summer 1953 collected in *Die Geschichtlichkeit der Kirche und ihrer Verkündigung als theologisches Problem* (1954), translated as *The Problem of Historicity: In the Church and Its Proclamation* in in 1967, *Das Wesen des christlichen Glaubens* (1959), translated as *The Nature of Faith* in 1961, *Word and Faith* (1963), and *Theologie und Verkundigung* (1962), translated as *Theology and Proclamation: A Discussion with Rudolf Bultmann* in 1966. In particular, in the collection, *Word and Faith*, in "The Question of the Historical Jesus and the Problem of Christology"—which is coincidently devoted to Bultmann and, at Ebeling's admission, dated to May 1959—Ebeling provides three questions that outline "a theological sketch on the subject of the problem of the 'historical Jesus.'"[12] These questions are predicated on the meaning of "historical Jesus" itself, "what came to expression in Jesus," and to what extent "faith in Jesus Christ" forms or becomes "a basis in Jesus himself."[13] What arises from these three questions, for Ebeling, is a broader proposition: "the question of the historical Jesus is manifestly grasped as a theological question only when we perceive that it is aimed at the problem of Christology."[14] Whatever degree, in Ebeling's words, "the question of the historical Jesus and the problem of Christology are bound up together,"[15] *the question of the meaning of Christology*, as such, provides what Ebeling calls a "connecting link."[16]

Hermeneutics," 305.

    12. Ebeling, "Question of the Historical Jesus and the Problem of Christology," 288.

    13. Ebeling, "Question of the Historical Jesus and the Problem of Christology," 288.

    14. Ebeling, "Question of the Historical Jesus and the Problem of Christology," 288.

    15. Ebeling, "Question of the Historical Jesus and the Problem of Christology," 288.

    16. Ebeling, "Question of the Historical Jesus and the Problem of Christology," 288.

For Ebeling, the connecting link between the question of the historical Jesus and the problem of Christology, as that which ultimately points
to what has been maintained as *the question of the meaning of Christology*
as I have prescribed it, is also brought to bear in another essay included in
Word and Faith, "Jesus and Faith," which Ebeling acknowledges, in a footnote, as "go[ing] back to lectures [he] first gave in the summer semester of
1957 in Zurich during a course on Christology and then in January 1958
as guest lectures at the *Kirchliche Hochschule* Berlin."[17] In this sense, "Jesus and Faith" stands in close ideological and methodological proximity to
the concerns of "The Question of the Historical Jesus and the Problem of
Christology," such that the former speaks to the latter, when Ebeling writes
very early in the former essay, "the question of the relation between Jesus
and faith affects the heart of Christology, and indeed the prime datum of
Christian dogmatics as such."[18] Ebeling goes so far as to conclude, "[Chris-
tology] is the cardinal point of the whole account of what Christianity really
means [since] there is no doubt that what makes a Christian is faith in Jesus
Christ."[19] Precisely because of this, Ebeling finds, "the task of Christology,
then, is to give an account of the statement, 'I believe in Jesus.'"[20] What
remains with this account is the question of what it means to "believe in Jesus," if that question, in itself, regulates and is regulated by *the question of the
meaning of Christology*—this is both promise and problem of Christology
itself. Ebeling articulates this promise and problem in the following way:

> The fact that we cannot, as the eighteenth and nineteenth centu-
> ries imagined, reconstruct from the sources a biography of Jesus
> surely must not be confused with the idea that the historical
> Jesus is completely hidden from us behind the New Testament
> witness and totally unknown to us.[21]

On this point, Ebeling provides a footnote that contextualizes how he perceives of *the question of the meaning of Christology* through a distillation of
the pervading sentiments *towards to the question of the meaning of Christology* during Ebeling's time. In this footnote, which Ebeling predicates as "the
now resuscitated question of the historical Jesus," Ebeling references a series
of texts dating from 1954 to 1957.[22] The first of these is Käsemann's "The

17. Ebeling, "Jesus and Faith," 201.

18. Ebeling, "Jesus and Faith," 201.

19. Ebeling, "Jesus and Faith," 201.

20. Ebeling, "Jesus and Faith," 202.

21. Ebeling, "Jesus and Faith," 205.

22. Ebeling, "Jesus and Faith," 205.

Problem of the Historical Jesus" (1954), followed by texts by Nils A. Dahl (1955)[23] and Ernst Heitsch (1956).[24] Next, Ebeling cites Fuchs' *"Die Frage nach dem historischen Jesus"* (1956) and Bornkamm's *Jesus von Nazareth* (1956), which is followed by references to Peter Biehl (1956/1957),[25] another to Heitsch (1957),[26] Ethelbert Stauffer (1957),[27] another to Fuchs (1957),[28] Hermann Diem (1957),[29] and finally Braun (1957).[30] In this regard, what is worth noting, here, is that Ebeling's references to the aforementioned texts are largely duplicated from Conzelmann's, since both cover relatively analogous time periods—while Stauffer and Braun appear, here, only in Ebeling's purview, figures such as Mussner, Schneider, and Jeremias appear only in Conzelmann's purview.[31] Nevertheless, in capturing the lay of the land before him—just as, to be sure, Conzelmann does too—what Ebeling surmises from "the now resuscitated question of the historical Jesus" is the sense that:

> If the quest of the historical Jesus were in fact to prove that faith in Jesus has no basis in Jesus himself, then that would be the end of Christology. On the other hand it is not meaningless for Christology, but can be of great critical and positive importance to it, if we can ascertain anything by historical means regarding the question how far faith in Jesus has a basis in Jesus himself.[32]

Certainly, Ebeling does not view "the quest of the historical Jesus" as becoming "the end of Christology." Rather, what makes it "of great critical and positive importance" is that it best positions us to an understanding, handling, and articulation of *the question of the meaning of Christology*, as that which is fundamentally oriented by Käsemann.

Given that Käsemann, in particular, remains in Ebeling's purview as the inflection point in the way that, just as Ebeling says, "the now resuscitated

---

23. Dahl's *"Der historische Jesus als geschichtswissenschaftliches und theologisches Problem"* (1956).

24. Heitsch's *"Die Aporie des historischen Jesus als Problem theologischer Hermeneutik"* (1956).

25. Biehl's *"Zur Frage nach dem historischen Jesus"* is, in actuality, published in 1957/1958.

26. Heitsch's *"Jesus aus Nazareth als Christus"* (1957).

27. Stauffer's *Jesus: Gestalt und Geschichte* (1957).

28. Fuchs' *"Glaube und Geschichte im Blick auf die Frage nach dem historischen Jesus"* (1957).

29. Diem's *"Der irdische Jesus und der Christus des Glaubens"* (1957).

30. Ebeling, "Jesus and Faith," 205.

31. Conzelmann, *Jesus*, 87–88.

32. Ebeling, "Jesus and Faith," 205.

question of the historical Jesus" speaks to *the question of the meaning of Christology* more broadly, Ebeling directly responds to Käsemann's "The Beginnings of Christian Theology" through Ebeling's *"Der Grund christlicher Theologie"* (1961), translated as "The Ground of Christian Theology" in the *Apocalypticism* collection. What Käsemann's refers to as "the beginnings" in the title of his essay becomes Ebeling's understanding of "the ground," insofar as Ebeling wishes to "rephrase [Käsemann's] title."[33] In terms of this rephrasing, Ebeling writes:

> This indicates the transition from the historical to the dogmatic approach and is in harmony with the trend of Käsemann's essay insofar as he not only puts questions explicitly to dogmatics but also plainly lets his own historical approach be guided by a dogmatic interest.[34]

What we see, here, is Ebeling's attention to the relationship between what he views as "the historical" and what he views as "the dogmatic." The extent that Ebeling views the two "in hanrmony with the trend of Käsemann's essay" speaks to a trajectory that Ebeling is witnessing since 1954 To be sure, though Ebeling is contributing to the lagging indicators of this trajectory— and he is undoubtedly aware of what his own contribution entails—Ebeling is also aware of his own participation in the leading indicators towards where the relationship between "the historical and "the dogmatic" will take, I submit, *the question of the meaning of Christology.*

The manner with which "the historical" informs "the dogmatic," and vice versa, comes to bear on how Ebeling positions himself to *the question of the meaning of Christology,* but, for Ebeling, what is also laid bare by how "the historical" informs "the dogmatic," and vice versa, is what he points out as:

> The fact that with the primitive Christian kerygma theology at once becomes a necessary task can be recognized from two closely interrelated symptoms: from the fact that Jesus (the proclamation of whom is the *one* concern of the primitive Christian kerygma) sets the problem of the language in the name of Jesus and through which reality in itself, that is, as it is before God, is revealed.[35]

From here, Ebeling adds:

33. Ebeling, "Ground of Christian Theology," 47.
34. Ebeling, "Ground of Christian Theology," 47.
35. Ebeling, "Ground of Christian Theology," 49.

But secondly, from the fact that this kerygma is a manifold interpretation from the start—*the* kerygma cannot be discovered
at all!—and therefore in need of interpretation, which means
that it is a controversial linguistic event wide open to confessional debate.[36]

Not only is it clear that Ebeling is in direct dialogue with Fuchs' notion
of the "language-event,"[37] but it is also clear that Ebeling's words are situated
firmly and contextually between two contemporaneously conceived texts: a
lecture, "Towards a Christology" (dated to Winter 1960/1961), and a lecture,
"*Wissenschaftliche Theologie und kirchliche Verkündigung*" (dated to April 19,
1961), which are both included in the *Theology and Proclamation* collection.
While "Towards a Christology" presents sixteen theses that seemingly construct Ebeling's approach to and understanding of *the question of the meaning
of Christology*, the three parts that make up the "*Wissenschaftliche Theologie
und kirchliche Verkündigung*" lecture provide a more thoroughgoing engagement with Bultmann, particularly, as Ebeling points out in the preface to the
Theology and Proclamation collection, given that "so many additions had been
made to the discussion with Bultmann in the third part that it had become the
major part of the work."[38] This third part, entitled "Kerygma and the Historical
Jesus," begins with Ebeling's assertion that, after with reckoning with the "tension" between matters of scientific theology and those of church proclamation
and, then, the relationship between historical and dogmatic theology, "we still
however have to consider the problem of proclaiming the Gospel today in the
acutest form in which it is raised for theology."[39] For Ebeling, "when we think
over the problem of proclamation today, our attention inevitably focuses on
the problem of Christology."[40] To this end, if the former problem points to the
latter problem, Ebeling questions "how can we hold ourselves accountable for
the basic [C]hristological claims which we make in our preaching today?"[41]
I find, here, that, in his approach to and understanding of *the question of the
meaning of Christology*, the Christological reflection necessary to even speak
to "the question" and formulate "a meaning" is fundamentally filtered through
one's handling of proclaiming "the question" and "a meaning." Essentially, if
proclaiming makes what it means to do Christology meaningful, one must lay
bare the meaningfulness of what it means to proclaim at all. Indeed, there are

36. Ebeling, "Ground of Christian Theology," 49.

37. Fuchs, *Studies of the Historical Jesus*, 222.

38. Ebeling, *Theology and Proclamation*, 7.

39. Ebeling, *Theology and Proclamation*, 32.

40. Ebeling, *Theology and Proclamation*, 32.

41. Ebeling, *Theology and Proclamation*, 32.

"questions which are raised," Ebeling writes, "when we consider the relation of proclamation to Christology."[42] These questions remain, Ebeling tells us, "in spite of the richness of thematic material" that should both direct what it means to proclaim and what that proclamation means to *the question of the meaning of Christology*.

All told, keeping in mind that "the richness of thematic material" holds a historical context and yields a historical significance, Ebeling arrives at this: the emphasis on historical thought in modern times has raised the gravest problems for theology precisely in the field of Christology."[43] This problem of historicity,[44] then, materializes, for Ebeling, into "the problem of the difference between the historical Jesus and the kerygmatic Christ remains, in spite of the fate of the enquiry into the life of Jesus."[45] The preponderance of these problems, as they come to bear on *the question of the meaning of Christology*, force Christology itself to appear, Ebeling says, "as no more than a later mythologizing of the person of Jesus, which it is no longer possible for us to accept."[46] Ebeling halts us here—thinking of Bultmann—to concede: "neither is it possible for us to recover that which lay behind the process of mythologizing."[47] What Ebeling is illustrating is the problem at the heart of *the question of the meaning of Christology*, as that which hinges on the "belief in the Person of the Son of God, as a necessary condition of the understanding of Christology," which Ebeling believes "is denied to modern man, and with it the possibility of an approach to the understanding of Christology."[48] In order to make *the question of the meaning of Christology* all the more accessible, Ebeling notes:

> Bultmann employed the concept of the kerygma in an attempt to come to grips with the problem of Christology faced with radically new difficulties in making itself intelligible to the modern world.[49]

---

42. Ebeling, *Theology and Proclamation*, 32.

43. Ebeling, *Theology and Proclamation*, 32–33.

44. This is the title of Ebeling's book (1967), as translated from *Die Geschichtlichkeit der Kirche und ihrer Verkündigung als theologisches Problem* (1954), which are based on lectures delivered in Summer 1953. In this text, how Ebeling describes the "problem of historicity" is in terms of our encounter with theological objects, such as "the exegesis of a biblical text, which cannot be encountered without encountering the historicity, or, Ebeling says, "the specific situation in the history of theology, or the discussion of a special doctrine of dogmatics" See Ebeling, *The Problem of Historicity*, 3.

45. Ebeling, *Theology and Proclamation*, 34.

46. Ebeling, *Theology and Proclamation*, 34.

47. Ebeling, *Theology and Proclamation*, 34.

48. Ebeling, *Theology and Proclamation*, 35.

49. Ebeling, *Theology and Proclamation*, 35.

This necessity of intelligibility, then, mitigates "the problem of Christology," but it also mitigates *the question of the meaning of Christology* as that which is projected and projects "the modern world." It is this contextualization, for Ebeling, that is ultimately situated by as much as it situates itself to the increasingly modernized role that the hermeneutical plays in the intelligibility of *the question of the meaning of Christology*. In this sense, if the intent is for the question of the meaning of Christology to be made meaningful for us and, in turn, exude a meaningfulness through us, Ebeling's understanding of what Bultmann contributes to this becomes all the more important—both as a way to assess Bultmann on Bultmann's terms, but also as a way for Ebeling to assess Bultmann on Ebeling's terms, for the sake of Ebeling's handling of *the question of the meaning of Christology* and what arises from Ebeling's own theologizing about the New Testament more generally. Along these lines, Ebeling gives an account of Bultmann in the following way:

> In Bultmann's view the existential interpretation which is required by his programme of demythologizing in no way leads to the mere discussion and examination of the general possibilities of understanding one's existence.[50]

Furthering this, if we to equate "the general possibilities of understanding one's existence" with *the question of the meaning of Christology*, Ebeling explains:

> Existential interpretation is much rather intended to bring out the theological significance of the mythological language of the New Testament, by interpreting it in such a way that the action of God in Christ and therefore the Person of Christ is stressed as the decisive saving event.[51]

By "existential interpretation," we are speaking of meaningfulness, for the sake of what is made meaningful and for that which must be meaningful. For us to "bring out the theological significance of the mythological language of the New Testament," something must be made meaningful, so that meaningfulness, through the interpretation of "the action of God in Christ" and "the Person of Christ," can make "the decisive saving event" just as meaningful as it is decisive, just as decisive as it is intelligible. In other words, meaningfulness, decisiveness, and intelligibility are one in the same, particularly when attending to *the question of the meaning of Christology*,

---

50. Ebeling, *Theology and Proclamation*, 36.
51. Ebeling, *Theology and Proclamation*, 36.

particularly by how we, to Ebeling's point, avoid "neglect[ing] the nature of the kerygma as 'word-event.'"[52] Here, just as Ebeling suggests:

> The decisive thing is the appearance of a challenge qualifying the situation of men and authorising them to deliver the kerygma; which not only makes kerygmatic statement intelligible in their particular form, but also explains the necessity of kerygma at all, and so enables is to understand kerygma as kerygma.[53]

How Ebeling situates the importance and decisiveness of kerygma certainly disagrees with, as Ebeling notes, the fact that "Bultmann has declared that any attempt to get behind the kerygma is illegitimate."[54] In particular, Ebeling finds that "[Bultmann's] polemic is directed against all attempts (liberal or positivist) to permit any question concerning the historical Jesus to be considered as theologically relevant to the kerygma."[55] Yet, for Ebeling, "the search for the historical Jesus is a search for the hermeneutic key to Christology,"[56] insofar as that "hermeneutic key" unlocks *the question of the meaning of Christology*. Consequently, Ebeling circumvents Bultmann's view of what the historical Jesus can mean for Christological reflection, by making it clear that "for the situation in which the [C]hristological kerygma can be understood, we shall have to concentrate on the encounter with the man Jesus who became subject to the law in order to free its subjects."[57]

FRIEDRICH GOGARTEN

Similarly rooted in the 1950s and grounded to Bultmann, Friedrich Gogarten becomes, as Vincent T. O'Keefe describes, a "protagonist for Bultmann's viewpoint,"[58] notably in terms of Bultmann's approach to Christology, particularly evident in Gogarten's *Entmythologisierung und Kirche* (1953), translated as *Demythologizing and History* in 1955, and later in *Jesus Christus Wende der Welt* (1967), translated as *Christ the Crisis* in 1970. Even so, to the best of my knowledge, Gogarten has remained relatively obscure, aside from one monograph dedicated to him, Larry Shiner's *The Secularization of History: An Introduction to the Theology of Friedrich Gogarten*

52. Ebeling, *Theology and Proclamation*, 44.
53. Ebeling, *Theology and Proclamation*, 52.
54. Ebeling, *Theology and Proclamation*, 57.
55. Ebeling, *Theology and Proclamation*, 61.
56. Ebeling, *Theology and Proclamation*, 55.
57. Ebeling, *Theology and Proclamation*, 80.
58. O'Keefe, "Book Review: Demythologizing and History," 588–90.

(1966)—though honest surveys of the 1960s[59] of German theology in the 1920s and 1930s place Gogarten as one of the co-founders of what has become known as "dialectical theology" alongside Barth and Brunner, Gogarten is especially important when situating his thought in close proximity of Bultmann. In *The Divided Mind of Modern Theology* (1967), James D. Smart characterizes Gogarten's relationship with Bultmann and Barth, acknowledging that Gogarten "[found] common cause much more with Bultmann than with Barth and he was later to be a major force in the thinking of some of the post-Bultmannians such as Fuchs and Ebeling."[60] Insofar as, Smart notes, "from the beginning there were tensions in [Gogarten's] relation with Barth,"[61] it is safe to say, then, that there was a comradery between Gogarten and post-Bultmannians Fuchs and Ebeling. Because Gogarten's tensions with Barth serve to position Gogarten closer to Bultmann and, by extension, the post-Bultmannian concerns of Fuchs and Ebeling in particular, it would be prudent to more keenly contextualize Gogarten's position, which Smart accomplishes in the following way:

> Friedrich Gogarten in the early twenties seemed to stand close to Barth in his Christology, but by making room for the orders of creation he was able to compromise for a time with Nazism[,] in spite of his Christology.[62]

Here, Smart's assessment of Gogarten is significant, as that which tells us that *the question of the meaning of Christology*, for Gogarten, is arguably at the heart of what draws Gogarten away from Barth, places Gogarten in a unthreatening position towards Nazi ideologically-construed theology, and brings Gogarten into Bultmann's theological orbit. If it is on *the question of the meaning of Christology* that Gogarten transitions from Barth to Bultmann, it is on the same question that brings Gogarten into the theological orbit of post-Bultmannians Fuchs and Ebeling, but, more broadly speaking, also into the theological orbit of Käsemann and Bornkamm and that which concerned the likes of Braun, Cullmann and Conzelmann.

59. Three notable surveys or discussions published in the 1960s are: John Macquarrie's *Twentieth-Century Religious Thought* (1963), James D. Smart's *The Divided Mind of Modern Theology: Karl Barth and Rudolf Bultmann, 1908–1933* (1967) and the James M. Robinson edited volume, *The Beginnings of Dialectic Theology: Volume 1* (1968). There is also the James C. Livingston co-edited volume, *Modern Christian Thought: The Twentieth Century: Volume 2* (1971).

60. Smart, *Divided Mind of Modern Theology*, 108.

61. Smart, *Divided Mind of Modern Theology*, 108.

62. Smart, *Divided Mind of Modern Theology*, 23.

Yet, before Gogarten becomes influential for post-Bultmannians, after Gogarten's own conflict and eventual distancing from Barth, and after Gogarten's kindred, Lutheran alignment with Bultmann, we must not forget the extent of Gogarten, to Smart's point, "[made] room" theologically, such that Gogarten "was able to compromise for a time with Nazism." This requires unpacking, which begins with situating Gogarten theologically in relation to Barth and Bultmann by 1933 on their respective proclivities to "dialectical theology"—this year not only follows the Barth-Gogarten relationship of the early 1920s, the development of the Bultmann-Gogarten relationship from the late-1920s to the early 1930s. One excellent, rare distillation of this is provided succinctly by Konrad Hammann's biography of Bultmann (2008), and translated in English in 2013:

> In 1933, the shared work and struggle of dialectical theology had collapsed. Karl Barth and [Rudolf] Bultmann had once again discerned commonalities in their theological intentions in the Confessing Church, and had made use of these in the struggle against the church politics of National Socialism, whereas in that same year Friedrich Gogarten has at times sided with the "German Christians" in 1933.[63]

The fact that Gogarten aligned himself with the "German Christians," comprised of thinkers and theologians seeking to rationalize and theologically appease National Socialism and the Nazi Party over the Confessing Church, which sought to defy and reject National Socialism is immensely important when ascertaining what eventually pulled Gogarten away from both Barth and Bultmann. It also allows us to place Gogarten alongside Käsemann's own (brief) involvement with the movement of the "German Christians"—coincidentally, Hammann notes that Käsemann "was the only one of [Bultmann's] students to join the 'German Christians' in 1933," but, by 1934, realized he had made a mistake, particularly by being "persuaded in large part" by Bultmann[64]—such that Gogarten became one of the Lutheran theologians, with the likes of Paul Althaus, Werner Elert, and Emmanuel Hirsch, Hammann notes:

> [Bultmann] distanced himself either explicitly or implicitly from [all of them] who in various ways accorded the priceless gift of theological legitimation to the Third Reich by interpreting the historical and natural realities of human life in an utterly

63. Hammann, *Rudolf Bultmann*, 218.
64. Hammann, *Rudolf Bultmann*, 282–83.

un-Lutheran way—that is, as direct or indirect manifestations
of the law of God."[65]

Yet, by 1951, Käsemann's Jugenheim lecture "triggered a lively debate"[66]
brought Bultmann and Gogarten together, just as, according to Hammann,
Bultmann discovered that "it had not been possible to settle the difference
that had arisen between him and Käsemann in Jugenheim."[67] What results
from this is an alignment between Bultmann and Gogarten against Käsemann (and a young Wolfhart Pannenberg[68]), when Bultmann and Gogarten, together, "held that the essence of history cannot be discovered by any
sort of empirical procedure like a historiography that engages in chronicling
or one that outlines the history of ideas."[69]

Gogarten's support of Bultmann up to Gogarten's death in 1967,
when,, Hammann tells us, "Bultmann was able to express his thanks for
what Gogarten had given him and his joy over their shared theological
achievements."[70] By way of these "shared theological achievements," if
considering that what Gogarten achieves on Bultmann's behalf towards *the
question of the meaning of Christology*, Gogarten's *Jesus Christus Wende der
Welt* serves as a culmination of Gogarten's co-efforts with Bultmann. It may
be possible to view Gogarten as a fundamental intermediary figure between
Bultmann and the "post-Bultmannians," insofar as, on *the question of the
meaning of Christology*, Gogarten brings Bultmann more fully and meaningfully into the Christological reflection of those interested in the "new quest"
in a way that Bultmann himself could not do after 1951. That is not to say,
though, that Bultmann did not directly influence how "post-Bultmannians"
such as Käsemann and Bornkamm approached *the question of the meaning
of Christology*—rather, Gogarten brings Bultmann into conversation with
Ebeling and Fuchs, who are just as influenced by Bultmann as they are by
the Christological reflection of Käsemann and Bornkamm.

In this sense, it stands to reason why, as Shiner explains in the introduction to *The Secularization of History*, that "in Germany[,] Gogarten's
work has been particularly influential among the 'post-Bultmannians,' especially Gerhard Ebeling and Ernst Fuchs."[71] Though Shiner points out,
in a footnote, the specific texts of Ebeling and Fuchs that lay bare Gogarten's

65. Hammann, *Rudolf Bultmann*, 283–84.

66. Hammann, *Rudolf Bultmann*, 458.

67. Hammann, *Rudolf Bultmann*, 458.

68. Hammann, *Rudolf Bultmann*, 458.

69. Hammann, *Rudolf Bultmann*, 458.

70. Hammann, *Rudolf Bultmann*, 519.

71. Shiner, *Secularization of History*, 18.

influences on them respectively, I submit that any influences upon Ebel-ing and Fuchs are also those of Käsemann and Bornkamm, though not as explicit, if for no other reason than because the latter two remain within a Bultmannian school, insomuch as all four are inextricably linked, "post-Bultmannians."

It is certainly not too much to say, then, that, if Gogarten's "central themes," as pointed out by Shiner, are "shown [in] the profound intercon-nection of [the] two problems"[72] of secularization and history, there is no doubt that all the "post-Bultmannians" wrestle with, in one form or another, issues of secularization and history, just as Bultmann himself is arguably concerned with the same issues. If, as Shiner notes, "Gogarten believes the need for thinking through the implications of a secular historical conscious-ness is nowhere more urgent today than in Christology,"[73] *the question of the meaning of Christology* orients itself towards and is oriented by Gogatern's Bultmann. Insofar as, Shiner cites, "Gogarten is still best known [. . .] as the author of one of the most influential defenses of Bultmann,"[74] it would be prudent to think of Gogarten's defensive comportment to Bultmann as ulti-mately predicated on how Gogarten wishes to work out and work through *the question of the meaning of Christology* on Bultmann's terms. Yet, if we are attending to how Gogarten understands and explains *the question of the meaning of Christology*, Shiner surmises that:

> [Gogarten's] Christology, therefore, is concerned with the his-torical character of the actual mystery of the revelation which the theologians of the early Church did not so much attempt to understand as to 'circumscribe while husbanding its character as mystery.'[75]

Nevertheless, Shiner warns us that:

> By refusing to speak of the divinity of Christ except in terms of the relation between the man Jesus and God, Gogarten leaves himself open to the charge of having repeated the liberal type of Christology in existentialist and personalistic garb.[76]

Even so, to whatever extent Gogarten's articulation of *the question of the meaning of Christology* is clothed in "existentialist and personalistic garb," what Gogarten is attuned to is a Christological reflection that, as John

72. Shiner, *Secularization of History*, 7.

73. Shiner, *Secularization of History*, 19.

74. Shiner, *Secularization of History*, 21.

75. Shiner, *Secularization of History*, 106.

76. Shiner, *Secularization of History*, 113.

Macquarrie notes, "was very much in sympathy with Bultmann's existentialist methodology."[77] This methodological "garb," as it were, is purposed towards construing what it means to be human as well as the degree to which Christological reflection grounds the meaning of human existence. It is, here, then, that we find that Gogarten is not simply dressing *the question of the meaning of Christology* in "existentialist and personalistic garb," even if this is something by which, to Shiner's point, leaves Gogarten open for criticism, but is interested in determining the meaningfulness of *the question of the meaning of Christology* to the modern situatedness of human existence. To this, Bultmann is a means to an end, particularly if, as Macquarrie briefly offers in *Jesus Christ in Modern Thought* (1990), Gogarten's understanding of what it means to be human is predicated on "the post-Enlightenment person for whom Christianity needs to be demythologized and related to human existence as it understands itself today."[78] In pointing this out, Macquarrie is highlighting not just Gogarten's use of Bultmann towards the existentializing of human existence, but that Gogarten is more focused and, in Macquarrie's words, "takes more trouble than Bultmann in analysing the changes which the Enlightenment has brought about."[79] For Gogarten, what the Enlightenment has laid bare, Macquarrie writes, "is the fact that metaphysics has been superseded by history."[80]

Because of this, we can find Gogarten engaging with what history means to *the question of the meaning of Christology* in two noteworthy texts originally published in the same year of 1953: *Demythologizing and History* (as it has been previously mentioned) and "*Theologie and Geschichte*," translated as "Theology and History" in the *History and Hermeneutic* collection in 1967. Given their respective theological proclivities, both are, undoubtedly, companion pieces. While the former is more specifically concerned with advancing Bultmann's demythologizing project, both are equally concerned with how theologizing makes sense of history and how, in turn, historicization informs what it means to do theology.

Let us consider "Theology and History" first. In it, Gogarten presents the relationship made between theology and history as a fundamental question as something to which Gogarten concedes requires "a neat and facile answer."[81] Recognizing that requirement, Gogarten acknowledges, "that I

---

77. Macquarrie, *Jesus Christ in Modern Thought*, 297–98.

78. Macquarrie, *Jesus Christ in Modern Thought*, 298.

79. Macquarrie, *Jesus Christ in Modern Thought*, 298.

80. Macquarrie, *Jesus Christ in Modern Thought*, 298.

81. Gogarten, "Theology and History," 37.

do not have, and I know of no place where it might be found today."[82] Nevertheless, in an effort "to attempt to determine the locus of the question with some exactitude,"[83] Gogarten proceeds to theologize about theology, as that which is calibrated by historicization. This is, in turn, a historicizing about history, as that which is, likewise speaking, calibrated by theology. There is an inextricability to what theology offers to historicizing and, conversely, what history offers to theologizing. To this point, Gogarten asserts:

> Theology has always been conscious of the fact that it has to do with history. It is not out of the question to ask whether it has always been conscious of how very much it has to do with history. In any case, it can be said without exaggeration that theology in its original form in which we find it in the writings of the Old and New Testaments, concerned itself almost exclusively with history.[84]

In beginning here, when thinking of history as "always [being] conscious of the fact" that it influences theologizing, it is possible to think of history as exorcising a similar influence on *the question of the meaning of Christology*. In other words, Christological reflection is not just a reflecting upon the ways in which one theologizes, but it also becomes a reflecting upon the ways in which one engages with history and historicizes. To be clear, *the question of the meaning of Christology*, as that which depends on a theologizing, is dependent on history, such that the question we must ask and the meaning we must seek is mitigated through a kind of historicizing. If this means, then, as Gogarten writes, is that "for theology there is no reality beyond or above the history with which it concerns itself,"[85] the same must be said about *the question of the meaning of Christology* construed through and by way of history—Christological reflection, as such, if rethinking and recasting Gogarten's point, since, for *the question of the meaning of Christology*, "there is no reality beyond or above the history with which [Christology] concerns itself."

Accordingly, at the point of Christological reflection through the articulation of *the question of the meaning of Christology*, Gogarten historicizes what it means to do Christology in the following way:

> The real difference between that which obtained before Christ and that which came after him and through him, lies elsewhere.

---

82. Gogarten, "Theology and History," 37.
83. Gogarten, "Theology and History," 37.
84. Gogarten, "Theology and History," 37.
85. Gogarten, "Theology and History," 39.

It lies in the fact that through Christ the historical world has come into being out of the mythical one.[86]

This relationship between "the historical world" and "the mythical one," for Gogarten, is most certainly drawn from Bultmann's influences on him. To this end, Gogarten suggests that "to speak of the mythical world means to speak of the world as it is experienced and, if one may use the expression here with all due reservation, conceived by means of myth."[87] In this sense, to approach *the question of the meaning of Christology* means to approach it as that which, when rethinking Gogarten, is "conceived by means of myth." What this means, I submit, is recognizing that the asking the question and seeking the meaning both come through, to Gogarten's point, "speak[ing] of the world as it is experienced." However, what is spoken to and experienced in terms of world requires a certain speaking to and experiencing of a mythical world—the relationship between "the historical' and "the mythical," as Gogarten considers it with respect to what is meaningfully carried forward from Bultmann, is what grounds *the question of the meaning of Christology.* This sort of Christological reflection, for Gogarten, comes to this:

> After Christ, this mythical piety is no longer possible, for in him the world has lost its enclosing character and has become historical; man, who has also become historical, has taken on the responsibility for the world being world and remaining world. After Christ, man can no longer withdraw from history; he must, whether he will or not, take the risk of history. For only in history does he have his reality.[88]

When we confront *the question of the meaning of Christology* through Christological reflection, we are situated fundamentally in an existential situation of "after Christ"—it is this state of existence, as that which existentializes "mythical piety," through how we ask about Christology and what we seek through the meaning of Christology that, to Gogarten's point, "the world has lost is enclosing character and has become historical." Once we are situated existentially to and by our Christological reflection, how we articulate *the question of the meaning of Christology* meaningfully "take[s] on the responsibility for the world being world and remaining world." That articulation in which we insert our meaning and allow ourselves to be made into meaning allows us to become "no longer withdraw[n] from history." The extent that we allow ourselves to become transformed by *the question of the meaning of*

86. Gogarten, "Theology and History," 43.
87. Gogarten, "Theology and History," 43.
88. Gogarten, "Theology and History," 59.

Christology becomes the means by which we can, if reconsidering Gogarten, "take the risk of history." The meaningfulness of *the question of the meaning of Christology* historicizes us, such that, just as Gogarten tells us, "for only in history" do we have our reality in the form and content of our Christological reflection, predicated on faith.

Yet, we see Gogarten wrestling with the proposition that—when slightly tempering Gogarten's language with a more inclusive one—"for only in history does [humanity] have [humanity's] reality" similarly in *Demythologizing and History*. Setting aside the fact that this text provides a more full-throated explicit defense of Bultmann than what can be gleaned contemporaneously from "Theology and History," Gogarten enters what he acknowledges as a "controversy" revolving around "the problem of demythologization, as it is called, of the New Testament."[89] To be sure, Gogarten recognizes that the demythologization project, through Bultmann, "is having such wide repercussions."[90] Insofar as Gogarten wishes to capture the controversies that have arisen with respect to "a radically different interpretation of history"[91] and how this interpretation of history "arose only with and as a consequence of the Christian faith,"[92] both becomes approaches by which Gogarten intends to problematize what history is and does. This problematizing is based, Gogarten tells us, on "two facts [that] must be clearly borne in mind."[93] To this end, Gogarten directs us in the following way:

> The problem of history reflects the original historical nature of the Christian faith and demands an understanding of it. It is only when this understanding is achieved, as it is originally implied in the Christian faith, that there is hope of solving the problems which this faith has encountered in history.[94]

This sense of history, for Gogarten, begins with what he calls a historical view of the Bible, such that the means by which "faith has encountered in history" and the role that theologizing fundamental plays in the larger encounter, Gogarten finds that:

> The problem of history, as it confronts modern theology, first became apparent in the historical view of the Bible, that is to say

89. Gogarten, *Demythologizing and History*, 7.
90. Gogarten, *Demythologizing and History*, 7.
91. Gogarten, *Demythologizing and History*, 10.
92. Gogarten, *Demythologizing and History*, 10.
93. Gogarten, *Demythologizing and History*, 10.
94. Gogarten, *Demythologizing and History*, 11.

in the interpretation of the Bible, both as regards [to] its origin and as regards [to] its contents, as a historical book like other historical books.[95]

In beginning here—with the relationship between meaningfulness of "the historical view" and "the interpretation" of the Bible—the problem of history not only affects the means by which we approach the task of theologizing, but also it affects the extent that theologizing is possible. What theology is as a kind of theologizing and what theology does as a task of theologizing are calibrated in terms of history , so that, when theologizing happens, if we can re-appropriate Gogarten's words, "faith [is] encountered in history." Yet, there arises a problem of theology as that which is related to the problem of history. These problems outline the kind of questioning necessary to make sense of "theology" and "history" through *the question of the meaning of Christology*, if we can say, of course, that faith is what ties "theology" and "history" together—if we are mindful of what Gogarten comparatively says in "Theology and History"—Gogarten concludes, "theology is confronted by the most difficult but also the most pressing question which exists for it today." From here, Gogarten surmises that "this is the question of the relation between faith and history."[96] Nevertheless, this question of what faith means to history and what means to faith is ultimately oriented towards *the question of the meaning of Christology*, particularly if Christological reflection theologizes matters of history with matters of faith, and vice versa.

Gogarten is careful to present "the question of the relation between faith and history"—as that which, I submit, construes and is construed by *the question of the meaning of Christology*—as, first, "the problem of history [as] an outcome of Christian belief,"[97] next as "the medieval conception of history,"[98] and then as "modern historical thought,"[99] all of which are fundamentally laid bare by Gogarten's understanding of "the suppression of [the] metaphysical by historical thought." Gogarten views this lattermost problem as a "translation."[100] What is translated, then, outstrips or compromises the extent that historical thought "returns a metaphysical and not a historical answer to the question which is always inseparable from the concept of history."[101] As far as this question is rooted in, Gogarten asserts,

95. Gogarten, *Demythologizing and History*, 12.

96. Gogarten, *Demythologizing and History*, 17.

97. Gogarten, *Demythologizing and History*, 18–20.

98. Gogarten, *Demythologizing and History*, 21–24.

99. Gogarten, *Demythologizing and History*, 25–33.

100. Gogarten, *Demythologizing and History*, 35.

101. Gogarten, *Demythologizing and History*, 34.

"the question of [history's] totality and unity and consequently of [history's] origin and purpose,"[102] it makes *the question of the meaning of Christology* all the more significant, necessary, and transformational. This seems so, both as a theological and Christological imperative, when, as Gogarten is right to say, "it is easy to see that [the concept of history] cannot satisfy the requirements of the historical character (*Geschichtlichkeit*) of the Christian faith."[103] Consequently, when thinking about what is translated away from "the metaphysical" to the very suppression of the meaningfulness of the metaphysical, Gogarten believes that "it is easy to see that not very much remains of the faith after this 'translation,' to which this historical approach subjects it in order to 'understand it,' a translation of its historical content into a suprahistorical truth."[104] If keeping Gogarten's advocation for reversal of how the metaphysical is suppressed by historical thought, and locating *the question of the meaning of Christology* as that which releases "the metaphysical" from its suppression, what must be encountered and combatted is, Gogarten says:

> [The] consequence of the historical interpretation of the Christian faith cannot satisfy a theology which is conscious of its task of taking as its 'object' the gospel of Jesus Christ as it is evidenced in the New Testament. But what is this theology to do? One course is certainly not open to it today. It cannot dispense neither with its critical historical techniques of investigation as they are applied to the historical tradition of the Christian faith nor with the historical approach to the faith itself or to the revelation upon which the faith knows itself to be founded.[105]

On this point, if maintaining that Gogarten is engaging in a Christological reflection that theologizes what faith means to the notion of historical and what the historical means to the notion of faith, he goes on to say:

> Theology can therefore no longer return to the metaphysical view which assumed its classical form in the old Church dogma. This metaphysical view was possible only so long as it comprised in the same manner not only the faith and the eternal divine reality which goes with it but also the temporal terrestrial reality of man.[106]

---

102. Gogarten, *Demythologizing and History*, 34.

103. Gogarten, *Demythologizing and History*, 34.

104. Gogarten, *Demythologizing and History*, 35.

105. Gogarten, *Demythologizing and History*, 35–36.

106. Gogarten, *Demythologizing and History*, 36.

Insofar as theology and the matter of theologizing itself can "no longer return to the metaphysical view," *the question of the meaning of Christology*, as Gogarten seemingly conceives it, does not "dispense" of any of the things that Gogarten warns us of. Instead, when asking *the question of the meaning of Christology*, this, in itself, if taking cue from Gogarten, is fundamentally cast by "its critical historical techniques of investigation as they are applied to the historical tradition of the Christian faith," and is oriented "with the historical approach to the faith." In a certain sense, too, the very articulation of *the question of the meaning of Christology* attends to, as Gogarten says, "the revelation upon which the faith knows itself to be founded," particularly when considering that faith situates and is situated by Christological reflection. Even so, Christological reflection, as such, is situated in and situates the historical view from which *the question of the meaning of Christology* articulates itself. All of this, then, with respect to what faith means to our historical view and what this historical view means to how we approach, understand, and formulate *the question of the meaning of Christology*, is problematized by Gogarten in the following way:

> If one separates the history of Jesus Christ from the proclamation in which alone it is transmitted to us, then, it is maintained, one is losing precisely the history upon which everything depends because without it there can be no genuine—that is to say justifying—faith.[107]

Here, as Gogarten describes, history, as that which comprises a historical perspective or a historical view, informs a "genuine" and a "justifying" understanding of faith, insofar as both history and faith inform *the question of the meaning of Christology*. The asking of that question and the seeking of that meaning through Christological reflection unites "the history of Jesus Christ" and "the proclamation in which alone it is transmitted to us," in a way that prevents the two from being separated—*the question of the meaning of Christology* grounds, if reconsidering Gogarten's point, "precisely the history upon which everything depends."

Given that Gogarten follows with two "historical views" of theologizing of the meaning of faith—one that is rooted is "the official 'theology' of the Church"[108] and the other (more expansive) rooted in "the theology of demythologization"—with the latter of the two providing a means, Gogarten says, "to express [demythologization] in positive terms, for the

---

107. Gogarten, *Demythologizing and History*, 38.
108. Gogarten, *Demythologizing and History*, 39–47.

existential interpretation of the New Testament."[109] What is existentialized, then, is "set[ting] history free from the objectivity which pervades it and in which it is deadened as soon as it is in one way or another thought of as an object."[110] This existentializing emanates in the theologizing that occurs through *the question of the meaning of Christology*, such that the existential interpretation of the New Testament becomes an existential interpretation of ourselves in accordance with how an existential interpretation of faith lays bare the meaningfulness of ourselves, the meaningfulness of our Christological reflection, and the meaningfulness of the New Testament itself. These degrees of meaningfulness—at the point of *the question of the meaning of Christology*—brings Gogarten to conclude:

> The freedom of man is founded upon the freedom of God, and this freedom comes to us in God's Word. The road to this freedom is precisely the road which is opened up by critical historical study and by reflection on history, in the sense, of course, in which it must be pursued in theology.[111]

This freedom is fundamentally theologized as much as it theologizes *the question of the meaning of Christology*, so that freedom, as that which provides for a means of us to existentialize, allows us to re-conceptualize and then recast Gogarten's final assertions, which are:

> It is necessary that all of [theology's] questioning and thinking should be directed to the reality and to the genus of the Word of God. This alone is and must be the purpose of the controversy concerning demythologization.[112]

The extent that "questioning and thinking should be directed to the reality and to the genus of the Word of God" is existentially laid bare by what is existentialized by Christological reflection and existentialized through *the question of the meaning of Christology*—to existentialize means to disclose the underlying metaphysics to what it means to do theology, if theologizing itself provides for a reckoning with what is metaphysical to *the question of the meaning of Christology*, as Gogarten informs us about how "metaphysics has been suppressed by history."

When characterizing Gogarten along the lines of proclaiming that "metaphysics has been superseded by history," Macquarrie surmises that "the problem for the modern theologian is to disengage theology and therefore

109. Gogarten, *Demythologizing and History*, 48.

110. Gogarten, *Demythologizing and History*, 80.

111. Gogarten, *Demythologizing and History*, 89–90.

112. Gogarten, *Demythologizing and History*, 90.

[C]hristology from its traditional metaphysical setting and express it anew in historical terms," insofar as Gogarten's emphasis on secularization as that which becomes historicization.[113]

While Shiner and Macquarrie agree with describing Gogarten's theologizing as, to credit Shiner, a "secularization of history," Gogarten's approach to *the question of the meaning of Christology*, as Macquarrie says, "has no interest in reconstructing the historical Jesus." This is certainly so, not just with respect to the stance Gogarten assumes in *Demythologizing and History*, but especially when considering Gogarten's *Christ the Crisis*. Rather than concerning himself with the historical Jesus contributing to the matters of "the new quest," as Macquarie rightly surmises, for Gogarten, "it is a question of reading the existential significance of Jesus' history in a way illuminates our own history and presents us with a possibility of existence [such that] Gogarten even uses Bultmann's term 'demythologizing' to designate the kind of interpretation he has in mind."[114] Insofar as *Christ the Crisis* is "a summation of the position set forth in Gogarten's earlier works and also the clearest statement of his thought,"[115] Peter C. Hodgson reviews *Christ the Crisis* as "an important book, for it ably summarizes the central themes in Gogarten's 'second' career and applies them to an interpretation of Jesus that is lucid and of intrinsic importance."[116] Hodgson's point, here, is important, when surmising what *Christ the Crisis* offers in relation to *Demythologizing and History*—the former presents a "second career" for Gogarten, when considering it as a second approach to and second conceptualization of *the question of the meaning of Christology*.

Gogarten begins Christ the Crisis with an acknowledgment that, as a means towards understanding early church theology in the purview of the Christology of Martin Luther, "the central question of [C]hristology is that of the unity of God and man in Jesus Christ."[117] In this way, "the essential thing about Luther's [C]hristology, the point indeed which alone males his thought [C]hristological," Gogarten is careful to tell us, "is that it asks not only about man, but also about God, whose unity with the man Jesus of Nazareth makes Jesus the Christ."[118] It is, here, that Gogarten takes us into the question of the historical Jesus, which, by the publication of Christ the

---

113. Macquarrie, *Jesus Christ in Modern Thought*, 298.

114. Macquarrie, *Jesus Christ in Modern Thought*, 298.

115. Review in *Choice*.

116. See Peter C. Hodgson's book review in *Theology Today*, which is reproduced, in brief, on the reverse of the paperback of *Christ the Crisis*.

117. Gogarten, *Christ the Crisis*, 1.

118. Gogarten, *Christ the Crisis*, 6.

Crisis, "has become one of the most important problems of theology, if not the most important of all."[119] Given that Gogarten is making this statement in 1967 (with the German edition), Gogarten is marking the state of the "new quest" as it stands more than decade after Käsemann's initiation of it—yet, Gogarten, nonetheless, is marking the state of Bultmann's influence in the late 1960s, as that which, Gogarten acknowledges, is based on "Bultmann's [C]hristological theses modify thee basic assumptions of modern [C]hristology in two very important ways."[120] While the first is "Jesus's preaching"[121] and the second is "the reduction of the history of Jesus to a *single* event,"[122] Gogarten clearly conceives of these two modifications as fundamentally modifying *the question of the meaning of Christology* more broadly. These modifications are what Gogarten pinpoints as "hav[ing] provoked the most fierce resistance to Bultmann's theology,"[123] in terms of positioning us to *the question of the meaning of Christology* by way of the meaningfulness of the kerygma.

Gogarten highlights "the most fierce resistance to Bultmann's theology" by providing Paul Althaus' theologizing as distinctly and explicitly representative of this. With Althaus' stance against Bultmann (and ostensibly against Gogarten) in 1958 having appeared since the publication of Gogarten's *Demythologizing and History*, Gogarten's challenging of Althaus in *Christ the Crisis* is relatively brief, but poignant. Speaking in terms of the question of the historical basis of kerygma, Gogarten directs the following at Althaus: "it is wrong to refuse to ask how this historical knowledge of the history and portrait of Jesus [. . .] is to be distinguished from the knowledge which Althaus repeatedly affirms is accessible only to faith."[124] To this end, Gogarten believes that:

> It is difficult to take what Althaus says to mean anything other than that the concrete portrait of Jesus [. . .] as something which can be shown historically to be a constituent part of the kerygma [which] gives it a power to "convince us and bring us to faith," is the historical element which is perceived by "reason."[125]

119. Gogarten, *Christ the Crisis*, 7.

120. Gogarten, *Christ the Crisis*, 15.

121. Gogarten, *Christ the Crisis*, 15.

122. Gogarten, *Christ the Crisis*, 15.

123. Gogarten, *Christ the Crisis*, 15.

124. Gogarten, *Christ the Crisis*, 20.

125. Gogarten, *Christ the Crisis*, 20.

Given that Gogarten critiques Althaus and suggests that Althaus unwittingly conceptualizes a "concrete portrait of Jesus," this allows Gogarten to enter the ongoing discussion about the "new quest" for the historical Jesus—this, in turn, allows Gogarten to reconceptualize and recast Althaus within the scope of the "new quest," such that, "in [Althaus'] work," Gogarten writes, "the historical quest beyond the kerygma unobtrusively becomes no longer a purely historical quest, but a theological and historical quest."[126] Consequently, according to Gogarten, "in [Althaus' work] he seeks the personality and life of Jesus as the real historical reality which Jesus has for faith."[127]

In this sense, if we tie Gogarten and Althaus—on Gogarten's terms, of course—to the same fundamental *question of the meaning of Christology*, Gogarten acknowledges a fundamental task that remains inherent to what it means to do Christology, what Christological reflection is, and what questions are asked and what meaning is sought Christologically. For Gogarten, what is ultimately laid bare by Christological reflection is that "the task of [C]hristology, which consists of bringing the faith of Jesus to expression in this way, has always existed since it came to expression in Jesus himself."[128] This speaks to *the question of the meaning of Christology*, and Gogarten, I submit, approaches and articulates this very question in the following way:

> The question which must first be decided is whether concrete historical reality only exists in the meaning given to it by Althaus and Bultmann's other opponents, and whether this is the reality which is meant in the confession of Jesus Christ. In order to answer this question, we ought first to try to find out what is the historical reality which is intended in New Testament [C]hristology.[129]

In an effort to work out the problem of historical reality and what historical reality means to *the question of the meaning of Christology*, Gogarten is careful to tell us that *Christ the Crisis*, if paying attention to the book's subtitle, "is not intended to put forward a comprehensive [C]hristology, which would be possible only within a complete dogmatic theology, nor to provide what might be called the 'outlines' of [C]hristology."[130] Gogarten is, instead, concerned with "basic questions, and how at least they should be posed, before it is possible at the present day to construct an honest [C]hristology."[131]

126. Gogarten, *Christ the Crisis*, 23.

127. Gogarten, *Christ the Crisis*, 23.

128. Gogarten, *Christ the Crisis*, 45.

129. Gogarten, *Christ the Crisis*, 50–51.

130. Gogarten, *Christ the Crisis*, 281.

131. Gogarten, *Christ the Crisis*, 281.

PAUL ALTHAUS

As a contemporary of Gogarten's, though acting as an antagonist to Gogarten's defense of Bultmann's demythologization project, Paul Althaus, a specialist on the theology of Martin Luther,[132] publishes *Das sogennante Kerygma und der historische Jesus: Zur Kritik der heutigen Kerygma-Theologie* (1958), translated as *The So-Called Kerygma and the Historical Jesus* in 1959 (alternately translated as *Fact and Faith in the Kerygma of Today* in 1959) —the book's "main contents," Althaus confirms, were "delivered by me as guest lecturer in the Universities of Tübingen and East Berlin in January-October 1957, and at the Hanover Whitsun Conference in June 1957."[133] Clearly, if contextualizing "the main content" of *The So-Called Kerygma and the Historical Jesus*, we find that Althaus comes to Bultmann not simply by way of Bultmann's work having appeared a handful of years before with German theological circles, but also, and more importantly, relatively contemporaneously (and certainly not coincidently) with Bultmann's work becoming available to the English-speaking world.

What also brought Althaus into an encounter Bultmann can be traced to an earlier essay, "*Der 'historische Jesus' und der biblische Christus: Zum Gedächtnis Kählers*" (1935), translated as "The Historical Jesus and the Biblical Christ"—as Althaus dedicates it to Kähler, Hans Schwarz writes the following about the 1935 essay in a profile of Althaus included in *Twentieth-Century Lutheran Theologians* (2013): "Althaus showed in that essay that the attempt of historicism to distinguish between the true words and actions of Jesus and those that were later additions creates a misleading juxtaposition."[134] From this characterization of Althaus, we find, on one hand, Althaus' understanding of the historical Jesus interestingly occupying an ideological space between what Schweitzer brought to an end for the first quest for the historical Jesus and what had yet to emerge with Bultmann. On the other hand, in terms of Althaus' use of Kähler, it is possible to view Althaus as re-asserting and re-conceptualizing the parameters for another quest, insomuch as, according to Schwartz:

> Althaus points out that it was through Kähler's theology that a new understanding was reached regarding what is true in the gospel, namely, each word and characteristic in which the realization at Easter expresses who Jesus Christ really is. The distinction

---

132. Althaus wrote two important books contributing to Luther studies: *The Theology of Martin Luther* (1966) and *The Ethics of Martin Luther* (1972).

133. Althaus, *So-Called Kerygma and the Historical Jesus*, 6.

134. Schwarz, "Paul Althaus," 150.

between historic and non-historic is therefore wrong if historic
does not also include that which the first believers understood in
the light of their experience with the resurrected Christ.[135]

This difference between "historic" and "non-historic," and the extent that,
for Althaus, any distinction "is therefore wrong," particularly if, by "historic," we ignore or minimize "that which the first believers understood" is
what brings Althaus into an eventual confrontation with Bultmann on the
conception of history. Within this vein, Schwarz writes:

In contrast to Bultmann and the purely kerygmatic Christ, Althaus asserts that the Easter faith is decidedly interested in the
historical issue because the question must be answered whether
the gospel is correct when it claims that it is founded on a historical fact.[136]

Schwarz reminds us, too, that, "before Althaus claimed the necessity of the
historical basis for the Christ event in his exchange with Bultmann," Althaus
challenged Barth's theologizing in 1925, grounded on Barth, as Schwarz
characterizes it, "juxtaposing the 'historical prof' and the 'testimony of revelation' by totally divorcing the Easter faith from the Easter history."[137]

In his own forward to *The So-Called Kerygma and the Historical
Jesus*, Althaus makes the following announcement: "Rudolf Bultmann's
theological project has roused interest and activity among theologians and
churchmen because of his programme of 'demythologising' and 'existential
interpretation.'"[138] As much as Althaus recognizes that Bultmann's theologizing along these lines is a fundamental aspect of Bultmann's overall
"theological project," Althaus, nonetheless, is concerned with Bultmann's
handling of *the question of the meaning of Christology*, as "another aspect to
[Bultmann's] theology closely connected with the existentialist approach."[139]
For Althaus, this other "aspect," so to speak, "is not less stimulating"[140]
than Bultmann's demythologization project. As that which speaks to how
Althaus understands Bultmann's understanding of *the question of the meaning of Christology*, Althaus concentrates on "[Bultmann's] severance of the
kerygma and consequently of Christology from the problem of the historical

---

135. Schwarz, "Paul Althaus," 150.

136. Schwarz, "Paul Althaus," 150.

137. Schwarz references Althaus on this matter, citing Althaus' "'Die Auferstehung
der Toten.' Zur Auseinandersetzung mit Karl Barth über die theologische Exegese" (1925).

138. Althaus, So-Called Kerygma and the Historical Jesus, 5.

139. Althaus, So-Called Kerygma and the Historical Jesus, 5.

140. Althaus, So-Called Kerygma and the Historical Jesus, 5.

Jesus."[141] Insofar as this serves as the chief impetus for how Althaus attends to Bultmann's theologizing on *the question of the meaning of Christology*, Althaus finds that, in this, "there is all the more prospect of entering into a fruitful discussion" with both Bultmann and Gogarten, when considering, as Althaus points out, how "[Gogarten] has come to [Bultmann's] support on the issue."[142]

Essentially, as much as Althaus is forthcoming about his confrontation with Bultmann and, by extension, what will be a confrontation with Gogarten, Althaus takes care to acknowledge, too, how *the question of the meaning of Christology*, as it is presented in the respective purviews of Bultmann and Gogarten, becomes the centrepiece of a kind of theologizing that springs forth from Bultmann. It is a broader confrontation which Althaus seeks, which focuses on the extent that, in Althaus' own Christological reflection, "the doubts and concerns which move me are also giving concern to theologians who stand near to Bultmann, like Günther Bornkamm and Ernst Käsemann."[143]

With direct references to Bornkamm and Käsemann, and the inclusion of Gogarten, Althaus is certainly envisions a confrontation with the "Bultmann School," or what we can simply think of "post-Bultmannians." Yet, though we know that this is an incomplete group, the fact that Althaus makes no mention of Fuchs nor Ebeling, nor even Robinson's contribution is understandably curious. Though the question that unavoidably arises is whether Althaus was aware of these unmentioned figures and, in turn, unaware of their participation in *the question of the meaning of Christology*, what arises is merely a rhetorical question of sorts Given that Althaus takes pains to provide a fairly thorough listing of works cited through *The So-Called Kerygma and the Historical Jesus*, there is no question that Fuchs, Ebeling, and Robinson—not to mention Cullmann's work—are out not on Althaus' radar. We can certainly speculate why this is the case for Robinson and Cullmann—in Robinson's case, *A New Quest of the Historical Jesus* first appeared in English in 1959, with a German version published in 1960, while Cullmann's *Christ and Time* first appeared in German in 1946—if, for Althaus, neither Robinson nor Cullmann actively figured into a Bultmannian theologizing of *the question of the meaning of Christology*. Though Fuchs and Ebeling were certainly engaging with Bornkamm and Käsemann throughout the 1950s, insofar as the former two—even as Bultmann's students, just as the latter two—are just as concerned with *the question of the*

141. Althaus, *So-Called Kerygma and the Historical Jesus*, 5.

142. Althaus, *So-Called Kerygma and the Historical Jesus*, 5.

143. Althaus, *So-Called Kerygma and the Historical Jesus*, 5.

meaning of Christology as that which is similarly comprised of the same "doubts and concerns which move [Althaus]," Fuchs' and Ebeling's respective contributions appear in May 1956 and Summer 1957. Though it may be possible to say that Ebeling's contribution in Summer 1957 is too contemporaneous to Althaus to have had any influence on "the main content" of Althaus' *The So-Called Kerygma and the Historical Jesus*, Fuchs' contribution should have influenced or, in the least, should have been in Althaus' purview, since Fuchs' lecture, "The Quest of the Historical Jesus" (the first text in Fuchs' *Studies of the Historical Jesus*) was delivered in lecture format the previous year before Althaus' lectures. It seems to me, too, that Althaus should have been aware of Braun's "The Meaning of New Testament Christology" from June 1956—also the year before.

What is only made all the more puzzling, I find, is that, given Althaus' dating of the lectures that make up "the main content" of *The So-Called Kerygma and the Historical Jesus* to 1957—with dating revolving around the summer of 1957—and Ebeling dating his "Jesus and Faith" text included in the *Word and Faith* collection to Summer 1957, there seems to be some thematic cross-pollination between Althaus and Ebeling, if we attend to Althaus' "Word of God and Faith" text in relation to Ebeling's "Jesus and Faith." Yet, neither mentions the other in these texts respectively—in fact, in Althaus' text, Althaus makes references largely to Gogarten, with a notable final reference to Hermann Diem. Even so, it remains difficult to determine what role—if any—other post-Bultmannians, such as Fuchs and Ebeling, and even (as an expansion of post-Bultmannians) Cullmann and Braun, figure into Althaus' Christological reflection.

Setting aside whatever degree—if any—Althaus' approach to *the question of the meaning of Christology* influences or is influenced by Ebeling's in particular (or Fuchs' or Braun's), Althaus is reckoning with Bultmann's theologizing of what it means to do Christology, by beginning, in the introductory section to *The So-Called Kerygma and the Historical Jesus*, with the following starting point:

> Christology is the theological doctrine of Jesus Christ the historical and exalted Saviour, the doctrine of His person and history. That is, in Christology the believer in Jesus Christ reflects theologically on the basis and content of his knowledge of Christ.[144]

As general as this appears to be, Althaus' concern is with what is meant by "His person" and what is meant by "history." The relationship between what the former means for the latter and, conversely, what the latter means for the

---

144. Althaus, *So-Called Kerygma and the Historical Jesus*, 13.

former is mitigated through Christological reflection, such that, as Althaus tells us, "the believer in Jesus Christ reflects theologically on the basis and content of his knowledge of Christ." At the very instance of what is "reflect[ed] theologically" through what can only be how we epistemologically comport ourselves to *the question of the meaning of Christology*, this holds true:

> We can accordingly speak of Christology only where Christian faith is unambiguously understood as faith in the person of Jesus Christ, i.e. where Jesus Christ in person is acknowledged as the revelation, as the truth disclosed to humanity by God, as salvation.[145]

This "speak[ing] of Christology," as acknowledged by Althaus, should remind us of Fuchs' "language-event" and Ebeling's "word-event," as that which is fundamentally attuned by a Christological reflection, to Althaus' point, "where Christian faith is unambiguously understood as faith in the person of Jesus Christ." However, what Althaus conceives of as a "language-event" or a "word-event" does not go as far as Fuchs and Ebeling, since the residual influence of Bultmann on Fuchs and Ebeling is absent from Althaus. Still, it is through "speak[ing] of Christology," then, that *the question of the meaning of Christology* is articulated and grounded to the event that makes it so. Faith—conceptually comparable to Ebeling's use of the term—attunes us to the manner with which we engage in Christological reflection and, in turn, when we are "reflect[ing] theologically," and are situated in such a way that "we can accordingly speak of Christology," our confrontation with *the question of the meaning of Christology*.

For Althaus, the extent that "Christian faith is unambiguously understood" certainly challenges the extent that Bultmann considers faith as ambiguously understood. While Bultmann's primary interest is in how faith in kerygma is foundational and an imperative for Christian faith, Althaus' contention is that "faith in the person of Jesus Christ" is the means by which "Christian faith is unambiguously understood." How Bultmann understands the concept of faith is precisely what Althaus points out a "so-called kerygma," when taking account of explicitness of the title of Althaus' work. Just as Althaus thinks of kerygma as "so-called," the same critique is directed at what role the historical Jesus plays in how we position ourselves to Christian faith—while the former is directed at Bultmann, the latter is undoubtedly targeting post-Bultmannians—Käsemann, in particular—and, in Althaus' view, the revival of the "so-called" *quest* for the "so-called" historical Jesus.

---

145. Althaus, *So-Called Kerygma and the Historical Jesus*, 13.

It is to this latter notion, in order to present what *the question of the meaning of Christology* should be, that Althaus proclaims:

> There is no theologically demonstrable necessity for Christianity's need of the person of Jesus. He is necessary as a cult-symbol, merely to fulfil some law of social psychology. Such a symbol does not need to have been a historical figure. In none of [this] can we speak of Christology in the strict sense of the word.[146]

Here, Althaus' sense of the "so-called" historical Jesus is made explicit. In this, there is also a straightforward rejection of "the new quest" initiated by Käsemann—speaking more broadly, it is a wholesale rejection of all post-Bultmannians attending to the significance of the historical Jesus towards *the question of the meaning of Christology*.

Yet, by decentering the historical Jesus from *the question of the meaning of Christology*, Althaus also wishes to decenter kerygma from *the question of the meaning of Christology*, which brings Althaus to make the following proposition: "for here we can say of faith that it is faith which believes in relation to Jesus, through Jesus like Jesus, yes, even for Jesus's sake, but it is no longer faith *in* Jesus."[147] Note the emphasis Althaus makes on "in"—for *the question of the meaning of Christology* to be meaningful, it garners its meaningfulness through "faith *in* Jesus." What we are questioning and from what are deriving meaning occurs through Christological reflection predicated on Althaus' understanding of "faith *in* Jesus." What defies Christological questioning and avoids Christological meaningfulness, for Althaus, is the historical Jesus, such that it dissolves *the question of the meaning of Christology* all-together. In Althaus' view:

> The dissolution of Christology can, however, simply arise from the fact that doubts have arisen as to whether the real Jesus of the gospels is able to support a Christology in the previously accepted sense of the term.[148]

Later, Althaus tells us:

> It is true that a distinction is no longer drawn between the Christ-principle and Christ's person, the latter being declared of merely relative importance in comparison with the former. But the *kerygma* and the historical Jesus are torn apart, and

---

146. Althaus, *So-Called Kerygma and the Historical Jesus*, 15.

147. Althaus, *So-Called Kerygma and the Historical Jesus*, 15.

148. Althaus, *So-Called Kerygma and the Historical Jesus*, 15.

the importance of the latter is minimised in comparison with the *kerygma*.[149]

Here, not only is Althaus addressing, with notions of "Christ-principle" and "Christ's person," the interdependence of the two, so that both are afforded an equivalent significance towards how we approach, understand, and articulate *the question of the meaning of Christology*, but he is also acknowledging the inseparability of Kähler's notions of "the so-called historical Jesus" and "the historic biblical Christ." Because Althaus sees that the two are fundamentally "torn apart," on the one hand by Bultmann's reverence for kerygma and, on the other hand, by those that seek a new quest for the historical Jesus (by Bultmann's followers), Althaus wishes to claim and align himself to Kähler's main, overarching argument in *The So-Called Historical Jesus and the Historic Biblical Christ*. This is over and against, as cited in Carl E. Braaten's lengthy introduction to Kähler's book, the extent that: "Bultmann and his followers have occasionally appealed to Martin Kähler as support for their characteristic theses concerning the relation between faith and the kerygma and between factual history (*Historie*) and existential history (*Geschichte*)."[150] In claiming and aligning himself to Kähler—countering what Althaus certainly considered as a misuse and abuse of Kähler by Bultmann and his followers—Althaus' intent is to reclaim and realign Kähler to what Althaus believes is a more legitimate, meaningful, and accurate approach to *the question of the meaning of Christology*.

Carrying forward Kähler's rejection of the "so-called historical Jesus" in such a way that it is offered, by Bultmann and his followers, "to the Christian Church as the ground and object if its faith,"[151] Althaus reiterates of an assertion Kähler makes in *The So-Called Historical Jesus and the Historic Biblical Christ*. That assertion is about the independence of faith and the necessity of "establish[ing] the right scholarly method," which Althaus cites from the 1892 German edition Kähler's text.[152] If considering Kähler's words more directly, as that which directly inspires Althaus, Kähler wishes to divide Christian faith from a notion of the historical Jesus, insofar, according to Kähler, "Christian faith and a history of Jesus repel each other."[153] Not only does Althaus certainly agree with this, Althaus is also undoubtedly in agreement with the following conclusion from Kähler:

149. Althaus, *So-Called Kerygma and the Historical Jesus*, 18.

150. Braaten, "Introduction," 3.

151. Althaus, *So-Called Kerygma and the Historical Jesus*, 19.

152. Althaus, *So-Called Kerygma and the Historical Jesus*, 19.

153. Kähler, *So-Called Historical Jesus and the Historic Biblical Christ*, 74.

> When we consider the relation of faith to its object, there seems
> to be no essential difference whether the content of faith derives
> from the substance of biblical accounts or from a scientifically
> produced picture of Jesus.[154]

Here, with Kähler proclaiming an independence of faith firmly in
mind, Althaus situates his use of Kähler to challenges what Althaus perceives
to be the misuse of Kähler. That misuse, in Althaus' view, misunderstands
Kähler's fundamental view on matters of faith and how these matters reject
the extent that, to Kähler's point, "'the Lives of Jesus' have supplanted [C]
hristological dogma or will have to do so."[155] This leads Althaus to proclaim,
in Kähler's stead, the following:

> In relation to faith, the claim of the historian that he alone can
> provide faith with its object and ground, is an assault upon
> faith's independence of theology. Faith in this manner becomes
> dependent on the scholars, and grows perplexed in view of the
> difference of their results. The ground and object of faith, Jesus
> Christ, must be immediately accessible to every Christian.[156]

Even if this can be viewed as Althaus recalibrating *the question of the meaning of Christology*, given that Kähler is a seminal figure grouped with Schweitzer and co-credited with asserting the impossibility of separating "the
so-called historical Jesus" from "the historic biblical Christ," Schwartz notes,
"Althaus later realized, especially through Rudolf Bultmann's conclusion
that one should not go behind the kerygma, that one must move beyond
Kähler's emphasis on the proclaimed Christ."[157]

What Althaus' need to move beyond what the "proclaimed Christ"
means for Althaus' approach to *the question of the meaning of Christology*
wishes to think more carefully about how one asks the question of Christology and one seeks the meaning of Christology. While that questioning
and meaningfulness takes Althaus further than what Althaus perceives
to be limitations in Bultmann's Christological and, in turn, limitations to
Kähler's Christological reflection seems to implicitly wrestle with the means
by which "the historical Jesus" informs what it means to do Christology at
all. If we can say that Althaus is wrestling with what sense can be made out
of "the new quest" at the close of the 1950s, Gogarten—even as Althaus'
interlocutor on Bultmann, demythologizing, and the appropriation of

---

154. Kähler, *So-Called Historical Jesus and the Historic Biblical Christ*, 74.

155. Kähler, *So-Called Historical Jesus and the Historic Biblical Christ*, 73.

156. Althaus, *So-Called Kerygma and the Historical Jesus*, 19.

157. Schwartz, "Paul Althaus," 150.

Kähler—seemingly wrestles with the same problem, couching his own critique of "the historical Jesus" with respect to Kähler in this manner: "it does not appear quite correct to me when Kähler says that there is no criterion for 'shelling' the historical Jesus out of the New Testament tradition."[158]

If the reverse is true, insofar as Gogarten can be taken to mean that there is, in fact, "criterion," Gogarten certainly questions what the notion of the historical Jesus means for *the question of the meaning of Christology* and, likewise, which of the two meaningfully contributes to the New Testament tradition. Like Althaus, Gogarten's interests with *the question of the meaning of Christology* lies with the extent that, as Althaus finds, "the ground and object of faith, Jesus Christ, must be immediately accessible to every Christian"—Gogarten seemingly agrees this in principle, but concludes:

> It is the problem that the Christian faith is faith is Jesus, as he meets us in history and only in it, and that this faith whose truth stands or falls with the fact that it is a work of God, is lost and becomes a human fabrication as soon as it is dedicated from its ground in history.[159]

Gogarten's emphasis, here, on history is challenged by Althaus in *The So-Called Kerygma and the Historical Jesus* in the section entitled "The Concept of History and the Historical," though Althaus chooses to "deal principally with" Gogarten's *Demythologizing and History*, rather than Gogarten's "Theology and History."

Working exclusively off of Gogarten's *Demythologizing and History*, Althaus characterizes Gogarten's stance on what history means to faith in the following way: "according to Gogarten it is only in the Christian faith that the historic character of man and the world has been disclosed."[160]From here, Althaus suggests that Gogarten's concept of history and the historical—still narrowed to Gogarten's *Demythologizing and History*—"can be comprehensively expressed as follows[:] history consists of those events which stand in relation to the historic character of human existence."[161] In Althaus' view, for Gogarten, history is predicated on "events which constitute a challenge to responsible man."[162] Not only does Althaus seemingly disregard what role Gogarten's understanding of faith plays in tandem with Gogarten's understanding of history, but, in concentrating on Gogarten's

---

158. Gogarten, *Demythologizing and History*, 63.

159. Gogarten, *Demythologizing and History*, 63.

160. Althaus, *So-Called Kerygma and the Historical Jesus*, 38.

161. Althaus, *So-Called Kerygma and the Historical Jesus*, 38.

162. Althaus, *So-Called Kerygma and the Historical Jesus*, 38.

handling of history and what that handling means towards how Gogarten and Althaus situate themselves towards *the question of the meaning of Christology*, Althaus finds that Gogarten's "conception of the historic is objectionable on two grounds"[163]—these two grounds directly tell us how well (or how poorly) Althaus understands, Gogarten's position.

Being mindful that neither of these grounds have anything to do with Althaus' characterization of Gogarten's conception of faith, one of the grounds, for Althaus, is the belief that Gogarten "departs completely from the concept of history and the historic current in scholarly usage."[164] This is objection is based on Althaus' suspicions with any articulation of history or any pronouncement of "the historical," since, according to Althaus, it "makes it hard to come to an understanding with the historian who investigates past history."[165] With this conceptually laid bare, with emphasis on who defines "history" and how one determines what is (or is not) "the historical," the second reason Althaus finds Gogarten's "history" objectionable arises from Althaus' sense that, in Althaus' view:

> The new concept [of demythologizing] as used by Bultmann and Gogarten serves to neutralise the historical-factual element inasmuch as in the case of the *kerygma* the question of historical fact is declared illegitimate.[166]

Setting aside Althaus tying Gogarten closely to Bultmann, we see that Althaus arrives at his understanding of Gogarten's understanding of history as that which is linked to and conflated, perhaps, with Bultmann. This is certainly so, of course, when attending only to *Demythologizing and History*, which Gogarten uses as a vehicle to defend Bultmann and rationalize the "reason for the controversy"[167] to which Bultmann's demythologizing emerges. Insofar as what constitutes the beginning section of *Demythologizing and History*, Gogarten wishes to firstly define "a radically different interpretation of history" and, secondly, understand "that history as a problem, in the sense in which we are here necessarily using the word, arose only with and as a consequence of the Christian faith."[168]

Viewing Gogarten outside Gogarten's espousal of Bultmann's demythologization, one might wonder whether Althaus and Gogarten—in

---

163. Althaus, *So-Called Kerygma and the Historical Jesus*, 39.

164. Althaus, *So-Called Kerygma and the Historical Jesus*, 39.

165. Althaus, *So-Called Kerygma and the Historical Jesus*, 39.

166. Althaus, *So-Called Kerygma and the Historical Jesus*, 40.

167. Gogarten, *Demythologizing and History*, 7–11.

168. Gogarten, *Demythologizing and History*, 10.

Althaus' view—are really that far apart on the role that history plays in the understanding and articulation of *the question of the meaning of Christology*. I submit that they are ultimately working on the same problem, but approaching the problem from difference positions—because of this, there may be more agreement than disagreement between Althaus and Gogarten, particularly what faith means for *the question of the meaning of Christology* and what this underlying Christological reflection means towards history, the historical, and fundamental historicization. If we delimit Althaus' rejection of "the so-called kerygma" and we keep in mind that Althaus never directly addresses Gogarten's "Theology and History," it will be prudent for us to wonder what Althaus would have thought about the following from Gogarten:

> It is the question how faith, which is the effect of Jesus, has to do with the historical reality of the man who believes in him. Faith can only have to do with that reality if Jesus, who brings this faith about, belongs to the same historical reality.[169]

Even here, in Gogarten's reference to "historical reality," as that which allows faith to ground *the question of the meaning of Christology*, we can certainly ask what Althaus would have made of it, given that, like Althaus, Gogarten seemingly agrees with Althaus' belief that, in Althaus' words, "the ground and object of faith, Jesus Christ, must be immediately accessible to every Christian."

---

169. Gogarten, *Demythologizing and History*, 71.

Chapter 5

The Question of the Meaning of Christology (V)

When considering the development of *the question of the meaning of Christology* beyond the 1950s and beyond the Bultmannians and those that are Christologically engaging with Bultmannians, I want to focus assessments of what it means to pose the question to and what it means to seek the meaningfulness of Christology in a way that attempts to provide a Christological reflection and the parameters for Christological thinking. Indeed, there has been many Christological projects and numerous Christological scholarship attendings to the task and the scope that Christology, generally speaking, presents to us—there are, to be sure, many that can be traced not just to the earliest years of Apostolic area but also, if we an honest broker of the matters of Christology, to what presents itself in the canonized texts of New Testament, setting aside the complexities of the canonization process itself and what message those involved with the canonization hopes to express about the relationship between Jesus of Nazareth and the Christ of faith.

What remains at the very core of what it means to Christology is what Jesus of Nazareth means to the Christ of faith and what the Christ of faith means to Jesus of Nazareth—the meaningfulness of the former to the latter and vice versa is just as much an issue for Bultmann, Bultmannians, and those that Christologically engage with Bultmannians as it is for individuals that can no more be characterized as Bultmannians than they can as those that are engaging strictly with Bultmannians. While the theologians that we can refer to as "Bultmannians" and theologians we can point to that confront these Bultmannians are a relatively closed groups of specific voices—even though, I admit, certain voices are more frequently pointed to than others, and there is a certain frequency grounded in and sprung forth from the 1950s—I want to, now, present just a handful of figures that contribute to a "post-Bultmannian" era, if I may use this term to speak about individuals that are not necessarily directly engaging with Bultmann, Bultmannians, or critics of Bultmannians or even, in an explicit sense, handling the landscape constructed by the "new quest." Rather, my intent to is provide a handful of voices that are chiefly concerned with *the question of the meaning of Christology* and, at times, attend to the perennial problem of the historical Jesus: Aloys Grillmeier (1910–98), Ferdinand Hahn (1926–2015), Reginald H. Fuller (1915–2007), Fred B. Craddock (1928–2015), Leonardo Boff (1938–present), Helmut Thielicke (1908–86), Edward Schillebeeckx (1914–2009), John B. Cobb Jr. (1925–present), John Dominic Crossan (1934–present), N. T. Wright (1948–present), Ben Witherington (1951–present), and Craig S. Keener (1960–present).

ALOYS GRILLMEIER

If we move a bit beyond Bultmann's successors, proponents, and critics and into the 1960s to further calibrate *the question of the meaning of Christology*, in Aloys Grillmeier's *Christ in Christian Tradition: Volume One: From the Apostolic Age to Chalcedon (451)*—translated in 1965—we are confronted with the notion that "ancient Christology puts Christ in the middle of time and sees in the development of faith in him a process which will only end with the Second Coming of the Lord."[1] For Grillmeier, as much as tradition plays a role in the development of *the question of the meaning of Christology*, focusing on the birth of Christology itself, we must reckon with a history predating and informing that tradition in the establishment of a culture around the Christological. Any Christological culture, as such, frames itself around a Christological tradition for the sake of a Christological history—similarly, history, tradition, and culture have a tripartite relationship within *the question of the meaning of Christology*, as a means of expressing *the what, the how, the why*, and the *for whom* this question and this meaning matters. Even though Grillmeier's *Christ in Christian Tradition*, as the title proposes, is more of a history of Christology than a methodology of Christology, sums

---

1. Grillmeier, *Christ in Christian Tradition*, xxiii.

all of this up what remains at stake for *the question of the meaning of Christology* in the following way:

> If we are to proclaim the *mysterium Christi* in the language of our time, we must first have understood what the Fathers wanted to say in the language of their time. The inward, intellectual struggles of the ancient church testify that the Christological writers of that church were concerned with something vital, namely the very nature of Christianity.[2]

Through Grillmeier, the relationship between *the question* of Christology, as such, and its *meaning*, as such—precisely as what is fundamental to *the question of the meaning of Christology*—is certainly contingent on *mysterium Christi*. What exactly is this, if we are to say, simply, that we speaking primarily about "the mystery of Christ"?

Let us consider the "mystery of Christ," first as a "mystery" to human existence about the complexities, intricacies, and transcendent qualities of what can be meant by "Christ." That mystery (or *mysterium*) is a Christological mystery of the meaning of *Christi* to human finitude. Yet, if following and recasting Soren Kierkegaard's notion of spirit at the opening of *Sickness Unto Death* (1849), it is a necessary mystery to humanity, as that which exists, by necessity, within infinitude, so that what we—as humans abiding by the temporal—can only perceive the Christological in reference to how we encounter the theological. How our temporal existences of necessity and finitude confronts "the mystery of Christ" is always in terms of, as Grillmeier points out, a *mysterium Christi* which exists, from our perspective, in an atemporal infinitude of freedom. In another sense, though, if maintaining a recasting of Kierkegaard, the very conceptualization of *mysterium Christi* presents us with Kierkegaard's question: "what is the self?"[3] How we existentially encounter the *mysterium Christi*, as that which is part of us and not part of us, is with respect to the matter of self, once that self is defined as a spirit and once that spirit is subsumed by human being.[4] What *mysterium Christi* means to us, from the standpoint of asking Kierkegaard's "what is the self" question, becomes, if reconsidering Kierkegaard's answer, a relation that relates itself to itself or is the relation's relating itself to itself in the relation."[5] Not only does Kierkegaard highlight the idiosyncratic relationship between human existence and *mysterium Christi*, but also the idiosyncrasy of *mysterium Christi* itself, as the juncture of *mysterium* and

2. Grillmeier, *Christ in Christian Tradition*, xxiii.
3. Kierkegaard, *Sickness Unto Death*, 13.
4. Kierkegaard, *Sickness Unto Death*, 13.
5. Kierkegaard, *Sickness Unto Death*, 13.

Christi. Even so, when considering *mysterium Christi* as "a self," when taking Kierkegaard's point that "the self is not the relation but is the relation's relating itself to itself,"[6] we find that *mysterium Christi* is "not the relation," but is, instead, attuned to what is "relating itself to itself."

The extent that we are even able to say that *mysterium Christi* is an entity of entities "relating itself to itself" points us towards a matter of language itself. What arises is how we articulate *mysterium Christi* and how what we articulate, as a matter of existential necessity, is a meaningful articulation. In Kierkegaard's handling of the extent and limits of language—even as a critique of Kierkegaard's own critique of the extent and limits of Hegel's use of language in what has become known as Hegel-speak in a work such as *Phänomenologie des Geistes* (1807)—Grillmeier's sentiment about the proclamation of *mysterium Christi* embodying "the language of our time" becomes another kind of mystery to human existence. It is through the proclaiming of *mysterium Christi*, as Grillmeier writes—the kerygma of *mysterium Christi*—that "we must first have understood what the Fathers wanted to say in the language of their time." In other words, how we articulate *mysterium Christi* in "the language of our time" is only as meaningful to us—and *the question of the meaning of Christology*—if that articulation is grounded on our own understanding of "what the Fathers wanted to say in the language of their time." It is by way of the task of what is articulated and the method through an articulation takes place bring forth, just as Grillmeier suggests, "the inward, intellectual struggles of the ancient church" that become our own struggles—these struggles "testify" to what "the Christological writers of [the ancient] church were concerned with," as that which testify to what we are also concerned with. Just as, to Grillmeier's point, the Christological writers of the ancient church "were concerned with something vital, namely the very nature of Christianity," we, too, are also concerned with that very vitality and "the very nature of Christianity" in terms of our *question of the meaning of Christology* now.

FERDINAND HAHN

How *the question of the meaning of Christology* becomes "something vital" and precisely permeates at "the very nature of Christianity" for Grillmeier can be contextualized contemporarily against Ferdinand Hahn's *The Titles of Jesus in Christology: Their History in Early Christianity* (1969), originally published as *Christologische Hoheitstitel: Ihre Geschichte im frühen Christentum* in 1963.

6. Kierkegaard, *Sickness Unto Death*, 13.

Before discussing Hahn's *The Titles of Jesus in Christology*, I want to contextualize Hahn, in order to allow me to situate Hahn not just to *the question of the meaning of Christology* and the perennial problem of the historical Jesus, but also to the "new quest" by way of influences that can be traced to Käsemann, Jeremias, Gogarten, and Bornkamm on Hahn's Christological thought. Indeed, as a student from 1947 to 1953 across universities in Mainz, Göttingen, and Heidelberg, Hahn was taught by Käsemann at Mainz and Göttingen (with Käsemann at Mainz from 1946 to 1951, then Göttingen from 1951 to 1959), then taught by Jeremias and Gogarten at the University of Göttingen (with both arriving in 1935, though Jeremias retired in 1968 and Gogarten retired in 1955). Thereafter, Hahn served as a teaching assistant to Bornkamm at the University of Heidelberg from 1956 to Hahn's completion of his doctoral degree in 1961, with Hahn's habilitation thesis completed in 1963. Viewed collectively, it is safe to say that Käsemann, Jeremias, Gogarten, and Bornkamm all shaped Hahn's understanding of Christology, especially as it explicitly lays bare in a text entitled "The Quest of the Historical Jesus and the Special Character of the Sources Available to Us," which is included in translation in the collection, *What Can We Know About Jesus?* (1969), though the collection originally appears as *Die Frage nach dem historischen Jesus* in 1962.

In one sense, what is significant about Hahn's "The Quest of the Historical Jesus and the Special Character of the Sources Available to Us" is that it appears with two other texts in the collection—one of these, notably, is by Bornkamm.[7] In another way, in a footnote to Hahn's text, we are informed that the text was originally a lecture, which Hahn delivered twice on separate occasions: at Tutzing on May 6, 1960 and, "in a somewhat expanded version" at Schwanenberg on April 15, 1961.[8] Though, as Hahn makes clear, the text has received "several minor changes," what we have in Hahn's "The Quest of the Historical Jesus and the Special Character of the Sources Available to Us" is a contribution to the perennial problem of the historical Jesus and, in a rather straight-forward way, a voice that speaks to the concerns raised conceptually by the "new quest"—this seems so, when placing Hahn's "The Quest of the Historical Jesus and the Special Character of the Sources Available to Us" at the very height of preoccupations of the Christological thinking and Christological thinking throughout the 1950s.

---

7. Bornkamm's "The Significance of the Historical Jesus for Faith" is dated to 1960, as a theological extension of Bornkamm's *Jesus von Nazareth* (1956). This text, Bornkamm notes, contains "some sections" originating in 1960, and "at a greater length" in another form of the text in the collection, *Der historische Jesus und der kerygmatische Christus* (1961). Bornkamm, "Significance of the Historical Jesus for Faith," 69.

8. Hahn, "Quest of the Historical Jesus," 9.

At the opening of "The Quest of the Historical Jesus and the Special Character of the Sources Available to Us," Hahn announces and historicizes the "new quest" in this way:

> The quest of the historical Jesus is typically a modern problem. It first arose in the period of the Enlightenment and during the late nineteenth and early twentieth centuries was discussed thoroughly by theologians. Later it was relegated to the background for several decades, but recently it has again come to the fore.[9]

What has "come to the fore, for Hahn, stands concurrently alongside the likes of Ebeling and Fuchs, as well as the likes of Conzelmann and Althaus. We can certainly contextualize Hahn's words in this manner, but, given Hahn's influences, we can see Hahn engaged with Käsemann and Bornkamm as his interlocutors. To this extent, in confronting the task and scope of the "new quest" by 1960, Hahn surmises:

> This quest has its basis in the insights and methods of modern historical science; in fact, it is founded upon the basic propositions of all modern thought, since it presupposes a different relationship to reality from that which held sway in past epochs. It is this quest which we must now take up if we really desire to make the biblical testimonies our own.[10]

The ability, Hahn says, "to make the biblical testimonies our own" comes by way of how we theologize those "biblical testimonies." How we theologize these "biblical testimonies," first as representations of the relationship between the historical Jesus and the Christ of faith, and then as representations of ourselves, is tempered by the means that Christological thinking leads us towards a Christological reflection about the what-ness, how-ness, and why-ness—when we pose the question to and seek the meaningfulness of Christology, we are guided by *the question of the meaning of Christology*. In fact, it is through Christological reflection that, as Hahn argues, "the picture which the Gospels give of the historical Jesus is not simply identical with the history of Jesus that historical investigation provides."[11]

What follows in Hahn's "The Quest of the Historical Jesus and the Special Character of the Sources Available to Us" is a "historical investigation" that proceeds through a careful consideration of the contributions sources that help shape *the question of the meaning of Christology*. Hahn makes it

9. Hahn, "Quest of the Historical Jesus," 9.
10. Hahn, "Quest of the Historical Jesus," 9.
11. Hahn, "Quest of the Historical Jesus," 9.

clear that "what is required is that we penetrate through the sources to the history that is reported in them."[12] To do this—to "penetrate through the sources" and lay bare "the history that is reported in them"—Hann gives accounts of the meaningfulness of non-Christian sources,[13] the apocryphal gospels,[14] the Gospel of John,[15] the synoptic gospels,[16] and "the substance of the oral tradition."[17] Each of these accounts—these that speak to how the historical Jesus and the Christ of faith disclose themselves through testimonies—form a composite account, or a composite testimony that gives an account of ourselves and "make the biblical testimonies our own." This brings Hahn to argue:

> What is involved here is not merely a historical continuity, and least of all a legitimation of the post-resurrection *kerygma* discovered by the aid of history [. . .] rather, what is involved here is the continuity in content, concerning the extent to which Jesus' own history and proclamation establish, require and already imply the early Christian *kerygma*.[18]

With the emphasis Hahn places on "kerygma," and this means not just to Bultmann, but also to the Bultmannians and to the extent that it reaches theologically and Christologically into the post-Bultmannian era which situates Hahn, Hahn makes the following conclusion:

> What is essential is that precisely in the quest of the historical Jesus our work must be coupled with knowledge of the ultimate ground of history (and this fact gives the quest its theological relevance). This knowledge is one that involves salvation and damnation, [insofar] as the history of Jesus brings us in contact with the reality of the living God.[19]

Here, the means by which "our work must be coupled with knowledge of the ultimate ground of history" explicitly lays bare *the question of the meaning of Christology*. For Hahn, I submit, there is an understanding of Christological thinking that informs and is informed by Christological reflection, insofar as both ground and are grounded by history. The knowledge that is

12. Hahn, "Quest of the Historical Jesus," 20.

13. Hahn, "Quest of the Historical Jesus," 20–25.

14. Hahn, "Quest of the Historical Jesus," 25–31.

15. Hahn, "Quest of the Historical Jesus," 31–34.

16. Hahn, "Quest of the Historical Jesus," 34–39.

17. Hahn, "Quest of the Historical Jesus," 39–44.

18. Hahn, "Quest of the Historical Jesus," 48.

19. Hahn, "Quest of the Historical Jesus," 48.

disclosed through "the ultimate ground of history" calibrates *the question of the meaning of Christology*, which, in turn, calibrates Hahn's *The Titles of Jesus in Christology*, given its subtitle "Their History in Early Christianity."

Even as Hahn's work in *The Titles of Jesus in Christology* shares a historical approach to what it means to do Christology—while Grillmeier chiefly considers the history of Christology alongside a tradition marked noticeably by key figures, movements, and events beginning with the Apostolic Age—Hahn's own history of Christology is tied more closely to a thematic representation of Christological titles ideologically-rooted in the pre-Apostolic era of Judaic and Hellenistic thought. Nevertheless, there remains a kindred spirit between Grillmeier's and Hahn's respective work, if we hold to the sense that both are ultimately and predominantly considered with *the question of the meaning of Christology*. Like Grillmeier, Hahn conceives of the relationship between "the inward, intellectual struggles" of those of the earliest days of the Church and ours—Hahn, too, seemingly locates a comradery between the earliest Christological writers and what can be said about Christology now. As with Grillmeier, what inevitably and necessarily ties us to the earliest Christological writers is the Christological tradition that has developed from them, providing an ideological lineage to us, insomuch as *the question of the meaning of Christology* contains its vitality as the very nature of Christianity. To this methodological point, Hahn's construes, "[. . .] to grasp the evangelist's thought we have to enter the field of Christology and, in doing so, to inquire what were the Christological traditions that have been worked up."[20] When entering the field of Christology, we do so, true enough, as Hahn suggests, in order to interrogate what has been traditionally "worked up," as a means of grounding what generally matters to what Christology has come to mean over time. But, that interrogation into what lies in antecedence to us also becomes a means of grounding what narrowly matters to what Christology has yet to become, if we are to project *the question of the meaning of Christology* into a new tradition of Christological ideas. On this, Hahn finds:

> The Christological ideas of the earliest church have nevertheless obtained far-reaching expression in the strata of tradition which are stamped with a definite title of majesty. Since a traditio-historical classification of the material that lay before the evangelist can be arrived at only if we do not confine ourselves to the Gospel of Mark—the pieces of evidence for the early period are as it is scanty enough—the constructive method of proceeding

20. Hahn, *Titles of Jesus in Christology*, 11.

has led to the problem of the beginnings of the formation of
Christological tradition in general.[21]

Hahn's point is quite salient here, given that Christological ideas, as such,
have an antecedence and, in themselves, set precedence, especially if these
ideas as always-already couched in a "traditio-historical classification." This
is not just the "material that lay before the evangelist," as Hahn suggests,
but, when more largely conceived of "if we do not confine ourselves to the
Gospel of Mark," it is also allows us to more firmly-crystallize and attune
ourselves to *the question of the meaning of Christology*.

Taking a closer look at the implications of what Hahn outlines as "the
constructive method of proceeding" in what Hahn classifies as "traditio-
historical," and attending to the notion that *the question of the meaning of
Christology* is precisely what, just as Hahn writes, "led to the problem of the
beginnings of the formation of tradition in general," what Christology is and
does requires a foundation that allows Christology to be a foundation in
itself. That is, when we speak of Christology, we must do so, not only from
a Christological standpoint of self-edifying *the meaning of Christology*, but
also as an edifying force that concretizes *the question of Christology*—for *the
question of the meaning of Christology* to be self-edifying and an edifying
force, the manner with which we construct what Christology is in terms of
constructing what Christology does behooves us to fundamentally attune to
Hahn's belief in a "constructive method of proceeding."

Yet, as clear as Hahn's position to and handling of *the question of the
meaning of Christology* may be, how Hahn position himself and handles
his own Christological reflection with respect to the "new quest" is grows
more complicated in the 1970s. At that time, two texts from Hahn[22]—one,
"*Probleme historishcer Kritik*" (1972), and the other, "*Methodologische
Überlegungen zur Rückfrage nach dem historischen Jesus*" (1974)—as Evans'
notes, Hahn "criticizes the methodology of the new quest [and] suggests a
new way of viewing the faith perspective of the New Testament writings."[23]

REGINALD H. FULLER

If following a traditio-historical constructive method to *the question of the
meaning of Christology*, we must apply a foundation that situates Christology

---

21. Hahn, *Titles of Jesus in Christology*, 11.

22. These two were published together, in translated form, as *Historical Investigation and New Testament* (1983).

23. Evans, *Life of Jesus Research*, 87.

in relation to the theology proper and projects Christology towards all which it directly influences. In *Foundations of New Testament Christology* (1965), Evans explains, Reginald H. Fuller "examines background, Jesus' self-understanding, and the development of New Testament Christology in the light of Easter faith."[24] To this extent, Fuller puts forth Hahn's suggestion of traditio-historical constructive method, by proposing, "in traditional dogmatics, Christology (the doctrine of Christ's person) precedes soteriology (the doctrine of Christ's work)."[25]

To tie Christology to soteriology is certainly not unique to Fuller—such a relationship, speaking systematically, within the larger scope of theologizing, is based on a proposition that the meaning of Christology is oriented towards the meaning of soteriology, such that the very nature of what Christ is, as one who is fully divine and fully human, is carried forth by the very nature of salvation. Just as the title of Fuller's work acknowledges, the foundation of New Testament theology is fundamentally constructed on the relationship between Christology and soteriology, to the extent that the latter provides validation for the former. In this way, the former always precedes the latter, insofar as, Fuller recognizes, "logically this is the true order."[26] For Fuller, in light of what Christology means to soteriology and vice versa, "it was because he was who he was that Jesus Christ did what he did."[27] Said another way, it is because of Christology that soteriology is made possible, as that which speaks to the traditio-historical importance of Christology itself.

As Fuller is right to point out, when considering that *the question of the meaning of Christology* is always-already one of traditio-historical importance, "Christology is essentially a response to a particular history."[28] Such a statement makes a critical observation that, in one sense, conceptualizes what Christology means for soteriology, if the former is "a response" to the latter as "a particular history" developing into a New Testament. In another sense, what Fuller brings to the fold is the notion that Christology itself is "a response to a particular history" grounded on the physical embodiment of Jesus as a consequential testament in relation to the Hebrew Bible as a previous testament. For Christology, then, to be "a response to a particular history" attunes it to a theologizing that is always historicizing what comes before and what follows. If, as Fuller claims, "[Christology] is a confessional

24. Evans, *Life of Jesus Research*, 51.
25. Fuller, *Foundations of New Testament Christology*, 15.
26. Fuller, *Foundations of New Testament Christology*, 15.
27. Fuller, *Foundations of New Testament Christology*, 15.
28. Fuller, *Foundations of New Testament Christology*, 15.

response,"[29] this is so primarily through an articulation of *the question of the meaning of Christology*—how one chooses to conceive of *the meaning* and articulate *the question* becomes a "confessional" undertaking.

When Christology, as that which is conceived of and articulated by *the question of the meaning of Christology*, is "a confessional response," it becomes so, as Fuller proposes, "since it is [humanity's] response to Jesus."[30] That response, in a confessional form, is existential—what is made meaningful through *the question of the meaning of Christology* has a meaningfulness that goes no further than the existentiality of the confessional meaning. Because of this confessional meaning, Fuller believes that "it follows that Christology is not itself a part of the original revelation or action of God in Christ."[31] What is important, here, both for Fuller and for *the question of the meaning of Christology* is one that meaningfully unfolds outside "the original revelation or action of God in Christ," especially if Christological ideas in themselves operate in a different space than any other theological ideas.

Here, if we can say that Fuller's understanding of "the original revelation or action of God in Christ" is not necessarily Christological, it is possible to ascertain from Fuller a reference to eschatological ideas, or even Trinitarian ideas—if so, it stands to reason that Christology is theologically beyond the purview of what Fuller describes as "the original revelation or action of God or Christ," when considering all that God is and does in relation to and within the scope of the meaning of Christ. The very meaning of Christ, in itself, as that which is predicated on *the question of the meaning of Christology*, cannot be interrogated meaningfully through the frameworks of, say, eschatology or Trinitarianism. Yet, it is precisely because of *the question of the meaning of Christology*—with its unique question and unique meaning—that matters of Christ are not explicitly self-evident, any more than matters of revelation or the functionality of the Trinity are explicitly self-evident in a monolithic way. As Fuller reminds us, "Jesus does not hand out a ready-made Christology on a plate."[32] Similarly, since God does not hand out a ready-made theology, nor a ready-made eschatology and Trinitarianism for that matter, what we can say theologically, or eschatologically, or in terms of the Trinity is also a confessional response.

The extent that *the question of the meaning of Christology* is a confessional response, if taking heed to Fuller, allows us to more fundamentally understand, Fuller points out, that "the church's Christology was a response

---

29. Fuller, *Foundations of New Testament Christology*, 15.

30. Fuller, *Foundations of New Testament Christology*, 15.

31. Fuller, *Foundations of New Testament Christology*, 15.

32. Fuller, *Foundations of New Testament Christology*, 15.

to its total encounter with Jesus, not only in his earthly history but also in its (the church's) continuing life."[33] In this way, just as much as *the question of the meaning of Christology* is a confessional response, *the question of the meaning of Christology* is relegated to and regulated by a "total encounter with Jesus." For this encounter to become a response, what arises is a confessional response to Jesus's "earthly history" and Christological ramifications of the Church's "continuing life," in terms of a response and an encounter explained through ecclesiology.

In a relationship between a response and an encounter—both that are equally confessional—*the question of the meaning of Christology* speaks to an underlying matrix of concerns that brings together Jesus's "earthly history" and the Church's "continuing life" into a meaningful foundation. The idea of a foundation is thematically at stake for Fuller, given the choice of title for his monograph—the same can be said about approaches made prior to Fuller respectively by Hahn, Grillmeier, Cullmann, and Braun, all of which, in their own way, provide a foundation of sorts for how they each surmise *the question of the meaning of Christology*. As Fuller makes explicit, what becomes apparent in the following scope and limits of his work, as that which, I submit, seemingly address the scope and limits of *the question of the meaning of Christology* itself:

> Since we are dealing with the "Foundations of NT Christology" we shall not take the story as far as the Christology of NT writers themselves. We are concerned rather with the Christological foundations of their theology.[34]

Insofar as the foundations for what it means to do New Testament Christology is not so much about the Christology as the New Testament writers—as thinkers contingently thinking through immediate thought of the New Testament era—but more about what Fuller describes as "the Christological foundations of their theology," *the question of the meaning of Christology* becomes a question and a meaning meeting not at the juncture of "the Christology of NT writers," but more meaningfully at "the Christological foundations of [NT writers'] theology."

FRED B. CRADDOCK

Like Fuller, Fred B. Craddock's *The Pre-existence of Christ in the New Testament* (1968) presents a similar understanding about how Christological

---

33. Fuller, *Foundations of New Testament Christology*, 15.
34. Fuller, *Foundations of New Testament Christology*, 16.

foundations serve New Testament theologizing, which Craddock first expresses in the following way: "Christology is central to the Christian faith."[35] In light of that centrality, Craddock suggests that "it is more directly helpful to say that Christology lies at the heart of the New Testament, and the New Testament has been, in our time, more directly and specifically a concern of theologians than is usually the case."[36] Even as much as Craddock understands how fundamental Christology is as that which "lies at the heart" of New Testament theologizing, Craddock also seems to recognize that the very relationship between Christological ideas and New Testament theologizing, by Craddock's time, has been influenced by the new quest for the historical Jesus. If this new quest is, indeed, in the purview of Craddock's sense that Christology is, in his words, "more directly and specifically a concern of theologians than is usually the case"—if we attend to the historical context of Craddock's text as the height of the new quest scholarship of the late 1960s—what Craddock undoubtedly acknowledges is a particular emphasis on *the question of the meaning of Christology* rooted in the question of the meaning of the New Testament and attuned to the question of the meaning of the historical Jesus. For Craddock, this three-fold question and three-fold meaning brings Craddock to advise the following about in the introduction section to his text, denoting a "problem" and "procedure":

> This book asks the reader to share in an investigation of the meaning of the pre-existence of Christ as it is expressed in the New Testament. This is an invitation to join in an exploration that may seem strange, perhaps even unreal, in that it focuses upon a category of being that does not correspond to reality as we experience it.[37]

What Craddock's "investigation" attempts to re-conceptualize *the question of the meaning of Christology* through what he refers to as "the meaning of the pre-existence of Christ." Yet, this re-conceptualization, for Craddock, is always-already baked into New Testament theologizing itself insomuch as it becomes infused into the very meaning of Christology, but it requires a recalibrated encounter that allows what is not explicitly, self-evident to become disclosed. Even so, Craddock concedes the following: "whether or not pre-existence remains in the language and thought structures of the Christian's creed, this idea and the doctrine framed upon it must be dealt with honestly."[38]

35. Craddock, *Pre-existence of Christ in the New Testament*, 7.

36. Craddock, *Pre-existence of Christ in the New Testament*, 7.

37. Craddock, *Pre-existence of Christ in the New Testament*, 11.

38. Craddock, *Pre-existence of Christ in the New Testament*, 16.

Here, the key for Craddock is the sense that what we deal with "honestly" is about what we deal with authentically, such that that authenticity allows for a more authentic understanding of *the question of the meaning of Christology*—if attend to this authenticity, matters of pre-existence are at the roots of the question of Christology and the meaning of it. Essentially, "this very honesty," Craddock writes, "demands an admission at the outset that we are not at home with the category of pre-existence."[39] There is an "uneasiness" in what Craddock hopes to explore, which, in dictating it as a problem and a procedure, embodies "one reason prompting this investigation."[40] The problem and the procedure, then, is one that confronts not just traditional New Testament theologizing but also Christological ideas—it is for this reason that Craddock recognizes that his view of pre-existence is not only non-traditional in the truest sense, but also becomes a radicalization of Christological ideas, which require an "honesty" unavoidably predicated on an "uneasiness." From this initial, prompting reason, Craddock provides what are distinctly four "specific reasons for our intellectual discomfort with this dimension of traditional Christology," as that which is based on the category of pre-existence.[41]

Having outlined what is essentially the problem, as Craddock details it, Craddock's procedure for re-conceptualizing *the question of the meaning of Christology* in terms of the pre-existence of Christ first unfolds with an "intellectual discomfort" with, Craddock finds, how "our civilization takes history seriously and within history finds meaning and value."[42] In this, Craddock contends, with the hope of establishing what meaning and value can be construed from "tak[ing] history seriously." Craddock explains: "this is to say that life is viewed in terms of time, having [a] beginning and [an] end."[43] On the point, Craddock envisions the meaning of the pre-existence of Christ through the meaning of history having been taken seriously, whereby history becomes a fundamental framework of more than just a forward projection, but also one of hindsight and precedence. To think of life, as Craddock does, as having beginnings and endings, means thinking about *the question of the meaning of Christology*, as I have posed it, as not strictly beginning with New Testament theologizing, but as a confessional response, precisely to Fuller's point, to that which exists before New Testament theologizing takes place. With an implied connection to Fuller, Craddock's

---

39. Craddock, *Pre-existence of Christ in the New Testament*, 16.
40. Craddock, *Pre-existence of Christ in the New Testament*, 16.
41. Craddock, *Pre-existence of Christ in the New Testament*, 16.
42. Craddock, *Pre-existence of Christ in the New Testament*, 16.
43. Craddock, *Pre-existence of Christ in the New Testament*, 16.

sense of a response is part and parcel of a more serious understanding of the framework of history. In Craddock's words:

> This framework is considered the valid structure within which the histories of men and institutions are to be understood, and to speak of a person or institution as having had an existence prior to the parenthesis of history is foreign and confusing.[44]

From this, *the question of the meaning of Christology*, as Craddock believes, points to "an existence prior to the parenthesis of history." Not only does this mean, for Craddock, that Christological ideas are not the beginning of the meaning of Christ, but both are, ultimately, when history is taken seriously, merely a response to the pre-existence of Christ. Conceiving of this "is foreign and confusing," Craddock notes, particularly given that "the biblical materials, through which the concept [of the pre-existence of Christ] comes to be a matter of concern for us, arose in the Near East, where Occident and Orient meet in the fusion of two world views."[45] These two worldviews come together in the Judeo-Christian tradition that, Craddock surmises, "is rather clearly fixed upon the linear view of history [while] it had been influenced by the cyclical view."[46] Because of this, Craddock concludes that there is a substantial and significant difference between the two views, insofar as "the concept of pre-existence has one meaning in terms of the historical line, but quite a different meaning in terms of the eternal cycle."[47] What arises from these two views are two implications for the pre-existence of Christ, as that which speaks to what I have referred to as *the question of the meaning of Christology*: "in the one case[,] pre-existence carries a temporal force, 'prior to,' whereas in the other it means 'suprahistorical,' implying not only 'prior to' but 'subsequent to' history."[48]

Craddock's outlining of the two views of the meaning of "pre-existence" is noteworthy, if we are to understand what "pre-existence" may have to do with *the question of the meaning of Christology* from Craddock's perspective. Yet, Cradock finds that there is a problem inherent in the very meaning of "pre-existence" in terms of what it possibly means. Craddock sees this problem as a "consequence" of what the linear view of history in relation to the cyclical view of history means for the notion of "pre-existence" as a term—the focus, here, is on how the prefix "pre-" can "signify priority in

---

44. Craddock, *Pre-existence of Christ in the New Testament*, 16.
45. Craddock, *Pre-existence of Christ in the New Testament*, 16–17.
46. Craddock, *Pre-existence of Christ in the New Testament*, 17.
47. Craddock, *Pre-existence of Christ in the New Testament*, 17.
48. Craddock, *Pre-existence of Christ in the New Testament*, 17.

time, space, or rank."[49] In this way, "a pre-existent Christ with reference to creation," Craddock writes, "might be temporarily defined as one having existence prior to the *act* of creation."[50] As a result, with an emphasis on "act," Craddock makes the following case:

> Creation refers not simply to the act of creating but to that which has been created. Therefore, in relation to the act, pre-existence carries a strong temporal connotation, but in relation to the created universe as such, pre-existence could easily carry the connotation of 'pre-eminence,' 'priority in rank,' 'superiority over,' 'noncontingency.' Immediately, therefore, the idea of pre-existence in such a discussion could carry the double force of involvement in creation as a process and yet pre-eminence over creation as a product.[51]

For Craddock, there is an ambiguity to "pre-existence," when defining the term's meaningfulness to the act of creation—the ambiguousness of what "pre-existence" means temporally for the act of creating and "that which has been created" brings about a "double force of involvement," as Craddock suggests, of the act of creation towards what can be rendered as *the question of the meaning of Christology*. What becomes ambiguous to the manner with which "pre-existence," in Chaddock's view, speaks to what occurs prior to creation and what occurs afterwards—in this way, to even incorporate "pre-existence" into *the question of the meaning of Christology* indicates an ambiguousness to it as well, which involves the possibility that *the question of the meaning of Christology* can point to what is being created Christologically just as much as it is to what has been created Christologically.

From this, Cradock proposes, "a final reason for confusion with reference to the concept of pre-existence lies in the ambiguity of language."[52] This ambiguity calls forth a variety of meaning of "pre-existence" or what can be meant by "pre-existent"—with its variety of meanings at hand, Craddock imports all into a "lexicography," by considering that "[it] leaves us this legacy with which to begin this study: pre-existence."[53]

For Craddock—and rightly so—how the broader legacy influencing the meaning of the pre-existence of Christ becomes integral to the "most current efforts to interpret and translate New Testament Christology so as to confront this generation with the gospel [which] are indebted to the pioneer

49. Craddock, *Pre-existence of Christ in the New Testament*, 17.
50. Craddock, *Pre-existence of Christ in the New Testament*, 17.
51. Craddock, *Pre-existence of Christ in the New Testament*, 17–18.
52. Craddock, *Pre-existence of Christ in the New Testament*, 18.
53. Craddock, *Pre-existence of Christ in the New Testament*, 18.

work of Bultmann."[54] In a footnote, Craddock extrapolates his reference to Bultmann as "especially [Bultnann's] programmatic essay of 1941," which is included in the collection, *Kerygma and Myth*.[55] Interestingly, Craddock's reference to Bultmann, as it is, comes very late in Craddock's work—what this seems to suggest, I find, is a purposeful minimization of Bultmann's Christological significance to Craddock's Christological thinking in a decidedly post-Bultmannian era, such that Craddock situates his Christological reflection on *the question of the meaning of Christology* beyond the concerns of the "new quest."

LEONARDO BOFF

By the 1970s, the "second quest," as it is called, having begun in the 1950s with Käsemann in the purview of Käsemann's Bultmannian influences, is waning in importance. Even so, *the question of the meaning of Christology* remains significant, especially as that which is asked and pursued over and against the concerns for the historical Jesus. Yet, the manner with which *the question of the meaning of Christology* is fundamentally cast, it is argued, is largely without any Bultmannian ideas—as largely as Bultmann looms over the theologizing of the 1950s and well into the 1960s towards the framing of Christological ideas, Bultmann's "towering influence,"[56] Witherington writes, subsides, as does "the enthusiasm for existentialism."[57]

As "the enthusiasm for the Second Quest"[58] falters in the 1970s, *the question of the meaning of Christology* intensifies hermeneutically in a way that incorporates a philosophizing to the theologizing of Christological ideas. An example of this occurs in Leonardo Boff's *Jesus Cristo Libertador. Ensaio de Cristologia Critica para o nosso Tempo* (1972), translated from the Spanish as *Jesus Christ Liberator: A Critical Christology for Our Time* in 1978. In it, Boff poses *the question of the meaning of Christology*, which, taking into account Boff's subtitle, addresses what can be taken to be "critical Christology" as well as to what extent Christological ideas speak to "our time." To this question, Boff defines Christology itself as "the Word of God that affects me today, now,"[59] insomuch as Christological ideas themselves

54. Craddock, *Pre-existence of Christ in the New Testament*, 174.
55. Craddock, *Pre-existence of Christ in the New Testament*, 174.
56. Witherington, *Jesus Quest*, 11.
57. Witherington, *Jesus Quest*, 11.
58. Witherington, *Jesus Quest*, 11.
59. Boff, *Jesus Christ Liberator*, 10.

are grounded on the extent that what it means "to believe in Christ as the Gospels preach him is to experience and achieve redemption."[60]

Yet, for Boff, *the question of the meaning of Christology* is ultimately tied to Bultmannian influences, even if those influences have—as it has been noted—gone out of vogue. It is with Bultmann in mind that Boff suggests that "we ought to demythologize the evangelical formulations and see their meaning for our existence."[61] Whether or not we can say that Bultmann stands behind Boff's understanding of *the question of the meaning of Christology* is beside the point—it is not so much that Boff is carrying forward Bultmann into the 1970s, or even that Boff hopes to necessarily resurrect Bultmann. Rather, I submit, Boff's is filtering his understanding of *the question of the meaning of Christology* through the "second quest" of the 1950s and the degree that that "second quest" owes its very existence to Bultmannian influences, especially when placing emphasis on Boff's confrontation with "evangelical formulations" and how he "see[s] their meaning for our existence." The relationship Boff envisions between "evangelical formulations" and what arises from "their meaning for our existence" is how Boff attunes himself to *the question of the meaning of Christology*, insomuch as the following proposition holds true: "to believe in the Crucified is to wrench oneself away from oneself."[62]

As much as it is clear that "believ[ing] in the Crucified" is construed through a belief in Christological ideas, what does Boff mean when saying that this Christological belief is equated with "wrench[ing] oneself away from oneself"? Can we say that the ability "to wrench oneself away from oneself," as Boff writes, requires existentially comporting oneself to oneself? Is this comportment, as that which allows oneself to be wrenched away from another oneself, based on an existential interpretation of what is wrenched away in relation to what remains? Can we say, then, that the manner with which an existential interpretation of this nature occurs is through "believ[ing] in the Crucified" as that which hinges on *the question of the meaning of Christology*? This certainly seems to be true, particularly if one's "[belief] in the Crucified" allows one's ability "to wrench oneself away from oneself" to the extent that, as Boff outlines, "salvation is to be found in this."[63] Insofar as salvation through soteriology is linked to *the question*

60. Boff, *Jesus Christ Liberator*, 10.

61. Boff, *Jesus Christ Liberator*, 10.

62. Boff, *Jesus Christ Liberator*, 10.

63. Boff, *Jesus Christ Liberator*, 10.

of the meaning of Christology for Boff, it stands to reason that, just as Boff concludes, "Christology is thus reduced to soteriology."[64]

In a certain sense, Boff's understanding of salvation grounds itself to the wrenching away of oneself from another oneself—the salvific value of Christological ideas is in the ability of situating oneself meaningfully away from that which prevents that meaningfulness. To confront *the question of the meaning of Christology*, in this way is to confront oneself, insomuch as what we wrench ourselves away promises a greater salvation for ourselves than what which we remain subjugated by. This, of course, is the task and method of an existential interpretation—it is not just the existential interpretation of the meaning of oneself as a whole, but it is also an existential interpretation of the meanings of selves, both wrenched away and unwrenched away. Similarly, when existentially considering the selves of "Jesus Christ," there is a oneself that must be wrenched away from another oneself, especially for the sake of *the question of the meaning of Christology*—for Boff, "to believe in the Crucified" carries two meanings: the self of Jesus and the self of Christ, so that, when we speak about Christology itself or soteriology itself, we must fundamentally orient ourselves to two directions that *the question of the meaning of Christology* takes us. Boff recognizes these directions—which undoubtedly hinge on the state of the quest for the historical Jesus in the 1970s—by noting that:

> Research now began to distinguish between two things: a 'Jesusology' (how Jesus understood himself and allowed others to understand him by his words and attitudes) and a Christology (the clarification done by the community afterwards). Christology is nothing more than going beyond that which emerged in Jesus.[65]

Even if *the question of the meaning of Christology* is, just as Boff says, "nothing more than going beyond that which emerged in Jesus," Christology, as such, has to be "wrenched away" from the matters of the historical Jesus, or what Boff refers to as "Jesusology."

What arises from the difference Boff makes between Christology and the historical Jesus (or "Jesusology") is pivotal to what sense we can make out of *the question of the meaning of Christology*. It is true that the very nature of Christological ideas wrestles with what *the question of the meaning of Christology* means to us now with respect to what the question meant for, to Boff's point, "how Jesus understood himself and allowed others to understand him by his words and attitudes." The latter concern is at the core

64. Boff, *Jesus Christ Liberator*, 10.
65. Boff, *Jesus Christ Liberator*, 13.

of the quest for the historical Jesus, as that which has the potential to inform what Boff calls "the clarification done by the community afterwards." What this "clarification" looks like for Boff's community in the 1970s is, in itself, wrenched away from what this "clarification" means for the community associated with the "second quest," just as this "clarification" holds a different meaning to the community around which Bultmann operates and the community with which Schweitzer brings an end to the "first quest."

Just as Bultmann wrenches away *the question of the meaning of Christology* from Schweitzer's ending of the "first quest" and Schweitzer does the same, wrenching away his own "clarification" from the 125-year history into the historical Jesus dating to Reimarus. If we can say that Boff, too, is wrenching away his own "clarification" from that of the 1950s to 1960s, as a means of Boff, when repurposing his words, "going beyond that which emerged in Jesus," it brings Boff to ask:

> How then can we know Jesus Christ? For most people[,] the answer presenting itself clearly: through the writings of the New Testament, especially the Gospels. We need only interpret them correctly (hermeneutics) to enlighten ourselves concerning Jesus. This reply, though it appears self-evident, contains a very intricate problem. It is called the hermeneutic (interpretation) problem, the central theme of modern philosophy and, as was always the case, of theology and exegesis.[66]

This hermeneutic problem, as Boff confronts it, is also "a very intricate problem" for every handling of *the question of the meaning of Christology* before Boff comes along. Insofar as the hermeneutic problem is "the central theme of modern philosophy and, as was always the case, of theology and exegesis," this problem is "the central theme" to *the question of the meaning of Christology*, just as much as it is "the central theme" to any quest for the historical Jesus. In a way, what Boff highlights as "the hermeneutic problem" precisely describes what is wrong, in Boff's view, with the situation of the quest for the historical Jesus by the 1970s.

HELMUT THIELICKE

Issues with hermeneutics (and the hermeneutic problem therein), in terms of how we approach *the question of the meaning of Christology* as an interpretive task with an underlying methodology of interpretation, become how Helmut Thielicke contributes what is essentially a counter-movement to

---

66. Boff, *Jesus Christ Liberator*, 32–33.

Bultmann, to existentialism, and to the "second quest"—this counter-movement, to which Boff can be included, is broadened by Thielicke, such that, like Boff, Thielicke's interest in what role the hermeneutic problem plays in the development of *the question of the meaning of Christology* becomes a re-appropriation of Bultmann, existentialism, and "the second quest." For Thielicke, hermeneutics—and the hermeneutic problem—orients the fundamental direction he takes *the question of the meaning of Christology.*

Having previously been a doctoral student of Althaus in 1934, being active in the Confessing Church in 1935, and publishing a strident critique of Bultmann's demythologization project with "The Restatement of New Testament Mythology" dated to 1943 (appearing in the Bultmann-focused collection, *Kerygma and Myth*), Thielicke publishes the three-volume, *Der Evangelische Glaube* (1974–1977), translated as *The Evangelical Faith*. In the second volume of the three, subtitled *The Doctrine of God and of Christ,* Thielicke's understanding of Christological ideas, according to Geoffrey W. Bromiley's editor's preface, can be described as the following:

> The approach to Christology is not through the two natures but through the three offices, so that the atonement and the resurrection can be treated as well as the traditional, if less important, [C]hristological themes of the virgin birth, the descent, and the ascension.[67]

What Bromiley notes is an ideological shift in Christological thinking in Thielicke from "two natures" to "three offices." Thielicke's shift moves from what Christology is to what Christology does, so that *the question of the meaning of Christology* is less about the theoretical relationship between "two natures" and more about the relationship between the "three offices." Thielicke's reference to the three Christological offices certainly expands upon earlier work in Hahn's *The Title of Jesus in Christology,* even though Hahn cites five offices (son of man, kyrios, christos, son of David, and son of God) and Thielicke condenses to three. As with Hahn, Thielicke's emphasis on the Christological offices attune *the question of the meaning of Christology* in such a way that, as Thielicke proposes, "the atonement and the resurrection can be treated." That is to say, matters of atonement (as that which is hamartiologically influenced and the bestowing of God's grace) and those of the resurrection (as that which influences eschatological concerns) attempt to mitigate the hermeneutic problem in the development of *the question of the meaning of Christology.* For Thielicke, the treatment of the atonement and the resurrection, as more important Christological themes,

---

67. Thielicke, *The Evangelical Faith: The Doctrine of God and of Christ,* v.

serves a systematic understanding of other themes that serve Christology more generally, such as the themes of "the virgin birth, the descent, and the ascension," even if, Thielicke finds, they are "less important."

What is clear for Thielicke, as we see also in Hahn, is that the Christological themes of atonement and the resurrection attend to an eschatological theme, insofar as the relationship between what matters for Christology and what matters for eschatology benefits *the question of the meaning of Christology* more broadly. Just as Hahn presents, in his appendix to The Title of Jesus in Christology, the notion that Hahn's enumeration of five Christological offices provide for an understanding of Jesus's role as an "eschatological prophet,"[68] Thielicke's preference of three offices—over and against "two natures"—ultimately point to eschatological significance hard-wired into the manner by which we pose *the question of the meaning of Christology*. With an eschatological theme attuning Thielicke's handling of Christological ideas, before asking *the question of the meaning of Christology*, Thielicke poses a preliminary question: "the first question, whether Christ may rightly be called *the* form of the divine self-disclosure, not just one form, can be answered only with an exposition of Christology itself."[69] That exposition, as Thielicke calls it, requires coupling what Christology is and does with Hahn's notion of the "eschatological prophet," so that *the question of the meaning of Christology* articulates, to Thielicke's point, "whether Christ may rightly be called *the* form of the divine self-disclosure, not just one form"—if our interest is with "*the* form of the divine self-disclosure" through what Christology is and does, the very nature of asking *the question of the meaning of Christology* must unconceal what "Christ may rightly be called" and, in turn, must be an unconcealment of an "eschatological prophet."

Yet, even in the pursuit of *the question of the meaning of Christology*, Thielicke takes care to warn us that:

> Every Christology faces the difficulty of making appropriate statements about its theme. Even a brief glance at the confused history of Christology, at the conflict over minor nuances, at the unstable and often non-existent balance between the divine and the human character of the figure of Christ, confirms this impression.[70]

Here, Thielicke's point is well-meaning, since *the question of the meaning of Christology* "faces the difficulty" of what it means to formulate the question itself in relation to the meaning itself, if we are to say, then, that the question

68. Hahn, *Title of Jesus in Christology*, 352.
69. Thielicke, *Evangelical Faith: The Doctrine of God and of Christ*, 264.
70. Thielicke, *Evangelical Faith: The Doctrine of God and of Christ*, 265.

and the meaning we hope to devise about Christology are both devoted to "making appropriate statement about [Christology's] theme." This goes to Boff's sense of clarification, when considering that *the question of the meaning of Christology* seeks to clarify what Christology is and does, in order to mitigate, Thielicke says, "the confused history of Christology" and "the conflict over minor nuances." To whatever extent there exists, Thielicke describes, "the unstable and often non-existent balance between the divine and the human character of the figure of Christ," the very task and method of *the question of the meaning of Christology* must adjudicate what is always-already unstable and non-existent about the balance traditionally struck between the two natures and that duality of character points to or becomes embodied in Christological offices. Even so, Thielicke suggests that:

> The contradictions and tensions with which every Christology has to wrestle [. . .] find their basis, not in faith itself, but in reflection on faith. They constitute a logical scandal so long as reflection 'goes it alone.'[71]

From this, according to Thielicke, what holds the questioning and meaningfulness within the framework of *the question of the meaning of Christology* is one's grounding "in reflection on faith." Through one's reflection, as that which is decidedly a Christological reflection through faith on *the question of the meaning of Christology*, Thielicke surmises that, with respect to the contradictions and tensions:

> [They] are reconciled—not dissolved—only when faith is understood as the fixed point around which reflection circles, so that faith and reflection are commentaries [of] the one on the other. To put it simply, the man who is unaffected by faith in Christ will not be able to understand [C]hristological reflection. The man who lives by believing contact with Christ will recognize him even in the most paradoxical leaps of reflection, for there is entrusted to him the reality of him who escapes rational comprehension and who thus makes those leaps necessary.[72]

What becomes apparent in Thielicke is that faith existentializes that which occurs in "reflection on faith," if we can say that, as Thielicke says, "faith is understood as the fixed point around which reflection circles." More importantly, because faith existentializes reflection, insofar as, to Thielicke's point, "faith and reflection are commentaries [of] the one on the other," this allows reflection on faith to existentialize *the question of the meaning*

71. Thielicke, *Evangelical Faith: The Doctrine of God and of Christ*, 268.

72. Thielicke, *Evangelical Faith: The Doctrine of God and of Christ*, 268.

of Christology. In this sense, if the reverse holds true to Thielicke's proposition, being affected by faith, such that faith existentializes as much as it is, in itself, existentialized, presents the possibility of faith in Christ and, in turn, that faith in Christ existentializes and is existentialized through what is understood through Christological reflection.

EDWARD SCHILLEBEECKX

If it is possible to view Thielicke as providing the task of Christological reflection, hinging on the extent that, just as Thielicke outlines, "the man who lives by believing contact with Christ will recognize him even in the most paradoxical leaps of reflection," the approach that Edward Schillebeeckx situates himself to *the question of the meaning of Christology* as the embodiment of a Christological methodology—how Schillebeeckx theologizes from the standpoint of faith with respect to a grounding in Christological reflection undoubtedly attempts to existentialize *the question of the meaning of Christology*, ultimately contributing to the continued waning interest in the historical Jesus.

Originally published in Dutch as *Jezus, het verhaal van een levende* (1974), then in German as *Jesus: Die Geschichte von einem Lebenden* in 1975, and translated as *Jesus: An Experiment in Christology* in 1979, this is the only Schillebeeckx work explicitly referenced in Evans' *Life of Jesus Research*, where Evans describes the work in the following way:

> Discussion of the historical Jesus [. . .] claims that behind the Church's proclamation is "the concrete person Jesus of Nazareth," which is "the one and only basis for an authentic [C]hristology [. . .] understands Jesus as a leader of a liberation movement, who offered himself as a servant and who remained silent when condemned in Jerusalem.[73]

Schillebeeckx's *Jesus: An Experiment in Christology* presents the first of a two-volume study—with the second volume, *Gerechtigheid en liefde, genade en bevrijding* (1977), translated as *Christ: The Christian Experience in the Modern World* in 1980—that, in one sense, contributes to the waning interest in the historical Jesus in the 1970s, but, in another sense, attends to *the question of the meaning of Christology*. Indeed, there are contradictions and tensions in this—if re-appropriating Thielicke here—to the extent that Schillebeeckx's broader theologizing from a Christological standpoint is predicated on faith and that faith is grounded on reflection. At the core

73. Evans, *Life of Jesus Research*, 72–73.

of this Christological reflection, Schillebeeckx notes that there are "two types of Christianity, based on two types of Christology."[74] The former two types, as they are "based" on the latter two types, arise from contradictions and tensions inherent in *the question of the meaning of Christology*—these contradictions and tensions allow Schillebeeckx to, in his first volume, "experiment in Christology," while, in the second volume, present a notion of "Christian experience," insomuch as the two volumes, in themselves, seemingly act in contradiction and tension with one another.

Yet, with respect to how the first volume, as an "experiment in Christology," addresses a specific and focused *question of the meaning of Christology*, as that which is "based on two types of Christology," Schillebeeckx goes to on to write:

> In the one case an explicit allergy to the word 'Christ' (in many a eucharistic canon of recent times the term is on the way out), in the other an obvious, sometimes aggressive and un-Christian aversion to the word "Jesus' (of Nazareth), as though our belief were not in a concrete person but in a gnostic mystery-cult.[75]

These two types, for Schillebeeckx, have a lineage traceable through a Christological tradition, to the extent that both types hail from the same origin of Christological ideas. Essentially, all of these Christological ideas spring forth from a Christological ideology grounded on the earliest understanding of what Christology is and what Christology does, both in task and method, carrying forward the fundamental *question of the meaning of Christology*. Schillebeeckx explains this in the following way:

> From the Council of Nicea onwards one particular Christological model—the Johannine—has been developed as a norm within very narrow limits and one direction; and in fact only this tradition has made history in the Christian churches.[76]

The extent that the Johannine Christological model "developed as a norm" certainly speaks to Schillebeeckx's awareness of the greater influence *the question of the meaning of Christology* expressed in the Gospel of John (which further delineated throughout the Johannine corpus) has in relation to the Christological ideas that can be teased from the Synoptic gospels or even from the Pauline letters. However, in another sense, Schillebeeckx's reference to what role the Johannine tradition plays in the development a normative Christological model also speaks to the manner in which

74. Schillebeeckx, *Christ*, 30.

75. Schillebeeckx, *Christ*, 30.

76. Schillebeeckx, *Christ*, 570.

Bultmann teases out *the question of the meaning of Christology* from his exegesis of the Gospel of John—as Bultmann accomplishes most notably in *Das Evangelium des Johannes* (1941)—in a way that challenges the traditional, normative Christological model. Even so, by Schillebeeckx's time, as radical as Bultmann's Christological approach was in the 1940s and how that radicalism bolstered the view of Christology throughout the 1950s and into the 1960s, Schillebeeckx notices that the development of *the question of the meaning of Christology* has become focused "within very narrow limits and one direction." We can certainly take this as commentary on Bultmann and those that followed into a Bultmannian school of thought, but it is also a commentary on the state of *the question of the meaning of Christology* as it exists in the waning influence of and interest in the historical Jesus. It is with respect to what Schillebeeckx recognizes as a constricted conceptualization of *the question of the meaning of Christology* that allows Schillebeeckx to engage in a Christological reflection that characterizes the following:

> The 'Christological' tendency [. . .] stands within an intellective horizon in which, according to the Enlightenment, human Reason is supposed to be able to set *a priori* limits to meaningful possibilities. Certainly, we in the twentieth century can no longer devise a Christology on pre-critical lines. The question is, though, whether this narrow rationality-principle of the Enlightenment does not itself call for criticism.[77]

Here, because Schillebeeckx wishes to resist the tendency to "devise a Christology on pre-critical lines," not only does this criticize the "pre-critical" nature of the quest for the historical Jesus, but it also similarly criticizes the "pre-critical" conception of Bultmann's demythologization project. What this means, for Schillebeeckx is that "pre-critical lines" ascribe to what he calls a "narrow rationality-principle of the Enlightenment," insofar as what is passed down from the Enlightenment era is a kind of thinking that "set[s] *a priori* limits to meaningful possibilities."

The question to which Schillebeeckx arrives is predicated on the limitless *posteriori* possibilities of *the question of the meaning of Christology*—this becomes part and parcel of Schillebeeckx's "experiment in Christology" (of his first volume) and the foundation for what necessitates what he inscribes as the "Christian experience in the modern world" (of his second volume, *Christ: The Christian Experience in the Modern World*). What results from this, then, is the need for clarifying *the question of the meaning of Christology*, so that, in this clarification, a new philosophical framework is gathered along the experiential lines of the Christological experience. Like Boff,

77. Schillebeeckx, *Christ*, 588.

Schillebeeckx's understanding of Christology is a "critical Christology," but one that adheres to the meaningfulness of the human experience, as that which must encounter and making meaning out of God's existence—the relationship between human existence and God's existence, once clarified, is what allows human existence, once clarified, to become the clarification of the human experience through *the question of the meaning of Christology.*

If building further upon Schillebeeckx's notion of experience as limit-less *posteriori* possibilities, with Boff's notion of clarification towards the hermeneutic problem, with Thielicke's notion of reflection as that which re-volves around faith, *the question of the meaning of Christology* is predicated on temporality. If we think of *the question of the meaning of Christology* as not just framing a temporal question, but also framing a temporal mean-ing, we find that Christological ideas, Christological reflection (Thielicke), and the Christological model (Schillebeeckx) are tempered by the temporal, particularly and most explicitly identified in Oscar Cullmann's *Christus und die Zeit* (1964) and Friedrich Gogarten's *Jesus Christus Wende der Welt* (1967). The temporal processes to *the question of the meaning of Christology,* when expanding upon Cullmann and Gogarten as well as expanding upon Thielicke, Boff, and Schillebeeckx, we arrive at the possibility of surmising a process to what it means to conceptualize and articulate *the question of the meaning of Christology*—that process, as such, can be explained in terms of process philosophy or, more specifically, process theology.

JOHN B. COBB JR.

The attunement of *the question of the meaning of Christology* through pro-cess theology is best exemplified by John B. Cobb Jr. in his *Christ in a Plu-ralistic Age* (1975)—the book represents lectures Cobb delivered in Winter 1972. Cobb's process theologizing, as that which lays bare Cobb's influences by Charles Hartshorne (1897–2000), and Hartshorne's own influences by Alfred N. Whitehead (1861–1947), seeks to add more nuance to his own Christological reflection of a decade earlier, where, as Cobb concedes in the preface to *Christ in a Pluralistic Age,* "I argued that Christology is possible only where the notions of God and man have been clarified."[78] Though he wishes to revise or perhaps amend that prior reflection after "the results of a long process of change within myself to which others have contributed in many ways."[79] Nevertheless, Cobb "still believe[s] that to speak to God as having become incarnated in a human being presupposes that we know

78. Cobb, *Christ in a Pluralistic Age,* 13.
79. Cobb, *Christ in a Pluralistic Age,* 13.

something of what we mean by the term 'God' and 'human being'"—this, in itself, points to the very "pre-critical lines" and "sets *a priori* limits to meaningful possibilities" that Schillebeeckx warns us about.

Even so, Cobb is able to position himself in a *posteriori* way, comporting himself to a Christological reflection on his previous publications, *A Christian Natural Theology* (1965), *The Structure of Christian Existence* (1967), and *God and the World* (1969) that allows him to conclude that "most of the time I was writing those books, the Christology I envisioned was little more than a Jesusology."[80] Cobb furthers this reflection by explaining that "the questions I had in mind were how God could be affirmed to have been incarnate in Jesus and how this historical figure is present and effective in our world."[81] What Cobb recognizes in this is a set of pre-critical lines, undoubtedly shaping how Cobb unknowingly continued to set "*a priori* limits to meaningful possibilities" of Cobb's understanding of *the question of the meaning of Christology*.

Following this, Cobb rather summarily concedes, "I thought that Christology could be largely worked out without relation to hope for the future."[82] This, too, just as Cobb seemingly suggests, offers more than a pre-critical question based on limited meaning of Christology—it is the sense that "hope for the future" grounds Christological thinking and projects one's Christological reflection. Similarly, it is how one works out how one establishes an individual, existentialized "hope for the future" that *the question of the meaning of Christology* discloses itself, particularly if Cobb's interest is to attend meaningfully and limitlessly to *the question of the meaning of Christology*. Indeed, it is Cobb's recognition of what arises through the "hope for the future" that construes more authentically what arises *posteriori* and what can be meant by "Christ" in a Christological reflection of pluralistic possibilities. Accordingly, Cobb tells us:

> The thesis of [*Christ in a Pluralistic Age*] is that Christ is no more bound to any particular system of religious belief and practice than is the creative power of art to any particular style, and the preliminary thesis [. . .] is that Christ himself is the creative power of art.[83]

Note that Cobb uses the phrase "the creative power of art" twice. The first time, of course, is with respect to Cobb's understanding that Christ—and

---

80. Cobb, *Christ in a Pluralistic Age*, 13.
81. Cobb, *Christ in a Pluralistic Age*, 13.
82. Cobb, *Christ in a Pluralistic Age*, 13–14.
83. Cobb, *Christ in a Pluralistic Age*, 33.

shall we add to this: Christology, and *the question of the meaning of Christology* itself—is not "bound to any particular system of religious belief." Where "the creative power of art" works in this is in its boundless aspect—similarly, for Cobb, *the question of the meaning of Christology* is boundless, not just in terms of the posing of the question to Christology, but also in terms of the seeking of the meaningfulness of Christology. In both cases, in construing the boundlessness of the question of the meaning of Christology, Cobb envisions what that boundlessness is and how it discloses itself through the fact that "the creative power of art" remains in a state of boundlessness "to any particular style."

Just as Cobb's approach to *the question of the meaning of Christology* is a "particular style," we know that, generally speaking, what it means to do Christology itself is not bound "to any particular style." This is evidenced by the trajectory of the development of *the question of the meaning of Christology* from Bultmann to Käsemann and from Käsemann to a series of Bultmannians throughout the 1950s and 1960s—Cobb comes to the ongoing conversation recognizing that what has developed up to Cobb's time has situated itself through "the creative power of art." This is only in part about Cobb's understanding of what *the question of the meaning of Christology* has been in its antecedence, but also what *the question of the meaning of Christology* can become, if we view Cobb's interest in setting a precedence, which grounds the second instance Cobb uses the phrase "the creative power of art."

As much as "the creative power of art" figures into the overall thesis of Cobb's *Christ in a Pluralistic Age*, there is an abiding Christological reflection to Cobb's use of the phrase, as that which is fundamental to Cobb's Christological thinking. This reflection and this thinking leads Cobb to present, as his guiding "preliminary thesis," the guiding proposition that "Christ himself is the creative power of art." It behooves us to parse this phrase, if our intent is to understand what the phrases means to Cobb's conception of the question of the meaning of Christology and how, in turn, the phrase fundamentally undergirds Cobb's Christological reflection and Christological thinking.

It will prove to be important for us to think through not just the meaning of "the creative power of art," but also the implications the phrases serve on how Cobb poses the question to and seeks the meaningfulness of Christology. Allow me to first ask a series of questions: generally speaking, what exactly does Cobb mean by this phrase? If it is parsed, what exactly does Cobb mean by "creative," by "power," and "of art"? What does any of this mean to theologizing? More specifically, what does any of it mean to how

Cobb positions himself Christologically in the mid-1970s, such that he arrives at the sentiment: "Christ himself is the creative power of art."

In asking these situational questions, we are, in effect, existentializing "Christ himself is the creative power of art." It seems to me that such an existentializing requires broadening our lenses beyond Cobb just a bit. That is to say, if we add a broader foundation to what Cobb is concerned with in the notion that "Christ himself is the creative power of art," we can, perhaps, acknowledge a purview to Cobb's Christological reflection and Christological thinking, which exists unsaid at the core of Cobb's approach to *the question of the meaning of Christology*. Indeed, though certainly not in the purview of how Cobb works out and works through Christology, I submit two thinkers to how I wish to construct Cobb's purview: the French philosopher, Gilles Deleuze (1925–95) and the Russian philosopher, Nicolai Berdyeav (1874–1948).

Let us consider Deleuze first, with respect to what is at stake in Cobb's notion that "Christ himself is the creative power of art." What helps us understand Cobb on this point is the degree that what Cobb constructs between "Christ himself" and "the creative power of art" is what Deleuze refers to as an "immanent event,"[84] as Deleuze argues in *Pure Immanence: Essays on a Life* (2001)—in it, Deleuze describes an "immanent event" as that which allows for the actualization "in a state of things" through the actualization of those "that make [the event] happen."[85] Insofar as Cobb's "Christ himself is the creative power of art" is an immanent event, this is made possible, Deleuze tells us, across a "plane of immanence [that] is itself actualized in an object and a subject to which it attributes itself."[86] Whether we view "Christ himself" as either the object or the subject—and, similarly, make "the creative power of art" as either the object or the subject—this of little consequence and needs no explicit specificity. This is because, as Deleuze explains, "however inseparable an object and a subject may be from their actualization, the plane of immanence is itself virtual, so long as the events that populate it are virtualities."[87] In this sense, when Cobb construes "Christ himself is the creative power of art," he does so across a "plane of immanence," such that the manner that *the question of the meaning of Christology* is laid bare, for Cobb, is as one of many "virtualities"—perhaps, we can go so far as to say that one's Christological reflection and one's

---

84. Deleuze, *Immanence*, 31.

85. Deleuze, *Immanence*, 31.

86. Deleuze, *Immanence*, 31.

87. Deleuze, *Immanence*, 31.

Christological thinking become, also, to Deleuze's point, "the events that populate" the immanent event as "virtualities."

In light of what has been disclosed about Deleuze, "the immanent event," "the plane of immanence," and the nature of "virtualities," Cobb's notion of "Christ himself is the creative power of art" can be further contextualized—let us consider, now, Berdyaev. In particular, let us call our attention to Berdyaev's *The Meaning of the Creative Act* (1955)—as the title prompts us, Berdyaev will allow us to connect Deleuze to Cobb, by existentialize Cobb's notion of "Christ himself is the creative power of art" along the lines of what Berdyaev calls a "creative act." For Berdyaev, the meaning behind the "creative act" is: "the creative act of knowledge [as] an act of loving choice, selecting the one good from among an evil multiplicity."[88] Insofar as Christological reflection and Christological thinking is, in itself, a "creative act of knowledge," when ascertaining the extent that "Christ himself is the creative power of art," what is accomplished arises, as Berdyaev tells us, from "an act of loving choice." To say, then, that "Christ himself is the creative power of art" means we are "selecting the one good from among an evil multiplicity," as that which becomes the immanent event of *the question of the meaning of Christology*—to Deleuze's point, this is grounded on the extent that "the events that populate [the immanent event] are virtualities." In this way, it stands to reason, Berdyaev concludes, that:

> The creative act always presupposes self-being, independence and freedom of personality, which is unknown to the pantheistic consciousness [. . .] the creative act presupposes a mono-pluralism, that is the existence of a multitude of free and independent beings; in other words, a concrete all-oneness.[89]

If Berdyaev's conception of "the creative act" can be viewed in terms of Cobb's notion of "Christ himself is the creative power of art," we find a clear analogy between the two, even if Berdyaev is not speaking about Christology, and Cobb does not explicit refer to his notion as a "creative act." Yet, we see that Cobb is implicitly thinking Christologically about a "creative act" that occurs when "Christ himself is the creative power of art," such that, across a "plane of immanence," what we know as "Christ himself" and what we know as "the creative power of art" make each other understandable.

Given that Berdyaev finds "the very desire to make the creative act understandable, to find a basis for it, is failure to comprehend it,"[90] and this

---

88. Berdyaev, *Meaning of the Creative Act*, 46.

89. Berdyaev, *Meaning of the Creative Act*, 133.

90. Berdyaev, *Meaning of the Creative Act*, 145.

certainly directly speaks to what Cobb is working through and working out Christologically, we encounter a complication in the connection between Berdyaev and Cobb on the matter of "the creative act." Even though Berdyaev provides something of a disclaimer with assertion that "to comprehend the creative act means to recognize that it is inexplicable and without foundation,"[91] Cobb contradicts this, suggesting that, in the relationship between "the creative act" and "Christ himself is the creative power of art," Christological reflection and Christological thinking incorporate a Christological "power of art" that makes "the creative act," for Cobb, all the more explicable and with a foundation. This is, indeed, essential to Cobb's approach to *the question of the meaning of Christology*, which grounds and is grounded by Cobb's notion of "Christ himself is the creative power of art," insofar as how we pose the question to and seek the meaningfulness of Christology allows, as Cobb makes explicit in *Process Theology: An Introductory Exposition* (1976) the meaning of "Christ himself" to make a way for "creative transformation."[92]

JOHN DOMINIC CROSSAN

Though it is certainly not at all difficult to see that *the question of the meaning of Christology* is what modestly ties Cobb to John Dominic Crossan, insofar as that connection, for both, is concerned with the posing of the question to and the seeking of the meaningfulness of Christology, the transition from discussing Cobb's process theologizing of *the question of the meaning of Christology*, I admit, could not be farther from the theologizing in which Crossan engages. We can think of the difference not only in terms of Cobb's work in the 1970s and Crossan's appearing in the 1990s, but also in terms of the theological lineages Cobb and Crossan respectively have—with Cobb, as an American, hailing from, as it has been noted, Hartshorne and influenced by Whitehead—with Crossan, a former Irish Catholic priest.

Even with the common thread of *the question of the meaning of Christology* firmly in mind, what also makes this shift from Cobb to Crossan

91. Berdyaev, *Meaning of the Creative Act*, 145.

92. This is key to a chapter devoted to Jesus Christ and the way that Christology unfolds through Cobb's understanding of process theology. Though the text itself, *Process Theology*, is co-authored by John B. Cobb Jr. and David R. Griffin, we are informed in the forward to the book that book's chapter focusing on Jesus Christ was among the chapters originally written by Cobb, with Griffin revising Cobb's chapters, just as Cobb revises the chapters Griffin originally writes. In addressing the relationship between Christology and process theology, Cobb is careful to term this as "process Christology." Cobb and Griffin, *Process Theology*, 95–106.

especially jarring, I admit, is Crossan's participation in the Jesus Seminar, founded in 1985 by Robert W. Funk (1926–2005)—while Cobb was not associated with the Jesus Seminar, Crossan can be viewed, more so than Cobb, as a direct contributor to what has arisen as though convening a collection of 150 laymen and scholars to provide a consensus agreement on the historicity of the historical Jesus in terms of the saying and deeds of Jesus of Nazareth, the Jesus Seminar hoped to attend to two frustrations with Life-of-Jesus research, which Robert J. Miller describes in *The Jesus Seminar and Its Critics* (1999) as: first, a lack of the disclosure of "the full range of evidence on which [numerous studies of the historical Jesus] are based,"[93] and secondly, "the failure of biblical scholars to educate the public about the historical Jesus."[94] Because of Crossan's participation in the efforts of the Jesus Seminar and the relative prominence with which Crossan had in it, Crossan is also at the forefront of what has come to the described as a "third quest" for the historical Jesus. As much as Crossan is important to this "third quest," just as Miller notes, there are critics that, though suspicious of the findings of the Jesus Seminar,[95] provide contributions that counter the Jesus Seminar and continue to cast *the question of the meaning of Christology* beyond the parameters of the earlier "quest" initiated by Käsemann—notable among the critics of the Jesus Seminar are: Craig A. Evans[96] and Carl E. Braaten (both of which, as I have detailed in earlier chapters, have played important roles in the development and documentation of Life-of-Jesus research), Darrell L. Bock,[97] and the contemporane-

---

93. Miller, *Jesus Seminar and Its Critics*, 10.

94. Miller, *Jesus Seminar and Its Critics*, 11.

95. Miller, *Jesus Seminar and Its Critics*, 65–77.

96. Craig A. Evans provides a fairly straightforward but still scathing indictment of the Jesus Seminar in "Fabricating Jesus: How Modern Scholars Distort the Gospels" (2006).

97. In *Studying the Historical Jesus: A Guide to Sources and Methods* (2002), Bock, coincidently, does not place Crossan within the third quest. Instead, and rather curiously, Bock places Crossan's *The Historical Jesus* within a list of works associated with the second quest. That list has one other work: Bornkamm's *Jesus of Nazareth*. Needless to say, Bock belongs to a minority opinion with how his classifies Crossan and, accordingly, Bock classifies Funk and the Jesus Seminar within the scope of the second quest as well. Because of this, the dividing line Bock places between the concerns of the "second quest" and those of the "third quest" is questionable and remains in disagreement with many other classifications of the two found in Life-of-Jesus scholarship dating back, perhaps, to at least the 1980s and 1990s.

ously published work of Luke T. Johnson,[98] Ben Witherington,[99] and N. T. Wright[100] (with Witherington and Wright, in particular, being discussed later, as counterpoints to Crossan).

Ascribing Crossan to the conception of a "third quest" and the extent to which Crossan remains concerned, I submit, with *the question of the meaning of Christology*, it will require giving an account of Crossan's significance theologically and Christologically. Let us first consider how the Theissen and Merz co-authored *The Historical Jesus* (1996)—in it, we are told that the "third quest," as such, "has split into different trends," with two referenced. The "trend" to which Crossan belongs, according to Theissen and Merz, is one that is focused on:

> A return to a "non-eschatological picture of Jesus" in which Jesus becomes the advocate of a paradoxical existential wisdom influenced by Cynicism—a "Jewish cynic" who, shaped by Hellenistic influences, moves to the periphery of Judaism.[101]

Theissen and Merz place Crossan as one of two leaders in this trend.[102] Witherington concurs with this characterization of Crossan's contribution to a "third quest," but expands the cast of voices much further than Theissen and Merz—for Witherington, Crossan's sense of Jesus as a cynic is one of eight trendlines, all under what Witherington refers to as a "third quest."

Still, in agreement with Theissen and Merz, Witherington views the strain of Christological thinking to which Crossan belongs is "one of the most distinctive and publicized portraits of Jesus [as] that of a type of wandering Cynic preacher."[103] Though Witherington places Crossan alongside two others aligning with this vein of thinking, Witherington maintains that Crossan's "work has made the largest impact and has the most to commend it."[104] Even so, Witherington tells us that this Crossan-led approach to the historical Jesus "ignores major portions of the Jesus tradition, especially the material in Mark, and in the end produces an essentially

---

98. Luke Timothy Johnson's main critique of the Jesus Seminar can be found in the explicitly-titled, *The Real Jesus: The Misguided Quest for the Historical Jesus and the Truth of the Traditional Gospels* (1996).

99. Ben Witherington's characterization of and problems with the Jesus Seminar can be found in *The Jesus Quest: The Third Quest for the Jew of Nazareth* (1995).

100. N. T. Wright's discussion of the Jesus Seminar can be found in *Jesus and the Victory of God* (1996).

101. Theissen and Merz, *The Historical Jesus*, 11.

102. The other is Burton L. Mack.

103. Witherington, *Jesus Quest*, 58.

104. Witherington, *Jesus Quest*, 58.

non-Jewish Jesus."[105] The reason for this, Witherington suggests, is partly "due to the methodological flaw of only dealing with material that is attested in more than one source, which leaves out an enormous amount of the Jesus material."[106] As careful as Witherington is with respect to how he characterizes Crossan's "historical Jesus," Witherington not only views the Jesus that Crossan depicts as "a wandering Cynic pundit,"[107] but he also considers Crossan's most important work, *The Historical Jesus: The Life of a Mediterranean Jewish Peasant* (1991) a "rather pretentiously titled book."[108]

However, given certain ideological proclivities towards Crossan, in *Jesus in Contemporary Scholarship* (1994), Marcus J. Borg[109] characterizes Crossan in a very different manner, believing that *The Historical Jesus* "could be the most important book on the historical Jesus since Albert Schweitzer's *Quest of the Historical Jesus* at the beginning of this century, both because of its brilliance, elegance, and freshness, and because of its likely effect on the discipline."[110] Borg incorporates Crossan's portrait of Jesus as a culmination of portraits, as well as a culmination of Jesus scholarship in the 1980s, which set the stage for what Borg presents as contemporary Jesus research and the issues inherent in it. For Borg, because Crossan is a significant voice that grounds and projects Borg's sense of "contemporary Jesus scholarship" by 1994—keeping in mind that Crossan's *The Historical Jesus* first appears only three years earlier—when speaking to the "picture of Jesus [that] emerges in Crossan's book,"[111] Borg encapsulates Crossan's Christological thinking to a single, fundamental proposition: "Jesus was a Jewish Cynic peasant with an alternative social vision."[112]

Insofar as Crossan's handling of the historical Jesus—as the perennial problem of the 1950s and 1960s—is tempered by Crossan's Christological thinking and from an undergirding Christological reflection, Crossan explains, at the outset of the prologue to *The Historical Jesus*, how he comports his thinking and reflection Christologically in the following way:

105. Witherington, *Jesus Quest*, 58.

106. Witherington, *Jesus Quest*, 58.

107. Witherington, *Jesus Quest*, 58.

108. Witherington, *Jesus Quest*, 58.

109. Like Crossan, Borg was a participant in the Jesus Seminar, producing one of the many publications presenting findings and conclusions off the work conducted in the Jesus Seminar: Borg's *Meeting Jesus Again for the First Time: The Historical Jesus and the Heart of Contemporary Faith* (1995).

110. Borg, *Jesus in Contemporary Scholarship*, 33.

111. Borg, *Jesus in Contemporary Scholarship*, 33.

112. Borg, *Jesus in Contemporary Scholarship*, 34.

> Historical Jesus research is becoming something of a scholarly bad joke. There were always historians who said it could not be done because of historical problems. There were always theologians who said it should not be done because of theological objections. And there were always scholars who said the former when they meant the latter. Those, however, were negative indignities. What is happening now is rather a positive one. It is the number of competent and even eminent scholars producing pictures of Jesus at wide variance with one another.[113]

Because of this, Crossan intends to pay attention to methodology, if we can say, then, that this methodology hopes to provide the parameters of Crossan's Christological thinking and his Christological reflection in how he comports himself to the state of search into the historical Jesus by 1991, with the intent on methodologically framing Crossan's approach to *the question of the meaning of Christology.*

On this point, Crossan contends that "methodology in Jesus research at the end of this century is about where methodology in archaeological research was at the end of the last."[114] Under these conditions, Crossan tells us that his "methodology for Jesus research has a triple triadic process: the campaign, the strategy, and the tactics, as it were," attending to the contextual levels of "cross-cultural and cross-temporal social anthropology," history, and literature.[115] For Crossan, "all three levels, anthropological, historical, and literary, must cooperate fully and equally for an effective synthesis."[116] What follows this is the second triad of "inventory," "stratification," and "attestation,"[117] which, in turn, lends itself to the third triad of "sequence of strata," "hierarchy of attestation," and "bracketing of singularity."[118]

Taken together, Crossan's methodology calibrates, I submit, how he wishes to pose the question to and how he wishes to seek the meaningfulness of Christology—this is accomplished, to be sure, by way of Crossan's own Christological thinking that informs and is informed by his own Christological reflection. To this end, Crossan's methodology is comprised of constituent pieces that comport Crossan to *the question of the meaning of Christology.* Crossan views this constituent pieces as follows:

113. Crossan, *Historical Jesus,* xxvii.

114. Crossan, *Historical Jesus,* xxviii.

115. Crossan, *Historical Jesus,* xxviii.

116. Crossan, *Historical Jesus,* xxviii–xxix

117. Crossan, *Historical Jesus,* xxxi.

118. Crossan, *Historical Jesus,* xxxii.

They are, of course, only *formal* moves, which then demand a *material* investment. Different scholars might invest those formal moves with widely divergent sources and texts, but historical Jesus research would at least have some common methodology instead of a rush to conclusion that could then be only accepted or denied.[119]

This point is essential to understanding what is at stake for Crossan, which ultimately hinges on, as Crossan writes in *Jesus: A Revolutionary Biography* (1994), the fact that the gospels are "interpretations."[120] Crossan goes on to say: "hence, of course, despite there being only one Jesus, there can be more than one gospel, more than one interpretation."[121] Here, Crossan eventually arrives at the following question, which, I submit, becomes the fullest representation of what *the question of the meaning of Christology* means to him:

> But what if you wanted to move behind the screen of credal interpretation and, without in any way denying or negating the validity of faith, give an accurate but impartial account of the historical Jesus as distinct from the confessional Christ?[122]

Crossan provides the following answer:

> That is what the academic or scholarly study of the historical Jesus is about, at least when it is not a disguise for doing theology and calling it history, doing autobiography and calling it biography, doing Christian apologetics and calling it academic scholarship. Put another way, no matter how fascinating result and conclusion may be, they are only as good as the theory and method on which they are based.[123]

We can note that this answer speaks to methodology, as that which Crossan casts *The Historical Jesus*. This methodology, as it is condensed and re-articulated in *Jesus*, is a "method [that] locates the historical Jesus where three independent vectors cross [. . .] like three giant searchlights coming together on a single object in the night sky," as, put more simply: "cross-cultural anthropology," "Greco-Roman and especially Jewish history," and "the literary or textual."[124]

---

119. Crossan, *Historical Jesus*, xxxiv.

120. Crossan, *Jesus*, xiv.

121. Crossan, *Jesus*, xiv.

122. Crossan, *Jesus*, xv.

123. Crossan, *Jesus*, xv.

124. Crossan, *Jesus*, xvi–xvii.

N. T. WRIGHT

If we are still attending carefully to *the question of the meaning of Christology*, how we can situate N. T. Wright to the posing of the question to and the seeking of the meaningfulness of Christology is by fundamentally situating Wright against Crossan's Christological thinking and Christological reflection. A good place to begin Wright-Crossan relations, I submit, is to first consider Wright's *The Challenge of Jesus: Rediscovering Who Jesus Was and Is* (1999). Just by the title alone, we can clearly see how Wright positions himself in relation to the perennial question of the historical Jesus, particularly if we characterize that positioning as firmly grounded in the concerns of the "third quest"[125]—while Crossan belongs to the third quest as well, how Crossan considers and discovers the historical Jesus becomes something, I argue, Wright wishes to reconsider and rediscover. As a Third Quester, concerned with the trajectory of the problem of the historical Jesus beyond that which has come to be understood, now, as the second quest—the likes of Käsemann, Bornkamm, assorted Bultmannians—Wright's confrontation with Crossan is, at the same time, a confrontation with the Jesus Seminar itself. As an opponent of the Jesus Seminar, Wright's concern with getting the problem of the historical Jesus "right."[126] Wright suggests that:

> When we get this right, we avoid at a stroke some of the extraordinary reductionism that has characterized the so-called Jesus Seminar, with its attempt to rule out the authenticity of most Jesus-stories on the grounds that people would only have remembered isolated sayings, not complete stories.[127]

Here, we find Wright's criticism of the Jesus Seminar in terms of its "reductionism"—we can infer from this that such a reductionism, for Wright, does not get the historical Jesus "right." This sort of critique of the Jesus Seminar, in Wright's footnote, is directed chiefly at what he calls "the Jesus Seminar's flagship product, *The Five Gospels*," which was published in 1993.[128] Though a more direct critique of this "flagship product" can be found, as Wright footnotes, in Wright's "Five Gospels but No Gospel: Jesus and the Seminar" (1999), we can view *The Challenge of Jesus* as an extended companion piece,

---

125. "The third quest" as it is characterized by Ben Witherington's *The Jesus Quest* (1997) and the Gerd Theissen and Annette Merz co-authored, *The Historical Jesus* (1998).

126. Wright, *Challenge of Jesus*, 26.

127. Wright, *Challenge of Jesus*, 26.

128. Wright, *Challenge of Jesus*, 198.

which certainly recognizes Crossan's prominent role in the Jesus Seminar and the presentation of its "flagship product."

While Wright's critique of the Jesus Seminar can be seen as fairly obvious and explicit, Wright's critique of Crossan himself is more subtle. Speaking of Crossan without mentioning Crossan by name, Wright makes the following assessment:

> There are those who see the peasant culture of ancient Mediterranean society as the dominant influence in the Galilee of Jesus' day, with the Jewish apocalyptic coloring decidedly muted; so that Jesus' announcement of the kingdom has less to do with specifically Jewish aspirations and more to do with the kind of social protest that might arise in any culture.[129]

Though Wright does not mention one of the most important terms in Crossan's characterization of the historical Jesus, which is "Cynic," Wright does inform us, in a footnote, that "I have in mind, among other writers, John Dominic Crossan" and Crossan's *The Historical Jesus*.[130]

> Let me stress *both* that this is a mistake *and* that showing it to be so does not lessen the element of social protest that is still to be found within the much wider-ranging and more theologically grounded kingdom-announcement that we can properly attribute to Jesus.[131]

The fact that Wright views Crossan's characterization of Jesus as a "mistake" should not be surprising, remembering Wright's belief that the Jesus Seminar engaged in "reductionism."

Yet, given Wright's substantive theological disagreements with the findings of the Jesus Seminar, Wright has maintained working relationships with Marcus Borg—as a prominent member of the Jesus Seminar and a frequent collaborator with Crossan, Borg and Wright collaborated on a text, *The Meaning of Jesus: Two Visions* (1999), in which the two discussed their theological differences. Similarly, Wright and Crossan have a collaborative relationship, despite their theological differences, which has been brought to bear by a text, *The Resurrection of Jesus* (2005), which includes a dialogue between Wright and Crossan on their difference of opinion on the resurrection as either a historical event or a theological explanation.[132] Even so, as is the case in Wright-Borg relations and Wright-Crossan relations, the

129. Wright, *Challenge of Jesus*, 26.

130. Wright, *Challenge of Jesus*, 198.

131. Wright, *Challenge of Jesus*, 26.

132. Wright and Crossan, *Resurrection of Jesus*, 16–47.

dialogues Wright respectively holds with both are Christological in nature, in terms of differences in Christological reflection and contrasting Christological thinking grounded in how *the question of the meaning of Christology discloses itself.*

What must be made explicit is that Wright, like Borg and Crossan, belong to what has now been referred to as the third quest, if we note how Wright is classified in Witherington's *The Jesus Quest*,[133] where Wright is categorized in terms of "Jesus and the reconstitution of Israel."[134] Witherington notes that "Wright's portrait of the historical Jesus is not yet finished."[135] Insofar as Wright "is another example of a work in progress, and it must be evaluated accordingly,"[136] with other key figures writing contemporaneously to Witherington, we see Witherington discuss two of Wright's works, *Who Was Jesus?* (1992) and *The New Testament and the People of God* (1996). With respect to the former, which is "written for a popular audience"[137]—as is *The Challenge of Jesus*—Witherington acknowledges that it provides "the program [Wright] is following in his multivolume work that has only begun to take shape."[138] At the time of Witherington taking note of this, which is circa 1997, the other volumes published since are out of Witherington's purview—because of this, Witherington is unable to see the complete picture of Wright's conceptualization of the historical Jesus. Nevertheless, Witherington gives the following impression of *The New Testament and the People of God*:

> Wright does not in fact directly discuss at any length the historical Jesus but deals with introductory issues such as the character and beliefs of early Judaism and the early church, the nature of ancient literature (especially biographies), the problems of studying ancient historical figures and the limits and possibilities of what we can know about them.[139]

Witherington's handling of what is essentially a first volume of a series of volumes that will collectively represent Wright's portrait of Jesus is fair. This is especially fair, of course, since Wright's second volume, *Jesus and the Victory of God* (1996) appeared in the year between the original publication of Witherington's *The Jesus Quest* and the revised edition. Though it is notable

---

133. It is notable that Wright is not included with the handful of "Third Questers" addressed in the Theissen and Merz co-authored, *The Historical Jesus*.

134. Witherington, *Jesus Quest*, 219–32.

135. Witherington, *Jesus Quest*, 219.

136. Witherington, *Jesus Quest*, 219.

137. Witherington, *Jesus Quest*, 219.

138. Witherington, *Jesus Quest*, 219.

139. Witherington, *Jesus Quest*, 219.

that, in the revised edition, Witherington cites Wright's *Jesus and the Victory of God* in the bibliography of *The Jesus Quest*, there remains, understandably, no direct reference to Wright's second volume. Commendably, Witherington frequently works through *The New Testament and the People of God*—indeed, this allows Witherington to provide the most up-to-date illustration of Wright's historical Jesus, even if it is largely based on the deeply contextual work Wright provides in *The New Testament and the People of God*.

Very early in *Jesus and the Victory of God*, Wright makes an assessment of the usefulness of the previous quests of the historical Jesus, first considering "Jesus through History,"[140] secondly, "The Rise of the Critical Movement" in the period from Reimarus to Schweitzer,[141] and, thirdly, "No Quest to New Quest" which briefly charts a period from Schweitzer to Schillebeeckx.[142] While it is certainly understandable that, as Wright notes in the "Jesus through History" section, that the "quest," as it were, begins before Reimarus, Wright wishes to situate this pre-Reimarus period in "the work and the theological position of the sixteenth-century reformers."[143] Though the section marked as "The Rise of the Critical Movement" works through how the approach to the historical Jesus culminates with Schweitzer, the highly-condensed section, "No Quest to New Quest," with a beginning marker of Schweitzer and an ending marker of Schillebeeckx is an interesting distillation of a large variety of voices, approaches, and interests in the historical Jesus from 1906 (with the original appearance of Schweitzer's *The Quest of the Historical Jesus*) to 1974 (with the original appearance of Schillebeeckx's *Jesus*). These markers are interesting, since, between them, Wright very briefly discusses Bultmann,[144] Käsemann,[145] and Bornkamm,[146] and manages to condense "the new quest" into its "main productions," which Wright believes are "of little value."[147]

With respect to this opinion—with which I disagree—within a rather short section entitled "Two Hundred Years of Questing," Wright asks an important and fundamental question: "what did the Quest achieve in the two hundred years between Reimarus and Schillebeeckx?"[148] This is an impor-

---

140. Wright, *Jesus and the Victory of God*, 13–16.

141. Wright, *Jesus and the Victory of God*, 16–21.

142. Wright, *Jesus and the Victory of God*, 21–25.

143. Wright, *Jesus and the Victory of God*, 13.

144. Wright, *Jesus and the Victory of God*, 22–23.

145. Wright, *Jesus and the Victory of God*, 23.

146. Wright, *Jesus and the Victory of God*, 24.

147. Wright, *Jesus and the Victory of God*, 24.

148. Wright, *Jesus and the Victory of God*, 25.

tant question, indeed—even if it limits itself to two contextual boundaries, it is a question that Wright is correct to ask, just the same. Wright answers it thusly: "it put the historical question firmly and irrevocably on the theological map, but without providing a definite answer to it."[149]

In Wright's answer, we should take care to note that, for Wright, what the Quest achieved, at its most fundamental manifestation, is that it placed "the historical question" in view, in such a way that allowed that question—what is invariably *the question of the meaning of Christology*—"firmly and irrevocably on the theological map." This speaks to the significance of "the historical question," if, as Wright suggests, "the historical question" manifests itself "without providing a definite answer to it." Yet, if we are truly concerned with *the question of the meaning of Christology*, as that which is a "historical question," that concern must not be allowed to have "a definite answer to it." The extent to which, if we follow Wright, we wish for "the historical question" to "provid[e] a definite answer," we do so at the concealment of "the historical question" itself and at the very peril of the meaningfulness of Christology itself—indeed, "a definite answer," as it were, only makes *the question of the meaning of Christology* all the more concealed, narrow, and void of its meaningfulness. This is because, I submit, "the historical question" is historical, and its historicity speaks to the various ways that the question has been posed from Reimarus to Schweitzer, and all points in between—it is because there is no way to a pose "the historical question," and because "the historical question" does not belong to any single moment in time. Insofar as, to Wright's point, one wishes for "definite answer" to the perennial "historical question," the historical aspect to the answer and the answer itself becomes immediately undermined, until *the question of the meaning of Christology* loses its existentializing elasticity.

All told, it is only through the continued significance and evolution of *the question of the meaning of Christology* that the following from Wright holds true:

> Looking simply, for now, at the period between Schweitzer and Schillebeeckx, we find many notable works in the field of systematic theology, and particularly Christology. All of them have made use, to a lesser or greater extent, of the figure of Jesus.[150]

Here, we see a contradiction in Wright's argument about "the main productions of the New Quest" having "little value." Though subtle, it must be pointed out. In particular, if, as Wright admits, there are "many notable

---

149. Wright, *Jesus and the Victory of God*, 25.
150. Wright, *Jesus and the Victory of God*, 25.

works [. . .] particularly Christology," this is laid bare by the fact that *the question of the meaning of Christology* does not have "a definite answer to it." For Wright to even acknowledge "many notable works" that have appeared "at the period between Schweitzer and Schillebeeckx" means he is acknowledging the various iteration of "the quest," such that *the question of the meaning of Christology* was broad enough to be approached in a multitude of ways, from post-Schweitzer to pre-Schillebeeckx. In effect, the fact that all these voices in between, to Wright's point, "have made use, to a lesser or greater extent, of the figure of Jesus," it speaks to the varied ways one can pose the question to Christology and, in turn, the varied ways one can seek the meaningfulness of Christology—these variations, I submit, must not be minimized any more than they should be marginalized.

Nevertheless, with the intent of defining and situating a post-Schillebeeckx conception of a third quest—which Wright spends much more time developing contextually than he does "the period between Schweitzer and Schillebeeckx"—Wright comes to the following conclusion:

> Two hundred years, then—surveyed swiftly here, because the story has been told so often—have demonstrated that the Quest is vital, but difficult. The sources are no less tricky to use now than they were at the start. The questions are no less pressing.[151]

Even if "the story has been told so often," the vitality of "the Quest," as Wright terms it, rests, ultimately, on the various voices that emerged in "the period between Schweitzer and Schillebeeckx." Because of this, "the story" cannot be told enough nor too often, lest the stories of Käsemann and Bornkamm—which Wright names—become overshadowed by Wright's prescribed bookends of Schweitzer and Schillebeeckx.

As "vital" as the ongoing "Quest" is, Wright is correct to see in that vitality a difficulty, and what makes it "difficult" is the complexity of *the question of the meaning of Christology*, insofar as this complexity and difficulty arise from an inherent and lasting value in what Wright recognizes as "the main productions of the New Quest." Even if we can say, of course, that these "main productions," which Wright views as "sources" marking numerous periods between Schweitzer to Schillebeeckx, are just as "tricky to use now than they were at the start," the perennial question of the meaning of Christology remains pivotal—the fact that there are so many variations of posing the question to and so many ways of seeking the meaningfulness of Christology is particularly why, as Wright tells us, "the questions are no less pressing."

---

151. Wright, *Jesus and the Victory of God*, 27.

BEN WITHERINGTON

The extent that there is a modern articulation to *the question of the meaning of Christology* can be marked by the acknowledgement and announcement of a "third quest" for the historical Jesus. The task and method of the "third quest," as it has come to be called, shares the conceptual and methodological concerns of what is now known as the "first quest" which was brought to an end by Schweitzer in 1906 and those of the "second quest" initiated Käsemann in the 1950s—the difference, however, is that, at the core of this very modern (even postmodern) "third quest," are new approaches, conceptualizations, and methodologies that set apart the modern direction that the "third quest" orients itself, as that which materializes over and against what arose in the two earlier quests. Insofar as all quests are concerned with how to approach and answer *the question of the meaning of Christology*, Witherington characterizes, in *The Christology of Jesus* (1990), what can be referred to as the Christological quest in the following way:

> Since the beginning of the new quest for the historical Jesus in the 1950s, both exegetes and theologians have been preoccupied with Christologies in and of the New Testament—the Gospels, Paul, Q, or other sources. Some have sought to isolate the Christologies of individual communities, even though there is little evidence that any community had a pure form of Christology as characterized by the use of one title or type of thinking or preaching. Exploring the Christologies of the New Testament is important, but doing this in place of a Christology of Jesus is a fundamental mistake.[152]

The point that Witherington is making here is with respect to *the question of the meaning of Christology* as something that is fundamentally cast by New Testament theologizing, but something that must also be fundamentally cast by theologizing Jesus, in terms of Christological themes, Christological experience, and Christological reflection. Though Boff, Thielicke, Schillebeeckx, and Cobb (and other like-minded theologians, thinkers, and scholars of the 1970s) all consider how Christology thematically informs our experience of Christology (individually and communally) and this, in turn, provides various possibilities for reflection on Christology, the manner with which *the question of the meaning of Christology* rears itself becomes too overly dependent on, as Witherington suggests, the exploration of "Christologies of the New Testament," to the de-emphasis of "a Christology of Jesus." For Witherington, this "is a fundamental mistake," particularly if a

---

152. Witherington, *Christology of Jesus*, 1.

quest—of some form or fashion—must undergird any *question of the meaning of Christology.*

With respect to the previous handlings of the understanding of *the question of the meaning of Christology* and to the varying degrees that it is predicated on the quest for the historical Jesus, as what plays out through Christological reflection, Witherington finds:

> In the vast majority of recent studies of Jesus there seemingly has been so much specialization, and so many attempts to rule the majority of available data out of bounds from the outset, that any progress in the discussion of Jesus and Christology has been rendered virtually impossible due to a too abrupt methodological foreclosing of the field of focus.[153]

What Witherington highlights as inherent problems in "recent studies of Jesus" is the issue with pre-critical lines, as similarly acknowledged by Schillebeeckx. The extent that "the majority of available data [is ruled] out of bounds from the outset," Witherington writes, equally speaks to Schillebeeckx's notion of "set[ting] *a priori* limits to meaningful possibilities." If the logic, here, is, to Schillebeeckx's credit, to ground Christological possibilities in "the Christian experience," doing otherwise, to Witherington's point, restricts "the discussion of Jesus and Christology" to the point that this discussion is "rendered virtually impossible due to a too abrupt methodological foreclosing of the field of focus." Our "field of focus," I submit, is *the question of the meaning of Christology,* as that which is fundamentally negotiated and adjudicated through "[a] discussion of Jesus and Christology," optimized and existentialized through Christological reflection.

If we are to say, then, that Christological reflection is what promotes how we discuss Jesus and Christology and, by extension, is what advances the means by which we conceive of and articulate *the question of the meaning of Christology,* we find ourselves able to imagine the most ancient and primitive conceptualizations of Christology and Christological themes— such an imagining, when rendered without pre-critical lines nor "*a priori* limits to meaningful possibilities," presents the unaffordable historicity that, as Witherington points out: "the first three evangelists were indeed interested in Christology, and the texts suggest they were also interested in Jesus' views on [C]hristological matters."[154]

Just as the three evangelists engaged in Christological reflection— those that are referred to as Synoptics—as it is thematically deployed in their respective texts, and, in doing so, to Witherington's point, sought to

153. Witherington, *Christology of Jesus,* 23.
154. Witherington, *Christology of Jesus,* 26.

thematically articulate their understanding of "Jesus' views on [C]hristo-logical matters," what remains noticeable and glaring in how Witherington conceives of *the question of the meaning of Christology* is his exclusion of the Gospel of John from that Christological conceptualization. Certainly, it is safe to say that Witherington's Christological conceptualization of the historical Jesus is, to some extent, influenced by that of the Jesus Seminar, even though Witherington remains critical of the Jesus seminar's own Christological conceptualization—we see, in Witherington's *The Jesus Quest*, a reference to Marcus Borg's *Meeting Jesus Again for the First Time* (1994) in which Borg argues, as Witherington cites himself, that "the contrast between the Synoptic and Johannine images of Jesus is so great that one of them must be nonhistorical."[155] Through Borg's sense that "both cannot be accurate characterizations of Jesus as a historical figure,"[156] we likewise find that the Jesus Seminar's Christological conceptualization of the historical Jesus, which is one that chooses to ground the historicity of the historical Jesus on the Synoptics over and against that of the Johannine tradition. For Witherington, such a decision "requires that Borg denude the Synoptics of all [C]hristologically focused passages or nuances, declaring them later accretions to the Jesus tradition."[157] From here, Witherington goes on to make the following assessment: "doubtless, the Jesus of the Jesus Seminar does not match up with the Jesus of the Fourth Gospel, but then the Jesus Seminar deliberately chose not to play with a full deck of Synoptic playing cards."[158] What we see, then, is that Witherington is not just critical of the discontinuity between the "Jesus" of the Jesus seminar and the "Jesus" disclosed in the Gospel of John, but he also just as critical of the incomplete representation of "Jesus" across the Synoptics themselves. To this end, Witherington tells us, declaratively: "yet, it must be admitted that there are *some* arguably authentic passages in the Synoptics where Jesus sounds very much like the Johannine Jesus."[159] It is to this final point, I submit, that Witherington makes his own decision about what is a meaningful Christological conceptualization, insofar as the Synoptics, rather than the Johannine tradition at large, become the best means of mining a sense of "historicity" to the historical Jesus, as that which is laid bare in Witherington's *The Christology of Jesus* as something that pre-dates *The Jesus Quest*.

---

155. Borg, *Meeting Jesus Again for the First Time*, 11.

156. Borg, *Meeting Jesus Again for the First Time*, 11.

157. Witherington, *Jesus Quest*, 103.

158. Witherington, *Jesus Quest*, 103.

159. Witherington, *Jesus Quest*, 103.

What is laid bare in *The Christology of Jesus* does not go unnoticed by J. Ramsey Michaels (1931–2020)—who authored an important commentary on the Gospel of John in 2010, as a replacement volume in the New International Commentary of the New Testament series the classic 1983 commentary on John by F. F. Bruce (1910–90)—in his 1992 review of Witherington's *The Christology of Jesus*. In one sense, while Michaels positions himself "as one heartily in agreement with Witherington's main contention," in another sense, Michaels tells us that he is "uneasy about some aspects of [Witherington's] method."[160] Michaels explains this unease in the following way:

> What I missed were his reasons for excluding as inauthentic those few passages in the Gospels which he did exclude. [. . .] Because these are the passages with the most direct bearing on the case Witherington is trying to make, it is surprising that he does not at least explain why he does not accept them as coming from Jesus.[161]

The excluded passages Michaels notes are, indeed, from the Gospel of John, which Witherington admits are excluded "because it is difficult to argue on the basis of the historical-critical method that go back to a *Sitz im Leben Jesu*."[162] Michaels directly cites Witherington on this point too—it is the idea that a Christological conceptualization, as it were, should be grounded on "a *Sitz im Leben Jesu*" which can be rendered as "a place in the life of Jesus." What it suggests is that, for Witherington's historical method and the extent that this method hopes to lay bare the historicity of the historical Jesus, Witherington's avoidance of the Gospel of John is oriented towards rendering "a place in the life of Jesus" in a way that is as authentic as possible. It is based on the idea that the Gospel of John, for Witherington—and, to a certain extent, those participating in the Jesus Seminar—makes it difficult to construct a reliable, plausible, and meaningful portrait of the historical Jesus, which authentically lends itself to and existentializes Christological thinking and Christological reflection, and, ultimately, allows one to adequately approach *the question of the meaning of Christology* itself.

CRAIG S. KEENER

Influenced by and currently belonging to the same faculty at Asbury Theological Seminary in Kentucky as Witherington, Craig S. Keener provides, I

---

160. Ramsey, "*Christology of Jesus* by Ben Witherington III," 142.

161. Ramsey, "*Christology of Jesus* by Ben Witherington III," 142.

162. Witherington, *Christology of Jesus*, 30.

submit, a fresh voice to the unfolding *question of the meaning of Christology*, with respect to Witherington, Wright, and Crossan. Suffice it to say, Keener undoubtedly belongs to the current "third quest," insofar as his approach to the historical Jesus certainly aligns with what chiefly defines the period—if we attend to the traits provided by Theissen and Merz, Keener's method is grounded on the criterion of "historical plausibility."[163]

Though Keener's body of work includes, most recently, probably the lengthiest and most comprehensive four-volume commentary on the Acts of the Apostles (2012–2015), equally comprehensive commentaries on Paul's Letter to the Galatians (2018) and the Gospel of Matthew (1999), and a two-volume commentary on the Gospels of John (2003), Keener's foray into *the question of the meaning of Christology* has a particular resonance in two works that are, I submit, companion pieces: *The Historical Jesus of the Gospels* (2009) and *Christobiography: Memory, History, and the Reliability of the Gospels* (2019). What allows these two works to stand out, especially in light of the comprehensive and exhaustive nature of Keener's work in general,[164] is that they attend to and make more declarative what Witherington brings forth in *The Christology of Jesus*. Like Witherington, Keener makes it clear in the introduction to *The Historical Jesus of the Gospels* that he has "elsewhere defended the likelihood of substantial historical information in the Fourth Gospel,"[165] and this can be found in Keener's commentary on the Gospel of John. Based on his work on that commentary, Keener tells us that *The Historical Jesus of the Gospels* will "draw on that argument very rarely here, for two reasons."[166] The first reason Keener provides is contingent on the length to which *The Historical Jesus of the Gospels* "has grown" and the extent that "readers have access to my arguments concerning John's Gospel elsewhere."[167] If we view this first reason of the literary context with which Keener perceives *The Historical Jesus of the Gospels* in relation to what he has previously argued about the Gospel of John and the resistance to

---

163. Theissen and Merz, *Historical Jesus*, 12.

164. For example, when considering *The Historical Jesus of the Gospels*, Keener's endnotes cover more than 200 pages, specifically enumerating pages 394–603 and his bibliography is more than 100 pages, enumerating pages 604–713. Similarly, *Christobiography* contains a more than 100-page bibliography paginated as pages 503–630— though *Christobiography* does not include endnotes, with the multitude of footnotes, it is possible to imagine the possibility of an endnote section just as lengthy as the one in *The Historical Jesus of the Gospels*.

165. Keener, *Historical Jesus of the Gospels*, xxxiv.

166. Keener, *Historical Jesus of the Gospels*, xxxiv.

167. Keener, *Historical Jesus of the Gospels*, xxxiv.

re-treading that territory, we can view his second reason as, perhaps, the more important one, which Keener expresses as follows:

> There is sufficient material in the more widely accepted Synoptic sources to make [this] book's point. John's Gospel is different from the others and poses special problems, and there are enough issues of controversy involved in the present discussion that it seemed superfluous to add another one.[168]

Here, the fact that Keener's preference for the Synoptics over John's Gospel, with the former "more widely accepted" than the latter speaks to, if we are reminded of Witherington, the fact that the former provides more authenticity than the latter. Insofar as, to Keener's point, the Gospel of John "is different from the others" and "poses special problems," what is implied, here, is that Synoptics share a relative sameness and, for that matter, are not as collectively problematic. Indeed, the Synoptic problem itself addresses the difficulties of aligning the three gospels and reveals inconsistencies across the texts—yet, as far as *the question of the meaning of Christology* is concerned and the extent that a portrait of the historical Jesus can be constructed, for there to be "historical Jesus of the gospels," the Synoptics provide a better chance at conceiving of historicity and grasping reliability in a way that the Gospel of John does not.

Given what is, ultimately, at stake for posing the question to and seeking the meaningfulness of Christology, in terms of what is projected by Christological thinking and laid bare in Christological reflection, Keener explains:

> As scholars often point out, claims based on research concerning the "historical Jesus" are not intended to be identical to claiming a complete or even representative knowledge of the Jesus who lived in the first century. What can be known of Jesus through historical methods, like what can be known of almost anyone by means of such methods, is only shadow of how the person would have been experienced by those who knew the person.[169]

Keener goes on to say:

> The historical enterprise proceeds based on probabilities and works from a limited base of evidence; it is therefore limited in the claims it makes [. . .] Beyond this observation, reconstructions vary widely based on whether we use minimalist historical criteria (admitting only the most certain evidence), a more

---

168. Keener, *Historical Jesus of the Gospels*, xxxiv.
169. Keener, *Historical Jesus of the Gospels*, xxxiv.

maximalist approach (admitting any evidence not clearly inadmissible), or some approach in between these two extremes.[170]

As a way of mitigating these "two extremes," in order to carefully attend to a "historical enterprise," Keener finds that the "Gospels are premeditated foundation documents."[171] As such, there are, Keener asserts, "foundation stories about the distant, legendary past were inevitably mythical."[172] Because of this, "schools tended to preserve information about more recent founders, a more appropriate comparison for first-century Gospels about the recent figure Jesus."[173] Being mindful of both what the first-century conceptualization of the "figure" of Jesus was and what became eventually "inevitably mythical," all while tending to the meaningfulness of the "foundation stories" and those which pose the question to Christology, Keener contends:

> Clearly the Gospels are not mythography, novels, or pure drama. As works focused on a single, historical character, drawing on significant amounts of historical tradition, the Gospels are most readily recognized as ancient biography.[174]

Insofar as Keener believes that the gospels, even as "foundation stories," are "not mythography, novels, or pure drama," Keener seems to suggest, though not explicit, that there is a narrative nature to what the gospels present about the "figure Jesus." In this way, if, as Keener purports, the gospels are "works focused on a single, historical character," they do so by historicizing Jesus—that historicization, to Keener's point, "draw[s] on significant amounts of historical tradition," such that what is laid bare is an overarching narrative that incorporates a narrative theologizing of Jesus. When viewing Keener's approach as that of narrative theology—or, perhaps, even a kind of narrative Christology—what we find in this is Keener's view that "the gospels are most readily recognized as ancient biography." Narrative theology, I submit, is what allows the gospels to be "most readily recognized" in the form of what Keener conceives of "as ancient biography." Yet, Keener understands this:

> Although ancient biography differed from its modern heir and namesake, it was supposed to deal in historical information rather than the fanciful creation of events. Some biographies were more historically reliable than others (typically, those about recent generations were much more reliable than those

170. Keener, *Historical Jesus of the Gospels*, xxxiv.
171. Keener, *Historical Jesus of the Gospels*, 83.
172. Keener, *Historical Jesus of the Gospels*, 83.
173. Keener, *Historical Jesus of the Gospels*, 83.
174. Keener, *Historical Jesus of the Gospels*, 84.

about the distant past). We must examine the Gospels in greater detail to see where on this spectrum they lie.[175]

The extent that the gospels, even "as ancient biography," becomes something that, to Keener's point, "was supposed to deal in historical information rather than the fanciful creation of events," how we characterize what sense can be made out of the gospels, then, becomes an essential benchmark of methodology. It is in this vein—in terms of method—that Keener acknowledges that "we must examine the Gospels in greater detail to see where on this spectrum they lie." That examination begins in *The Historical Jesus of the Gospels* and continues in *Christobiography*.

Though published ten years apart, Keener's argument about the gospels embodying a form of ancient biography has a natural continuity from *The Historical Jesus of the Gospels* to *Christobiography*, with the title of the latter seemingly more explicitly referring to Keener's overarching theme. The two works are, to a certain extent, even to Keener's admission, companion pieces.[176] However, in the introduction to the latter, Keener qualifies the title of *Christobiography* in this way:

> [*Christobiography*] is not about the historical reliability of the details of the Gospels, although it should contribute to challenging frequent assumptions of their overall unreliability. Instead, more precisely, I explore here the degree of historical intention in comparable works from the era of the Gospels, as well as the sort of prior information to which the Gospel writers could possibly have had access.[177]

Essentially, with these disclaimers in mind, there is a noticeable difference Keener wishes to make between "historical reliability" and "historical intention"—it is through the latter that Keener approaches what he means by "ancient biography," such the former charts a very different path of Christological reflection. In this way, through an attention to "historical intention," Keener views *Christobiography* as "a prolegomenon to using the Gospels as historical sources, rather than an examination of the Gospels themselves."[178] From this, Keener further contextualizes the text as something that:

> Draws attention to an old and yet sometimes neglected insight for historical-Jesus research: in terms of recognizable ancient genres, the Gospels are like ancient biographies. That is, the type

175. Keener, *Historical Jesus of the Gospels*, 84.

176. Keener, *Christobiography*, 20.

177. Keener, *Christobiography*, 1.

178. Keener, *Christobiography*, 1.

of literary work from the Gospels' era that they most closely re-
semble is the *bios*, or "life," of a subject—what we call (and this
book regularly titles) ancient biography.[179]

This idea of "ancient biography," here, and in the prior *The Historical Jesus
of the Gospels*, brings to the forefront, just as Keener argues, "an old and
yet sometimes neglected" approach to the problem of the historical Jesus.
When viewing the Gospels as "ancient biographies," we assume a path on
the quest for the historical Jesus that is not as well-charted as other paths.
For that matter, as much as Keener is certainly influenced by Witherington,
Keener ventures further methodologically than Witherington, insofar as
Keener's conceiving of the Gospels as "ancient biographies" does not necessary solve the problem of the historical Jesus—as perennial a problem it is—
but, rather, what Keener conceives of presents a "an old and yet sometimes
neglected" way of posing the question to and seeking the meaningfulness of
Christology itself, as that which can have as its task and as its scope something other than the historical Jesus. Subsequently, Keener writes:

> I reiterate here that this is not a book about the historical Jesus
> himself, nor a survey of the evidence in the Gospels. It is the
> latter that ultimately must decide where on the spectrum of
> memories of Jesus the Gospels lie. Examination of the evidence
> in the Gospels, however, is a well-worn path.[180]

Even so, Keener maintains:

> My objective in this book is not to construct a portrait of the
> historical Jesus, thereby adding to a surfeit of publications on
> that subject (including my own), but to contribute to the episte-
> mology of historical-Jesus research.[181]

Here, Keener makes an excellent point that certainly worth elucidating. In
particular, Keener's point is important since, with respect to *the question of
the meaning of Christology*, the purpose of posing the question to and seeking the meaningfulness of Christology may seem, on the surface, intent on
conceptualizing a portrait of the historical Jesus. Yet, such a conceptualization, or construction, insinuates that there is a particular way to, if attending to Keener, "construct a portrait of the historical Jesus." Just as Keener's
objective is not to do this, *the question of the meaning of Christology* also
wishes to "not to construct a portrait of the historical Jesus"—what wishes

179. Keener, *Christobiography*, 1.

180. Keener, *Christobiography*, 20.

181. Keener, *Christobiography*, 20.

to disclose itself through the posing of the question to and the seeking of the meaningfulness of Christology comes by way of a Christological reflection and through Christological thinking, which, once laid bare, are both not about "constructing" but more explicitly about existentializing the historical Jesus in the form of a portrait for the sake of existentializing. As with Keener, to simply "construct a portrait of the historical Jesus" merely attempts to assume that there is a certain way to make sense out of the historical Jesus and, in turn, a certain way to make sense out of what the historical Jesus means to the Christ of faith, and, furthermore, a certain way to make sense out of what makes the Christ of faith Christological. In this sense, such a construction assumes that there is right way to tread the path from the problem of the historical Jesus to one's own Christological reflection and Christological thinking—it is the sense that there is something systematic to Christology. This is, indeed, not the case, which is only made all the more apparent if we are reminded of the long, nearly 70-year arch of Christological reflection and Christological thinking from Käsemann to, now, Keener.

Given these end-points and all points in between, we need not think of *the question of the meaning of Christology* as a systematizing of the problem of the historical Jesus, as I have endeavoured to explore it from Käsemann to Keener, but, instead, only as a way to approach "the problem," confront "the historical," and understand what "Jesus" meets us existentially in the ever-evolving now. To this end, if being reminded of the extent that Keener wants *Christobiography* "to contribute to the epistemology of historical-Jesus research," I submit *the question of the meaning of Christology* similarly in its task and its scope—it contributes to "the epistemology of historical-Jesus research" just as much as all that has been presented from Käsemann to Keener have contributed—to varying degrees and differing extents—to an undergirding epistemology to *the question of the meaning of Christology*.

Chapter 6

Derrida's Philosophical Question of Love as Christology

As *the question of the meaning of Christology* has unfolded in the previous chapters from Bultmann and Bornkamm to Robinson through Conzelmann, from Dahl through Jeremias to Ebeling, Gogarten and Althaus, and across the landscape from Hahn to Keener, what is posed in terms of a question and what is sought in terms of a meaningfulness informs what Christology is. What remains an important part of the what-ness of Christology is the how-ness of it—how we pose the question to and seek the meaningfulness of Christology. Because the what-ness of Christology is differently approached in different contexts and for different reasons, the how-ness of Christology is, indeed, about how Christology is approached differently, and how it is laid bare in different contexts, and how the different reasons for approaching the various contexts frame how Christology comes to mean anything for anyone. That how-ness of Christology directly speaks to an inherent why-ness: why Christology is—that is to say, why is Christology "Christology" and why must it be approached differently, and why must it be laid bare in different contexts and why must it be brought to the fold for different reasons.

For us to even think of *the question of the meaning of Christology* as grounded in a what-ness, a how-ness, and a why-ness, where we expressly locate the meaning of Christology becomes all the more important. The where-ness of Christology is, I submit, part and parcel of any "quest" for the historical Jesus, and any quest, in turn, for the Christ of faith. It is the where-ness of Christology, as it has been laid bare in the earliest manifestations of the relationship between the historical Jesus and the Christ of faith, has its origins in what the disciples thought of the historical Jesus and what sense the disciples made out of the Christ of faith. Starting here, the disciples, essentially, at the first to be confronted with *the question of the meaning of Christology* in the what-ness, how-ness, and why-ness of the First Century C.E.—they are confronted with *the question of the meaning of Christology* in Jesus's ministry and the Christ that remained after Jesus's crucifixion and ascension.

All of the theologizing that has historically posed the questions to Christology and historically sought the meaningfulness of Christology has always conceived of *the question of the meaning of Christology*, however implicitly, as the intersection of a what-ness, a how-ness, and a why-ness. Schweitzer is at that intersection—it is only by being there that Schweitzer is able to argue for an end to the quest for the historical Jesus, given all that the various intersections antecedent to Schweitzer that inform Schweitzer's contextualization of the intersection on his own terms. Bultmann is at that intersection, situating himself in terms of a "no quest." All the Bultmannians and those that are contemporarily engaged in dialogues with the Bultman-nians are each, in their own way, at that intersection. The same can be said about the period from Hahn to Keener, which traverses the Jesus Seminar, and those in agreement and disagreement with its findings—insofar as the what-ness, the how-ness, and the why-ness of Christology remains con-ceptually and methodologically significant, *the question of the meaning of Christology*, in all its various articulations, is fundamentally attuned by the "where-ness" of Christology.

It is the "where-ness" of Christology—where we locate our Christo-logical reflection and where we locate our Christological thinking—that becomes the means by which the posing of the question to and the seek-ing of the meaningfulness of Christology can be cast. For the purposes of casting a specific task to and a specific scope for Christology, the way that we can attune ourselves to *the question of the meaning of Christology*, as that which runs through various traditions, various contexts, various lenses, various Christological thought, and various Christological reflections, from the First Century C.E. up to the present, I will consider *the question of the meaning of Christology*, now, through a philosophizing about Jacques Der-rida (1930–2004).

Speaking more generally, given that we are placing Christology in a relationship with Derrida and, therein, we are developing a relationship between theology and Derrida, I am mindful of previous considerations of

Derrida's theology or the manner with which one might theologize through Derrida at the careful juncture of theology-Derrida relations and, similarly, Derrida's religion or the manner with which one might conceive of religious through Derrida at a juncture of religion-Derrida relations. Perhaps, to either approach, the most notable of these studies include: the Harold Coward and Toby Foshay co-edited, *Derrida and Negative Theology* (1992), Walter J. Lowe's *Theology and Difference: The Wound of Reason* (1993), John D. Caputo's *The Prayers and Tears of Jacques Derrida: Religion without Religion* (1997), Steven Shakespeare's *Derrida and Theology* (2009), Andrew Shepherd's *The Gift of the Other: Levinas, Derrida, and a Theology of Hospitality* (2014), the Edward Baring and Peter E. Gordon co-edited, *The Trace of God: Derrida and Religion* (2015), Hugh Rayment-Pickard's *Impossible God: Derrida's Theology* (2018), and Clayton Crockett's *Derrida after the End of Writing: Political Theology and New Materialism* (2018).

BETWEEN FORCE AND SIGNIFICATION

In *"Force et signification"* (written in 1963), included in the collection, *L'écriture et la différence* (1967), and translated as "Force and Signification" in the 1978 translation of the collection as *Writing and Difference*, Derrida views structuralism itself as an "invasion," which, as such, "might become a question for the historian of ideas, or perhaps even an object."[1] Similarly, if we think of the problem of the historical Jesus and the conceptualization of the Christ of faith as representations of structuralism and, in turn, embodying an "invasion," what becomes clear, I argue, is that the same holds true: *the question of the meaning of Christology*, as such, as a kind of "invasion," through Derrida, also "might become a question for the historian of ideas, or perhaps even an object." In one sense, as it has been laid bare from Bultmann to the Bultmannians to Keener, all, to a certain extent, as "historian[s] of ideas," since, history often dictates not just how one poses the question to Christology, but also how one seeks the meaningfulness of Christology— what also becomes apparent is that in this posing of the question and this seeking of the meaningfulness, Christology, in itself, becomes, to Derrida's point, "perhaps even an object."

However, Derrida warns us, though, that "the historian would be deceived."[2] In the same sense, we can certainly come to the conclusion that every approach to *the question of the meaning of Christology* is, in fact,

---

1. Derrida, "Force and Signification," 3.
2. Derrida, "Force and Signification," 3.

grounded on being "deceived." This seems so, when "[the historian] came to this pass," as Derrida explains:

> By the very act of considering the structuralist invasion as an object [the historian] would forget its meaning and would forget that what is at stake, first of all, is an adventure of vision, a conversion of the way of putting questions to any object posed before us, to historical objects—his own—in particular. And, unexpectedly among these, the literary object.[3]

Here, if maintaining a connection between Derrida's notion of "the structuralist invasion" and what "invasion" of *the question of the meaning of Christology*, insofar as both are respectively explained "as an object," the need to pose the question to and seek the meaningfulness of Christology is also about "forget[ting] its meaning." By that, the Christological thinking and Christological reflection that remains necessary to approaching the problem of the historical Jesus is grounded on, in fact, "forget[ting] its meaning," since it is only through that forgetting that the question remains posed and the meaningfulness remains sought.

Indeed, when looking at the trajectory of Christological reflection and Christological thinking from Käsemann to Keener, what Keener does is certainly influenced by Witherington, and Witherington by the findings of the Jesus Seminar, and, for that matter, the findings of the Jesus Seminar owes its existence to the conceptualization of a third quest which, itself, is a reaction to the second quest as that which is enumerated by Bultmannians and those that were critical of the Bultmannians, and those that can be ascribed to a "Bultmannian" era throughout the 1950s and 1960s speak to what Bultmann, himself, laid bare in the 1940s. We can go on, of course, to what lies antecedently to Bultmann—what we find is a certain kind of forgetting of the meaning that can be traced to the earliest articulations of Christology in the First Century C.E., if we can situate the earliest conceptualizations of the problem of the historical Jesus and the Christ of faith to the Gospels, Paul's epistles, and other contemporary texts (some of which, we know, was not canonized in what has come down as the New Testament canon). It is only through this "forget[ting] its meaning" that *the question of the meaning of Christology* remains a perennial question of meaningfulness—it is about implicitly forgetting in order to find new ways to pose questions and seek meaningfulness to what Christology is.

Moving from quest to quest, from Bultmann to the Bultmannians, from the Bultmannians to the third quest, from the findings of the Jesus Seminar to the critics of those findings, each "Quester," to an extent, "would

3. Derrida, "Force and Signification," 3.

forget that what is at stake," Derrida tells us, "is an adventure of vision." We can see this in the full scope of the history behind *the question of the meaning of Christology*—we see in this history "an adventure of vision." In each instance, from all that influences Schweitzer to all that are influenced by Schweitzer to Bultmann's influences on the likes of Käsemann and Bornkamm to the various voices emerging from Ebeling to Fuchs, and so on, the iterations of *the question of the meaning of Christology* becomes, in Derrida's words, "a conversion of the way of putting questions to any object posed before us." That question "before us" is not only about what Christology is, but it also about what Christology does—that is, the questions and meanings about the problem of the historical Jesus. This, then, is the "historical object"—it is to which questions are posed and from which meaningfulness is sought. Yet, if we are to continue using Derrida on this point, we find, too, that, if the problem of the historical Jesus is a "literary object," *the question of the meaning of Christology* is as well—what we pose as a question and what we seek as a meaningfulness is predicated on the extent that the problem of the historical Jesus is laid bare as a "literary object" and, in turn, the Christological reflection and Christological thinking necessary to devise *the question of the meaning of Christology* is dependent on how we handle the "literary object" that is laid bare "before us."

Inherent in how the "literary object" is handled as something that is "before us" is what Derrida calls "an anxiety of language."[4] Consider Derrida's assertion here:

> By way of analogy: the fact that universal thought, in all its domains, by all its pathways and despite all differences, should be receiving a formidable impulse from an anxiety of language—which can only be an anxiety of language within language itself—is a strangely concerted development; and it is the nature of this development not to be able to display itself in its entirety as a spectacle for the historian, if, by chance, he were to attempt to recognize in it the sign of an epoch, the fashion of a season, or the symptom of a crisis.[5]

Essentially, *the question of the meaning of Christology* presents itself "in all its domains, by all its pathways and despite all differences." In doing so, what grounds every approach to the posing of the question to and the seeking of the meaningfulness of Christology is an "anxiety of language"—the extent that this, as Derrida says, "can only be an anxiety of language within language itself" arises through Christological reflection and through Christological

4. Derrida, "Force and Signification," 3.
5. Derrida, "Force and Signification," 3.

thinking. Yet, whether we are speaking about Schweitzer or Bultmann, Käsemann or Bornkamm, Ebeling or Fuchs, or all that has disclosed itself in the Jesus Seminar, in Crossan, from Witherington and Keener, there remains "a strangely concerted development." In this way, through "the nature of this development" in *the question of the meaning of Christology* not being "able to display itself in its entirety," what is posed as a question and what is sought as a meaningfulness becomes "a spectacle for the historian."

If we continue to operate "by way of analogy," as Derrida does, we find that every approach to *the question of the meaning of Christology* is an "attempt to recognize in it the sign of an epoch, the fashion of a season, or the symptom of a crisis." Though, in moving from quest to quest, every Quester, as it were, acknowledges, through Christological reflection and Christological thinking that the problem of the historical Jesus is "the sign of an epoch" as much as it is "the fashion of a season." Perhaps, more importantly, the problem of the historical Jesus is "the symptom of a crisis"—this crisis is symptomized by *the question of the meaning of Christology*, as that which is especially laid bare by either an "anxiety of language" or an "anxiety about language."

This "anxiety"—predicated on "the sign of an epoch," and "the fashion of a season," and "the symptom of a crisis"—theologically unconceals itself through *the question of the meaning of Christology*, but does so within a particular structure: the question and the meaning. What is also within this structure is the relationship between the historical Jesus and the Christ of faith. When Christologically thinking about what is "within structure," Christological reflection dictates that, as Derrida surmises, "there is not only form, relation, and configuration."[6] Derrida goes on to say: "there is also interdependency and a totality which is always concrete."[7]

Given that there is an "interdependency" between the meaning of the historical Jesus and the meaning of the Christ of faith and a "totality" in what is represented by *the question of the meaning of Christology* "which is always concrete," there is a problem that unfolds not just "within structure" but in terms of what structure articulates. It is not so much a problem of the historical Jesus or even a problem of the Christ of faith—it is about the problem of "interdependency" and what occurs "within" the structure of *the question of the meaning of Christology*. To this end, Derrida ascertains, "since we take nourishment from the fecundity of structuralism, it is too soon to dispel our dream."[8] Because of this "fecundity," the structuralism

6. Derrida, "Force and Signification," 5.

7. Derrida, "Force and Signification," 5.

8. Derrida, "Force and Signification," 4.

of *the question of the meaning of Christology* is from what "we take nourishment" and, for that matter, it is from this that it becomes "too soon to
dispel our dream"—if we are to say, of course, that, though each quest for
the historical Jesus wishes to "take nourishment" in what has come before
and towards what they wish to project what is made meaningful, each quest
hopes to "dispel" the dream arising from the problem of the historical Jesus
and the necessity for defining the Christ of faith and "dispel" how either is
problematized and defined moving forward.

Consequently, if we hold to the situatedness of *the question of the
meaning of Christology*, Derrida finds:

> We must muse upon what it *might* signify from within it. In
> the future it will be interpreted, perhaps, as a relaxation, if not
> a lapse, of the attention given to *force*, which is the tension of
> force itself. *Form* fascinates when one no longer has the force to
> understand force from which itself. That is, to create.[9]

Setting aside the fact that Derrida draws his understanding of "form" from
Jean Rousset's *Forme et Signification* (1962), Derrida's intent is on expli-
cating "form" as "force"—which we see are both emphasized—such that
"force" and signification grounds the relationship Derrida defines. What
arises from this is the extent that force brings about signification, rather
than form. It is not so much that *the question of the meaning of Christology*
is a form that must be signified—rather, it is that *the question of the meaning
of Christology* embodies a force that discloses "what it *might* signify from
within it." Whether we think of what "might" be signified from *the question
of the meaning of Christology* or from force itself—if we are carefully attending to what is meant by "it"—the significance Derrida places on the concept
of force, as that which makes signification possible, suggests that there is an
excess meaning to what is provided by structure. Indeed, there is an excess
to *the question of the meaning of Christology*—the force of the posing of the
question to and the seeking of the meaningfulness of Christology, as what
is signified by the relationship between the historical Jesus and the Christ
of faith, brings about an excess from which something otherwise than *the
question of the meaning of Christology* must be existentialized through, to
Derrida's point, what is ultimately created.

In effect, if *the question of the meaning of Christology* harbors a "force"
that discloses—or unconceals—something beyond the posing of the question and the seeking of the meaningfulness, what is signified must arise
beyond the explicit nature of the structure itself. If this excess is in the

9. Derrida, "Force and Signification," 4–5.

relationship between the historical Jesus and the Christ of faith, through Derrida's "Force and Signification," we must reckon with what is laid bare in excess.

BETWEEN STRUCTURE, SIGN, AND PLAY

Insofar as "Force and Signification" presents Derrida's assessment of the general inadequacy with what is signified by structure and, in a narrow sense, the extent that force "within" brings about an "excess" that is more meaningful than the structure itself, Derrida revisits these preoccupations in "Structure, Sign, and Play in the Discourse of the Human Sciences."

Originally delivered on October 21, 1966 under the title "*La structure, le signe et le jeu dans le discours des sciences humaines*" at the International Colloquium on Critical Languages and the Sciences of Man at The Johns Hopkins University, and also included in the *Writing and Difference* collection—given that "Force and Signification" and ""Structure, Sign, and Play in the Discourse of the Human Sciences" are companion pieces, with the latter seemingly proceeding where the former leaves off—Derrida enters into a conversation about structuralism and, more specifically, critiques the extent to which there is a "structure" governed by the concept of the linguistic sign, as argued by Ferdinand de Saussure (1857–1913). For Derrida, the Saussure's correspondence between signifier and signified within the overarching concept of structure becomes especially problematic—this problem remains problematized in *the question of the meaning of Christology*, which, in itself, contains a direct correspondence, as it were, between the meaning of the historical Jesus and the meaning of the Christ of faith.

Previously, as Derrida argues in "Force and Signification," that which allows excess to be laid bare is how Derrida conceives of the meaning of structure. In the earlier text, Derrida locates an "imbalance"[10] and a "preponderance"[11] in what makes structure "structure"—the extent that these issues point to an excess of meaning by way of the extent that "force" makes signification possible, Derrida surmises that the "imbalance" and the "preponderance" of what makes structure "structure" is "more actualized than acknowledged"[12] is in terms of what "seems to be *double*."[13] The emphasis Derrida places on the notion of "double" towards how he conceives of the concept of structure is, I submit, also what needs to be emphasized in the

---

10. Derrida, "Force and Signification," 15.

11. Derrida, "Force and Signification," 15.

12. Derrida, "Force and Signification," 15.

13. Derrida, "Force and Signification," 15,

problem of *the question of the meaning of Christology*—like with structure, to even conceive of the concept of *the question of the meaning of Christology* "seems to be *double*" not only from the standpoint of the posing of the question to and the seeking of the meaningfulness of Christology, but also from the standpoint of the problem of the historical Jesus and the problem of the Christ of faith. Just as Derrida tells us in "Force and Signification," with respect to what "seems to be *double*," structure can be thought of "*on the one hand*" as "becom[ing] the object itself, the literary thing itself,"[14] while, Derrida explains, "*on the other hand* (and consequently), structure as the literary thing is this time taken, or at least practiced, *literally*."[15]

Insofar as what "seems to be *double*" in Derrida's understanding of structure arises from Derrida's recognition of "force," how Derrida enters "Structure, Sign, and Play in the Discourse of the Human Sciences" is with an overture to what has already been laid bare in "Force and Signification"— "Structure, Sign, and Play in the Discourse of the Human Sciences" begins with an acknowledgement that "perhaps something has occurred in the history of the concept of structure that could be called an 'event.'"[16] This event, according to Derrida, will have an "exterior form," which "would be that of a *rupture* and a *redoubling*."[17]

Similarly, I would argue, "something has occurred" in the history of the concept of Christology, as that which is expressed in *the question of the meaning of Christology*. What has "occurred" is an "event"—we can think of this "event" as the ever-evolving relationship between the problem of the historical Jesus and problem of the Christ of faith. All Questers, as such, recognize that this "event" exists and attempt to explain what is at stake with this "event" across the various approaches to *the question of the meaning of Christology*. That "event," of course, begins with what the historical Jesus lays bare in the First Century C.E. and how the disciples and others, influenced by the historical Jesus, sought to explain the Christ of faith. In all the centuries since these earliest days, well before the growth and development of the Church, this "event" has remained potent, existentializing the very history of the structure of Christianity itself and, in turn, how the question is posed to and the meaningfulness is sought for Christology. In effect, *the question of the meaning of Christology* acknowledges that an "event" has occurred and, essentially, embodies, to Derrida's point, an "exterior form"— this "exterior form," as such, becomes the very "rupture" and "redoubling"

14. Derrida, "Force and Signification," 15.
15. Derrida, "Force and Signification," 15.
16. Derrida, "Structure, Sign, and Play," 278.
17. Derrida, "Structure, Sign, and Play," 278

that *the question of the meaning of Christology* grounds and is grounded the very nature of structure.

By beginning with the implications of the "event," with the evocation of *"rupture"* and *"redoubling,"* Derrida proposes that "the history of concept of structure" must be reinterpreted, or even deconstructed, especially at the point of the *event*, particularly when any understanding of what *structure* is—conceptually, that is—must be focused on "structure itself," rather than what *structure* looks like in the world—similarly, if we see *the question of the meaning of Christology* as a concept of structure, we must focus on the meaning of Christology itself, rather than what Christology looks like in the world.

Derrida's approach to structure takes a Heideggerian line of inquiry—the same is inherent in my approach to *the question of the meaning of Christology*, which, in itself, mirrors Heidegger's own construction of *the question of the meaning of being*. In other words, like Heidegger's task in *Being and Time* about the history of the concept of "being," Derrida is concerned with rethinking what has been thought about the history of the concept of structure and, my intent, too, through Derrida, is to rethink what has been thought about the history of *the question of the meaning of Christology*.

What that means, moreover, is that, in light of the method by which *the concept of structure* has been historically conceptualized, Derrida proposes a new method—Derrida's new method involves accepting that the word "structure" is inadequate, since it is bogged down with assumptions carried forward through the Western philosophical tradition. In the same way, Christology, I submit, is also inadequate, since it, too, is bogged down with assumptions, especially all of the preconceived notions and presumptions that have been carried forward from the earliest reactions to the historical Jesus and interpretations of the Christ of faith.

Like Heidegger's focus on "being," Derrida focuses on *structure*, paying special attention to what *structure* is on one hand, and on the other, what *structure* does. My interest is the same: focusing on Christology from the standpoint of what Christology is and what Christology does.

To be clear, in terms of *what structure is* and *what structure does*, Derrida views these two aforementioned things as vastly different concerns and, in a manner reminiscent of Heidegger approach to "being," Derrida's intention is to redefine "structure." My intent is, too, is to redefine "Christology." For Derrida, the word "structure" as well as *the concept of structure* is "as old as the epistémé—that is to say, as old as Western science and Western philosophy—and that their roots thrust deep in the soil of ordinary language."[18] The same can be said, too, of Christology, as that which is "as old as the epistémé" of Christianity and Christian thought, insofar as the very concept of Christology as, so to speak, "as old as Western science and Western philosophy," if taking into account certain arguments in the theologizing of the Hebrew Bible to say that there is a Christology to the Old Testament.[19] In a certain sense, then, if attending to what Derrida says about the concept of structure, Christology itself and *the question of the meaning of Christology* has its "roots thrust deep in the soil of ordinary language," when recognizing that Christological thinking and Christological reflection is laid bare in Christological language.

To this end, Derrida is concerned with the relationship between ordinary language and the concept of structure and how, by way of that relationship, there has been a "metaphorical displacement,"[20] not just in how ordinary language functions but how the concept of structure has skewered ordinary language with the "deepest recesses" of epistémé.[21] These deepest recesses involve what Derrida calls an "event" Here, Derrida's "epistémé"—or what, for Plato and Aristotle is "ἐπιστήμη"—is about a system of knowledge. That is to say, a system that has its most full-throated origins in Plato, especially exemplified in Plato's *Theaetetus* with the argument about knowledge as neither perception, explanation, or true judgment (according to Socrates).[22] Viewed this way, given that there is a system of knowledge is "skewed" by way of what the concept of structure exerts over ordinary language, the same holds true, I argue, for certain system of Christological knowledge, which, itself, is "skewed" by way of what *the question of the meaning of Christology* exerts over Christological language.

If "epistémé" is, indeed, a system, then Derrida finds that "system" to be a problematic structure, which is built upon subtle connotations and implicit assumptions that can, if following Alfred N. Whitehead's notion, be ultimately footnoted to Plato.[23] Derrida's approach to the history of metaphysics begins here with Plato—like Heidegger's preliminary considerations in *Being and Time*, Derrida recognizes that the center of structure is conceptualized in the center of Platonic metaphysics and, in turn, *structure*, as it has been perpetuated conceptually, must be delinked and decentered

18. Derrida, "Structure, Sign, and Play," 278.

19. Here, I am thinking about Ernst W. Hengstenberg's *Christology of the Old Testament* (1829).

20. Derrida, "Structure, Sign, and Play," 278.

21. Derrida, "Structure, Sign, and Play," 278.

22. Plato, *Theaetetus*, 92.

23. Whitehead, *Process and Reality*, 39.

from its Platonic origins by way of an event, through *rupture* and *redoubling*. With this in mind, for Derrida, "the whole history of the concept of structure, before the rupture [. . .] must be thought of as a series of substitutions of center for center, as a linked chain of determinations of the center."[24]

With all of this now in mind, Christological knowledge—or Christological "ἐπιστήμη"—is also problematic, indeed, if we can say that Christological knowledge is built upon subtle connotations and implicit assumptions that can be ultimately footnoted to Plato by way of Augustine and the earliest Christological reflections and Christological thinking that grounded the Early Church. More importantly, though, Christological knowledge can be footnoted to the historical Jesus and to those during those all too critical years before the Early Church that sought to articulate the Christ of faith in terms of the historical Jesus. Yet, how we approach to the question of the meaning of Christology invariably requires beginning with, like Derrida, a history of metaphysics—only insofar as the posing of the question to and the seeking of the meaningfulness of Christology is always about the tracing of the history of metaphysics. Though this does, to be sure, begin with the historical Jesus, I have placed the origins of *the question of the meaning of Christology* within a specific context that is framed in terms of Bultmann.

To this end, Bultmann—even with the antecedence of Schweitzer—I argue, must be recognized as the center of modern Christological thought and Bultmann's demythologization project, then, must be conceptualized in the center of Christological metaphysics, when concerning ourselves with Bultmannians, those that are interlocutors with the Bultmannians, and how Life-of-Jesus research itself develops throughout the 1960s, 1970s, the Jesus Seminar of the 1980s, and up to the present-day. As it has been perpetuated conceptually, *the question of the meaning of Christology* must be delinked and decentered from its Bultmannian origins by way of an "event" through *rupture* and *redoubling*. Consider a recasting of Derrida's sentiment that: "the whole history of the concept of structure, before the rupture [. . .] must be thought of as a series of substitutions of center for center, as a linked chain of determinations of the center"—we find in this, now, when attending to matters of Christology, that "the whole history" of *the question of the meaning of Christology* "before the rupture," as in before Bultmann perhaps, also "must be thought of as a series of substitutions of center for center, as a linked chain of determinations of the center." We can see Schweitzer's conclusion in *The Quest of the Historical Jesus* coming to bear on this point, just as much as we can see Bultmann's interest in a "no quest" period as a

24. Derrida, "Structure, Sign, and Play," 279.

reaction to what Schweitzer lays bare—yet, we see, through all the various handlings of *the question of the meaning of Christology* from Käsemann to Keener as, in Derrida's words, "as a series of substitutions of center for center, as a linked chain of determinations of the center."

From Schweitzer to Bultmann, from the Bultmannians to their critics, and from various voices throughout the 1970s to the Jesus Seminar of the 1980s, the question of the meaning of Christology is a "structure" with which many have constantly and perpetually wrestled.

This "structure," as Derrida recognizes it, "has always been neutralized or reduced, and this by a process of it a center or referring it to a point of presence, a fixed origin."[25] That center, as such—a historical-ideological position in *the concept of structure*—has a function, which Derrida points out as: "not only to orient[,] balance, and organize the structure [. . .] but above all to make sure that the organizing principle of the structure would limit what we might call the *play* of the structure."[26] Because of this, Derrida views the center as "clos[ing] off the *play* which it opens up and makes possible."[27] That is to say, through the stabilization of the center on the whole concept of structure, the center both closes and opens the possibility of "play"—the center confines and liberates "play." Through the closeness and restrictions of the center, the center, according to Derrida, "is the point at which the substitution of contents, elements, or terms is no longer possible."[28] This means, then, that "play"—at least in the truest sense of the term, containing the possibility of "the substitution of contents, elements, or terms"—does not allow for the free and open exchange of what can be "signified" and what can be "signifiers."

If the "center" is always the relationship between the problem of the historical Jesus and the problem of the Christ of faith, it is possible to conceive of this relationship, at its most fundamental, as something that, to reuse Derrida's words, "has always been neutralized or reduced," in an effort to make sense of what has been Christologically laid bare. Yet, to Derrida's point, though I am repurposing Derrida a bit, "by a process of" Christological reflection and Christological thinking, "a center or referring {Christology] to a point of presence, a fixed origin." That center, again—as a historical-ideological position grounded on *the question of the meaning of Christology*—is something that means, reconsidering Derrida's words, "not only to orient[,] balance, and organize the structure [. . .] but above all to

25. Derrida, "Structure, Sign, and Play," 278.
26. Derrida, "Structure, Sign, and Play," 278.
27. Derrida, "Structure, Sign, and Play," 279.
28. Derrida, "Structure, Sign, and Play," 279.

make sure that the organizing principle of the structure would limit what we might call the *play* of the structure." Essentially, the question of the meaning of Christology, while orienting, balancing, and organizing "Christology" in terms of the posing of a question and the seeking of a meaningfulness, we are able, again, "to make sure that the organizing principle of the structure would limit what we might call the *play* of the structure," which I have referred to as *the question of the meaning of Christology.*

Derrida's notion of "play"—which is not just captured in "Structure, Sign, and Play in the Discourse of the Human Sciences," but it is also acknowledged in "*Différance*" (1968) in the *Bulletin de la Société française de philosophie,*[29] as well as expressed in *La Dissémination* (1972), translated as *Dissemination* in 1981[30]—becomes Derrida's primary concern and, likewise, it will become mine.

Let us, for the moment, consider Derrida's characterization of "play" first. Derrida's problem with *the concept of structure*, ordinary language, and the relationship between signifiers and the signified is that "signs"— things by which we interpret, assign value, and make meaning in the world are not given "play." Derrida sees "play" as being indicative of more than just one signifier relating to a signified. Disagreeing with Saussure, Derrida conceives of the "sign" as engaging in much more than just bilateral hermeneutics—or *one* thing always being interpreted as *one* other thing. Not only is this kind of bilateral hermeneutics greatly limiting to what a "sign" is and what a "sign" can do, but it ultimately buys into the overarching understanding of structure as binary. This is the subject-object problem, which Heidegger wishes to "*destrukt*" in *Being and Time,*[31] and Derrida also wishes to "deconstruct" particularly in *Of Grammatology*. If the "sign" has been approached as something binary—something that can be traced most notably to not just Saussure but also to Claude Levi-Strauss (1908–2009)[32]—then any understanding of the "sign" itself has been constricted/restricted to the pairing of signifiers to the signified. What this seems to suggest is that "freeplay" makes it possible for signifiers to point towards a variety of signified things.

29. The article also appears as part of the English translation, *Speech and Phenomena* collection (1973), and in the English translation, *Margins of Philosophy* collection (1982).

30. Refer to the section entitled "Play: From Pharmakon to the Letter and from Blindness to the Supplement."

31. Heidegger, *Being and Time*, 193.

32. Here, if we tie Saussure and Levi-Strauss together, we do so under the broader theme of structuralism.

LOVE AS CHRISTOLOGY AND CHRISTOLOGY AS LOVE

Co-directed by Kirby Dick and Amy Ziering Kofman, the 85-minute documentary, *Derrida* (2002),[33] appeared just two years before Derrida's death. In it, the filmmakers incorporate a variety of interviews with Derrida, various public footage from Derrida's lectures and speaking engagements during the time of filming, as well as private footage of Derrida's family and friends, including, most notably, Derrida's wife, Marguerite (1932–2020),[34] who was, in her own right, a noted psychoanalyst and translator.[35] Notably, in a number of scenes, Kofman reads excerpts from Derrida's body of work, as a means of illustrating Derrida's academic life and, in other instances, illustrates various aspects of Derrida's personal life. Given the film's purposeful relationship between Derrida's academic persona and what can be known about Derrida's private and personal life, the two converge frequently throughout the course of the film, particularly in occasions when Kofman conducts one-on-one interviews with Derrida. One such interview, as with many others in the film, occurs as improvisation, when Kofman asks Derrida a question on the subject of love.

With respect to this, Kofman tells Derrida: "just whatever you want to say about love."[36] Prompted, Derrida questions "about what" is Kofman referring—Derrida, speaking in French, questions whether Kofman is asking him about "love" or about "death"[37]—noting, of course, that the two, for Derrida, sound roughly similar in cadence in French as "*l'amour*" for love and "*mort*" for death. Kofman clarifies, "love, not death [since] we have heard enough about death."[38] Still, Derrida questions: "love?"[39] Kofman, then, affirms that she is asking about love—to this, Derrida contends: "I have nothing to say about love," continuing with a subtle chide: "at least pose a question [since] I can't examine 'love.'"[40] Indeed, Kofman, to Derida's credit, does not necessarily pose a question about love, insomuch as

33. It was released at the Sundance Film Festival in January 2002 and released theatrically on October 23, 2002.

34. Coincidentally, not only was Marguerite married to Jacques Derrida from 1957 to his death in 2004, but she also died in Paris, France, from complications due to COVID-19.

35. She was trained at the Paris Psychoanalytic Society, which, founded in 1926, is the oldest psychoanalytical organization in France.

36. Kofman, Dick, and Derrida, *Derrida*, 78.

37. Kofman, Dick, and Derrida, *Derrida*, 78.

38. Kofman, Dick, and Derrida, *Derrida*, 78.

39. Kofman, Dick, and Derrida, *Derrida*, 78.

40. Kofman, Dick, and Derrida, *Derrida*, 78.

Kofman merely prompts Derrida in an open-ended way to say whatever he wishes to say about love—Derrida's problem with this is, in one sense, that Kofman does not adequately frame her inquiry, even if it is an implied question, and, in another sense, due to Derrida's necessity to approach such an inquiry in a philosophical way that more explicitly poses a question and seeks a meaning. To Derrida, it is not enough to simply say "whatever you want to say about love"—rather, the only way to approach love is to, first, approach it as *the question of the meaning of love.*

For Derrida, *the question of the meaning of love,* as I have construed it, becomes, in itself, a structure that must be deconstructed—given what Derrida argues in "Force and Signification" and "Structure, Sign, and Play in the Discourse of the Human Sciences," Derrida puts his prior theorizing about structure in general into a practical approach to the specificity of love. In this way, Derrida handles *the question of the meaning of love,* as it were, in the following manner:

> One of the first questions one could pose [. . .] is the question of the difference between "the who" and "the what." Is love the love of someone or the love of something? Okay, supposing I loved someone, do I love someone for the absolute singularity of who they are? I love you because you are you. Or do I love your qualities, your beauty, your intelligence? Does one love someone, or does one love something about someone? The difference between "the who" and "the what" at the heart of love separates the heart. It is often said that love is the movement of the heart. Does my heart move because I love someone who is an absolute singularity, or because I love the way that someone is? Often love starts with some type of seduction. One is attracted because the other is like this or like that. Inversely, love is disappointed and dies when one comes to realize the other person doesn't merit our love. The other person isn't like this or that. So at the death of love, it appears that one stops loving another, not because of who they are, but because they are such and such. That is to say, the history of love, the heart of love, is divided between "the who" and "the what."[41]

Here, what Derrida outlines, I submit, as a Heideggerian-like[42] *the question of the meaning of love,* hinges on another question—essentially: *what is love,* or perhaps, *how can love be defined as something knowable and*

41. Kofman, Dick, and Derrida, *Derrida,* 78–108.

42. By "Heideggerian-like," we can certainly compare how Derrida construct the question as a philosophical inquiry in much the same manner as what we see in the opening pages of Heidegger's *Being and Time.*

explainable?—which seems rather off-hand. It seems, too, as unplanned a question by Kofman as much as it is un-thought an answer by Derrida. Though the former possibly holds true—that is to say, the extent to which Kofman likely did not plan to ask the question—the latter cannot completely be considered as an un-thought by Derrida. In other words, though it appears impromptu, that appearance may merely be a red herring, if appearances do not match reality. But, what, exactly, is reality here?

Though Derrida is speaking about love and carrying forward *the question of the meaning of love*, it is possible to read more into Derrida than simply just his impromptu thoughts on the structure of love. What Derrida appears to be saying about love, I argue, becomes something that, in reality, allows us to explicate Derrida's handling of the question of the meaning of Christology—if we take one structure for another structure, "Christology" can become a stand-in for love and, for that matter, Derrida's question of the meaning of love can be substituted for *the question of the meaning of Christology.*

The question, now, is this: in what way can Derrida's handling of love be an expansion of Derrida's earlier handling of structure in "Force and Signification" and "Structure, Sign, and Play in the Discourse of the Human Sciences"? Posed differently, is it possible to say that Derrida's seemingly extemporaneous grappling with the meaning of love is not at all un-thought, but merely an epistemology that has already been framed in Derrida's earlier works?

Think of it this way: can we say that, through "Force and Signification" and "Structure, Sign, and Play in the Discourse of the Human Sciences," these earlier texts lay a foundation for what brings Derrida to say what he says about love in the *Derrida* film?

Indeed, there is a connection between Derrida's two earlier texts and what is said in the *Derrida* film. Even if it seems as if Derrida's answer about love is extemporaneous, and the thinking is thought out in real-time over the course of the formulation of his answer—I wish to emphasize "seem"—there is clearly, I argue, a concerted effort on Derrida's part to directly draw from what he has written about structure in his earliest writings in the 1960s. This seems so, I believe, because his answer in the film is undoubtedly thoughtful and formulated—this is clear by Derrida's lengthy response, which I have let stand in its totality—given the measured performance of it and the fact that it yields the possibility that Derrida thought about *the question of the meaning of love* prior to the positing of the question. The thinking necessary to think the kind of thought into *the question of the meaning of love* "always-already" exists in the lexicon of Derrida's epistemology of love, as that which is drawn from Derrida's epistemology about structure, insofar as we can say, too, that Derrida's thinking the thought of *the question of the meaning of love* is "always-already" about the question of the meaning of structure and, in turn, it attends to *the question of the meaning of Christology.*

The question of the meaning of love, as it is presented by the interviewer, merely prompts Derrida to narrow the generalities of the question into a question that interrogates and existentializes *the meaning of love*—the narrower question is grounded on more than just the general question itself, but, rather, it points to the "meaning" in the question as a teleology about *the meaning of love* beyond its mere conceptualization. By teleology, I mean that *the meaning of the love* refers to a "meaning" that has teleological implications to *the question of the meaning of love.* That is, the "meaning" in *the meaning of love* is not its "concept," if agreeing that, by a "concept of love," we are referring to the general hermeneutics about love. We must do more than simply interpret what the "meaning" is in *the meaning of love*—the hermeneutics necessary to interpret *the meaning of love* through *the question of the meaning of love* only takes the "meaning" and the "question" so far. In either case, we reach a limit in what we can understand. What is interpreted by either questioning or meaning-making will not bring us to *the meaning of love*, even if *the question of the meaning of love* appears to carry us there.

Similarly, *the question of the meaning of Christology* merely prompts us to narrow the generalities of the question into a question that interrogates and existentializes the meaning of Christology. Again, the narrower question is grounded on more than just the general question itself—rather, it points to the "meaning" in the question as a teleology about the *meaning of Christology* beyond its mere conceptualizations. Teleologically speaking, *the meaning of Christology* refers to a "meaning" that has teleological implications to *the question of the meaning of Christology.* That is, the "meaning" in *the meaning of Christology* is not its "concept," if still agreeing that, by a "concept of Christology," we are referring to the general hermeneutics about Christology. We must, again, do more than simply interpret what the "meaning" is in *the meaning of Christology*—again, the hermeneutics necessary to interpret *the meaning of Christology* through *the question of the meaning of Christology* only takes the "meaning" and the "question" so far. Consequently, what is interpreted by either questioning or meaning-making will not bring us, I argue, to *the meaning of Christology*, even if *the question of the meaning of Christology*, in terms of what is posed and what is sought, only appears to carry us there: the relationship, in reality, between the historical Jesus and the Christ of faith.

BETWEEN QUESTION, MEANING, AND CENTER

Appearances and reality, in themselves, hold specific relevance between how Christology looks outside its worldhood, as a phenomenon,[43] and what Christology truly is when encased in its worldliness, as a noumenon.[44] Quite often, the former is what we believe Christology is and, accordingly, it becomes what we believe we are experiencing as "Christology-Itself." This cannot be so. *Christology-Itself* is not a *noumenon* at all—it is not an entity that can be authentically experienced in its worldliness, since the worldhood of *the meaning of Christology* is simply "a way" of answering *the question of the meaning of Christology*. The World[45] presents only one way of interpreting *the meaning of Christology*—and, as only one way, we are experiencing the appearances of Christology in the world, which never bring us to *Christology-Itself*. Rather, what we are experiencing are a multitude of concepts of Christology as it appears to us in a multitude of possibilities in our worldhood. If *the meaning of Christology* is not grounded in our experiences of the concept of Christology in its multiplicity in the World as either a *noumenon* or a *phenomenon*, what we believe we are interpreting is really a misinterpretation of *the meaning of Christology*, yielding misunderstanding and misdirection.

Misdirection, misunderstanding, and misinterpretation are all inevitable consequences of locating *the meaning of Christology* by the question of *the meaning of Christology*. This is partly because "the question" we are attempting to pose never authentically asks the right question into *the meaning of Christology*. By suggesting that there is a "meaning of Christology," we are assuming that there is a "center" to the "structure" of Christology—this "center," then, becomes something accessible and assessable, in order to say that the "Structure of Christology" is knowable, as long as "the meaning" is in/within the center. However, finding the "center" is not the answer to the question we must pose about *the meaning of Christology*. In fact, when we search for the "center" as *the meaning of Christology* and conclude that this "meaning" and "center" are authentic epistemologies towards our conceptualizations of Christology, we are always-already looking in the wrong place. When we concede "meaning" as having a presence on the "center," we are deceiving ourselves—the web of belief we have about *the meaning of Christology* is restricted to an inauthentic relationship between "meaning" and "center" that is a false epistemology about *the meaning of Christology*.

---

43. Husserl, *Ideas*, 101–2.

44. Husserl, *Ideas*, 101–2.

45. Husserl, *Ideas*, 101–2.

We never "know" *the meaning of Christology*, at its most authentic, when believing that any "meaning" about "Christology" permeates from the meaningfulness of a "center." There is no true "center," in such that it can be the correct grounding for *the meaning of Christology*. The "center" is only an arbitrary entity that does nothing meaningful for *the meaning of Christology*, any more than it is even interpretable as *the meaning of Christology*. I do not mean to say that the "center" is meaningless, or that it lacks interpretation. There is a meaningfulness to what the "center" holds, to the extent that *the meaning of Christology* merely chooses to conceal itself in/ within the center. There is, indeed, "meaning" to what is "interpreted" from the "center," when thinking of the "center" as a meaningful *concealment of the meaning of Christology*. Though the "center" is arbitrary as a meaning-maker for *the meaning of Christology*—with respect to a meaninglessness to it—there remains a meaningfulness to it as an entity, just as there is an interpretation to the "meaning" of what has been concealed meaningfully. We cannot interpret the "center" by locating the "meaning" of Christology in it, because, whatever "meaning" the "center" holds, the center's "meaning" is always-already inauthentic and imaginary—the "center" only misdirects us from *the meaning of Christology* in its real authenticity, since what we think we understand about *Christology-Itself* is a misunderstanding and misinterpretation of *the meaning of Christology*.

All of this makes us misidentify *the meaning of Christology* by thinking a thought that proceeds no further than *the concealment of the meaning of Christology*. At its most concealed inauthenticity, *the meaning of Christology* is always-already unanswerable, unknowable, and uninterpretable. The very moment we pose a question about *the meaning of Christology*, we are intentionally directed towards an arbitrary and mythical "center." What makes this "center" so arbitrary is that it mythologizes *the meaning of Christology* into a "meaning" that is created and perpetuated from a meaningless point of reference—to refer to *the meaning of Christology* as something answerable, knowable, and interpretable, at all, means, then, holding onto a "center" from which the concept of Christology must be anchored. The "question" about *the meaning of Christology* superficially interrogates not just the "meaning" of "Christology," but it also generally searches for a "center" that validates and confirms what is being asked. The interrogation and the search proceeding from a "question" about *the meaning of Christology* never provides a "meaning" that adequately works out *the question of the meaning of Christology*. The arbitrariness of whatever "meaning" we think we discover when presenting a "question" into the "meaning" of "Christology" is not an authentic "meaning" at all—it is always-already a misdirection that misunderstands, until it is utterly misinterpreted. Because of this, *the meaning of Christology*, at its most authentic and unconcealed, always-already hides itself in the questions that frame the problem of the historical Jesus and the problem of the Christ of faith—*the question of the meaning of Christology* operates at the juncture of "question," "meaning," and "center."

CHRISTOLOGY OF SOMEONE AND CHRISTOLOGY OF SOMETHING

Setting aside Derrida's presentation of the question of the difference between "the who" and "the what," let us concentrate, again, on the following questions, as Derrida poses them:

> Is love the love of someone or the love of something? Okay, supposing I loved someone, do I love someone for the absolute singularity of who they are? I love you because you are you. Or do I love your qualities, your beauty, your intelligence? Does one love someone, or does one love something about someone?[46]

In each case, every answer, as it is solicited by every question Derrida poses, is always-already unanswerable, unknowable, and uninterpretable. This is because, as posed, each question solicits a body of knowledge about the concept of love, as that which is centralized in a structural understanding of *the meaning of love*. This holds true, I submit, for how each question solicits a body of knowledge about the concept of Christology, as that which is, in turn, centralized in a structural understanding of *the meaning of Christology*.

If we continue to substitute "Christology" for "love," there remains something important in Derrida's words to ask, when continuing with our substitution: "is [Christology] the [Christology] of someone or the [Christology] of something?" When recast, we come to the issue at the very heart of *the meaning of Christology*: the problem of the historical Jesus as the Christology of someone and the problem of the Christ of faith as the Christology of something. Hence, this allows us to reconsider the question that follows this in this way: "okay, supposing I [Christologized] someone, do I [Christologize] someone for the absolute singularity of who they are?" By making Christology into a verb—something we do—we are asking what it means to Christologize the historical Jesus, and if we do so to Christologize the historical Jesus "for the absolute singularity of who" Jesus is? From this question, if following our recasting of Derrida, we suppose: we Christoogize Jesus because Jesus is Jesus—said differently, perhaps, we Christologize the historical Jesus because the historical Jesus is the historical Jesus, just as we

---

46. Kofman, Dick, and Derrida, *Derrida*, 78–108.

Christologize the Christ of faith because the Christ of faith is the Christ of faith. Proceeding from here, we can ask, just as Derrida does, but in a recasting: do we Christologize Jesus' "qualities, [his] beauty, [his] intelligence"? To this end, we arrive at the same sort of question to which Derrida arrives, though recasting it: "does one [Christologize] someone, or does one [Christologize] something about someone?"

What makes this structural understanding inadequate is that, on one hand, it assumes that there is a structure of Christology which has, as its center, a delineable "meaning." Yet, on the other hand, this supposed delineable "meaning" is not delineable into anything meaningful, since *the meaning of Christology* cannot be answered with rhetorical questions. It is here where the biggest problems lie with Derrida's questions, and our own, if they can, indeed, be considered as "rhetorical" in nature: they presuppose that, through an apparent answerability, knowability, and interpretability, each question corresponds to an answer. Not only is this correspondence between question-answer erroneous, if, through Derrida's intentions, we are to locate *the meaning of Christology*, but it also navigates us to a "rhetoric" of Christology—that is, to say, it is a way that we can speak of Christology meaningfully, so that, through how we speak about Christology, the meaningfulness of what Christology is and what Christology does is declaratively laid bare.

To be sure, even if we can say that there is a rhetoric at play grounded in Plato's *Symposium*, in a general sense, argumentation about *the meaning of love* as that which we recast as *the meaning of Christology*, leads us into defining that "meaning" as rooted fundamentally in language. Though Plato tells us in *Theaetetus*, through Socrates, that knowledge is neither perception, nor an account nor a justified belief,[47] *the meaning of Christology* attends to perception as much as it attends to an account and as much as it attends to a justified belief, such that what we can perceive, what we can give an account towards, and what we can form a justified belief about *the meaning of Christology*—all are rooted, one way or another, on the limits of language itself and what, exactly, makes language a fundamental component of the limits of what can be perceived and what justified belief can be formed about *the meaning of Christology*. While this is true to a certain extent, especially if we can affirm that *the meaning is Christology* is housed in language, just as Heidegger affirms about "Being," there is a meaningfulness in *the meaning of Christology* that is beyond language quo "Being"—it is a meaningfulness that is meaningful for the sake of itself, and verges on the ineffable in its latent inauthenticity. So, if this meaningfulness is meaningful

47. Plato, *Theaetetus*, 92.

for the sake of itself without argumentation about it—that is, without logical propositions, truth-claims, or acts of persuasion—what can we actually ask about *the meaning of Christology*? Can we even ask a question about *the meaning of Christology* without misdirecting ourselves away from what it is we wish to find about *Christology-Itself*? Is there even a question that can possibly work out the problem of *the meaning of Christology* adequately enough to not become meaningless the moment we utter it? And, can we de-problematize *the meaning of Christology* with questions such as Derrida's? I do not believe we can—rather than de-problematizing *the meaning of Christology*, we, instead, re-problematize it. In fact, if we are true to the problem itself, as it pertains to unconcealing *the meaning of Christology* and the inadequacy certain questions provide, Derrida is, unknowingly, misdirecting himself with each question, since every answer, if there can be any, never authentically answers *the meaning of Christology*.

When asking "is love the love of someone or the love of something," what exactly is being asked by Derrida, when reconstructing it into: is Christology the Christology of someone or the Christology of something?

Does such a question actually unconceal *the meaning of Christology* at all? Or, rather, does it assume something about *the meaning of Christology* that only, ultimately, conceals what we can know about *the meaning of Christology* in the concealment of the meaninglessness of a "center"? Is Derrida, then, assuming that there is a "center" to *the meaning of Christology*? Does this "center," then, account for a structure to *the meaning of Christology*, which, assumedly, presents us with an epistemology of Christology regulated structuralized *the meaning of Christology*? And by this assumption, is Derrida unnecessarily limiting himself to thinking a thought about *the meaning of Christology* which is, undoubtedly, tied to a meaningless structure (in all its meaninglessness)—a structure with a "center" that does not liberate *the meaning of Christology*, but confines it to a meaninglessness?

Derrida is certainly assuming this: a "center" to *the meaning of Christology*. Moreover, Derrida is suggesting that this "center" contains and expresses *the meaning of Christology*, particularly through a containable "meaning" that gives forth an expressible "meaning." This suggestion, as such, must be teased carefully out of Derrida's question, when reconstructed: is Christology the Christology of someone or the Christology of something?"

What this question proposes, first, is that "Christology" is contained and expressed either in "the Christology of someone" or "the Christology of something," as entities capable of the containment and expression of *the meaning of Christology*. Again, if we can say that this containment and expression attempts to locate *the meaning of Christology* as residing in either "the Christology of someone" or "the Christology of something," we are saying, secondly, that such a containment and expression centralizes *the meaning of Christology* —it is the centralization of *the meaning of Christology* in the situations of either "the Christology of someone" or "the Christology of something."

To even pose this question, as Derrida does, he is undoubtedly implying that, depending on how we answer this question—the notion that *the meaning of Christology* is in either "the Christology of someone" or "the Christology of something"—we must decide which best represents what we can say is the "center" of *the meaning of Christology*. In either case, "someone" and "something" must have a "meaning" inherently centralized in them for us to be able to even answer such a question in the first place.

For us to say, in either case, that *the meaning of Christology* is contained and expressed in "the Christology of someone" or "the Christology of something" both become fraught with epistemological errors—the choice between them becomes an ethical stance, rather than a deontological stance, towards our ability to conceive of and grasp *the meaning of Christology* as *Christology-Itself*, when it becomes limited to explanations of "the Christology of someone" and "the Christology of something." That is not to say, however, that both cases do not contain nor express *the meaning of Christology*. Whether we are speaking ethically or deontologically about *the meaning of Christology*, we are always-already conceptualizing a kind of containment and expression quo *Christology-Itself* —we speak, in a way, about *Christology-Itself* by referring to *the meaning of Christology* as a bracketing[48] of what is contained and expressed in that "meaning." The bracketing, as such, brackets not just an ethics we must apply to *the meaning of Christology*, if we are to say, to any extent, that *Christology-Itself* is even knowable and referable, but also a detontological, or moral commitment to *the meaning of Christology*, if we are to know, to any extent, how we Christologize and why we encounter what is Christologized. This "how-ness" and "why-ness" develops from an ethics, but must be grounded on deontology—we use that "how-ness" and "why-ness" to construct more than just rules, regulations, and standards to *the meaning of Christology* for us (and for others), since these rules, regulations, and standards must be steeped in a deeper "meaning" invested in morality and commitment for us (and for others).

To be clear, "the Christology of someone" and "the Christology of something" are merely ethical constructions—neither employ the necessary deontology of *the meaning of Christology*. Rather, both are unavoidably contingent on the ethical contexts of "the Christology of someone" and "the Christology of something," as two understandings of *the meaning of Christology*.

---

48. This refers to Husserl's use of the term. Husserl, *Ideas*, 110–11.

These contexts are merely ethical pretexts too, since they both presume that the only means by which we can ethically point to *the meaning of Christology* arises in a certain "someone," or a certain "something"—that is, to any extent to which we can say that "someone" and not some other one is Christologized, and "something" and not some other thing is Christologized.

Here, the underlying is-ness and not-ness merely pivots on a preferred "center" that remains, for worse, ethical and never deontological—when we mythically[49] engage in an ethics about *the meaning of Christology*, we never authentically confront *Christology-Itself* as it always-already is in its most unconcealed authenticity. *Christology-Itself*, then, does not have a "center" in an ethical sense, even when adjudicating whether *the meaning of Christology* is "the Christology of someone" or "the Christology of something." This is because, more specifically, *the meaning of Christology* does not have a "center" either, in an ethical sense. In an ethical sense—an ethics constructed around rules, regulations, and standards providing an overall framework—we are not speaking of a "center" to *Christology-Itself* nor *the meaning of Christology*. Neither is oriented, balance, nor organized by a "center," but, instead, a concealed deontology orients, balances, and organizes both.

To this end, we have a moral commitment to the mere ontology of *Christology-Itself* and *the meaning of Christology*, in order to authentically confront these ontologies as epistemologies and, then, as an always-already-ness through inherent understandings of an extendedness in the appearances of "the Christology of someone" and "the Christology of something." And yet, for Derrida to propose that *the meaning of Christology*—and *Christology-Itself*, for that matter—is a question between "the Christology of someone" and "the Christology of something," he misunderstands what is at stake in the question itself, by assuming that *the meaning of Christology*, as an always-already, concealed entity, is unconcealed in "the Christology of someone" and "the Christology of something." Instead, in its purposeful concealedness, *the meaning of Christology* is always-already inauthentic as "the Christology of someone" and "the Christology of something." Since, as Heidegger suggests about "Being" liking to hide itself in a concealedness, *the meaning of Christology* as it appears to us in either "the Christology of someone" or "the Christology of something," in their respective always-already-ness, is not *Christology-Itself*. Both "the Christology of someone" and "the Christology of something" are merely concealments of *Christology-Itself*—both, ultimately, misdirect us from what *Christology-Itself* is in its most

---

49. By "mythically," I am conjuring Bultmann's notion of "myth" as what is essential to Bultmann's demythologization.

unconcealedness, so that what we think we are interpreting as *Christology-Itself* are only appearances of inauthenticity. Not only does Derrida assume otherwise, but he also assumes that *the meaning of Christology* does not (or cannot, or even would not) conceal itself to us at all.

Through Derrida, what appears to us through "the Christology of someone" and "the Christology of something" are unconcealments of *the meaning of Christology*. What this means, then, is that, in Derrida's view, when we locate *the meaning of Christology* in either "the Christology of someone" or "the Christology of something," we can "know" *Christology-Itself* by way of an apparent unconcealment—it is the idea that "the Christology of someone" and "the Christology of something" are unconcealments of *the meaning of Christology* and *Christology-Itself.*

What do we exactly "know" about *the meaning of Christology* through "the Christology of someone" and "the Christology of something"? Can we even say we "know" anything at all, if what we must "know" is *the meaning of Christology*?

However, neither "the Christology of someone" nor "the Christology of something" ever really unconceal what we wish to "know" about *the meaning of Christology* and *Christology-Itself*. If our goal is to unconceal *the meaning of Christology*, we can never achieve this when focuses exclusively on "the Christology of someone" and/or "the Christology of something." This is because what we "know," essentially, is only "knowing" in the loosest sense of the word through—we never really "know" *the meaning of Christology* any more than we "know" *Christology-Itself.*

Yet, for Derrida, *the meaning of Christology*, as it exists in "someone" or "something," has no other option but to unconceal *Christology-Itself* in what can be called: the act of Christologizing someone or the act of Christologizing something. These acts, as they are, especially as Derrida seems to contend, are events of immanent importance[50] that unconceal *Christology-Itself*. I will concede, of course, that there is a pure immanence[51] at play in the acts of Christologizing someone and Christologizing something—these events do orient us, if nothing else, to *the meaning of Christology* through the inauthentic ontologies of "someone" and "something." Nevertheless, Derrida seems to assume otherwise about *Christology-Itself*, proposing, at its most authentic, that it is always based on an organized structure of ontologies, by which *the meaning of Christology* is always either "the Christology of someone" or "the Christology of something."

50. Deleuze, *Pure Immanence*, 31.
51. Deleuze, *Pure Immanence*, 31.

Clearly, this assumption about *the meaning of Christology* and *Christology-Itself* in relation to "the Christology of someone" or "the Christology of something," as it can be adapted from Derrida in 2002, fundamentally disagrees with Derrida's "Structure, Sign, and Play in the Discourse of the Human Sciences" from 1966, wherein he, firstly, contends that:

> The function of [a] center was not only to orient; balance, and organize the structure—one cannot conceive of an unorganized structure—but above all to make sure that the organizing principle of the structure would limit what we might call the *play* of the structure. By orienting and organizing the coherence of the system, the center of a structure permits the play of its elements inside the total form. And even today the notion of a structure lacking any center represents the unthinkable itself.[52]

From this, how can this early-Derrida be reconciled with the later one from the film? If Derrida's earlier remarks hold true, and if "one cannot conceive of an unorganized structure," do the assumptions Derrida ultimately makes, with his remarks from 2002, attempt to conceive of an organized structure between "the Christology of someone" and "the Christology of something," since he "cannot conceive of an unorganized structure"?

In my view, Derrida does, in fact, envision an organized structure between the two—through him, *the meaning of Christology* functions by way of a "center" between "the Christology of someone" and "the Christology of something" epistemologically-grounded upon *Christology-Itself* as a kind of compass which means "not only to orient; [but to] balance, and organize the structure" of *Christology-Itself*. More importantly, when considering his 1966 remarks in relation to those in 2002, does Derrida come to view *the meaning of Christology* as an "organizing principle of the structure" of *Christology-Itself*? This is certainly true as well, particularly if we can interpret Derrida's understanding of the relationship between *the meaning of Christology* and *Christology-Itself* as one that is based on "an organizing principle" of what might be called "Structure-Itself."

To this end, what is contingently true, too, is that *the meaning of Christology*, through Derrida in 2002, becomes, contradictorily to his words in 1970, "the organizing principle of the structure [that] would limit what we might call the *play* of the structure" of *Christology-Itself*. There is no "play of the structure" of *Christology-Itself*, when *the meaning of Christology* is limited between "the Christology of someone" and "the Christology of something." Consequently, because, as Derrida argues in 1966, "the notion of a structure lacking any 'center' represents the unthinkable itself," Derrida

---

52. Derrida, "Structure, Sign, and Play," 278.

seemingly presupposes, by way of 2002, that there is a "center" to his "notion of a structure" between what I have reconstituted as "the Christology of someone" and "the Christology of something." I say "presupposes," since Derrida is not clear about what he means by "the love of someone" and "the love of something," insofar as his notions of both inform my own conceptions of "the Christology of someone" and "the Christology of something."

We can only presuppose, likewise, that his contention is not only that *the meaning of Christology* is contained in the "center" between "the Christology of someone" and "the Christology of something," but, more importantly, that "the "the Christology of someone" and "the Christology of something," of someone" and "the "the Christology of someone" and "the Christology of something," of something" have respective "centers" that are existentially-drawn to one another's otherness by a "center"-driven intendedness[53] that allows both to recognize one another's "center" as that which draws them immanently together.

There is, true enough, a dialectic[54] here: it is *the meaning of Christology* between "the Christology of someone" and "the Christology of something." I do not mean this to say that there is *Christology-Itself* between the two. Rather, what I mean is that, through Derrida, posing a question about the meaning of *Christology-Itself* as either one thing or another—as either "the Christology of someone" or "the Christology of something"—one must dialectically-construe the two as extremes rooted in an extendedness from a "center."

At that "center," we find, through the reconstructing of Derrida's question, that, to some extent, problems with asking: is Christology "the Christology of someone" or "the Christology of something"? This question is inadequate, when simply posed as it is, and leads us down an impossible pathmark, if our intention, as it has been to this point, is to investigate into *the meaning of Christology* by locating *Christology-Itself.* If we answer Derrida's question as either one or the other—by saying that *the meaning of Christology* is either "the Christology of someone" or "the Christology of something"—our "meaning" is always-already moot. The "meaning" we uncover only conceals what it is we wish to unconceal—to conclude that *the meaning of Christology* is "the Christology of someone," or *the meaning of Christology* is "the Christology of something" means arriving at an arbitrary meaning that is more meaningless than it is meaningful, since such an inquiry unknowingly cleaves itself to a "center" that is also more meaningless than it is meaningful.

53. I am thinking about "intendedness" in terms of Hegel's notion of "being acknowledged" or "the process of Recognition." Hegel, *Phenomenology of Spirit*, 111.

54. We can think of this "dialectic" with respect to Hegel, in terms of a Lordship and a Bondage. Hegel, *Phenomenology of Spirit*, 111–19.

THE ONE WHOM CHRISTOLOGIZES
AND CHRISTOLOGY-ITSELF

For there to even be "the Christology of someone" and "the Christology of something," it means that there is undoubtedly a "center," of some sort, bringing the two together within an "immanent," epistemological space.[55] To say "center," at all, means we are beholden to acknowledge the space between "the Christology of someone" and "the Christology of something"— this space simply separates the two, so that neither is immanently like the other, and, more importantly, so that the underlying concepts of "Someone" and "Something," to which *Christology-Itself* is respectively directed, sustained, and redirected, provide different epistemologies about *the meaning of Christology*. This "center," as a space, does not make-meaning for *the meaning of Christology* immanently and epistemologically denoted in either "the Christology of someone" or "the Christology of something."

There is no real centralization to what the "center" does for and to "the Christology of someone" and "the Christology of something"—the "center," in this case, is always-already contrived and invented as a contingency of representation, which is necessary for us to differentiate "the Christology of someone" from "the Christology of something" as intentionalities[56] through which *the meaning of Christology* interprets to what extent either "Someone" or "Something" embodies *Christology-Itself*.

The "center," if we can still use this term loosely, is not a force of centralization meant to organize "the Christology of someone" and "the Christology of something" in epistemological positions in a structural sense. Rather, the "center," as an immanent epistemological space, merely allows us the ability to arrive at different interpretations about *the meaning of Christology* through "meanings" always-already inherent and pre-wired in "Someone" and "Something."

Even though there are always-already "meanings" in "Someone" and "Something," as respectively providing "the Christology of someone" and "the Christology of something" as possibilities toward *the meaning of Christology*, the "center" is not a real entity, since it has nothing to do with *the meaning of Christology*. Furthermore, when interrogating the Husserlian realness[57] of "center" in relation to *the meaning of Christology*, we find that the "center" is always-already unreal. If its functionality, in Derrida's words,

---

55. Deleuze, *Pure Immanence*, 31.

56. This is another version of the term "intendedness," in terms of Hegel's notion of "being acknowledged" or "the process of Recognition." Hegel, *Phenomenology of Spirit*, 111.

57. Husserl, *Ideas*, 297.

"was not only to orient; balance, and organize the structure," what we call "structure," in itself, is also always-already unreal, since, by "structure," we are only referring to the immanent epistemological space—a kind of Heideggerian clearing, so to speak[58]—in which "the Christology of someone" and "the Christology of something" unconceals themselves. Once in the unconcealment of the clearing, either "Someone" or "Something," for the sake of interpretation, attunes themselves to *the meaning of Christology* in its always-already-ness, and, in turn, indicates modes of Husserlian Worldhood[59] for *Christology-Itself.*

The "meaning" in the "center" is dubious and misleading, with respect to the "meaning" of the "center." Note the difference here: in the "center" against of the "center." That is to say, because we can never epistemologically locate "meaning" in the "center," whatever "meaning" exists, it surely exists out of the "center" instead. Nevertheless, "meaning," as in *the meaning of Christology*, is more associated with an in-ness of the "center" rather than with the out-ness.

The problem here, then, is that we often phenomenologically assume that the "meaning" that arises out of the "center" is, in fact, the epistemological residue of a "meaning" in the "center"—this is a basic problem of phenomenology, especially when we inadvertently invent a web of belief about the interconnectedness of the "center," the concept of "structure," and *the meaning of Christology*, which inappropriately relies on an assumed extendedness of "meaning" from a meaningless "center." What makes the "center" meaningless is not just due to the manufactured relationship between its in-ness and out-ness, but, more specifically, it is due to the extent to which *the meaning of Christology* extends itself out of the "center" meaningfully in its always-already-ness.

However meaningless this "center" is to the meaningfulness of *the meaning of Christology*, to denote a "center" means, first and foremost, providing an anchor by which we can even discuss *the meaning of Christology* at all. That anchor allows us to construct the meaningfulness of *the meaning of Christology* as it always-already is—this anchor only serves to build-up what we always-already phenomenologically-know about *the meaning of Christology*, until we can encounter and stabilize what we can epistemologically-know about the "center"-grounded interpretations of "Someone" and "Something" as epistemologically-sound representations of *Christology-Itself.* Relatively speaking, the "center(s)" of both "structures" (of "the Christology of someone" and "the Christology of something") respectively

58. Heidegger, *Being and Time*, 171.
59. Husserl, *Ideas*, 101–2.

centralize themselves meaningfully and meaninglessly on an arbitrary "center" of an immanent space[60] that has always-already determined the meaningfulness and meaninglessness of "Someone" or "Something" in relation to *the meaning of Christology* and *Christology-Itself.*

There is nothing more than an available epistemology in this space—as immanent and necessary as it is—which always-already attunes us to bracketing[61] "the Christology of someone" and "the Christology of something" as *the meaning of Christology.* Through a Husserlian phenomenological εποχη,[62] we only phenomenologically-fashion "the Christology of something" and "the Christology of someone" as *the meaning of Christology,* and apparent representatives of *Christology-Itself,* through meaningful attunement. What becomes fashioned, then, are merely meaningless phenomenological stand-ins for what always-already is meaningful epistemologically. Still, this kind of fashioning occurs as a contingency for us when phenomenologically encountering the "immanence"[63] of "the Christology of something" and "the Christology of someone"—since *the meaning of Christology* is always-already at an epistemological distance, we always-already phenomenologically approximate *Christology-Itself* as either as fashioning of *Something* or *Someone,* in order to bridge the gap between the phenomenology of Christology and the epistemology of Christology.

To be sure, this gap, at its most fundamental, is more than just grounded in subject-object distinctions, or even in dialectics—neither of which prove to be helpful—because what is bridged between "the one whom Christologizes" *Something* or *Someone* and directs that epistemology towards the phenomenological intendedness of "the Christology of something" or "the Christology of someone" is a sense/reference as well as reference/sense.[64]

In effect, when approaching this Fregean relationship between sense and reference, that which is sensed always-already refers, just as much as that which refers always-already senses. How does this figure into and affect "the one whom Christologizes," with respect to "the Christology of something" and "the Christology of someone"?

To put this another way, if we are always-already confronting "the Christology of something" and "the Christology of someone" in their respective phenomenological intendedness toward "the one whom Christologizes," in

---

60. Deleuze, *Pure Immanence,* 31.

61. Husserl, *Ideas,* 110–11.

62. Husserl, *Ideas,* 110–11.

63. The functionality of an Immanent event. Deleuze, *Pure Immanence,* 31.

64. Frege, "On Sense and Reference," 56–78.

what manner, at all, do *Something* and *Someone* embody a simultaneous sensing-reference and referring-sense?

The sense of "the one whom Christologizes" is grounded in the referents of either *Something* or *Someone* as much as the sense of either *Something* or *Someone* is grounded in the referent of "the one whom Christologizes"—the phenomenological and epistemological intersectionality, here, makes it difficult for us, as "the one whom Christologizes," to ever separate ourselves from *Something* or *Someone*, once we ascribe to these entities the respective titles of either "the Christology of something" or "the Christology of someone." These titles define *Something* in its something-ness and *Someone* in its some-one-ness,[65] but it also allows us to define ourselves by proxy—that is to say, our existence and the existences of *Something* and *Someone* harbor a bilateral significance. This can be, perhaps, thought of in a Hegelian[66] and Sartrean[67] way, with respect to the inter-significance and intra-significance of "being-for-itself," "being-in-itself," and "being-for-others."[68] In this, existentiality, I call it, has a Hegelian reflective and abstract significance[69] on one hand, and yet, on the other, it yields a reflecting significance. How we, as "the one whom Christologizes," are able to both have a sense and a reference of either *Something* or *Someone*—in both a sensing-reference and referring-sense—is by how being-in-itself is housed not just "for-itself," but it is always-already housed "for-others." The "in-itself," the "for-itself," and the "for-others" create an inextricable web of belief at a point of intersectionality.[70] This point, as such, contains an inter-significance as well as an intra-significance, when "the one whom Christologizes" recognizes that their inherent being-in-itself is not just limited to a being-for-itself as intra-significance, but, rather, their being-in-itself has extendedness as being-for-others as inter-significance. By intersectionality, what we can ever conceive of (or grasp) and what we can ever know—respectively in phenomenological and epistemological contexts—is always-already deferred in immanence.

Since the way in which we conceive of and grasp *Christology-Itself* is always-already linked to what we can know about *Christology-Itself*,

65. While "something-ness" is the situation or condition in which "Something" finds its being, "someone-ness" denotes another, analogous situation or condition in which "Someone" finds its being.

66. Hegel, *Phenomenology of Spirit*, 111–19.

67. Sartre, *Being and Nothingness*, 49–81.

68. Hegel, *Phenomenology of Spirit*, 111–19.

69. Hegel, *Phenomenology of Spirit*, 111.

70. I am using the term "intersectionality" here to express the underlining relationship between "in-itself," "for-itself," and "for-others," as contributive to a network of epistemology about selfhood.

what kind of significance is there in *the meaning of Christology*, either as intra-significance or inter-significance? What is it that makes *the meaning of Christology* significant? When we say *the meaning of Christology* exists, at all, are we fundamentally orienting that conceptualization, either phenomenologically or epistemologically, to ourselves (reflectively), as "the one whom Christologizes," or to *Something* or *Someone* (reflectingly) as the embodiments of either "the Christology of something" or "the Christology of someone"?

The question is, then, what happens when "the one whom loves" separates themselves from *Something* or *Someone*? Is such a separate even possible? That is to say, what happens when we, as part and parcel of our inquiry into the unconcealment of *the meaning of Christology* and *Christology-Itself*, overcome the Platonic humanism[71] inherently always-already wired into the relationship—a relatedness of inter-significance and intra-significance—between "the one whom Christologizes" and *Something* or *Someone*? This relatedness relates us to either *Something* and *Someone* in an inter- and intra-signifying relation of selves, when we assume the role of "the one whom Christologizes" and direct that intendedness towards "the Christology of something" and "the Christology of someone."

Here, intersectionality becomes our anthropocentric web of belief—the intentionalities of *Something* and *Someone* have an intendedness towards us as "the one whom Christologizes," by either a something-ness or a someone-ness narrowly relative to the immanent situatedness of our humanistic being-in-itself. If there is a situated intersectionality between being-in-itself, being-for-itself, and being-for-others, does this intersectionality fundamentally limit our perspective, as "the one whom Christologizes," through what it means to be human, about what we can conceive of or grasp or know about *Something* or *Someone* the moment we become "the one whom Christologizes"? To what extent, with respect to *what it means to be human*, is there an inescapable humanistic intra- and extra-understanding of *Something* or *Someone* by "the one whom Christologizes"?

For Derrida, *what it means to be human* is a "meaning" that is, ultimately, linked to *the meaning of Christology* —his differentiation between "the Christology of something" and "the Christology of someone" seems implicitly tethered to *what it means to be human*. The issues and concerns of *Something* and *Someone* is respectively unfounded in "the Christology of something" and "the Christology of someone," because these states of existence for both are always-already oriented towards "the one whom Christologizes."

71. Heidegger, "Letter on Humanism," 240.

While "the Christology of something" is not really *Something*, "the Christology of someone" is not really *Someone*—if we say, too, that Derrida's approach to *the meaning of Christology* seemingly views *Christology-Itself* as the Anthropocene, "the Christology of" and that which is Christologized are anthropocentrically contingent on "the one whom Christologizes." Is this logical? If we wish to sort out *what it means to be human*, is the Anthropocene where we adjudicate, in any authentic way as "the one whom Christologizes," how *Something* is "the Christology of something" or how *Someone* is "the Christology of someone"? Is it actually, then, "the one whom Christologizes" that regulates either the something-ness of *Something* or the someone-ness of *Someone*? In other words, if we find that *Something* and *Someone* do not authentically exist in their particular states of existence, does this lead us away from Derrida's logic all together? Will we arrive, once taking this path-mark, at the notion that "the one whom Christologizes" locates *the meaning of Christology* in either *Something* or *Someone*, at any given immanent moment, regardless of what hold "the one whom Christologizes" has on either conceptually? Is because there is "play," as Derrida calls it?

Yes, because, despite of "the one whom Christologizes," differentiation always-already occurs, particularly on two levels of deferring-difference/differing-deference. On one hand, the differentiation must be made between the two, but, on the other, it becomes another differentiation that must be made between the is-ness and not-ness of the two—"the one whom Christologizes" acts as a Sovereign wielding a sovereignty.[72] Not only does this sovereignty allow "the one whom Christologizes" to recognize *the meaning of Christology* through either *Something* or *Someone*, but it, too, brings forth the ability to meta-recognize, at yet another level, a human stain from either *Something* or *Someone* is oriented towards *what it means to be human*.

It is certainly true, though, when invoking *what it means to be human*, we are surely undertaking a decidedly anthropocentric perspective of not just human being, in a general sense, but we are presupposing that the entire stock of the World, in all its Worldhood[73] and Worldliness,[74] is narrowly skewed towards the issues and concerns of "The Human."

Yet, when, in this narrow sense, only *The Human* is "the one whom Christologizes," *the meaning of Christology* is never fully recognized in "the Christology of something" or "the Christology of someone." Nothing meaningful is unconcealed. There is only the anthropocentric meaningless-ness of *The Human* as "the one whom Christologizes"—*The Human* and

---

72. Agamben, *Homo Sacer*, 15–29.

73. Husserl, *Ideas*, 101–2.

74. Heidegger, *Fundamental Concepts of Metaphysics*, 196–97.

the Anthropocene already-always conceal *the meaning of Christology*, to the extent that what we can say is "the Christology of something" or "the Christology of someone" is, in actuality, an untruth about *Something* or *Someone* as *Christology-Itself*. The Human both liberates *the meaning of Christology* and, still, confines it—and *what it means to be human* confines and liberates *Christology-Itself*, since what it means to human, at the point of humanism, constrains what questions can be posed to and what meaningfulness can be made for Christology.

For *Christology-Itself* to fully unconceal itself in *the meaning of love* through either "the Christology of something" or "the Christology of someone," our Recognition[75] of either *Something* or *Someone* must be a meta-recognition. That is, for us to even "know" the meaning of Christology at all, and "know" what we mean to say when we say, "the Christology of something" or "the Christology of something," we must devote ourselves not to *The Human*, the Anthropocene, or Humanism, but to a posthumanism about *the meaning of Christology*.

In effect, *the meaning of Christology* is always-already Posthuman, and its posthumanism (or the condition of its posthumanity) is always-already something that must be adequately worked out, just as this must be for Heidegger's "being." To be clear, *the meaning of Christology*, in its always-already-ness, has never been anything other than being-Posthuman. The kind of thinking necessary to think this kind of thought has not aligned with what always-already is, since our conceptualization of *Christology-Itself* is weighed down by metaphysical Humanism or humanistic metaphysics.

When we "post-" ourselves from the restraints of Humanism and constraints of humanistic thinking about *Christology-Itself*—which always-already conceals more than it actually unconceals, and inauthenticates more than it actually authenticates—*the meaning of Christology* is authentically unconcealed in a meaningful unconcealment of what it always-already is: *Christology-Itself*. By that, we are speaking about *the meaning of Christology*, as that which poses a question and seeks a meaningfulness which must be cast beyond the bounds of Humanism and must be cast into a posthumanity where Christologizing is made possible.

THAT WHICH EXISTS BETWEEN "THE WHO" AND "THE WHAT"

Now, let us consider a relationship which Derrida sets up towards framing the meaning of love, which undeniably and explicitly speaks to *the question*

75. Hegel, *Phenomenology of Spirit*, 111.

of the meaning of Christology. I will provide it here again, with less relevant elements cropped out:

> One of the first questions one could pose [. . .] is the question of the difference between "the who" and "the what." [. . .] The difference between "the who" and "the what" at the heart of love separates the heart. It is often said that love is the movement of the heart.[76]

What we have here, when considering, again, Derrida's notion that there is "first questions [that] one could pose," is Derrida's conceptualization about how one engages and critiques the concept to love. For Derrida, the meaning of love is expressed, framed, and existentialized between "the who" and "the what." It is this fundamental difference between the two—the fact that we are, indeed, speaking of different experiences of and directedness towards the meaning of love—but, what, exactly, can we take Derrida to mean by this? Essentially, how can this conception, though situated in Derrida's approach to how we come to the question of the meaning of love, become a necessary way to cast *the question of the meaning of Christology*?

A great place to start—to begin recasting Derrida for our purposes—is with Derrida's sense that "the difference between 'the who' and 'the what' at the heart of love separates the heart," which we can reconsider and repurpose Derrida's words, for our purposes, *the question of the meaning of Christology*, as that which exists "at the heart of [Christology] separates the heart." In this way, through Derrida, "the difference between 'the who' and 'the what'" allows us to existentialize *the question of the meaning of Christology*, not only as the posing of a question and the seeking of a meaningfulness— which remains important—but, more importantly, as a representation of difference as it lays itself bare.

In one sense, can we say that Derrida literally considers that the way we approach the concept of love is by posing a question grounded in the "difference" between "the who" and "the what"? That means, if taken literally, while recasting our interests, *the question of the meaning of Christology* is based on a "difference" made between the Who-ness of "the who" and the What-ness of "the what." Either *the meaning of Christology* is literally about Who-ness or literally about What-ness—*the meaning of love*, then, is an adjudicated "meaning," in which we must decide that *Christology-Itself* is either more meaningfully represented by "the who" as Who-ness or "the what" as What-ness. When this choice is made literally, not only do we "decide" that one is more meaningful than the other, but we "decide," too, that the one not

---

76. Kofman, Dick, and Derrida, *Derrida*, 78–108.

chosen is not meaningful and verges on a meaninglessness with respect to *the meaning of Christology*. I say "decide" because what we are deciding is rather arbitrary—*the meaning of Christology*, even in this literal sense, has already-decided itself for us before we "decide" between "the who" and "the what." What we "decide" between Who-ness and What-ness is a decision made after-the-fact, since what we "decide" is more meaningful between the two as a primordial meaningfulness, remaining always-concealed in the choice we make. Nevertheless, to arrive at a "decide" between that which is meaningful and that which is not meaningful means, literally, determining what "difference" we find in the two.

Indeed, "the who" and "the what" are merely stand-ins for this determination—they are merely rhetorical entities upon which two arguments about *the meaning of Christology* are temporarily and contextually affixed to the canvases of Who-ness and a What-ness. Who-ness and What-ness, then, function as separate texts. To this end, Who-ness is not What-ness, no more than What-ness is Who-ness—that "difference" is not strictly associated with one not being the other, but, rather, verges more towards what they individually are self-evidently. Both entitles have a self-evident "difference." That is, for us to say that there is a "difference," at all, it is more about using the one that we do not choose to make the one that we do choose meaningful through a differing-deference/deferring-difference. The act of choosing does this, certainly, but the is-ness of the one we choose only goes so far, since it is also the not-ness that further enframes[77] the meaningfulness of the one that we choose—*the meaning of love*, as such, is both literally represented by either the is-ness of the Who-ness or the is-ness of the What-ness that we have chosen and, simultaneously, always-already literally represented by either the not-ness of the Who-ness or the not-ness of the What-ness we have not chosen.

Taken literally, "the difference between 'the who' and 'the what'" is not only not meaningfully about "difference," but it is also not meaningfully about "a question." To say "not meaningfully" suggests that meaning itself— *the meaning of Christology*, that is—can never be located in any "difference" made between two entities nor in any "question" made about the "difference" between two entities: Who-ness and What-ness. In this case, the Who and the What are literally non-literal, since both literally do not serve *the meaning of Christology* in any authentic manner and, to a greater extent, are merely non-literal points of misdirection and allow us to misunderstand what *the meaning of Christology* is.

---

77. Heidegger, "Question Concerning Technology," 3–35.

The moment we, as Derrida does, propose that the meaning of love is "a question of the difference between 'the who' and "the what,'" we have contaminated the meaning of the question asked with the meaning of *a* difference. Derrida seemingly conflates the two, working under a presupposition that, when we question difference, that "difference" itself unconceals the meaning of Who-ness and What-ness.

In other words, when Derrida uses terms such as "difference" and "question," both terms, themselves, are meaningless. To be sure, I do not wish to presume that both terms, especially as Derrida appropriates them, literally have no meaning in them. There is "meaning" in the terms, but it is "a meaning" that does not unconceal *The Meaning* that needs to be unconcealed about Who-ness and What-ness. In fact, Derrida's use of the two terms, in a literal sense, generalizes *The Meaning*—or *the meaning of Christology* itself, at its most existential—so that it would seem that there is a directedness in the choice made between Who-ness and What-ness. That is, The Choosing does not direct us towards *The Meaning*, and, in that regard, the act of choosing either the Who-ness or the What-ness offers us meaninglessness and misdirection. What this means, then, is that "the who" and "the what" are phenomenological signposts of disorientation, situating the situatedness of Who-ness and What-ness predicated on an arbitrary "difference" and an arbitrary "question." The arbitrariness of "difference" and "question" misdirect us from *the meaning of Christology* —both, in their respectively arbitrariness, conceal *the meaning of Christology* beneath the "difference between 'the who' and 'the what'" on one hand, and, on the other, the choosing of one over the other. What Derrida misses here, then, is the extent that "difference" only separates Who-ness from What-ness, while never accomplishing anything more than authentic than arbitrary aesthetic grounds.

Yet, in another sense, if we take a more figurative route, the "difference" between Who-ness and What-ness—for the sake of "the who" and "the what"—is not really about "difference" at all. In effect, "difference" is a form of Negation,[78] since any "difference" we make between Who-ness and What-ness negates both across an immanent plane of understanding. In this way, when "difference" negates Who-ness and What-ness, the Negation[79] prevents "the who" and "the what" from ever existing in a state other than absolute Abstraction.[80]

78. Hegel, *Phenomenology of Spirit*, 51.

79. Hegel, *Phenomenology of Spirit*, 51.

80. Hegel, *Phenomenology of Spirit*, 51.

"Différance,"[81] as a form of Negation, prevents the Concretization[82] of Who-ness and What-ness, if we hold to the presupposition that *the meaning of Christology*, through Concretization, must be unconcealed in a meaningful unconcealment. When we speak of Abstraction, Negation, and Concretization, we find that *the meaning of Christology* does not naturally unconceal itself, since it figuratively resides in an Abstraction—because of this, Negation always-already conceals *the meaning of Christology* so that it cannot actualize itself to the point of Concretization. This concealment is figurative.

Though *the meaning of Christology* must confront and overcome Negation in order to concretize and unconceal itself, it is always-already actualized in its primordiality and, thusly, it becomes concretized in a meaningful unconcealment. The entities of Who-ness and What-ness do not unconceal the meaning of love, even though their appearances to us make it seem so. Instead, Who-ness and What-ness function as forces of Negation, from their situatedness as absolute Abstractions, which must be confronted and overcome to unconceal *the meaning of Christology* as it always-already is in its primordiality. Since the Who-ness of "the who" and What-ness of "the what" are absolute Abstractions, neither meaningfully fulfills what must be necessarily unconcealed about *the meaning of Christology*.

Though Derrida believes, if modifying him, that "one of the first questions one could pose [about Christology] is the question of the difference between 'the who' and 'the what,'" the question of difference ultimately, in an always-already-ness, negates the question of meaning. "Difference" and "question," as Derrida has employed them, cancel out one another, and, in turn, conceal any possible meaning either holds individually or dialectically.

Figuratively speaking, there is no meaningful "difference" between Who-ness and What-ness, since *the meaning of Christology* never truly resides in either. As such, neither unconceals *the meaning of Christology*. That is to say, *the meaning of Christology* does not and cannot unconceal itself through either entity, since both entities are always-already forms of concealment. To focus on the "difference" means misrecognizing this concealment as unconcealment. In suggesting that *the meaning of Christology* is "the question of the difference between 'the who' and 'the what,'" Derrida misrecognizes that "difference" always-already conceals any "question" that means to be asked about Who-ness and What-ness. Derrida's "question" is

---

81. Derrida, "Différance," 1–27.

82. I use "Concretization" in the way Hegel uses the term "determinate." Hegel, *Phenomenology of Spirit*, 51.

rooted in what kind of state "the who" and "the what" exist in and how this relates to *that which exists between.*

Since "the who" and "the what" are forms of concealment by nature, locating "difference" between their respective Who-ness and What-ness obscures both states of existence to us, primarily because these states of existence conceal *the meaning of Christology* at its most primordial. We cannot perceive or conceive of Who-ness or What-ness without "the who" and "the what" standing-out to us in reserve.[83] The ek-sistence[84] of both, as a standing-reserve,[85] is nothing more than what we think/believe we see ontologically—when we perceive "the who" and "the what" beyond their respective ontics, what we conceive of, at the core of their metaphysics, in states of Who-ness and What-ness, become stand-ins for *that which exists between,* predicated on *the question of the meaning of Christology.* In this, there are issues of "difference" and "question," which oscillate between matters of meaningfulness and unconcealment. Nevertheless, neither "difference" nor "question" can authentically unconceal or bring forth *that which exists between* from concealment and its concealedness and into the clearing of unconcealment.[86]

When *that which exists between* is unconcealed in the clearing, we authentically encounter *the meaning of Christology,* as it wants to be encountered by us. The "Meaning" of *the meaning of love,* at its most primordial and authentic, is only meaningful in the clearing: this becomes *that which exists between.* The clearing, as the means by which *that which exists between* unconceals itself, allows us to confront *the meaning of Christology.* To do so, we do it without the service of questioning the "difference between 'the who' and 'the what.'" If the "question" is indubitably about *the meaning of Christology,* the "difference" made between Who-ness and What-ness always-already conceals *the meaning of Christology,* to the extent that this concealment fools us into thinking/believing that "difference" between Who-ness and What-ness orients us to an unconcealment of *Christology-Itself*—that is, *Christology-Itself,* as another name for *that which exists between,* is never (and can never) be unconcealed from/by/through states of Who-ness or What-ness. "The who" and "the what" are markers pointing to these meaningless states of existence and, essentially, are only as meaningful as their respective standing-in-reserve of Who-ness and What-ness allows.

83. Heidegger, "The Question Concerning Technology," 3–35.

84. Heidegger, "Letter on Humanism," 249.

85. Heidegger, "Question Concerning Technology," 3–35.

86. Heidegger, *Being and Time,* 171.

If both are merely meaningless stand-ins, when we adjudicate the "difference" between Who-ness of "the who" and What-ness of "the what," the act of choosing itself becomes an arbitrary act of deontology. That is not to say that what is deontological is arbitrary—rather, the choice we make is unavoidably deontological, since we feel morally obligated to choose and, in turn, believe that what we have chosen is morally obligated to us. What we choose also chooses us. We choose out of moral obligation towards "the who" and "the what" for the sake of difference, but also through a morality to *the question of the meaning of Christology* in relation to this "difference." The Choice that is made between Who-ness and What-ness is fundamentally meaningless, with respect to what *the meaning of Christology* is. We assign meaningfulness to the Choice (as that which is made between "the who" and "the what"), because we cannot believe/think, in a morally-obligated way, that the Choice can really ever be meaningless.

To this end, we merely believe/think that there is always a meaningfulness over/above any meaninglessness, especially as signifiers in relation to the Choice and its deontology as the signified. When approaching the Choice and its deontology, the Choice is never meaningless, if the Choice, as such, is deontological. Through believing/thinking, they are inextricable and mutually-existential entities—the Choice and its deontology—to the extent that both are independently-dependent and dependently-independent on one another. The Choice as an act of choosing and the deontological as an act of deontology become so arbitrary in their inextricability and existentiality that we believe/think that the Choice by way of its deontology is *the meaning of Christology*. Because of this, through believing/thinking in/with the Choice, we are so morally-obligated to meaningfulness over/above meaninglessness that we believe/think that either "the who" or "the what" is *the meaning of Christology*.

To be clear, the deontology we infuse into the Choice, and how the act of choosing becomes deontological, gives us an epistemological space to believe/think that either "the what" or "the who" is actually *the meaning of Christology*. This "actually" is a problem that entraps us and subjects us to an arbitrary kind of believing/thinking that is fraught with what we believe we are believing and what we think we are thinking. Frankly, what we believe we are believing about the Choice, and what we think we are thinking about the Choice's deontology entraps/subjects us in/with "Meaning"—we are always-already interpolated by "Meaning" until our ideology about/towards *the meaning of Christology* is always-already delineated into the superstructure of meaningfulness and the infrastructure of meaninglessness.

This interpolation of "Meaning" always-already leads us towards believing/thinking that the Choice we make between "the who" and "the what" is about a deontology of either meaningfulness or meaninglessness, pivoting on *that which exists between*, so that what is "Meaningful" is *the meaning of Christology* and what is "Meaningless" is not *the meaning of Christology*.

This is never so, if *that which exists between* is more aligned with *the meaning of Christology* than with "the who" or "the what." *That which exists between* the Who-ness of "the who" and the What-ness of "the what" is not contingent on the extent to which it is aligned or misaligned with *the meaning of Christology*. When we say, then, that *that which exists between* is "more aligned" with *the meaning of Christology*, this means that, in terms of meaningfulness and meaninglessness, "Meaning" occurs at different levels for *that which exists between, the meaning of love*, and the Who-ness of "the who" and the What-ness of "the what." In effect, *that which exists between* is made more meaningful in comparison and juxtaposition to *the meaning of Christology* than it is with the Who-ness of "the who" and the What-ness of "the what." Because the Who-ness of "the who" and the What-ness of "the what" can never be *the meaning of Christology*, the same can be said about how they inadequately embody *that which exists between*. To even say the Who-ness of "the who" and the What-ness of "the what" means, fundamentally, that we are engaging these entities as phenomenon—what we can know (and can ever know) about the Who-ness of "the who" and the What-ness of "the what" are translated/interpreted by our senses. The senses, or sense-perception,[87] allows us to experience the Who-ness of "the who" and the What-ness of "the what." What exactly do we experience by way of the senses? The senses, on one hand, translate/interpret the Who-ness of "the who" and the What-ness of "the what" in terms of difference, but, on the other hand, the senses translate/interpret all things that separately align with the Who-ness of "the who" and the What-ness of "the what." To put it another way: when experiencing the phenomenon of the Who-ness of "the who" and the What-ness of "the what," we come to "know" what Who-ness is in relation to "the who"—and What-ness in relation to "the what," for that matter—and believe/think that we "know" *that which exists between*.

That which exists between the Who-ness of "the who" and the What-ness of "the what" is not strictly involved in making either entity what it individually is or separately is. Though *that which exists between* is not strictly involved in the metaphysics of either entity, it is still loosely involved in making the ontological space in which both entities exist—if it were not for the metaphysical presence of *that which exists between*, the Who-ness of "the who" and the What-ness of "the what" would not be able to ontologically situate themselves as entities upon which we make our Choice. The

87. Husserl, *Ideas*, 119–20.

way in which the Who-ness of "the who" and the What-ness of "the what" stand out to us is an ek-sistence that is partially build upon that which exists between. Our Choice and the deontological nature of that Choice builds up "the who" and "the what" beyond their respective Who-ness and What-ness. *That which exists between* grounds the deontology of the Who-ness of "the who" and the What-ness of "the what," so that, when we choose between "the who" and "the what," we are not only believing/thinking we have created either "the who" or "the what" through our Choice, but we believe/think that we "know" what makes the Who-ness of "the who" and the What-ness of "the what."

Essentially, "the who" and "the what" ek-sist[88] in such a way that we never have complete access to the Who-ness or the What-ness that lies beneath. Who-ness and What-ness are shadows structurally dependent on "the who" and "the what" that they shadow—they are no more "knowable" to us when we choose between "the who" and "the what" than *that which exists between* is "knowable." That is so, at least in part, because, while "the who" and "the what" are always-already our phenomenon, Who-ness and What-ness are always-already noumenon. What makes either so is not because of our experience of "the who" and "the what," or even the extent to which we can say we "know" either, but because of their status as Kantian things-in-themselves.

For example, let us take a closer look at "the who," with the hope that, by extension, we can shed light on "the what" as well. Certainly, "the who," as a phenomenon, is an entity that I can experience as rudimentarily as "knowing" that it is not "the what." What am I saying when I say "experience"? This requires thinking more critically through what experience means—and, of course, what experience is not. Consider this: in despite of what I experience or "know" about "the who," what makes it so is not my experience of it. I do not create "the who" when I experience it—it is always-already created/invented prior to my experience of it, such that it is *a priori* and I only believe, to certain extent, that what is laid bare is *posteriori*. The Choice that I make between it and "the what" merely references an always-already ek-sistence. What makes this possible, then, is the stand-out-ability[89] of "the who" from its Who-ness—a Who-ness that I do not experience first-hand, or even "know" in any narrow sense. What I experience or "know" about Who-ness is only always in the general sense, as metaphysical residue beneath/behind the ontology of "the who," insofar as "the who" announces

---

88. Heidegger, "Letter on Humanism," 249.

89. This is a modification of Heidegger's term "ek-sistence," which, in itself, Heidegger argues, "means standing out into the truth of being." Heidegger, "Letter on Humanism," 249.

itself to me as Who-ness in terms of the difference between it and "the what" and its What-ness, all within the broader ontology of *the question of the meaning of Christology*.

Whether speaking about "the who" and its Who-ness, or applying the same method to exemplify "the what" and its What-ness, we are attending to *the meaning of Christology*, as that which construes itself through *the question of the meaning of Christology*. The only way to pose the question to and seek the meaningfulness of Christology requires venturing beyond *the question of the meaning of Christology* to situates ourselves towards *the meaning of Christology* through Christological reflection and Christological thinking. This reflection and thinking hinges on the questions we can respectively pose to "the who" and "the what" and the meaningfulness we ca respectively seek in Who-ness and What-ness—how we existentialize *that which exists between* is in terms of viewing the problem of the historical Jesus as a matter of "the who" brought forth by Who-ness and in terms of viewing the problem of the Christ of faith as a matter of "the what" brought forth by What-ness. The difference that arises between the two, the tension that arises between "The Meaning" and "The Choice" (or the Choosing), and how the need to existentialize one over the other grounds what it means to Christologize all attend to the ways and means by which we can unconceal *the question of the meaning of Christology*, even though, at its very utterance, *the question of the meaning of Christology* becomes more of a concealment, concealing what we wish to Christologize—though we must articulate *the question of the meaning of Christology* to pose questions to and seek the meaningfulness of Christology, and these endeavors lay our Christologizing bare, *the question of the meaning of Christology* remains an Abstraction and maintains a Negation to what wishes to be Christologized, since the deontological grounds by which we speak about *the meaning of Christology* inevitably makes the ontological grounds all the more elusive and the metaphysical grounds of *that which exists between* our concerns with the historical Jesus and those of the Christ of faith all the more posthuman.

Postscript

The perennial *question of the meaning of Christology*, as that which pits the historical Jesus against the Christ of faith, remains our ultimate concern from the moment those that sought to make sense out of the ministry of Jesus committed themselves theologically to a Christology. What arose, as early as the first century C.E., through Christological thinking and Christological reflections remains what situates us now to pose the question to and seek the meaningfulness of Christology—what we are perennially engaged with is *that which exists between*, or what allows, according to the Chalcedonian Creed, two natures (divine vs. human) to have one existence. We know, of course, that the Chalcedonian Creed only perpetuates the development of the problem of the historical Jesus and, in turn, the difficulties with how we conceptualize the full existentiality of the Christ of faith.

Indeed, since the Council of Chalcedon, we have been wrestling with *that which exists between*. We can think of this as what ties the concerns of historical Jesus and those of the Christ of faith into a single "problem." Similarly, we can think of *that which exists between* as the dialectic—Hegel's notion of "unity"[1]—which philosophically brings together the two natures into one existence, into a phenomenological conglomeration of Husserlian "bracketing."[2]

While *that which exists between* makes it possible to both dialectically and phenomenologically understand what the existence of Jesus Christ is, it leaves us with the perennial problem of the historical Jesus, as what is passed down through the centuries and framed by "the first quest" that Schweitzer brings to an end, framed by the period of "no quest" ushered by Bultmann, and framed by the commencement of a "second quest" by Käsemann, Bornkamm, and other, for the sake of simple categorization,

1. Hegel, *Phenomenology of Spirit*, 110.
2. Husserl, *Ideas*, 110–11.

"Bultmannians." Because the problem of the historical Jesus makes *that which exists between* explicit, it is the problem of the historical Jesus, as a notion, that comes to represent and embody *that which exists between*. In this sense, those involved in the development of the "first quest" and Bultmann's period of "no quest" and what propels those engaged in the "third quest" are all wrestling with *that which exists between*—to this end, *that which exists between* is the focus of all Questors.

Because of this, *that which exists between* is also always-already noumenon: its existence is not dependent on our experience of it. In particular, the "Meaning" in *that which exists between* is not the "Meaning" in *the meaning of Christology*, since the former precedes the latter. The essence of *that which exists between* precedes the existence of *the meaning of Christology*. The only way we can know what *the meaning of Christology* is, then, is based on the account of the being-ness of *that which exists between*. What makes either of them meaningful is grounded in an individualized meaningfulness, which is made more meaningful by the meaninglessness of the other. What this means, then, is that *that which exists between* is not *the meaning of Christology*—essentially, the former is *a priori* and the latter is *posteriori*.

From what Derrida says about the meaning of love, and the extent that we can cast it in terms of *the meaning of Christology*, what we find, then, is that *what it means to be human* is always-already the theoretical starting point to what *the meaning of Christology* is to us. We cannot conceive of *the meaning of Christology*, at all, without the predicate of *what it means to human*—in this way, *that which exists* between, in its always-already *a priori*, is what situates us towards *the meaning of Christology*, such that it appears that *the meaning of Christology* is known to us *posteriori*. The sense that what *the meaning of Christology* is—well before we are able to confront and make sense out of *the question of the meaning of Christology*—is projected from *that which exists between* and translated through *what it means to be human*.

Yet, *what it means to be human*, as the theoretical starting point, for what *the meaning of Christology* is for us becomes a human construction, predicated by human finite epistemology. What we are able to know about Christology—in terms of what Christological thinking and Christological reflection tells us—is merely captured by a humanism, which acts as an epistemological foundation that allows us to construct for ourselves the questions we wish to pose to and the meaningfulness we wish to seek about Christology.

The humanistic framework allows *the meaning of Christology* to have a "meaning" that becomes "Christological," insofar as what lies *posteriori* tells us—it is humanism, at the juncture of *what it means to be human*, that

makes it possible for us to meaningfully account for the concerns of Christology, as that which we can fundamentally make sense of as a relationship
between the historical Jesus and the Christ of faith. However problematic
this relationship is—such that what unfolds is as much about the problem
of the historical Jesus as it is about the "problem" of the Christ of faith—
humanism, as its humanistic framework, allows us to adjudicate what is
problematized Christologically, so that *what it means to human* actualizes,
reifies, and solves what *the meaning of Christology* is.

We must take care to note what is actualized, what is reified, and what is
solved. We must think of this simply and merely from the humanistic standpoint, rather than from a natural standpoint—that is to say, if we make use
of Husserl's "bracketing," we not only bracket the meaning of Christology,
but we also bracket what sense we make out of the relationship between the
problem of the historical Jesus and the "problem" of the Christ of faith. This
humanistic standpoint allows us to best position ourselves to *the question of
the meaning of Christology*, in terms of what questions we can pose and what
meaningfulness we can seek—humanism makes *the question of the meaning
of Christology* possible, when we "bracket" *the meaning of Christology* out of
its natural standpoint of *that which exists between*, so that what *the meaning
of Christology* is, then, is grounded on our phenomenology of it and the
degree to which we can articulate *the question of the meaning of Christology*
is phenomenological.

What is made expressible in *the question of the meaning of Christology*
comes by way of difference—what is substantive between two things—such
that *the question of the meaning of Christology* is, in itself, a by-product of
what Hegel's notion of "unity" means and what Husserl's "bracketing" does.
To a certain extent, when we utter the question of the meaning of Christology, we are uttering a dialectic: between "question" and "meaning," between
what is posed and what is sought, between the historical Jesus and the
Christ of faith, between what is *a priori* and what is *posteriori*, and between
meaningfulness received and meaningfulness presented. What guides all
these issues of difference is the difference, as Derrida refers to it, between "a
who" and "a what."

If there is, as Derrida argues, a "difference between 'a who' and 'a
what,'" *the question of the meaning of Christology*, at its most authentic and
unconcealed, attempts to sort out issues of a "Who-ness" and a "What-ness."

To start here means starting with a relationship between humanism
and *Christology-Itself*, and assuming that this relationship is grounded on an
always-already-ness of both "The Human" and *the meaning of Christology*.
Starting with *The Human* means assuming that *The Human* always-already
invents, extends, sustains, and translates *the meaning of Christology*, like a

painting upon a canvas, in order to invent, extend, sustain, and translate *what it means to be human* towards the Christ of faith over and against the problem of the historical Jesus.

When thinking about where Derrida begins with a framework upon which *the meaning of love* is constructed as a structure, perpetuated by *what it means to be human,* and stratified into the superstructure of "the who" and the infrastructure of "the what"—Humanism is this structure, which becomes constituted by a metaphysical tension in *the meaning of Christology* between *The One Whom Christologizes* as "the who" and either *Something* or *Someone* as "the what."

Insofar as Derrida's humanistic understanding of *the meaning of love* yields an inauthentic and concealed approach to the question of Love-Itself, so, too, is the concealedness of the question of *Christology-Itself*. If, to be clear, what we can conceive of/grasp and know, as *The One Whom Christologizes*, is "[a] question of the difference between 'a who' and 'a what,'" *the meaning of Christology,* as its itself is, always-already begins at the starting point of *what it means to be human,* based on an overarching Humanism.

In saying that there a Humanism or a humanistic understanding behind how "the one whom Christologizes" embarks on *the meaning of Christology* through an intendedness towards *Something* or *Someone,* respectively as "the Christology of something" or "the Christology of someone," as phenomenological stand-ins for *Christology-Itself,* I mean to denote that there is a framework of thinking always-already freeing and confining how "the one whom Christologizes" conceives of, grasps, and explains *the meaning of Christology.* To what extent Plato—and Aristotle and Descartes, for that matter—are to blame for how we can explain Christology at all is certainly worth keeping in our purview. To whatever degree, at this point, that we say that Heidegger recognizes the influence Plato/Aristotle has had on what we know, at all, about anything that conceals or unconceals itself and what role The Clearing plays in the possibility of unconcealment is important—essentially, for us to say that what is laid bare is the difference between "a who" and "a what," if making use of Derrida, is fundamentally due to what has unconcealed itself to us.

What must be first addressed, when acknowledging what Heidegger contributes, is the manner in which Derrida falls into a metaphysical trap, by even suggesting that "love" should be asked about in terms of being either "the love of something" or "the love of someone." In effect, if we ask, as Derrida does, *is love the love of something or the love of someone,* we are presupposing something not just about Christology, "the Christology of something" and "the Christology of someone" as mere unconcealed interpretations of *the meaning of Christology,* but we are assuming, too, that "the one whom Christologizes" is always-already intended towards *Something* or *Someone* before any authentic thinking/thought is ever accomplished, since the underlying intendedness, within the way we think about *the meaning of Christology*, is an escapable intentionality. The always-already-ness of Christological thinking is a kind of metaphysical thinking that must be overcome, but certainly not eliminated. Similarly, Christological reflection, in its always-already-ness, is a kind of metaphysical reflection that must be overcome, but certainly not eliminated.

To be clear, though it is important that we overcome metaphysics in the Heideggerian sense, we certainly cannot do away with it entirely. That ladder, so to speak, cannot be realistically kicked away and cast off. All that we can ever "know" in the World, including *the meaning of Christology* and *Christology-Itself*, has its Worldhood inextricably attached to metaphysics. By that, I mean that the only way we can "know" *the meaning of Christology* and *Christology-Itself* is with respect to the metaphysics that undergird them, even though these very metaphysics condemn us to a way of thinking about the World and Worldhood, which, in turn, condemns us to a kind of metaphysical thought that conceals more than it can unconceal, especially with respect to how we pose the question to and seek the meaningfulness of Christology, as *the question of the meaning of Christology*.

Is our main interest—our ultimate concern, as Paul Tillich surmises[3]—in ensuring that what we "know" exists in an unconcealment? Our main interest can be with nothing else. In other words, our main interest, as *The One Whom Christologizes*, is certainly with that which is unconcealed to the extent that it has unconcealed itself authentically in an epistemological unconcealment. And, furthermore, if we pose another question about "our main interest," through such an unconcealment, are we not seeking a meaningful authentication of *Christology-Itself* through what we meaningfully identify in "the Christology of something" and "the Christology of someone," insofar as either are mere interpretations of *the meaning of Christology* at its most meaningfulness?

Nevertheless, the way we think about *the meaning of Christology* and *Christology-Itself* must be deconstructed—overcome, but not eliminated—so that we can fully understand what is being concealed and unconcealed through "the Christology of something" and "the Christology of someone." Both "the Christology of something" and "the Christology of someone" are propositional statements we make when addressing either *Something* or *Someone*, in order to capture, in an immanent way, what it is that we intended-towards as a sensing-reference and a referring-sense. Within language,

---

3. Tillich, *Dynamics of Faith*, 1–4.

the meaning of Christology is translated through *Someone* or *Something*, through the time-tempered "the Christology of someone" and "the Christology of something." Because of this, *The One Whom Christologizes* recognizes either *Something* or *Someone* as phenomenological stand-ins that lean toward an epistemology, even if that epistemology is inextricably linked and served by an underlying phenomenological authenticity. Not only do these stand-ins always-already present us, as *The One Who Christologizes*, with meaningless phenomenological unconcealments, but what is apparently unconcealed in the unconcealedness of a *Someone* or a *Something* is an apparent-epistemological inauthentic *Christology-Itself.*

Since *the meaning of Christology* tends to always-already conceal itself to us in either a *Someone* or a *Something* towards which we always direct the already-ness of our understandings about *Christology-Itself.* Because these already-understandings about *Christology-Itself* are always more phenomenological than epistemological, we substitute *the meaning of love* for either "the Christology of someone" or "the Christology of something," to the extent that we both knowingly and unknowingly refer to either *Someone* or *Something* as *Christology-Itself.*

Let us return to Derrida's questions concerning "the love of someone" and "the love of something" as what has been recast as "the Christology of someone" and "the Christology of something." Reconsider Derrida's questions here:

> Is love the love of someone or the love of something? Okay, supposing I loved someone, do I love someone for the absolute singularity of who they are? I love you because you are you. Or do I love your qualities, your beauty, your intelligence? Does one love someone, or does one love something about someone?[4]

Yet, more specifically, then, this means that even when "lov[ing] someone for the absolute singularity of who they are," as Derrida suggests, there remains a "center" to this "absolute singularity of who they are." We could call this the Who-ness of "someone"—this Who-ness allows "someone" to have an "absolute singularity," to the extent that no other Who-ness in a World of innumerable Who-nesses, embodies the Same of the "absolute singularity of who they are." There is a resoluteness in this "absolute singularity," which suggests that "who they are" is like no other "Who"—it is such that "the absolute singularity of who they are" becomes meaningful to the one that does the meaning-making about the Who-ness of "someone." Similarly, this kind of meaning-making allows, if following Derrida a little further, for the

---

4. Kofman, Dick, and Derrida, *Derrida*, 78–108.

What-ness of "something," where I can say that I am "lo[ving] some[thing] for the absolute singularity of wh[at] they are."

What is apparent in Derrida's explanation about love is that there are no general hermeneutics of love. To only generally interpret love, then, means applying an interpretation "to love," "from love," or even "by love." None of these arrive at love's about-ness, or *the meaning of love*. This holds true, of course, to *the meaning of Christology*—there is no general hermeneutics to it, since interpreting Christology generally means applying an interpretation "to Christology," working "from Christology," or even situating oneself "by Christology."

In this narrow sense, *the meaning of Christology* refers to an epistemology of Christology—what we know that we know about the *meaning* of Christology—as that which always-already imposes itself upon us before we are ever aware of its imposition. Arriving at *the meaning of Christology* in a narrow sense involves a narrow hermeneutics of *Christology-Itself*, especially if we can say, with certainty, that *Christology-Itself* contains a "meaning" that refers to something meaningful, and, in that meaningfulness, we can conclude, with certainty, that a certain something meaningfully expressed *the meaning of Christology*.

To say that *the meaning of Christology* can be answered with a general question means suggesting, fundamentally, that *Christology-Itself* is a generality that can be conceived of, grasped, and explained in a general sense. This is untrue. In this general sense, the question of *Christology* is not based/grounded on the generalities of *Christology*—*Christology* is this or *Christology* is that, or *Christology* is not this or not that—because generalities do not give an account of *Christology*. A generality of *Christology*, then, places *Christology-Itself* in a structure that, in turn, suggests that there is a structure of *Christology* and any meaning of *Christology-Itself* is encased in *the meaning of the center of the structure of Christology*. Referring to *Christology-Itself* as something that carries a general meaning never "unconceals" *the meaning of Christology* at all. Generalities only further "conceal" *the meaning of Christology* in an existential concealment at the "center" of a manufactured structure. If generalities are general claims and propositions, *Christology-Itself* is more than just a general claim or proposition that results from a general question. To say that someone loves someone else "generally" proceeds from a general claim—more importantly, in arriving at such a general claim, one merely poses a general question about *Christology* that only "conceals" *the meaning of Christology-Itself* in the generalities of the questioning.

This is what Derrida points out, when judging his initial reaction to the generalities of question from the off-screen interviewer. Not only does Derrida obviously react to the generality of the question itself, but we also see how the generality of the question legitimately (and noticeably) takes him by surprise. If it is a surprise towards the generality of the question itself, or a surprise at the specificity required to focus on the meaning of the question, Derrida's answer, again, is thoughtful and formulated—his response attempts to isolate *the question of the meaning of Christology* as a relationship between "the who" and "the what."

This is, in fact, a philosophical and theoretical divide, as Derrida suggests, between "the who-ness" and "the what-ness" of *Love-Itself* in relation to *the question of the meaning of love*. Yet, "the meaning," here, seems to point to a divide between *the subject of love* and *the object of love*—in other words, it is a divide between *love's subjectivity* in terms of how love is defined through essentialized subjectification and the degree to which *love's objectivity* defines love as that which necessitates existentialized objectification. It is a divide between "essence" and "existence" as issues that must be respectively worked out between *love's subjectivity* and *love's objectivity*, which can be similarly construed, in terms of "essence" and "existence," and in terms of *Christology's subjectivity* and *Christology's objectivity*.

Now, the divide itself poses the problem, as a hermeneutical problem—the "problem," to be clear, is with what can be essentialized as "essence" and what can be existentialized as "existence" through the question of and the meaning of *Christology's subjectivity* and *Christology's objectivity*. That which becomes essentialized as "essence" and that which becomes existentialized as "existence" present a "problem" for *Christology's subjectivity* and *Christology's objectivity* alike.

And yet, by "problem," I do not mean that, in what must be worked out, the "problem" solves itself. The divide as "Divide" between *Christology's subjectivity* and *Christology's objectivity* makes any working out of the "problem" only arbitrary—it is solved only arbitrarily enough. I do not mean say, of course, that, in this arbitrariness, we are doomed to never work out the "problem" satisfactorily. In fact, we do "work out," adequately, what divides *Christology's subjectivity* from *Christology's objectivity* by problematizing both through the respective situatedness of the two on either side of the "Divide." The "being" of both stand out for us, when we posit their respective.

Because *Christology's subjectivity* and *Christology's objectivity* are mutually-exclusive entities—not entirely dependent on the other's essence" or "existence"—the "problem" always remains inevitable to *the question of the meaning of love*. Any "meaning," here, is bound to/by *the question of Christology* itself as a "problem" between the mutual exclusivity of *Christology's subjectivity* and *Christology's objectivity*. The to/by-ness of what binds "meaning" to *the question of Christology* is a "meaning" that is never really ascertained beyond simply ascribing meaningfulness and meaninglessness. For us to even suggest that there is a "meaning" in *the question of the meaning of Christology* means to propose that, first, there is a "meaning" in the question, and, secondly, that *the question of Christology* harbors "meaning" by *extensa*.

In other words, *Christology's subjectivity* and *Christology's objectivity* "extend" towards one another, soliciting a "meaning" from the other, across the "Divide" that is *the question of the meaning of Christology*. In this divide, there is a differing-deference as much as there is a deferring-difference between *Christology* as subject and *Christology* as object. Between *Christology's subjectivity* and *Christology's objectivity*—the differing-deference and deferring-difference between "the who-ness" and "the what-ness"—Derrida is right to suggest that there is "the question of the difference between 'a who' and 'a what.'" Yet, Derrida does not go far enough in discussed what "the question of the difference" is—the "difference," as such, between "the who" and "the what" is a question of hermeneutic significance.

What is significant in the question of hermeneutic significance is this: the *Difference*—or *that which exists between*—which existentially divides *the subject of Christology* and *the object of Christology* in a differing-deferring difference/deference. In this, there is a Hegelian independence and dependence of *Christology's subjectivity* and *Christology's objectivity*, insofar as what links them is the Recognition of the other.[5] Not only does *the subject of Christology* recognize the Otherness of *the object of Christology*, but *the object of Christology* also recognizes *the subject of Christology* similarly. What is recognized is otherness—something that one is not through the process of othering in a subject-object relation—but also the extent to which The Other holds a power over what it is not. This is so by a Play of Forces[6] dictated through an independent-dependence and dependent-independence—each has an independence from the other, but each is dependent on the other. This "play" between Independence and Dependence is rooted on the extent to which *the object of Christology* and *the subject of Christology* have a "force" in themselves and between themselves, across the overall structure of Christology as *what Christology is*. In a loose sense, this construction reveals a "play" between *the subject of Christology* and *the object of Christology* within an overarching conceptualization of Structuralized *Christology* unconcealed by *the question of the meaning of Christology*.

Therein lies a Hegelian self-consciousness between the two grounded in a Lordship-Bondage dialectic,[7] but that self-consciousness, when cast in a Husserlian way, is not just inwardly-oriented for *the subject of Christology*

5. Hegel, *Phenomenology of Spirit*, 110.

6. Hegel, *Phenomenology of Spirit*, 110.

7. Hegel, *Phenomenology of Spirit*, 110.

to assume *Christology's subjectivity*. Rather, it is projected outwardly to the Other, *the object of Christology* as *Christology's objectivity*. However, the self-consciousness of *the object of Christology* as *Christology's objectivity* functions the same way. What arises, then, through a dialectical self-consciousness between the two, is *a difference in the question of the meaning of Christology* and, more narrowly, the means by which we can locate a definition of love in either the *subject of Christology* or the *object of Christology*. That is, when we pose the question about *Christology* (for example: *What is Christology?*), in an effort to define it, we are attempting to locate *the meaning of Christology* in a question that indubitably suggests a *difference in the question of the meaning of Christology*—we are formulating an epistemology about *Christology*.

If we say, if following Derrida, that any definition of *the meaning of Christology* employs a notion of the difference between "the who" and "the what," we must conceptualize the *Who-ness* and *What-ness*, perhaps not strictly as separate entities of irreconcilable difference, but as two differing entities of deference that point to the same entity. Essentially, the extent to which there is a Who-ness and What-ness is due to a same-difference, or a different-sameness. Here, it is not a rigid structural difference between a subject and an object—especially if we wish, too, to move beyond typical subject-object restrictions and utterly abide by a Structure of love—but an arbitrary difference of *Difference*. It is a *Difference* that does nothing more than propose that *Who-ness* is not *What-ness* and *What-ness* is not *Who-ness*.

Any definition of *the question of the meaning of Christology* as *Difference*, at all, places "the subjectified one" against "the objectified one," and, in particular, presents the *difference in the question of the meaning of Christology* as a problem of situated knowledge.

Is the definition of *Christology*, as a question that must be posed and a meaningfulness that must be sought, a definition that defines itself as situated knowledge? Put differently, if we are to define *Christology* as *something knowable and explainable*, do we situate what we know and what we explain about *the question of the meaning of Christology* in *the subjectified one* that knows and explains *the objectified one*? Or, rather, do we utilize what *the objectified one* knows and explains as a way to trace *the subjectified one*? In effect, is it *the one whom Christologizes* or that which is Christologized?

The only way this line of inquiry unconceals anything for us, in terms of posing the question to and seeking the meaningfulness of Christology, is to approach *the question of the meaning of Christology* as an engagement between *the one whom Christologizes* and that which is Christologized, both of which permeate at the existential intersection of *that which exists between*.

Appendix A

Telling the Tale: The Narrative of Jesus Christ

This paper examines the "Narrative of Jesus Christ" not only as it appears in the canonical gospels of Matthew, Mark, Luke, and John, but also in certain non-canonical gospels and other apocryphal texts. The overall trajectory of the events that make up the "Narrative of Jesus Christ" is ripe with problems, contradictions, and multiple instances of editing and revision, all of which present a rather unconventional narrative. Its unconventionality is evident in the Synoptic problem between the gospels of Matthew, Mark, Luke, and John, where each includes and excludes different Jesus events as much as they do differ in Jesus sayings. This Synoptic problem makes it possible to consider that the four canonical gospels borrowed from one another and, to that end, makes it all the more apparent that the writers of each gospel viewed their respective texts as being the most accurate and true. Not only is this problematic in itself, since none of the four gospels were written during the lifetime of the historical Jesus—which can be roughly dated from 7–2 B.C. to 30–36 C.E.—but is particularly challenging when considering that the gospels that bear the names of Matthew, Mark, Luke, and John were not authored by the said disciples that they purport to be. What becomes even more problematic is the extent to which the four canonized gospels were deemed as canon-worthy, particularly over various non-canonical gospels and other apocryphal texts—some of which can be dated to the same time of the canonical Four—that incorporated the same literary license, but sought to edit and revise the "narrative" by including events that do not occur anywhere in the canonical Four. So, in a sense, this editing and revising was meant to be corrective in order to present the most logical chain of events in the "narrative," but, more importantly, meant to reflect changes in the Christian Church as it went through a theological transformation over the course of five hundred years since Jesus' death.

TRADITION-SCRIPTURE VS. SCRIPTURE-TRADITION

I find that the "Narrative of Jesus Christ" is about as much tradition as it is scripture. In terms of tradition, it is important to account for the fact that the "narrative" began exclusively from the oral tradition. That is, telling the tale of Jesus Christ passed from early Christian community to community in the decades after Jesus' crucifixion. Nothing was written down. Instead, through the oral tradition, the "narrative" was shaped by particular noteworthy events that were deemed essential in understanding the life of Jesus and the nature of Jesus' Christology and relation to the Trinity. These events influenced the depiction of Jesus Christ, and they formed a theological foundation for what would eventually become the Christian faith. As a "narrative" rooted in the oral tradition, early Christian storytellers did not have the foresight to predict any theological ramifications but, rather, simply told and re-told the "narrative" under the assumption that the "narrative" originated with people that had lived in Jesus' lifetime and knew Jesus personally. It is, of course, impossible to say with any degree of certainty if the oral tradition can be traced back to the original twelve disciples, since there is no documented evidence to suggest that any of Jesus' followers actually wrote anything.

Because the "narrative" began exclusively from an oral tradition, eventually texts had to be produced, since the "narrative" had to be preserved for posterity. I would argue that the contingency of this situation arose due to the letters of Paul. These letters were written to Christian communities that Paul founded in the mid-First Century—only the following seven have been considered as inarguably Pauline: 1 Thessalonians, Philippians, Philemon, 1 Corinthians, Galatians, 2 Corinthians, and Romans.[1] For Paul, this correspondence was simply a case of pastoral care, where Paul wrote in response to the questions and problems these early communities had with regards to issues of faith, issues of character, and issues of lifestyle. I would venture to say that Paul would not have expected his letters to be circulated through these communities as pseudo-scripture. But, before Paul's letters—that is, to

---

1. Though there are other letters ascribed to Paul, the seven mentioned here are largely considered authentic. The others, in turn, have been debated, as having been written by others and only using Paul's name for authority.

say in the fifteen to twenty years after Jesus' death –there was no scripture to follow beyond that of the Hebrew Bible. As the Followers of the Way,[2] which was what these early Christians called themselves, since the term "Christian" was a label applied by the Roman Empire, scripture was needed for the purposes of preaching to potential converts and teaching to the converted.

Paul's letters put forth a theology that did a lot to shape the Christian faith in mid-First Century, but did so in a way that, perhaps, overshadowed Jesus, the man. What I am suggesting is that Paul's letters present a theology that is Christ-centric, functioning as if excluding Jesus the man from its overall conceptual framework. Much of this can be credited to Paul's conversion story that can be arguably dated from 31 to 36 C.E. As the story goes—as it has been told through Christian tradition and with varying degrees of care in his letters—Paul received a vision of Jesus Christ on the Road to Damascus. At the time, Paul went by the name Saul, and was embarked on a merciless pursuit of Christians. In effect, Saul/Paul was a mercenary, or bounty-hunter that obtained the authority of Hebrew priests and officials to arrest Christians in the years immediately following Jesus' death. It has been debated, of course, to what extent Saul/Paul had this authority and to what degree did those that gave Saul/Paul this authority have the authority to do so. Nevertheless, Saul/Paul pursued and persecuted Christians and, at his own admission, "persecuted the church of God."[3] Some historians have suggested that what Paul admitting is that he killed or murdered Christians, which can be gleaned from Acts 9. There is no way to know if that is true, since Paul is not completely clear as what he means when he says, "persecuted the church of God." But, what remains clear is that Saul/Paul was a persecutor of Christians, and the conversion experience he had changed his life.

Paul's conversion is particularly important to way he does theology, since Paul sought to express the fact that anyone can have a life in Christ. This, in fact, was in direct opposition to the way that the disciples did their theology. For Paul, a man did not need to be circumcised as a prerequisite to becoming a Follower of the Way. In effect, Paul was taking an inclusive approach to his theology that was completely at odds with the disciples that felt that circumcision was a critical component to pushing away from Judaism.

However, I find that the opposition between Paul and the original twelve disciples stemmed from something much simpler and straightforward: their disbelief in Paul's conversion experience. In other words, the twelve disciples did not trust that Paul's conversion experience had

---

2. This is in relation to what Jesus mentions in John 14:6. Followers of "The Way" were deemed as followers of Jesus.

3. 1 Corinthians 15:9

actually happened and, to that end, were suspicious of his taking authority as an "apostle" in the Christian movement. For them, since Paul had not known Jesus and had not walked with Jesus as they had, Paul did not have the authority to preach and teach. In their minds, only the twelve of them were authentic and Paul was, for lack of a better word, a con-man. This is particularly so when the Twelve reconciled Paul with the Saul that had persecuting Christian communities, which broadened their suspicions of him. To a greater extent, though Paul founded many Christian communities during his missionary journeys and his letters were founding documents extrapolating and articulating the Christian faith, tradition dictated a wider scope beyond Paul in order to include the life of Jesus, the man. Though Paul was important to the Christian tradition, the life of Jesus the man was immensely more important.

So, the "Narrative of Jesus Christ" developed not just from oral tradition, but also, I would argue, as a counter-tradition to Paul's. Perhaps, this can be best represented as concentric circles, where the events of Paul's life and his letters form an outer concentric circle, to the extent that the Jesus "narrative" embodies the centermost core. That is, the "narrative" of Jesus the man is at the core of Paul's theological message, since Paul's teachings are meant to be tangential to Jesus' teachings. Tradition, then, dictated a need to present scriptures that employed Jesus' own teachings in Jesus' own words –teachings that could be compared to Paul's in terms of content and theme. I believe that this explains why, when considering the four canonized gospels, the earliest-dated Gospel of Mark is not written until sometime between 66–70 C.E., with the Gospel of Matthew, Gospel of Luke, and Gospel of John arriving shortly thereafter in about 80 C.E., about 90 C.E. and between 90–100 C.E. respectively.

HISTORICITY AND TEXTUAL TRANSMISSION

To truly understand the "Narrative of Jesus Christ" means to do so beyond the four canonical gospels to what was produced before and after their production between 66 and 100 C.E. First, I would like to focus on the "before" period. Here, I am not referring to Paul's letters but, instead, to a lost gospel that can be dated to a time as early as a year before Paul's first dated letter to the Church of Thessalonica in about 51 C.E. This lost gospel is referred to as "Q." Admittedly, not much is known about what the "Q" text contained, since it is, of course, lost.[4] However, it is possible to ascertain what

---

4. Some historians would even suggest that "Q" was not actually a text but, in fact, circulated orally.

"Q" might contain, particularly since "Q" was a source in the compositions of both the Gospel of Matthew and the Gospel of Luke. The relevance in the existence of "Q" is that, when considering the commonalities between the Gospel of Matthew and the Gospel of Luke, "Q" contains information that cannot be found in the Gospel of Mark.

If "Q" is the earliest telling of the "Narrative of Jesus Christ," then I would contend that the author of the Gospel of Mark sought to tell the "narrative" in a different, more specialized way. One important way that Mark author did this was by excluding the events in the childhood of Jesus as well as Jesus' familial connection to John the Baptist. The fact that the Gospel of Matthew and the Gospel of Luke both contain these elements not only provides circumstantial evidence that they both utilized "Q," but that they may have been aware of each other's existence.[5] I find this particularly apparent since the gospels of Matthew and Luke can be dated to the same relative period in time: about 90 C.E. Another important example is the relative overlap between the two in reference to their sharing of Jesus events as they are told in the Gospel of Mark.

Now, I would like to discuss the "after" period—the period after the canonical gospels, which include the production of various non-canonical gospels and other relevant texts that sought to further edit and revise the "Narrative of Jesus Christ." The first text worth noting can be dated to about 93–94 C.E. entitled *The Antiquities of the Jews* by the Jewish historian Josephus (37 C.E.–100 C.E.). I find Josephus to be immensely important since his *Antiquities* is the earliest reference to Jesus that is distinctly non-Christian. In Book 18 Chapter 3 Section 3 of his *Antiquities*, Josephus mentions Jesus as "Christ" and the crucifixion at the orders of Pilate, but he does so with scant detail. In this very short section of Antiquities, Josephus concludes his mention of Jesus with "those that loved him at the first did not forsake him, for he appeared to them alive again the third day, as the divine prophets had foretold these and ten thousand other wonderful things concerning him; and the tribe of Christians, so named from him, are not extinct at this day."[6] In terms of the histories of antiquity, the reference Josephus makes to name "Christians" is one of the earliest. Another prominent and equally important historian of antiquity, Philo (20 B.C.E.–50 C.E.), makes no explicit mention of Jesus, even though Philo was a Jew, as was Josephus, and lived much closer to Jesus' lifetime.[7]

5. This has been greatly debated among New Testament scholars, and merely based on quantifying similar statements and scriptures between the gospels of Matthew and Luke.

6. Josephus, *The Works of Josephus*, 480.

7. Philo, *The Works of Philo*, x.

In the century following Philo and Josephus, there are essentially five texts that play a role in revising or editing some aspect of the overall "Narrative of Jesus Christ," but do so in ways that guaranteed their exclusion of the New Testament canon at large. In order of their dating, there are as follows: The Gospel of Peter (circa early 2nd century), The Gospel of Judas, (sometime between 130 C.E.), The Dialogue of the Savior (circa 150 C.E.), The Infancy Gospel of James (circa mid-2nd century), and the Infancy Gospel of Thomas (circa at least 185 C.E.).

First, In The Gospel of Peter, Mary Magdalene is presented as "a disciple of the Lord" in 12:1.[8] This, of course, goes against the traditional depiction of Mary of Magdala being a prostitute, at worst, or, at best, being nothing more than one of the many Jesus followers that existed outside the sphere of importance of the twelve disciples. Again, in The Dialogue of the Savior, Mary of Magdala is bestowed with a position of importance within Jesus' ministry, an importance equal to those of the disciples—in this text, Mary is a complex theological conversation with Jesus, Judas, and Matthew.[9] Something similar happens to a revision of the role of Judas in Jesus' ministry, which occurs in The Gospel of Judas: Judas is depicted as being a 'beloved" disciple that was taught secret teaching by Jesus, where Jesus says to Judas, "Move away from the others, and I shall explain to you the mysteries of the kingdom. You can attain it, but you will go through a great deal of grief."[10] And finally, the Infancy Gospel of James and the Infancy Gospel of Thomas both attempt to respectively add significant detail to the childhoods of Mary, the mother of Jesus, and Jesus. While the Infancy Gospel of James is focused mostly on the circumstances of Mary's birth, the years of her infancy and childhood,[11] The Infancy Gospel of Thomas "attempts to fill the gap between Jesus' birth and his visit to Jerusalem recorded in Luke 2:41–52."[12] What becomes, then, important about the five texts of the 2nd century is that they each contribute something to the Jesus narrative by—with the exception of The Infancy Gospel of Thomas –revising the depictions of three of the most important people in the life of Jesus: Mary, Judas, and Mary Magdalene.

There is more of the same character revision in the two texts dating in following the 3rd century, but these two texts tend to move in more radical direction by depicting Mary Magdalene as a pseudo-love interest of Jesus.

8. Miller, *The Complete Gospels*, 407.

9. Miller, *The Complete Gospels*, 343–56.

10. Meyer, *The Nag Hammadi Scriptures*, 755–69.

11. Miller, *The Complete Gospels*, 380.

12. Miller, *The Complete Gospels*, 369.

These two texts are The Gospel of Mary and The Gospel of Philip. I am certainly not over-radicalizing the theme of these two texts. The degree to which they were so radical allowed The Christian Church to condemn them both as heretical, not just because the two authors of the respective texts elevated Mary Magdalene's relevance in Jesus' ministry to a position of equality with the other disciples, but because they hinted to a secret relationship between Mary of Magdalene and Jesus. In effect, the two texts use the word "love" to explain the nature of that relationship and what Jesus feels for Mary. The Gospel of Mary mentions Mary of Magdala receiving a special teaching by Jesus which she tries to relay to Andrew, Peter, and others. The others refuse to believe the "truth" in her teaching, even though the following is conveyed in 6:1–2: "Sister, we know that the Savior loved you more than any other woman. Tell us the words of the Savior that you know, but which we haven't heard."[13] Now, The Gospel of Philip takes what The Gospel of Mary proposes a bit further by mentioning the following in its verses 63 to 64:

> And the companion of the [. . .] Mary Magdalene. [. . .loved] her more than [all] the disciples [and used to] kiss her [often] on her [. . .]. The rest [of the disciples. . .]. They said to him, 'Why do you love her more than all of us?' The savior answered and said to them, 'Why do I not love you like her? When a blind man and one who sees are both together in darkness, they are no different from one another. When the light comes, then he who sees will see the light, and he who is blind will remain in darkness.[14]

What this does, of course, is suggest that Mary of Magdalene may have been Jesus' wife. Though it is only implicit in the above sample, I would argue that, since Jesus does not directly answer the question about "why do you love her more than all of us," the answer Jesus' does give seems flippant and passive. Perhaps, I would suggest, as if, by not answering question, Jesus is simply affirming something he is unwilling to admit, something that lurks mysteriously in Jesus' character and personality.

This, then, leads me into mentioning the next two texts that both add something to Jesus' character and personality in a way that fills a gap in the "narrative" as it is presented in the canonical gospels. These two texts are The Gospel of Nicodemus that dates to sometime between the 3rd and 4th centuries, and The Apostles' Creed that can be relatively dated at around 600 C.E. Though these two texts are, at a minimum, two centuries apart, they focus on a particularly important aspect of Jesus' "life." I say "life" because

13. Miller, *The Complete Gospels*, 363.
14. Robinson, *The Nag Hammadi Library in English*, 149.

the two texts consider the period of three days between the crucifixion and the resurrection, between what eventually became the Christian traditional days of Good Friday and Easter Sunday. This three-day period in the Jesus "narrative" is a time when Jesus has already died and been buried in his tomb, but has not yet been resurrected. The canonical gospels simply make no mention of Jesus' whereabouts during this three-day period, if it is to be considered that Jesus was "somewhere." It would seem, perhaps, to be an omission on account of the four authors of the canonical gospels. What makes this omission particularly problematic is in the Christological implications in it –the fact that Jesus states, "I am the way, and the truth, and the life. No one comes to the Father except through me."[15] The issue here is, as I mention, Christological. It involves the theological plight of the Old Testament patriarchs and prophets such as Adam and Eve, Noah, Abraham, Joseph, Jacob, David, Solomon, Jeremiah, and Isaiah, just to name a few. If Jesus is taken for his word, then this would mean that all the important people of the Hebrew Bible would be condemned to hell, simply because they lived and died before the birth of Jesus. So, what The Gospel of Nicodemus did was make an allowance for this, and suggest that Jesus "descends" into hell to save all who have died since the beginning of the world.[16] The same allowance is written in the Apostle' Creed,[17] which is an early Christian doctrinal creed meant to define a formula for the functioning of the Trinity –though an early version is different, the later version included the following at its statements #4 and #5: "suffered under Pontius Pilate, crucified, dead and buried; he descended into hell, rose again the third day."[18] By interjecting Jesus descending into hell, both The Gospel of Nicodemus and the Apostles' Creed edit and revise a particularly important part of the "Narrative of Jesus Christ" in an attempt to uphold theology.

LITERARY HAVES AND HAVE-NOTS

Aside from the aforementioned non-canonical and other texts relevant to the creation of the "Narrative of Jesus Christ," it remains important to note that, generally, the canonical gospels are viewed as the "canonized" story of Jesus. In this sense, they are deemed as productively and effectively

---

15. John 14:6.

16. Barnstone, *The Other Bible*, 374–78.

17. It was coincidently meant to represent the twelve disciples having come together after the ascension of Jesus at the end of Luke 24, when Jesus commissions them to go forth and preach the gospel.

18. Bettenson and Maunder, *Documents of the Christian Church*, 26.

advancing the events of the life of Jesus in a way that promotes the overall message of the Christian faith. But, as true as that might be, the fact that there are inconsistencies among the four gospels becomes an issue of concern in New Testament studies. This is the Synoptic problem. Moreover, it is a problem of a lack of continuity among the four gospels in terms of what Jesus said, when he said what he said, and where he said what he said. The way that I apply this specifically to my understanding of the Jesus "narrative" as a composition of the gospels of Matthew, Mark, Luke, and John is on three essential fronts: content, structure, and authorial intent—respectively, what is being said, how is the "what" being said, and why is the "what" being said.

The following events in the Jesus "narrative" seem to best illustrate the synoptic problem along with what I mean by examining content, structure, and authorial intent: (1) the baptism of Jesus by John the Baptist in the Jordan River, (2) the Appointment of the "Twelve," (3) Jesus calming the storm on the Sea of Galilee, (4) the Crucifixion and Jesus' Last Words, and (5) the Resurrection.

First, I would like to take a look at the baptism of Jesus by John the Baptist in the Jordan River. This event occurs in the gospels of Matthew, Mark, and Luke, represented respectively in Matthew 3:13–17, Mark 1:9–11, and Luke 3:21–22. The differences between how these three gospels describe the event occur particularly between Matthew's depiction and that of a similar one in Mark and Luke. While Mark and Luke similarly describe the event in similar language, where John does not interact with Jesus, Matthew includes an interaction. The interaction is as follows: John tells Jesus "I need to be baptized by you, and do you come to me?" But Jesus answered him, "Let it be so now; for thus it is fitting for us to fulfill all righteousness." In my view, this interaction in Matthew supposes that Jesus and John knew each other, which supports tradition. Mark and Luke seem to present Jesus as being someone foreign to John.

Next, the event that I call the Appointment of "The Twelve" occurs exclusively in Mark 3:13–19 and Luke 6:12–16. It is absent from the gospels of Matthew and John. The chief difference between Mark's and Luke's listing of Jesus' disciples is that Mark lists a disciple named Bartholomew, while Luke names a disciple Judas in addition to Judas the traitor.

The event where Jesus calms the storm on the Sea of Galilee can be found in the gospels of Matthew, Mark, and Luke respectively in 8:25–27, 4:38–41, and 8:24–25. One difference is that only Mark and Luke make mention of Jesus having been asleep and awakened by his disciples in response to their impending danger—Matthew does not mention Jesus having been asleep. Matthew is the only one of the three where Jesus speaks before "rebuking" the wind and calming the sea.

In the event depicting Jesus' crucifixion and his last words, Jesus' demeanor and emotional state is represented very differently among all four gospels in Matthew 27:45–50, Mark 15:33–37, Luke 23:44–46, and John 19:28–30. Matthew and Mark similarly depict Jesus as crying "My God, my God, why hast thou forsaken me?" I would argue that such a cry seems to suggest fear and despair, where Matthew's and Mark's Jesus is noticeably afraid in the final moments of his life. Luke's Jesus is more fearless and defiant, where Jesus cries with a loud voice and says, "Father into thy hands I commit my spirit." I find there to be a great deal of heroism in this, which seems to suggest that Luke wants to depict his Jesus as a tragic hero. The same can be said of John's Jesus, where Jesus is not only heroic and poised, but seems more interesting in calming others that are witnessing his crucifixion. John's Jesus, then, says that he thirsts, and, when he dies, simply says, "It is finished" with a heroic emphasis.

Finally, in the event of the resurrection, which occurs in all four of the gospels in Matthew 28:1–2, Mark 16:1–4, Luke 24:1–3, and John 20:1–2, Mary Magdalene plays a different role in each. In Luke, Mary Magdalene is not mentioned as finding Jesus' body missing from the tomb –Luke seems content with using "they" through, stating "they went to the tomb," "they found the stone rolled away," and "when they went in, they did not find the body." This, of course, is in contrary to tradition. John, on the other hand, suggests that Mary Magdalene, alone, came to the tomb and "saw the stone had been taken away," which prompts her to tell the disciples that Jesus' body is missing. Matthew and Mark not only present a narrative of Mary Magdalene coming to the tomb to find Jesus' body missing, but they also do so in the company of another Mary. In both Matthew and Mark, an "angel of the Lord" appears to confirm that Jesus' body is missing.

CANONIZATION OF JESUS AND THE NEW TESTAMENT CANON

I believe that the four gospels of Matthew, Luke, Mark, and John were chosen to be canonized over the many other gospels and other religious texts in order to consolidate, systematize, and streamline the Jesus narrative. This means perpetuating the legacies of Judas as traitor and Mary Magdalene as prostitute. But, also, the canonization process meant keeping dubious texts away, and labeling them as heretical because they over-complicated the life of Jesus and the theological understanding of the Christian faith. I say this to suppose that the canonization process—the idea of choosing appropriate texts and authorizing them—was about reaching as many converts as possible rather than sustaining the converted. To a certain extent, I would call this a case of advertising and message packaging, where the narrative of Jesus was pivotal to substantiating the Christian faith by placing Jesus as the Christian movement's central figure. In my view, this is why the four gospels appear first in the New Testament canon prior to Paul's letters, even though Paul's letters can be dated earlier than the four gospels.

WHAT IS THE "WHAT"?

I argue that there are essentially three things that are at stake in the development of "Narrative of Jesus Christ" that serve as major implications due to the editing and revising process that the "narrative" has endured throughout its textual history: historical, literary, and theological. In terms of the "history," I am referring to the dated history of the texts that have been produced, essentially, to continually write and re-write the events of Jesus' life—I would include in this the ramifications of Paul's letters on the Jesus tradition. In terms of the "literary," I argue that the authors that produced the canonical gospels and all of the non-canonical texts did so with the purpose of presenting them as factual accounts written by the names that the texts' bear –the most extreme example of this is with the Apostles' Creed, which was composed under the guise that the twelve disciples each wrote one of the statements that the Apostles Creed is composed of. In terms of the "theological," I contend that the overall "narrative" is shaped to present a certain theology about Jesus Christ, which is rooted in Christological and Trinitarian themes.

Appendix B

A Commentary on Luke 2:25–32

The passages of Luke 2:25–32, which are traditionally ascribed to Paul's companion Luke,[1] present a narrative about righteous and devout man named Simeon,[2] who not only has it "revealed to him that he would not see death before he had seen the Lord's Messiah,"[3] but also takes part in the baptism of the infant Jesus Christ which, ultimately, fulfills Simeon's

---

1. Note this: "The tradition that the author was Luke, who was a companion of Paul, mentioned in Colossians 4:14, Philemon 24, and 2 Timothy 4:2, originates in the second century. While not all second- century ascription of this kind can be relied upon, strong evidence exists regarding this particular tradition as being trustworthy, because the man to whom the gospel is ascribed was not otherwise a prominent figure in the apostolic church. The authorship of the work by a member of an apostle's staff correlates suffi- ciently with the Prologue's statement as to the writer's relation to men and things, but there are more precise grounds for regarding the tradition as accurate. These grounds are found largely in conclusions drawn from certain sections of Acts, where the writer, who must, in any case, by the evidence of language and style, be identified with the author of the gospel, uses the first personal pronoun plural 'we,' thereby seeming to indicate that he was, at certain times, an associate of Paul and a witness of events described in Acts 16:10–17, 20:5–15, and 21:1–18." Manson, *Gospel of Luke*, xvii–xviii.

2. Though Simeon is also referred to in Acts 15:13–14, which states, "After they fin- ished speaking, James replied, 'My brothers, listen to me. Simeon has related how God first looked favorably on the Gentiles, to take from among them a people for his name.'" It is impossible, therefore, to know if the Simeon in James' speech in Acts and the one of Luke's gospel are the same person. This is, in part, due to the fact that Peter also had another name, which was either Simon or Simeon. Riesner, "James's Speech," 272.

3. Luke 2:25.

prophetic vision from the Holy Spirit.[4] This eschatological[5] tale is an integral portion of Luke's Infancy Narrative[6] of Jesus beginning at 2:1, culminating in the immediately preceding 2:21–24 with a depiction of an eight-day-old infant Jesus being presented for circumcision and purification required by the law of Moses.[7] The Simeon narrative as well as the larger Infancy Narrative comprised within the whole of the Gospel of Luke are historically-contextualized, as stated in the Luke's Prologue from 1:1–4, by Luke's intent to provide Theophilus[8] with "an orderly account of the events [in the life of Jesus as they] have been [experienced] by those who[,] from the beginning[,] were eyewitnesses and servants of the word."[9] Specifically, however,

4. At the beginning of the first scene with Simeon, details are provided about the presentation of firstborn males in the temple and the terms of the offering. From this, there is a brief sketch of Simeon and his dreams, which are grounded on the Holy Spirit having already altered him and guiding him into the temple and up to the child Jesus. The spirit becomes, in this case, the facilitator of Simeon's gnosis. Wojcik, *Road to Emmaus*, 112–113.

5. Conzelmann defines "eschatological" in this manner: "Eschatology as an imminent hope belonging to the present cannot by its very nature be handed down by tradition. It is only the ideas concerning what is hoped for, not the hope itself, that can be transmitted." Conzelmann, *Theology of St. Luke*, 97.

6. Note the following: "Though much of The Gospel of Luke is indebted to three sources: the Q source (information common to The Gospels of Luke and Matthew), the L source (material that is special to The Gospel of Luke), and the M source (information from The Gospel of Mark), the Infancy Narratives are, perhaps, drawn from still another source. In particular, the narratives of the circumcision and the presentation of the child in the Temple suggest that Jesus himself is accepting his role in the Jewish covenantal community." Danker, *Jesus and the New Age*, 16; Franklin, *Christ the Lord*, 82.

7. Consider the following: "Under Moses' law, also known as Mosaic Law, a woman was ceremonially unclean and strictly segregated for seven days after the birth of a son. For a month longer she could neither visit nor take part in religious services, as stated in Leviticus 12:1–8. At that time, she was to offer a dove or pigeon –as described in Luke 2:24 –to expiate her uncleanness and a lamb as a burnt offering of general worship. For the latter sacrifice, the poor might substitute a dove. Since they were near Jerusalem, Mary performed these rites personally in the temple. In this setting, Simeon utters his prophetic oracle from Luke 2:29–32." Ellis, *New Century Bible Commentary: The Gospel of Luke*, 82.

8. Note this: "If Theophilus, whom the Luke addresses with "Most Excellent" in 1:3 was, as is usually assumed, a Roman official of rank who was interested in Christianity, the Lukan writings may be regarded as the earliest apology for the Christian religion. In other words, it may be contended that Luke hoped by his presentation of the Christian facts to abolish in official circles the suspicion which, since Nero's days (64 C.E.), had fallen on the hapless Christians of the Empire, and to win for the followers of Christ the same measure of toleration as was already granted to the Jews." Manson, *Gospel of Luke*, xx–xxi.

9. Consider: "Luke 1:1–2; Luke intended to give not only a truthful, full, consistent view, but also a somewhat different view from what others had attempted in writing of the history of Jesus and, ultimately of the Christian cause." Hovey, *American Commentary on the New Testament: Luke*, 11.

when considering 2:25–32, the Simeon narrative functions as more than just an orderly account of the life of Jesus for Theophilus but, instead, represents a systematic positioning of Jesus as a Messianic figure foundationally grounded in the customs and traditions of Judaism that transitions philosophically into the break-away religion of Christianity.

When considering Luke's authorship[10] of the Gospel that bears his name, it is important to note the background of the author as being born a Gentile and joining Paul at Troas to share Paul's journey into Macedonia.[11] But also, there exists the unique circumstances which prompt Luke to write, which arise out of "[Paul's imprisonment in Caesarea, which is the] circumstance [that] would furnish [Luke with the] opportunity for the research he mentions with such fine literary style and classical flourish in 1:1–4."[12] It is during Paul's imprisonment in Caesarea, occurring somewhere between 58 and 60 C.E., that Luke composed the Gospel of Luke.[13] In light of these circumstances, Luke[14] wants to write "an orderly account of the events [in the life of Jesus as they] have been [experienced] by those who[,] from the beginning[,] were eyewitnesses and servants of the word."[15] This orderly account, as indicated in the following 1:3–4, is directed towards Theophilus.[16] Though the role Theophilus plays in the composition of Luke's Gospel could be of Luke's patron,[17] it becomes more distinctly apparent that Luke is addressing a

10. Refer to this: "The identification of the evangelist with Luke makes it possible to form some fairly accurate conception of his experience and, in particular, his opportunities of obtaining knowledge of established facts of Christianity. Apart from Paul, Luke –though Luke had, in 50 C.E., the acquaintance, for a time, of the Jewish-Christian Silvanus (Silas), who would have been qualified to speak about the early church history –was excellently qualified to speak of the early days of the Jerusalem church as described in Acts 16:10. Moreover, Luke spent the years 57–59 C.E. in Palestine, chiefly in Jerusalem and Caesarea, and his opportunities of investigating not merely the early history of the Church, but the current tradition of the Saviour's life would be abundant." Manson, *Gospel of Luke*, xxvii.

11. Consider: "He was born at Antioch in Syria, and he was taught the science of medicine. He was not born a Jew, for he is not reckoned among those of the circumcision by Paul. The date of his conversion is uncertain. He joined Paul at Troas, and he shared his journey into Macedonia." Peloubet and Peloubet, *Smith's Bible Dictionary*, 367.

12. Unger, *Unger's Bible Dictionary*, 671.

13. Having been written before Acts of the Apostles, it remains uncertain about how much earlier it can be dated. Peloubet and Peloubet, *Smith's Bible Dictionary*, 367.

14. Luke, or Lucas, is an abbreviated form of Lucanus, which means "light-giving." Peloubet and Peloubet, *Smith's Bible Dictionary*, 366.

15. Luke 1:1–2.

16. It is noted that: "Theophilus was probably a native of Italy, and perhaps an inhabitant of Rome." Peloubet and Peloubet, *Smith's Bible Dictionary*, 367.

17. It is noted that: "Some New Testament scholars think that Theophilus acted as a patron for the production of Luke's Gospel." Unger, *Unger's Bible Dictionary*, 671.

broader community of Gentiles[18] specifically concerned with the Parousia.[19] To that end, Luke himself is not just concerned with Parousia[20] but with greater eschatological concerns between Christianity and Judaism,[21] where his ultimate motivation is to confront the false teachings of Gnosticism[22] and "persuade the authorities in the Gentile world of the respectability of the Christian Way and to convince them of its international appeal."[23]

Therefore, from 1:1 through 2:24, Luke "sets the story of Jesus within th[ese] larger [contexts, where], in Luke, unlike the other gospels, Jesus is not the prime mover of the narrative, though he is, of course, its central figure [because] it is God who determines the course of events in the story."[24] This span of the Gospel, including 2:25–32, represent Luke's Infancy Narrative, which contains material that is unique to Luke, not just within Luke's own body of work, but in the greater landscape of New Testament writings to which Luke's work belongs.[25] But, more importantly, the uniqueness of this special material in Luke, particularly with respect to 2:21–24 involving the infant Jesus' circumcision, purification, and presentation in the Temple, is ideologically rooted in the positioning of Jesus first within Judaism by the

18. Consider: "Whatever the ethnic composition of Luke's community, it is certain that they faced the question of how Gentile Christianity relates to Judaism. Many scholars believe that Luke himself was a Gentile and that in his day Christianity had become, by and large, a Gentile religion." Powell, *What Are They Saying About Luke?*, 51.

19. The term means "presence" or "arrival," and was used to describe the visits of gods and rulers. In this case, it refers to the "second coming" of Jesus. Ferguson and Wright, *New Dictionary of Theology*, 230.

20. It is noted that: "Luke downplays Parousia, or the belief in the imminence of the return of Jesus and the end of the world." Miller, *Complete Gospels*, 117.

21. Consider: "Luke's eschatology, compared with the original conception of the imminence of the Kingdom, is a secondary construction based on certain considerations which with the passage of time cannot be avoided. It is obvious what gives rise to these reflections –the delay of the Parousia. This explains the analogy between the Jewish and the Christian development. The primitive Christian hope, which at first had an immediate bearing, suffers a similar fate to its Jewish predecessor, Judaism: salvation is delayed." Conzelmann, *Theology of St. Luke*, 97.

22. Powell, *What Are They Saying About Luke?*, 45.

23. MacGregor, *Dictionary of Religion and Philosophy*, 389.

24. Miller, *Complete Gospels: Annotated Scholars Version*, 115.

25. Consider this: "The first two chapters of Luke's Gospel are not only without parallel in the rest of the New Testament, but they are somewhat unique even within Luke's own work. Scholars have long noted the unusual style that sets these chapters apart from the rest of Luke. The infancy account is written in Greek that more closely resembles that of the Septuagint, and, as in the Old Testament, the narrative is frequently interrupted by the insertion of hymns, insofar as theological distinctions can be made between this section of the Gospel, and the rest of Luke's work." Powell, *What Are They Saying About Luke?*, 32.

covenant of Abraham[26] before projecting the purpose of Jesus' life as being an eschatological engine for universal salvation, as is evident in the Simeon's hymn, Nunc Dimittis.[27]

What occurs, subsequently, at 2:25, is a transition into "now there was a man in Jerusalem whose name was Simeon," which might be considered as rather coincidental in its appropriation.[28] Despite that possibility, the significance of Simeon is far from coincidental and, alternately, lies in his status[29] in the community of Jerusalem as being "righteous and devout,"[30] which seem to intentionally invoke the same righteousness of Job and Zechariah[31] while representing a distinctly devout character[32] that responds to "walking in the commandments and ordinances of the Lord blameless[ly]."[33] In this regard, the fact that Simeon is "looking for the consolation of Israel,"[34] suggests that, as a "righteous and devout" man of God,

26. It is noted that: "Although Jesus was sinless, he was subjected to the rites which symbolized the putting off of the sinful lusts of the flesh. Although Jesus was the Son of God, it behooved him to be made a child of God through the covenant of Abraham." Dummelow, Commentary on the Holy Bible, 742.

27. Refer to this: "Prophetic hymn, which, in traditional liturgy, is called the 'Nunc Dimittis,' which is from the opening words in Latin. The main point of the poem is that salvation has now come and that this salvation is for all people." Laymon, Interpreter's One-Volume Commentary on the Bible, 676.

28. Consider the following: "Rather than the RSV's "now," the KJV uses the term "and behold," which, perhaps, calls attention to there being a remarkable coincidence of a man residing in Jerusalem, who was well-known for his piety and his great age." Laymon, Interpreter's One-Volume Commentary on the Bible, 50.

29. It is noted that: "Simeon is illustrated in terms that would suggest to both Jews and Greco-Romans that he was an ideal member of the community." Danker, Jesus and the New Age, 63.

30. It is noted that: "Simeon being 'righteous and devout' allowed for him to experience a revelation from the Spirit of God that he would live to see the Messiah." Summers, Commentary on Luke, 41.

31. Consider this: "When compared to the stories of Job and Zechariah, which are described respectively in Job 1:1 and Luke 1:6, Simeon is depicted as being anxious to conform to God's will and showed himself conscientious in his religious practices." Danker, Jesus and the New Age, 63.

32. It is noted that: "Belonging to the same class of worshipers such as Zachariah and Elizabeth from Luke 1:39–55, and Joseph of Arimathea as found in Mark 15:43, who was "waiting expectantly for the Kingdom of God." Hovey, American Commentary on the New Testament: Luke, 50–51.

33. Hovey, American Commentary on the New Testament: Luke, 50.

34. Consider this: "Temple, law, and prophecy witness to the outpouring of the Spirit which accompanies the birth of Jesus, so enabling representatives of what they have produced to acknowledge Jesus as the answer to those "looking for the consolation of Israel" and "to all who were looking for the redemption of Jerusalem" (2:25, 38). This episode shows Luke's belief that the instruments of the old covenant, when

he wants "consolation," or comfort,[35] indicated through a "yearning and waiting for the messianic deliverance anticipated in Israel."[36] Not only does this echo the similar sentiments of Genesis 49:18[37] and Isaiah 40:1–2,[38] but, in Simeon, specifically, it is apparent that, because "the Holy Spirit rested upon him,"[39] he was "empowered by God to understand what God was doing at this hour in Israel's history."[40] This means that the presence of the Holy Spirit,[41] as evidenced within Simeon, "habitually qualif[ied] him for the revelation next spoken of [in 2:29–32], and for the special discernment which he now displayed."[42]

It is through the presence and the power of the Holy Spirit acting in Simeon that, as 2:26 reports, "It had been revealed to him by the Holy Spirit that he would not see death before he had seen the Lord's Messiah." What becomes "revealed" to or "seen by"[43] Simeon does not come by way of any "independent knowledge of the peculiar circumstances surrounding the birth of the infant Jesus,"[44] but, instead, is something divinely communi-

---

they are rightly understood, should gather up their adherents and lead them over to Jesus, in whom they find fulfillment and before whom they recognize their role to be but preparatory, but this same episode shows too that Luke sees Jesus as in some sense bound to the Jewish covenant so that he is controlled by its expectations which are to find their realization in him." Franklin, *Christ the Lord*, 82.

35. The great relief to Israel from their prostration, ungodliness, and suffering. (Compare to Genesis 49:18, Isaiah 40:1; 49:23), which Simeon looked for as coming through the Messiah. Hovey, *American Commentary on the New Testament: Luke*, 50–51.

36. Summers, *Commentary on Luke*, 41.

37. This verse states, "I wait for your salvation, O Lord."

38. These verses express the following: "Comfort, O comfort my people, says your God. Speak tenderly to Jerusalem, and cry to her that she has served her term, that her penalty is paid, that she has received from the Lord's hand double for all her sins."

39. Luke 2:25D.

40. Danker, *Jesus and the New Age*, 63.

41. In other words, Holy Spirit can be interpreted as "a spirit which was holy," where, in Jewish tradition, the Holy Spirit was equated with the "spirit of prophecy." Ellis, *New Century Bible Commentary: The Gospel of Luke*, 83.

42. The term "habitually" indicates Simeon's unwavering righteousness and doggedly devout character through adherence to Jewish tradition expressed through religious practices. Hovey, *American Commentary on the New Testament: Luke*, 50–51.

43. Utilizing the word "see" through the implementation of "seen by" parallels wording in 9:27, which states "But, truly I tell you, there are some standing here who will not taste death before they see the Kingdom of God," suggesting that Luke relates the two promises. To that end, he may imply that Simeon "saw" the kingdom of God. Ellis, *New Century Bible Commentary: The Gospel of Luke*, 83.

44. Danker, *Jesus and the New Age*, 64.

cated to Simeon through Simeon's prophesy.[45] This prophesy by the Holy Spirit communicates to Simeon that "he would not see death before he had seen the Lord's Messiah," meaning that not only has Simeon "received the supernatural assurance that he will live to see the Lord's Messiah,"[46] but that, through divine revelation, the Lord's Messiah would be physically embodied in something that would already know.[47]

Consequently, as 2:27 describes, being "guided by the Spirit, Simeon came into the temple; and when the parents brought in the child Jesus, to do for him what was customary under the law." The fact that Simeon is "guided by the Spirit" to come to the temple suggests divine inspiration[48] that is "not of his own personal impulse but moved by the Spirit of God to visit the temple just at that time."[49] In this capacity,[50] Simeon "do[es] for [the child Jesus] what was customary under law,"[51] since it may have been that, when Jesus' parents brought their child to the temple for an aged rabbi to bless and pray for their child, the infant Jesus was placed in Simeon's arms,[52] which is conveyed explicitly in 2:28A.

By 2:28B, Simeon has "praised God," which, undoubtedly, intends to express that Simeon is "returning thanks with praise"[53] due to the dual realization that the infant he is holding is the Lord's Messiah and that his death once having seen the Lord's Messiah is a promise that will imminently come to pass. In other words, once "[Simeon] recognizes in [the infant] Jesus

45. According to biblical and rabbinic tradition, the Holy Spirit would make his presence known especially in the messianic age as imparted in Isaiah 40:1 and Joel 2:28, which asserts, "Then afterward, I will pour our my spirit on all flesh; your sons and your daughters shall prophesy, your old men shall dream dreams, and your young men shall see visions."

46. Manson, *Gospel of Luke*, 21.

47. Consider the following: "Just how that revelation was made to him is not indicated in The Gospel of Luke. More importantly, perhaps, it is not indicated just how the Spirit made it known to him that the baby boy named Jesus was the Messiah from his revelation. In some way, he knew." Summers, *Commentary on Luke*, 41.

48. It is noted that: "The Spirit had given Simeon hope and now leads him to its realization, for he comes to the temple inspired by the Spirit." Danker, *Jesus and the New Age*, 64.

49. Hovey, *American Commentary on the New Testament: Luke*, 51.

50. Being there in the temple around the arrival of Jesus and his parents and, more importantly, being in the pious position to receive and transmit a blessing to the infant Jesus.

51. Luke 2:27 corresponds to 2:22 which states that: "when the time came for their purification according to the law of Moses, hey brought him up to Jerusalem to present him to the Lord."

52. Manson, *Gospel of Luke*, 83.

53. Hovey, *An American Commentary on the New Testament: Luke*, 51.

the fulfillment of [God's] promise, [he, therefore,] utters a prayer which, [when placed within its] context, clearly is to be regarded as prophetic."[54] What, then, is evidenced in 2:29–32 is known as the *Nunc Dimittis*,[55] or Simeon's hymn, which "signifies that [,] in the coming of Jesus[,] the prayer of Israel's saints is answered, and they can depart with a satisfied mind."[56] This is precisely what Simeon is addressing in 2:29, where he says "Master, now, you are dismissing your servant in peace, according to your word." Here, Simeon recognizes that, "according to your word" or according to God's promise to him, he has his righteous and devout life has afforded him to opportunity to the Lord's Messiah represented in the infant Jesus. Furthermore, in the fulfillment of that prophesy, he will be "dismissed," or allowed to die, as God's servant "in peace," which is correlates semantically with Luke 1:79 and 2:14.[57] How Simeon is able to be dismissed[58] in peace is through personal salvation that is illustrated in "for my eyes have seen your salvation" in 2:30.

The "salvation" Simeon refers to in 2:30 is, undoubtedly, "a term applied to the messianic deliverance"[59] as evidenced in Simeon first seeing[60] the coming of the Messiah through the Holy Spirit, then actually seeing the infant Jesus in the flesh. But, for Simeon, as he further extrapolates, this "salvation" is something "which [God has] prepared in the presence of all people"[61] Not only does Simeon recognize that this universal salvation is available to all people contingent on their acceptance[62] of the infant Jesus as being the Lord's Messiah and the subsequent messianic deliverance that comes by way of that, but that "the good news comes to all nations by way of Israel and that no one nation, not even Israel, has a monopoly on salvation."[63]

54. Ellis, *New Century Bible Commentary: The Gospel of Luke*, 82.

55. This is Latin for "now lettest thou depart," which are the first words of Simeon's prayer as translated in the King James Version of Luke 2:29.

56. Manson, *Gospel of Luke*, 21.

57. Luke 1:79 says, "To give light to those who sit in darkness and in the shadow of death, to guide our feet into the way of peace" and Luke 2:14 says, "Glory to God in the highest heaven, and on earth peace among those whom he favors."

58. Consider this: "Perhaps, as a slave (or servant of the Lord) addressing his sovereign (God), what Simeon requests is dismissal from duty (service to God as a righteous and devout man)." Ellis, *New Century Bible Commentary: The Gospel of Luke*, 83.

59. Ellis, *New Century Bible Commentary: The Gospel of Luke*, 83.

60. This could be considered as "seeing" through the mind's eye, or as an internalized vision that occurs through the lens of prophesy.

61. Luke 2:31.

62. Hovey, *American Commentary on the New Testament: Luke*, 51.

63. Danker, *Jesus and the New Age*, 66.

The reason that this is the case is because Simeon further acknowledges that the infant Jesus, as the Lord's Messiah, will be "a light for revelation to the Gentiles and for glory to [God's] people Israel."[64] This language echoes Isaiah 49:6–7 and suggests that Jesus, as "a light for revelation," will allow for a revealed religion to spread to the non-Jewish world.[65] When this occurs, when unpacking Simeon's statement of "for glory to your people Israel," the term "glory" stands with "light" in relation to salvation to the degree that "Jesus is Israel's glory and the means whereby she can achieve her ultimate purpose as God's people."[66]

If Luke's Gospel is, on the whole, "not concerned with the eschatology of Jesus or with that of the primitive Christian community [but, instead,] with the eschatological conceptions [of the] description of the life of Jesus and of the work of the Spirit in the life of the Church,"[67] the function of the Gospel is to present what might be called an "inaugurated eschatology."[68] In this, Luke hopes to explain the birth of Christianity through the birth of Jesus, subjugating the theological inception of the faith with the theological inception of its central theological figure, in order to define Christianity as not a break-away religion of Judaism but, instead, as Judaism's legitimate descendant.[69] Bearing this in mind, in order to teach from this passage in a church setting, it is important to, first, contemporize the circumcision, purification, and presentation of infant Jesus as it occurs in 2:21–24 as a traditional practice common to that historical period, then objectify how this practice, as being important not just to Jesus but to Judaism, is enacted analogously within modern church liturgy. More importantly, however, the passage should be further utilized in reference to the importance of prophesy and destiny, and the roles both play in our lives everyday.

64. Luke 2:32.
65. Manson, *Gospel of Luke*, 21.
66. Danker, *Jesus and the New Age*, 67.
67. Conzelmann, *Theology of St. Luke*, 95.
68. Soards, *Passion According to Luke*, 111.
69. Manson, *Gospel of Luke*, xxi.

Appendix C

A Commentary on 1 Thessalonians 5:1–8

In 1 Thessalonians 5:1–8, Paul not only addresses the Thessalonians' concerns about the precise time of the Parousia,[1] but he also presents the need for them, as Christians, to remain active in their faiths and lifestyles with the intent of being "awake and sober" for what will be imminent. This imminence, in the Parousia, is an extension of the argument Paul makes in 4:13–18, where he discusses the eschatological mechanics of the Parousia in distinctly pastoral terms to, in part, assure them that those that have already died will not be restricted from receiving a blessing at the time of the Parousia. What Paul responds to, then, are the impatient uncertainties of a young church, which was founded only months prior to the composition of the First Epistle, still shaping their Christian faith against relative poverty and persecution with only Paul's teachings as guidance, in order to prevent themselves from backsliding into paganism and Judaism. The passage in 5:1–8, consequently, functions as Paul's epistolary surrogate, embodying an extrapolation of his teachings to them with first-person pluralistic, inclusive language and further indoctrinating them as believers to adhere to their Christian faith as they await the Parousia.

Though the exact date of Paul's founding of the Thessalonica church is highly debated among scholars due to insufficient historical documentation,[2]

---

1. The term "parousia" is imperial, referring to "the arrival of an imperial official, general, or emperor," but Paul applies this term, instead, "to Jesus and the establishment of God's purposes." Carter, *Roman Empire and the New Testament*, 88.

2. Stevens supposes the Church was founded in 52 CE, which seems to be a dissenting opinion among a majority of scholars placing the date in the year 50. Stevens,

there are two very important facts that aid in surmising that the church was a young church: first, Paul wrote to them from Corinth,[3] and secondly, the letter, itself, can be dated, perhaps, somewhere within the year 50 CE.[4] So, based on what is depicted in Acts 18:13 of Paul's travels upon leaving Thessalonica[5] and what can be historically gleaned from his presence in Corinth,[6] this, subsequently, presents a rather narrow window of time in which Paul would have written the letter to the Thessalonica church. To juxtapose this with the founding of the Thessalonica church sometime in early 50 CE,[7] it is evident that there also exists another, rather narrow window of time: the period between the composition of Paul's first letter to the Thessalonians and the founding of the Thessalonica church. That period, then, could have been "nearly half a year after [Paul, Silas, and Timothy] had fled from Thessalonica to Beroea."[8] In turn, what this means is that the Thessalonica church was a young church, having been in existence over such a short period of time that Paul, in his inability to return personally,[9] would have been rightly concerned about "the scoffing and ridicule which the [Thessalonian] church-members would have to endure from their relatives and neighbors, [as well as how] the temptation to drift back into

---

Commentary to the Thessalonians, 8.

3. Consider this: "The most widely accepted theory holds that 1 Thessalonians was written by Paul on his first visit to Corinth." Best, *Commentary on the First and Second Epistles to the Thessalonians*, 7.

4. This is in reference to the notion that "there is remarkable consensus among scholars that I Thessalonians was written in the year 50." Elias, *1 and 2 Thessalonians*, 28.

5. It is noted that: "The route Paul, Timothy, and Silas took upon leaving from Thessalonica involved the following sequence of events: the three of them fled to Beroea from Thessalonica, shortly thereafter, Paul left Silas and Timothy at Beroea when Paul was taken to Athens by some Beroean brethren, sending a message by the Beroean brethren to Silas and Timothy instructing them to follow as soon as possible, and, after relative failure in Athens and rendezvousing with Timothy to instruct Timothy to visit the Thessalonian church, Paul left for Corinth, where Silas and Timothy eventually met him after returning from Macedonia." Whiteley, *Thessalonians*, 2.

6. It is noted that: "Though, in the First Epistle to the Thessalonians, Paul makes no explicit reference to writing from Corinth, this can be ascertained from Acts 18:12–17, where Paul is brought before Gallio, the proconsul of Corinth, for a hearing on the accusation that Paul was "persuading people to worship God in ways that are contrary to the law." See, in particular, Acts 18:13. More accurately, then, it can be surmised from the historical records relating to Gallio's pro-consulship, that "Paul was probably in Corinth at some point during spring 51 CE and summer 52 CE. . .[with the "hearing" taking] place in late summer 51 CE. . .[and] Paul would have then arrived in Corinth in the spring of 50." Jones, *Epistles to the Thessalonians*, xiv.

7. Moore, *Century Bible: 1 and 2 Thessalonians*, 1.

8. Jones, *Epistles to the Thessalonians*, xiv.

9. 1 Thessalonians 2:17–18.

paganism or Judaism might prove to be overpowering."[10] This would have been attributed to the number of Jews being larger in Thessalonica than in any other Macedonian city and the possibility that "their malignity was [so] unrelenting [that] the church was from the very first a suffering church."[11] Also, too, aside from obvious persecution[12] from the time of its founding, since the Thessalonica church was a poor church composed of people that worked with their hands,[13] Paul would have been equally worried about that poverty being "no ordinary poverty [which would have] tested [their] patience and fidelity [to Paul's teachings and indoctrination]."[14]

Not only was this among the news Silas and Timothy brought back from Thessalonica to Paul in Corinth but they also brought back questions about the Parousia that began to circulate in the congregation in reaction to the deaths of some of the Thessalonian brethren.[15] On the whole, however, what Silas and Timothy brought Paul was relatively good news of the faith and love of the Thessalonica church,[16] by which Paul was moved to write a letter that "[assumed] an instructed faith, a more or less fully developed body of Christian teaching; in other words, a theology."[17] This instructed faith or theology Paul presents is eschatological, which, after legitimating himself as being pure in the motives of his presentation of the Gospel to them,[18] culminates in 4:13–18, when Paul directly addresses their concerns about family and friends that have already died before the Parousia, as being inaccessible to a blessing that has yet to come.[19] In response to this, Paul proceeds to reassure them that "since we believe that Jesus died and rose again, even so, through Jesus, God will bring with him those who have died [so that] we who are alive, who are left until the coming of the Lord, will by no means precede those who have died."[20] It is here, as a result, that

---

10. Hendriksen, *New Testament Commentary: Exposition of I and II Thessalonians*, 11.

11. Stevens, *Commentary to the Thessalonians*, 9–10.

12. Paul mentions "persecution" several times in 1 Thessalonians, beginning in 1:6, where he writes, "And you became imitators of us and of the Lord, for in spite of persecution you received the word with joy inspired by the Holy Spirit."

13. 1 Thessalonians 4:11.

14. Stevens, *Commentary to the Thessalonians*, 9.

15. Harris, *1 and 2 Thessalonians*, 69.

16. 1 Thessalonians 3:6.

17. Stevens, *Commentary to the Thessalonians*, 10.

18. 1 Thessalonians 2:1–8.

19. As Moore suggests, "Paul explains how [Parousia] will happen [and] that those alive at the Parousia will in fact not enjoy some blessing denied [to] those who beforehand have died." Moore, *Century Bible: 1 and 2 Thessalonians*, 70.

20. 1 Thessalonians 4:14–15.

Paul not only promises that the Parousia "may be trusted [but] cannot be predicted [because] it comes quickly, with no one's knowledge, and under no one's control. In other words, having confidence in Jesus' return is one thing, but naming a day is another,"[21] but begins 5:1 working under the assumption that the question of "when" will arise.

Therefore, in response to this contingency, Paul asserts "now concerning the times and the seasons, brothers and sisters, you do not need to have anything written to you."[22] Here, at the beginning of this verse, Paul pivots from the subject of 4:18 with the transitional "now concerning," in order to directly address "the times and the seasons" of the Parousia as the eschatological event previously described in 4:16–17. Not only, then, does Paul's premise that the Thessalonians "need not have anything written to [them]" hark back to an earlier statement Paul makes in, "you do not need to have anyone write to you, for you yourselves have been taught by God to love one another,"[23] but it is evident that Paul believes his initial teachings to the Thessalonians do not require any appendices or ratifications.

What Paul wants to do, subsequently, at the start of 5:2, is provide pastoral comfort and reassurance with "for you yourselves know very well."[24] From there, by proceeding with, "that the day of the Lord will come like a thief in the night," which rounds out 5:2, Paul is working with three distinct eschatological concepts fused into the singular eschatological phrase: "the day of the Lord," "will come," and "like a thief in the night." First, "the day of the Lord," as an expression originating in the Old Testament in the Book of Amos,[25] embodies the same eschatological connotations of the term, Parousia. The semantic verbiage of the Parousia and "the day of Lord" is, undoubtedly, in the notion of "will come," which, in Greek, "uses the present tense which not only gives vividness to the thought but aptly expresses something of the New Testament insistence on the nearness of the Parousia."[26] When considering the "nearness of the Parousia," Paul's use of "like a thief in the

21. Gaventa, *First and Second Thessalonians*, 69.

22. 1 Thessalonians 5:1.

23. 1 Thessalonians 4:9.

24. Consider the following: "Some, finding it difficult here, suggest that Paul is replying to a letter from Thessalonica and giving them credit for accurate knowledge at this point, while other would suggest that he simply means that they know accurately a word of Christ's on this matter." Moore, *Century Bible: 1 and 2 Thessalonians*, 73.

25. Moore cites the Book of Amos 5:18–20, where "the day of the Lord" is synonymous with the Lord's presence in relation to three particular events: the judgment of the nations, the blessing of the righteous, and the restoration and renewal of all things by the overthrow of evil. Moore, *Century Bible: 1 and 2 Thessalonians*, 73.

26. Moore, *Century Bible: 1 and 2 Thessalonians*, 73.

night" not only expresses the suddenness of the Parousia but, more aptly, utilizes the eschatological language of Jesus in Matthew 24:42–43.[27]

For 5:3, Paul carries forward the analogy from 5:2 as much as he further operates within what Jesus says in Matthew 24:42–43. To operate this way, Paul begins with "when people say," which, perhaps, attempts to personify the counterargument of Thessalonian Jews persecuting Thessalonian Christians. But, more importantly, Paul uses it a rhetorical device contextualizing Jesus' "owner of the house" parable by way of a "metaphorical picture [of] the real world [that] paint[s] a picture of people at large"[28] saying "there is peace and security." This, as Paul presents it, acts as the causality to the effect of "then sudden destruction will come to them," where, "those who do not reckon with the coming of the Parousia possess a false security which will be rudely shattered."[29] In an effort to further the argument of unpreparedness and the suddenness of destruction, Paul explicates his point into "as labor pains come upon a pregnant woman, and there will be no escape," which not only provides "an image of sudden, inevitable, dreaded anguish,"[30] but seems to connect ideologically to the writings of Old Testament prophet Isaiah, which the Thessalonians would have known well, in reference to the destruction of Babylon.[31]

From this, Paul makes another significant transition in 5:4a with, "But you, beloved, are not in darkness" as a means of imparting the notion of inclusivity. This part of the verse, then, performs two duties: first, "but you" can be translated from the Greek as an "emphatic 'you' [to] contrast with the general 'people' in verse 3,"[32] in addition to the "beloved" embodying an inclusiveness not evident in "people," and secondly, "not in darkness" draws a systematic distinction by which "Paul likens the present world to [a] sphere of darkness"[33] peopled with Thessalonian Jews and other non-Christians. Consequently, when Paul further postulates in 5:4b that "for

---

27. Jesus says, in Matthew 24:42–43, "Keep awake therefore, for you do not know on what day your Lord is coming. But understand this: if the owner of the house had known in what part of the night the thief was coming, he would have stayed away and would not have let his house be broken into."

28. Marshall, *New Century Commentary: 1 and 2 Thessalonians*, 134.

29. Moore, *Century Bible: 1 and 2 Thessalonians*, 74.

30. Stevens, *Commentary on the Epistles to the Thessalonians*, 59.

31. In Isaiah 13:6-8c, the Old Testament prophet similarly writes, "Wail, for the day of the Lord is near; it will come like destruction from the Almighty! Therefore all hands will be feeble, and every human heart will melt, and they will be dismayed. Pangs and agony will seize them; they will be in anguish like a woman in labor."

32. Moore, *Century Bible: 1 and 2 Thessalonians*, 74.

33. Moore, *Century Bible: 1 and 2 Thessalonians*, 75

that day to surprise you like a thief," Paul is working within the inclusive-ness belief that "participation in the light of the approaching day through faith in Christ is the first requisite for the [Parousia] not to come upon one unawares"[34]—essentially, when Christians "are not in darkness," they "are not in the state in which the thief may surprise them as he surprises the unwary householder."[35]

Not only does Paul continue his inclusive language of 5:4a in 5:5 with the terms "all" and "we" within "for you are all children of the day; we are not of the night or of darkness," but what Paul does, specifically, in 5:5 is "[use] the eschatological oriented imagery of light and darkness but now in a Semitic idiom."[36] This Semitic idiom of "children of the day" represents, in effect, an eschatological inclusiveness, where the Thessalonian Christians, "by [their] faith in Christ, the Light of the World, become [children] of light and [children] of the day,"[37] a distinction in which Paul includes himself through first-person plurality.

Paul advances his inclusive, first-person pluralistic language in 5:6 by suggesting "so then let us not fall asleep as others do, but let us keep awake and be sober." Here, more poignantly, though "the times and the sea-sons" of the Parousia can never be predicted, Paul engages in exhortation, where "what matters is readiness for [the Parousia] that may happen at any time."[38] The contrast Paul makes, then, is between being "asleep as others do" implying a lack of readiness among the Jews of Thessalonica and being "awake and sober" describing the state of mind that Christians should be in, as a "broad maxim of Christian duty, summing up in itself the temper and attitude appropriate to the life of faith."[39]

What Paul does, then, in 5:7 with "for those who sleep sleep at night, and those who are drunk get drunk at night" is not only expound on the importance of a life of faith against "immoderate and immoral behavior belong[ing] to the realm of night and darkness [which is] quite inappropri-ate to the realm of light and day,"[40] but he also indicts the Thessalonian Jews living lives "at night" that are "asleep" and "drunk" until they will not be prepared for the Parousia.

---

34. Moore, *Century Bible: 1 and 2 Thessalonians*, 75.

35. Best, *Commentary on the First and Second Epistles to the Thessalonians*, 209.

36. Best, *Commentary on the First and Second Epistles to the Thessalonians*, 210.

37. Harris, *1 and 2 Thessalonians*, 70.

38. Marshall, *1 and 2 Thessalonians*, 136.

39. Stevens, *Commentary on the Epistles to the Thessalonians*, 60.

40. Moore, *Century Bible: 1 and 2 Thessalonians*, 76.

In juxtaposition, Paul employs more inclusive language and first-person plurality to argue in 5:8a, "But since we belong to the day, let us be sober." The Thessalonian Christians, as "children of the day," undoubtedly, "belong to the day" through their faith in Christ. To maintain this faith at the time of the Parousia, Paul declares the importance of "[being] sober," which proposes not only sobriety physically through a morality, but spiritually through a righteousness. But, for Paul, the Christian's ability to "be sober" presents a challenge against persecution by Jews as indicative of persecution evident in the world. In light of these struggles, in 5:8b, Paul believes they should "put on the breastplate of faith and love, and for a helmet the hope of salvation," which not only contains the similar Old Testament imagery found in Isaiah 59:17,[41] but repeats the eschatological triad of faith, love, and hope evident in 1:3 which are deemed necessary so that the Christian may "be sober" at the time of the Parousia.

When considering that "Paul does not write his first Thessalonian letter in response to an acute crisis but [. . .] to give support to the work already done [. . .] exhorting the Thessalonians,"[42] the function of the letter is to provide pastoral encouragement to the Christians against persecution in a larger Jewish-majority Thessalonica community and to exhort them to uphold their faith in Christ as they await the Parousia, rather than re-vert to Paganism or Judaism. With this in mind, in order to teach from this passage in a church setting, it is important to, first, contemporize the Parousia-concept, then objectify the notions of poverty and persecution. Rather than presenting the Parousia-concept as being imminent,[43] this passage's use of "Parousia" could be deconstructed into a revelatory event that, when still upholding faith in Christ and adhering a Christian lifestyle, will reward Christians who suffer from social or cultural poverty and religious persecution. Utilizing the passage this way, then, allows for the same pastoral encouragement Paul wished to give the Thessalonians and, on the same note, underscore the relevance of faith.

41. In Isaiah 59:17, "He put on righteousness like a breastplate, and a helmet of salvation on his head."

42. Johnson, *Writings of the New Testament*, 261.

43. This is based on Paul's eschatological belief that the Parousia would occur within his own lifetime. See Whiteley, *Thessalonians*, 25.

Appendix D

Paul's Letter to the Galatians

Paul's Letter to the Galatians serves chiefly as his response to a crisis occurring in Galatia after his departure involving a group of Jewish Christians that spread through the churches of Galatia a teaching on faith in terms of Mosaic Law that directly conflicted with Paul's teaching. What Paul puts forth in his letter to the churches of Galatia, then, is a justification of faith arguing for a specialized depiction of Christianity's "gospel" and what it means to be a Christian without the restraints of Mosaic Law.

For Paul, Christianity's "gospel" is, conceivably, that of inclusion. This, of course, is in direct contrast to Mosaic Law communicating the necessity of all Christians being circumcised and observant of Mosaic Law in order to partake in the benefits of Christianity, particularly as a means of becoming descendants of Abraham through the act of circumcision. Paul disagrees with this. Paul's belief in inclusion, in contrast to what can only be perceived as the Mosaic Law's exclusion, purposefully transcends Mosaic Law by presenting the supposition that "we know that a [Christian] person is justified not by the works of the law but through faith in Jesus Christ."[1]

Having faith in Jesus Christ is Paul's inclusive message. It is within the framework of Christianity's "gospel" in order to not just suggest the inadequacies and limitations of Mosaic Law since "for the whole of law is summed up in a single commandment, 'You shall love your neighbor as yourself,'"[2] but to further propose that "the law does not rest on faith [but

1. Galatians 2:16.
2. Galatians 5:14.

310

through] Christ [who] redeemed us from the curse of the law by becoming a curse for us."[3]

As a result, the inclusiveness of Paul's interpretation of Christianity's "gospel" rests explicitly on the ideal that faith is the only prerequisite of Christianity, whereby the importance of having faith in Jesus as Christ is more inclusive than the requirements of Mosaic Law to be circumcised. While Mosaic Law contends that a Gentile must be circumcised in order to be accepted into the Christian faith, Paul paradoxically asserts that the act of circumcision is unnecessary, particularly when considering the powerful, transformational experience of the Spirit through faith. For Paul, perhaps, his central thesis is that the crucifixion of Jesus serves as a spiritual circumcision, which is more in line with God's covenant with Abraham.

Here, in Paul's version of Christianity's "gospel," it is evident that Paul is much more concerned with unequivocal faith in Jesus as Christ rather than the beholding of Gentiles to the regulations of Mosaic Law as an avenue into the benefits of Christianity. By doing this, Paul makes the Christian faith more accessible through making the ability to receive the "gospel" Paul interprets more comprehensible and the benefits less restrictive.

3. Galatians 3:12–13.

Appendix E

The Didache Interpretation

Dated to sometime in the First Century C.E., *The Didache*, also known as "The Lord's Teaching Through the Twelve Apostles to the Nations," is a relatively short Greek text of only about 2,300 words in length. The exact dating of the text remains questionable—while, traditionally speaking, biblical scholars have dated the text to the late Second Century, an increasingly view that has arisen contemporarily is that the text was more likely written in the First Century C.E. To be sure, it remains difficult to date *The Didache*—what further complicates the dating of the text is in that it has, since the earliest second generation of Christian writings, remained non-canonical, having been excluded from the official canonization of the New Testament in the Fourth Century C.E.

Given its exclusion from the canonization of the New Testament and the possibility of dating the text alongside the general dating of Paul's letters—if we date Paul's epistolary corpus roughly from 50 C.E. to 64 C.E—it is believed that *The Didache* shares some similarities with the Gospel of Matthew (composed sometime between 80 C.E. and 90 C.E.), insofar as both texts, it has been argued, have a shared origin in similar communities. Yet, even if *The Didache* can be understood in terms of other texts that can be reasonably dated contemporaneously, what remains notable about *The Didache* is that, in one sense, the author of the text is still unknown and, in another sense, the source from which the text's opening chapters are probably derived is a still unknown Jewish source.

Though these problems are certainly not unique to *The Didache*, in terms of its First Century context, they do make it all the more difficult to conceptualize what sort of "gospel" does *The Didache* espouse—this is only made all the more elusive, given that the earliest reference to *The Didache* can be found in *Historia Ecclesiastica* by Eusebius (c.265–340 C.E.), which carefully attends to a chronological account of church history up to 324 C.E. Just as Eusebius cites *The Didache* as non-canonical, Athanasius (c.296–373 C.E.), by 367 C.E. considers the text as belonging to apocrypha. Remaining largely non-canonical and apocryphal—with the exception of its inclusion in the *Apostolic Constitutions* collection, dated from 375 C.E. to 380 C.E.—the Greek manuscript was considered lost for centuries until its rediscovery by Philotheos Bryennios (1833–1917) in 1873 in the *Codex Hierosolymitanus*, itself, dated to sometime in the 11th Century C.E. Nevertheless, *The Didache* captures a particular meaning of the "gospel"—unlike what is captured by Paul's letters and the similarities it shares with the Gospel of Matthew—which poses particular questions and seeks particular meanings, if we can say, then, that The Didache ascribes to *the question of the meaning of Christology.*

When approaching an understanding of the interpretation of the "gospel" as imparted in the *Didache*, it is essential to, first, contextualize its perspective of the "gospel" in terms specified teachings of tradition. Accordingly, the "gospel" extrapolated in the *Didache* is chiefly substantiated in what Christians should do by virtue of appropriate actions and attitudes and the specific way of life they should live to be considered righteous, honorable, and holy.

The *Didache* defines this ideal Christian lifestyle in three very distinct categories: ethics and standards, rituals and liturgy, and ministry and false prophets –by turns, the ethics involve simple doctrines beginning with "bless them that curse you, and pray for your enemies,"[1] then in terms of rituals regarding fasting and baptismal practices, then in the election of bishops and deacons as church community leaders, and then, finally, framing the importance of recognizing the teachings of false prophets conflicting those of authentic apostles. Each of these categories confronts Christian issues from four distinct societal fronts and, on the whole, seemingly point out that these four fronts must be actively engaged unambiguously in order to give the necessary balance a Christian needs, in order to fulfill a Christian lifestyle.

Therefore, the "gospel" mostly represented in the *Didache* is contingent on all the followers of the Christian faith maintaining certain ethical

---

1. *Didache* 1:3.

standards within their communities outside the church in addition to participating in certain ritualized habits within the community of the Christian church itself. Together, according to the teachings of the *Didache*, it can be surmised that a certain type of Christian can be crafted, upheld, and traditionalized over subsequent Christian generations. To lead such a specified lifestyle regulated by restrictions and regulations is to acknowledge the notion in the *Didache* of "there [being] two paths, one of life and one of death,"[2] whereby the optimal Christian lifestyle gives tangible evidence of having followed the first path: the path of life. Essentially, the *Didache* ascertains Christianity's "gospel" as, perhaps, the fundamental goal of living a path of life dependent, in part, on how well "thou shall love the God who made thee, thy neighbour as thyself, and all things that thou wouldest not should be done unto thee, do not thou unto another."[3]

To accept the interpretation in the *Didache* of Christianity's "gospel" as the personal receipt of a specified communitarian lifestyle as the path of life is to, in essence, enjoy the benefits of the Christian faith knowing that a life lived well results in a well-lived life.

2. *Didache* 1:1.
3. *Didache* 1:2.

Appendix F

Three Key Features of Church Orthodoxy (70–300 CE): Canon, Creed, and Monarchical Episcopacy

When considering the orthodoxy of the early church, there are three key features that each play a significant role in the establishment of the Church during the period of 70–300 C.E., those being the purpose and creation of the canon, the implementation of creeds, and the function of the monarchical episcopacy.

THE PURPOSE AND CREATION OF THE CANON

The formation of the New Testament canon from a collection of documents that were probably written before the end of the first century[1] became an essential duty of the early Christian church. Not only was the canonization process an important means of defining a doctrinal rule of faith for the early church and its early Christians, but it also provided an ideological orthodoxy since "the [early] church existed under the threat of false teaching and [ultimately] found it necessary to protect the truth of the gospel from heresies such as Gnosticism and Docetism and from other heterodox movements of the late first and early second centuries."[2] While Gnosticism presented a "serious threat to Christianity throughout the second century [because church leaders] saw in it a denial of several crucial Christian

---

1. Patzia, *Making of the New Testament*, 166.
2. Patzia, *Making of the New Testament*, 171.

doctrines, such as creation, incarnation, and resurrection,"[3] Docetism[4] was a collective representation of various Christian-Gnostic arguments about the earthly Jesus being different from the heavenly Christ. The threats from the Gnostics wasn't the only threat to the early church's ability to fashion a coherent, canonized message within a definitive doctrine because Marcion[5] "posed an even greater threat to the church," because, like the Gnostics, "he rejected or radically reinterpreted the doctrines of creation, incarnation, and resurrection [and, by extension] went beyond [the doctrines of the Catholic church] in that he organized a church with its own bishops and its own scripture."[6] What makes the efforts of Marcion significant is that Marcion's list was the first attempt to put together a canon that could read in churches and used as the basis of Christian instruction –this distinctly Marcionite canon was "compiled of a list of books that [Marcion] considered true Christian Scriptures. These [being] the epistles of Paul, [who Marcion believed was] one of the few who had really understood Jesus' message] and the Gospel of Luke."[7] The Marcionite canonization, then, put pressure on the Catholic church to respond and counter the Marcionite movement, and "thus the church at large began to compile a list of sacred Christian writings [but did so, in contrast to Marcion's Paul-biased, Luke-redacted[8]

3. Gonzalez, *Story of Christianity: The Early Church to the Dawn of the Reformation: Volume 1*, 60–61.

4. These were considered Christian Gnostics because they rejected the notion that Christ had a body like ours. On this account, some of them believed that the body of Jesus was an appearance, or perhaps a sort of ghost that miraculously seemed to be a real body. This was the means by which these Christian Gnostics distinguished the difference between the heavenly Christ and the earthly Jesus, going so far as to believe, consequently, that Jesus did not have a body, but was a spiritual matter different from ours and, in some cases, denying the birth of Jesus all together. In effect, this Gnostic influenced Christological doctrine believed that the suffering and death of Jesus was only an appearance. The church ruled many of these notions under the moniker "Docetism." Gonzalez, *Story of Christianity: The Early Church to the Dawn of the Reformation: Volume 1*, 59–60; Reese, *Dictionary of Philosophy and Religion*, 134.

5. It is noted that: "By developing an understanding of Christianity that was both anti-Jewish and anti-material, Marcion, who emphasized Pauline principles and stressed salvation by faith, crafted doctrines that contradicted several fundamental points in Christian doctrine." Reese, *Dictionary of Philosophy and Religion*, 331; Gonzalez, *Story of Christianity: The Early Church to the Dawn of the Reformation: Volume 1*, 61–62.

6. Gonzalez, *Story of Christianity: The Early Church to the Dawn of the Reformation: Volume 1*, 62.

7. Gonzalez, *Story of Christianity: The Early Church to the Dawn of the Reformation: Volume 1*, 62.

8. In using the Gospel of Luke, Marcion deleted all references to Judaism or to the Hebrew Scriptures. This was done because Marcion not only viewed "the Old Testament as being the word of an inferior god" but, also, thought of it as being representative of

canonization,] in a formal manner, through a council or special meeting."[9] What arose from the debate in these councils or special meetings[10] about the Christian canonized doctrine "not [being] based on the supposed witness of a single apostle or Gospel, but [instead] on the consensus of the entire apostolic message"[11] was the necessity of crafting a creed as another element for the church to respond to Marcionism and other heresies, most notably Montanism.[12]

THE IMPLEMENTATION OF CREED

The first significant creed that the church implemented along with the crafting of a canonized collection of documents was called the "Apostle's Creed," which arose from the "notion that the apostles gathered before beginning their mission and composed this creed [where] each [apostle] suggest[ed] a clause." What must be understood, first, is that the "Apostle's Creed" wasn't put together by the apostles but, rather, that it was probably created in Rome around the year 150 C.E. as a "symbol" or recognition of faith, by which "Christians could distinguish true believers from those who followed the various heresies circulating at the time, particularly Gnosticism and Marcionism [so that] any who could confirm [a belief in] this creed were neither

---

"the handiwork of Judaizers seeking to subvert the original message" of the Hebrew scripture. Gonzalez, *Story of Christianity: The Early Church to the Dawn of the Reformation: Volume 1*, 61–62.

9. Gonzalez, *The Story of Christianity: The Early Church to the Dawn of the Reformation: Volume 1*, 62.

10. The first significant meeting was at the Council of Nicaea in 325 C.E., which was called by Constantine, with the final meeting occurring in Constantinople in 381 C.E. Reese, *Dictionary of Philosophy and Religion*, 389.

11. Gonzalez, *Story of Christianity: The Early Church to the Dawn of the Reformation: Volume 1*, 63.

12. This is the name given to the religious movement in the name of its leader Montanus, who had been a pagan priest until his conversion to Christianity in 155 C.E. Like Marcionism, Montanism provided a significant challenge to the early church. The movement of Montanism, then, was otherworldly, stressing the importance of martyrdom and awaiting the coming of the Lord. More poignantly, Montanists taught the separation from the world, which directly contrasted with the early church leaders wanting to keep the Church as open as possible to those outside it. In response to Montanism, which spread rapidly beyond Asia Minor and entered Europe and North Africa, the Church became Catholic, coming to terms with the world and leaving to live within it. Boer, *Short History of the Early Church*, 63–65; Reese, *Dictionary of Philosophy and Religion*, 367–368; Gonzalez, *Story of Christianity: The Early Church to the Dawn of the Reformation: Volume 1*, 76.

Gnostics nor Marcionites."[13] This creed, undoubtedly, under the guise of an invented link to the historical apostles of Jesus, is directed against Marcion and the Gnostics. The second clause of the creed, specifically, stating that "Jesus is the Son of the God who rules over this world and over all reality,"[14] meant to draw a Christological dividing line between what the Church believed and what Marcion and the Gnostics espoused. Not only does the second clause go further to refute the Marcionite and Gnostic belief that Jesus simply appeared on earth but to explicitly state that Jesus was born to Mary by a virgin birth. Also, within the same second clause, the creed also seeks to deny Docetism by referring to Pontius Pilate as a means date the event of Jesus' crucifixion and "insist on the fact that [Jesus' crucifixion] was a historical, datable event."[15] More importantly, to oppose Docetism further, the Apostle's Creed proceeds to declare that Jesus "was crucified [. . .] and was buried. The third day he rose from the dead; he ascended into heaven; and sitteth on the right hand of the Father; from thence he shall come to judge the quick and the dead. And in the Holy Ghost; the Holy Church; the forgiveness of sins; the resurrection of the body."[16]

Another important creed was the Nicene Creed, being developed from the Council of Nicaea held in 325 C.E., is "the most widely accepted Christian creed [and] is acknowledged both by Western churches [such as Roman Catholic and churches created by the Protestant Reformation] and by those of the east—Greek Orthodox, Russian Orthodox, and the like."[17] Not only does the Nicene Creed differ from the Apostle's Creed due to the latter "[being] Roman in origin [and] known and used only in churches of Western origin," but in purpose and content. The Nicene Creed, then, as approved by the bishops of Nicea, sought to communicate a "main concern [that] reject[ed] any notion that the Son or Word—Logos—was a creature, or a being less divine than the Father."[18] The subject of this proclamation is within the concept of the Trinity: God the Father, God the Son, and God the Holy

13. Gonzalez, *Story of Christianity: The Early Church to the Dawn of the Reformation: Volume 1*, 63.

14. Gonzalez, *Story of Christianity: The Early Church to the Dawn of the Reformation: Volume 1*, 64.

15. Gonzalez, *Story of Christianity: The Early Church to the Dawn of the Reformation: Volume 1*, 64.

16. This is the old Roman form of the Apostle's Creed from lines 4–11. Refer to Schaff, *The Creeds of Christendom: Volume 1*, 21–22.

17. Gonzalez, *Story of Christianity: The Early Church to the Dawn of the Reformation: Volume 1*, 165.

18. Gonzalez, *Story of Christianity: The Early Church to the Dawn of the Reformation: Volume 1*, 165.

Ghost. It is here that the Nicene Creed advances a systematic definition of the relationship in the Trinity through *"homoousios,"* which "intended to convey that the Son was just as divine as the Father."[19]

THE FUNCTION OF THE MONARCHICAL EPISCOPACY

While the creation of the canon and the implementation of creeds both sought to consolidate the Christian faith against outside religious movements such as Marcionism and Montanism, as well as other Gnosticisms, the Church also found a need to develop a hierarchical structure within church leadership. What this meant, then, was that the development of the monarchical episcopacy would function "by persons of immense symbolic nature, who bear full responsibility for maintaining integrity of the church as an institution."[20] But, more importantly, when considering the Church as being an institution, the function of the monarchical episcopacy, or papacy, gave unity and continuity by way of tradition[21] and succession, and, as a result, provided the frameworks of authority and Episcopal leadership roles. Chiefly, in the highest leadership position is the pope, who becomes "the first bishop among bishops [with a] role [that] can't be understood as that of an official who sets policy at will and gives orders to all other bishops, nor be understood as that of one who chairs a parliamentary process for making decisions."[22] In the early church, the pope was defined as "first among equals rather than a head over subordinates"[23] and, by tradition, is associated to Peter as being the first to hold this role.[24] In addition to the

19. *"Homoousios"* is translated as "of one substance." Reese, *Dictionary of Philosophy and Religion*, 231; Gonzalez, *Story of Christianity: The Early Church to the Dawn of the Reformation: Volume 1*, 166.

20. Long, *Patterns of Polity*, 13.

21. The monarchical structure of the church does not eliminate personal variations among bishops. But such variations are usually about matters peripheral to the doctrinal orthodoxy and institutional orthopaxis, which it is the bishop's duty to defend and advance. Moreover, the monarchical bishop's role is one of preserving rather than changing the customary patterns and fundamental convictions of the church. Long, *Patterns of Polity*, 17.

22. Long, *Patterns of Polity*, 15.

23. Long, *Patterns of Polity*, 15.

24. Though, Gonzalez explains, the origins of episcopacy in Rome are not clear, "most scholars agree that Peter did visit Rome, and that there is at least a very high probability that he died there." Nevertheless, there is a significant disagreement about various lists of early bishops, particularly whether "Clement was Peter's successor" or "the third bishop" after Peter's death." Gonzalez, *Story of Christianity: The Early Church to the Dawn of the Reformation: Volume 1*, 242.

pope, the rest of church leadership were to, among many duties, "exemplify Christian fidelity in its most rigorous form [and] expected to perform sacramental and ceremonial functions, not only the Eucharistic celebration reserved for the priesthood, but also ceremonies like confirmation and ordination over which [the bishop] precedes"[25] and, essentially, uphold and represent canonical law.

25. Long, *Patterns of Polity*, 19.

Appendix G

Christology of Touching the Passion

In *Touching the Passion: Seeing Late Medieval Altarpieces through the Eyes of Faith* (2018), Donna L. Sadler begins by asserting that, in the late medieval period, "the divisions between the five senses were not as zealously maintained," especially with respect to the intersectionality of religious experiences mediated by the role of the altarpiece.[1] Not only does the altarpiece physically frame the meaning of sacramental experience, it also becomes a transcendent frame for the overall meanings of Christological, theological, liturgical, and ecclesiastical experience—this becomes integral, I submit, to the manner by which Christological reflection and Christological thinking work.

In this way, Donna Sadler finds that the altarpiece, as "a devotional object,"[2] is experienced by touching it—that is, touching the passion is inherent in what the altarpiece is physically, metaphysically, and theologically. To touch the altarpiece means not just experiencing the passion tactilely as that which aids Christological thinking, but also allowing Christological reflection through "belief [that] has become contingent on seeing."[3]

Essentially, if we read Sadler's understanding of the late medieval relationship between "passion" and the altarpiece, if "vision was a corporeal experience,"[4] Sadler's argument is certainly bolstered by the influence of Thomism on late medieval theology as it comes to bear on religious

---

1. Sadler, *Touching the Passion*, 1.

2. Sadler, *Touching the Passion*, 1.

3. Sadler, *Touching the Passion*, 1.

4. Sadler, *Touching the Passion*, 1.

experience. Sadler's chief focus, in this regard, in Chapter 1, is to see the altarpiece through the eyes of faith, both as a historical medium between the late medieval worshiper and God, and as a contemporary medium between us and our understanding of medieval faith. To do so, when the altarpiece is placed in its historical context, Sadler "probe[s] the effect that medium has upon the worshiper."[5] Sadler poses a series of questions about the functionality of altarpieces, as well as if the choices made to "use paint or sculpture [was] purely an economic one, or did geographic predilections come into play?"[6]

In answering these questions, in Chapter 2, Sadler presents a geographical study of altarpieces and their associated retables found in Burgundy and Champagne. Though both depict the narrative of the Passion of Christ, the religious communities of Burgundy and Champagne make aesthetic choices in how both depict the Virgin Mary, such that, as Sadler posits, the difference between Burgundy and Champagne resides in their respective glorifications of Mary, and how the two works of art are experienced *a posteriori* (with the senses). Sadler explores this further in Chapter 3 by suggesting that the relationship between altarpieces and their accompanying retable expressing the Passion of Christ is ultimately grounded on an "aesthetics of immersion."[7]

For Sadler, this immersion solicits all the senses collectively, so that the worshiper does not just receive the altarpiece as a mediator between the worshiper and "the passion," but engage the altarpiece itself as trans-corporeally as the extension of the worshiper. This very trans-corporeality of the retable's "Passion" presents the worshiper with an unavoidable visual experience that also becomes an extension of the worshiper, particularly, as Sadler notes, when the "carved surfaces of the retable alone possess[es] tantalizing kinetic potential for the viewer."[8]

With this in mind, in Chapter 4, Sadler examines the retables of Lhuitre, Géraudot, Vievigne, Saulx-le-Duc, Ray-sur-Saône, and Vignory, as examples of how different religious communities contingently engage with the pathos of Passion of Christ[9]—this pathos is predicated on the goals of each composition, where each begins in telling "the passion," the directions

---

5. Sadler, *Touching the Passion*, 6.
6. Sadler, *Touching the Passion*, 6.
7. Sadler, *Touching the Passion*, 71.
8. Sadler, *Touching the Passion*, 10.
9. Sadler, *Touching the Passion*, 11.

each takes with its depiction, and how these elements are embodied in a visual language that "capture[s] the mind's attention."[10]

Though the late medieval worshiper touched "the passion" and was touched by "the passion" differently, in Chapter 5, Sadler argues that the relationship between the altarpiece, the retable, and the "passion" depicted are all relegated to and regulated by "the role of the frame."[11] Sadler explores this role in two ways: "the dynamics of the frame and the framed"[12]—on one hand, Sadler regards the frame as an expression of anthropomorphism of carved altarpieces as embodiment of "the worlds they conjure into existence,"[13] and on the other hand, she views the frame as capturing the overall structure of the narrative of the Passion of Christ, even if what is captured is only one of many possible frames of the narrative.

Additionally, Sadler views the role of the frame as that which frames the altarpiece as a "house of memory," since the altarpiece and its accompanying retable frames the Passion of Christ for the late medieval worshiper more than a thousand years after the historical event "The Passion" depicts. More importantly, now, the altarpiece frames for us, as Sadler rightly concludes, the meaning of the altarpiece as "the basis of faith during the late medieval period."[14] In this way, the altarpiece becomes a "house of memory" for the worshiper—inasmuch as it both encapsulates first-century religious culture and late medieval religious culture—but it is also a "house of memory"[15] for us, as provided in the subtitle of Touching the Passion, to contemporarily see late medieval altarpieces through the late medieval eyes of faith.

10. Sadler, Touching the Passion, 10.
11. Sadler, Touching the Passion, 10.
12. Sadler, Touching the Passion, 11.
13. Sadler, Touching the Passion, 11.
14. Sadler, Touching the Passion, 11.
15. Sadler, Touching the Passion, 4.

Appendix H

Karl Barth and Christology

KARL BARTH'S DIALECTICAL CHRISTOLOGY: BRONDOS VS. KÄRKKÄINEN

Central Arguments: Brondos and Kärkkäinen

Allow me to first consider the argument David A. Brondos makes in *Fortress Introduction to Salvation and the Cross* (2007). When Brondos assesses Barth's doctrine of reconciliation, he predicates that assessment on an understanding of the functional or practical problems inherent in Barth's conception of Christology. What Brondos considers as the most serious problem is that, for Barth, "human salvation and reconciliation appear to be automatic and mechanical."[1] This leads Brondos to further argue that Barth's idea of human salvation is something that is accomplished only by God—from the situatedness of God's transcendence and Otherness—in Christ to the extent that Barth, as Brondos surmises, "reduces humanity virtually to nothingness."[2] In this sense, then, Brondos suggests that, in Barth's view of Christology and the parameters of human salvation, "human beings are totally passive in their salvation and do not even have a say in it."[3]

---

1. Brondos, *Introduction to Salvation and the Cross*, 140.

2. Brondos, *Introduction to Salvation and the Cross*, 140.

3. Brondos, *Introduction to Salvation and the Cross*, 140.

Now, in moving on to Veli-Matti Kärkkäinen's *Christology: A Global Introduction* (2003), Kärkkäinen's argument begins by outlining Barth's theoretical framework about God as God being "totally Other."[4] This is a very important starting point for Kärkkäinen, since it is here that Kärkkäinen is able to assert the following about Barth's conception of God and the human-God dialectic: "there is no contact point between humankind and God apart from that which God has created, that is, the person of Jesus Christ."[5] As such, this dialectic that Kärkkäinen describes is one where God "stands over and against humanity and everything human"[6] and, subsequently, situates God's existence, in relation to human existence, as a "wholly other God."[7] Like Brondos, Kärkkäinen has identified Barth's God as a transcendent God. Because of this, Kärkkäinen argues that Barth's theology is Christ-centered,[8] since the role of Christ is one as "mediator between the transcendent God and humankind [which] comes to focus in Christ's dual role as the agent of revelation and of reconciliation."[9] Christ's "dual role" particularly comes to bear in how Barth conceives of election—his Doctrine of Election—where, Kärkkäinen writes, "all God's elective actions are centered on Christ and Christ only."[10]

Critical Analysis

Brondos and Kärkkäinen's view of Barth's God as being "wholly Other" seems to suggest, I would argue, that God is existentially encased in ideality, where the infinitude of God's existence embodies a meaning that, ultimately, transcends finite human understanding. In this sense, because of God's ideality, God's Otherness is "wholly" in itself apart from humanity. I find that this is particularly important to note because this notion of "Otherness" has an exoticism to it—it denotes not just a kind of Orientalism, or "foreign-ness," argued by Edward Said, but also a kind of distancing effect of the "Other," as theorized by Gilles Deleuze. This also leads me to assess the "Other" in another way: I find that the "Other" puts forth the possibility that, as Hegel notes in *Phenomenology of Spirit*, the nature of self-consciousness is formed reflectively. In the former case, I am thinking particularly

4. Kärkkäinen, *Christology*, 112.
5. Kärkkäinen, *Christology*, 112.
6. Kärkkäinen, *Christology*, 112.
7. Kärkkäinen, *Christology*, 112.
8. Kärkkäinen, *Christology*, 115.
9. Kärkkäinen, *Christology*, 115.
10. Kärkkäinen, *Christology*, 117.

of post-modernism and post-colonial theory: the sense that the "Other" is something "wholly" apart from the mainstream of "sameness" that the "Other's otherness" is misunderstood, marginalized, compartmentalized, and deemed as "meta-human." Now, in the latter sense, the presence of the "Other," through the Hegelian perspective, allows for humanity to conceptualize their self-consciousness through a "human-Other" dialectic—this is precisely what Hegel argues with his "lordship-bondage" dialectical analogy. So, if understanding what the "Other" is and how the "Other" exudes an "otherness," it becomes clear about Barth's God as being "wholly Other." For Barth, "God in His deity is human."[11] This is a key to understanding Barth's conception of God. By humanizing God, Barth is, essentially, suggesting that God's "Otherness" is so distanced from humanity that humanity has no direct access to God. In my view, Barth is channeling Plato's "Theory of Forms."

But, Barth is, of course, going a step further than Plato and the Forms, in order to suggest that the only way humanity has access to God, as an object of understanding, is through Jesus Christ. The "human-God" dialectic, as Brondos and Kärkkäinen describe, is not necessarily "dialectical" in the traditional sense of the term –perhaps, this is precisely why Barth was never comfortable with the term being applied to his theology. Instead, Barth's dialectical Christology, as a kind of tripartite relationship, Christ embodies an equalizing force. For Barth, then, Christ is the "bracketing" force within a Husserlian "phenomenological εποχη"[12]—thinking this way, Christ allows the human finite mind to "bracket" a "wholly Other" God that exists in ideality.

KARL BARTH'S *CHRIST AND ADAM*

Inarguably, two of Barth's most important works are: *Der Römerbrief* (1918/1919)[13] and the four volumes of *Kirchliche Dogmatik* (1932–1967).[14] Though both, to a certain extent, provide Barth's approach to Christology—if we can say, of course, that it is possible to locate in Barth's thought a specific articulation of *the question of the meaning of Christology*—a lesser-known and much smaller text, *Christus und Adam nach Römer 5* (1952), provides, I argue, the best and most concentrated representation of Barth's posing of the question to and seeking the meaningfulness of Christology.

11. Barth, *Humanity of God*, 55.

12. Husserl, *Ideas*, 110–12.

13. This can be translated into English as *The Epistle to the Romans* in 1933.

14. This can be translated as *Church Dogmatics*.

Translated as *Christ and Adam: Man and Humanity in Romans 5* in 1956, it is notable that the text originally appeared in German a year after the publication of the fourth and final part of the third volume of *Kirchliche Dogmatik*, subtitled as, in English, "The Doctrine of Creation: The Command of God the Creator." What is notable, here, is that *Christ and Adam* provides a smaller and more concentrated treatment of what is "extensively treated"[15] in the second part of the third volume of *Kirchliche Dogmatik*, which, itself, first appeared in 1948. While sharing a relationship with what is thematically at the heart of the third volume, "The Doctrine of Creation," and, as Wilhelm Pauck notes in the introduction to *Christ and Adam*, another relationship with the first part of the fourth volume, "The Doctrine of Reconciliation," that first appeared in 1953, we can certainly explicitly see a connection, in terms of content, to Barth's earlier *Der Römerbrief*—given these connections, it becomes understandable that *Christ and Adam* would largely become obscure and marginalized. Yet, when we attend to the very narrow scope of *Christ and Adam* towards only the fifth chapter of Romans—made explicit in the subtle to the work—we find that the task of the work is just as narrow, looking, particularly, at a series of verses: Romans 5:12–21.

Pauck acknowledges that Romans 5:12–21 represents the centerpiece of the "Pauline conception of the two humanities, one headed by Adam and the other by Christ,"[16] insofar as this conception has, as a point of assumption, a "special significance in relation to the doctrine of the atonement,"[17] Pauck characterizes the handling of these verses in Barth's *Christ and Adam* in the following way:

> In [*Christ and Adam*], Barth does not deal with all these doctrines. His interest is concentrated upon the relation between Christ and Adam as the Apostle understood it. By-passing the entire exegetical and theological tradition built upon this chapter of the Pauline Epistle, Barth offers an entirely new and unprecedented interpretation of the conception of man implied in the Apostle's view of the relation between Christ and Adam.[18]

With respect to this "unprecedented interpretation," Pauck suggests that *Christ and Adam* can be viewed in terms of three key "considerations"—first, it provides a "contribution"[19] to the traditional and historical interpretations

---

15. Barth, *Christ and Adam*, 17.
16. Barth, *Christ and Adam*, 8.
17. Barth, *Christ and Adam*, 8.
18. Barth, *Christ and Adam*, 8.
19. Barth, *Christ and Adam*, 9.

of Romans and chapter five therein, secondly, "it is an example of Barth's distinctive exegetical method,"[20] and thirdly, "it illumines the significance of a theme that is central in Barth's crowning systematic achievement, the *Church Dogmatics*."[21] Together, these three considerations speak to a reconsideration, I submit, of Barth's handling of what theological anthropology can mean for *the question of the meaning of Christology*, particularly when situating Christ and Adam thematically between the third and fourth volumes of *Church Dogmatics*, respectively delineating Barth's doctrines of "creation" and "reconciliation." In a way, Barth's doctrines, as they are expressed across *Church Dogmatics*, are meant to rethink tradition and, in turn provide a countertradition to not just the relationship between humanity and Adam anthropologically, but also between humanity and "the Christ of faith" Christologically. What ties these two relationships together, I argue, is Barth's working through the problem of the historical Jesus, which, of course, is cast in the 1930s as a reaction to Bultmann's work in the 1920s and what Schweitzer lays bare in 1906, but also, by the time *Christ and Adam* appears, as a reaction to the landscape of the "new quest" initiated by Käsemann" in 1951.

Even so, even with respect to these two contexts, Barth confronts a broader context, situated on wider tradition that informs the meaning of Christology at the juncture of the relationship between Adam to us and "the Christ of faith" to us. What is at stake for Barth, then, is the very manner with which we engage with theological anthropology and how it conceptually calibrates what is "theological" and what is "anthropological" in terms of our hamartiology. To this end, Pauck writes:

> In the course of Christian history, Barth implies, these ideas linking man's predicament of sin with Adam, the first man, and their hope of freedom from sin with Christ, came to receive a stress far removed from the intention and meaning of Paul: Adam, as the father of the race, was viewed as the originator of sin.[22]

Though Pauck acknowledges that "Barth makes no direct reference to this historic teaching,"[23] what holds true nonetheless, for Pauck, is that: "[Barth] evidently has it in mind throughout his commentary."[24] Subsequently,

20. Barth, *Christ and Adam*, 9.
21. Barth, *Christ and Adam*, 9.
22. Barth, *Christ and Adam*, 10.
23. Barth, *Christ and Adam*, 11.
24. Barth, *Christ and Adam*, 11.

Pauck explains, "Barth's prime purpose is to correct this age-old tradition by pointing out that Paul is not correctly understood unless one recognizes that the Apostle sees Christ as the true head of *all* humanity."[25] This sort of reconceptualization, then, is Barth's approach to *the question of the meaning of Christology*. In it, Pauck tells us: "we must realize that [Barth's] Christological view of man implies a radical departure from all ordinary general doctrines of man, including the traditional theological 'anthropologies.'"[26]

Insofar as Barth moves away from "traditional" theological anthropology, and ventures away from "all ordinary general doctrines"—which is certainly evident in *Church Dogmatics*—we are able to come to the conclusion, as Pauck does, that, in the *Christ and Adam* text:

> According to Barth, man and mankind must not be interpreted in terms of Adam, that is, in the light of biological or historical or philosophical conceptions of human nature. Rather, the only indispensable precondition for an understanding of human nature is the fact of God's revelation of Himself in the man Jesus.[27]

While this represents Barth's handling of Romans 5:12–21 in *Christ and Adam*, when we place this alongside Barth's previous handlings of the same span of verses in *The Epistle to the Romans* commentary in 1918/1919, we can see, to an extent, that Barth remains true to the notions of a "new world" and "new men,"[28] as two conditions that are existentalized by *the question of the meaning of Christology*.

25. Barth, *Christ and Adam*, 11.

26. Barth, *Christ and Adam*, 15.

27. Barth, *Christ and Adam*, 15–16.

28. Barth, *Epistle to the Romans*, 164–87.

Appendix I

Rudolf Bultmann and Christology

RUDOLF BULTMANN'S MYTHOLOGICAL
CHRISTOLOGY: BRONDOS VS. KÄRKKÄINEN

Central Arguments: Brondos and Kärkkäinen

In considering David A. Brondos' *Fortress Introduction to the Salvation and the Cross* (2007) first, Brondos evaluates Bultmann's interpretation of the New Testament and, then, Bultmann's view of Christology as that of "participation." Brondos takes this idea as a way to understand how Bultmann's Christology is based on "the salvific significance of Jesus' death and resurrection primarily in terms of believer participating in this event."[1] However, Brondos highlights what he considers as the most common objection to Bultmann's Christology, which is Bultmann's treatment of history. Brondos suggests that this treatment grounds Christian faith "no longer in historical events, but only in the meaning that we give to what was and is proclaimed regarding Christ and the cross."[2]

This is precisely what Bultmann's "demythologization" is all about: it is essentially about myth or history from the present lived experience—for Bultmann, as Brondos ascertains, "salvation appears not to consist of a

---

1. Brondos, *Introduction to Salvation and the Cross*, 153.
2. Brondos, *Introduction to Salvation and the Cross*, 153.

future life or world which we now await, but only something to be experienced in the present as we live authentically in openness to the future."[3]

Now, directly in line with the argument Brondos makes, in *Christology: A Global Introduction* (2003), Kärkkäinen describes Bultmann's mythological Christology as viewing Jesus through the lens of mythology. The approach of "demythologization" that Bultmann employs, as Kärkkäinen rightly clarifies, "does not mean stripping away the mythical expression of the gospel in the spirit of liberalism," as a way, perhaps, to examine a more "pure" perspective of the life and times of Jesus.[4] So, as Kärkkäinen further clarifies, demythologizing is a matter of experience, in order to reinterpret the myths in the Gospel. For Kärkkäinen, what this means, then, is that the purpose of demythologization is to reinterpret a myth existentially, so that "the message of the New Testament can be made intelligible to a modern person."[5]

Critical Analysis

After reflecting on Brondos and Kärkkäinen's description of Bultmann's mythological Christology and reading the selection from Bultmann, I believe that a very helpful way to understand Bultmann's demythologization is along the two rather analogous approaches of Paul Tillich and John Macquarrie. The Tillich and Macquarrie approaches reflect –as does Bultmann with his demythologization—the sense that the authentication of human existence comes through careful consideration of both temporal and spatial limitations as well as the power of personal experience to shape "being."

For Tillich, whose theology is just as influenced by Heidegger as Bultmann's is, human existence comes into being as a result of "being thrown"[6] into existence. From this, Tillich asserts, in brief, that humanity is encased in an existential predicament, where it must seek authentic existence through conceiving and grasping the concept of God and God's "Being." Now, Macquarrie is operating from much the same Heideggerian-influenced perspective, suggesting that the fulfillment of human selfhood is contingent on "Being." Macquarrie goes a bit further and more explicitly

3. Brondos, *Introduction to Salvation and the Cross*, 153.

4. Kärkkäinen, *Christology*, 122.

5. Kärkkäinen, *Christology*, 122.

6. This is a Heideggerian term that is used in a variety of ways: "thrown-ness," "being-thrown-towards-death," "thrown-ness into the there," and "being thrown through abandonment." "Thrown-ness into existence" is one of these ways. Heidegger, *Being and Time*, 321.

than Tillich—though I think Tillich would agree by way of his notion of New Being[7]—and asserts that the historical symbol of Jesus has "ontological import" of personal existential ramifications, which "gives to our minds the fullest disclosure of the mystery of Being that we can receive.[8] What becomes essential about Macquarrie and Tillich's sense of human existence in reference to God's existence is that humanity must be concerned with the present, the here and now. In other words, humanity cannot authenticate its existence by historicizing Jesus, but, instead, through applying ontological-existential meaning what Christ is and what Christ does—the theory and praxis, respectively—to fully understand what human existence is and what God's Being is. Here is where Bultmann's argument lies: the sense that humanity must tease out meaning through the reinterpretation and demythologization of Scripture, in order to apply that meaning experientially to our current, contemporary lived situation. What this means, furthermore, is that humanity's encounter with Scripture must be delineated along two lines: the historical event and the personal event. The latter is the most important, as I am sure Bultmann would agree, since the personal event—the individualized experience—opens the possibility for the greatest amount of meaning to be uncovered through the immanence of the event.[9]

7. Tillich, *Systematic Theology Volume 2*, 119.

8. Macquarrie, *Principles of Christian Theology*, 272.

9. I am thinking, here, of Gilles Deleuze's notion of the "immanent event" as an event that humans bring their lived experiences into and become changed by that event after the encounter.

Appendix J

Rudolf Bultmann's Jesus

Appearing about twenty years following the 1906 German publication of Albert Schweitzer's *Geschichte der Leben-Jesu-Forschung*—itself, translated in English as *The Quest of the Historical Jesus* in 1910—Bultmann's *Jesus* (1926) is an important, but often overlooked explication of Bultmann's conceptualization of Christology. Much of the reason for this is, I submit, the fact that *Jesus* is situated in a blind-spot in Bultmann's body of work—it appears just a few years after Bultmann's *Die Geschichte der synopischen Tradition* (1921)[1] and fifteen years before the publications of the essay collection *Neues Testament und Mythologie* (1941)[2] and *Das Evangelium des Johannes* (1941),[3] both of which frame Bultmann's theologizing from the standpoint of form criticism. In light of the expansive nature of *Die Geschichte der synopischen Tradition* before and *Das Evangelium des Johannes* after, the *Jesus* text is a much smaller work comparatively—nevertheless, in spite of that, *Jesus* marks a critical point in Bultmann's early career at the University of Marburg, of which Konrad Hammann provides a rare account in, to the best of my knowledge, only comprehensive biography of Bultmann, translated in English in 2013.[4]

---

1. Translated as *History of the Synoptic Tradition* in 1976.

2. Translated as part of the collection, *Kerygma and Myth* in 1953, and as *The New Testament and Mythology and Other Basic Writings* in 1984.

3. Translated as *The Gospel of John* in 1971.

4. Hammann, *Bultmann*, 186–201.

It may be possible to view Jesus as a turning point, not just in Bultmann's theologizing from the 1920s to how he situates himself in the 1940s, but also in Bultmann's stance on Christology which directly informs, for example, *Das Evangelium des Johannes*. Perhaps, more importantly, it must not be lost on us that Bultmann's *Jesus* first appears in Germany in the same year as Heidegger's *Being and Time* does—this should not be viewed as a coincidence, given that Bultmann and Heidegger had a strong personal and professional relationship as colleagues at Marburg, with Bultmann being part of the faculty of Marburg's theology department, and Heidegger belonging to Marburg's philosophy department. Though I have given an account of the relationship between Bultmann and Heidegger in *Heideggerian Theologies* (2018),[5] I want to reiterate here that it is through this relationship that Heidegger influences Bultmann philosophically as much as Bultmann influences Heidegger theologically.

Insofar as Heidegger becomes a philosophical influence on Bultmann's theologizing, Bultmann's *Jesus* text approaches the problem of the historical Jesus, as that which is laid bare by Schweitzer in 1906, by approaching the "problem" through more carefully understanding what is and can be meant by "historical." The co-translators of the 1958 edition of the original 1934 English translation describe the text in the following way:

> Professor Rudolf Bultmann's *Jesus*, here translated, is a strictly historical presentation of the teaching of Jesus in the setting of the thought of his own time. Its aim is to free that teaching from certain accretions and re-interpretations, often superficial and inaccurate, which have grown up around it in modern times.[6]

This characterization of *Jesus* is, perhaps, more relevant to what *Jesus* means to Bornkamm's *Jesus von Nazareth* (1956)—we can look at this 1958 account of *Jesus* as not in anticipation of or as an influence on Bornkamm's key work that appears some twenty years after *Jesus* originally appeared, but, instead, I would argue, as a deft reaction to provide a better understanding and context to *Jesus* in light of Bornkamm's *Jesus von Narareth*. It is to this degree that, as the co-translators assert, *Jesus* "has not lost value."[7] That value, in many ways, is evident in the work of Bultmannians such as Käsemann, Bornkamm, and even Ebeling and Fuchs, and still others that were absorbed into the orbit of the Bultmann-led "Old Marburgers" group. Given that *Jesus*, in terms of its value, set a tone for not only Bultmann's

---

5. Woodson, *Heideggerian Theologies*, 58–91.

6. Bultmann, *Jesus and the Word*, 5.

7. Bultmann, *Jesus and the Word*, 5.

work that followed, but also the work of both Bultmannians and those that theoretically challenged the assertions of Bultmannians, the co-translator further contextualize *Jesus* as this:

> It serves, moreover, to correct the impression sometimes gained by readers of certain of his other works—that the author is one of those who emphasize Pauline and Johannine theology at the expense of the teaching of Jesus of the Synoptics.[8]

While this is certainly true, when considering *Jesus* in the 1950s, situating *Jesus* more firmly within the 1920s reveals a much different impression of Bultmann. Bultmann's approach to Christology in the 1920s is less about Pauline and Johannine theology—Bultmann in the 1920s is more concerned with the problem of the historical Jesus, as that which is best represented by the Synoptic gospels. By placing *Jesus* in its proper context of the 1920s, we find, as the co-translators tell us, that:

> It forces recognition of the fact that Jesus' teaching did not centre around such ideas as the infinite worth of personality, the cultivation of the inner life, the development of man toward an ideal, that Jesus spoke rather of the coming Kingdom of God, which was to be God's gift, not man's achievement, of man's decision for or against the Kingdom, and of the divine demand for obedience.[9]

From here, the co-translators conclude:

> Bultmann recognized in the thought of the past certain essential, lasting truths which in later sophisticated times were often missed; and he has certainly and critically separated these truths from the accretions of later misinterpretations.[10]

Here, though the co-translators tell us that, through this context, Bultmann's sense of what was "often missed," particularly by Schweitzer, in terms of Bultmann's assertion that "the ethical teaching of Jesus is inseparable from [Jesus'] eschatology,"[11] it is certainly possible to see Bultmann's dialogue with Schweitzer as also a dialogue with Heidegger.

Just as Heidegger, speaking generally, in *Being and Time*, was also interested in what was "often missed" in the history of being,[12] Bultmann's

8. Bultmann, *Jesus and the Word*, 5.

9. Bultmann, *Jesus and the Word*, 5–6.

10. Bultmann, *Jesus and the Word*, 6.

11. Bultmann, *Jesus and the Word*, 6.

12. Heidegger, *Being and Time*, 19.

interest is in what was "often missed" in the history of Jesus. With this in mind, when taking into account Bultmann's introduction to *Jesus*, subtitled "View-Point and Method," it stands to reason that, Bultmann writes:

> For a fundamental presupposition of this book is that the essence of *history* cannot be grasped by "viewing" it, as we view our natural environment in order to orient ourselves in it. Our relationship to history is wholly different from our relationship to nature. [. . .] Hence, there cannot be impersonal observation of history in the same sense that there can be impersonal observation of nature.[13]

Note here Bultmann's emphasis on history, and the impossibility of an "impersonal observation of history." This emphasis speaks to, I submit, the inextricable relationship between us and history. That is, history is always a personal observation, since the only way anything can be observed is by engaging in an observation grounded on history. Essentially, for Bultmann, history informs and is informed by what can be observed. It is through understanding what we mean to history and what history means to us that "lead to our seeing Jesus as a part of the history in which we have our being, or in which by critical conflict we achieve being."[14] Consequently, in order to come to terms with the problem of the historical Jesus, Bultmann suggests that we "must be in the nature of a continuous *dialogue with history*."[15] This dialogue is at the heart of Bultmann's approach to *the question of the meaning of Christology*—the way in which he poses the question to and seeks the meaningfulness of Christology is grounded on a "dialogue with history," which is made more explicit in Bultmann's Shaffer Lectures and Cole Lectures delivered respectively in October 1951 and November 1951, collected in *Jesus and Mythology* (1958).

13. Bultmann, *Jesus and the Word*, 11.
14. Bultmann, *Jesus and the Word*, 11.
15. Bultmann, *Jesus and the Word*, 11.

Appendix K

Dietrich Bonhoeffer and Christology

Though Dietrich Bonhoeffer's better-known writings include: *The Cost of Discipleship* (1937, translated in English 1954), *Life Together* (1939, translated in English in 1948), *Letters and Papers from Prison* (posthumously translated in 1953), and *Ethics* (posthumously translated in 1955), perhaps the best representation of Bonhoeffer's approach to Christology can be found in the text, *Christ the Center*—unlike the other writings, *Christ the Center* is, as Edwin H. Robertson explains in the preface to the 1978 English translation of the text, "contains reconstructed lectures given by Bonhoeffer in 1933 on the theme of [C]hristology."[1] Because of this, Robertson acknowledges that *Christ the Center*, as a "reconstructed" text, "needs justifying,"[2] insofar as "there are two obstacles to be overcome."[3]

The first "obstacle," as a means to justify the importance of *Christ the Center* to Bonhoeffer's corpus and the extent that it represents a significant articulation of Bonhoeffer's take on Christology as it can be "reconstructed," is explained by Robertson in the following way:

> First, this is not Bonhoeffer's text—it has been reconstructed from notes by [Bonhoeffer's] students. With so much genuine Bonhoeffer material still not translated, why pick on this doubtful text? The answer is that [C]hristology is at the heart of Bonhoeffer's

1. Bonhoeffer, *Christ the Center*, 7–8.
2. Bonhoeffer, *Christ the Center*, 8.
3. Bonhoeffer, *Christ the Center*, 8.

theology and that Eberhard Bethge is better qualified than any man living to reconstruct what Bonhoeffer really said.[4]

We need not take Robertson's characterization of *Christ the Center* as "not Bonhoeffer's text" lightly. It speaks as much to the degree to which Bonhoeffer himself was not involved in the construction of *Christ the Center* as it speaks to the fact that *Christ the Center* is, at best, an approximation of what Bonhoeffer "really said." The problem here—which revolves mostly around the text having been "reconstructed"—is that the text is based on "notes by his students," rather than an actual text in Bonhoeffer's own hand. Consequently, just as Robertson rightly raises, there is something of a tension between what sense can be made out of the textual transmission of *Christ the Center* and "genuine Bonhoeffer still not translated." While this seems to suggest, more broadly, is that *Christ the Center* eludes any possibility of being a "genuine Bonhoeffer"—yet, Robertson concedes that what has been "reconstructed" by Eberhard Bethge comes as close as possible to "reconstruct[ing] what Bonhoeffer really said."

Given that Bethge "reconstructs" the lecture notes from Bonhoeffer's students into what we now have as *Christ the Center* is, itself, notable, since Bethge is an authority on Bonhoeffer's life and thought and, to Bethge's credit, what is "reconstructed" attempts to represent the original manuscript that, Bethge tells us, "was not discovered."[5] For that matter, keeping in mind that Bethge's 1967 biography is widely-considered as the most authoritative and comprehensive, Bethge's cooperation in the translation of the lecture notes into *Christ the Center* seems to corroborate Robertson's assertion that *Christ the Center*, as a text, is at the heart of Bonhoeffer's Christology just as "Christology is at the heart of Bonhoeffer's theology." As such, Robertson finds, in *Christ the Center*, as a text:

> We can listen to Bonhoeffer, not talking about Bonhoeffer's contribution to [C]hristology, but Bonhoeffer lecturing on [C]hristology and making his contribution as he goes along. There is much in these lectures that we should expect to find in any lectures on [C]hristology, but through an examination of this material we come very close to the mind of Bonhoeffer.[6]

As much as "we come very close" to Bonhoeffer's mind, we do so by examining what is, essentially, representative of Bonhoeffer's early career by 1933. As Bethge notes that "the lectures were given in 2-hour sessions in

4. Bonhoeffer, *Christ the Center*, 8.

5. Bonhoeffer, *Christ the Center*, 118.

6. Bonhoeffer, *Christ the Center*, 8.

the summer of 1933, in Berlin,"[7] we should take care to note that, around the same time, Bonhoeffer has become actively involved in the Confessing Church movement and participates in co-authoring the "Bethel Declaration" by August 1933. It is in this context that Robertson locates a second obstacle to *Christ the Center*—it is the fact that the content of the text comes "before most of the great events in [Bonhoeffer's] life had taken place, and before he had matured his thought about the Church."[8]

Nevertheless, if we maintain the idea that *Christ the Center*, as a text—which is referred to as "Lectures on Christology" in Bonhoeffer's *Gesammelte Schriften*—is "at the heart" of Bonhoeffer's broader theology, Robertson characterizes how Bonhoeffer comports himself to *the question of the meaning of Christology* in the following way:

> In these lectures on [C]hristology, Bonhoeffer is not prepared to find a category for Christ. His questions are not, "How is it possible for Christ to be both man and God?" His question about Christ is never, "How?," but always, "Who?" He will not even have a disguised "What?" or "How?" in the form of a "Who?" Every avenue of his thinking leads him to confront Christ and ask, "Who art thou, Lord?" or to be confronted by Christ and hear his question, "Whom do you say that I am?"[9]

Insofar as Bonhoeffer's approach to Christology is in terms of "who," this concern with "who-ness," I submit, is at the heart of the Christology that is at the heart of Bonhoeffer's theology. If Bonhoeffer, indeed, is always focused on "who," this becomes essential, as it is expressed in the introduction to *Christ the Center*, to Bonhoeffer's "unfolding of the Christological question."[10]

As Bonhoeffer allows "the Christological question" to unfold, he concludes that, when approaching Christology, "only the question, 'Who are you?,' will do."[11] Subsequently, "the phenomenon is opened up only by this [question]," Bonhoeffer argues, whereby "[Christ] answers only to the question, 'Who?'"[12] The who-ness of Christ, then, becomes, for Bonhoeffer "the question about transcendence," rather than that of "immanence," which, as such, is more concerned with "how."[13] This distinction is important, since:

7. Bonhoeffer, *Christ the Center*, 118.
8. Bonhoeffer, *Christ the Center*, 8.
9. Bonhoeffer, *Christ the Center*, 15.
10. Bonhoeffer, *Christ the Center*, 27.
11. Bonhoeffer, *Christ the Center*, 30.
12. Bonhoeffer, *Christ the Center*, 30.
13. Bonhoeffer, *Christ the Center*, 30.

It is because the one questioned is the Son that the immanent question is not adequate [. . .] The question, "Who?," expresses the strangeness and the otherness of the one encountered and at the same time it is shown to be the question concerning the very existence of the questioner.[14]

To this end, Bonhoeffer continues:

[The questioner] is asking about the being which is strange to his being, about the boundaries of his own existence. Transcendence places his own being in question. With the answer that his logos has reached its boundary he faces the boundary of his own existence. So the question of transcendence is the question of existence, and the question of existence is the question of transcendence. In theological terms: it is only from God that man knows who he is.[15]

Indeed, the manner with which we know ourselves comes from "the question of transcendence," which is grounded on the question of "who-ness," if the larger intent is for us to approach the Christological question at its most meaningful. Yet, Bonhoeffer recognizes "so long as the [C]hristological question is the question of the human logos, it remains imprisoned in the ambiguity of the question, 'How?'"[16]

Bonhoeffer outlines "the ambiguity of the question" of "how," as that which is "imprisoned" in the relationship between "the person and work of Christ." Part of this ambiguity, it seems, is in the extent that, Bonhoeffer notes, "Christology is not soteriology"[17]—insofar as the former situates "the Person of Christ" and the latter discloses "the Work of Christ," Bonhoeffer asks: "how are the two related to each other?"[18] This relationship, as Bonhoeffer considers it, brings Bonhoeffer to the following conclusion:

Thus the priority in theology of the [C]hristology question over the soteriological has been established. When I know who he is, who does this, I will know what it is he does. However, it would be wrong to conclude from this that the Person and the Work can be separated. We are concerned here with the epistemological connection between Person and Work, as we know it, not as it is in reality. The separation of the question

14. Bonhoeffer, *Christ the Center*, 30.

15. Bonhoeffer, *Christ the Center*, 30–31.

16. Bonhoeffer, *Christ the Center*, 36.

17. Bonhoeffer, *Christ the Center*, 37.

18. Bonhoeffer, *Christ the Center*, 37.

of [C]hristology from that of soteriology is necessary only to establish a theological method.[19]

Bonhoeffer goes on to say:

> For the [C]hristological question, by its very nature, must be addressed to the one complete Christ. This complete Christ is the historical Jesus, who can never in any way be separated from his work. He is asked and he answers as the one, who is his own work. But [C]hristology is primarily concerned with who he is rather than what he does. To put that into an academic formula: the subject of [C]hristology is the personal structure of being of the complete historical Jesus Christ.[20]

Though this rounds out the end of the introduction to *Christ the Center*, and, as Robertson tells us, *Christ the Center* represents Bonhoeffer's theologizing that had not yet matured, *Christ the Center* does, at the same time, embody a more mature Christologizing, when viewing Bonhoeffer's arguments in 1933 in relation to Bonhoeffer's notion of "Being in Christ"[21] articulated in Bonhoeffer's 1930 *habilitationsschrift* at the University of Berlin, entitled, in its 1996 English translation, *Act and Being: Transcendental Philosophy and Ontology in Systematic Theology.*

---

19. Bonhoeffer, *Christ the Center*, 39.
20. Bonhoeffer, *Christ the Center*, 39.
21. Bonhoeffer, *Act and Being*, 150–61.

Appendix L

Paul Tillich and Christology

PAUL TILLICH'S HEIDEGGERIAN CHRISTOLOGY

In *Heideggerian Theologies* (2018), I discuss the relationship between Heidegger and Tillich in a way to especially lay bare Heidegger's philosophical influence on Tillich's theologizing.[1] Indeed, there is no question to the extent that Heidegger's *Sein und Zeit* (1926) fundamentally shapes the three volumes of Tillich's *Systematic Theology* (1951, 1957, 1963), which can be ultimately traced to the mid-1920s, when Heidegger and Tillich initially developed a professional relationship at the University of Marburg—with Heidegger being part of the philosophy faculty and Tillich being part of the theology faculty (which included Bultmann). Though Tillich's encounter with Heidegger is relatively brief (and not as extensive as Bultmann's, for instance), the fact that the influence is so lasting is significant, particularly if acknowledging that Tillich's first volume of *Systematic Theology* does not appear until 1951—by this time, of course, Heidegger's reputation had waned from his 1920s professional exaltation, due to Heidegger's active relationship with the Nazi Party in the 1930s and, by the end of World War II, the condemnation of the Denazification Hearings that decreed Heidegger a "Nazi follower" and banned Heidegger from teaching from 1946 to 1951.

We need not see it as just a coincidence that Tillich's the first volume of *Systematic Theology* appears just as Heidegger reappears professionally at

1. Woodson, *Heideggerian Theologies*, 92–121.

the University of Freiburg with lectures delivered in the Winter 1951/1952 and the Summer 1952 semesters, entitled *Was Heißt Denken?* This is not to say that Heidegger's *Was Heißt Denken?* lecture had a direct influence on Tillich's first volume of Systematic Theology—rather, Heidegger's concentration on Nietzsche in 1936 through 1944/1945 exerts a significant influence on Heidegger's preoccupations by the time he returns to teaching at the end of 1951, which, similarly, seemingly exerts an influence on how Tillich theologically comports himself to his own theological preoccupations in the years leading up to the appearance of the first volume of *Systematic Theology*. Yet, it is, perhaps, possible to see that Heidegger's *Was Heißt Denken?* lecture serves some kind of influence on Tillich's second volume of *Systematic Theology*, published in 1957—it is this second volume, more so than the first, that Tillich presents his approach to Christology, which makes it all the more possible to view Heidegger's philosophical influences as shaping Tillich's Christological thinking and Christological reflection in the second volume of *Systematic Theology*, subtitled "Existence and the Christ."

To say that Heidegger influences how Tillich constructs what Christology is and what Christology, I submit, does require a certain amount of care. Indeed, Tillich only mentions Heidegger by name three times in the second volume of *Systematic Theology*—with six in the first volume, and three times in the third volume. These three name-droppings often sort Heidegger either within Tillich's understanding of existentialism or fundamentally situate Tillich's argumentation to align Heidegger with Nietzsche. Not only does this help us come to terms with what Tillich means by "existence," it also informs his use of the term "the Christ." Consider the term "existence" first. Tillich, undoubtedly, conceptualizes the term within, again, a broader view of the school of existentialism, as that which enjoys a particular relevance in the 1950s. This is made explicit from the beginning of the main section of the second volume of *Systematic Theology*, when Tillich outlines an "etymology of existence," which makes sense of "the existentialist problem"[2]and conceptualizes "existentialism against essentialism" from Hegel to Schelling to Schopenhauer to Kierkegaard to Nietzsche to Heidegger to Jaspers to Sartre, insofar as Tillich is interested in drawing a distinction between atheistic existentialism and theistic existentialism.[3] What follows is a working through of notions of "existential" and the extent of "existentialist thinking" in a small section,[4] before Tillich arrives at the

2. Tillich, *Systematic Theology Vol. 2*, 21–24.

3. Tillich, *Systematic Theology Vol. 2*, 24–26.

4. Tillich, *Systematic Theology Vol. 2*, 26.

pivotal section, "Existentialism and Christian Theology,"[5] in which Tillich begins with the following:

> Christianity asserts that Jesus is the Christ. The term "the Christ" points by marked contrast to man's existential situation. For the Christ, the Messiah, is he who is supposed to bring the "new eon," the universal regeneration, the new reality. New reality presupposes an old reality; and this old reality, according to prophetic and apocalyptic descriptions, is the state of estrangement of man and his world from God.[6]

Here, we note a relationship—or perhaps a distinction—that Tillich makes between two kinds of existence: one that exists in relation to "the Christ" and another that exists in relation to an "existential situation." These two kinds of existence are, essentially, laid bare respectively as two kinds of reality: a new and an old. The extent that "the Christ" brings the "new eon," Tillich explains, what also comes is a new reality—what the "new eon" accomplishes, then, is it brings "man's existential situation" grounded in an "old reality," in order to provide a re-existentializing out of—or away from—what Tillich denotes as "the state of estrangement of man and his world from God."

For Tillich, insofar as "existentialism has analyzed the 'old eon,' namely the predicament of man and his world in the state of estrangement,"[7] and existentialism, we can say, is concerned with making a philosophical account for the "old reality," Tillich wishes to make a Christological account for a new reality in relation to "the Christ" by theologizing and construing an answer to *the question of the meaning of Christology*. In this way, Tillich's handling of existentialism, however rooted in a 1950s now-antiquated conceptualization, becomes no more than a philosophical foundation upon which Tillich can construct a theological frame with Christological eaves— yet, even if we can say that existentialism is simply a means to a particular end for Tillich, there remains a philosophical bent to Tillich's theologizing, which owes its assumptions and preoccupations to Heidegger's brand of "existentialism."

It is important to be clear here when associating Heidegger with existentialism. Such an association does not do Heidegger's philosophizing any justice any more than it allows us to make sense out of existentialism itself. However, if we are to remain honest to Tillich's articulation of "existentialism," we must acknowledge Tillich's assumptions about Heidegger and existentialism and, for that matter, recognize that, when Tillich speaks

5. Tillich, *Systematic Theology Vol. 2*, 27–28.

6. Tillich, *Systematic Theology Vol. 2*, 27.

7. Tillich, *Systematic Theology Vol. 2*, 27.

of existentialism, Tillich is preoccupied with Heidegger's philosophizing. Indeed, Tillich gathers his understanding of Heidegger's philosophizing into Tillich's own understanding of existentialism, such that what we have, then, is Tillich's view of Heidegger's brand of "existentialism—if we attend to the theological language Tillich uses, which is calibrating philosophically, it is impossible to not notice a Heideggerian bent to what Tillich theologizes from the standpoint of what Tillich calls "man's existential situation" and "the state of estrangement of man and his world from God."

The difference Tillich makes between an "old reality" and a "new reality" certainly has a Heideggerian sort of difference, when contextualizing the difference against Heidegger's argument in *Being and Time* about the degree to which we have forgotten the meaning of Being. To forget the meaning of Being means, essentially, we are in an "existential situation" and an "old reality." To more fundamentally come to terms with the question of the meaning of Being, as Heidegger does from the outset of *Being and Time*, means, essentially, we are orienting ourselves to "the Christ" and a "new reality," so that Tillich, thusly, comes to terms with *the question of the meaning of Christology*. Tillich's approach to *the question of the meaning of Christology*, through a kind of Heideggerian understanding of "man's existential situation" and the "old reality." It is through Christological thinking, as that which thinks through the meaning of Being, and Christological reflection, as that which thinks through the "new reality and "the Christ" that brings Tillich provide a theologizing in the section entitled, "The Marks of Man's Estrangement and the Concept of Sin."[8]

From the outset of what is a pivotal section for how Tillich wishes to express what it means to do Christology and what is, ultimately, at stake with *the question of the meaning of Christology*, Tillich explains:

> The state of existence is the state of estrangement. Man is estranged from the ground of his being, from other beings, and from himself. The transition from essence to existence results in personal guilt and universal tragedy."[9]

Here, to this point, Tillich provides the following question: "what is the relation of the concept of estrangement to the traditional concept of sin?"[10] If we focus, first, on Tillich's "concept of estrangement," as that which brings about the extent that "man is estranged from the ground of his being," Tillich makes it clear that his use of the term "estrangement" is derived from "a

8. Tillich, *Systematic Theology Vol. 2*, 44–59.

9. Tillich, *Systematic Theology Vol. 2*, 44.

10. Tillich, *Systematic Theology Vol. 2*, 45.

philosophical term [that] was created and applied by Hegel, especially in his doctrine of nature as estranged man (*Geist*)."[11] Though not explicit, Tillich's approach to "Geist" is in terms of Hegel's *Phänomenologie des Geistes*, often translated as *Phenomenology of Spirit*.

If we remain true to Heidegger's influence on Tillich, it is possible to view Tillich's approach to "estrangement" through Heidegger's, even if Tillich chooses to not make it explicit. While Heidegger delivers a lecture on Hegel's Phenomenology of Spirit in Winter 1930/1931 is starting point that becomes a possible influence on Tillich, I submit another text that is in closer proximity to Tillich's second volume of *Systematic Theology*, which seems to be, I argue, Heidegger's *Hegels Begriff der Erfahrung* (1950), which is included in the collection, *Holzwege*. In it, Heidegger works through Hegel's introduction to *Phänomenologie des Geistes*, wherein Hegel speaks of the experience of consciousness,[12] and Heidegger suggests that "the essential nature of Spirit resides in self-consciousness."[13] In this way, we can view consciousness—or self-consciousness—as something that informs "estrangement," which allows Tillich come to the conclusion that:

> Estrangement points to the basic characteristic of man's predicament. Man as he exists is not what he essentially is and ought to be. He is estranged from his true bring. The profundity of the term "estrangement" lies in the implication that one belongs essentially to that from which one is estranged.[14]

For this to occur, as, to Tillich's point, "the basic characteristic of man's predicament," it means that consciousness not only allows us to be aware of what our "predicament" is or that our existence "is not what [it] essentially is and ought to be," but also a fundamental component of that which allows us to recognize that we are "estranged from [our] true being."

The extent that, as Tillich argues, it is possible to conceive of the fact that "one belongs essentially to that from which one is estranged" speaks to the presence of consciousness. Similarly, the presence of consciousness, as what Heidegger suggests, again, "the essential nature of Spirit resides in self-consciousness," makes it possible to acknowledge how sin is, Tillich says, "not implied in the term 'estrangement,' namely, the personal act of turning away from that to which one belongs"[15]—to make sense out of the relationship

---

11. Tillich, *Systematic Theology Vol. 2*, 45.

12. Heidegger, *Hegel's Concept of Experience*, 26.

13. Heidegger, *Hegel's Concept of Experience*, 27.

14. Tillich, *Systematic Theology Vol. 2*, 45.

15. Tillich, *Systematic Theology Vol. 2*, 46.

between "sin" and "estrangement" Christologically denotes, Tillich says, "the element of personal responsibility in one's estrangement,"[16] which can be viewed as a Heideggerian conceptualization, not just in terms of Heidegger's reading of Hegel in 1950, but also, earlier, in *Being and Time* itself, when Heidegger discusses notions of "being-guilty" and "being responsible for."[17] When attending to Heidegger's terms, we find a particular resonance in how they become foundational to what Tillich means by "personal responsibility" and how this unfolds as part of "one's estrangement." To this, if "one's estrangement" is always-already linked to one's "sin," what links them is, as Heidegger devises it, notions of "being-guilty" and "being responsible for."

Yet, if we consider Tillich's approach to "estrangement" as integral to how he approaches *the question of the meaning of Christology*, what we invariably find is an implicit use of Heidegger's "thrownness," particularly in terms of the relationship between "thrownness" and "abandonment"[18] and "thrownness" and "conscience."[19]

PAUL TILLICH'S EARLY CHRISTOLOGY

As early as 1911—just after the original German publication of Albert Schweitzer's *Geschichte der Leben-Jesu-Forschung* in 1906, translated as *The Quest for the Historical Jesus* in 1910, but before the original German publication of Rudolf Bultmann's *Jesus* in 1926—it has been acknowledged by both Glyn Richards (1974) and Anne M. Reijnen (2009) that Paul Tillich's earliest handling of *the question of the meaning of Christology* was rooted in attempting to make sense out of the problem of the historical Jesus. To this point, Richards notes in "Paul Tillich and the Historical Jesus" (1974):

> In a set of propositions presented to a group of theological friends as early as 1911, [Tillich] attempted to answer the question how it might be possible to interpret Christian doctrine if the non-existence of Jesus as a historical person were to become a probability.[20]

Indeed, Tillich does confirm this in his *On the Boundary: An Autobiographical Sketch* (1967). In light of what Tillich conforms, Richards contextualizes Tillich early interests, from the very beginning sentence of the piece, by

16. Tillich, *Systematic Theology Vol. 2*, 46.

17. Heidegger, *Being and Time*, 327.

18. Heidegger, *Being and Time*, 397–98.

19. Heidegger, *Being and Time*, 337–38.

20. Richards, "Paul Tillich and the Historical Jesus," 120.

asserting that "the problem of the relation of history to faith and of the effect of historical criticism on Christian belief was a matter of continuing concern" for Tillich.[21] This sense of their being a "problem of the relation of history to faith" speaks to a grappling with the relation between the historical Jesus and the Christ of faith—the degree to which there exists, to Richards' point, " the effect of historical criticism on Christian belief was a matter of continuing concern" speaks to, I feel, *the question of the meaning of Christology*, as that which "was a matter of continuing concern" for the trajectory of Tillich's thought well into 1950s across the three volumes of Tillich's *Systematic Theology*, but particularly in the second volume, subtitled, "Existence and Christ" (1957).

Though this second volume is often the first place one might look for Tillich's account of his Christology, which Richards and Reijnen cite—and rightfully so—both Richards and Reijnen, nonetheless, recognize that Tillich's specific handling of the problem of the historical Jesus Christologically is actually antecedent to volume two of *Systematic Theology*. However, it can be noted that, interestingly, D. Moody Smith's "The Historical Jesus in Paul Tillich's Christology" (1966), by way of its title, wishes to provide an account of Tillich's Christological reflection on and Christological thinking through the historical Jesus, but does works exclusively from the standpoint of the second volume of *Systematic Theology*—this is certainly noteworthy, given that Moody is writing in such a close proximity to the publication of the third and last volume of *Systematic Theology*, and does not mention Tillich's earliest handling of Christology.

Yet, when setting aside Moody's account, we can certainly broaden Richards' and Reijnen's contextualization of Tillich in 1911 to include the research Tillich conducted while at the University of Breslau and then at the University of Halle-Wittenberg, culminating respectively in two dissertations on Schelling: "The Conception of the History of Religion in Schelling's Positive Philosophy: Its Presuppositions and Principles" (1911) and "Mysticism and Consciousness of Guilt in Schelling's Philosophical Development" (1912). Through Schelling, Tillich explored the meaning of history—this conception of history, particularly with respect to the 1911 dissertation, allowed Tillich to situate himself to the problem of the historical Jesus philosophically.

It is also during this time, when, Richards notes, "Tillich's attention was focused on the historical problem by the work of Martin Kähler, one of [Tillich's] theological teachers."[22] Richards cites Tillich's reference to Kähler

21. Richards, "Paul Tillich and the Historical Jesus," 120.
22. Tillich, *On the Boundary*, 47.

in *On the Boundary*.[23] Given that Kähler died in 1912, Tillich's attention to Kähler is all the more significant, with Kähler's *Der sogenannte historische Jesus und der geschichte, biblische Christus* (1892) having a heavy influence on Tillich.[24] That influence, Richards presents, was grounded on:

> Kähler attempt[ing] to solve the problem of how to be sure of the truth of the Christian message by equating the Jesus of history with the Christ of faith and making the Christ of faith independent of the uncertainties of historical research. [. . .] he believed that we have to ground our certainty concerning the Christian message in the Christ of faith. Faith guarantees what historical research cannot reach.[25]

That which "grounds" and "guarantees," then, is that which existentializes us, as Richards says, to "the Christian message in the Christ of faith," insofar as faith bridges the gap between "historical research" and what eludes that historical research. That gap must also be existentialized, so that *the question of the meaning of Christology*, for Tillich, allows for a question to the posed and a meaningfulness to be sought—it is *the question of the meaning of Christology* that allows us, to Richards' point, "to be sure of the truth of the Christian message." How we are even able to equate "the Jesus of history"—or the historical Jesus—with the Christ of faith, such that it involves, Richards writes, "making the Christ of faith independent of the uncertainties of historical research" is by attending to *the question of the meaning of Christology*. It is through the necessary Christological reflection and Christological thinking, for Tillich, that brings Tillich towards a meaning of Christology influence, first, by Kähler, and then, working existentially alongside Bultmann, until Tillich is able to articulate *the question of the meaning of Christology* through, eventually, Heidegger's philosophizing of the question of the meaning of Being in the 1920s.

---

23. Richards, "Paul Tillich and the Historical Jesus," 120.

24. Manning, *Cambridge Companion to Tillich*, xix.

25. Richards, "Paul Tillich and the Historical Jesus," 120.

Appendix M

Karl Rahner and Christology

KARL RAHNER'S TRANSCENDENTAL CHRISTOLOGY: TRANSCENDING KÄRKKÄINEN

Here, I intend to examine Karl Rahner's "transcendental Christology" from the perspective of Veli-Matti Kärkkäinen and, then, I will outline Kärkkäinen's argument in the form of a critique. From there, I will use Kärkkäinen's argument about Rahner's "transcendental Christology" as a means to understand the whole of Rahner's theological endeavors constructed around notions of the "transcendental." In this regard, I find that Rahner's "transcendental Christology" is only part of a broader view of theology and a kind of theological "transcendental," which extends Heideggerian onto-theology and Kantian transcendental theology. As such, my intent is to suggest that Rahner's "transcendental Christology" speaks to what I will refer to as "phenomenological theology," where Rahner's chief theological concerns is with the "transcendental" as a point of phenomenological value.

Kärkkäinen's Understanding of Rahner's Transcendental Christology

In *Christology: A Global Introduction* (2003), when Veli-Matti Kärkkäinen sets forth a description of Rahner's Christology, he makes a very important first move, which is to frame Rahner's theological task as "holding together two seemingly contradictory premises: the universal saving action of God and the necessity of supernatural revelation and faith in Christ."[1] What Kärkkäinen cites as key to what Rahner is "holding together" is the two premises of revelation and faith and how, essentially, they must occur "at a universal, transcendental level."[2] In this regard, Kärkkäinen notes that Rahner is concerned with how "God reveals Godself" to humanity through the human experience,[3] but, also, based on the extent to which Rahner wanted to respond to the challenge of modern Western culture's hesitance to believe in a transcendent God.[4] With this in mind, according to Kärkkäinen, Rahner's the crux of challenge was to confront any "talk about God mainly in immanental terms."[5]

So, the transcendental method Rahner employs is, as Kärkkäinen describes, a philosophical tool used to show that by definition a human being is 'spirit,' open to receive revelation from God."[6] This "openness" is particularly predicated on transcendental experiences, which Kärkkäinen defines as occurring "whenever a human being acknowledges that human life is more than just what one sees in everyday life."[7] It is through these transcendental experiences that, for Rahner, an openness to revelation becomes revealed evidence and, as Kärkkäinen further asserts, the grace of God in Christ [becomes] nothing foreign to the structure of the human being but belongs to its core."[8]

This is particularly important to how Rahner appropriates the term "transcendental." Rahner applies the term, according to Kärkkäinen, as a way to suggest that "human beings transcend the limits of 'nature' and are oriented towards the Holy Mystery that Christian theology calls God." Rahner's "transcendental" view of God plays itself out in Rahner's approach to Christology, where Kärkkäinen identifies Rahner's main Christological task as the following: "to inquire into the possibility of an absolute God-man, an absolute Savior."[9] Accordingly, Kärkkäinen notes that Rahner's Christology situates the role of Jesus as one that is situated in "mediation"

1. Kärkkäinen, *Christology*, 140.
2. Kärkkäinen, *Christology*, 140.
3. Kärkkäinen, *Christology*, 140.
4. Kärkkäinen, *Christology*, 141.
5. Kärkkäinen, *Christology*, 141.
6. Kärkkäinen, *Christology*, 141.
7. Kärkkäinen, *Christology*, 141.
8. Kärkkäinen, *Christology*, 141.
9. Kärkkäinen, *Christology*, 142.

—Kärkkäinen makes this particularly explicit by ascertaining: "in [Jesus's] person, Christ is the historical presence of God's disclosure to humans."[10]

What ultimately—and rather logically—arises from this "disclosure" is the sense that Christ is the absolute Savior. This means, then, if following Kärkkäinen's discussion very carefully, that Christ's absolutism as Savior encompasses salvific value that, in turn, ushers forth a perpetual salvific trajectory in its existential meaning for all of humanity. Here, Kärkkäinen argues, through Rahner's view of soteriology, that "salvation encompasses not only our 'divinization' but also the beginning of the process of the divinization of the whole world."[11] Consequently, Kärkkäinen suggests that Rahner's notion of Christ's divinity is "accentuated by [a] larger soteriological vision."[12] Salvation as human "divinization" comes to bear specifically in Kärkkäinen's understanding of Rahner's Christological-soteriological perspective in the following manner:

> Human beings, while finite, are also able to transcend themselves as "spirit." For Rahner, this is also a crucial Christological affirmation. It was God who willed this transcendental nature of humanity to make room for a genuine self-expression of God in the form of humanity. . . Salvation for Rahner is participation in the divine life to which the entire structure of the human being is naturally oriented, over and above that which human nature is able to ascend to on its own.[13]

As an extension of this, Kärkkäinen makes a great final assessment that, in brief, explains Rahner's "transcendental Christology" as this: "in [Christ's] person is the self-communication of God's presence to humanity and the opportunity for human participation in the divine nature."[14]

Transcending Kärkkäinen's Rahner

In order to truly grasp Rahner's appropriations of the terms "transcendent," "transcendence," and "transcendental," I find it essential to discuss them as Immanuel Kant does in his *Critique of Pure Reason*. I find that, in beginning with Kant, I can offer a different way of considering how Rahner uses the aforementioned terms theologically.

10. Kärkkäinen, *Christology*, 141.
11. Kärkkäinen, *Christology*, 141.
12. Kärkkäinen, *Christology*, 141.
13. Kärkkäinen, *Christology*, 143.
14. Kärkkäinen, *Christology*, 144.

For Kant, these terms are embodied in the "transcendental idea," which is a pure concept of reason.[15] The "pure" aspect to any concept, or object –that is, when it is a "transcendental idea" —is one predicated on being *a priori*. As such, this kind of object of understanding is something that is represented, or objectified, prior to all experience. This is very important to understanding how Rahner uses "transcendental" —something that is, in fact, predicated on *a priori* concepts. These *a priori* concepts, through the process of a more rigorous experiential objectification, according to Kant, "indicate the synthetic unity which alone makes possible an empirical knowledge of objects."[16] What this means, then, is that, when there is an encounter with an object of understanding, particularly one that is a transcendental idea, there is an initial knowledge of it as a "mere logical form" before there is a deeper, deliberative knowledge of it as an "empirical form." Knowledge of an *a priori* object of understanding, as Kant argues, "[is] not to be obtained by mere reflection but only by inference."[17] So, what arises here is the relationship between sense and reference,[18] where what can be logically inferred about an a priori object of understanding becomes an empirical point of reference.

Kant's notion of the "transcendental idea" is particularly concerned with the dialectic, as is Rahner's use of the term. Like Rahner's "transcendental Christology," Kant assertion about the transcendental dialectic, then, is based on the extent to which reason— "pure" reason, as it were—is a natural and unavoidable component of any dialectic formed between a subjective being and an object of understanding. Let me be clear here: this is a dialectic pitting the knower against the known. This knower-known dialectic is where I would argue Rahner is framing his "transcendental": it is the situatedness of the knower, the situatedness of the known, and the degree to which the knower is "oriented" towards the known.

This orientation, of course, is, as Kärkkäinen describes, grounded on transcending the limits of nature. As I am sure Rahner would agree, these "limits of nature" are encased in the human existential predicament. Paul Tillich illustrates this "predicament" as one of estrangement in his *Systematic Theology Volume 2*: it is the extent to which, when human existence comes into being by being-thrown in the Heideggerian sense, humanity's being recognizes that they are "estranged" from God's Being and, in fact, the

---

15. Kant, *Critique of Pure Reason*, 315.

16. Kant, *Critique of Pure Reason*, 315.

17. Kant, *Critique of Pure Reason*, 308.

18. I am thinking particularly of Gottlob Frege's notions of "sense" and "reference," which, of course, owe their theory and praxis to Kant. Frege, "On Sense and Reference," 61.

true ground of humanity's own being itself.[19] In this respect, it becomes possible to say that, once humanity's being recognizes that the "ground" of their being is not in the facticity of that being, humanity seeks a facticity that is, as Emmanuel Levinas would contend, "otherwise than being."[20]

In light of Tillich's specific argument about estrangement, Rahner is also concerned with the "ground" of human being. I find that Rahner is keenly aware of onto-theology, not just Kantian, but Heideggerian –the sense that "being" and "Being" are inextricably linked through issues of ontological value, existential meaning, and theological ramifications. Like Heidegger specifically, Rahner seems to be operating under the assumption that the connectedness of being and Being is as much an ontological concern as it is a theological one.[21]

But, of course, Rahner offers some very important nuances that deviate from Heidegger, Kant, and Tillich. Rather than being concerned with seeking outwardly for the ground of humanity's being, Rahner focuses the seeking inwardly—I would argue that Rahner conceives of this ground as being intrinsic, not extrinsic. That is, in order to "transcend" the finitude of Tillich's human existential predicament, Rahner, as Kärkkäinen argues, suggests that the human "spirit" is the "ground." But, more importantly, if taking Rahner a bit further, it is possible to suggest that the facticity of humanity's "spiritual" side is contingent on having been "grounded" in God's "Being," even if there is some sense of estrangement evident in what is "grounded.

Though there is "estrangement" in Tillich's view, that estrangement is not one where humanity's being is mutually exclusive from God's Being. Instead, regardless of estrangement, God is within us. In other words, I would argue that what Rahner is precisely articulating –that is to say, through the notion that God "willed" the spiritual nature of humanity within humanity—is that the "transcendental nature of humanity" is what makes it possible for God to "self-communicate" God's "Being" in the form of Jesus's humanity.

As Rahner suggests, the way that this "self-communication" occurs is through, as I have interjected with Kant, a transcendental dialectic. Here, with the transcendental dialectic, it is possible to argue that Rahner's self-communication is based on the situatedness between two that share a dialectic with one another. Specifically, in regard to what Rahner proposes as "communication" between humanity and God's "Being" —of course, through the form of Jesus's humanity—the Kantian transcendental dialectic

---

19. Tillich, *Systematic Theology Vol. 2*, 44.
20. Levinas, *Otherwise than Being*, 3.
21. Heidegger, *Identity and Difference*, 59.

is one that is between humanity's being and God's "Being," or, as I will argue further, a "being-Being" dialectic.

KARL RAHNER'S "CHRISTOLOGY TODAY"

Just four years before his death in 1984, Karl Rahner published the text entitled, "Christology Today," along with two other texts, which appeared in a co-authored work with Wilhelm Thüsing, *A New Christology* (1980), though "Christology Today" seemingly appeared earlier in *Theologie aus Erfahrung des Geistes* (1975) as Volume 12 of his *Schriften zur Theologie*, then, again, within Volume 17 of *Theological Investigations* as part of *Jesus, Man, and Church* in 1981. Given that the text, most notably, in 1980 and again in 1981, it suggests, I submit, that Rahner viewed "Christology Today" as, perhaps, his most declarative and succinct expression of *the question of the meaning of Christology*—this certainly seems so, when, for that matter, viewing what is said in "Christology Today" with the *"Jesus Christus"* chapter in the original German publication of *Grundkurs des Glaubens: Einführung in den Begriff des Christentums* (1976),[22] subsequently translated as *Foundations of Christian Faith: An Introduction to the Idea of Christianity* in 1978.[23]

If attending to the textual transmission of "Christology Today," its contextual origins, according to Rahner's notes in *Schriften zur Theologie*, can be traced to a December 1973 lecture delivered at Saarbrücken, which was entitled *"Christologie heute?"*[24] We will note, though, that the title of the original version of the text poses a question in 1973 and 1975, and this punctuation is dropped by 1980. Though this could just be simply an editorial decision, there is certainly more to it—the two texts are fundamentally different in terms of form and different in terms of how Rahner presents his argument between the two. If we think of the December 1973 lecture as initiating a point of inquiry, the 1980 text seems more declarative, insofar as it is possible to see the latter as a revised version of the former. This is certainly confirmable from copyright page of *A New Christology*, which declares that the Rahner material included within has a new material copyright. Taken literally, the implication is that "Christology Today," in its specific form, does not appear anywhere else prior to 1980—nevertheless, "Christology Today," as a 1980 text, represents a culmination of Rahner's handling of *the question of the meaning of Christology*, with certain contextual origins rooted in the 1973 *"Christologie heute?"*

22. Rahner, *Grundkurs des Glaubens*, 180–312.

23. Rahner, *Foundations of Christian Faith*, 176–321.

24. Pekarske, *Abstracts*, 460.

Yet, it is possible to trace Rahner's sense of Christology in his time—in terms of his "today"—as far back as the first volume of his *Schriften zur Theologie* (1954), translated as *God, Christ, Mary and Grace* in 1961 within the *Theological Investigations* series, with the text entitled, "Current Problems in Christology."[25] In it, Rahner considers what the Chalcedonian formula is and does, indeed, for *the question of the meaning of Christology*. Consequently, Rahner writes:

> We shall never cease to return to this formula, because whenever it is necessary to say briefly what it is that we encounter in the ineffable truth which is our salvation, we shall always have recourse to the modest, sober clarity of the Chalcedonian formula.[26]

Rahner, then, provides what he intends to problematize:

> But we shall only really have recourse to it (and this is not at all the same thing as simply repeating it), if it is not only our end[,] but also our beginning. We must say something here about this incompleteness which the formula does not resolve but in fact preserves.[27]

The extent that the Chalcedonian formula, in its "incompleteness," becomes something that "does not resolve" *the question of the meaning of Christology*, but, instead, merely "preserves" it, for Rahner, becomes a Christological problem that affects one's Christological thinking and one's Christological reflection on the way towards posing the question to and seeking the meaningfulness of Christology. To this point, when reckoning with what is laid bare by "our beginning," Rahner comes to the conclusion: "if we are always at the beginning, then the first step is always the uneasy feeling of a need to ask whether it might not be possible to give this or that matter closer attention and find a better solution."[28]

Given Rahner's desire "to give this or that matter closer attention and find a better solution"—a solution that resolves the incompleteness of the Chalcedonian formula—the account of Christology he eventually gives in the 1973 lecture, *Christology Today?* In a certain sense, though the lecture wishes to confront classical Christology, as that "which stresses the descent of the pre-existent Logos and tends towards monophysitism"[29] Rahner's

25. Rahner, *Theological Investigations: Volume 1*, 149–200.

26. Rahner, *Theological Investigations: Volume 1*, 150.

27. Rahner, *Theological Investigations: Volume 1*, 150–51.

28. Rahner, *Theological Investigations: Volume 1*, 151.

29. Pekarske, *Abstracts*, 460.

intent in "find[ing] a corrective in modern, horizontal [C]hristology which takes as its starting point the full humanity of Jesus,"[30] as with "Current Problems in Christology" from 1954, wants to resolve the incompleteness of the Chalcedonian formula. Needless to say, Rahner "find[s] a better solution" by the time he writes *Foundations of Christian Faith*, especially when noting that his account of Christology, by 1976, spans about one-third of both *Grundkurs des Glaubens* and *Foundations of Christian Faith* texts.

As much as *Foundations of Christian Faith* is undoubtedly Rahner's magnum opus, and, for that matter, how Rahner handles Christology in it becomes the most extended concentration on the subject, one would think that Rahner had said all that he wished to say about what I have called *the question of the meaning of Christology*. Indeed, *Foundations of Christian Faith* is a cumulative work, which articulates, at various turns, Heidegger's influences on Rahner—this can be traced, as I have argued in *Heideggerian Theologies* (2018), to Rahner's relationship with Heidegger in the 1930s.[31] However, whatever we can say *Foundations of Christian Faith* accomplishes Christologically for Rahner, if we are to say that Rahner hoped it would "find a better solution" to the perennial problem of the incompleteness of the Chalcedonian formula and how this continues to stunt *the question of the meaning of Christology*, it is possible to view the text, as seminal as it is to Rahner's body of work, as just the beginning.

As Rahner writes in 1954, "if we are always at the beginning," what we must ask is what kind of beginning does Rahner provide by 1980 in "Christology Today," when we are reminded, of course, that it encompasses new material? If we take "Christology Today" as, to some extent, Rahner's final testament on *the question of the meaning of Christology*, given that it incorporates a cumulative effect, does it outline a manner in which Rahner found "a better solution" to the posing of the question to and the seeking of the meaningfulness of Christology?

From the outset of "Christology Today," Rahner begins with four preliminary remarks, which not only allows himself to be situated what he believes is at stake for Christology "today," but he also allows himself to think through the problems inherent in Christology itself as a beginning. The first preliminary remark is to the impossibility "to exhaust the subject in the present work,"[32] while the second preliminary remark works from the assumption that one "would fail to do justice to the subject-matter if [one] did not appeal to the whole mystery of human existence and approached

30. Pekarske, *Abstracts*, 460.

31. Woodson, *Heideggerian Theologies*, 122–54.

32. Rahner and Thüsing, *New Christology*, 3.

the question simply as one special object of man's curiosity alongside other objects of equal status."[33] The third preliminary remark, Rahner indicates, affirms that "it is possible to approach Christology today in many different ways,"[34] while the fourth preliminary remark makes it clear that: "it would be impossible to delineate the whole of the Church's official Christology in all its fulness and many distinctions at a high theological or even at a traditional catechetical level within this framework."[35] Cumulatively, with an emphasis on the final preliminary remark, Rahner asserts the following:

> We do not begin by saying that Jesus is God, the Word of the eternal God made flesh, existing with the Father from eternity. Nor do we begin by speaking of the hypostatic union of the divine and human nature in the one person of the divine Logos.[36]

Here, we see Rahner, again, confronting the "incompleteness" of the Chalcedonian formula, in terms of what it fails to resolve through *the question of the meaning of Christology*. Such an "incompleteness" confirms, for Rahner, that "we are always at the beginning." To venture outside of this perpetual beginning, and in an effort, as Rahner says, "to make it possible to give this or that matter closer attention and find a better solution," calibrates himself Christologically in the following way:

> Our point of departure is not the Christological formulations of Paul and John in the New Testament, providing a highly developed reflection about faith [. . .] Let us therefore begin by examining what is meant by what might perhaps be called a searching Christology.[37]

This idea of "searching Christology" is important to Rahner's Christological thinking and Christological reflection, which, as Pamela D. Young points out in "Rahner's Searching Christology" (1987), is predicated on "when we are searching for something which will guarantee or assure us of that salvation, we are searching for a saviour, for the Christ."[38] While Rahner validates this characterization, he also explains, "we must now move from a searching Christology, which seeks to discover the absolute bringer of salvation in history, to a Christology which has really found this bringer of salvation in

---

33. Rahner and Thüsing, *New Christology*, 3.
34. Rahner and Thüsing, *New Christology*, 4.
35. Rahner and Thüsing, *New Christology*, 4.
36. Rahner and Thüsing, *New Christology*, 4.
37. Rahner and Thüsing, *New Christology*, 4–5.
38. Young, "Rahner's Searching Christology," 438.

history."[39] For that matter, Rahner comes to the conclusion that "it is in this conviction that the bringer of salvation has been found that the very heart and substance of Christianity subsists." Subsequently, this suggests that it is through this "conviction" that *the question of the meaning of Christology* is possible in its "very heart and substance," as that which poses the question to and seeks the meaningfulness of Christology, which, in itself, grounds how "Christianity subsists."

39. Rahner and Thüsing, *New Christology*, 7.

Appendix N

John Macquarrie and Christology

Macquarrie's approach to *the question of the meaning of Christology,* as that which explicates the problem of the historical Jesus and that of the Christ of faith, can be located, to varying extents, in the following six works: *Principles of Christian Theology* (1966), *In Search for Humanity: A Theological and Philosophical Approach* (1982), *In Search of Deity: An Essay in Dialectical Theism* (1984), *Jesus Christ in Modern Thought* (1990), *Christology Revisited* (1998), and *Stubborn Theological Questions* (2003). Given that Macquarrie's Christological thinking and Christological reflection covers the theological landscape of these six texts, it stands to reason that what is laid bare Christologically for Macquarrie can be best illustrated when attending to each of the texts in a chronological fashion, beginning with what is, inarguably, Macquarrie's most important work, *Principles of Christian Theology,* and, then, carefully determining how this seminal work—as early as it is in Macquarrie's career—undoubtedly informs the other four works, as we proceed through what the meaning of Christology is for Macquarrie from the 1980s to the 1990s to the 2000s.

What remains contextual to how we situate Macquarrie theologically and, in turn, come to an understanding of what *the question of the meaning of Christology* is in his theologizing is acknowledging Macquarrie's relationship with Heidegger and Bultmann. In *Heideggerian Theologies* (2018), I devote a chapter to the Macquarrie-Heidegger relationship and Macquarrie's 1954 dissertation grounding Heidegger-Bultmann relations.[1] Indeed,

---

1. Woodson, *Heideggerian Theologies,* 23–57.

given that Macquarrie can be considered as a specialist in both Heidegger's and Bultmann's thought—in one sense, with Macquarrie's co-translation of the English version of *Being and Time* in 1962 and, in another sense, Macquarrie's deft handling of Bultmann's demythologization project in the 1954 dissertation, published in 1955, and a monograph devoted to Bultmann in 1960—both Heidegger and Bultmann, to certain degrees, influence Macquarrie's *Principles of Christian Theology* (1966), even if we can say, of course, that Heidegger leaves more of a fingerprint in Macquarrie's theologizing by 1966 than Bultmann.

To be sure, to the extent that *Principles of Christian Theology* is a work of systematic theology with a philosophical bent allows us to think of Macquarrie's Heideggerian influences over his Bultmannian. This seems so, since Bultmann is not a systematic theologian.[2] Even if Macquarrie approaches the first part of *Principles of Christian Theology* in terms of "The Tasks of Philosophical Theology"[3] and "Human Existence,"[4] as much as these can be construed generally from Bultmann—particularly aspects of the "existential" to human existence—both are specifically Heideggerian constructions for Macquarrie, insofar as Macquarie's section on "human existence" makes two strategic uses of *Being and Time*. Though Macquarrie;s subsequent chapter "Being and God"[5] makes explicit and frequent use of Heidegger, the chapter that follows it, entitled "The Language of Theology,"[6] interestingly enough, makes more use out of Bultmann than Heidegger.

While varying uses of Bultmann and Heidegger fundamentally ground Macquarrie's task and scope of what he considers as philosophical theology in the first part of *Principles of Christian Theology*, the second part of the book, denoting "Symbolic Theology," proceeds through theological themes such as "the triune God,"[7] "creation,"[8] the relationship between "providence,"[9] "miracles,"[10] "natural evil,"[11] and "sin,"[12] before Macquarrie provides two successive chapters on Christology: "the person of Jesus

2. Woodson, *Heideggerian Theologies*, 88.

3. Macquarrie, *Principles of Christian Theology*, 43–58.

4. Macquarrie, *Principles of Christian Theology*, 59–83.

5. Macquarrie, *Principles of Christian Theology*, 104–22.

6. Macquarrie, *Principles of Christian Theology*, 123–48.

7. Macquarrie, *Principles of Christian Theology*, 190–210.

8. Macquarrie, *Principles of Christian Theology*, 211–38.

9. Macquarrie, *Principles of Christian Theology*, 239–46.

10. Macquarrie, *Principles of Christian Theology*, 247–53.

11. Macquarrie, *Principles of Christian Theology*, 253–59.

12. Macquarrie, *Principles of Christian Theology*, 259–67.

Christ" and "the work of Christ." Together, Macquarrie's chapters on Christology acknowledge, on one hand, the problem of the historical Jesus in terms of "person" and, on the other, the Christ of faith in terms of "work."

Macquarrie begins his Christological thinking through a Christological reflection that asserts, through the relationship between "reconciliation" and "historical revelation" through an existentialized understanding that "man needs some concrete manifestation of God's activity, some manifestation that can seize him and bring him to the attitude of faith."[13] This "concrete manifestation" that concretizes—or existentializes—what is reconciled and historically revealed for us, as that which is a climatic existential experience, is rooted, Macquarrie explains, in the fact that "the New Testament claims that this climax of God's reconciling work did come with the historical revelation in Jesus Christ."[14] What this means, then, for Macquarrie's conceptualization of *the question of the meaning of Christology* is in the conclusion that "Jesus Christ then is for Christian faith the decisive or paradigmatic revelation of God."[15] If what is made "decisive" or "paradigmatic" is the posing of the question to and the seeking of the meaningful of Christology, what is posed and what is sought is Jesus Christ as, Macquarrie says, "the focus where the mystery of Being is disclosed."[16] Insofar as "the mystery of Being" grounds and is grounded by *the question of the meaning of Christology*, as that which is both decisive" and "paradigmatic," Macquarrie decisively proclaims, "in Christ, as the paradigmatic existence, we receive a renewed understanding of ourselves that amounts to a new possibility of existence."[17] In this respect—"the new possibility of existence" laid bare by "the paradigmatic existence" of the Christ of faith—Macquarrie locates, he acknowledges:

> The type of [C]hristology that begins, as it were, from below up, from the human career that is received as the manifestation of God rather than from the notion of the pre-existent Logos that has then to be conceived as taking a body and appearing as a particular existent.[18]

Given that the meaning of Christology, for Macquarrie, existentializes "from below up," the two companion texts, *In Search for Humanity: A Theological*

13. Macquarrie, *Principles of Christian Theology*, 270.

14. Macquarrie, *Principles of Christian Theology*, 270.

15. Macquarrie, *Principles of Christian Theology*, 271.

16. Macquarrie, *Principles of Christian Theology*, 271.

17. Macquarrie, *Principles of Christian Theology*, 272.

18. Macquarrie, *Principles of Christian Theology*, 274.

and *Philosophical Approach* and *In Search of Deity: An Essay in Dialectical Theism* outline what is at stake in posing the question to and what is at stake in seeking the meaningfulness of Christology: language. While Macquarrie recognizes the importance of language to theologizing in *Principles of Christian Theology*, by the 1980s, with *In Search for Humanity* and *In Search of Deity*, Macquarrie comes to the questionability and meaningfulness of language differently. Perhaps this difference is due to a turn and preoccupation in Macquarrie's theologizing that mirrors, in a way, Heidegger's own turn and preoccupation with language by 1950—with Macquarrie's earliest encounter with Heidegger in the 1950s with his dissertation and the translation of *Being and Time* in the 1960s, and Heidegger's shift from early concerns of the 1920s to the matters of his own later thought, Macquarrie's shift to language in the 1980s as seminal to theologizing makes use of Heidegger's eventual preoccupation with the importance of language to philosophizing.

It is in this way that, by *In Search for Humanity*, Macquarrie arrives at: "language isolates and brings to notice that about which the speaker wishes to say."[19] Such a statement is certainly not out of the scope of what he says in *Principles of Christian Theology* in terms of the "language of theology." What is different, however, is that Macquarrie decidedly channels the terminology indicative of Heidegger's later period, by supposing: "language does bring what we talk about out of its hiddenness into light, then it has a claim of truth, which the Greeks called aletheia, precisely 'unhiddenness.'"[20] Not only do we see Heidegger's notion of unconcealment in this, but we also see, through Macquarrie's own notion of "*aletheia*," the sense that, Macquarrie supposes, "perhaps language can articulate and bring into intelligible relations the swirling chaos of experiences only because there is some order there to be discovered."[21] This understanding of what language does for "the swirling chaos of experiences" is seemingly addressed again in *In Search of Deity*, when Macquarrie discusses "God-language," as that which "arose from the sense of affinity that human beings had with the cosmic forces around them."[22] Even with a "sense of affinity" in tow, Macquarrie surmises, "we can apprehend [God] up to a point, we can make some affirmations about him, we can even say (and we shall have to ask how this is possible) that God *must* be such and such, if he is a reality at all."[23]

19. Macquarrie, *In Search of Humanity*, 103.
20. Macquarrie, *In Search of Humanity*, 103.
21. Macquarrie, *In Search of Humanity*, 104.
22. Macquarrie, *In Search of Deity*, 19.
23. Macquarrie, *In Search of Deity*, 25.

What Macquarrie presents in the companion texts, *In Search of Humanity* and *In Search of Deity* was, Macquarrie tells us in the preface to *Jesus Christ in Modern Thought*, meant to be the first two parts of a trilogy with *Jesus Christ in Modern Thought*, as "originally planned," intended to be a "third part."[24] However, what became of *Jesus Christ in Modern Thought* is much broader than what Macquarrie planned, insofar as Macquarrie, he explains, would have "draw[n] on the findings of the two earlier books on humanity and deity," such that what the book he had planned to write "would have attempted to make sense in modern times of the conception of the God-man, as applied to Jesus Christ."[25]Nevertheless, what we have in Macquarrie's *Jesus Christ in Modern Thought* is more than just a "third part" to Macquarrie's handlings of Christology in the two companion texts, *In Search of Humanity* and *In Search of Deity*—rather, the Christological thinking and the Christological reflection that grounds *Jesus Christ in Modern Thought* makes it, I submit, inarguably, Macquarrie's most comprehensive statement on *the question of the meaning of Christology*. From the outset of the text, in which Macquarrie concentrates on the "problems of Christology," Macquarrie makes the following assessment:

> Christology is the study which has for its subject-matter Jesus Christ, his person and his work, or, to put it in a slightly different way, who he was (or is) and what he did (or does). Christianity, as the name implies, has Jesus Christ at its very centre, so that if [C]hristology is concentrated on a study of Jesus Christ, it is not so much a branch of Christian theology as its central theme; or, at least, it shares the centre with the equally fundamental doctrine of God.[26]

By beginning here, what follows, throughout *Jesus Christ in Modern Thought*, is largely a historical look at the development of *the question of the meaning of Christology*. Macquarrie proceeds from what he calls "the prehistory of Christology"[27] to what he denotes as "the rise of classical Christology,"[28] by traversing how Christology is witnessed by Paul,[29] the Synoptists,[30] John,[31]

---

24. Macquarrie, *Jesus Christ in Modern Thought*, ix.

25. Macquarrie, *Jesus Christ in Modern Thought*, ix.

26. Macquarrie, *Jesus Christ in Modern Thought*, 3.

27. Macquarrie, *Jesus Christ in Modern Thought*, 27–47.

28. Macquarrie, *Jesus Christ in Modern Thought*, 147–72.

29. Macquarrie, *Jesus Christ in Modern Thought*, 48–68.

30. Macquarrie, *Jesus Christ in Modern Thought*, 69–96.

31. Macquarrie, *Jesus Christ in Modern Thought*, 97–122.

and other New Testament texts.[32] Subsequent to these characterizations, Macquarie gives an account of various critiques of classical Christology through what he surmises as "attempts at reconstruction"—these attempts include, as Macquarrie defines them: "rationalist Christology,"[33] "humanistic Christology,"[34] "idealist Christology,"[35] "mid-century misgivings,"[36] "positivist Christology,"[37] "critical responses and theological renascence,"[38] and Christologies of the late twentieth century."[39] Given all these attempts, as such, Macquarrie comes to the following conclusion:

> We have followed a long path on which we have had to take note of a quite bewildering variety of responses provoked through the centuries by the figure of Jesus Christ. Yet it has all been preparation for the decisive question that now faces us—what do we make of Jesus Christ in our time?[40]

Thematically, still attending to the significance of "our time" to Christology, what follows *Jesus Christ in Modern Thought* is a relatively smaller work, *Christology Revisited* (1998)—as small as *Christology Revisited* is, there is a tendency to consider it a minor Macquarrie work, particularly if we compare the size and breadth of *Jesus Christ in Modern Thought* to *Christology Revisited*. It may not necessarily be inappropriate to think of *Christology Revisited* as a minor text, insofar as it is, indeed, a more obscure text in Macquarrie's body of work. Despite its obscurity as a work that could be easily overlooked, *Christology Revisited* represents an important step in Macquarrie's handling of *the question of the meaning of Christology*. In the preface to *Christology Revisited*, Macquarrie tells us that the text, as it is constructed, "contains the substance" of Macquarrie's Albert Cardinal Meyer Memorial Lectures for 1998.[41] The title of these lectures is the same given to the book.[42] The context of the book, then, must be situated with respect to *Jesus Christ in Modern Thought* that, he acknowledges:

32. Macquarrie, *Jesus Christ in Modern Thought*, 123–46.

33. Macquarrie, *Jesus Christ in Modern Thought*, 177–91.

34. Macquarrie, *Jesus Christ in Modern Thought*, 192–211.

35. Macquarrie, *Jesus Christ in Modern Thought*, 212–34.

36. Macquarrie, *Jesus Christ in Modern Thought*, 235–50.

37. Macquarrie, *Jesus Christ in Modern Thought*, 251–68.

38. Macquarrie, *Jesus Christ in Modern Thought*, 269–92.

39. Macquarrie, *Jesus Christ in Modern Thought*, 293–335.

40. Macquarrie, *Jesus Christ in Modern Thought*, 339.

41. Macquarrie, *Christology Revisited*, 7.

42. Macquarrie, *Christology Revisited*, 7.

Trie[s] to put together the results of many years of teaching and study in the field of [C]hristology, paying special attention to the difficulties which have been felt since the time of the Enlightenment in acknowledging Jesus Christ as the God-man.[43]

Even so, Macquarrie concedes:

As soon as [*Jesus Christ in Modern Thought*] was finished and fixed in print, I began to realize that some things that might have been said had not been said, that many things could have said better, while still other things should perhaps not have been said at all.[44]

The extent that, for Macquarrie, *Jesus Christ in Modern Thought* left his Christological thinking and Christological reflection towards *the question of the meaning of the Christology* unfinished, it stands to reason, then, that Macquarrie would say:

So I feel the need to go back and revisit [C]hristology, and I believe that as long as there are Christian theologies, they will still be revisiting [C]hristology and seeking better understandings of what Kierkegaard called the "absolute paradox of the God-man.[45]

We need not take Macquarrie's reference, here, to Kierkegaard lightly. To a certain extent, given that Macquarrie pinpoints a connection between how he defines "existentialism" and his approach to theologizing through the philosophizing of Kierkegaard,[46] insofar as, for Macquarrie, Kierkegaard acts in "the service of theology,"[47] this informs Macquarrie's existentializing an "absolute paradox" in the God-man relationship. As a result, Macquarrie begins his revisiting of Christology by attending to "the absolute paradox" that is fundamental, I submit, to *the question of the meaning of Christology*. What becomes paradoxical to what it means to do Christology—in terms of what Christological thinking means to Christological reflection and what Christological reflection means to Christological thinking—is this:

There are clearly limits as to how far we can go in the quest for understanding. I do not think that, if we remain Christian, we can ever escape the fundamental paradox, that Jesus Christ is

43. Macquarrie, *Christology Revisited*, 7.

44. Macquarrie, *Christology Revisited*, 7.

45. Macquarrie, *Christology Revisited*, 7.

46. Macquarrie, *Existentialism*, 271.

47. Macquarrie, *Studies in Existentialism*, 22.

both human and divine. There are no devices that would eliminate it, short of the destruction of Christianity itself.[48]

This leads Macquarrie to eventually view this issue—what is paradoxical—
as steeped in "metaphysical questions," such that, to even ask something
so paradoxical means that, Macquarrie finds, "we have to ask about the
range of human cognition."[49] That range and that human cognition are
both grounded on "purely objective knowledge, knowledge of facts whether
natural or historical."[50] All told, Macquarrie questions what knowledge is
and what knowledge affords us in various contexts, particularly with which
the way it allows us to comport ourselves to the *question of the meaning of
Christology*—essentially, Christological thinking is a kind of knowledge in
much the same way as Christological reflection is another kind of knowledge, and both pose different questions and seek different meanings. These
questions and these forms of seeking allow Macquarrie to traverse engagements with "the humanity of Jesus Christ,"[51] the question: "how do we
know Jesus Christ,"[52] and what he describes as "the metaphysical Christ."[53]

Given where Macquarrie leaves off at the conclusion of *Christology
Revisited*, these issues find their way in the aptly-titled, *Stubborn Theological
Questions* (2003). From the standpoint of Macquarrie's own Christological
thinking and Christological reflection, he considers three Christological
questions as "stubborn questions." The first two questions Macquarrie presents are "the cosmic Christ"[54] and "the pre-existence of Jesus Christ"[55]—
the two questions, in Macquarrie's view, are antiquated in the respective
questions they pose and the meaningful that they seek, respectively. Both
remain "stubborn" to what it means to do Christology today, if it is only
from what matters today that questions can be adequately posed and meaningfulness can be adequately sought. What it means to do Christology today
is laid bare in the third "stubborn" question Macquarrie provides: "Christology from above or from below?" It is within this question, as "stubborn" as it
is, that Macquarrie comports himself to both distance himself from the first
two "stubborn" questions and outline a stance towards what he has given us
as an either/or. He begins by saying:

48. Macquarrie, *Christology Revisited*, 17.
49. Macquarrie, *Christology Revisited*, 25.
50. Macquarrie, *Christology Revisited*, 25.
51. Macquarrie, *Christology Revisited*, 26–42.
52. Macquarrie, *Christology Revisited*, 81–97.
53. Macquarrie, *Christology Revisited*, 98–114.
54. Macquarrie, *Stubborn Theological Questions*, 123–33.
55. Macquarrie, *Stubborn Theological Questions*, 134–39.

Jesus Christ is at the centre of Christian faith, and it stands or falls him with. But how are we to think of hum today? The theological world is itself divided on the question, and the ancient creeds are being called in question by many modern theologians. What is Christ's meaning for us, two thousand years after he lived and taught and died in Palestine?[56]

Needless to say, Macquarrie sees himself as one of the "many modern theologians" and, if we are reminded of what Macquarrie asserts in *Principles of Christian Theology*, he views Christology and the means by which one handles *the question of the meaning of Christology* "from below up."

56. Macquarrie, *Stubborn Theological Questions*, 140.

Appendix O

On Christology: Between Wolfhart Pannenberg and Jürgen Moltmann

As contemporaries, the relationship between Wolfhart Pannenberg (1928–2014) and Jürgen Moltmann (1926-present) is just as significant professionally as it is personally, which Moltmann, when interviewed at the Emergent Village Theological Conversation in 2009, confirms, "[Pannenberg] is a dear friend and opponent." Similarly, in *A Broad Place: An Autobiography* (2007), Moltmann gives an account of Pannenberg, suggesting that their relationship can be traced to their time together as colleagues on the faculty at Wuppertal seminary from 1959 to 1961, when, Moltmann writes, "our theological discussions occasionally escalated into sharp disputes."[1] As a result, Moltmann explains:

> We were not unknown to each other, and we had exchanged theological ideas. Consequently, in periodicals and newspapers we were later often made jointly responsible for the new eschatological orientation of Protestant theology. But whether in spite of that we were still worlds apart is a question that may be left to the judgment of keen-eyed doctoral students.[2]

Perhaps, it is a little strong to suggest that only the "judgment of keen-eyed doctoral students" can ascertain how Moltmann and Pannenberg are "worlds apart." Perhaps, it is simply "a question" that is transparently laid

---

1. Moltmann, *A Broad Place*, 105–07.
2. Moltmann, *A Broad Place*, 105–07.

bare, when carefully attending to Moltmann's and Pannenberg's respective "eschatological orientation" within the context of "Protestant theology," insofar as what grounds both Moltmann and Pannenberg is, I submit, *the question of the meaning of Christology.*

To the extent that, as Moltmann tells us, he and Pannenberg "exchanged theological ideas," what informs the exchange and their respective "theological ideas" is the fact that both Moltmann and Pannenberg theologize from a Protestant standpoint—Moltmann as a Reformed, and Pannenberg as a Lutheran. As such, both theologize a Trinitarian God, and with the help of how they both theologize the resurrection and from the standpoint of situating themselves in a post-Barthian fashion, both construct a "theology of hope."

Indeed, when Moltmann writes *Theologie der Hoffnung* (1964), translated as *Theology of Hope* in 1967, Moltmann admits that it served as a reaction to Pannenberg's edited volume of essays, *Offenbarung als Geschichte* (1961), translated as *Revelation as History* in 1968—Moltmann's text wished to criticize the Pannenberg-led text.[3] Given Moltmann's criticizing of *Offenbarung als Geschichte*, Moltmann recounts that "Pannenberg, however, felt not so much wounded as taken over."[4] Just as Moltmann notes, Pannenberg reacted to Moltmann's *Theologie der Hoffnung* as a "contribution to the Bloch Festschrift of 1965,"[5] entitled "*Der Gott der Hoffnung*," translated as "The God of Hope" (1968) in the journal, *CrossCurrents.*

Pannenberg's contribution to the "Bloch Festschrift" is notable, insofar as Pannenberg is influenced by Ernst Bloch and, for that matter, so too is Moltmann—in this way, Moltmann and Pannenberg draw their respective *Theologie der Hoffnung* and "*Der Gott der Hoffnung*," by theologically attuning their approach to a "*Hoffnung*" as it is philosophically construed by Bloch in his three-volume, *Das Prinzip of Hoffnung* (1954, 1955, and 1959), translated as *The Principle of Hope* in 1986. As with Bloch's handling of decidedly Hegelian constructions of the subject-object dialectics, as that which is evidenced in the unfolding of human history, Moltmann's and Pannenberg's take on "*Hoffnung*" employ Bloch's philosophical foundations.

It is for this reason, we can certainly better understand why, as Moltmann explains, "I was linked with Pannenberg over the years,"[6] particularly with respect to their respective theologizing in the 1960s. It is due, Moltmann acknowledges, "through [their] similar approach in the

3. Moltmann, *A Broad Place*, 105–07.

4. Moltmann, *A Broad Place*, 105–07.

5. Moltmann, *A Broad Place*, 105–07.

6. Moltmann, *A Broad Place*, 105–07.

eschatology of history and a parallel development of Trinitarian thinking."[7] Even so, Moltmann goes on to say:

> We both, each in his own way, tried to do theology in light of Christ's resurrection. But although my idea of promise and his idea of anticipation show theoretical correspondences, the practical consequences we drew in politics could unfortunately be completely contrary to each other.[8]

The fact that, as Moltmann tells us, he and Pannenberg "tried to do theology in light of Christ's resurrection," the two of them differed, I submit, on what the resurrection means for *the question of the meaning of Christology*. While Moltmann's understanding of the resurrection is an "idea of promise" and Pannenberg, as characterized by Moltmann, views the resurrection as "anticipation," they differ on what the resurrection means to history and what history means to the resurrection—for Moltmann, history is qualitative, insofar as we must think beyond whatever history we experience or whatever history means to historians, while, for Pannenberg, history is quantitative, insofar as we can verify and measure history historically.

As much as both Moltmann and Pannenberg are influenced by Hegel, if we are to say that their respective understandings of the meaning of history owe their construction to Hegelianism, this influences how Moltmann and Pannenberg do eschatology. What history means eschatologically and what eschatology means historically becomes, for Moltmann, the beginning of a new era, while, for Pannenberg, history-eschatology relations offer a sense of fulfilment. It is along these lines that Moltmann and Pannenberg approach *the question of the meaning of Christology*—Pannenberg does Christology "from below,"[9] while Moltmann resists assuming either a "from below" or a "from above" stance.

---

7. Moltmann, *A Broad Place*, 105–07.

8. Moltmann, *A Broad Place*, 105–07.

9. Pannenberg, *Jesus—God and Man*, 33–37.

Appendix P

Hans W. Frei's Unfinished Christology Book

Though primarily known for *The Eclipse of Biblical Narrative: A Study in Eighteenth and Nineteenth Century Hermeneutics* (1974), Hans W. Frei (1922–1988) published very little in the 1950s, 1960s, and up to the mid-1970s, including his 1956 dissertation at Yale Divinity School, entitled, "The Doctrine of Revelation in the Thought of Karl Barth, 1909–1922: The Nature of Barth's Break with Liberalism."

As central as *The Eclipse of Biblical Narrative* is to Frei's body of work, it helps to note that it arrives late in Frei's career—yet, it is important to be reminded that the text occupies an important place in what is known about Frei and Frei's theological contributions to the state of theology in the 1970s. Similarly, as seminal as the text has now become to studies in hermeneutics, guided by, as Mike Higton explains, "trac[ing] changes in biblical interpretation that took place in the eighteenth and nineteenth centuries," insofar as Frei "claimed that there had been, prior to that period, something of a consensus in Christian biblical reading,"[1] the text, according to Cornel West, did not receive enough attention in the final decade of Frei's life.[2] Given that, West rightly acknowledges, "[Frei] text is the best historical study we have in English of developments from Post-Renaissance hermeneutics to the modern hermeneutics of Schleiermacher and Hegel,"[3] and in light of one of the earliest criticisms of the text, particularly by

---

1. Higton, "Forward," xi.
2. West, "On Frei's *Eclipse of Biblical Narrative*," 299.
3. West, "On Frei's *Eclipse of Biblical Narrative*," 299.

Leander E. Keck in 1975, which unmistakeably reviews the text as providing a significant contribution to the "exploratory and critical analysis of the change of the tide,"[4] the fact that Frei is primarily known for *The Eclipse of Biblical Narrative* understandably overshadows the only other book-length monograph Frei produced in his lifetime: *The Identity of Jesus Christ: The Hermeneutical Bases of Dogmatic Theology* (1975).

While *The Eclipse of Biblical Narrative*, at the time of its publication, has been described as, by Justin Kelly (1975), "an exact and exacting scrutiny of some major interpretative efforts from the age of the deists to that of Schleiermacher, Hegel, and D. F. Strauss,"[5] or, by F. W. Dillistone (1975), as a means of "record[ing] the history of [the] hermeneutical quest during a critical period of the development of Protestant theology,"[6] or, by George Steiner (1977), as "an investigation of the breakdown of the realistic and figural interpretations of the biblical stories,"[7] Leslie Brisman (1976) draws a thematic through-line from Frei's concerns in *The Eclipse of Biblical Narrative* and what is laid bare in his concerns in *The Identity of Jesus Christ*. For Brisman, the former assesses the extent that figures such as Herder, Schleiermacher, and Hegel "still hover over and cloud what passes for most of modern theology and modern literary interpretation,"[8] such that the latter, Brisman continues, "offers the proper cure for the blindness of the past."[9] With respect to this, and the other characterizations of *The Eclipse of Biblical Narrative*, Mike Higton mentions, in the 2013 Forward to *The Identity of Jesus Christ*, the latter text allows Frei to pursue "not a generalized reversal of that eclipse of biblical narrative, but one localized response."[10] Subsequently, further elucidates what the former means for the latter in the following way:

> *The Eclipse of Biblical Narrative* had itself not been about the Bible as a whole, but about specific narrative portions of it. In *The Identity of Jesus Christ*, Frei's focus narrows still further: he offers a post-critical reading of the Gospels that takes seriously the fact that—at least in the passion-resurrection sequences in the Synoptics—they contain a certain kind of realistic narrative.

4. Keck, "Eclipse of Biblical Narrative," 367.

5. Kelly, "Book Review: The Eclipse of Biblical Narrative," 155.

6. Dillistone, "Eclipse of Biblical Narrative," 223.

7. Steiner, "Eclipse of Biblical Narrative," 238.

8. Brisman, "Eclipse of Biblical Narrative," 369.

9. Brisman, "Eclipse of Biblical Narrative," 369.

10. Higton, "Forward," xii.

Frei argued that these particular narratives render the identity of their central character, Jesus Christ.[11]

Here, what we find, essentially, is the degree to which *The Eclipse of Biblical Narrative* becomes a foundational text to what becomes known as narrative theology—or postliberal theology—and "narrative theology" is, such that it situates *The Identity of Jesus Christ* as an expression of what "narrative theology" does. In this way, the former theorizes precisely what the latter puts into explicit practice.

This certainly holds true, when, as Higton tells us, "[*The Identity of Jesus Christ*] is not a book about 'story,' nor about 'narrative theology.'"[12] To this end, Higton maintains, "this is a book about the way in which Jesus of Nazareth's identity is rendered by the Gospels [...] by means of a certain kind of narrative."[13] To even say that Frei attends to "a certain kind of narrative" suggests that, in the resulting rendering of "Jesus of Nazareth's identity," Frei is attending to a means of doing Christology. Particularly, if we understand that *The Identity of Jesus Christ*, as a 1975 text, is a revised version of two long articles Frei published in 1967 as "The Mystery of the Presence of Jesus Christ," we can say that what culminates in 1975 is the fuller expression of Frei's Christological thinking and Christological reflection. For that matter, if, Frei acknowledges in the preface (written in 1974) to the 1975 text, it is "a theological experiment,"[14] we have to ask: what kind of experiment is it, and what did it accomplish for Frei? If we say, then, as Frei tells us, that *The Identity of Jesus Christ* was an experiment not only in the sense of how much of Frei's "thinking developed in the process of writing,"[15] but also "because [the experiment] tested out,"[16] the conclusions Frei reaches, interestingly, are in terms of a basic conviction that:

> Christian faith involves a unique affirmation about Jesus Christ, that is to say, not only that he is the presence of God but also that knowing his identity is identical with having him present or being in his presence.[17]

Nevertheless, the fact that Frei does, indeed, view the work conducted in *The Identity of Jesus Christ* as an "experiment," insofar as it carries forward

11. Higton, "Forward," xii.
12. Higton, "Forward," xi.
13. Higton, "Forward," xi.
14. Frei, *The Identity of Jesus Christ*, 3.
15. Frei, *Identity of Jesus Christ*, 3.
16. Frei, *Identity of Jesus Christ*, 3.
17. Frei, *Identity of Jesus Christ*, 3.

the foundational theorizing seen in *The Eclipse of Biblical Narrative*, it stands to reason that Frei would have remained interested in furthering the connection between the two texts.

Thanks to Higton's chronology of Frei provided in *Christ, Providence and History* (2004), we know that, by April 1975, Frei gave a talk on what can only be presumed to be the relationship and connection between *The Eclipse of Biblical Narrative* and *The Identity of Jesus Christ* as, perhaps, companion strands of thought—the exact contents of the talk are unknown. With respect to critiques, criticisms, and responses to *The Identity of Jesus Christ* throughout the rest of 1975, by 1976, in a letter to William Placher, Frei expresses a shift in his thinking about *The Identity of Jesus Christ* "on a number of issues," which seem to have been reflected, most notably, in the marginal annotation Frei makes to his personal copy of Leslie Brisman's joint review of *The Eclipse of Biblical Narrative* and *The Identity of Jesus Christ* published in Fall 1976—by November 1976, Frei makes it clear in another letter that he "is engaged in trying to push the project of *The Identity of Jesus Christ* a little further, both by working on the exegesis of the parables, and by taking further his 'Wittgensteinian' reflections," which become part and parcel of Frei's Greenhoe lectures,[18] delivered at Louisville Seminary.[19] These interests are furthered, it seems, in a colloquium Frei presents on *The Eclipse of Biblical Narrative* and *The Identity of Jesus Christ* at Emory University at the Candler School of Theology in November 1978—unfortunately, the contents of this colloquium are unknown.[20] By September 1979, in a latter to Van Harvey, Frei proclaims his "ambition is really to write a history of modern Christology, but to do so utilizing recent reworking of intellectual history."[21]

Yet, even though Frei is exceedingly interested in writing what he calls "a history of modern Christology," as, perhaps, a means of taking *The Identity of Jesus Christ* further, Higton takes care to note that, by February 1976, Frei's Curriculum Vitae had as his only "writing in progress or projected" a project that Frei tentatively-titled, *German Religious Thought between Enlightenment and Romanticism: Aesthetics, Language and Religious Thought in Lessing, Kant and Herder*—this planned project was to be based on Frei's Rockwell Lectures delivered at Rice University in 1974.[22] Though this planned project remained in Frei's purview at least until 1981,

18. Higton, *Christ, Providence and History*, 252.

19. Frei, *Reading Faithfully: Volume 1*, 68

20. Higton, *Christ, Providence and History*, 255.

21. Higton, *Christ, Providence and History*, 256.

22. Higton, *Christ, Providence and History*, 251.

when, as Higton notes, Frei taught the lecture course, "The Formation of German Religious Thought in the Passage from Enlightenment to Romanticism," to which there are associated lecture notes in Frei's papers at Yale Divinity School,[23] it seems, judging from Higton's chronology, that Frei abandons plans for the *German Religious Thought* project by the 1980s. Indeed, though it can be presumed that some of the material for the proposed *German Religious Thought* project found its way notably into Frei's Shaffer Lectures of 1983, an article on David Strauss as part of the collection, *Nineteenth Century Religious Thought in the West* (1985), a paper Frei presents at a conference in New York in May 1986, and Frei's Cadburt Lectures at the University of Birmingham in 1987, by 1987, in a revised version of Frei's Curriculum Vitae, Frei lists two new projected books: "a book on theological typology and *sensus literalis* in modern theology," to be based on his Shaffer and Cadbury Lectures, and "a book on Christology in Germany and England from 1700 to 1950."[24] While the former is largely posthumously represented, as co-edited by George Hunsinger and William Placher in *Types of Christian Theology* (1992), Frei's proposed Christology book remains unaccounted for.

In the Forward to *Types of Christian Theology*, co-written by David Kelsey, George Lindbeck, and Gene Outka, we are informed that:

> Hans W. Frei's projected history of Christology in the modern period was cut short by his death on 12 September 1988. It was to be a major project for which he had been preparing through most of his academic career, and those who knew him and his scholarship looked forward to it with high anticipation.[25]

From this, we are confronted with unavoidable questions, in spite of what the *Types of Christian Theology* text is and does for Frei posthumously. Given the "high anticipation" and the extent that Frei's "projected history of Christology" had the potential to be a magnum opus, a cumulative work that Frei for which "had been preparing through most of his academic career," the questions we must ask about the unfinished Christology book must speak to both the what and the how—what would the project have been, and how would Frei have proceeded from what he projected to what was possible to execute.

In outlining what is essentially the question of the meaning of Frei unfinished Christology book, we must be guided by more specific and

---

23. Higton, *Christ, Providence and History*, 258.

24. Higton, *Christ, Providence and History*, 266.

25. Frei, *Types of Christian Theology*, vii.

localized questions. The first question we must ask, then, remains this: what kind of work would Frei's unfinished book on Christology have been, had Frei lived to complete what he explicitly planned as late as 1987? Secondly, in building on the first, we have to ask: what role does *Types of Christian Theology*, as a posthumous text based on "the book Frei wished to write [that] could no longer be written,"[26] as well as *The Eclipse of Biblical Narrative* and *The Identity of Jesus Christ* play, if any, in what we can possibly surmise to be Frei's handling of Christology in general, and to what degree we can even conceptualize what his unfinished book on Christology would have looked like, given Frei's Christological proclivities? Lastly, if it is even possible to reasonably map Frei's concerns Christologically, is it even possible to do reasonable justice to what Frei wished to accomplish in his unfinished Christology book, if, as with what *Types of Christian Theology* embodies posthumously, and we repurpose the words from Hunsinger and Placher co-authored editorial introduction to *Types of Christian Theology*, "we [remain] acutely aware that the book Frei wished to write could no longer be written" still holds true?

A good starting point for approaching these questions can be through Higton's *Christ, Providence and History*—as the first full-length study of the whole of Frei's theology—which largely argues, in Higton's words, that Frei "painstakingly calls Christian theologians to a public task, providing us with tools which make that task easier and exposing confusions which have too often prevented us from carrying it out with conviction."[27] Higton builds a means of characterizing Frei's public task as grounded on the fact that:

> Christian believers have been able to hold together in their lives and in their theology the reading of the Gospel narratives about Jesus of Nazareth in which the focus of God's history is displayed, the reading of their newspapers in which the bewildering scope of God's history is opened up, and theological commentary which seeks to clarify something of what it means to find both to be God's history.[28]

Higton goes on to say:

> That these things *can be* held together is not the result of any esoteric technology that lies only in the hands of experts, but is a gift of God's spirit distributed more widely than we might think; that they *have been* held together is demonstrated by the

26. Frei, *Types of Christian Theology*, ix.

27. Higton, *Christ, Providence and History*, 1.

28. Higton, *Christ, Providence and History*, 2.

fact of Christian lives lived fallibly but well in the public world; that they *will be* held together is a hope and a task to which Frei dedicated all his theological and historical work.[29]

Notice the emphasis Higton makes about what is held together—in this, there is a certain declarative manner, for Higton, with which Frei holds together "the reading of the Gospel narratives about Jesus of Nazareth." Yet, as Higton concedes, "*how* Frei held those things together is not so quickly stated."[30] Even so, Higton attends to the following:

> We will begin with the various forms of the question of faith and history which Frei posed to himself. He did not simply ask how faith fosters the discernment we need for Christian life in the public, historical world, but also asked how contemporary faith is related to the history of Jesus of Nazareth, and how we might understand faith as true faith in God without claiming it as an aspect of our lives somehow immunized against history's fallibility.[31]

Insofar as there is, indeed, a question of faith and a question of history, as two questions "which Frei posed to himself," Higton draws a necessary connection between the two in Frei's theologizing. That connection, then, is what holds together "the reading of the Gospel narratives about Jesus of Nazareth" for Frei's theologizing. To this point, Higton explains, "such a theology is made attentive to history—to Christ's history and to the history that is providentially ordered in him."[32] Higton expands this a bit further:

> The question of an historical faith, of faith's own historical consciousness, turns out therefore to be a dual question. On the one hand, it is a question about the incarnation. [. . .] On the other hand, it is a question about the providential ordering of history in Jesus.[33]

This becomes integral to understanding Higton's title, which suggests a three-fold significance to "Christ," "providence," and "history," as three things that Frei theologizes as a means of holding together "the reading of the Gospel narratives about Jesus of Nazareth." At the juncture of this three-fold significance is Frei's Christological reflection and Christological thinking, such that the very question of the meaning of Christology hinges on the

29. Higton, *Christ, Providence and History*, 2.

30. Higton, *Christ, Providence and History*, 4.

31. Higton, *Christ, Providence and History*, 4.

32. Higton, *Christ, Providence and History*, 6.

33. Higton, *Christ, Providence and History*, 6.

three-fold significance between questions directed towards Christ, questions associated with providence, and questions concerned with history.

In a certain sense, what arises in Higton's *Christ, Providence and History*, through which Higton devises a means of understanding Frei's theologizing and how, then, that theologizing calibrates Frei's undergirding approach to Christology, has its origins in Higton's "Frei's Christology and Lindbeck's Cultural-Linguistic Theory" (1997)—though Higton is comparing Frei with Lindbeck, Higton's sense that Frei's "method for theology is considerably more subtle and Christologically focused than that of Lindbeck" is an important point,[34] to the extent that Higton bases his reading of Frei's Christology on Frei's *The Identity of Jesus Christ*. From it, Higton is able to suggest, "in a fully Christological way, the tail of Frei's argument is eaten by its head, and it becomes properly circular." More specifically, Higton writes:

> It is precisely because the Church is the earthly-historical form of Jesus Christ now in the time between his direct presence in some unguessable mode in the eschaton, that we are justified in looking to the church and its talk of "presence," to its pointing to the Bible as its source of knowledge of Jesus Christ, as the starting point of our Christology.[35]

Just as Higton highlights this as the starting point of Frei's Christology, we can think of Higton as providing a starting point for any account we can give about Frei's unfinished Christology book—because Higton provides us with a means to approach how Frei oriented himself Christologically, we will need to venture further than Higton through Hunsinger's understanding of Frei's Christology as a way to make sense out of what is at stake with Frei's unfinished Christology book that Frei, in his own right, seems to have considered as a project that would take the main thread of argument in *The Identity of Jesus Christ* further.

Let us now turn to Hunsinger. In the Afterword to *Theology and Narrative: Selected Essays* (1993),[36] a set of Frei's papers published the year following the publication of *Types of Christian Theology*, as a co-editor of the volume, Hunsinger considers *The Identity of Jesus Christ* as Frei's "principal work whereby [Frei] is known to us not as an intellectual historian or as a commentator on the theology of others, but as a theologian himself."[37]

34. Higton, "Frei's Christology and Lindbeck's Cultural-Linguistic Theory," 83.

35. Higton, "Frei's Christology and Lindbeck's Cultural-Linguistic Theory," 90.

36. The contents of Hunsinger's Afterword appeared the previous year, in 1992, as "Hans Frei As Theologian: The Quest for a Generous Orthodoxy."

37. Frei, *Theology and Narrative*, 235.

If we attend to this, and make clear that Frei is operating as a theologian and, in doing so, the task of theologizing, with which he gives an account of himself, is laid bare by what Christology means to him "as a theologian himself." In short, it is by asserting that Frei is a theologian, as Hunsinger does, that it becomes possible to make sense of the theologizing behind the Christological concerns of *The Identity of Jesus Christ*.

To acknowledge Frei thusly, and with the dominant, pervading theme of "presence," it is possible, then, to consider Frei as a theologian of presence. Hunsinger speaks to this, recognizing that the notion of "presence" runs through Frei's 1956 dissertation—though in the form of the term "coinherence"[38]—through *The Identity of Jesus Christ*, of course, and possibly through "something that [Frei] perceived in his mentor," H. Richard Niebuhr.[39] With this in mind, Hunsinger asserts, "Frei regarded the concept of 'presence' as the Achilles' heel of modern Christology."[40] Even so, with respect to how Frei reckons with "presence" in *The Identity of Jesus Christ*, Hunsinger makes three important assessments:

> First, that Frei thinks his *Identity* book offers a high Christology; second, that he does not succeed in this project; and finally, that at the end of his career he does succeed in showing how a high Christology can be based on an interpretative scheme that avoids his earlier deficiencies.[41]

Speaking more specifically, Hunsinger outlines the "deficiencies" as this:

> Frei offers a convincing account of the Jesus's irreducible particularity, but fails to establish Jesus's universal saving significance, because he fails to establish that Jesus is truly God. [. . .] Therefore, although in his *Identity* book Frei wishes to propound a high Christology, he succeeds in establishing only one of its three defining elements by means of a narrative analysis.[42]

Even so, what Frei lays bare in *The Identity of Jesus Christ*, coupled with Frei's "five types"[43] in *Type of Christian Theology*, becomes the best estimation we have as to how far Frei proceeded towards a definitive, historical view of Christology, even if, to Hunsinger's point, it, ultimately, falls short. Yet, even if the "deficiencies" in *The Identity of Jesus Christ* cause the text

38. Hunsinger, "Frei's Early Christology," 25.

39. Hunsinger, "Frei's Early Christology," 27.

40. Hunsinger, "Frei's Early Christology," 27.

41. Hunsinger, "Frei's Early Christology," 31.

42. Hunsinger, "Frei's Early Christology," 34.

43. Frei, *Types of Christian Theology*, 1–7.

to fundamentally fail to "propound a high Christology," perhaps it is best that we view *The Identity of Jesus Christ*, with its companion text of *Types of Christian Theology*, as a transitional work that brings Frei incrementally closer to the problem of Christology that he wishes to interrogate, as what can only be construed as *the question of the meaning of Christology* itself.

Given that Frei eventually returns, Hunsinger tells us, to "the problem of Christology in accord with Chalcedon," he does so by leaving behind the concerns of *The Identity of Jesus Christ*.[44] In this way, then, Hunsinger recognizes, "the Chalcedonian formula thus authorizes and ensures the kind of high Christology with a narrative orientation that the early Frei had sought but never found."[45] Even if it is possible to say, as Hunsinger does, that *The Identity of Jesus Christ* is merely "a book of detours" that Frei navigated in order to ultimately arrive "at Chalcedon as his hermeneutical home,"[46] we can certainly say, by the end of Frei's life, the unfinished Christology book he had been planning to write—perhaps at its most vigorous around the time of his 1986 lectures delivered at Princeton Theological Seminary[47]— would have found a way that "holds together" the two strands of thought from *The Eclipse of Biblical Narrative* and *The Identity of Jesus Christ*, with the two strands of thought mitigating a decidedly high Christology with a decidedly low Christology, as a way to overcome the "eclipse" in the history of Christology itself.

44. Hunsinger, "Frei's Early Christology," 35.
45. Hunsinger, "Frei's Early Christology," 36.
46. Hunsinger, "Frei's Early Christology," 36.
47. Higton, *Church, Providence and History*, 264.

Bibliography

Agamben, Giorgio. *Homo Sacer: Sovereign Power and Bare Life*. Translated by Daniel Heller-Roazen. Stanford: Stanford University Press, 1995.

Althaus, Paul. *Das sogenannte Kerygma und der historische Jesus: Zur Kritik der heutigen Kerygma-Theologie*. Gütersloh: Berlesmann, 1958.

———. *Fact and Faith in the Kerygma of Today*. Westport: Greenwood, 1959.

———. *The Ethics of Martin Luther*. Translated by Robert Schultz. Minneapolis: Fortress, 1972.

———. *The So-Called Kerygma and the Historical Jesus*. Translated by David Cairns. London: Oliver and Boyd, 1959.

———. *The Theology of Martin Luther*. Translated by Robert Schultz. Minneapolis: Fortress, 1966.

Anderson, Charles C. *Critical Quests of Jesus*. Grand Rapids: Eerdmanns, 1969.

———. *The Historical Jesus: A Continuing Quest*. Grand Rapids: Eerdmanns, 1972.

Anderson, Paul N. "Foreword." In *The Testament of Jesus: A Study of the Gospel of John in the Light of Chapter 17*, translated by Gerhard Krodel, xi–xxxviii. Eugene: Wipf & Stock, 2017.

Barnikol, Ernst. *Das Leben Jesu der Heilsgeschichte*. Halle: Niemeyer, 1958.

Barnstone, Willis, ed. *The Other Bible*. New York: Harper Collins, 1984.

Barth, Karl. *The Epistle to the Romans*. Translated by Edwyn C. Hoskyns. New York: Oxford University Press, 1968.

———. *Christ and Adam: Man and Humanity in Romans 5*. Translated by T. A. Smail. New York: Collier, 1962.

———. *Church Dogmatics: The Doctrine of Reconciliation: Volume IV: Part 2*. Translated by G. W. Bromiley. Edinburgh: T. & T. Clark, 1958.

———. *The Humanity of God*, Translated by John Newton Thomas and Thomas Wieser Louisville: John Knox Press, 1960.

Bettenson, Henry and Chris Maunder, ed. *Documents of the Christian Church*. New York: Oxford University Press, 1999.

Berdyaev, Nicolai. *The Meaning of the Creative Act*. Translated by Donald A. Lowrie. New York: Harper and Brothers, 1955.

Best, Ernest. *A Commentary on the First and Second Epistles to the Thessalonians*. New York: Harper and Row, 1972.

Biehl, Peter. "*Zur Frage nach dem historischen Jesus*" *Theologische Rundschau* 24.1 (1957/1958) 54–76.

Bock, Darrell L. *Studying the Historical Jesus: A Guide to Sources and Methods*. Grand Rapids: Baker, 2002.

Boer, Harry R. *A Short History of the Early Church*. Grand Rapids: Eerdmans, 1976.

Boff, Leonardo. *Jesus Christ Liberator: A Critical Christology for Our Time*. Maryknoll: Orbis, 1978.

———. *Jesus Cristo Libertador. Ensaio de Cristologia Critica para o nosso Tempo*. Petrópolis: Vozes, 1972.

Bonhoeffer, Dietrich. *Act and Being: Transcendental Philosophy and Ontology in Systematic Theology*. Translated by Hans-Richard Reuter. Mineapolis: Fortress, 1996.

———. *Christ the Center*. Translated by Edwin H. Robertson. New York: Harper, 1978.

Borg, Marcus. *Jesus in Contemporary Scholarship*. Harrisburg: Trinity, 1998.

———. *Meeting Jesus Again for the First Time: The Historical Jesus and the Heart of Contemporary Faith*. New York: Harper, 1994.

Borg, Marcus, and N. T. Wright. *The Meaning of Jesus: Two Visions*. New York: Harper, 1999.

Bornkamm, Günther. *Bibel: Das Neue Testament. Eine Einführung in seine Schiften im Rahmen der Geschichte des Urchristentums*. Berlin: Kreuz, 1971.

———. "End-Expectation and Church in Matthew." In *Tradition and Interpretation in Matthew*, translated by Percy Scott, 15–51. London: S.C.M., 1963.

———. *Early Christian Experience*. Translated by Paul L. Hammer. London: S.C.M., 1969.

———. *Jesus of Nazareth*. Translated by Irene McLuskey, Fraser McLuskey, and James M. Robinson. Minneapolis: Fortress, 1960.

———. *Jesus von Nazareth*. Berlin: Kohlhammer, 1956.

———. "Myth and Gospel: A Discussion of the Problem of Demythologizing the New Testament Message." In *Kerygma and History*, translated and edited by Carl E. Braaten and Roy A. Harrisville, 172–96. Nashville: Abingdon, 1962.

———. *The New Testament: A Guide to Its Writings*. Translated by Reginald H. Fuller. Philadelphia: Fortress, 1973.

———. *Paul*. Translated by D. M. G. Stalker. New York: Harper and Row, 1971.

———. *Paulus*. Berlin: Kohlhammer, 1969.

———. "Preface." In *Tradition and Interpretation in Matthew*, translated by Percy Scott, 9–10. London: S.C.M., 1963.

———. "The Significance of the Historical Jesus for Faith." In *What Can We Know About Jesus?: Essays on the New Quest*, translated by Grover Foley, 69–86. Philadelphia: Fortress, 1969.

———. "The Stilling of the Storm in Matthew." In *Tradition and Interpretation in Matthew*, translated by Percy Scott, 52–7. London: S.C.M., 1963.

Bornkamm, Günther, Gerhard Barth, and Heinz Joachim. *Überlieferung und Auslegung im Matthäusevangelium*. Neukirchen: Wageningen, 1961.

Braaten, Carl E. "A Critical Introduction." In *Kerygma and History: A Symposium on the Theology of Rudolf Bultmann*, translated and edited by Carl E. Braaten and Roy A. Harrisville, 9–24. Nashville: Abingdon, 1962.

———. "Introduction: Revelation, History, and Faith in Martin Kähler." In *The So-Called Historical Jesus and the Historic Biblical Christ*, edited by Carl E. Braaten, 1–38. Philadelphia: Fortress, 1988.

Braun, Herbert. "*Der Sinn der neutestamentlichen Christologie*" Zeitschrift für Theologie und Kirche 54.3 (1957) 341–77.

———. *Die Problematik einer Theologie des Neuen Testaments.* Tübingen: Mohr, 1961.

———. *Jesus, der Mann aus Nazareth und seine Zeit.* Stuttgart: Kreuz, 1969.

———. *Jesus of Nazareth: The Man and His Time.* Translated by Everett R. Kalin. Philadelphia: Fortress, 1979.

———. "The Meaning of New Testament Christology." In *God and Christ: Existence and Province*, edited by Robert W. Funk, 89–127. New York: Harper and Row, 1968.

———. "The Problem of a New Testament Theology." In *The Bultmann School of Biblical Interpretation: New Directions?*, edited by Robert W. Funk, 169–83. New York: Harper and Row, 1965.

Brisman, Leslie. "The Eclipse of Biblical Narrative: A Study in Eighteenth and Nineteenth Century Hermeneutics by Hans W. Frei; The Identity of Jesus Christ: The Hermeneutical Bases of Dogmatic Theology by Hans W. Frei." *Comparative Literature* 28.4 (1976) 368–72.

Brondos, David A. *Fortress Introduction to Salvation and the Cross.* Minneapolis: Fortress, 2007.

Brown, Colin. *Jesus in European Protestant Thought: 1778–1860.* Grand Rapids: Baker, 1985.

Brown, Raymond. *An Introduction to New Testament Christology.* New York: Paulist, 1994.

Bultmann, Rudolf. "*Das Problem der Hermeneutik*" Zeitschrift für Theologie und Kirche 47.1 (1950) 47–69.

———. "*Das Verhältnis der urchristlichen Christusbotschaft zum historischen Jesus.*" In *Exegetica*, edited by Erich Dinkler, 445–69. Tübingen: Mohr, 1967.

———. *Die Geschichte der synoptischen Tradition.* Göttingen: Vandenhoeck and Ruprecht, 1921.

———. *Glauben und Verstehen II.* Tübingen: Mohr, 1952.

———. "*Heilsgeschichte und Geschichte.*" Theologische Literaturezeitung 73 (1948) 659–66.

———. "History of Salvation and History." In *Existence and Faith: Shorter Writings of Rudolf Bultmann*, edited by Schubert M. Ogden, 226–40. New York: Meridian, 1960.

———. *History of the Synoptic Tradition.* Translated by John Marsh. Peabody: Hendrikson, 1963.

———. *Jesus Christ and Mythology.* New York: Scribner, 1958.

———. *Jesus and the Word.* Translated by Louise P. Smith and Erminie H. Lantero. New York: Scribner, 1958.

———. "The Primitive Christian Kerygma and the Historical Jesus" In *The Historical Jesus: Volume 1: The History of the Quest: Classical Studies and Critical Questions*, edited by Craig A. Evans, 211–32. New York: Routledge, 2004.

Carter, Warren. *The Roman Empire and the New Testament: An Essential Guide.* Nashville: Abingdon Press, 2006.

Craddock, Fred B. *The Pre-existence of Christ in the New Testament.* Nashville: Abingdon, 1968.

Cobb, John B. *Christ in a Pluralistic Age.* Philadelphia: Westminster, 1975.

Cobb, John B., and David R. Griffin. *Process Theology: An Introductory Exposition.* Philadelphia: Westminster, 1976.

Conzelmann, Hans. "Bultmann, Rudolf, Die Geschichte der synoptischen Tradition." *Theologische Literaturzeitung* 84 (1959) 189.

———. *Die Mitte der Zeit: Studien zur Theologie des Lukas.* Tübingen: Mohr, 1954.

———. "Gegenwart und Zukunft in der synoptischen Tradition." *Zeitschrift für Theologie und Kirche* 54.3 (1957) 277–96.

———. *Jesus.* Translated by Raymond Lord. Philadelphia: Fortress, 1982.

———. "Jesus Christus." *Die Religion in Geschichte und Gegenwart: Handwörterbuch für Theologie und Religionswissenschaft.*3 (1959) 619–53.

———. "Present and Future in the Synoptic Tradition." In *God and Christ: Existence and Province,* edited by Herbert Braun and Robert W. Funk, 26–44. New York: Harper and Row, 1968.

———. *The Theology of St. Luke.* Translated by Geoffrey Buswell. New York: Harper and Row, 1960.

———. "Zur Methode der Leben-Jesu-Forschung." *Zeitschrift für Theologie und Kirche* 56.1 (1959) 2–13.

Crossan, Dominic. *The Historical Jesus: The Life of a Mediterranean Jewish Peasant.* San Francisco: Harper, 1991.

———. *Jesus: A Revolutionary Biography.* New York: Harper, 1995.

Cullmann, Oscar. *Christ and Time: The Primitive Christian Conception of Time and History.* Translated by Floyd V. Wilson. London: S.C.M., 1951.

———. *The Christology of the New Testament.* Translated by Shirley C. Guthrie and Charles A. M. Hall. Philadelphia: Westminster, 1959.

———. *Die Christologie des Neuen Testaments.* Tübingen: Mohr, 1957.

———. *Christus und die Zeit: Die urchristiche Zeit und Geschichtsauffassung.* Zollikon-Zürich: Evangelischer-Verlag, 1946.

———. *Heil als Geschichte: Heilsgeschichtliche Existenz im Neuen Testament.* Tübingen: Mohr, 1965.

———. "Out of Season Remarks on the 'Historical Jesus' of the Bultmann School." *USQR* 16 (1961) 131–48.

———. *Salvation in History.* Translated by Sidney G. Sowers. London: S.C.M., 1965.

Dahl, Nils A. "Der historische Jesus als geschichtswissenschaftliches und theologisches Problem." *Kerygma und Dogma* 1 (1955) 105–32.

———. "Problemet den historiske Jesus." In *Rett laere og kjetttske meninger,* edited by Nils A. Dahl, 156–202. Oslo: Land og Kirke, 1953.

———. "The Problem of the Historical Jesus." In *Kerygma and History,* edited by Carl E. Braaten and Roy A. Harrisville, 138–71. Nashville: Abingdon, 1962.

Danker, Frederick W. *Jesus and the New Age: A Commentary on St. Luke's Gospel.* Philadelphia: Fortress, 1988.

Dawes, Gregory W. *The Historical Jesus Quest: Landmarks in the Search for the Jesus of History.* Louisville: Westminster John Knox, 2000.

———. *The Historical Jesus Question: The Challenge of History to Religious Authority.* Louisville: Westminster John Knox, 2001.

Deleuze, Gilles. *Pure Immanence: Essays on a Life.* Translated by Anne Boyman. New York: Zone Books, 2001.

Derrida, Jacques. "Différance." In *Margins of Philosophy,* translated by Alan Bass, 1–27. Chicago: The University of Chicago Press, 1982.

———. *Dissemination*. Translated by Barbara Johnson. Chicago: The University of Chicago Press, 1981.

———. "Force and Signification." In *Writing and Difference*, translated by Alan Bass, 3–30. Chicago: The University of Chicago Press, 1978.

———. *Of Grammatology*. Translated by Gayatri C. Spivak. Baltimore: The Johns Hopkins University Press, 1976.

———. "Structure, Sign, and Play in the Discourse of the Human Sciences." In *Writing and Difference*, translated by Alan Bass, 278–93. Chicago: The University of Chicago Press, 1978.

Diem, Hermann. *Der irdische Jesus und der Christus des Glaubens*. Tübingen: Mohr, 1957.

———. *Dogmatics*. Translated by Harold Knight. Edinburgh: Oliver and Boyd, 1959.

———. *Dogmatik: Ihr Weg zwischen Historismus und Existenzialismus*. München: Kaiser, 1955.

———. "The Earthly Jesus and the Christ of Faith." In *Kerygma and History*, edited by Carl E. Braaten and Roy A. Harrisville, 197–211. Nashville: Abingdon, 1962.

Dillistone, F. W. "The Eclipse of Biblical Narrative: A Study in Eighteenth and Nineteenth Century Hermeneutics." *The Journal of Theological Studies* 26.1 (1975) 223–24.

Dinkler, Erich. "Comments on the History of the Symbol of the Cross." In *The Bultmann School of Biblical Interpretation: New Directions?*, edited by Robert W. Funk, 124–46. New York: Harper and Row, 1965.

———. *Signum crucis: Aufsätze zum Neuen Testament und zur christlichen Archäologie*. Tübingen: Mohr, 1967.

———. "Zur Geschichte des Kreuzsymbols." *Zeitschrift für Theologie und Kirche* 48.2 (1951) 148–72.

Drews, Arthur. *Die Christusmythe*. Jena: Diederichs, 1909.

———. *The Christ Myth*. Translated by C. Delisle Burns. London: Unwin, 1910.

Dummelow, J. R., ed. *A Commentary on the Holy Bible: By Various Writers*. New York: The Macmillan Company, 1949.

Ebeling, Gerhard. *Das Wesen des christlichen Glaubens*. Tübingen: Mohr, 1959.

———. "Die Frage nach dem historischen Jesus und das Problem der Christologie." *Zeitschrift für Theologie und Kirche* 56.1 (1959) 14–30.

———. "Der Grund christlicher Theologie." *Zeitschrift für Theologie und Kirche* 58.2 (1961) 227–44.

———. *Die Geschichtlichkeit der Kirche und ihrer Verkündigung als theologisches Problem*. Tübingen: Mohr, 1954.

———. "The Ground of Christian Theology." In *Apocalypticism*, edited by Robert W. Funk, 47–68. New York: Herder and Herder, 1969.

———. "Jesus and Faith." In *Word and Faith*, translated by James W. Leitch, 201–46. Philadelphia: Fortress, 1963.

———. "Jesus und Glaube." *Zeitschrift für Theologie und Kirche* 55.1 (1958) 64–110.

———. *The Nature of Faith*. Translated by Ronald G. Smith. Philadelphia: Fortress, 1961.

———. *The Problem of Historicity: In the Church and Its Proclamation*. Translated by Grover Foley. Philadelphia: Fortress, 1967.

———. "The Question of the Historical Jesus and the Problem of Christology." In *Word and Faith*, translated by James W. Leitch, 288–304. Philadelphia: Fortress, 1963.

————. *Theologie und Verkundigung: Ein Gespräch mit Rudolf Bultmann*. Tübingen: Mohr, 1962.

————. *Theology and Proclamation: A Discussion with Rudolf Bultmann*. Translated by John Riches. Philadelphia: Fortress, 1966.

————. "Word of God and Hermeneutic." In *The New Hermeneutic*, edited by James M. Robinson and John B. Cobb Jr., 78–110. Evanston: Harper and Row, 1964.

————. "Word of God and Hermeneutics." In *Word and Faith*, translated by James W. Leitch, 305–32. Philadelphia: Fortress, 1963.

————. *Wort und Glaube*. Tübingen: Mohr, 1960.

Ehrman, Bart. *The Orthodox Corruption of Scripture: The Effect of Early Christological Controversies in the Text of the New Testament*. New York: Oxford University Press, 2011.

Elias, Jacob W. *1 and 2 Thessalonians*. Scottdale: Herald, 1995.

Ellis, Edward E. *The New Century Bible Commentary: The Gospel of Luke*. Grand Rapids: Eerdmans, 1980.

Erickson, Robert P. *Complicity in the Holocaust: Churches and Universities in Nazi Germany*. New York: Cambridge University Press, 2012.

Evans, Craig A. *Life of Jesus Research: An Annotated Bibliography*. Leiden: Brill, 1996.

Evans, Craig A., ed. *The Historical Jesus: Critical Concepts in Religious Studies: Volume 1: The History of the Quest: Classical Studies and Critical Questions*. New York: Routledge, 2004.

————. *Routledge Encyclopedia of the Historical Jesus*. London: Routledge, 2010.

Fallet, Marcel. "*Témoignage de l'évangile de Matthieu: Pour une histoire de Jesus II* by Béda Rigaux." *Reve de Théologie et de Philosophie* 20.2 (1970) 120–21.

Ferguson, Sinclair B., and David F. Wright, eds. *New Dictionary of Theology*. Downers Grove: InterVarsity Press, 1988.

Feyne, Sean. *Jesus, a Jewish Galilean: A New Reading of the Jesus Story*. London: Bloomsbury, 2010.

Franklin, Eric. *Christ the Lord: A Study in the Purpose and Theology of Luke-Acts*. Philadelphia: Westminster, 1975.

Frege, Gottlöb. "On Sense and Reference." In *Translations from the Philosophical Writings of Gottlob Frege*, edited by Peter Geach and Max Black, 56–78. Oxford: Blackwell, 1960

Frei, Hans W. *The Eclipse of Biblical Narrative: A Study in Eighteenth and Nineteenth Century Hermeneutics*. New Haven: Yale University Press, 1974.

————. *The Identity of Jesus Christ: The Hermeneutical Bases of Dogmatic Theology*. Eugene: Cascade, 2013.

————. *Reading Faithfully: Volume 1: Writings from the Archives: Theology and Hermeneutics*. Edited by Mike Higton and Mark A. Bowald. Cambridge: Clarke, 2017.

————. *Types of Christian Theology*. Edited by George Hunsinger and William C. Placher. New Haven: Yale University Press, 1992.

Fuchs, Ernst. "*Das Neue Testament und das hermeneutische Problem*." *Zeitschrift für Theologie und Kirche* 58 (1961) 198–226.

————. "*Die Frage nach dem historischen Jesus*." *Zeitschrift für Theologie und Kirche* 53 (1956) 210–29.

————. "*Die Theologie des Neuen Testaments und der historische Jesus*." *Zeitschrift für Theologie und Kirche* 57 (1960) 296–301.

———. *Gesammelte Aufsätze.* Tübingen: Mohr, 1965.

———. *"Glaube und Geschichte im Blick auf die Frage nach dem historischen Jesus: Eine Auseinandersetzung mit G. Bornkamms Buch über 'Jesus von Nazareth.'"* *Zeitschrift für Theologie und Kirche* (1957) 117–56.

———. *Hermeneutik.* Tübingen: Mohr, 1970.

———. *"Jesu Selbstzeugnis nach Matthäus 5."* *Zeitschrift für Theologie und Kirche* 49 (1952) 14–34.

———. *"Muß man an Jesus glauben, wenn man an Gott glauben will?"* *Zeitschrift für Theologie und Kirche* 58.1 (1961) 45–67.

———. "Must One believe in Jesus if He wants to Believe in God?" In *The Bultmann School of Biblical Interpretation,* edited by Robert W. Funk, 147–68. New York: Harper and Row, 1965.

———. "The New Testament and the Hermeneutical Problem." In *The New Hermeneutic,* edited by James M. Robinson and John B. Cobb Jr., 111–45. Evanston: Harper and Row, 1964.

———. "On the Task of a Christian Theology." In the *Apocalypticism,* edited by Robert W. Funk, 69–98. New York: Herder and Herder, 1969.

———. *Studies of the Historical Jesus.* Translated by Andrew Scobie. London: S.C.M., 1964.

———. *"Uber die Aufgabe einer christichen Theologie: Zum Aufsatz Ernst Käsemanns über 'Die Anfänge christlicher Theologie.'"* *Zeitschrift für Theologie und Kirche* 58.2 (1961) 245–67.

———. *"Warum fordert der Glaube an Jesus Christus von un sein Selbstverständnis?"* *Zeitschrift für Theologie und Kirche* 48.3 (1951) 342–59.

———. *"Was wird in der Exegese des Neuen Testaments interpretiert?"* *Zeitschrift für Theologie und Kirche* 56 (1959) 31–48.

———. *Zum hermeneutischen Problem in der Theologie: Die Existentiale Interpretation.* Tübingen: Mohr, 1965.

———. *Zur Frage nach dem Historischen Jesus.* Tübingen: Mohr, 1960.

Fuller, Reginald H. *Foundations of New Testament Christology.* London: Lutterworth, 1965.

Funk, Robert W. "Forward." In *The Bultmann School of Biblical Interpretation,* edited by Robert W. Funk, ix–xi. New York: Harper and Row, 1965.

———. *Language, Hermeneutic, and Word of God: The Problem of Language in the New Testament and Contemporary Theology.* New York: Harper and Row, 1966.

Gaventa, Beverly R. *First and Second Thessalonians.* Louisville: John Knox Press, 1998.

Gogarten, Friedrich. *Christ the Crisis.* Translated by R. A. Wilson. Richmond: John Knox, 1970.

———. *Demythologizing and History.* Translated by Neville H. Smith. London: S.C.M., 1955.

———. *Entmhyhologisierung und Kirche.* Stuttgart: Vorwerk, 1953.

———. *Jesus Christus Wende der Welt.* Tübingen: Mohr, 1966.

———. "Theology and History." In *History and Hermeneutic,* edited by Robert W. Funk, 35–81. New York: Harper and Row, 1967.

Gonzalez, Justo L. *The Story of Christianity: The Early Church to the Dawn of the Reformation: Volume 1.* New York: Harper Collins, 1984.

Grillmeier, Alois. *Christ in Christian Tradition: Volume One: From the Apostolic Age to Chalcedon (451).* Translated by John S. Bowden. London: Mowbrays, 1965.

Grundmann, Walter. *Die Geschichte Jesu Christi.* Berlin: Evangelische Verlagsanstalt, 1956.

———. *Jesus der Galiläer und das Judentum.* Leipzig: Wigland, 1941.

———. "Schneider, Johannes, Die Frage nach historischen Jesus un der neutestamentlichen Forschung der Gegenwart." *Theologische Literaturzeitung* 84 (1959) 103–05.

———. "Stauffer, Ethelbert, Jesus: Gestalt und Geschichte." *Theologische Literaturzeitung* 83 (1958) 837–40.

———. *Wer ist Jesus von Nazareth?* Weimar: Verlag Deutsche Christen, 1940.

———. "Who is Jesus of Nazareth?" In *A Church Undone: Documents from the German Christian Faith Movement,* edited by Mary M. Solberg. 453–69. Lantham: Fortress, 2015.

Hahn, Ferdinand. *Christologische Hoheitstitel: Ihre Geschichte im frühen Christentum.* Göttingen: Vandenhoeck und Ruprecht, 1963.

———. "The Quest of the Historical Jesus and the Special Character of the Sources Available to Us." In *What Can We Know About Jesus?: Essays on the New Quest,* translated by Grover Foley, 9–48. Philadelphia: Fortress, 1969.

———. *The Titles of Jesus in Christology: Their History in Early Christianity.* Translated by Harold Knight and George Ogg. London: Lutterworth, 1969.

Hammann, Konrad. *Rudolf Bultmann: A Biography.* Salem, OR: Polebridge, 2013.

Harrelson, Walter J., Donald Senior, Abraham Smith, Phyllis Trible, and James C. VanderKam, eds. *The New Interpreters Study Bible: New Revised Standard Version with the Apocrypha.* Nashville: Abingdon, 2003.

Harris, William B. *1 and 2 Thessalonians.* London: Epworth Press, 1968.

Hegel, Georg W. F. *Phenomenology of Spirit.* Translated by A. V. Miller. New York: Oxford University Press, 1977.

Heidegger, Martin. *Being and Time.* Translated John Macquarrie and Edward Robinson. New York: Harper and Row, 1962.

———. *The Fundamental Concepts of Metaphysics: World, Finitude, Solitude.* Translated by William McNeill and Nicholas Walker. Bloomington: Indiana University Press, 1995.

———. *Hegel's Concept of Experience.* Translated by Kenley R. Dove. New York: Harper and Row, 1970.

———. *Identity and Difference,* Translated by Joan Stambaugh. Chicago: The University of Chicago Press, 1969.

———. "Letter on Humanism" In *Pathmarks,* edited William McNeill, 239–76. Cambridge: Cambridge University Press, 1998.

———. "The Question Concerning Technology." In *The Question Concerning Technology and Other Essays,* translated by William Lovitt, 3–35. New York: Harper Collins, 1982.

Heitsch, Ernst. "Die Aporie des historischen Jesus als Problem theologischer Hermeneutik." *Zeitschrift für Theologie und Kirche* 53.2 (1956) 192–210.

———. "Jesus aus Nazareth als Christus." In *Der historische Jesus und der kerygmatische Christus: Beiträge zum Christusverständnis in Forschung und Verkündigung,* edited by Helmut Ristow and Karl Matthiae, 62–86. Berlin: Evangelische Verlagsanstalt, 1960.

Hendriksen, William. *New Testament Commentary: Exposition of I and II Thessalonians.* Grand Rapids: Baker, 1964.

Heschel, Susannah. *The Aryan Jesus: Christian Theologians and the Bible in Nazi Germany.* Princeton: Princeton University Press, 2008.

―――. "Confronting the Past: Post-1945 German Protestant Theology and the Fate of the Jews." *Studies in Contemporary Jewry* 24 (2010) 46–70.

―――. "Nazifying Christian Theology: Walter Grundmann and the Institute for the Study and Eradication of Jewish Influence on German Church Life." *Church History* 63.4 (1994) 587–605.

Higton, Mike. *Christ, Providence and History: Hans W. Frei's Public Theology.* New York: T. & T. Clark, 2004.

―――. "Foreword." In *The Identity of Jesus Christ: The Hermeneutical Bases of Dogmatic Theology*, xi–xix. Eugene: Wipf & Stock, 2013.

―――. "Frei's Christology and Lindbeck's Cultural-Linguistic Theory." *Scottish Journal of Theology* 50.1 (1997) 83–96.

Hodgson, Peter C. "Christ the Crisis, by Friedrich Gogarten, translated by R. A. Wilson. 308 pp. Richmond, John Knox Press, 1970. $7.95" *Theology Today* (1971) 361–64.

Hoole, Charles, trans. *The Didache, or Teaching of the Twelve Apostles.* London: Nutt, 1894.

Hovey, Alvah. *An American Commentary on the New Testament: Luke.* Philadelphia: American Baptist Publication Society, 1884.

Hunsinger, George. "Afterword: Hans Frei as Theologian." In *Theology and Narrative: Selected Essays*, edited by George Hunsinger and William C. Placher, 233–70. New York: Oxford University Press, 1993.

―――. "Frei's Early Christology: The Book of Detours." *Pro Ecclesia* 24.1 (2015) 24–36.

―――. "Hans Frei as Theologian: The Quest for a Generous Orthodoxy." *Modern Theology* 8.2 (1992) 103–28.

Husserl, Edmund. *Ideas: General Introduction to Pure Phenomenology.* Translated by W. R. Gibson. New York: Macmillan, 1931.

Jeremias, Joachim. "The Present Position in the Controversy Concerning the Problem of the Historical Jesus." *Expository Times* 69 (1958) 333–39.

―――. *The Problem of the Historical Jesus.* Translated by Norman Perrin. Philadelphia: Fortress, 1964.

Johnson, Luke T. *The Writings of the New Testament: An Interpretation.* Philadelphia: Fortress Press, 1986.

Jones, Ivor H. *The Epistles to the Thessalonians.* Peterborough: Epworth Press, 2005.

Josephus, Titus F. *The Works of Josephus.* Translated by William Whiston. Peabody: Hendrickson Publishers, 1987.

Kähler, Martin. *Der sogenannte historische Jesus und der geschichtliche, biblische Christus.* Leipzig: Deichert, 1892.

―――. *The So-Called Historical Jesus and the Historic Biblical Christ.* Translated by Carl E. Braaten. Philadelphia: Fortress, 1964.

Kant, Immanuel. *Critique of Pure Reason.* Translated by Norman Kemp Smith. New York: St. Martin's, 1929.

Karkkainen Veli-Matti. *Christology: A Global Introduction.* Grand Rapids: Baker, 2003.

Käsemann, Ernst. "A Critical Analysis of Philippians 2:5–11." In *God and Christ: Existence and Province*, edited by Robert W. Funk, 45–88. New York: Harper and Row, 1968.

―――. "The Beginnings of Christian Theology." In *Apocalypticism,* edited by Robert W. Funk, 17–46. New York: Herder and Herder, 1969.

———. "Blind Alleys in the 'Jesus of History' Controversy." In *New Testament Questions of Today*, translated by W. J. Montague, 23–65. London: S.C.M., 1969.

———. *Der Ruf der Freiheit*. Tübingen: Mohr, 1968.

———. "Die Anfänge christlicher Theologie." *Zeitschrift für Theologie und Kirche* 57.2 (1960) 162–85.

———. *Exegetische Versuche und Besinnungen: Band 1*. Göttingen: Vandenhoeck und Ruprecht, 1960.

———. *Exegetische Versuche und Besinnungen: Band 2*. Göttingen: Vandenhoeck und Ruprecht, 1968.

———. "Gottesgerechtigkeit hei Paulus." *Zeitschrift für Theologie und Kirche* 58.3 (1961) 367–78.

———. *Jesus Means Freedom*. Translated by Frank Clarke. London: S.C.M, 1969.

———. "Neutestamentliche Fragen von Heute." *Zeitschrift für Theologie und Kirche* 54.1 (1957) 1–21.

———. "New Testament Questions of Today." In *New Testament Questions of Today*, translated by W. J. Montague, 1–22. London: S.C.M., 1969.

———. "On the Topic of Primitive Christian Apocalyptic." In *Apocalypticism*, edited by Robert W. Funk, 99–113. New York: Herder and Herder, 1969.

———. "The Problem of the Historical Jesus." In *Essays on New Testament Themes*, translated by W. J. Montague, 15–47. London: S.C.M., 1964.

———. "Righteousness of God in Paul." In *New Testament Questions of Today*, translated by W. J. Montague, 168–82. London: S.C.M., 1969.

———. *The Testament of Jesus: A Study of the Gospel of John in the Light of Chapter 17*. Translated by Gerhard Krodel. Eugene: Wipf & Stock, 2017.

———. "Zum Thema der urchristlichen Apokalyptik" *Zeitschrift für Theologie und Kirche* 59.3 (1962) 257–84.

Keck, Leander E. "The Eclipse of Biblical Narrative: A Study in Eighteenth and Nineteenth Century Hermeneutics: By Hans W. Frei: New Haven, Yale University Press, 1974. 355pp. $15.00." *Theology Today* 31.4 (1975) 367–70.

Keener, Craig S. *Christobiography: Memory, History, and the Reliability of the Gospels*. Grand Rapids: Eerdmans, 2019.

———. *The Historical Jesus of the Gospels*. Grand Rapids: Eerdmans, 2009.

Kelly, Justin J. "Book Review: The Eclipse of Biblical Narrative: A Study in Eighteenth and Nineteenth Century Hermeneutics." *Theological Studies* 36.1 (1975) 155–58.

Kierkegaard, Soren. *Sickness Unto Death*. Translated by Howard V. Kong and Edna H. Kong. Princeton: Princeton University Press, 1980.

Koester, Helmut. "Forward." In *Jesus of Nazareth*, translated by Irene McLuskey, Fraser McLuskey, and James M. Robinson, 3–6. Minneapolis: Fortress, 1995.

Kofman, Amy Z. Kirby Dick, and Jacques Derrida. *Derrida: Screenplay and Essays on the Film*. Manchester: Manchester University Press, 2005.

Kryvelev, Iosif A. *Christ: Myth or Reality*. Translated by S. Kotlobye. Moscow: USSR Academy of Sciences, 1987.

Laymon, Charles M. *The Interpreter's One-Volume Commentary on the Bible*. Nashville: Abingdon, 1982.

Levinas, Emmanuel. *Otherwise than Being, or Beyond Essence*. Translated by Alphonso Lingis. Norwell: Kluwer, 1991.

Long, Edward L. *Patterns of Polity: Varieties of Church Governance*. Cleveland: Pilgrim, 2001.

MacGregor, Geddes, ed. *Dictionary of Religion and Philosophy*. New York: Paragon, 1989.

Macquarrie, John. *Christology Revisited*. Harrisburg: Trinity, 1998.

———. *Existentialism*. New York: World, 1972.

———. *In Search of Deity: An Essay in Dialectical Theism*. New York: Crossroad, 1984.

———. *In Search of Humanity. A Theological and Philosophical Approach*. New York: Crossroad, 1982.

———. *Jesus Christ in Modern Thought*. London: SCM, 1990.

———. *Principles of Christian Theology*. New York: Scribner, 1966.

———. *Stubborn Theological Questions*. London: SCM, 2003.

———. *Studies in Existentialism*. Montreal: McGill, 1965.

Manning, Russell R., ed. *The Cambridge Companion to Paul Tillich*. Cambridge: Cambridge University Press, 2008.

Manson, William. *The Moffatt New Testament Commentary: Gospel of Luke*. New York: Harper and Brothers, 1930.

Marshall, I. Howard. *1 and 2 Thessalonians: The New Century Bible Commentary*. Grand Rapids: Wm. B. Eerdmans Publishing Company, 1983.

McEleney, Neil J. "Béda Rigaux, *Témoignage de l'évangile de Matthieu (Pour une histoire de Jesus II*: Bruges: Desclée de Brouwer, 1967)" *The Catholic Biblical Quarterly* 31.4 (October 1969) 601–02.

McGrath, Alister E. *A Scientific Theology: Volume 3: Theory*. London: Bloomsbury, 2014.

———. *The Making of Modern German Christology: 1750–1990*. Eugene: Wipf & Stock, 2005.

Metts, Michael B. "Neglected Discontinuity between Early Form Criticism and the New Quest with Reference to the Last Supper." In *Jesus, Skepticism and the Problem of History: Criteria and Context in the Study of Christian Origins*, edited by Darrell L. Bock and J. Ed Komoszewski, 67–90. Grand Rapids: Zondervan, 2019.

Meyer, Marvin, ed. *The Nag Hammadi Scriptures*. New York: Harper Collins Publishers, 2007.

Michaels, J. Ramsey. "*The Christology of Jesus* by Ben Witherington III." *Journal of Biblical Literature* 111.1 (1992) 141–43.

Miller, Ed. L., and Stanley J. Grenz. *Fortress Introduction to Contemporary Theologies*. Minneapolis: Fortress, 1998.

Miller, Robert J. *The Jesus Seminar and Its Critics*. Santa Rosa: Polebridge, 1999.

Miller, Robert J., ed. *The Complete Gospels: Annotated Scholars Version*. Sonoma, CA: Polebridge, 1994.

Moltmann, Jürgen. *A Broad Place: An Autobiography*. London, SCM, 2007.

———. *Theologie der Hoffnung*. Munich: Christian Kaiser, 1964.

———. *Theology of Hope: On the Ground and the Implications of a Christian Eschatology*. Minneapolis: Fortress, 1967.

Moore, Arthur L. ed. *The Century Bible: 1 and 2 Thessalonians*. Camden: Thomas Nelson and Sons Ltd., 1969.

Mussner, Franz. "*Der 'historische' Jesus*." *Trierer Theologische Zitschrift* 69 (1960) 321–37.

———. "*Der historische Jesus und der Christus des Glaubens*." *Biblische Zeitschrift* 1 (1957) 224–52.

———. *Die Johanneische Sehweise und die Frage nach dem historischen Jesus*. Freiburg: Herder, 1965.

———. *The Historical Jesus in the Gospel of St. John*. Freiburg: Herder and Herder, 1966.

———. "Methodologie der Frage nach dem historischen Jesus." In *Rückfrage nach Jesus: zur Methodik und Bedeutung der Frage nach dem historischen Jesus*, edited by Karl Kertelge, 118–47. Freiburg: Herder, 1974.

O'Keefe, Vincent T. "Book Review: Demythologizing and History." *Theological Studies* 17.4 (1956) 588–90.

Pannenberg, Wolfhart. "The God of Hope." *CrossCurrents* 18.3 (1968) 284–95.

———. *Grundzüge der Christologie*. Gütersloh: Gütersloher Verlagshaus, 1964.

———. *Jesus-God and Man*. Translated by Lewis L. Wilkins and Duane A. Priebe. London: SCM, 1968.

Pannenberg, Wolfhart, ed. *Revelation as History*. New York: Macmillan, 1968.

Patzia, Arthur G. *The Making of the New Testament: Origin, Collection, Text, and Canon*. Downers Grove: InterVarsity, 2011.

Pekarske, Daniel T. *Abstracts of Karl Rahner's Theological Investigations 1–23*. Milwaukee: Marquette University Press, 2002.

Peloubet F. N., and M.A. Peloubet, eds. *Smith's Bible Dictionary*. Grand Rapids: Zondervan, 1948.

Perrin, Norman. *Rediscovering the Teaching of Jesus*. New York: Harper and Row, 1967.

Philo. *The Works of Philo*. Translated by C.D. Yonge. Peabody: Hendrickson Publishers, 1987.

Plato. *Theaetetus*. Translated by M. J. Levett. Indianapolis: Hackett, 1992.

Pokorný, Petr. "Jesus as the Ever-Living Lawgiver in the Letter of Mara bar Sarapion." In *The Letter of Mara bar Sarapiom in Context*, edited by Annette Merz and Teun L. Tieleman, 129–39. Leiden: Brill, 2012.

Porter, Stanley E. *Criteria for Authenticity in Historical-Jesus Research: Previous Discussions and New Proposals*. Sheffield: Sheffield, 2000.

Powell, Mark A. *What Are They Saying About Luke?* Mahwah: Paulist, 1989.

Rahner, Karl. *Foundations of Christian Faith: An Introduction to the Idea of Christianity*. Translated by William V. Dych. New York, 1978.

———. *Grundkurs des Glaubens: Einführung in den Begriff des Christentums*. Freiburg: Herder, 1976.

———. *Theological Investigations: Volume 1: God, Christ, Mary and Grace*. Translated by Cornelius Ernst. Baltimore: Helicon, 1961.

———. *Theological Investigations: Volume 17: Jesus, Man and Church*. Translated by Margaret Kohl. New York: Crossroad, 1981.

Rahner, Karl, and Wilhelm Thüsing. *A New Christology*. New York: Seabury, 1980.

Reese, William L. *Dictionary of Philosophy and Religion: Eastern and Western Thought*. Atlantic Highlands: Humanities, 1980.

Reijnen, Anne M. "Paul Tillich's Christology." In *The Cambridge Companion to Paul Tillich*, edited by Russell R. Manning, 56–73. Cambridge: Cambridge University Press, 2008.

Reumann, John. "Introduction." In *The Problem of the Historical Jesus*, translated by Norman Perrin, v–xviii. Philadelphia: Fortress, 1964.

———. Translation of Conzelmann's Jesus

Richards, Glyn. "Paul Tillich and the Historical Jesus." *Studies in Religion* 4.2 (1974) 120–128.

Rieger, Paul. "Foreword." In *What Can We Know About Jesus?: Essays on the New Quest*, translated by Grover Foley, 7–7. Philadelphia: Fortress, 1969.

Risener, Rainer. In *Jesus of Nazareth: Lord and Christ: Essays on the Historical Jesus and New Testament Christology.*, edited by Joel B. Green and Max Turner, 263–279. Grand Rapids: Eerdmans, 1994.

Rigaux, Béda. *Jésus-Christ devant l'histoire et la dialectique*. Bruxelles: Goemaere, 1958.

———. "L 'historicité de Jésus devant l'exégèse récente." *Revue Biblique* 65.4 (1958) 481–522.

———. *Témoignage de l'évangile de Jean: Pour une histoire de Jesus 5*. Bruges: Desclée De Brouwer, 1974.

———. *Témoignage de l'évangile de Luc: Pour une histoire de Jesus 4*. Bruges: Desclée De Brouwer, 1970.

———. *Témoignage de l'évangile de Marc: Pour une histoire de Jesus 1*. Bruges: Desclée De Brouwer, 1965.

———. *Témoignage de l'évangile de Matthieu: Pour une histoire de Jesus 2*. Bruges: Desclée De Brouwer, 1967.

———. *The Testimony of Saint Mark*. Translated by Malachy Carroll. Chicago: Franciscan Herald, 1966.

———. *The Testimony of Saint Matthew*. Translated by Joseph Oligny. Chicago: Franciscan Herald, 1968.

Robinson, James M. *A New Quest for the Historical Jesus*. London: S.C.M., 1959.

———. "For Theology and the Church." In *The Bultmann School of Biblical Interpretation*, edited by Robert W. Funk, 1–19. New York: Harper and Row, 1965.

———. "Hermeneutic Since Barth." In *The New Hermeneutic*, edited by James M. Robinson and John B. Cobb Jr., 1–77. Evanston: Harper and Row, 1964.

———. "The Quest of the Historical Jesus Today." *Theology Today* 15.2 (1958) 183–197.

Robinson, James M. ed. *The Nag Hammadi Library in English*. New York: Harper Collins, 1990.

Sadler, Donna L. *Touching the Passion: Seeing Late Medieval Altarpieces through the Eyes of Faith*. Boston: Brill, 2018.

Sartre, Jean-Paul. *Being and Nothingness: A Phenomenological Essay on Ontology*. Translated by Hazel Barnes. New York: Citadel, 2001.

Schaff, Philip S. *The Creeds of Christendom: Volume 1: The History of Creeds*. New York: Harper and Brothers Publishers, 1877.

Schillebeeckx, Edward. *Gerechtigheid en liefde, genade en bevrijding*. Bloemendaal: Nelissen, 1977.

———. *Christ: The Christian Experience of Jesus as Lord*. Translated by John Bowden. New York: Seabury, 1980.

———. *Jesus: An Experiment in Christology*. Translated by Hubert Hoskins. New York: Seabury, 1979.

———. *Jezus, het verhaal van een levende*. Bloemendaal: Nelissen, 1974.

Schilling, Sylvester P. *Contemporary Continental Theologians* London: SCM, 1966.

Schleiermacher, Friedrich. *Das Leben Jesu*. Berlin: Reimer, 1864.

———. *The Life of Jesus*. Translated by S. Maclean Gilmour. Philadelphia: Fortress, 1975.

Schneider, Johannes. *Baptism and Church in the New Testament*. London: Carey Kingsgate, 1957

———. *Das Evangelium nach Johannes*. Berlin: Evangelische Verlagsanstalt, 1976.

————. *Die Frage nach dem historischen Jesus in der neutestamentlichen Forschung der Gegenwart.* Berlin: Evangelische Verlagsanstalt, 1958.

Schwarz, Hans. "Paul Althaus." In *Twentieth-Century Lutheran Theologians*, edited by Mark C. Mattes, 136–54. Göttingen: Vandenhoeck und Ruprecht, 2013.

Schweitzer, Albert. *Geschichte der Leben-Jesu-Forschung: Von Reimarus zu Wrede.* Tübingen: Mohr, 1913.

————. *The Quest of the Historical Jesus.* Translated by W. Montgomery. London: Black, 1910.

Shiner, Larry. *The Secularization of History: An Introduction to the Theology of Friedrich Gogarten.* Nashville: Abingdon, 1966.

Smart, James D. *The Divided Mind of Modern Theology, Karl Barth and Rudolf Bultmann: 1908–1933.* Philadelphia: Westminster, 1967.

Solberg, Mary M. Introduction to "Who is Jesus of Nazareth?" In *A Church Undone: Documents from the German Christian Faith Movement: 1932–1940*, edited by Mary M. Solberg, 453–69. Minneapolis: Fortress, 2015.

Soards, Marion L. *The Passion According to Luke: The Special Material of Luke 22.* Sheffield: JSOT Press, 1987.

Stauffer, Ethelbert. *Christ and the Caesars: Historical Sketches.* Translated by R. Gregor Smith. Philadelphia: Westminster, 1955.

————. *Christus und die Caesaren.* Hamburg: Wittig, 1948.

————. *Die Botschaft Jesu.* Bern: Francke, 1959.

————. *Die Theologie des Neuen Testaments.* Stuttgart: Kohlhammer, 1941.

————. "*Entmythologisierung oder Realthelologie?*" In *Kerygma und Mythos II: Ein theologisches Gesprach*, edited by Hans W. Bartsch, 13–28. Hamburg-Bergstedt: H. Reich Evangelischer Verlag, 1965.

————. "Grundmann, Walter, Die Geschichte Jesu Christi." *Theologische Literaturzeitung* 84 (1959) 186–88.

————. *Jesus and His Story.* Translated by Dorothea M. Barton. London: SCM, 1960.

————. *Jesus: Gestalt und Geschichte.* Bern: Francke, 1957.

————. *Jesus war ganz anders.* Hamburg: Wittig, 1967.

————. "*Neue Wege der Jesusforschung.*" In *Gottes ist der Orient*, edited by Otto Eissfeldt, 161–86. Berlin: Evangelische Verlagsanstalt, 1959.

————. *New Testament Theology.* Translated by John Marsh. London: SCM, 1963.

Stevens, William A. *Commentary on the Epistles to the Thessalonians: An American Commentary on the New Testament.* Chicago: The American Baptist Publication Society, 1890.

Steiner, George. "The Eclipse of Biblical Narrative: A Study in Eighteenth and Nineteenth Century Hermeneutics." *Philosophy and Literature* 1.2 (1977) 238–43.

Stone, Howard W., and James O. Duke. *How to Think Theologically.* Minneapolis: Fortress, 2006.

Strauss, David F. *Das leben Jesu kritisch bearbeitet.* Tübingen: Osiander, 1835.

————. *Der Christus des Glaubens und der Jesus der Geschichte: eine Kritik des Schleiermacher'schen Lebens Jesu.* Berlin: Duncker, 1865.

————. *The Christ of Faith and the Jesus of History: A Critique of Schleiermacher's Life of Jesus.* Translated by Leander E. Keck. Philadelphia: Fortress, 1977.

————. *The Life of Jesus, Critically Examined.* Translated by George F. Eliot. Cambridge: Cambridge University Press, 1846.

———. *In Defense of My 'Life of Jesus' Against the Hegelians.* Translated by Marilyn C. Massey. Hamden: Archon, 1983.

———. *Streitschriften zur Verteidigung meiner Schrift über das Leben Jesu und zur Charakteristik der gegenwärtigen Theologie* Tübingen: Osiander, 1837.

Summers, Ray. *Commentary on Luke.* Waco: Word Books Publishers, 1972.

Theissen, Gerd, and Annette Merz. *The Historical Jesus: A Comprehensive Guide.* Translated by John Bowden. Minneapolis: Fortress, 1998.

Thielicke, Helmut. *The Evangelical Faith: The Doctrine of God and of Christ.* Translated by Geoffrey W. Bromiley. Grand Rapids: Eerdmans, 1977.

———. "The Restatement of New Testament Mythology." In *Kerygma and Myth: A Theological Debate,* edited by Hans W. Bartsch, 138–74. New York: Harper, 1961.

Tillich, Paul. *Dynamics of Faith.* New York: Harper, 1957.

———. *On the Boundary: An Autobiographical Sketch.* New York: Scribner, 1966.

———. *Systematic Theology Vol. 2: Existence and the Christ.* Chicago: University of Chicago Press, 1957.

Unger, Merrill F. *Unger's Bible Dictionary.* Chicago: Moody Press, 1972.

Van Til, Cornelius. *The New Hermeneutic.* Nutley: Presbyterian and Reformed, 1974.

Vorgrimler, Herbert, ed. *Exegese und Dogmatik.* Mainz: Matthias-Grünwald, 1962.

———. *Dogmatic vs. Biblical Theology.* Baltimore: Helicon, 1965.

Wells, George A. *Cutting Jesus Down to Size: What Higher Criticism Has Achieved and Where It Leaves Christianity.* Chicago: Open Court, 2009.

West, Cornel. "On Frei's *Eclipse of Biblical Narrative.*" *Union Seminary Quarterly Review* 37.4 (1983) 299–302.

Whitehead, Alfred N. *Process and Reality: An Essay in Cosmology.* New York: Free Press, 1978.

Whiteley, D. E. H. *Thessalonians.* London: Oxford University Press, 1969.

Witherington, Ben. *The Christology of Jesus.* Minneapolis: Fortress, 1990.

———. *The Jesus Quest: The Third Search for the Jew of Nazareth.* Downers Grove: InterVarsity, 1997.

———. *The Many Faces of the Christ: The Christologies of the New Testament and Beyond.* New York: Crossroad, 1998.

Wojcik, Jan. *The Road to Emmaus: Reading Luke's Gospel.* West Lafayette, IN: Purdue University Press, 1989.

Wood, Laurence W. *Theology as History and Hermeneutics: A Post-Critical Conversation with Contemporary Theology.* Lexington: Emeth, 2005.

Woodson, Hue. *A Theologian's Guide to Heidegger.* Eugene: Wipf & Stock, 2019.

———. *Heideggerian Theologies: The Pathmarks of John Macquarrie, Rudolf Bultmann, Paul Tillich, and Karl Rahner.* Eugene: Wipf & Stock, 2018.

Wright, N. T. *The Challenge of Jesus: Rediscovering Who Jesus Was and Is.* Downers Grove: InterVarsity, 1999.

———. *Jesus and the Victory of God.* Minneapolis: Fortress, 1996.

Wright, N. T., and John D. Crossan. "The Resurrection: Historical Event or Theological Explanation?: A Dialogue." In *The Resurrection of Jesus: John Dominic Crossan and N. T. Wright in Dialogue.* edited by Robert B. Stewart, 16–47. Minneapolis: Fortress, 2006.

Young, Pamela D. "Searching Christology." *New Blackfriars* 68.809 (1987) 437–43.

Index

Made in the USA
Middletown, DE
17 December 2022

18958061R00235